THE INDEPENDENT REGULATORY COMMISSIONS

THE

INDEPENDENT REGULATORY

COMMISSIONS

ROBERT E. CUSHMAN

1972

OCTAGON BOOKS

New York

Reprinted 1972
by special arrangement with Oxford University Press, Inc.

OCTAGON BOOKS
A DIVISION OF FARRAR, STRAUS & GIROUX, INC.
19 Union Square West
New York, N. Y. 10003

LIBRARY OF CONGRESS CATALOG CARD NUMBER: 71-159176

ISBN 0-374-92019-2

Manufactured by Braun-Brumfield, Inc.
Ann Arbor, Michigan

Printed in the United States of America

THIS BOOK IS DEDICATED TO

CHARLES AUSTIN BEARD

WITH THE ADMIRATION, GRATITUDE, AND
AFFECTION OF THE AUTHOR

PREFACE

In the spring of 1936 I was asked to join the staff of the President's Committee on Administrative Management which had just been set up, and to prepare for the committee during the ensuing four months a memorandum on the independent regulatory commissions. It was suggested that this memorandum should set forth the statutory basis of the commissions, should attempt some analysis of their relations to the three major departments of the federal government, and finally should attempt to formulate any possible alternatives to the independent commission as an administrative device for carrying on the work of regulation. Out of this assignment emerged the proposal for the possible reorganization of the independent regulatory commissions which is discussed on pages 709 ff. of this volume and which was incorporated by the President's committee into its final report to the President in January 1937.

There also emerged from this endeavor a realization that little or nothing was known about the commissions as administrative agencies or about their relations to Congress or the President. Regulatory commissions had been more or less taken for granted and no information was readily available about why they had been created in their present forms or how they were supposed to fit into the general framework of the national government. Nor had any comprehensive attempt been made to explore in this connection the parallel experience of Great Britain in dealing with analogous problems. It seemed clear that a wide and highly important area in the field of public administration lay almost entirely unexplored. The members of the President's committee, Louis Brownlow, Charles E. Merriam, and Luther Gulick, were all keenly interested in promoting research in the field of public administration, particularly in this area. It was accordingly suggested that I should undertake to direct a thoroughgoing and comprehensive study of the independent regulatory commissions if funds could be found to underwrite it. Dr. Luther Gulick, Director of the Institute of Public Administration, assumed responsibility in the matter, and through the Institute of Public Administration a generous grant was secured from the Rockefeller Foundation for financing the preparation of the study and its final publication. The writer accordingly has produced this volume under the auspices of the Institute of Public Administration. This has meant concretely that the work has gone forward under the watchful eye of Dr. Luther Gulick, to whom, as an old friend, a wise counsellor, and a shrewd critic, I am deeply grateful.

One of the major conditions under which this work was undertaken, and a condition obviously essential to its permanent value, was that it should be an objective and thorough research undertaking quite unrestricted by any *a priori* assumptions. Consequently the President's committee's proposal is dealt with, not as the culminating conclusion of the study, but as one of the steps in the development of ideas and proposals for dealing with the independent regulatory commission problem. This volume, in other words, was not written as a brief to support my earlier proposals.

The completion of this task would have been impossible without the help generously extended by a very large number of persons. Not all of these can be mentioned here. I feel a certain sense of embarrassment in acknowledging my debt of gratitude to certain friends, among them a number of distinguished public officials, for their kindness in reading and commenting upon sections of the manuscript or proof of this book. This is because most of these men were sharply critical, some of them publicly, of my proposals to the President's committee for the reorganization of the independent regulatory commissions, and if any of them have since been converted to the merits of that proposal they have not made that fact known to me. I wish therefore to make it most emphatic that no one but myself is responsible for the inferences and conclusions which are drawn in this study. Having said this, I wish to acknowledge with keen gratitude the counsel and aid of the following persons.

The long chapter on the Interstate Commerce Commission was read in proof by Chairman Joseph B. Eastman and Commissioner Clyde B. Aitchison; the section on the Federal Reserve Board was read in manuscript by my colleague, Professor Harold L. Reed; the section on the Federal Trade Commission was read in proof by Colonel William H. England, the chief economist of the commission; Professor Paul M. Zeis of the University of Akron, read the manuscript of the section dealing with the Shipping Board and Maritime Commission, and I used freely his excellent study, *American Shipping Policy*. Dr. Lester V. Plum of Princeton University read the material dealing with the Federal Power Commission and allowed me to make free use of his unpublished doctoral dissertation on the commission. The section on the Radio and Communications Commissions was read in proof by Mr. Louis G. Caldwell, the first general counsel of the Radio Commission, and also by Dr. Irvin Stewart, a former member of both commissions. Dean James M. Landis of the Harvard Law School read the material dealing with the Securities and Exchange Commission, of which he was formerly chairman. My colleague, Professor Royal Montgomery, read the proof of the chapter on the National Labor Relations Board. Dr. Ralph H. Baker, of the New York State College for Teachers, read the proof of the section on the National Bituminous Coal Commission, and I also made free use of his forthcoming volume on the commission. Mr. Clinton M. Hester, the first Administrator of Civil Aeronautics, read the proof of the section dealing with the Civil Aeronautics Authority.

The chapter on the state regulatory commissions is grounded in its entirety upon the studies made by Professor James W. Fesler of the University of North Carolina. His inquiry was planned in consultation with me in the expectation that such a study of the state commissions would throw light upon the problems relating to the federal commissions. Professor Fesler's studies will, however, have very great value as independent contributions. I owe much to his criticism and suggestion, in addition to the wholesale appropriation of his material in Chapter VII.

I am under heavy obligations to friends in London for aid in collecting and appraising the material dealing with British agencies in the field of economic regulation. I am especially indebted to Dr. William A. Robson of the London School of Economics who gave me continuous assistance and extended innumerable courtesies. Similarly Professor Harold J. Laski,

Dr. Herman Finer, and Dr. Ivor Jennings, all of the London School of Economics, rendered invaluable aid. Dr. Finer, now in this country, read the proof of the section dealing with British experience. This portion of the proof was also read by Professor Marshall E. Dimock of the University of Chicago.

George Allen & Unwin Ltd. kindly granted permission to reprint the quotations appearing on pages 564, 598, 611, and 613 from W. A. Robson's *Public Enterprise;* and those on pages 579 and 601 from T. O'Brien's *British Experiments in Public Ownership and Control;* and the Manchester University Press gave me permission to print the passage on page 547 from D. N. Chester's *Public Control of Road Passenger Transport.*

Finally I wish to put on record my gratitude to several younger friends and scholars who, as research associates, made major contributions to the production of this book. My task in London was made infinitely lighter and pleasanter by the exceedingly able assistance of Alec Nove, my research assistant, now in the British army. I was similarly aided in the American end of the study by Professor David O. Walter of the University of New Hampshire, John F. Miller, now with the National Resources Planning Board, Dr. Robert W. Anderson, Dr. George Manner, Henry H. King, and Worth Sharpe. I am under very special obligations to Dr. Miriam Drabkin for invaluable assistance in helping push the book to completion and for making the index.

R. E. C.

Ithaca, New York
June 1941

CONTENTS

THE INDEPENDENT REGULATORY COMMISSIONS

'Our national commission octopus is already too large; his legs are too long. I am in favor of lopping them off instead of trying to grow more.'—Mr. Larsen of Georgia in debate in the House of Representatives on the radio bill of 1927.

'Efficiency in the processes of governmental regulation is best served by the creation of more rather than less agencies.'—James M. Landis, *The Administrative Process*, 24.

I

INTRODUCTION

THE term 'independent regulatory commission' is not a self-explanatory label. Every one of the three words which comprise it is a variable, having no definitely fixed meaning. To make clear, therefore, the scope of this study, it is necessary to say at the outset just what is meant by an independent regulatory commission.

A commission or board is 'independent,' for our purposes, when it is entirely outside any regular executive department. It is isolated from the integrated administrative structure of the executive branch. It is subject to no direct supervision or control by any Cabinet Secretary or by the President. The members of some 'independent' commissions can be removed from office by the President at his pleasure. This is true of the Securities and Exchange Commission and the Federal Communications Commission. The President may remove members of other commissions only for specific causes stated in the statutes creating them. The term 'independence' is sometimes used to refer to this immunity of a commission from the President's discretionary removal power. It is not so used in this study. It is used here rather to denote a location in the governmental system outside the ten executive departments.

Not all independent commissions are 'regulatory.' A commission is regulatory when it exercises governmental control or discipline over private conduct or property interests. This control may take different forms and use different methods, but there is always present an element of coercion. It is this coercion which distinguishes the regulatory Federal Trade Commission from the non-regulatory Reconstruction Finance Corporation.

3

The former polices interstate commerce in an effort to prevent businessmen from indulging in unfair trade practices; the latter lends government money, but places coercion on no one. Occasionally a governmental agency which is in the main non-regulatory is given some minor and incidental regulatory power. This is true of the United States Employees Compensation Commission. The present study does not include such agencies but confines itself to those that are exclusively or predominantly regulatory.

The word 'commission' is used in a non-technical sense to include any agency made up of a group of administrators having essentially equal power. If there are any reasons other than those of euphony which lead Congress to call an independent regulatory agency a 'commission' rather than a 'board' or an 'authority,' those considerations have no meaning for the purposes of this study, which includes all such agencies regardless of which label they bear.

By an 'independent regulatory commission,' then, is meant any commission, board, or authority which lies outside the regular executive departments and which has for its major job the exercise of some form of restrictive or disciplinary control over private conduct or private property.

This study deals with the problem of the independent regulatory commission, rather than with the commissions as such. Some commissions are much more interesting and important than others. No two are identical and each makes its own contribution to the general problem. It is arguable that certain other agencies might reasonably have been included. However, this study has been primarily based on the following agencies of the federal government. Some, it will be noticed, no longer exist, or no longer exist as independent agencies, but they are entitled to their places in the broad picture:

Interstate Commerce Commission
Federal Reserve Board (now the Board of Governors of the Federal
    Reserve System)
Federal Trade Commission
United States Shipping Board (defunct)
Federal Power Commission
Federal Radio Commission (defunct)
Securities and Exchange Commission

Federal Communications Commission (supplanting the Federal
    Radio Commission)

National Labor Relations Board

National Bituminous Coal Commission (transferred in 1939 to the
    Department of the Interior)

United States Maritime Commission

Civil Aeronautics Authority (transferred in 1940 to the Department
    of Commerce)

A glance at this list shows that there are no more important
tasks being done by the federal government than those which
have been assigned to the independent regulatory commissions.
None affect more vitally the economic life of the nation. The
success with which this work is done will depend largely upon
the soundness and suitability of the administrative organization
and procedure of the regulatory commissions. The importance
of the job itself justifies a far closer inquiry into the administrative problems inherent in regulation than has thus far been
made. Until fairly recently, in fact, the administrative aspects
of the independent regulatory commissions have attracted only
the most casual attention of students and writers. Economists
have explored with care the nature and range of the regulatory
powers conferred on these bodies; lawyers have been obliged to
concern themselves with the legal limitations on the powers of
the independent agencies and the confused and uncertain efforts
of the courts to stabilize the law in regard to the judicial review
of the work of the commissions. But the commissions as units of
government, as cogs in the vast federal governmental machine,
as administrative devices, have been more or less taken for
granted. Certainly they have never been subjected to any serious critical examination. Attention has been riveted on the job
rather than on the specific tool selected to perform it.

Another reason for studying the administrative phases of the
independent regulatory commissions is that their growth and
multiplication have been so haphazard. Congress began creating
these agencies fifty years ago and the movement steadily increases in momentum. In any recent Congress it will be found
that at least a hundred bills providing for the creation of independent federal agencies have been introduced and that from
ten to twenty of these are to be given regulatory power. Most
of these are sidetracked, but they show a Congressional partial-

ity for the independent regulatory commission technique. Thus the list increases in length. It is often an easier legislative task to create a new and independent governmental body than to fit a new job into the existing administrative structure with its confusing network of jurisdictional lines. Also when there is a new governmental task of a relatively minor nature which seems to have some relation to the work of an existing independent regulatory commission, there is a wholly natural Congressional disposition to give the new task to the commission. This is often done without considering whether the new job is intrinsically of the kind that ought to be assigned to an independent agency. Thus many purely executive tasks have been given to the Interstate Commerce Commission and other similar federal agencies. No judgment is passed at this point upon whether the multiplication of independent regulatory commissions in the federal government is good or bad, or whether the assignment to such agencies of widely heterogeneous tasks is good or bad. If we are to answer these questions, however, with intelligence and reasonable assurance, we must study more thoroughly than has thus far been done the nature of the independent regulatory commissions and the nature of the work they are fitted to do. After fifty years of experience it is high time we take an objective and comprehensive view of the independent regulatory commission movement as a movement in the field of federal administration, appraise its results, scrutinize the assumptions upon which it has proceeded, discover if there be limitations upon it or changes in it which would increase its usefulness, and, in short, make an effort to stabilize the position of these commissions in the federal governmental structure. The present study makes no ambitious claim of accomplishing all this, but this is the goal toward which it is directed.

Such an inquiry seems peculiarly timely. The problem of administrative reorganization in the federal government in the interests of efficiency and economy has been and remains before the country. If the progress made in that direction is meager, it is because responsible statesmen cannot agree upon the means to be used, not because they doubt the need for reform. Certainly no thoroughgoing reorganization plan can leave out of account the confused legal and administrative status of the independent regulatory commissions, even though no change be proposed in that status. Furthermore, some of these independent agencies are charged with the duty of administering federal regulatory statutes in fields in which the clashes of economic interest are so sharp that action must often be taken in an atmosphere of bitter and deep-rooted antagonism. This is true, at the time of writing, of the National Labor Relations Board, and in lesser degree of the Federal Trade Commission. Steady criticism is directed against the policies which these agencies are administering, against the way in which they are organized, and against the procedures which they employ. It is possible to judge the soundness of such criticism only if we have a thorough understanding of the nature of the independent regulatory commission as a regulatory device, the degree of flexibility possible in its internal administrative management, and the availability of other possible devices or procedures for doing the same work.

The problem is one which deeply concerns the states. While the onward march of federal centralization has increased the range of federal regulatory power over business and industry at the expense of the states, the states themselves have pushed forward the outposts of their regulatory power. They too have used the independent regulatory commission along with other administrative devices, and have thus created another important area in which full knowledge of the independent regulatory commission, its limitations and relations, is of great importance. The experience of the states can be made to throw light upon the broader problem presented, and effective analysis of the problem itself will aid the states.

The problem of the independent regulatory commission is challenging not only because of its intrinsic practical importance, but also because of its great complexity. This complexity arises in the first place from the number and variety of the powers which have been conferred upon these bodies. Not only do the clearly regulatory powers assigned to the independent commissions differ sharply in purpose and in method, but, as has already been stated, many incidental and even irrelevant duties have been given to these agencies. This may be made clearer by a brief summary of the chief types of power now possessed by our independent regulatory commissions, powers which in some cases have no descriptive names.

First, most of the commissions exercise what is called 'quasi-judicial' power. This is illustrated by the power of the Interstate Commerce Commission to fix just and reasonable railroad rates, and by the power of the Federal Trade Commission to issue cease and desist orders forbidding unfair competitive trade practices. The use of the term 'quasi,' for which the best synonym is 'not exactly,' is a confession of vagueness, an announcement that precise definition is impossible. The quasi-judicial function, however, is of vital importance in the administration of regulatory power. If it cannot be defined with precision, it can, at least, be explained in concrete terms. The term describes the application by administrative officers of a broadly stated legislative policy to concrete cases by a procedure patterned after that used by a court of law. Congress by statute enacts the policy that railroad rates shall be just and reasonable. It confers on the Interstate Commerce Commission the duty of determining what railroad rate in a particular situation and its surrounding circumstances is just and reasonable, and of making its determination by a procedure roughly judicial in character. In the same way the Federal Trade Commission Act announces the policy of banning 'unfair methods of competition' and directs the Federal Trade Commission to determine in concrete cases which acts of businessmen do constitute such unfair methods of doing business. The procedure required in both cases seeks to guarantee the fairness and objectivity of the judicial mind in dealing with the conflicting interests involved; but the inescapable vagueness and generality of the legislative standard or policy—i.e. 'just and reasonable' or 'unfair'—compel the regulatory body enforcing the law to exercise a discretion, to form a policy judgment, which, under our constitutional system, can not validly be conferred upon a judicial court. Most of the federal agencies covered in this study exercise in varying degrees some kind of quasi-judicial power. The Board of Governors of the Federal Reserve System is an exception. Its control, direct and indirect, over banking and currency is enormous; but that control is exercised not by any quasi-judicial procedure, but rather by the direct exercise by the board of certain fiscal and banking functions—a direct participation in certain phases of the activities to which the basic regulatory statute applies.

In the second place, probably every independent regulatory

agency exercises what is sometimes called 'quasi-legislative' power. This might also be called the power of 'sub-legislation.' For the purposes of our study this means the power to issue rules and regulations of a legislative nature which have the force of law. Thus the Interstate Commerce Commission issues rules requiring railroads engaged in interstate commerce to install a particular safety appliance on locomotives. Or the Securities and Exchange Commission issues elaborate rules under which information regarding corporate securities must be filed with the commission. In each case the basic statute must state with reasonable clearness the policy Congress is furthering, and must delegate to the agency the sub-legislative power. The issuance by the latter of the rules or regulations is regarded as merely filling in the details of the legislative policy embodied in the statute. This rule-making function is not confined to independent regulatory commissions. It is exercised in varying degree by nearly every major executive officer in the national government. It is a function indispensable to the process of modern administration.

Thirdly, some of the agencies under review exercise broad administrative or managerial powers, powers actually to conduct or closely direct the conduct of business operations. The important duties of the Board of Governors of the Federal Reserve System are of this variety and have already been mentioned. The United States Maritime Commission under the Act of 1936 administers the construction and operating subsidies given by the government to private shipping interests, and owns and operates the government's merchant fleet. These are business operations, and in many analogous situations they have been placed under the control, not of independent commissions, but of government-owned corporations.

In the fourth place, several of the independent regulatory agencies exercise functions which are purely executive. These usually take the form of the direct enforcement of penal statutes. The Interstate Commerce Commission not only promulgates many of our safety-appliance rules applicable to railroads, but also enforces them. Its agents search out violations and report them to the federal district attorneys, who institute prosecutions. The commission, in short, functions here in exactly the same way as do the agents of the Department of Justice in the enforcement of countless other penal statutes. It is a simple executive function.

A fifth function exercised by most of our federal regulatory bodies is inquisitorial—the function of investigation. Congress has armed these agencies with the authority to compel witnesses to testify and to produce documentary evidence. They may not be given the independent power to punish for contempt recalcitrant witnesses, but Congress usually allows them to ask the aid of a federal court in securing such evidence and the court furnishes the compulsion. These powers of investigation have been of tremendous importance in some cases. Some of the inquiries conducted by the Federal Trade Commission have had far-reaching consequences.

Finally, the commissions have often been charged with responsibility in the field of policy planning. They have been directed to carry on appropriate studies and to recommend to Congress new legislation or changes in existing laws. This power is usually conferred in general terms and authorizes the commission to make such proposals to Congress whenever it deems it desirable to do so. In other cases the mandate has been more specific. The Interstate Commerce Commission was directed to bring in after appropriate study specific proposals for consolidations of the railroads. The Federal Communications Commission was directed to report to Congress on a specific date such changes in the basic statute as the commission's experience led it to think desirable.

A second element of complexity is added to the independent regulatory commission problem by the fact that Congress has followed no consistent principle in assigning regulatory functions to independent agencies rather than to other units in the national government. There seems to be nothing about the regulatory job which makes it imperative that it be handled by the same kind of administrative body. Some forty regulatory statutes—of widely varying importance, it is true, but all regulatory—are administered by the Department of Agriculture. When the Packers and Stockyards Act was passed in 1921, its enforcement was placed in the hands of the Secretary of Agriculture, rather than with the Federal Trade Commission as was currently proposed, and that officer accordingly exercises, under the statute, powers analogous to those of the Interstate Commerce Commission and the Federal Trade Commission combined. Federal regulation of merchant shipping has never been very drastic, but it has been shunted about from one kind of administrative agency to another and back again. It was first given to the independent United States Shipping Board; later it was transferred by executive order, but with tacit Congressional approval, to the United States Shipping Board Bureau in the Department of Commerce. In 1936 it went to a newly created independent regulatory body, the United States Maritime Commission. In 1940 it was divided, and part went to the Interstate Commerce Commission and part remained with the Maritime Commission. The National Bituminous Coal Commission began life as an independent regulatory body, though with the rather ambiguous status of being 'in the Department of the Interior.' In 1939 that ambiguity of status was removed by an executive order which took away the commission's 'independence' and made it an integral unit in the Department of the Interior. This all suggests that the independent commission is only one of several ways in which regulatory functions may be implemented, and this leaves us with the problem of deciding under what conditions the independent commission, rather than another type of administrative unit, should be employed for this purpose.

The concrete problems raised by the independent regulatory commission as it exists today cluster around four major points. First, there are intensely interesting problems of a constitutional and legal nature. Viewed superficially the independent commission appears to be a complete negation of the orthodox constitutional doctrine of the separation of powers. To what extent, if any, is this true? Are there constitutional limits upon the use which may be made of the independent regulatory commission technique, or limits upon the kinds of powers which may validly be given to such agencies? To what extent and in accordance with what principles do the courts review the work of the commissions?

Second, very important practical problems result from the 'independence' of these regulatory agencies. In what sense and to what extent are they independent? To what extent are they responsible to Congress or to the President for what they do? Can they be made responsible for part of their work and retain complete independence with respect to the rest? Ought their independence to restrict the kinds of functions assigned to them? Can important determinations of policy be safely left to an independent agency? These questions may have vital importance. Here is an illustration. Under the Merchant Marine Act of 1936 the United States Maritime Commission has authority to authorize the transfer of ships from American to foreign registry. The commission is independent and its members can be removed from office by the President only for incompetence or misconduct. In time of peace the transfer of ships may be a fairly routine matter which may safely be left to an independent administrator. With the outbreak of war in Europe, however, it instantly became a matter intimately tied in with the nation's policy of neutrality, a policy determined in varying degrees by Congress and by the President. The commission in this situation sagaciously adapted its policy with reference to the transfer of American ships to foreign registry to the President's policy of neutrality. The question remains what could have been done, if anything, had the commission stubbornly insisted on transferring the ships over the President's protest. Many problems, perhaps less spectacular but equally arresting, grow out of the actual results of the independence of these regulatory agencies, and upon their relations with other departments of the government. Many of these problems have never been adequately explored.

A third problem concerns the merger in the hands of the independent regulatory bodies of powers which many critics and students have believed to be incompatible. Legislative, executive, and judicial powers, it is alleged, are combined in the commissions in violation of our American tradition of the separation of these powers as well as in violation of the principles of fair play. From the time of the debates on the Interstate Commerce Act in 1886 to the latest newspaper blast against the National Labor Relations Board, there has been no let-up in the attack on the independent commissions because of this merger of powers. That the problem is a real one is evidenced by the number and variety of concrete proposals which have been made to effect some kind of segregation of the regulatory function into its component parts and to take away from the commissions the powers that are not clearly regulatory. Whether any such segregation is possible, or desirable if possible, remains a matter of controversy after fifty years; and it would be even more difficult to secure any agreement upon the precise method for making such a segregation. These are problems upon which too much light cannot be thrown.

Finally, there are numerous problems relating to the actual structure and organization of the independent regulatory commissions as well as to the vitally important unsolved problem of commission personnel. How large ought a commission to be? How long should its members serve? Should it choose its own chairman or should he be chosen by the President? What internal divisions of labor in the commission would produce the best results? Ought there to be specific statutory qualifications and disqualifications for membership on the commission? These matters intimately concern the efficiency of the commission and merit careful study.

In thus summarizing the problems that fall within the scope of this study it should be stated that one important group of problems will not be dealt with save incidentally. These are the basic problems of social and economic policy which determine the concrete nature of the powers assigned to the commissions. We shall, in other words, deal with the Federal Trade Commission as an administrative body designed to perform a certain job; we shall not discuss or pass judgment on the question whether Congress was wise in giving to the Federal Trade Commission the particular powers which it now has. The question how far the federal government ought to go in subjecting business and industry to regulation lies outside the scope of this inquiry. That is a broad question of politics and economics. The study does deal, however, with the question of what administrative techniques and procedures are best adapted to the carrying out of any specific program of regulation on which the government decides to embark.

The present study undertakes to do certain definite things. A preliminary word may be said to indicate what these are, why they were chosen, and the method and relative emphasis with which each is handled. In the first place, it attempts to present a comprehensive and accurate survey of the legislative history of the independent regulatory commission movement. This story has never before been told. There are fragments here and there which throw light on the legislative histories of particular commissions, but there is no complete and accurate account of the commission movement as such. The history of a fifty-year development must hew rigidly to the line, and certain things have somewhat arbitrarily been excluded. The complete story of the regulatory commissions would comprise a very substantial part of the economic history of the United States for the last sixty years. No effort is here made to paint this broad picture, or to trace the evolution of the concrete economic policies which the independent regulatory agencies have been set up to administer. It has not been either possible or useful to present the whole story of the federal government's policy toward monopoly and unfair competition, merely because the Federal Trade Commission has been an important instrument in dealing with these problems. This broader historical background may be found in other writings. It is, furthermore, not wholly relevant to the general purpose of this study.

The historical material in this study is more the history of an idea and a method, and is presented to throw light on the origin and development of that idea and that method. It seeks to explain why Congress regarded the independent regulatory commission as a suitable device for handling the various jobs given to it. What did Congress and other responsible leaders think was the relation of these independent agencies to the other departments of government? What did they conceive their status in the constitutional system to be? Why have the independent regulatory commissions varied so widely in organization, in powers, and in their relations to the other agencies of government? Why were some tasks of government regulation given to independent commissions while other similar or analogous jobs were confided to bureaus or divisions in the executive departments? What, in general, did those responsible for setting up these agencies think about them and expect from them in the way of administrative service? How have the independent commissions been appraised by legislators who have had occasion to examine their work? What judgments have been expressed about them? What proposals have from time to time been made to alter their structure, their powers, or their procedure?

This historical study should have substantial value. It should have value as history, in so far as it tells a story which has not been told before. There is value, too, in presenting the views, conflicting as they have been, of legislative leaders groping with the vastly important problems bound up in the independent commissions. These men have often been men of ability, experience, and practical wisdom. What they thought about the agencies they were creating will throw important light upon the real nature of those agencies. Furthermore, the independent regulatory commission problem, after fifty-odd years, still remains a problem. Analysis and recital of the ideas, proposals, criticisms, and discussions which have emerged in the course of the legislative history of these commissions may easily aid somewhat in the solution of that problem.

There are, however, definite and inescapable limitations on the value of any such survey of the legislative history of an important movement. Ideas about administration which are fifty years old, thirty years old, or even twenty years old may easily lack any large intrinsic value. We are also faced with the fact that what Congress thought it was doing in creating some of these independent agencies has been rendered somewhat irrelevant by decisions of the Supreme Court holding that something quite different was actually done. Nor is there any accurate way of appraising the influence of speeches, committee reports, and debates upon the actual course of legislation. The views of a dominant majority may be presented with casual brevity, since their case is safely won. The views of a protesting minority defending a hopeless cause may be expressed with an elaboration and cogency which tend to exaggerate their actual influence. Finally, as every student knows, the only way to capture the real atmosphere of an important legislative debate is by reading the debate itself. There is no way of compensating for the loss involved in telling a second-hand tale and in the drastic compression required by limits of space. And the writer freely admits that the device used of presenting the substance of what was said in Congress and before legislative committees under more or less orderly subject-matter headings gives an impression of a coherence and thoroughness which were seldom there.

A second major division of the study puts on record the more important facts about the independent regulatory commissions as they now exist. The chapter on the Constitutional Status of the Independent Regulatory Commissions is a descriptive and analytical summary of the existing legal status of the commissions. It is not an argument for any particular legal theory nor does it attempt to demonstrate what the status of the commissions would have been (and perhaps ought to be) had the Supreme Court decided certain cases differently. There is also a rapid-fire summary of the highlights in a much more elaborate study by Professor James W. Fesler of the University of North Carolina, of the organization, relations, and procedure of the regulatory agencies in a selected group of states.

A third division of this study presents a bird's-eye view of those British administrative agencies and devices which have been set up to do work similar or roughly analogous to that assigned to our own independent regulatory commissions. Many of these British agencies, singly or in groups, have been studied in elaborate detail by English and American scholars and those studies are readily available. No attempt is made here to do over again this careful work, although these books and monographs have been freely used. What has been sought here is rather an evaluation of English experience in this field and an understanding of the objectives of English regulatory policy, the principles upon which it is set up, the structure and organization of the governmental units used and their relation to the rest of the English government, and the general methods and procedures employed. The material here presented was collected in the main in London, by the asking of countless questions and trespassing upon the time and patience of a very large number of public officials and scholars, who with unvarying courtesy put their experience and judgment in these matters at the writer's disposal. If this portion of the study is open to the charge of superficiality, it may be countered that it is the first systematic effort to focus on the American regulatory problem the methods and results of British experience.

The concluding part of the study is devoted to an analysis of certain basic problems relating to the independent regulatory commissions. In separate chapters are discussed the problems which grow out of the independence of the commissions, the merger in them of several kinds of powers, their relation to the important task of policy planning in the field, and their structure and personnel. In respect to each of these topics the experience in England and in this country is summarized, proposed changes are catalogued, and an effort is made to appraise the results of this complicated trial and error process and to venture some tentative conclusions.

Apart from the historical sections, the study here presented is frankly exploratory in nature. To have dealt exhaustively with all the matters touched upon would have required many volumes and many years. In a field in which the experimental method is being so openly employed it is much too early to expect definitive answers to many of the problems presented. But there is great gain in cataloguing such findings as may reasonably be made, in the hope that later studies may fill in the gaps and fortify or correct the conclusions.

In conclusion mention may be made of certain matters which have been excluded from this study even though they have relevance. In the first place, certain areas in the field have been left untouched because recent exhaustive studies have made further treatment superfluous. In the comprehensive and detailed studies of the executive agencies of government made by the Brookings Institution for the Byrd committee and published in 1937, there is an admirable summary of the organization and functions of these executive agencies, including the independent establishments. This places on record all the general facts about those parts of the executive branch of the federal government to which regulatory functions have been assigned. Here, for instance, can be found the things which one might wish to know about the agencies engaged in administering the forty-odd regulatory statutes confided to the Department of Agriculture. This was followed in 1938 by the publication of Dr. F. F. Blachly's *Working Papers on Administrative Adjudication,* prepared for the Senate Committee on the Judiciary. This presents a painstaking analysis of nearly one hundred federal administrative tribunals, setting out with respect to each its (a) legal basis, (b) organization, (c) functions, (d) procedures, (e) enforcement methods, and (f) appeals.[1] Finally, no attempt has been made to study with care the vastly important problems relating to the

1. See also the admirable study, *Federal Regulatory Action and Control,* by F. F. Blachly and Miriam E. Oatman, published by the Brookings Institution, 1940.

procedure of federal regulatory agencies and the judicial review of their work, since in 1939 there was set up the Attorney General's Committee on Administrative Procedure, which, under the direction of Professor Gellhorn, has made a most exhaustive inquiry in this field.[2]

It has, furthermore, been impossible to broaden this study to include an appraisal of the government-owned corporation (such as the TVA) as an instrument for carrying on some of the functions usually assigned to the regulatory commissions. Nor could there be included any treatment of the many important lending and spending agencies in the federal government, even though in a number of instances they exercise incidental functions which are regulatory in character.

2. S. Doc. 8, 77th Cong., 1st sess. (1941).

II

PRECEDENTS AND BACKGROUND—
STATE EXPERIENCE

REGULATORY commissions were not invented in 1887 when the Interstate Commerce Commission was created. That invention was the normal outgrowth of a broader state commission movement which dated back to the early nineteenth century. However, it was more than a new bud on an old branch. It was a new limb of such major importance that it pointed the whole tree in a new direction. The extension in 1887 of federal regulatory power to the nation's railroads was indeed an important exercise of economic control; but it was much more than that: it was a shift in the center of control in the federal system. The crucial problem in 1887 was not whether railroads ought to be regulated; it was whether the time had come for the national government to take over the task of regulation. The Interstate Commerce Commission was an innovation not because it was endowed with a new type of power, but because it represented a new location of power in the federal system.

When Congress approached the difficult task of establishing a federal regulatory commission in 1887, it had before it the diversified experience of more than twenty states in which somewhat similar commissions were then operating. It had also rather vague and not wholly accurate impressions of English experience in the field of railway control. Beginning in 1846 there had been a number of British experiments with commissions set up to deal with British railroads. But it is a fallacy to assume that lawmakers and statesmen always benefit from past experience and that existing precedents are fully known and

19

properly evaluated by them. It is hard to prove that any particular body of experience influenced legislators to pass a particular law; difficult to judge how much weight to attribute to past experience as against current ingenuity in the solution of any legislative problem. But in spite of these uncertainties it is useful to present a rough picture of what had been going on in the field of regulation by commissions which may have influenced Congress in setting up the Interstate Commerce Commission. We shall, therefore, explore the commission movement in the American states down to 1887, and mention the main facts relating to regulation of British railroads. These matters must be dealt with briefly, but it seems safe to assume that only the major facts could possibly have influenced federal regulatory policy.

Early State Experience with Commissions and with Administrative Regulation

The early history of the commission movement in the American states is bound up with the problem of railroad supervision and control. There was a limited and unspectacular body of experience in dealing with canals, but this experience was not carried over to railroads. Canals dropped into the background as the railroads expanded.

The attitude of the American state toward the railroad was at first one of encouragement and support. The railroad was a vital element in the broad program of public improvements which was to bind the country together and increase its prosperity. One or two states embarked upon programs of government ownership of railroads. These in the main were not successful and were ultimately dropped. But with unanimity and enthusiasm state legislatures granted charters and franchises to railroad corporations and subsidized by loans of money and credit these enterprises which were to do so much for the material welfare of the state.

It shortly became clear that this open-handed generosity upon the part of the states was being rewarded in many cases by callous disregard, if not outright exploitation, of the public interest. Some kind of regulation became imperative, and in the eastern states, particularly in New England, steps began to be taken in this direction. These early methods of regulation were both legislative and judicial. The legislatures began to embody increasingly sharp restrictions in the charters of railroad companies, restrictions which in some cases undertook to fix maximum railroad rates. Provisions in charters, however, failed to meet adequately the problems presented by railroad abuses. It was hard to foresee just what provisions ought to be included. At the same time, the granting of valuable rights to private corporations by special legislative act undermined official integrity and ushered in some of the most unsavory chapters in state political history. This legislative control of railroads was supplemented by a limited and rather routine judicial control which arose from the fact that the railroads were common carriers and subject as such to various common law restrictions and responsibilities. By the late '40's and early '50's most of the states, aware of the abuses incident to special charters, passed general laws under which railroads might be incorporated and their rights and obligations defined. The statutes were highly detailed, their enforcement was by action brought in the courts, and the results were far from adequate. Even with these general laws the pressure for the granting of special charters did not wholly abate, and in some states the practice of granting them was not wholly abandoned. Such efforts at railroad regulation were the results of legislative groping, attempts by legislative bodies to deal with a new and increasingly complicated problem. The results were far from satisfactory, and even before 1850 there emerged the beginnings of what we may call the commission movement, the setting up of occasional, somewhat embryonic commissions to aid the legislatures in the work of railroad control.

A number of factors inherent in the railroad problem itself account for the breakdown of direct legislative regulation by either special or general statutes. In the first place, railroad corporations, even in these early days, were relatively large and powerful. Their management was highly centralized and changes in their policies could be made quickly. The ordinary legislature had no expert knowledge of the railroad problem, and its clumsy attempts to deal with it could often be easily evaded by the railroads. Secondly, the railroad industry was undergoing rapid change and vast expansion. Neither special charters nor general laws could be kept up to date. They needed almost constant amendment in order to cope with the ever-shifting problems presented and with the rapidly changing railroad practices. Third, the general laws set up for railroad control were of necessity uniform in their provisions. They could not adjust their provisions to what Charles Francis Adams called 'the natural differences between railroad enterprises.' Not all railroads could successfully be treated alike. In short, twenty-odd years of experience made it abundantly clear that the job of railroad regulation could not be effectively handled by the legislature itself.

The early commissions just referred to were created to aid the legislature in dealing with certain *ad hoc* situations, and to give it necessary information which it could not secure by its own efforts. The functions of these early commissions fell into four groups. First, they were set up to supervise the carrying out of charter provisions: to see, in other words, whether a railroad was living up to the provisions of its charter. As early as 1832 Connecticut had granted a special railroad charter and had then created a special commission to assure compliance with its terms. In 1849 Connecticut set up a permanent commission for this purpose, the first permanent railroad commission to be established. Commissions charged with this duty of supervision were directed to report their investigations to the legislature and to make recommendations. Second, the commissions were given the important duty of inspecting the roads in the interests of safety. Early roads had in many instances been poorly built and accidents occurred with appalling frequency. In 1844 New Hampshire established the first commission definitely assigned to the job of safety inspection. Third, commissions were set up to arbitrate disputes between the railroads and others with whom they had dealings. These disputes related to such matters as the condemnation of land and the assessment of damages resulting from railroad construction. It seemed desirable to take these disputes out of the hands of the local courts, and accordingly *ad hoc* commissions were set up to do the work. Such a commission was created in New York as early as 1850. Finally, commissions were created in the hope of preventing discrimination in rates and services. Rhode Island set up a commission for this purpose in 1844. Usually, however, this function was not specifically assigned to the commissions but was more commonly merged in the general authority to investigate compliance with the terms of a charter.

Viewed generally, therefore, these earliest commissions were occasional, and created for the handling of special or *ad hoc* situations. They had a variety of functions, but mainly they were to serve as fact-finding agencies for the legislature and to handle tasks which that body had undertaken and in which it had failed. They were looked upon as agents of the legislature and not in any sense as part of the executive branch. There was no tendency to confer on the governor or any other state executive officer the powers of supervision assigned to these commissions. It should be remembered that this was a period in the development of state government in which the executive was still pretty well submerged under the dominating power and prestige of the state legislature. It may be noted that all of these early commissions, with the exception of the Vermont commission of 1855, were composed of more than one officer.

We may turn now to the emergence of permanent state commissions set up to deal with the railroad problem, a movement which may be placed roughly between 1869 and 1887. It is true that a few permanent commissions had been set up earlier, and it should have been easy to foresee that permanent bodies were going to be necessary to deal with the railroad problem. The disturbances incident to the Civil War probably delayed the emergence of more stable commissions. The coming of the permanent commissions did not, however, mean an end of experimentation. There was perhaps even more of it than before, for railroad development continued to present new and challenging problems. In the main the commissions tended to fall into two major groups. The first was the advisory or 'weak' commission, which appeared first in the New England states and tended to dominate the eastern picture; the second was the 'strong' or definitely regulatory commission, first set up in Illinois and utilized more extensively in the Middle West. Each of these made its contribution to the broader problem in which we are interested.

The advisory commissions in the East exercised no rate-making or other regulatory powers. It was probably natural that the scattered *ad hoc* bodies and the uni-functional agencies just mentioned should be replaced by one permanent commission to which all these tasks and problems could be assigned. It was also inevitable that the problem of railroad rates should force itself to the front. It was not a problem which could be indefinitely side-stepped. In 1869 Massachusetts created a railroad commission which served as a model for commissions of the advisory type. According to Hadley, the Massachusetts railroad system had by this time acquired a substantial degree of stability. 'Many abuses incident to a period of rapid growth had passed away, or were in a fair way to regulate themselves. These same abuses, in newer sections of the country, might baffle all attempts at regulation.'[1] Charles Francis Adams comments in the same vein on 'a more composed state of the public mind'[2] prevailing in the East, and these less acute and pressing situations probably explain why an advisory commission seemed adequate to the task of handling the Massachusetts railroad problem.

The Massachusetts commission had no real disciplinary power over the roads. This is far from saying, however, that its powers and influence were negligible. It had sweeping authority to investigate the financial and physical conditions of the railroads and to report its findings either to the legislature or to the attorney general for appropriate action. It had the power to determine what were just and reasonable railroad rates and to recommend these rates to the railroads. But it could not compel a railroad to adopt these rates, and the only sanction its recommendations had was that of public opinion. It had the authority to make reports to the legislature upon any phase of the railroad situation and to propose legislation. It was, in short, an 'arm of the legislature,' an agency set up to supply the legislature with detailed information and expert advice. It started its work under auspicious circumstances. Its three members were men who commanded public confidence. One of them, Charles Francis Adams, was one of the best-known figures in the railroad world. It was left undisturbed in its personnel, only two changes being made in nine years; and thus it was able to build up a body of experience and a sound tradition which greatly enhanced its prestige. In fact, as Hadley

1. A. T. Hadley, *Railroad Transportation* (1885), 138 f.
2. C. F. Adams, Jr., *Railroads: their Origin and Problems* (1878), 137.

pointed out, writing in 1885, 'It would be a mistake to suppose that because the system worked so well in Massachusetts, it must work equally well elsewhere.' [3] But the Massachusetts commission, with its early and marked success, proved an attractive model to other states struggling with the railroad problem.

By 1887 when the Interstate Commerce Commission was created, fifteen states had set up state railroad commissions of the advisory type. These states were Colorado, Connecticut, Iowa, Kentucky, Maine, Massachusetts, Michigan, Nebraska, New York, Ohio, Rhode Island, Vermont, Virginia, and Wisconsin, and the territory of Dakota. It will be seen that the list includes all of the New England states except New Hampshire, and a substantial scattering of other states. There were, of course, wide variations in the details of organization and function. But none of these commissions could fix a railroad rate and enforce it, or compel compliance with any other finding or order.

The second type of permanent state railroad commission was the 'strong' commission, a commission having legal power to fix rates and to enforce orders. The strong commission originated in the Middle West, where the railroad problem had become both unique and acute. The period of railroad expansion had continued in this section of the country longer and more actively than in the East. Sparsely settled agricultural states, relying upon railroad building to increase their population and their prosperity, extended generous favors to railroad companies. The result was the serious overdevelopment of the railroad system. Railroad lines penetrated into areas which could not possibly support them, and collapse seemed inevitable. To meet the acute financial difficulties in which they found themselves, the railroads resorted to unscrupulous cutthroat competition where competition existed, and to the charging of exorbitant rates where it did not. The middle-western farmer, dependent upon the railroad for the moving of his crops, found himself at its mercy. Out of his resentment came what was known as the Granger movement, the immediate objectives of which were the prompt and effective correction of the railroad abuses of which the farmer was the victim. Thus arose an organized group wielding great political power, acutely conscious of rail-

3. A. T. Hadley, op. cit. 138.

road misconduct and firmly bent upon drastic regulation. Here was a wholly different situation from that which had produced the much milder legislation creating the Massachusetts commission of 1869.

The state of Illinois was a pioneer in this drive for effective railroad control. In 1869 the legislature passed an Act which declared that rates should be 'just, reasonable, and uniform,' but the Act provided no special arrangement for its enforcement. In 1871 Illinois created its Board of Railroad and Warehouse Commissioners. This was a body of three, charged with the duty of enforcing the laws of the state relating to railroads and grain elevators and of reporting to the governor. Again no special procedure was set up for the enforcement of the commission's powers. Two years later, in 1873, this Act was substantially stiffened. The provisions forbidding discriminations in rates and services were sharpened and the Railroad and Warehouse Commission was given power to prosecute violations of the Act. Furthermore, the commission was directed to issue a schedule of maximum rates, and these rates were declared to be *prima facie* reasonable in all rate suits. Here was an important advance in the technique of railroad regulation, a precedent which was ultimately to form the basis for our permanent national system of railroad control.

When the Interstate Commerce Commission was created in 1887, ten states had set up 'strong' commissions of the Illinois type, possessing actual rate-making powers. These states were Alabama, California, Georgia, Illinois, Kansas, Minnesota, Mississippi, Missouri, New Hampshire, and South Carolina. Here again this type of commission was arrived at by a good deal of trial and error. The record shows much uncertainty from time to time and some fluctuation from 'weak' control to 'strong.' This is shown in the experience of three of the states which by 1887 had joined the Illinois group. Minnesota in 1871 established a railroad commissioner to collect statistics and enforce railroad laws, but left the task of fixing maximum rates to the legislature. This law had proved ineffective and in 1874 a board of railroad commissioners was set up, having powers of rate control and prosecution similar to those of the Illinois commission. The following year the pendulum swung back and this powerful board was replaced by a single elective commissioner who had power only to investigate and report. In 1885 Minnesota returned to a mandatory or strong commission. In 1874 Iowa passed a statute fixing maximum rates. The railroads themselves urged the creation of a commission and in 1878 a 'weak' commission was created with power to investigate, recommend action, and report to the governor and legislature. In 1888 Iowa established a commission with substantial power. Wisconsin in 1874 provided by statute a schedule of maximum rates and gave to a commission of three the power to reclassify freight and to reduce rates. Two years later this commission was abolished and a single commissioner with advisory powers was set up. It was not until 1907 that Wisconsin established a strong commission.

The powers of the strong commissions of this period fall into two groups. The first and most important of these was the power to set up reasonable and non-discriminatory rates. This power was enforceable in two ways. First, a rate so established was declared by law to be *prima facie* reasonable in any suit between the railroad and any shipper. Second, the attorney general, and in a few cases the commission itself, could bring suit to have these rates enforced. It is apparent from this that the rates thus set up by the commission were in all cases subject to review by the courts, and this came to be held an essential requirement of due process of law. The second group of powers which the strong commissions possessed comprised all of those the weak commissions had. They were to see if railroad laws were being enforced, to inspect railroads for safety, to investigate accidents, and to examine the accounts of railroad companies; they were also authorized to compel disputants and witnesses to testify under oath.

THE STATE COMMISSIONS IN 1887

We may comment briefly on the state commission movement in 1887:

In the first place, it had been characterized by a high degree of experimentation. It had not grown out of any *a priori* concept nor was it based upon any carefully worked out philosophy. It had run more or less counter to the orthodox conception of the doctrine of the separation of powers. It had moved along the lines deemed necessary to meet concrete situations. The problem presented by the railroads in our state and national economy had been shrewdly recognized to be a dynamic one, and American legislators had groped around for a dynamic solution to it.

In the second place, we have seen that two different lines of attack had emerged. One had resulted in the weak commission, the other in the strong commission, and in the year 1887 the relative merits of these two types of organization were being vigorously discussed. We can see now, what was less clear at that time, that the two types of commission really represented attacks upon two different problems. The advisory commission had been set up to deal with a much less acute need. If one compares the best type of advisory commission, as in Massachusetts, with the contemporary strong commission, one gets the impression that the former was more efficient and was securing much better results. These weak commissions had by their nature fewer difficulties; being less under fire they were better organized, had greater continuity, more experienced personnel, and less trouble with corrupt political pressure. They had friendlier relations with the railroads because the roads knew that the commission was legally powerless. They were forced to rely upon public opinion for the achievement of any results, and must, consequently, present their cases impartially and fairly. But they were bodies set up to study and inspect and not to act, and it is obvious that these weak commissions could not have met successfully the demands that were imposed upon the strong ones. The comparison lies, not between two forms of administrative organization, but between two economic philosophies. The strong commissions were assigned a difficult task which no one had yet learned how to do. They were created to accomplish results and to accomplish them promptly. They were obliged to deal with a situation in which powerful interests were lined up against each other and passions ran high. They did much of their work in an atmosphere of antagonism. They were regarded by the railroads as natural enemies to whom no co-operation was to be extended, and information frequently had to be extracted with great difficulty. All these circumstances, furthermore, contributed to make the problem of personnel on the commissions a peculiarly difficult one.

Charles Francis Adams summarizes the difficulties and short-comings of the strong commissions in the following paragraph:

It was from the beginning, therefore, obvious that no high stand-ard of success could reasonably be hoped for from the Granger com-missions. They were far too heavily handicapped. In the first place the executives of the states in selecting their members not infre-quently seemed to regard any antecedent familiarity with the rail-road system as a total disqualification. So afraid were they of a bias, that they sought out men whose minds were a blank. Farmers, land-surveyors, men of business and politicians were selected. There were, of course, exceptions to this remark, and some very competent men were appointed who did excellent work so long as they remained in office. But a long continuance in office was again looked upon as un-desirable, and these men were either speedily removed to make way for incompetents, or they voluntarily passed into the employ of the railroad corporations before they had fairly mastered the situation. Above and beyond all this, however, these commissions began their work in a false position, and they never extricated themselves from it. They were not judicial tribunals. They ever reflected the angry complexion of the movement out of which they had originated. They were where they were, not to study a difficult problem and to guide their steps by the light of investigation. Nothing of this sort was, as a rule, expected of them. On the contrary they were there to prosecute. The test of their performance of duty was to be sought in the degree of hostility they manifested to the railroad corpora-tions. In a word they represented force.

That under these circumstances they succeeded at all is the true cause of astonishment; not that they succeeded but partially. That they did succeed was due solely to the incorrigible folly and passion-ate love of fighting which seems inherent in the trained American railroad official.[4]

It must be remembered in reading Adams's indictment that he himself had been a leader in organizing the Massachusetts commission, was perhaps its outstanding member, and certainly its most conspicuous advocate. In comparing the two types of commissions we may safely conclude that the strong commission had fallen far short of solving its problems, but we must also remember that it was still struggling manfully with an exacting and difficult job which the advisory commission could never hope to do.

4. C. F. Adams, Jr., op. cit. 133 ff.

In the third place, one may observe certain general tendencies in the matter of the structure and organization of the state commissions. Along with an inevitable variety in matters of detail there was a striking similarity of major organizational features and, interestingly enough, very little difference in basic structure between the weak commissions and the strong. The commissions usually had three members, although in some cases, where powers were limited fairly closely to problems of inspection, a single commissioner was created. The terms of office varied from two to six years, and frequently the terms of members were staggered in order to secure continuity of membership. In more than half of the states the commissioners were appointed by the governor with the advice and consent of the state senate; in a few cases the legislature itself chose them; and as time went on there appeared a drift toward the popular election of commissioners. As a rule there were no specific provisions for removal of members of commissions of the weak type. Doubtless the question of removal was not important in the case of a body which had no drastic regulatory powers. In eight of the ten strong commissions, however, there were specific provisions with respect to removal, most of them designed to protect the independence of the commission. It should be remembered in this connection that the American state governor does not as a rule have a power to remove officers similar to that of the President of the United States. Such removal power as the governor has is given to him specifically by either the state constitution or the state statutes. Most of the states had special provisions fixing the qualifications of members of the commissions. It was customary to disqualify all persons who had any railroad interests, either as employees or officials. Charles Francis Adams criticized this rule on the ground that it excluded from membership on the state commissions all the persons who might possibly have expert railroad knowledge. Geographical distribution of members on the commissions was required in some states, and even more commonly the members had to be chosen from both political parties. In one or two cases a statute required special kinds of experience as, for example, legal training, business experience, or familiarity with railroad affairs. Finally, in the matter of annual reports the general rule was to have the state commission report to the governor, although in some instances the report was sent to the legislature.

In the fourth place, how did these new and hybrid agencies fit into the general structure of American state government? What relation did they have in practice and in legal theory to the legislature, the governor, and the courts? It is not easy to answer these questions with assurance. They are not questions which were asked when the commissions were set up. The problems involved were not clearly thought out, and the relations created were mixed and complex. We may, however, make some general observations on this important point:

The relation between the commission and the legislature was a fairly close one. The commission was set up to do a job which the legislature in many cases had tried to do and found impossible. It was a servant of the legislature in securing information for that body, and an adviser in making recommendations to it. The strong commissions had, furthermore, the important quasi-judicial function of applying legislative standards to concrete situations. By a legislative standard we mean a not-too-definite formulation of legislative policy to be applied to *ad hoc* situations. Thus these commissions were to determine 'just and reasonable rates' in the light of their detailed study of concrete railroad problems.

The relation of the commissions to the governor or to other executive officers was somewhat haphazard in character, and tended to become less and less close. The governor enjoyed in many states the power of appointment and a restricted power of removal. He had, however, no general authority and no state commission was in any sense responsible to him. Some of the functions of some of the commissions were, of course, executive or administrative in character, including wide powers of investigation and powers of instituting prosecutions; but while these are duties commonly given to a district attorney or to a state attorney general, when the commissions carried on these duties they did so wholly free of any supervision by the state governor.

The relation of the commissions to the courts varied with the degree of authority which the commission had over private rights. When the commission was advisory in character it naturally had no contact with the courts. When the commission was strong and had power to establish rates and issue orders, it was dependent upon the courts for the enforcement of its findings. These findings were often made *prima facie* correct, but even in this early period the courts were beginning to build up the present doctrine that due process of law requires the findings of an administrative tribunal to be subject to judicial review on all vital points affecting the interests of private parties.

The question has recently been widely discussed in connection with the federal regulatory commissions whether the federal legislature, in setting up a commission of this type and giving it a status of independence, has in any way trenched upon the executive department or usurped executive power. Early state experience throws no light on this point. The doctrine of the separation of powers has seldom been worked out in American state constitutions with the thoroughness that characterizes it in the federal Constitution. Furthermore, the separation of powers may be modified or even abandoned by any American state by constitutional amendment. Finally, in the American state of 1887 there was no executive department headed by a governor who had powers comparable to those of the President; on the contrary there were numerous executive and administrative officers, many of them elected directly by the people and none of them, as a rule, subject to any control by the state governor. The powers of the governor had been construed by the state courts with great rigidity. General clauses in state constitutions describing him as the chief executive of the state had been held to give him no concrete powers whatever. His were delegated powers, and powers not to be enlarged by implication. He had, as a rule, no power to see 'that the laws be faithfully executed,' and had such clauses existed in any state constitution they would have been interpreted as conferring no substantive power. The legislature, in short, was free to make and remake the concrete lines bounding the executive department, if there could be said to be an executive department. It could freely add or subtract agencies without any constitutional worry that it might be invading the governor's prerogative in this field, since he had no such prerogative. In fact, it is not impossible that the freedom with which state legislatures, under a very different set of legal conditions, could create administrative commissions and make them independent of the executive may have influenced Congress to assume powers which later, because of the President's much more sweeping range of executive authority, raised interesting and difficult questions of constitutional law. This, however, is speculation, and not history.

Returning to the general discussion of state commissions in 1887, it seems clear, in the fifth place, that the rapid multiplication of these agencies indicates a general acceptance in all parts of the country of the principle of commission regulation. It was natural, however, that there should be sharp differences of opinion about the relative merits of the weak and the strong commissions. Those wishing a minimum of railroad regulation very naturally favored the advisory commission. Chauncey M. Depew, president of the New York Central Railroad, was outspoken in his praise of the Massachusetts commission. In a speech made in 1886 he declared:

In Massachusetts, which gives us the most conspicuous example of State control that we have in this country, and where the problem has passed beyond the realm of experiment and is an established success, the powers of the commission are limited to investigation, recommendation, and report to the Legislature, except as to certain obvious powers. No scandal of any kind has ever attached to their action, no road has ever defied their recommendation, however extensive or burdensome it may have been. The people are entirely satisfied, the roads are doing reasonably well, and the railway problem in that State has entirely disappeared from politics.[5]

Depew's high opinion of the weak commission was shared, as we have seen, by the two leading writers on railroad problems, Charles Francis Adams and Arthur T. Hadley, men whose interests and experience had lain in the East where the weak commissions mainly prevailed; men who were understandably shocked by the drastic powers wielded by some of the western commissions.

Nevertheless it was beginning to be recognized that the weak commissions, however well they might be working, were not going to be permanently satisfactory. Railroad abuses were not being effectually dealt with. The public interest was not being adequately protected. Corruption and political pressure prevailed in some of the states and some of the commissions

5. *The New York Times,* Dec. 17, 1886, p. 1, col. 3.

appeared to be dominated by the railroads. We may sum up the current opinion of 1887 on commissions by saying that they had won general acceptance as a mode of attack on the problem of railroad regulation, but that most of the major problems of functions, structure, and procedure had still to be worked out.

Finally, what influence did this experience with state commissions have upon Congress? Obviously this is extremely difficult to measure. It was unquestionably important in moving Congress in the direction of regulation by commission. Congress could hardly ignore the varying experience of twenty-five states dealing more or less actively with the railroad problem through commissions. It is not safe, however, to generalize on the influence of particular forms of state commission organization, power, or procedure. It is interesting to note that Senator Cullom, chairman of the Senate committee responsible for the Interstate Commerce Act of 1887, had been Speaker of the House of Representatives in Illinois in 1873 and had taken a keen interest in the work of the Illinois Railroad and Warehouse Commission. His powerful influence was behind the creation of a federal commission. It may also be observed that Mr. Reagan, the leader of the forces for railroad control in the House of Representatives, was bitterly opposed to the creation of a federal regulatory commission for that purpose. Reagan was congressman from Texas and in 1887 Texas had no state railroad commission.

THE INFLUENCE OF BRITISH EXPERIENCE WITH RAILWAY REGULATION

Parallel developments in the field of railroad regulation had been going on in Great Britain.[6] What influence, if any, did they have upon the shaping of our own policy and methods in the same field?

We may first summarize what these developments had been. In 1840 and in 1842 the British Board of Trade was given some limited powers over English railways. In 1846 Parliament created a commission of five persons to examine proposed railway amalgamations, encourage competitive schemes, and take over

6. See *infra*, 510 ff., for a more elaborate analysis of British experience.

the limited supervisory powers of the Board of Trade. This first British commission appears to have failed miserably. It was abolished in 1851 and the Board of Trade was again given authority over the problem. A Royal Commission to investigate the railway situation reported in 1865, but it made no constructive proposals nor did it intimate that the situation called for any. It expressed an opinion that there would be no substantial changes in the field of railway control for a considerable period of time. In 1873 Parliament passed the Regulation of Railways Act, which created the Railway Commissioners. This board of commissioners was given certain very limited powers over the railways, but it, too, proved to be inadequate and unsatisfactory. As Hadley described it in 1885, 'It has power enough to annoy the railroads, and not power enough to help the public efficiently.' [7] Another Royal Commission, reporting in 1882, exposed the obvious shortcomings of the arrangement, and in 1888, the year after the enactment of our own Interstate Commerce Act, Parliament created the Railway and Canal Commission.

What influence did this not very inspiring record have upon the American states as they groped for a solution of their own railroad problems? It seems fairly clear that the influence was negligible. New Hampshire created a commission to inspect railroads in the interests of safety in 1844, two years before the first English commission was set up. It is unlikely that the New Hampshire legislature knew anything about, or was influenced by, the previous activities of the British Board of Trade, and one is inclined to feel that American intelligence could produce the idea that railroads should be safe for the traveling public without borrowing it from England. It has been suggested that the report of the British Royal Commission of 1865 influenced the passage of the Massachusetts Act of 1869. There is no actual evidence that this is true. The report, as we have seen, was not constructive or particularly informing, nor did it propose the establishment of a new British commission. Most of the powers given to the Massachusetts commission in 1869 had been exercised earlier in some form or other, and it was not until 1873 that England created a commission even remotely similar to

7. A. T. Hadley, op. cit. 173.

that of Massachusetts. Charles Francis Adams was perhaps the most distinguished and voluminous writer on railway problems during this period. He was familiar with British experience. At the same time most of his writing was done after 1870 so that what he had to say about British railway regulation could hardly have influenced a state commission movement which was already well established. In short, it would appear that the state commissions set up to deal with railroad problems were created in response to local needs to deal with local problems. There is no convincing evidence that the movement was influenced by British experience.

Congress was more exposed to the influence of English precedents than were the early state legislatures. By the time Congress had come to grips with the problem of railroad control on a national scale, British experiments in that field had been going on for a substantial period of time and had attracted attention on this side of the Atlantic. The writings of men like Adams and Hadley, both of whom had written accounts of English railway regulation, would undoubtedly be part of the evidence which at least some members of Congress would consider. The fact that a good deal of Adams's description of British experience was far from accurate and presented British achievements in a much more favorable light than they deserved would not, of course, diminish the influence of the British precedents which he described. Great Britain had established a commission to deal with its railway problem and that single fact would by itself carry weight with the American Congress. But there is no evidence by which to measure the extent of that influence. It seems reasonable to conclude that the members of Congress, all of whom came from American states, would be more actively influenced by the fact that twenty-five of those states had created railroad commissions of one sort or another, commissions the character and functioning of which they knew first hand, than by the fact that England had created a railway commission about which their ideas were necessarily vague.

III

THE INTERSTATE COMMERCE
COMMISSION

A. The Railroad Problem of 1887

THE emergence and growth of the Interstate Commerce Commission can be understood and appraised only against the background of the vitally important railroad problem which the commission was created to meet. This problem can be briefly sketched. Railroads began in the United States in the 1830's. They presented at first a state rather than a federal problem, and a problem, furthermore, not of regulation but of promotion. Early state legislatures encouraged railroad construction by liberal company charters, loans of money, and grants of land. The federal government paid little or no attention to railroads until the Civil War, when its policy also became one of promoting railroad expansion. This state and federal generosity, unaccompanied by any effective disciplinary restrictions, generated serious abuses in the railroad industry. These abuses were accentuated in volume and variety by the ruinous collapse of the railroad construction boom in the late '60's and '70's. Overexpansion in railroad building produced this collapse, and there ensued an era of cutthroat competition among the railroads, carried on by every objectionable practice which ingenuity could devise. In reporting to the Senate in 1886, the famous Cullom committee [1] presented eighteen 'causes of complaint' against the railroads. Without setting forth all the refinements of this indictment, it is enough to say that railroad rates were in many cases exorbitant, that these rates were not matters of

1. S. Rept. 46, 49th Cong., 1st sess. (1886).

public record, that they fluctuated at the will of the carriers, that discrimination in rates and service was ruthlessly indulged in, that this discrimination was directed not only against shippers in the same territory but also against localities, that rebates and other illicit forms of unfair competition were resorted to, that pooling and monopoly were unrestrained, that the problem of long and short hauls had created vital inequalities, and that through their vicious practices the railroads were contributing to the growth of industrial monopoly in other fields.

These abuses did not arise all at once, but they became acute long before effective federal regulation was thought of. We have already mentioned the efforts of the various states to deal with the railroad problem, and have described the state railroad commissions set up for this purpose, ranging from the weak advisory commissions of Massachusetts and New York to the powerful and belligerent commissions in the Granger states of the Middle West.

The railroad problem, however, extended far beyond the reaches of state power. It was by its very nature an interstate problem and demanded federal control. In 1877 the Supreme Court in the Peik case [2] had intimated that as long as Congress did nothing about railroad rates the states might regulate interstate railroad business within their own borders, even though interstate commerce was thereby affected. Even within the narrow lines thus drawn, state power fell far short of giving effective relief; and in 1886 in the famous Wabash case [3] the Supreme Court decided with bluntness and finality that the states could not regulate interstate railroad traffic within their own limits even in the absence of Congressional regulation. Federal legislation to deal with the whole broad problem of interstate railroad transportation had been simmering for a dozen years. The Wabash decision injected into the picture what someone has called the categorical imperative. Its precise and immediate effect upon Congressional leaders remains in doubt; but it made federal regulation clearly imperative, and the Interstate Commerce Act of 1887 was passed within a few months.

2. *Peik* v. *Chicago & N. W. Ry. Co.,* 94 U.S. 164 (1877).
3. *Wabash, St. L. & P. R.* v. *Illinois,* 118 U.S. 557 (1886).

B. STAGES IN THE GROWTH OF THE STRUCTURE AND POWERS OF THE INTERSTATE COMMERCE COMMISSION

In tracing the legislative history of the Interstate Commerce Commission it will be convenient to have a framework upon which to hang the story. While more than thirty amendments have been added to the original Interstate Commerce Act of 1887 and many separate laws affecting the railroads have been passed, the evolution of the commission itself may be recorded in terms of six major legislative debates and the statutes in which they culminated. These will be listed below, and then discussed in detail.

The Interstate Commerce Act of 1887. The original Act of 1887 did two things: it forbade certain objectionable railroad practices such as rate discriminations, rebating, pooling, and the charging of unjust and unreasonable rates; and it created the Interstate Commerce Commission to aid in the enforcement of these prohibitions. The commission had no power to fix a railroad rate. It could, however, upon complaints duly filed, find a rate to be unreasonable and unjust, issue an order against it, and then seek from the courts their aid in enforcing its order.

The Hepburn Act of 1906. This important statute rehabilitated the weakened commission, which had been pretty well emasculated by various Supreme Court decisions interpreting its powers. It gave the commission power to establish joint rates, and to fix a reasonable rate upon complaint that rates were too high. The rate orders of the commission were made presumptively correct, were made immediately effective, and could be set aside only by court injunction upon complaint of the carriers.

The Mann-Elkins Act of 1910—*Commerce Court.* The rate power of the commission was extended by this law to all rates. The commission could suspend new rates announced by a railroad, and the carrier must assume the burden of proving such rates to be reasonable. A Commerce Court was created to hear all appeals from the orders of the commission.

War-Time Control of Railroads—1918. Under emergency war legislation the government took over the operation of

American railroads and by the Act of 1918 the President was empowered to fix rates subject to review by the Interstate Commerce Commission.

The Transportation Act of 1920. This Act undertook quite frankly to unify the entire railroad system of the country. The Interstate Commerce Commission was given power to initiate new rates and was charged with the duty of seeing that the new rate structures were such as to produce a self-sustaining railroad system. It could establish joint rates and minimum rates. The famous recapture clause was included. State discriminations against interstate commerce by rail were forbidden, and the commission was authorized to prepare far-reaching plans for railroad consolidations.

The Emergency Transportation Act of 1933 *and Subsequent Amendments.* The Act of 1933 sought to pull the railroads out of the depression. The methods employed to accomplish this were the elimination of overlapping services, the establishment of the joint use of facilities, the repeal of the unworkable recapture clause, and the formulation of far-reaching plans for future development. It set up on an experimental basis the Co-ordinator of Transportation, who was given important responsibilities relating to the unification of the railroad system and the elimination of some of the more serious results of competition. The Federal Communications Act of 1934 relieved the Interstate Commerce Commission of its jurisdiction over the telephone and telegraph, while the Motor Carrier Act of 1935 gave to the commission the vastly important and complicated job of regulating interstate commerce by motor vehicles. In 1940 domestic water carriers were put under its jurisdiction.

We now take up these major phases in the establishment and development of the commission and summarize the legislative history bearing upon each one.

C. SETTING UP THE COMMISSION—THE ACT OF 1887

1. STEPS IN THE LEGISLATIVE HISTORY OF THE ACT

The Act of 1887 [4] was the culmination of a demand for legislation extending back nearly twenty years. Between 1868 and

---

4. Act of Feb. 4, 1887, 24 Stat. at L. 379.

1886 more than 150 bills were introduced in Congress providing for some variety of federal control over railroads. The idea that this control should be exercised by some sort of federal commission appeared as early as 1871 in the Cook bill, in the House, providing for a railroad bureau. In 1873 the Hawley bill proposed a federal commission to collect information and recommend legislation relating to railroads. In the same year Senator Windom and Representative Negley introduced other bills providing for commissions. During nearly every session thereafter such bills were introduced. Finally, in 1874 the House passed the McCrary bill. This bill utilized common law principles as a basis of railroad regulation. It forbade unreasonable and extortionate rates and it provided for the creation of a commission of nine, appointed by the President, to investigate and prepare schedules of maximum rates, to secure necessary relevant information by the calling of witnesses, to watch for violations of the law, and to institute suits in court for its enforcement.

The McCrary bill failed to pass the Senate. While the impact of the Granger drive for effective railroad regulation was very strong, and it looked for a time as though some sort of federal legislation would be forced through Congress, the Senate managed to side-step the issue. It did this by creating a select committee under the chairmanship of Senator Windom to investigate and report on transportation routes to the seaboard. In 1874 the Windom committee brought in a somewhat conservative set of proposals.[5] It asserted the existence of federal power to regulate interstate railroads but doubted the wisdom of its drastic use. It emphasized the value of competition in the railroad industry. It proposed the establishment of a bureau of commerce in one of the executive departments, to serve as a fact-finding agency to provide Congress with the information necessary to intelligent legislation. The railroads would be required to report relevant information once a year. The committee also proposed a government-owned railroad to provide a yardstick for the fixing of railroad rates. No action was taken upon the report.

The legislative drive which culminated in the passage of the

5. S. Rept. 307, 43d Cong., 1st sess. (1874).

Act of 1887 may be said to begin with the Reagan bill,[6] which passed the House in 1878 by a vote of 139 to 104, but which died in a Senate committee. Judge Reagan, from Texas, introduced this bill with changes and improvements every year thereafter through 1886. It was modeled upon earlier proposals. It forbade discriminations and rebates; it contained a strong prohibition against pooling, and a rigid long-and-short-haul clause; it required the posting of all railroad rates; and it set up heavy penalties for violations of the Act. It did not provide for a commission but relied upon ordinary court process for its enforcement. The Reagan bill did not contemplate the fixing of rates. It sought merely to put an end to objectionable competitive practices which had come to be serious abuses.

While Judge Reagan was able over a period of years to solidify his leadership of the House on this railroad legislation, he met temporary setbacks. In 1882 the House Committee on Interstate and Foreign Commerce brought in a report[7] which rejected the major provisions of the Reagan bill. It stated that of the thirteen railroad bills before it, at least half proposed some kind of commission, and it urged the creation of a board of three commissioners 'as a branch of the Interior Department.' Its reasons for doing so will be discussed later on.[8] This commission was to have power to investigate and to make findings and reports. It had no power to enforce its findings but could merely make public and report to Congress refusal by the carriers to obey them. It was, in other words, an advisory or weak commission, patterned after those of Massachusetts and New York. Judge Reagan filed a minority report attacking the proposals of the committee, and reintroduced his own somewhat modified bill. The House rejected the report of its committee and again passed the Reagan bill.[9]

In the meantime the Senate had not ignored the railroad problem. In 1883 Senator Cullom of Illinois introduced a bill[10] providing for a federal railroad commission. The Cullom bill did not contain the specific and drastic prohibitions of the

6. H.R. 3547, 45th Cong., 2d sess. (1878).
7. H. Rept. 1399, 47th Cong., 1st sess. (1882).
8. *Infra,* 55.
9. H.R. 5461, 48th Cong., 2d sess. (1884).
10. S. 840, 48th Cong., 1st sess. (1883).

Reagan bill, but set up much more generally stated standards to be applied to railroad practices and gave the administration of these to the proposed federal commission. Pooling, for example, was not absolutely forbidden, but pooling agreements could be lawfully made only under commission supervision. The Senate was by no means enthusiastic over the Cullom bill and its committee on commerce returned an adverse report. However, the bill passed the Senate in January 1885.

Thus there existed a deadlock between the two houses, which legislative leaders saw small chance of breaking. The Senate demanded a federal regulatory railroad commission; the House vigorously opposed the whole commission idea. In 1885 Senator Cullom, to strengthen his position, induced the Senate to create a select committee of five members under his chairmanship to explore the whole controversial problem and bring in a report. This body is commonly referred to as the Cullom committee and its report as the Cullom report.[11] The committee took its task seriously. It sent out to railroads, business leaders, and other interested parties an elaborate questionnaire. It traveled about, it conducted hearings in a number of important cities, and in 1886 it presented its report. The views presented in its hearings and expressed in its report will be discussed later.[12] The Cullom report was accompanied by a bill [13] embodying the committee's recommendations. This bill did not materially differ from the original Cullom bill; and while we cannot know the extent to which the whole Cullom inquiry was loaded in favor of Senator Cullom's own views, the fact remains that those views prevailed. Though delayed by a strong opposition, the Cullom bill passed the Senate in 1886 by a vote of 47 to 4. The House referred the Cullom bill to its Committee on Interstate and Foreign Commerce, of which Judge Reagan was chairman. This committee promptly substituted the Reagan bill for the Cullom bill, and reported it back to the House, which passed it by a vote of 192 to 41. The deadlock between the two houses, much more acute than before, was referred to a conference committee, which set about what seemed to be the hopeless task of working out a compromise. When Congress ad-

11. *Supra*, note 1.   13. S. 1532, 49th Cong., 1st sess. (1886).
12. *Infra*, 46 ff.

journed in the summer of 1886 little or no progress had been made in this direction.

In October 1886 the Supreme Court handed down its decision in the Wabash case, already referred to.[14] The Court announced in substance that the states must keep their hands off interstate railroad regulation even though Congress had not succeeded in setting up any regulation of its own. Since 75 per cent of the railroad business of the country was interstate in character, this meant that only a minor fraction of it could be validly regulated unless Congress should act. Commissioner Aitchison draws attention to the fact that earlier in 1886, in the Railroad Commission cases,[15] the Court had 'recognized as consonant with the Constitution a regulatory scheme which involved creation of a regulatory commission, charged with the duty of supervision of railroads.'[16] Though the case dealt with state commissions, it gave the regulatory-commission technique a clean bill of health. These two important decisions exerted a profound influence upon the conferees struggling to effect a legislative compromise between the Senate and House bills.

On December 15, 1886, the conference committee reported back to each house a complete bill representing concessions from both sides. The Senate conferees had accepted the rigid anti-pooling provisions of the Reagan bill and certain other sharply drawn prohibitions. The House conferees accepted an interstate commerce commission as a proper agency for the administration of the Act and also a more flexible provision with regard to long and short hauls. The conference report took the railroads completely by surprise. They had grown so accustomed to the deadlock between House and Senate that the possibility of an agreement had ceased to worry them. They at once brought terrific pressure to bear to defeat the bill, but public opinion, aroused by the crisis created by the Wabash decision, demanded action. Early in 1887 the Senate passed the bill by a vote of 43 to 15 with 17 Senators absent, and the House passed it by a vote of 219 to 41 with 58 absent. President Cleveland signed it on February 4, 1887.

14. *Supra,* 38
15. 116 U.S. 307 (1886).
16. C. B. Aitchison, 'The Evolution of the Interstate Commerce Act: 1887-1937,' *George Washington Law Review,* vol. v (March 1937), p. 300, note 27.

2. TOPICS AND ISSUES IN HEARINGS AND DEBATES

Following are the main ideas presented upon the major issues and problems that emerged during the legislative proceedings which produced our first federal regulatory commission.

a. *Shall there be a railroad commission?—Legislative versus administrative regulation*

The first major problem and also the last which confronted those working for the federal regulation of railways was whether or not a commission should be set up to administer the law. It was generally agreed that federal control had become imperative, but those supporting such control were divided into two camps. The first, led by Judge Reagan of Texas, the chairman of the House Committee on Interstate and Foreign Commerce, demanded drastic regulation by statute to be enforced directly by the Department of Justice and the courts. Reagan was able to carry the House with him down to the very last. The other group, headed by Senator Cullom, a former governor of Illinois, insisted that federal regulation of railways should be administered through a commission set up for that purpose. This vital difference of opinion persisted throughout the entire period of discussion and was only adjusted, as we have seen, in conference committee a few weeks before the actual passage of the Act of 1887. The long and full discussions make clear the opinions held with regard to the independent commission as a technique for regulation. It is interesting to note that when Congress three years later passed the Sherman Antitrust Act [17] it did not set up an independent commission to aid in its enforcement. It will be well to bear in mind, further, that those who wanted a commission did not agree in wanting the same kind of commission.

The arguments and influences which supported the setting up of a commission may be grouped roughly under six headings. In the first place, a commission would provide flexible and expert administration of railroad regulation. The House committee which reported in 1882 sharply criticized the attempt 'to

17. *Infra*, 177.

solve the problem by means of iron-clad rules and special legislation.'[18] The witnesses before that committee testified to the
'vastness and intricacy' and 'complexity' of the railroad business
and urged that it would be impossible to deal effectively with
it by the simple and traditional mechanism of passing penal
laws and enforcing them by court process. The same view had
been expressed before the Cullom committee. Many problems
of railroad regulation were both vague and complex, and these
would be much better handled by a body of experts. Railroad
statutes ought to embody general standards of conduct and the
commission should be charged with the delicate task of administering those standards. This whole position was well summed
up in the House debate in 1886 by Mr. Hitt of Illinois:

> There is a softening discretion allowed to the commissioners by
> the Cullom bill, and it is the better for it . . . How much better
> this is than to fix in advance by inflexible law the whole body of
> rules to govern the most complex business known to our civilization
> and the most extensive, involving the largest amount of property
> and the greatest number of individual interests in the whole world.
> It is well to have five wise, able, experienced men of reputation,
> commanding general confidence, clothed with a limited discretion
> in applying and enforcing a law that touches every man and every
> interest so closely.[19]

A second advantage of the commission lay in the field of
policy planning. It would serve as an expert body to aid Congress in formulating its legislative policy toward the railroad
industry. This point was urged vigorously and often. The experimental nature of the whole problem was recognized on
every hand. Congress was not equipped to inform itself on the
intricacies of the subject, but a continuing administrative body
could accumulate experience and ideas which could be passed
along in the form of legislative recommendations. The advantage of this had been emphasized in 1874 by the Windom
committee, which had declared that one of the purposes of a
commission would be 'the procuring and laying before Congress
and the country such complete and reliable information concerning the business of transportation and the wants of commerce, as will enable Congress to legislate intelligently upon

18. *Supra,* note 7, op. cit. vol. v, 2.
19. 17 Cong. Rec. 7290.

the subject.' [20] The same view had been taken by the House committee in 1882. Charles Francis Adams had declared before the Cullom committee in 1885:

I have always thought that if Congress would provide for a commission of men who were at once honest, intelligent and experienced, whose business it should be to observe this question very much as a physician would observe the progress of disease, the results of their observations might be of value in leading gradually to the building up of legislation . . .[21]

He was supported by another witness who declared:

. . . We believe the railroad question is comparatively in its infancy and is an exceedingly complex one. We believe that the laws which will ultimately govern it have hardly begun to come to the surface, and that those laws would be evolved and made equal more quickly through a commission whose attention would be directed to the examination of complaints and the suggestion of remedies than by any method now in vogue.[22]

It was urged particularly that specific legislative action with regard to the difficult problem of long and short hauls might well wait upon the experience and recommendations of a commission. The whole case for a commission as a planning agency was admirably presented by the minority of the House committee in 1886 in its protest against the Reagan bill and its plea for the passage of the Cullom bill. It said:

It is the province of legislators to ascertain by intelligent experience the legislation required, and that experience can best be secured through the proposed commission. It should be a permanently-established bureau of an appropriate department; should be composed of the ablest men of the country; salaries should be large enough to attract men from the very highest and most lucrative positions of the varied business life of our citizens . . .

We desire to impress the House with our implicit belief in the present advantage of a board of interstate-commerce commissioners. We ask you to defer radical legislation until we have tried the commission, which, with powers to hear grievances, will also be required to report annually to Congress, and to suggest from time to time

20. *Supra,* note 5, op. cit. vol. I, 241.
21. *Supra,* note 1, op. cit. Part II, 1208.
22. Wm. B. Dean, St. Paul Jobbers Union, ibid. 1292.

the legislation necessary to create harmony between shippers and transporters.[23]

In the third place, a commission would provide a protector against the railroads both for the public and for shippers. It was urged before the Cullom committee that the individual shipper was often quite incapable of protecting his rights. He had small means and little influence. The railroads, if attacked in court, could rally to their defense unlimited resources and could bring about delays which were costly and even ruinous to small litigants. A commission set up to act upon complaints would protect the rights of those whose resources left them otherwise defenseless. This argument loomed large in the House and Senate debates in 1886. As one congressman graphically put it, 'Pygmies do not invite giants to combat'; [24] and without aid the small shipper was at the mercy of the railroads. Mr. Hepburn of Iowa thus described the shipper's position:

> . . . He stands there alone, weak and poor and ignorant though he may be, with a ten-dollar case or a one-hundred-dollar case. He must make his own case against a wealthy corporation. He must do that, too, without technical knowledge of the matters litigated. He has no witnesses who are better informed than himself. The witnesses which must establish his case are the experts that belong to the other side of the question. The employés of the carrier are the only experts he can secure.[25]

A federal commission set up to handle shippers' complaints would serve therefore as 'the poor man's court.' [26] Mr. La Follette, then in the House, said:

> . . . Few indeed dare enter into litigation with railways . . . Those who can afford to fight the railways are those usually who enjoy their favor . . .
> To meet this necessity the bill provides for the creation of a commission . . . Every citizen of the United States is given the right to present his grievance and have his case tried without the attendant cost which now practically closes the courts to him.[27]

23. 17 Cong. Rec. 7285.
24. Rep. Rowell, Ill., ibid. Appendix, 444.
25. Ibid. 457.
26. Rep. Hermann, Ore., 18 Cong. Rec., Appendix, 35.
27. Ibid. 187.

Mr. Peters of Kansas emphasized particularly that no public agency was in a position to secure accurate statistical information about the railroads:

But the grand part of this bill, to my mind, is the commissioner part of it . . . Railroads have employed statisticians and managers and lawyers to look up the statistics of this great transportation question from the railroad side of the case. But the people have never had any parties under their own control or in their employ exclusively for the purpose of looking up the facts of the transportation question from their side of the case. That is just what this commissioner system will give to them . . .[28]

It was urged in the fourth place that an administrative commission would serve as an arbitral body to adjust the conflicting interests of the railroads themselves. This advantage was pointed out by the railroads' own witnesses before the Cullom committee. The carriers were suffering acutely from the ruinous consequences of cutthroat competition. Many of them looked with no disfavor upon a tribunal which would force that competition onto a higher plane.

In the fifth place, a commission would render valuable service to the courts. It was nowhere suggested that the commission should exercise any final regulatory power. It would, however, present expert findings of fact upon which its tentative orders would be based and upon which the courts might rely when the cases came to them for final decision. The chairman of the New York Railway Commission testified before the Cullom committee on this point:

There are many who believe that a new and distinct tribunal needs to be created for the determination of cases involving transportation, labor, telegraph, telephone, and such like questions, with an appeal from the decision thereof to the Supreme Court. There are serious objections to such an increase of the judicial department of the Government. It may come in the future, but it is at present unnecessary. As has been shown, the fault lies neither in the common law nor in the courts; the one needs only to be clearly declared as the law with some supplementary provisions growing out of the changed aspects of the transportation question in modern times; the other should have the help of a board with time and opportunity to unravel and clearly present the facts.[29]

28. 18 Cong. Rec. 860. 29. *Supra,* note 1, op. cit. Part I, Appendix, 23.

Finally, the experience of the American states and of England was weighted in favor of a commission. As we have seen, railroad commissions of various kinds existed already in some twenty-five states, and members in both House and Senate were familiar with them. The success of the weak Massachusetts commission under the leadership of Charles Francis Adams was impressive. Senator Cullom as governor of Illinois had had intimate experience with commission regulation of Illinois railways and Illinois congressmen took pride in the successful operation in their state of the strong commission. The belief prevailed, also, that in England railroad regulation had moved successfully along the same lines. This was not the case; but the ineffectiveness of the English tribunal established in 1873 was not fully appreciated even by the British public, and knowledge of its workings was still more vague and inaccurate over here, as the comments in the Congressional debates show. However, it was less important that British railway regulation had not been, in fact, very successful than that it was currently believed in Congress that British experience justified commission regulation.

The major arguments against the creation of a commission may also be listed under six headings. First, a commission would soften the force of statutory regulation, since it would have broad powers to suspend or abrogate the law. Judge Reagan and his supporters did not wish railroad regulation to be flexible. They wished it to be specific, rigid, and drastic. They looked with distrust upon any agency to which might be confided any discretion in softening or lightening the force of these rigorous penal provisions. This position had been presented to the Cullom committee by the representatives of the Grange:

> The people want no board of railroad commissioners. They want just and wholesome laws, with well defined provisions for enforcing them. Several of the States have created 'commissions,' but with unsatisfactory results. The people prefer to trust the courts rather than a commission.[30]

> We want an absolute law, if you can consistently give it to us, and we do not want our justice strained through a commission, because our experience with a commission . . . is that they are not only worthless, but worse than worthless.[31]

30. Ibid. 109.   31. Ibid. Part II, 1284.

In the House debate this argument was urged with great vigor. Mr. Grosvenor of Ohio declared:

. . . They [the commission] are to have more power than has the President of the United States—more power for evil or good than has the Congress of the United States; for they may do what neither the President nor Congress may do; they may suspend the operation of law; they may enforce the operation of law upon one man and withhold its operation from another. They may give whatever is good of this law to one section of the country and deprive another section of its benefits.[32]

Mr. Campbell of Ohio was particularly eloquent:

. . . Was ever legislation stretched so far? Not the President, nor the Cabinet, nor the governors of the States, nor the highest courts have ever been intrusted with power to suspend, repeal, or annul the law. Yet this commission, which may be ignorant, willful, or corrupt, can abrogate the law as to one road and enforce it upon another, being all the while responsible to nobody for their actions! . . .

. . . The absurdity consists in describing an offense, forbidding its practice, decreeing its punishment, and then serenely permitting it to be committed with impunity by the consent of a commission who are empowered by law to grant the privilege of sinning. Nothing like it has been known since the sale of indulgences, which Martin Luther thundered against and which disrupted the all-powerful Roman Church. If this principle is to be ingrafted upon our jurisprudence it would be next in order to establish a commission to modify or annul the decalogue and prescribe upon what terms certain favored persons might steal, covet, and commit other offenses prohibited in that fundamental moral law.[33]

It was particularly feared that the commission's discretion in the enforcement of the long-and-short-haul provisions would prove objectionable. Mr. Brown of Georgia, speaking on this point, protested vigorously:

. . . In other words, the proviso in the fourth section of this act arms the commission appointed by the President, under the authority conferred by the act of Congress, with a greater power than that which is wielded by any sovereign in Europe where anything like constitutional government prevails. Indeed, the Czar of Russia could not have a more arbitrary power.

32. 18 Cong. Rec., Appendix, 49.   33. Ibid. 29 f.

The commission in its discretion has the power to suspend the law in case of one railroad company and to refuse to suspend it in case of another railroad company located by the side of the one relieved if it chooses to do so, and there is no appeal from its decision.[34]

A second major attack upon the commission charged that appointments to it would be influenced by the railroads and that the commission would therefore represent railroad interests. In his minority report in the House in 1882 Judge Reagan had stated this argument:

. . . My fear as to a commission is that it would be more likely to represent the interests of the railroad companies than those of the general public. The railroad companies can always combine their influence, either directly, or, if thought more provident, indirectly, to influence the making of the appointment of such commissioners, by whomsoever to be appointed.[35]

In the House debate in 1886 he stressed this view still more strongly:

. . . I shall fear that the railroad interests will combine their power to control the appointment of the commissioners in their own interest. We all understand how easy it is for a few persons controlling large interests to unite their influence to carry out their wishes. However honest and patriotic a President of the United States may be, and however anxious he might be to secure a good and faithful commission, he would in a large measure have to depend on the information of others in appointing them. The great body of the people would be poorly qualified to give advice about such appointments, and if they were able to give good advice it is not practicable for them to unite in the recommendation of proper persons.

The notorious facts as to how railroad managers have corruptly controlled Legislatures, courts, governors, and Congress in the past give us sufficient warning as to what may be expected of them in the future. It is not to be supposed that they would directly approach any President of the United States and corruptly propose to secure the appointment of commissioners in their own interest; but the vast resources which they control, with the power of levying any tribute they please on the commerce of the country to secure means

34. 18 Cong. Rec. 571.
35. H.R. Misc. Doc. 55, 47th Cong., 1st sess. (1882), 261.

for the employment of men, enables them to control the best legal and business talent of the country, and would enable them to procure influential men in their interest to appeal to the President in the name of justice and on account of capacity to appoint such men as would serve their purposes.[36]

Mr. Campbell of Ohio sarcastically charged, 'this bill creates a sort of railway syndicate, designated as "The interstate-commerce commission," ' and went on to say that 'this bill ought to be entitled "A bill to more completely give over the control of the business and political interests of the people into the hands of . . . monopolists." ' [37]

It was objected, thirdly, that the commission would be 'the foot-ball of politics.' [38] It would permit the President through his power to appoint the members of the commission to exert vast and dangerous authority over the business of the country. By the juggling of these appointments he could strengthen his chances for re-election. It was further charged that the provision requiring that not more than three of the five commissioners be of the same party definitely imposed political bias upon the commission and that that bias would dominate the commission's work.

A fourth argument was that the job of railroad regulation was too big for a single administrative body to perform. Those who presented this argument seemed to have assumed that the commission would be required to examine and pass upon all of the individual rates of all the railroads of the nation. This would be, as Senator Aldrich put it, a physical impossibility.[39] Mr. Campbell of Ohio declared, 'to take charge of this bill under its present terms I do not think fifty commissioners would be able the first year to transact the business that will be thrown on their hands'; [40] and Senator Sherman of Ohio stated that 'there will not be time in the twelve months between January and January to act upon one-tenth of the cases that will be presented to it.' [41]

It was objected, in the fifth place, that the establishment of a commission would result in delays, obstructions, and hin-

36. 17 Cong. Rec. 7283.
37. 18 Cong. Rec., Appendix, 28.
38. Rep. Campbell, Ohio, ibid.
39. Ibid. 21.
40. Ibid. 30.
41. Ibid.

drances to the effective process of regulation. Mr. O'Ferrall of Virginia forcefully urged this point:

> . . . Speaking with due deference, I must say that in my judgment a more troublesome and intricate . . . piece of legal machinery was never suggested. If the more fertile minds in either House of Congress could have been employed to devise means to retard, embarrass, mystify, hinder, and delay the redress of wrongs and the punishment of violations of law they could not in my opinion have succeeded better than the distinguished framer of the Senate bill. It is the very thing that railroads want, since they are convinced that Congress intends to act upon the subject of regulating interstate commerce, for their favorite mode of warfare is to delay, embarrass, and hinder.[42]

Finally those who were eager for clear-cut and drastic regulation were inclined to discount the eulogies pronounced upon the state commissions. Especially in the West, where the Populists were gaining strength and where railroad abuses had been most acute, there was argumentative ammunition for those who opposed a federal commission. The state commissions had fallen far short of an adequate solution of the railroad problem and, in certain cases, had laid themselves open to serious criticism.

b. *The nature of the commission's powers—legislative, executive, or judicial*

There was no imperative reason why the statesmen who were proposing an interstate commerce commission and discussing the problems connected with it should feel it necessary to apply a descriptive label to the job which the commission was to do. It was generally recognized that the commission must do several different kinds of work, legislative, executive, and judicial; and that fact caused a few people some distress of mind. But those who now seek to describe the Interstate Commerce Commission as a legislative body or an executive body will find little support or illuminating comment in the debates or hearings on the original Act of 1887. But while descriptive words were not then used, because it did not seem important to use them, there is

42. 17 Cong. Rec. 7296.

evidence that Congress did have some fairly definite ideas on the nature of the tasks it was assigning to the new commission and these we may briefly summarize.

In the first place, Congress appears to have regarded the new commission's task of planning and of advising Congress with regard to legislation as functions properly belonging to executive officers. The Windom report of 1874 emphasized the importance of this advisory job. At the same time it recommended that the commission which was to do it be set up as 'a Bureau of Commerce, in one of the Executive Departments of the Government.' [43] When the House committee reported in 1882 [44] in favor of the creation of a commission one of the principal tasks of which would be to propose legislation to Congress, it also urged that the commission should be set up as a board in the Department of the Interior. These recommendations seem to run counter to the current theory that an agency set up to provide Congress with information must by virtue of that fact be a part of the legislative branch and therefore dissociated from executive control.

In the second place, there is a good deal of general discussion in the hearings and debates indicating that the proposed commission was viewed as an executive agency endowed with quasi-judicial powers. The Cullom report appears to have regarded the commission as primarily an agent—an executive agent—of law enforcement. It said:

In the light of all the evidence and the facts before it, the committee has become satisfied that no statutory regulations which may be enacted can be made fully effective without providing adequate and suitable machinery for carrying them into execution. 'What is everybody's business is nobody's business,' and the conclusion seems irresistible that specific enactments must inevitably fail to remedy the evils they are designed to cure unless an executive board be organized for the special purpose of securing their enforcement. Such enactments cannot possibly be self-enforcing, and whenever attempts have been made to control or regulate commercial transactions it has been found necessary to do so through a special instrumentality.[45]

43. *Supra,* 41   45. *Supra,* note 1, op. cit. Part 1, 213.
44. *Supra,* 42.

Senator Edmunds referred to the commission as exercising 'executive, discretionary power,' [46] while Mr. La Follette referred to its 'supervisory and executory' [47] powers.

While there may have been uncertainty whether the proposed commission possessed legislative or executive authority, there was little disposition to describe its power as judicial. It had no final authority to enforce its orders or to do anything else except under ultimate judicial scrutiny, and Senator Platt pointed out in defense of the validity of the bill that Congress had been careful not to give the commission any judicial power.[48]

The Act of 1887 gave the commission no direct power to fix railroad rates, a power now uniformly regarded as legislative in character. While opponents of the commission even then charged that legislative power had been delegated to it under cover of its authority to exercise some discretion in the application of the standards set up in the Act, we find no clearly expressed opinion that the major functions confided to the commission were legislative in character.

Congressional leaders not only saw no necessity for labeling the commission's powers, but they felt that it would be undesirable to try to do so. This was brought out in an interesting debate in the Senate precipitated by an amendment proposed by Senator Morgan of Alabama, which read: 'The commissioners appointed under this act shall be considered and regarded as being executive officers, and shall not exercise either legislative or judicial powers.' [49] The Senator was obviously worried by the failure of the bill to indicate clearly just what kind of animal the new interstate commerce commission was supposed to be, and he proposed that Congress should classify it. The debate on the Morgan amendment was very illuminating. It ran as follows:

MR. MORGAN: I have heard a great variety of expressions among Senators in regard to the functions of these officers, whether they are executive, or whether they are legislative, or whether they are judicial. My judgment is that we have combined very skillfully powers derived from each of these departments of the Government in the hands of these commissioners; and I merely wanted to under-

46. 17 Cong. Rec. 4422.
47. 18 Cong. Rec., Appendix, 187.
48. 17 Cong. Rec. 4422.
49. Ibid.

stand whether they were executive officers, or whether they were legislative officers, or whether they were judicial officers . . .

I think that in passing this bill we ought to give the courts some guide as to whether we are conferring these powers upon executive officers, or upon judicial officers, or upon legislative officers. I think I have seen in this bill decided evidences of legislative powers, and I suppose the Senate is prepared either to express its opinion or not to express it. I do not care which way so that we have a definite expression.

MR. EDMUNDS: This bill confers upon these commissioners powers, much or little, great or small; and to undertake to say that they shall exercise no power of one kind or another is entirely unique in the history of legislation. I should suppose that an amendment of this kind would be offered in order to trammel the exertion of the powers that we confer upon the President of the United States all the time and upon the Secretary of the Treasury and everybody else, to exert in respect to executive and administrative affairs a discretion applied to circumstances. I think, therefore, that the amendment ought not to be adopted.

MR. MORGAN: . . . Now, if these commissioners have a right to exercise any judicial function, to sit in judgment on the rights of men, then they are judicial officers, and I want to know merely whether we are conferring that power upon them. If they have the right to change the rights of men by their decrees, whether arbitrary or not, whether just or not, then they are legislative officers. Perhaps they are even more than that; they are autocrats. But we ought to know what they are.

The Senator from Vermont says we have given them powers. Well, we have given them powers, a large admixture of powers, quite a voluminous array of powers. We have given them contradictory powers, I am afraid. I believe we have, and I think it is our duty to be able to expound what is our view of their authority that we are conferring in this bill, and not to leave it as a matter of litigation and dispute to be fought out at the expense of people who go before these commissioners hereafter. It is the first bill I have ever known to be brought into the Senate—and in that respect this bill is unique—where the authors of it were not willing to enter into a definition as to whether the powers they conferred by the bill were conferred upon officers of the executive department, officers of the legislative department, or officers of the judicial department of the United States.

MR. MAXEY: I only want to say that it is not a matter of the slightest consequence to me whether the powers are called executive, judicial, legislative, or ministerial. We have defined on the face of the bill the powers which are to be exercised by the commissioners, and if those powers are not constitutional, that fact ought to be pointed out. Therefore I see no necessity whatever for the amendment proposed by the Senator from Alabama.[50]

The Morgan amendment was not passed.

c. *Problems arising under separation of powers*

There was little general or philosophical discussion of the separation of powers in connection with the establishment of the commission, but some of the more practical aspects of the doctrine and its corollaries were discussed. In the first place, the new statute delegated powers to a new type of agency. It was suggested in the House debates that the discretion given to the commission under the long-and-short-haul clause would amount to a delegation of legislative power. It was further suggested that one reason why positive rate-making power was not given to the commission was that Congress could not lawfully delegate that power to anyone else. The provisions of the Act, however, give little support to any serious charge of an unconstitutional delegation of legislative power. The contention was once or twice made that invalid delegations of judicial power were being made to the new commission. This was effectively answered by pointing out that the commission had no final authority, that its findings of facts were subject to review, and that it was dependent upon the courts for the enforcement of its orders.

Much more fully discussed was the question whether the proposed statute did not merge in the commission powers of government which under the separation of powers ought to be kept separate. It was obvious that the functions of the commission would necessarily be varied. It was being set up to deal in an administrative manner with a problem so complicated as to call for the exercise of different functions and the use of different procedures. The Cullom committee felt strongly that the task assigned to the commission could not be effectively divided up or distributed amongst several agencies. The regulatory prob-

50. Ibid.

lem must be dealt with as a whole, and state experience supported that view. Those attacking the commission, however, were quick to point out this merger in one body of several kinds of powers. A prominent railway witness before the Cullom committee declared:

Judicial power should not be vested in a commission without first establishing more specific laws under which it can act. Such commission must not be allowed to first make the law, and then, without any knowledge on the part of those who are to comply with it, decide the law and execute it. Commissions, or courts, or any body of men, who are at the same time law-makers, judges, and sheriffs, are not to be tolerated in a free country . . .

Unfortunately Congress can pass no definite laws under which the railroad property can be managed; in the absence of a well-defined law, and the commissioners making their own laws, no judicial power should be given to them . . .

. . . I am in favor of establishing special tribunals to try railroad cases, but they must be purely judicial tribunals and must act under well-defined laws.[51]

Changes were rung upon this same argument throughout the debates. Senator Morgan charged that the bill 'combined very skillfully powers from each of these [three] departments'[52] and protested against encroachment by the legislative and executive branches on the judicial.[53] In the House debate Mr. Oates of Alabama declared:

I believe that it is absolutely unconstitutional and void, because to my mind it is a blending of the legislative, the judicial, and perhaps, the executive powers of the Government in the same law.[54]

Mr. Little of Ohio defended the bill against this charge particularly in its relation to the long-and-short-haul provision:

But this authority is of a judicial character . . . Aside from this one feature it is really interesting to note how little power the commission has. Its other authority is, I believe, entirely of an inquisitorial, advisory, or ancillary character.

It may investigate, advise, complain, and sue.[55]

51. Albert Fink, head of New York Trunk Lines Pool, *supra*, note 1, op. cit. Part 2, 124 f.

52. 17 Cong. Rec. 4422.   54. Ibid. 848.
53. 18 Cong. Rec. 399.   55. Ibid. Appendix, 73.

However, it was not until the powers of the commission had been strengthened by later legislation that this attack on the objectionable merging in its hands of incompatible powers gained substantial strength.

d. *Relation of the commission to the three branches of government*

What light, if any, do the hearings and debates throw upon the actual relation of the new commission to Congress, to the President, and to the courts?

There was virtually no discussion of the commission's relation to Congress. Congress was, of course, creating the commission and assigning its powers, but there is nothing to suggest that the legislative leaders looked upon the commission as having a relation to Congress different from that of any other administrative agency. There is no evidence that they regarded it as in any special way an 'arm of Congress'; but it should be borne in mind that the Act of 1887 did not give to the commission the broad rate-making powers which it was later to enjoy. It was assumed that the commission would aid Congress directly by giving it expert information on railroad problems, and it was also assumed that the commission would remain under the supervision of Congress in the sense that its status and duties would be subject to legislative revision from time to time.

Equally vague was the view taken of the commission's relation to the President. There was, in fact, no discussion of this relation in terms of direct responsibility or control. There was no assumption that there would be any actual working relation between the President and the commission nor was it suggested that the commission owed any obedience or responsibility to the White House. There was no discussion of the President's power to remove members of the commission or of the restrictions in the statute upon that power of removal. It was recognized that the President would control the commission's personnel through appointment. There was much comment upon the political implications arising from this fact, and the opponents of the bill described in highly imaginative terms the vast power the President would wield in appointing commissioners and in removing them from office. Representative Call of Florida referred to the commission inaccurately as 'amenable to the President' who is, in turn, 'amenable to the people,' [56] but it is clear that any Presidential domination of the commission in its normal activities was neither contemplated nor discussed.

The commission's relation to the courts was touched upon but briefly. There could be no delegation of judicial authority for constitutional reasons, and every effort was made to avoid what could possibly be looked upon as such a delegation of judicial power. The commission had no final authority and was dependent upon the courts for the enforcement of its orders. The idea was suggested, though not thoroughly developed, that the commission in making its expert findings of fact, findings which would otherwise have to be made by the courts, was serving as an aid or auxiliary to the courts, in a capacity like that of a referee. The real struggle over the relation between courts and commission was reserved for a later stage in the evolution of the Act.

e. *The independence of the commission*

It is an interesting fact that the legislative leaders did not discuss the question of the independence of the commission. The Cullom inquiry throws no light upon the problem. The witnesses appearing before the committee seem not to have been interested. The word independence does not appear in the legislative debates and the problem itself escaped any direct consideration. There were, however, certain views expressed and certain assumptions made which are of interest in this connection.

In the thinking of those responsible for the Act, independence, if it meant anything, appears to have meant bipartisanship, as a guarantee of impartiality. Independence of executive domination seems not to have been thought of and was certainly not discussed, but independence of one-sided partisan control was a matter of great moment. There was, in fact, some facetious comment in the debates on whether an 'independent' in politics could qualify for a seat on the commission.[57]

In the second place, while freedom from Presidential domination was probably assumed, the clause in the statute provid-

56. Ibid. 570.   57. Ibid. Appendix, 50.

ing for the removal of commissioners by the President for inefficiency, neglect of duty, or malfeasance in office was looked upon more as a protection to the public by providing a way to get rid of objectionable commissioners than as a limitation on Presidential authority.

Finally, whatever independence the new commission was supposed to have was not incompatible with the location of the commission in the Department of the Interior. This appears to have been a sort of carry-over from earlier proposals and a reflection of the idea that the new agency ought not to be left in a vacuum. The Windom report of 1874 [58] had called for a commission set up in an executive department, and the report of the House committee of 1882 [59] had similarly suggested a railroad board which should be a bureau in the Department of the Interior. The Act of 1887 gave to the Secretary of the Interior general supervision over the Interstate Commerce Commission's budget, offices, and supplies, and the appointment and compensation of its employees. It provided that the annual report of the commission should be filed with the Secretary who should transmit it to Congress. There was practically no discussion of this anomalous arrangement. Mr. Oates of Alabama in the House debate mentioned the authority of the Secretary of the Interior over the salaries to be paid to the commission's staff and declared that 'the veto power which the bill gives to the Secretary of the Interior is an inadequate safeguard to the Treasury.' [60] There was no other comment on this point. It may be recalled that the Federal Civil Service Act was in its fourth year, sound traditions regarding appointments and salaries were yet to be established, and it no doubt seemed appropriate to place the new commission under departmental supervision with respect to its 'housekeeping' functions.

f. *Problems of personnel and qualifications of commissioners*

It was steadily assumed throughout the debates that if the commission was to serve the purpose set for it, it must be staffed by men of high calibre. The salary of $7,500 was larger than that of any United States judges except the members of the

---

58. *Supra*, 41.   60. 18 Cong. Rec. 849.
59. *Supra*, 42.

Supreme Court, and the salutary results expected were thus summarized by Mr. Hermann of Oregon:

They receive generous salaries, even larger than any of the judges of the United States courts, excepting of the Supreme Court, and they are thus rendered greatly independent of temptation. Their tenure of office continues for six years. And still more. Should either of them prove corrupt, inefficient, negligent, or false to duty, his immediate removal from office by the President is authorized. Five eminent men are thus appointed and thus guarded and thus rewarded. And further still. Even their proceedings are subject to review and enforcement by the higher courts. Can human affairs be more honestly, more efficiently, and in the ultimate more perfectly conserved by human effort than this? Our boasted trial by jury is not more perfect while frequently it falls far short.[61]

We have already mentioned the importance attached to the requirement of bipartisanship stated in the proviso that not more than three members of the commission should be chosen from the same political party. Impartiality, or at least neutrality, was looked upon as more important than expertness. There was no suggestion that men of specialized training ought to be placed on the commission. It was assumed that the commissioners would acquire expertness in their complicated tasks through experience; but it was believed that the honesty and fairness so essential to adequate railroad regulation could be guaranteed only by preventing partisan domination. Of course views varied on this point. It was urged that politics was actually being legislated into the commission by the very requirement of bipartisanship, and Mr. Grosvenor of Ohio expressed the belief, with rather shrewd foresight, that 'lame ducks' would be appointed to the commission without serious consideration of ability.[62]

An interesting discussion took place on the provision disqualifying for membership on the commission those having immediate railroad affiliations. Mr. Grosvenor took the lead in attacking this:

. . . Who are they to be? They are to be five gentlemen who know nothing whatever of their business. That is the first requisite; that is a qualification not to be varied from under any circumstances. Men who know anything about this business upon which

61. Ibid. Appendix, 35.   62. Ibid. 50.

the commission is to embark are to be disbarred from appointment. The commissioners are to hold no stocks in railroads or any other carrier by land or water, are not to be officers or attorneys of railroads, are not to be interested directly or indirectly in the railroads of the country or any of the carriers of the country.

. . . These commissioners are to be 'tramps' without any visible means of support.[63]

Mr. O'Neil of Pennsylvania declared:

Believing that holding stock or bonds in a railroad company should not disqualify a man from accepting the office of a commissioner, I would strike out that inhibition in the Cullom bill and provide in its place that a commissioner should not take part in the decision of any complaint against such company of whose stock or bonds he might be an owner. Many of the wisest and purest men of the country might be prevented from taking such an office because of his legitimately owning railroad securities, while an upright man in any judicial position would decline to hear or decide a case in which he might have even a remote interest.[64]

The disqualification, however, was kept in the bill.

It may be mentioned to keep the record complete that some of the witnesses before the Cullom committee advocated specialized or regional sections or panels on the commission with the full commission acting as an appellate body. These proposals, however, received no serious consideration at this time.

g. *Experimental nature of the commission and of the problem*

Finally it should be emphasized that throughout the entire history of the bill it was clearly recognized that the important problem of federal railroad regulation would have to be solved by trial and error. A major purpose in creating a commission was to provide machinery to secure the accurate and expert information necessary to the solution of that problem. Congress felt it wise to move slowly. The powers first granted to the commission seem now to have been meager indeed, but the expansion of those powers in the light of future experience was not foreclosed. Speaking in the House, Mr. Rowell of Illinois said,

63. Ibid. 49 f.   64. 17 Cong. Rec. 7286.

'The Senate bill is not all that will be required, in my judgment, but it is a beginning. Eventually we shall go further.' [65] And this probably expressed the views of all those who were not definitely opposed to rigorous regulation.

D. RESCUING THE COMMISSION FROM FUTILITY—THE HEPBURN ACT OF 1906

1. DEVELOPMENTS CULMINATING IN THE HEPBURN ACT

It took nearly twenty years and much bitter humiliation for the Interstate Commerce Commission to impress upon Congress the necessity of strengthening that body and equipping it to deal effectively with the increasingly acute railroad problems which were confronting the country. We may summarize roughly the events which led to the passing of the Hepburn Act of 1906,[66] which was to give to the commission a positive rate-making power and free it to some extent from the strangling grip of the courts.

The commission had started off auspiciously. President Cleveland made an outstanding contribution to its success by naming Judge Thomas M. Cooley its first chairman. Cooley's distinguished name lent prestige to the new body and his shrewd management of its early organization and methods left a lasting influence. He set about at once the judicialization of the commission's procedure and the development of a body of case law embodied in carefully written opinions. An impression of high efficiency and distinterestedness was created.

However, the commission was weak; and the law under which it operated was feeble in its provisions and vague in its language. The commission could take no action with finality. At every crucial point it had to rely upon the courts for aid and sanction. The statute imposed upon it the task of interpreting such general standards as 'just and reasonable rates,' the precise meaning of which had nowhere been declared. Its work would have been difficult enough under favorable circumstances, but the attitude and tactics of the railroads rendered the circumstances peculiarly trying. The carriers looked upon the commis-

65. Ibid. Appendix, 444.   66. Act of June 29, 1906, 34 Stat. at L. 584.

sion as a natural enemy and fought, harassed, obstructed, and delayed it at every possible point. They refused to obey the orders of the commission regardless of their reasonableness, and invoked every technicality which their highly paid lawyers could discover. Particularly did they obstruct the commission's work and weaken its prestige by refusing to present to it all of the pertinent evidence in the hearings held before it. The commission's record and findings thus built on an inadequate presentation of facts came in due course to the courts for review. The courts thereupon took the case *de novo,* allowed the new evidence to be presented, reached their own conclusions and rendered their decisions with scant respect for the earlier findings of the commission itself.

The courts, in fact, were themselves far from friendly to the commission. They showed a steady and increasing disposition to do over again the commission's job of finding facts, thereby undermining the prestige of the commission and the effectiveness of its orders. Furthermore, the commission found its efficiency weakened and its substantive powers reduced by a series of Supreme Court decisions. *Counselman* v. *Hitchcock* [67] held that the provisions of the Act relating to the immunity from prosecution of witnesses before the commission inadequately protected the constitutional rights of those witnesses, and until the enactment of the Compulsory Testimony Act [68] the commission was seriously crippled in its legal right to secure evidence. Of much greater importance was the decision in the Maximum Rate cases,[69] decided in 1897. For a decade the commission had acted on the assumption that the statute authorized it not only to declare a railroad rate to be unjust and unreasonable but to announce a just and reasonable rate to replace it. The Supreme Court now held that the statute gave the commission no authority whatever to fix any railroad rate. At the same time the Court in the Alabama Midland case [70] emasculated the long-and-short-haul clause of the Interstate Commerce Act, one of the commission's most effective weapons against

67. 142 U.S. 547 (1892).

68. Act of Feb. 11, 1893, 27 Stat. at L. 443.

69. *Interstate Commerce Commission* v. *Cincinnati, N.O. & T.P.R. Co.,* 167 U.S. 479 (1897).

70. *Interstate Commerce Commission* v. *Alabama Midland Ry. Co.,* 168 U.S. 144 (1897).

railroad discrimination against localities. Mr. Justice Harlan, dissenting in that case, summed up the results of these decisions in the following statement:

> . . . Taken in connection with other decisions defining the powers of the Interstate Commerce Commission, the present decision, it seems to me, goes far to make that Commission a useless body for all practical purposes, and to defeat many of the important objects designed to be accomplished by the various enactments of Congress relating to interstate commerce. The Commission was established to protect the public against the improper practices of transportation companies engaged in commerce among the several States. It has been left, it is true, with power to make reports, and to issue protests. But it has been shorn, by judicial interpretation, of authority to do anything of an effective character.[71]

Congress was not wholly oblivious to the needs of the commission during this period, and passed a number of laws effecting minor improvements and making minor additions to the commission's power. While none of these went to the root of the pressing problems involved, the more important ones should be mentioned. In 1889 at the twice-repeated request of the Secretary of the Interior Congress took the commission out of that department, abolished all of the Secretary's supervisory authority over the commission, and made it for the first time completely independent and self-sufficient.[72] In 1893, in the Compulsory Testimony Act already mentioned,[73] Congress restored to the commission an effective power to compel testimony. In 1903 Congress passed the Elkins Act.[74] This imposed heavy penalties upon the railroads for deviations from their posted rates by rebating and similar practices; this legislation was sponsored by the carriers themselves in self-defense against the discriminatory practices induced by cutthroat competition. Beginning in 1893 Congress gave the commission the task of enforcing the Safety Appliance Acts,[75] which a public opinion aroused by numerous railroad accidents had forced through the national legislature. The job assigned was that of inspection

71. Ibid. at 176.
72. Act of Mar. 2, 1889, 25 Stat. at L. 855.
73. *Supra,* 66.
74. Act of Feb. 19, 1903, 32 Stat. at L. 847.
75. Act of Mar. 2, 1893, 27 Stat. at L. 531. These laws are set forth in Aitchison, *supra,* note 16, op. cit. p. 348, note 174.

and supervision and the subsequent reporting of violations of the Safety Appliance Acts to federal district attorneys for criminal prosecution. Thus began the practice of imposing upon the Interstate Commerce Commission duties which are purely executive in character.

Finally we may borrow from Professor Ripley [76] his suggestive summary of the four major incentives which led Congress finally to rehabilitate the Interstate Commerce Commission by passing the Act of 1906. First, the spread of railroad consolidations with the consequent elimination of competition. Second, sharp increases in freight rates on practically all railroads beginning about 1900. These fell with increasing pressure upon the shippers. Third, the concentration of financial control over railroad systems in the hands of a few men. This amounted to complete dominion without any effective responsibility. In the public mind it was represented by Mr. E. H. Harriman and his domination of the Southern Pacific. Fourth, various disclosures which had shown the extent to which industrial monopoly was promoted by vicious railroad rate discriminations; the part which rebates had played in the building up of the Standard Oil Company was a case in point. These factors ultimately produced an aroused public opinion which Congress could not defy or evade.

2. STEPS IN THE LEGISLATIVE HISTORY OF THE HEPBURN ACT

The movement which resulted in the passage of the Hepburn Act of 1906 may be traced back to the '90's. In 1894 the Senate Committee on Interstate Commerce reported favorably a bill giving the Interstate Commerce Commission the positive power to establish railroad rates and expediting judicial procedure on appeal. No action was taken. In 1899 Senator Cullom and Senator Chandler introduced similar bills which met a similar fate. In 1901 outside organizations began to be active, and various programs for reform were discussed. The next year the Industrial Commission made its famous report [77] and recommended the strengthening of the Interstate Commerce Commission.

76. Wm. Z. Ripley, *Railroads: Rates and Regulation* (1912) 487 ff.
77. Final Report of the Industrial Commission (1902), vol. XIX of the commission's *Reports.*

Railroad opposition, accordingly, began to organize itself effectively and line up for the fight against further governmental regulation. In that year, in response to heavy pressure from the public, Senators Cullom and Nelson introduced new bills which died in committee. At the same time the House Committee on Interstate and Foreign Commerce under the chairmanship of Mr. Hepburn held elaborate hearings on a number of railroad bills and spread upon the record much useful information. No action, however, took place in either house. In 1904 President Theodore Roosevelt came into the game. His annual message to Congress made adequate railroad regulation a 'paramount issue' and he began to line up his forces to secure effective legislation. During the following year things began to happen. The Esch-Townsend bill,[78] an Administration measure, passed the House on February 9, 1905, by the overwhelming vote of 326 to 17. This bill gave the Interstate Commerce Commission the power to fix reasonable railroad rates which were to remain in effect until set aside by judicial process, and it established a transportation court to hear all railroad cases on review. The bill, however, died in the Senate committee. But while the Senate continued to delay, it dared not wholly ignore the growing public pressure. It met it by instructing the Senate Committee on Interstate Commerce to hold hearings and report on various proposals for amending the law. These hearings under the chairmanship of Senator Elkins filled five large volumes,[79] but the actual report of the committee, made verbally to the Senate, consisted principally of an expression of the committee's hope that it would be able to present a bill later on.[80] At this juncture the House Committee on Interstate and Foreign Commerce, citing at length the annual report of the Interstate Commerce Commission for 1904 strongly urging corrective legislation, again reported the Esch-Townsend bill. The Democratic minority of the committee supported the proposed increase in the powers of the commission but objected to the creation of a transportation court. President Roosevelt again brought pressure to bear on Congress in his annual message in 1905, and

78. H.R. 18588, 58th Cong., 3d sess. (1905).

79. Hearings before the Senate Committee on Interstate Commerce Pursuant to S. Res. 288, 58th Cong., 3d sess. (1905).

80. 40 Cong. Rec. 387.

public opinion was further aroused by the disclosure of attempts made by certain railroads to influence public opinion by the bribing of newspaper editors and by other unsavory devices. These various influences at last brought action. Early in 1906 the House passed the Hepburn bill by an almost unanimous vote, 346 to 7. The Senate, still reluctant, was forced into line. It amended the bill in many parts but finally passed it with only three dissenting votes. The bill went to conference, which lasted a month; passed the two houses again on June 28, 1906; and was signed by the President the following day.

3. PROVISIONS OF THE HEPBURN ACT

The major provisions of the Hepburn Act as they relate to the Interstate Commerce Commission are as follows:

a. The commission was empowered to prescribe future maximum railroad rates and practices.

b. The orders of the commission were to be immediately effective. The burden rested on the carrier of testing the validity of these orders in court.

c. The commission's power to enter an award of reparation was clarified.

d. The commission was enlarged from five to seven members and was authorized to appoint examiners and agents.

e. The scope of the Interstate Commerce Act was extended to include express companies, sleeping-car companies, and pipeline companies transporting oil.

f. The famous commodities clause was added, a provision which prevented the ownership by railroads of goods and products which they themselves transported.

4. TOPICS AND ISSUES IN HEARINGS AND DEBATES

a. *Delegation of rate-making power to the commission*

The Hepburn Act gave the commission power to establish reasonable railroad rates for the future, but this power could be exercised only upon complaint by those affected by unreasonable rates. The commission could not initiate a new rate upon its own responsibility. The new power was, however, a

genuinely significant one and represented a long step in advance. Several aspects of it came in for active discussion before
committees and in Congressional debates.

In the first place, was such a grant of power to the commission
desirable? On this point there was little discussion. Public opinion demanded this action; the President was urging it. It was
too late to make a convincing argument that it would be objectionable. Lack of control over railroad rates had produced far
too serious results to be ignored. Many large manufacturing interests joined the railroads in opposing the grant of the new
power, and they presented before the Elkins committee of 1905
a long list of arguments against it; but in the debates in Congress no voice was raised to urge that effective rate regulation
was not necessary and desirable. No congressman cared to risk
his political future by opposing the new legislation on its merits.

Granting that the delegation of rate-making power was desirable, the question remained, was it constitutional? Could Congress validly grant to the commission this important authority?
The constitutional attack on the Hepburn bill was in large part
a smoke screen for those who for much more practical reasons
opposed giving the commission the power to fix rates. But even
on constitutional grounds their cause was hopeless. The commission had for nearly ten years exercised the rate-making
power on what turned out to be the erroneous assumption that
the Act of 1887 conferred it. The Supreme Court itself had
spoken with approval in the Railroad Commission cases [81] of
rate-making by administrative commissions, and in the Maximum Rate cases [82] it had clearly implied that while Congress
had not given the commission this power it might do so if it
wished. A strong opinion by the Attorney General [83] also supported the constitutionality of this delegation of power. The
constitutional objections were nevertheless aired with thoroughness. Fundamentally they all rested upon a simple syllogism:
rate-making is a legislative power; legislative power cannot constitutionally be delegated; therefore rate-making cannot be delegated. This position had been ably presented by Richard Olney
in 1905 in the *North American Review,* and to this position
Mr. Olney's standing as a lawyer lent weight in the Congres-

81. *Supra,* 44.   83. *Infra,* 73.
82. *Supra,* note 69.

sional debates. Mr. McCall of Massachusetts stated the argument with force:

> . . . If that does not make a legislature of the Commission, then the hitherto accepted notions of the function of legislation will need to be radically revised . . . If the making of railroad rates is a legislative function which can be delegated by calling it administrative, why may we not in a bill originating in the House confer upon a commission the power to fix tariff rates? [84]

Senators Elkins and McCumber objected that the proposed bill gave to the commission a discretion with regard to the policy of its action which was not controlled by any sufficiently definite standard. As Senator Elkins put it:

> The language of the bill seems designed to turn the entire subject of regulation, which is within the power of Congress, over to the discretion of the Commission. The Commission is given full authority to act not merely when rates in fact violate the law but whenever the Commission 'shall be of opinion' that the rates are unjust or unreasonable.
> They determine their own jurisdiction by their own opinion. Thus the Commission's opinion is sought to be made the sole basis of its jurisdiction . . . This turns over to the Commission all the discretionary power that Congress itself could exercise. [85]

The vagueness of the standards set up to guide the commission's discretion was also criticized by Senator Foraker:

> . . . All that Congress can do, if it has power to make rates at all, is to fix just and reasonable rates. If we confer that power on the Commission, we have divested ourselves of every particle of the rate-making power we have and given it all to the Commission. And yet Senators tell me there is no delegation by this provision of legislative power. [86]

These constitutional arguments pushed to the foreground a consideration of the nature of the rate-making power. If the power to fix rates can be delegated to the commission, and if legislative power cannot be delegated, what, then, is the rate-making power? The answer was that it is 'administrative' power.[87] The commission makes an administrative application

84. 40 Cong. Rec. 1972.   86. Ibid. 5134.
85. Ibid. 4841.   87. Sen. Rayner, Md., ibid. 3782.

of a standard fixed by Congress in the statute. Weight was given this view by no less an authority than the Attorney General:

. . . The courts have held, that where the legislature has enacted that railway rates shall be impartial and reasonable, the duty of executing this law and determining the rates for the future in detail in conformity with it, may be conferred constitutionally upon an administrative body, and that a grant of such power is not a delegation of the legislative authority.[88]

. . . Rate making is purely a legislative function, in the performance of which the legislative body may avail itself of the aid of an administrative body for the execution in detail of general rules which have been enacted in law. This is only another way of saying that the rate-making power is not a judicial function.[89]

Senator Simmons expressed this as follows:

. . . The Hepburn bill . . . settles and declares the legislative policy with respect to this question by prescribing the rule and standard of rates, and simply directs the Commission to find the facts, apply to them this rule and standard, and declare the result.[90]

Commissioner Prouty, a member of the Interstate Commerce Commission, wrote to a member of the Senate:

. . . It seems to me extremely important that there should be some language in the bill which clearly shows that the Commission in making the new rate is exercising its administrative judgment, and not merely deciding the question of fact as a judge or a jury.[91]

It remained for Mr. Mann of Illinois to describe the rate-making process in terms which involved almost metaphysical refinements:

. . . We do not give to the Interstate Commerce Commission the power to fix rates. We say by legislative act what the rate shall be. The Legislature defines what the rate shall be. The rate shall be just, reasonable, and fairly remunerative. That is a legislative declaration as to the rate just as much as though we said the rate shall be 50 cents a hundred pounds. We make the declaration ourselves, we do not confer upon the Interstate Commerce Commission any legislative authority or any judicial authority. We say as a matter of legislative act that the rate shall be just, that the rate shall be reason-

---

88. 25 Op. Att'y Gen. (1905), 424.
89. Ibid. at 428.

90. 40 Cong. Rec. 3730.
91. Ibid. 7065.

able, that the rate shall be fairly remunerative, and then we leave
to the Commission the administrative power to determine what in
each particular case is the just, reasonable, and fairly remunerative
rate . . . The Legislature finds what the rates shall be and puts
those rates into force; and all the Commission is given power to
do is the administrative act of making the computation . . .[92]

Thus it was emphasized in the debates that the commission in
fixing rates would be acting for Congress, performing a function
which Congress might itself perform but only with great inconvenience. This appears to be the beginning of the idea that the
commission is an 'arm of Congress.' Mr. Bankhead of Alabama
expressed this as follows:

The legislature has power to fix rates. Were it to do so it would
do it through the aid of committees appointed to investigate the
subject, to acquire information, to cite parties, to get all the facts
before them, and, finally, to decide and report. No one can say this
is not due process of law, and if the legislature can do this, acting
by its committee and proceeding according to the usual forms
adopted by such bodies, why can it not delegate the duty to a board
of commissioners charged to regulate and fix charges so as to be
equal and reasonable? [93]

Mr. Clay of Georgia said, 'the rates put in operation by the
Commission are, in effect, rates fixed by Congress . . . This
Commission represents Congress . . .' [94] And Senator Elkins in
opposing the Act declared that the commission would, in effect,
be 'acting for Congress.' [95]

b. *New relation of commission to courts—Immediate*
effectiveness of rate orders—Scope of judicial review

Much more hotly discussed than the delegation of rate-making power was the relation between the commission and the
courts with reference to the commission's new rate orders. If
the commission was to establish future rates, at what point
ought the courts to be permitted to intervene to suspend or
set aside those rates, and how broad should be the scope of this
judicial review? These were problems of great practical importance since the weakness of the commission had been largely

92. Ibid. 2245.
93. Ibid. 2231.
94. Ibid. 4443.
95. Ibid. 4838.

due to the strangling influence of the courts. The discussions on this problem turned roughly around two major points.

In the first place, there was a sharp clash between those who advocated broad judicial review of commission rulings and those who demanded narrow judicial review. Even today this remains a highly controversial issue. Those anxious to see the commission's authority extended urged 'narrow' review. To allow the courts to supervise the discretion of the commission in fixing a rate was to allow the court to exercise legislative power. If the courts were limited in reviewing rate orders to constitutional questions alone, that was sufficient to protect essential rights and yet would prevent the courts from doing over again the commission's job. One of the serious difficulties under the existing Act had been the suppression of important evidence by the railroads in the hearings before the commission, a strategy which had led the reviewing court to try the entire case *de novo*. It was therefore urged that the law require that any new evidence presented to the court on review should be sent back to the commission for finding and report, thus breaking up the objectionable practice described. Those urging broad judicial review of the commission's orders argued that only in this way could the rights of all parties concerned be properly protected and that any attempt to narrow judicial scrutiny would be a denial of due process of law.

Another issue arose regarding the procedure under which judicial review should be exercised. Under the new Act the rate orders of the commission were to be effective immediately, in contrast to the old arrangement under which they were effective only when supported by court decision. At what point, then, and by what procedure were the courts to be permitted to intervene? Could a federal district judge on his own responsibility set aside the commission's rate order by injunction and thus leave the situation for practical purposes exactly where it was under the old statute? Friends of the bill sought to restrict the power of the courts to issue such injunctions, and there were long debates on both the propriety and the constitutionality of doing this. The constitutional argument was participated in by many of the leading lawyers in the Senate. It was urged that Congress could not prevent a federal court from issuing an injunction, and there ensued a long and informing debate on the important distinction between federal judicial power and jurisdiction.[96] In reply it was pointed out that Congress had more than once restricted the power of injunction by statute and that the courts had held these restrictions valid. It was plausibly argued that it was unfair and anomalous to allow a single district judge to tie up for an almost indefinite period an order issued by an independent expert agency which was devoting its entire time to the study of the problems involved. It was urged in answer to this that it was unfair to the railroads to subject them even temporarily to a suspension or abrogation of their rights by a commission order which might be *ultra vires* or unconstitutional. A middle ground between these two positions permitted the issuance of injunctions but under certain safeguards. These safeguards in the main comprised notice and hearing and a reasonable delay before the issuance of an injunction, in order to permit the commission to present its case to the court. In addition, the railroad seeking the injunction should file with the court an adequate deposit for the compensation of the shippers in case the injunction should not be sustained. It was also suggested that the orders of the commission should remain in force until the decision of the court of last resort could be secured.

c. *Merger in the commission of powers which should be kept separate*

We have seen that in 1886 some concern was expressed at the merging in the hands of the commission of powers which under the orthodox theory of the separation of powers should be kept separate. This became an acute issue in the discussions on the Hepburn bill. The commission was to have rate-making power; and while this for convenience was labeled administrative, it was regarded as fundamentally legislative in character. At the same time, the *prima facie* validity of the commission's findings of fact smacked strongly of judicial authority. As a result there was a barrage of criticism against the bill because of this supposedly objectionable combination of powers. Much of the attack came from the railway witnesses appearing before the Hep-

96. See Senate debates from Feb. 28, 1906, to May 18, 1906, and particularly Senator Bailey's speech, 40 Cong. Rec. 4977 ff.

burn committee and later before the Elkins committee. Mr. Walker D. Hines, vice-president of the L. & N. Railroad, stated this point cogently:

> It has been admitted before the committee by one of the commissioners that that Commission is a partisan body to some extent, and I think that that grows out of the very nature of the tribunal, that it has so many different functions to perform that are incompatible with each other. It has considerable administrative supervision over the railroads, it is constantly coming into contact with them on that side, of controlling them in police matters and things of that sort, and I think it will be conceded that a person who occupies that attitude is not a proper person to assume a far-reaching quasi-judicial jurisdiction over the corporation . . .
>
> Although the Commission has judicial functions of the very highest importance, it is not only not a court, but it has so many incompatible functions to propose that it cannot be a judicial or impartial tribunal . . . It is supervisor, detective, prosecutor, plaintiff, attorney, and court. No tribunal charged with such functions can have the attributes which ought to characterize a judicial tribunal.[97]

It was repeatedly emphasized before the Elkins committee in 1905 that the Interstate Commerce Commission was a partisan body which represented the shippers against the railroads and that it ought not therefore to be given quasi-judicial duties. It was further urged that this merger of different powers would result in inefficiency, and that therefore the commission's powers ought to be sharply limited.

It is interesting to note that two members of the Interstate Commerce Commission, Messrs Prouty and Fifer, supported the views just expressed. Mr. Fifer declared:

> . . . The railroads do not want to have their civil rights submitted to a tribunal that is spying on them and whose duty it is to convict them in the courts of the country and to obtain fines and imprisonment to be imposed.[98]

Mr. Prouty emphasized this merger of powers and the inescapable partisanship of the commission as a basis for his plans for segregating the functions of the commission.[99]

97. Hearings before the House Committee on Interstate and Foreign Commerce on Bills to Amend the Interstate Commerce Law, 57th Cong., 1st sess. (1902), 469, 493.

98. *Supra,* note 79, op. cit. vol. IV, 3364.   99. *Infra,* 78 f.

In the Congressional debates this combination of powers evoked sharp attack. Senator Lodge of Massachusetts referred to the commission as a body 'who are to be in the operation and discharge of their functions judge, jury, and prosecuting officer, resembling nothing that I can think of except the French juge d'instruction.' [100] Mr. Littlefield of Maine charged that the commission would be 'a detective agency, a prosecuting attorney, and a lord high executioner.' [101]

d. *Proposals for segregation of commission powers*

Most of those who objected to the merging of varied powers in the commission were those who not only opposed strengthening that body but opposed any effective railroad regulation. They were content to play up this supposedly objectionable merging and let it go at that. But many friends of the commission, including the two commissioners just mentioned, were honestly worried about the problem and anxious to correct the difficulty. Accordingly, a number of interesting schemes were suggested for preventing the commission from exercising what were deemed to be incompatible powers.

In the first place, it was proposed that these powers be distributed among several agencies rather than merged in the hands of one. This was Mr. Prouty's idea and over a period of years he threw his influence behind it, although his concrete proposals for working out this segregation underwent considerable change. Appearing before the Hepburn committee in 1902 he said 'the only proper way and only possible way to deal with it is to create a special court which shall . . . enforce the orders of some commission.' [102] Before the Elkins committee in 1905 he elaborated this much more fully:

The Interstate Commerce Commission at the present time is an executive body. It is charged with the duty within certain limits of executing this law. It is our duty to enforce the criminal features of the law.

Now, I am perfectly clear in my own way that those powers should be taken away from the Interstate Commerce Commission. In the first place, a body of five men is too cumbersome to act as an

---

100. 40 Cong. Rec. 4104.
101. Ibid. 2071.

102. *Supra,* note 97, op. cit. 236.

executive. It does not do things. It does not get anywhere. In the
next place, I do not think you ought to combine in the same body
the executive, the administrative and the judicial functions. That is
my attitude as a commissioner. If it is my duty as a commissioner to
investigate, to unearth criminal violations of the law, I think I am
very likely to get into a frame of mind which unfits me to dispas-
sionately pass upon the rates made by the defendant; so I say now,
and I have always said, that you should take away from the Interstate Commerce Commission and put either in the Department of
Justice or in the Department of Commerce and Labor what I may
call the executive functions of the commission. Now, the Commission has certain judicial functions. It is allowed in certain cases to
award damages. I think those judicial functions should be taken
away from the Commission. I do not think that the Commission as
now constituted, hearing cases as it hears them, receiving testimony,
as it receives testimony, ought to be charged with the judicial duty
of trying a damage suit.[103]

Senator Dolliver asked Mr. Prouty the following question:

. . . I have been wondering whether it would not be policy to
continue the Commission with substantially the same powers and
duties which it now exercises and to create in addition to the Interstate Commerce Commission a tribunal to sit in judgment upon
these questions of rates for the future and discriminations, leaving
this higher commission a commission which might be called a 'commission of interstate commerce appeals,' in a quiet atmosphere, undisturbed by the business of the detective, the prosecutor or the in-
quisitor of any sort—just to pass judgment on the rate question.
What would you say to that idea?

Mr. Prouty replied:

That meets my suggestion exactly. Only, it must be a commission.
It cannot be a court.[104]

In the debates in the House, Mr. Stevens of Minnesota made
a similar suggestion though the terms of his proposal were less
clearly thought out. He said:

. . . Of course this bill does not and could not confer strictly
judicial authority and does not make the Commission into a court.
It very carefully avoids that by requiring only the opinion of the
Commission to find a rate unreasonable as a basis for action. We all

103. *Supra,* note 79, op. cit. vol. IV, 2893.   104. Ibid. 2896.

realize that strictly legislative power is not conferred, but only power is delegated to work out the details of the legislative will and make it effective. But quasi-judicial and quasi-legislative powers are conferred upon an executive tribunal, and it is not an effective or satisfactory policy to be pursued. The investigation and prosecutions should be definitely committed to an executive officer and bureau who should have no other duties and the full responsibility. The full judicial power should be committed to the courts, and the legislative power should be worked out by a separate tribunal having no other duties and reporting to Congress, its sole authority.[105]

A similar plan was proposed by Mr. Sulzer of New York:

First, there must be a body like the Interstate Commerce Commission, clothed with the right and authority to make just, fair, and reasonable rates in place of unjust, unfair, and unreasonable rates, and have these rates take effect immediately, and remain in full force and effect until modified or set aside by the Commission; or modified or set aside by the court of last resort. This is an administrative function and should be the sole and only power under the constitutional limitations of our Government conferred on the Interstate Commerce Commission.

Second. There must be a body clothed with authority to determine controversies, review the orders of the Interstate Commerce Commission, and interpret the laws of Congress governing and regulating transportation. This is a judicial function, and should properly be vested in the courts of our country.

Third. There should be an executive department in the National Government, with a Cabinet officer at its head, charged with the responsibility and the sole duty of the prompt and thorough enforcement of the laws of the United States concerning companies and corporations doing an interstate-commerce business. My bill creates this department. This is an executive function, and belongs to the executive branch of the Government; and these three functions should always be kept separate and distinct.[106]

Even more interesting was the colloquy between Senator Newlands and Commissioner Fifer, during the hearings of the Elkins committee, regarding the possibility of an effective internal segregation of the commission functions believed to be incompatible with each other. This is set forth in full:

SENATOR NEWLANDS: Is there not some way of organizing this Interstate Commerce Commission in such a way that you could have

105. 40 Cong. Rec. 2086.   106. Ibid. 2191.

one part that will attend entirely to the quasi-judicial functions of hearing and determining, and another branch of the Commission to transact the detective and police duties?

MR. FIFER: So far as I can see now, I would answer, no.

SENATOR NEWLANDS: Would not that work better than putting them as far apart as giving these powers to the Attorney General's office would involve?

MR. FIFER: It is altogether likely that it would. That is a matter of detail, however, that nobody can tell in advance just what would be best to do.[107]

The same suggestion was made by a representative of the New York Produce Exchange, Mr. James F. Parker, who said:

. . . Give the Commission increased powers of investigation, if that is possible. Increase the number of its members so that its business can be facilitated by dividing it; also that all preliminary investigations can be conducted by one part of the Commission, whilst another part is engaged in considering testimony, and deciding questions submitted, so that complaints can be disposed of more expeditiously.[108]

e. *Proposal for a transportation court*

As early as 1904 Mr. Hearst of New York had introduced a bill providing for an interstate commerce court,[109] and an unsuccessful attempt was made to incorporate in the Act of 1906 a provision for a transportation court. This had been a controversial feature of the Esch-Townsend bill and the idea was favored by Mr. Hepburn himself. It was dropped out of the Hepburn bill as finally introduced and discussion of it was accordingly confined to the Congressional committees. This transportation court was to be a constitutional court much like the later Commerce Court of 1910. The railroads took no strong stand with regard to it. If the powers of the commission were to be drastically increased, the carriers were inclined to favor such a court. Otherwise they did not care.[110] Most of those who wanted the commission strengthened opposed the transportation court for fear it would increase the judicial throttling

107. *Supra,* note 79, op. cit. vol. IV, 3364.
108. Ibid.
109. *Infra,* 85.
110. *Supra,* note 79, op. cit. vol. II, 816.

of the commission.[111] Commissioner Prouty expressed his approval of such a court before the Hepburn committee [112] and he was supported by A. T. Hadley,[113] who referred to the successful experience with such a tribunal in England. The House committee of 1905 recommended such a court, while the Democratic minority of the committee opposed it. We shall examine the merits of the proposal more fully in considering the Commerce Court of 1910.

f. *The Interstate Commerce Commission as an administrative agency*

We have seen that in the debates on the Act of 1887 there was little disposition to try to classify the commission according to its essential nature, to label it as legislative, judicial, or executive, or to apply these terms to the functions assigned to it. It is interesting therefore to note the unanimity with which the commission is referred to throughout the hearings and debates on the Hepburn bill as an 'administrative' agency. The reason for·this is not hard to find. Those sponsoring the new legislation were under heavy fire over the alleged delegation of legislative and judicial powers to the commission. It was agreed on all sides that legislative and judicial powers could not constitutionally be delegated and it was accordingly of the first importance to show that the powers given to the commission were neither legislative nor judicial but administrative. The following comments drawn from the Congressional debates in 1906 are typical:

. . . The Commission is an administrative body to whom is delegated certain duties in carrying out the will of Congress . . . In so far as the Commission is administrative it becomes a part of the executive arm of the Government . . .[114]

. . . Then we leave to the Commission the administrative power to determine what in each particular case is the just, reasonable, and fairly remunerative rate.[115]

111. Ibid. 2063 f., 2636.
112. *Supra*, 78.
113. *Supra*, note 79, op. cit. vol. II, 1889 ff.
114. Rep. Hogg, Colo., 40 Cong. Rec. 2029.
115. Rep. Mann, Ill., ibid. 2245.

. . . The power now sought to be conferred upon the Commission to condemn an existing rate and to fix a future rate is essentially administrative . . .[116]

Senator Rayner of Maryland took special pains to make this clear. He emphasized strongly that the new rate-making power 'is an administrative function' and declared that the difficulty had arisen from 'the unfortunate—I ought not to say "unfortunate"; "inadvertent," perhaps—expression of the court in the Maximum Rate cases, in 167 United States, where it uses the word "legislative" instead of "administrative." '[117] President Roosevelt had repeatedly referred to the commission as an administrative tribunal or an administrative body, and that terminology seems to have been accepted as correct.

g. *Proposals for consumer protection against railroads*

Through the debates runs comment on the fact that unless the shippers or other roads complained, the commission had no power to intervene and protect the public interest against exploitation by the carriers. It was suggested therefore that the commission be allowed to act on its own initiative. Mr. La Follette strongly urged either that the commission be given independent power to protect consumers or that some special agency be set up to represent them and to press actions on their behalf.

h. *Planning functions and advisory duties*

There was no general discussion of the commission's responsibility in advising Congress on new legislation or in planning a transportation policy. We have seen, however, that the report of the commission for 1904 had had substantial influence in the movement for new legislation.[118] Mr. La Follette criticized the commission's recommendations for new legislation, and charged that the commission proposed to Congress only the things which it felt reasonably sure would be passed.[119]

116. Rep. Simmons, N. C., ibid. 3730.   118. *Supra,* 69.
117. Ibid. 3782.   119. 40 Cong. Rec. 5695.

E. Further Strengthening of Commission—The Commerce
Court Experiment—The Mann-Elkins Act of 1910

1. BACKGROUND OF THE MANN-ELKINS ACT OF 1910

Problems left unsettled by the Hepburn Act of 1906 soon
began to press for solution. Under the statute the commission
could establish a new railroad rate only on complaint. It could
neither initiate a new rate action nor suspend a new rate established by a carrier. The long-and-short-haul clause, which had
been emasculated by the Supreme Court, remained unchanged
and the commission's power under it was negligible. There
was a growing feeling that railroad mergers and traffic agreements between carriers ought to be permitted if adequate protection to the public could be guaranteed. Finally it was recognized that the problem of railroad capitalization would have to
be dealt with sooner or later. The principle of government regulation of railroads had been won, but it was clear that it would
need to be greatly extended if certain major problems were to
be successfully met.

For two years after the enactment of the Hepburn Act the
commission had relatively smooth sailing. It proceeded dis-
creetly in the use of its new powers and the railroads appeared
to acquiesce. In 1908, however, a large number of attacks upon
commission rate orders were instituted, and a flood of litigation ensued. There were conflicting court decisions and the
courts showed a definite tendency to poach upon the administrative discretion of the commission.

In the Presidential campaign of 1908 the Democratic platform proposed that the commission should be given the power
to initiate rate orders and demanded the physical valuation of
railroads. The Republican platform proposed that the carriers
be permitted to establish tariff agreements subject to the approval of the commission, and also that the commission be
given authority over the issuance of railroad securities. In this
campaign there appeared a new party, the Independence
Party, led by Mr. William Randolph Hearst, its candidate for
the presidency. His platform contained this plank: 'We favor
the creation of an Interstate Commerce Court, whose sole func-

tion it shall be to review speedily and enforce summarily the orders of the Interstate Commerce Commission.' [120] After his election President Taft threw his influence in favor of a commerce court. More than any other President he was interested in the judiciary and in problems of judicial administration, and he sponsored the commerce court proposal with wholehearted enthusiasm. However, no aroused public opinion appeared to be back of it.

2. STEPS IN THE LEGISLATIVE HISTORY OF THE MANN-ELKINS ACT AND COMMERCE COURT PROPOSAL

The focus of interest in the new legislation was its proposal of a commerce court. The basic idea was by no means new. As early as 1893 it had been suggested that a specialized court of commerce be set up in each judicial district. In 1904 Mr. Hearst introduced a bill in the House proposing a commerce court, and reintroduced it annually through 1908. Mr. Hearst's proposal, which differed from that finally embodied in the Mann-Elkins Act, was as follows: The commerce court was to be composed of three judges appointed for life by the President and not drawn from the existing federal courts. It was to have broad powers to pass upon the reasonableness of rates fixed by the commission. It could suspend those rates if it believed them to be 'clearly unjust, unreasonable, or unlawful.' The Attorney General was to defend the orders of the commission before the commerce court. The court's jurisdiction in all cases affecting railroads was to be final, save where the Supreme Court or the commerce court believed that constitutional questions were involved.[121]

In 1905, as we have seen, railroad bills including proposals for a commerce court were introduced in the House by Townsend, Esch, and Hepburn; and the House Committee on Interstate and Foreign Commerce reported favorably the Esch-Townsend bill with its accompanying court proposal. The commerce court plan was dropped out of the Hepburn bill but it was kept pretty steadily before Congress until its enactment in 1910.

120. K. H. Porter, *National Party Platforms* (1924), 291.
121. H. Doc. 422, 58th Cong., 3d sess. (1905), 119-38.

Early in 1910 President Taft sent to Congress a special message dealing with the railroads.[122] He had already discussed this problem and commented upon the commerce court idea in various public speeches. This special message urged the establishment of a commerce court 'for reasons precisely analogous to those which induced the Congress to create the Court of Customs Appeals.' An Administration railroad bill was at once introduced into each house drafted by a group composed of Attorney General Wickersham, Secretary of Commerce and Labor Nagel, Commissioners Knapp and Prouty of the Interstate Commerce Commission, the Solicitor General, and Representative Townsend. This bill, which later emerged as the Mann-Elkins bill, contained the following provisions: It legalized traffic agreements between competing roads subject to the approval of the commission. It gave the commission supervision over railroad capitalization. It created a commerce court of five judges to be selected from the circuit courts by the President for five-year terms. The court was to review on appeal all orders made by the commission, and its decisions were to be final except on constitutional points. The Attorney General was to defend the commission's orders before the commerce court.

Hearings were held on the bill by the Senate and House committees on interstate commerce in 1910, but there was very little discussion of the court plan. Certain members of the Interstate Commerce Commission were questioned at length and expressed themselves as favoring a commerce court provided certain changes could be made in President Taft's proposal. The bill was debated in the House and the Senate, and substantially amended through the efforts of the powerful insurgent group in Congress. Differences between the bills finally passed by the House and Senate were ironed out in conference and the measure was enacted June 18, 1910.

3. SUMMARY OF THE PROVISIONS OF THE ACT

The major provisions of the Mann-Elkins Act of 1910 [123] were as follows: First, it gave to the Interstate Commerce Com-

---

122. 45 Cong. Rec. 378 f.   123. Act of June 18, 1910, 36 Stat. at L. 539.

mission power to suspend proposed increases in railroad rates by carriers, and placed upon the railroads the burden of defending the reasonableness of such rates. The commission could prosecute inquiries upon its own initiative and could establish freight classifications. Secondly, the much contested long-and-short-haul clause was rehabilitated and the commission's jurisdiction under it was restored. Thirdly, the commission's jurisdiction was extended to telegraph, telephone, and cable companies. Fourthly, the Commerce Court was established. The judges of the court were to be selected from the circuit judges not by the President but by the Chief Justice of the United States, and the jurisdiction of the court was to be no greater than that then possessed by the federal courts.

The original proposal to legalize traffic agreements was dropped out completely. The Interstate Commerce Commission was not given the proposed authority to supervise railroad capitalization; instead, a Railroad Securities Commission was set up to investigate the whole subject and report to Congress.

4. TOPICS AND ISSUES IN HEARINGS AND DEBATES

a. *Increase in substantive powers of the commission*

There was no very animated discussion of the new powers given to the commission. The new legislation in fact attracted little attention outside of Congress. It was overshadowed by other important political developments. The new powers given to the commission were, however, of great practical importance. To allow the commission to suspend proposed rate increases and to restore its authority over long-and-short-haul discrimination was to make it a potent agency of public control. These powers were not, however, essentially different in kind from those which the commission already enjoyed. While it took a struggle to secure their enactment, that struggle was mild when compared with the bitter fight on the Hepburn bill. The progressive insurgent movement was getting into swing and the forces working for effective railroad regulation were powerful and well organized.

b. *Should a commerce court be established?*

The place of the Commerce Court in our judicial system and the problems impinging upon our whole jurisprudence which arose in connection with it are matters that fall outside the scope of this study. We may summarize briefly, however, the main arguments for and against the establishment of the court, as some of these have a measure of relevance to the status and powers of the Interstate Commerce Commission.

Arguments for a commerce court. Between the introduction of Mr. Hearst's proposal in 1904 and the abolition of the Commerce Court in 1913 the case for such a tribunal was thoroughly elaborated. The main arguments may be summarized as follows:

1. Railroad litigation will be speeded up by a specialized court. Intermediate courts of appeal are eliminated. There will be fewer appeals from a five-man court than from a one-judge district court.

2. Uniformity of decision will result. Railroad cases will no longer be handled in eighty-odd judicial districts but in one centralized court. Under the old arrangement there was much confusion. Conflicts arose between district courts sometimes affecting the same railroad. This confusion will disappear.

3. There will be expert judges to deal with highly technical cases. Railroad problems are beyond the capacity of most federal judges. A specialized court will acquire expertness by experience. At the same time new blood will be brought into the court by the rotation of its members and this will prevent undue bias.

4. The regular federal courts will be relieved of the heavy burden of railroad litigation. Many federal judges are incompetent to deal with these complicated problems and intensely dislike them. They tend, where possible, to postpone consideration of them.

5. The judges of the new court will be completely free from local influences and prejudices.

6. Railroads will no longer be able to choose the court in which to bring a case. Certain federal judges are more favor-

able to railroad interests than others, and the carriers have been alert to take advantage of this fact.

7. The new duties imposed upon the Interstate Commerce Commission by recent legislation will produce many more appeals from commission orders. The commerce court is needed to handle this new mass of litigation.

8. The establishment of the Court of Customs Appeals in the Tariff Act of 1909 provides a sound precedent for the new court. It shows that specialized courts are a proper part of our judicial system and are not contrary to basic American traditions and principles. Any fear of dangerous specialization should be allayed by the provision for the rotation of judges.

9. All questions affecting railroads are of national importance. It is therefore highly desirable that they be dealt with by a national court, rather than by district or circuit courts.

10. Finally the commerce court will be able to build up a body of law relating to railroad regulation. As Mr. Madden of Illinois put it in the House, there ought to emerge a 'harmonious, consistent, and justly proportioned system of laws, rules, and regulations, governing interstate commerce in all its branches and phases.' [124]

Arguments against a commerce court. Opposition to a commerce court came chiefly from the group of progressives who were suspicious of any attempt to curb the Interstate Commerce Commission and who feared that the proposed court would have that effect. Their argument ran as follows:

1. The new court will be a 'railroad' court. It will unconsciously and inevitably develop a bias favorable to the railroads. As Mr. Hardy of Texas expressed it:

. . . Environments affect us all. Our opinions gradually take a tinge from our association. I do not know that this amounts to very much, but when you get your court set aside for the trial of one class of cases only, with the representatives of the United States, far removed from the people, upon one side, and the representatives of the great railroads and other corporations immediately and vitally interested on the other, after a while your impartial judge begins to see things in a little different light from what he did before.[125]

2. A commerce court will usurp the discretion of the Interstate Commerce Commission and tend to supplant it as the real

124. 45 Cong. Rec. 4939.   125. Ibid. 5162.

authority in the fixing of railroad rates. It will follow the bad practice of other federal courts in trying railroad cases *de novo,* and the rate-making power of the commission will be undermined.

3. There is no clear necessity for such a court. There is no serious demand for it except upon the part of the President. There will not be enough business to keep it occupied. It will be 'a fifth wheel to the judicial wagon.' [126] Furthermore, the recent decision of the Supreme Court in the Illinois Central case [127] in which the commission's findings of fact were held to be final if supported by evidence has eliminated any need for a new tribunal which might have existed before.

4. The claim that the commerce court will be composed of experts is specious. The judges are to be drawn from the existing circuit courts. They will be no wiser on a commerce court than they were before. If expertness is expected to be developed by experience the short terms of office and the principle of rotation operate to preclude it.

5. But expert judges are undesirable. Justice comes from law not from experts, as Mr. Adamson of Georgia [128] put it; and what is needed is not technical knowledge but broad judgment like that exercised by the Supreme Court. The only justification for having a court of experts would be on the assumption that the judges are to do over again the job already done by the Interstate Commerce Commission. Experts may be desirable on the commission; they are out of place on a court of review.

6. It is undesirable to restrict railroad litigation to a court sitting in Washington. Litigants will be subjected to inconvenience and expense. Furthermore, local judges familiar with local conditions are in a better position to decide railroad cases fairly.

7. Long delay and much litigation will be needed to settle the jurisdiction and the powers of the new court. After twenty years the powers and status of the Interstate Commerce Commission have been reasonably well established by decision. All

126. Rep. Richardson, Ala., 39 Cong. Rec. 2009.

127. *Interstate Commerce Commission* v. *Illinois Central R. Co.,* 215 U.S. 452 (1910).

128. 48 Cong. Rec. 6152.

of these problems will be reopened and a period of confusion and uncertainty will ensue.

8. Instead of speeding up litigation the new court will inject delays, technicalities, and complications into the picture. The normal delays involved in railroad cases would be as substantial in one court as in another, and railroad lawyers will be able to exploit the new system and make it more complicated than the old. Mr. Shull of Pennsylvania charged that the court 'is hedged in by and tinctured with all the technical traps and pitfalls of inglorious judicial practice, a court constructed for the purpose of making litigation before it difficult, uncertain, and indeterminate.' [129]

9. Uniformity of decision will not come through the decisions of a commerce court but, in the very nature of the case, can come only through the Supreme Court of the United States.

10. The new court will be a judicial body, but its broad powers of review endow it with legislative and administrative powers as well. This is an unconstitutional merging of incompatible powers.

11. A specialized court is contrary to the spirit and tradition of our institutions. It is 'un-American' and violates the principle of the republican form of government.

12. The selection of the judges of the commerce court by the Chief Justice of the United States will inject politics into the Supreme Court and subject it to unwholesome pressure.

13. The supposed analogy between a commerce court and the Court of Customs Appeals is imaginary. The latter is not really a court at all but is essentially a board of appeals, reviewing administrative decisions.

c. *The relation of the commerce court to the commission*

While this study is not concerned with the established Commerce Court as a judicial body, we should, however, analyze its relations with the commission and what its sponsors and opponents deemed those relations to be. Following is an analysis of the discussions on two aspects of this important relationship.

129. 39 Cong. Rec., Appendix, 52.

The commerce court's review of Interstate Commerce Commission discretion. One of the chief arguments of those opposing a commerce court was that it would be likely to usurp the essential job already being done by the commission. Whether this was true, and the extent to which it might be true, were subjects of bitter dispute throughout the entire history of the commerce court idea. There was a substantial body of opinion which desired a commerce court with power to review all orders of the Interstate Commerce Commission substantially on their merits. As early as 1902 Mr. Prouty, a member of the commission, had urged the creation of a tribunal to review Interstate Commerce Commission orders.[130] These orders, he stated, were not produced by judicial process, and ought not, therefore, to be reviewed by the regular federal courts. He later came to believe that they should be reviewed by a quasi-judicial body exercising its judgment and passing upon the merits of the commission's rulings; that what was needed was not a court but an appellate administrative board. Mr. Hearst began in 1904 to advocate a commerce court. This court was to review the reasonableness of rates fixed by the commission. The House committee which reported the Esch-Townsend bill in 1905 favored a transportation court which would decide what is a just and reasonable rate.[131] The minority report attacked this arrangement because it permitted that court to re-try commission orders on their merits and thereby established a complete review *de novo* of all commission orders. This broad court review was defended in the House by Mr. Hepburn. The railroads took a lukewarm attitude toward the establishment of a commerce court but they had definite views on one point: if a court was to be established they wished it to have the broadest possible power to review commission orders. President Taft in his message in January 1910 urging the creation of a commerce court proposed that it have power

130. American Economic Association *Publications,* series 3, vol. IV, no. 1 (1903), 80. With regard to Mr. Prouty's later views, Commissioner C. B. Aitchison in a letter to the writer states: 'In fairness to Commissioner Prouty, who advocated the creation of a separate commerce court, it ought to be stated that Prouty (who was a hard-headed New England pragmatist) changed his mind when he saw the court, headed by his old colleague Knapp, undertaking to act as an appellate commission.'

131. *Supra,* 69.

to review all orders of the Interstate Commerce Commission. He referred to the Court of Customs Appeals as an analogy and the inference is that he expected the commerce court to exercise broad powers of review on the merits.

Those who favored a strong commission and drastic railroad regulation sharply attacked the proposal to give the commerce court this broad supervisory authority over the commission. The commission's experience with the regular federal courts had been unhappy. They had assumed broad authority to review commission orders on their merits and their policy of trying commission cases *de novo* had seriously weakened the commission's powers. In 1904 and 1905 the power of the commission itself had been comparatively small; yet even then there had been sharp criticism from those who feared that a commerce court would substitute its own judgment for that of the commission and would essentially nullify any rate-making power which that body might enjoy. Mr. Norris of Nebraska strongly urged this point [132] and Mr. Davis of Minnesota declared that to give the new court power to determine the lawfulness, justness, and reasonableness of rates was to give it powers greater than those of the regular federal courts; to create in substance two juries to pass upon factual matters.[133] It was also argued that the delegation of these broad powers to the commerce court amounted to an unconstitutional delegation of legislative power.

The 1910 attack on the broad grants of authority to be given to the commerce court was much sharper than in the earlier debates. The commission had been strengthened by the Hepburn Act of 1906, and in the Illinois Central case [134] the Supreme Court had given needed relief by holding that the commission's determinations of fact were to be treated by the lower courts as *prima facie* correct. Any change which threatened to dissipate the salutary results of these gains was bound to be bitterly opposed. The Interstate Commerce Commission itself, at least those members who appeared on its behalf, were definitely worried on this point. Mr. Knapp, the chairman, while favoring a commerce court urged before the House committee:

132. 39 Cong. Rec. 1413.
133. Ibid. 2110 ff.
134. *Supra*, 90.

. . . We strongly recommend that the bill be so amended as to contain the explicit statement that the commerce court shall have no jurisdiction or power over the orders of the commission not now possessed by circuit courts of the United States as defined and limited by the Supreme Court in the 'car distribution cases,' so called, which were recently decided. Therefore we desire to have the language of the bill expressly limit the jurisdiction of the circuit courts under the present law, by holding in substance that orders of the commission involving the exercise of judgment and discretion are not open to review by the courts unless (a) the commission has acted without jurisdiction, or (b) made an order which operates to deprive the carrier of its property without due process of law.[135]

Senator Dolliver expressed the same point of view more forcibly:

. . . In 1906 it was very strongly urged that we ought to have two interstate commerce commissions—one for the purpose of trying the cases, and the other for the purpose of seeing that the cases were correctly decided. That was rejected by the good sense of both Houses of Congress practically without debate. Yet I fear we have introduced into our present proposed legislative programme exactly that absurdity . . .

I warn Senators that, if the Interstate Commerce Commission is to have these cases transferred to a court of commerce, there should be no discretion lodged anywhere to review the wisdom of the order of the commission or to exercise an appellate jurisdiction over the discretion which the law confides to the Interstate Commerce Commission. I think that ought to be guarded by common consent.[136]

Senator Newlands believed that the commerce court would hamstring the Interstate Commerce Commission,[137] and the fears of the court's opponents were not allayed by the amendment to the bill which provided that the jurisdiction of the commerce court should be no greater than that of the existing courts. It was trenchantly pointed out in a resolution submitted by the Nevada Railroad Commission that the commerce court was bound to override the commission. If it did not do so there would be no need for its existence, and so for its own preservation it must reverse the commission if possible.[138] As

---

135. Hearings before the House Committee on Interstate and Foreign Commerce on Bills Affecting Interstate Commerce, 61st Cong., 2d sess. (1910), 1173.

136. 45 Cong. Rec. 5324.

137. Ibid. 8371.   138. 48 Cong. Rec. 450.

we shall see later, one of the major reasons for the abolition of the Commerce Court in 1913 was that the worst fears of its opponents had been realized on this particular point. The court stood convicted of having usurped the prerogatives and discretion of the commission.

The unsuccessful effort to give the commerce court power to pass on railroad consolidations. On the President's suggestion the original Mann-Elkins bill sought to authorize railroad consolidations under careful restrictions. The consolidations permitted were to be those which involved roads 'not directly and substantially competitive,' [139] and the question whether the roads were directly and substantially competitive was to be referred to the proposed commerce court for decision. The Interstate Commerce Commission was given no authority to pass on the question. In presenting the bill in the House, Mr. Mann admitted that this arrangement was highly debatable, but explained it on the ground that the commerce court could be given power to enter a final judgment authorizing a consolidation, whereas the commission could merely present a finding which would have to be reviewed later in some court.[140] Mr. Mann later opposed giving the court this power and urged that the commission itself should have final power to authorize these consolidations.[141] The commission, he declared, was more familiar with the problems which would have to be considered and, not being a judicial body, could consider evidence which could not properly be presented to a court of law. This position was supported by many others during the debates. As Mr. Kennedy of Ohio put it, the fact of competition between railroads could be settled by a court, but the wisdom and desirability of a consolidation should be determined by the commission.[142] The general temper of Congress at this time toward trusts and monopolies was not to tolerate railroad consolidations in any circumstances. There was an underlying fear voiced by Mr. Sims of Tennessee that if the commerce court permitted railroads to consolidate, the government would be estopped from all subsequent proceedings under the antitrust laws and vital protection to the public interest would be sacri-

139. 45 Cong. Rec. 4719.
140. Ibid. 4718.
141. Ibid. 5891.
142. Ibid. 5010.

ficed.[143] The consolidation clause was finally dropped out of the bill.

d. *Merger of powers in the commission—Defense of commission orders before commerce court by Attorney General*

The first proposals for a commerce court in 1904 and 1905 carried the provision that when orders of the Interstate Commerce Commission came before the court for review, the defense of those orders should be handled by the Attorney General rather than by the commission's own attorneys. The proponents of the commerce court regarded this as a highly desirable scheme, the main argument for it being that it would avoid the merging in the commission of incompatible powers. In his message in 1910 President Taft defended this arrangement as a means of preserving the impartiality of the commission. He stated:

Under the existing law, the Interstate Commerce Commission itself initiates and defends litigation in the court for the enforcement, or in the defense, of its orders and decrees, and for this purpose it employs attorneys who, while subject to the control of the Attorney-General, act upon the initiative and under the instructions of the commission. This blending of administrative, legislative and judicial functions tends, in my opinion, to impair the efficiency of the commission by clothing it with partisan characteristics and robbing it of the impartial judicial attitude it should occupy in passing upon questions submitted to it. In my opinion all litigation affecting the Government should be under the direct control of the Department of Justice; and I recommend that all proceedings affecting orders and decrees of the Interstate Commerce Commission be brought by or against the United States *eo nomine,* and be placed in charge of an Assistant Attorney-General, acting under the direction of the Attorney-General.[144]

Chairman Knapp told the House committee that 'it is not for the Commission to go into court and defend its own action.' [145] Mr. Mann of Illinois, speaking in the House, declared:

143. Ibid. 4841.
144. Ibid. 379.

145. *Supra,* note 135, op. cit. 1237.

. . . So that in such a case the commission becomes, as it were, the grand jury, its attorneys the prosecuting attorneys, and itself the judge trying the case.

. . . We think that practice has very largely led to the undue criticism against orders of the commission by railroads and their attorneys. They say that the commission packs itself. It inaugurates litigation before itself; it determines upon litigation; and then, in its own name, defends it in the courts.[146]

Mr. Townsend of Michigan supported this view, stating:

. . . It was the opinion of many people, including the President and some, if not all, of the commissioners, that the dual, triple, and, perhaps, quadruple character of the commission in investigating, trying, administering, and enforcing matters subject to its control was at times embarrassing to the commission and in a way obnoxious to American notions of justice. The greatest and most beneficial function of the commission, as I understand it, is its power to investigate, advise, and settle, but it was discovered that carriers hesitated to make statements in matters in controversy and to submit matters in the nature of compromise to a tribunal which might, if a settlement failed, afterwards prosecute them before the court.[147]

Mr. McCall of Massachusetts charged that the commission was a whole government in itself with legislative, executive, and judicial powers.[148] He therefore favored this proposal. In the Senate, Senator Elkins declared:

Since the adoption of the first regulation of commerce the Interstate Commerce Commission has been by law placed in a most unenviable position. It was made the prosecutor, the judge, and was required to assume the position of plaintiff or defendant in litigation affecting its orders. To give confidence to those whose interests are affected by its judgments it is essential that it should be disassociated, as far as the nature of the subject of its duties will permit, from occupying any attitude that, through pride of opinion, bias in its investigations, or partiality of judgment, by reason of active participation in litigation, may prejudice its conclusions . . .

With such power conferred, affecting such vast interests, both property and commercial, is it unwise, as proposed under the scheme of this bill, to segregate that tribunal, as far as their duties will per-

146. 45 Cong. Rec. 4574.
147. Ibid. 5234.
148. Ibid. 8481.

mit, from occupying the position of prosecutor, judge, and litigant? [149]

There were other arguments for the proposal. Senator Root felt that it was desirable to centralize in the Department of Justice all of the legal activities of the government in the interests of efficiency and economy.[150] Mr. Madden of Illinois believed that better legal ability would be found in the Department of Justice than in the commission.[151] But in the main the authority given to the Attorney General to defend the commission's orders before the projected commerce court was justified on the theory that it was improper for a body which had reached a conclusion by a quasi-judicial process to appear in the role of a prosecutor before an appellate court to defend that decision.

The attack on this arrangement was vigorous. It was urged that the Attorney General could substitute his judgment for that of the commission and assume the role of a reviewing tribunal passing upon commission orders. Mr. Hitchcock of Nebraska declared that the whole tendency was 'to belittle the Commission . . . We detract from its dignity and subordinate it not only to the court of commerce but to the Attorney-General.' [152] Senator Cummins stated the objections more elaborately in these words:

. . . It is proposed to convert the Department of Justice into a court of review without publicity, without appeal, without redress of any sort whatsoever . . .

But that is not all. Here is a case brought before the Interstate Commerce Commission, with its great detail of evidence and volumes of rate sheets and of business and transportation conditions. It finally reaches an end in an order of the commission. The commission is thoroughly familiar with the case, because it has taken every step from the beginning to the end of it. Then comes the suit in the court of commerce by the railway company affected by the order, and instantly the whole forum changes. The Attorney-General is to defend the case. He knows nothing about it. It is impossible for him to become as familiar with it as those who have been in at the beginning and who have pursued it step after step. The attorneys for the railway company have collected this testimony; they

149. Ibid. 3469.   151. Ibid. 4938.
150. Ibid. 4104.   152. Ibid. 5517.

have brought it together for the purpose of arguing the case before the Interstate Commerce Commission, and they are with the case in the court as well as before the commission.

But not one person who is either financially interested in the outcome or one person who has any familiarity with the proceedings is allowed to take any part in its after conduct.[153]

Senator Clapp of Minnesota expressed the same view in a slightly mixed metaphor when he declared that as a result of the proposal the commission would 'be emasculated by being bound hand and foot.'[154] The Attorney General, unfamiliar with the rate cases in their earlier stages, would be less competent to present them than the commission's own attorneys, and there would be serious delay as a result of this transfer of responsibility. As the bill finally passed, the Attorney General retained the authority originally given to him, with the proviso that the Interstate Commerce Commission might, if it wished, be represented before the commerce court through its own lawyers.

e. *The nature of the commission's powers and its relation to other departments*

The authority given to the Attorney General in the provision just discussed stimulated a wholly different line of thought. For the first time a definite legal relation was established between the Interstate Commerce Commission and an executive officer, and this led to a reconsideration of the nature of the commission's powers and its relation to the other departments of government. We have seen that in the debates on the Hepburn bill emphasis was placed on the 'administrative' character of the commission and its duties, a designation designed to meet the constitutional criticism that the commission had invalidly been given legislative power.[155] In 1910, in the face of what was thought to be an attempt to subordinate the commission to an executive officer, emphasis was placed on the 'legislative' character of the commission, on its complete independence from the executive, and on its status as an 'arm of Congress.' Let us summarize briefly this analysis:

153. Ibid. 3350.
154. Ibid. 3539.

155. *Supra*, 71 ff

In the first place, it was felt highly objectionable to subordinate a nonpartisan and independent commission to a political officer such as the Attorney General. This was stressed in the minority report of the House committee as follows:

We object to the fourth and fifth sections of the bill, because they practically transfer the important and essential work of the Interstate Commerce Commission to the Department of Justice. The commission is now, and was intended to be from its organization, an independent tribunal of the rights of the people and the carriers. The Department of Justice is a political department of this Government, and its appointees who direct the policies of the department are the representatives and the supporters of the present political administration of the country.[156]

Mr. Richardson of Alabama in the House debate demanded:

. . . Why is it that there is any necessity to transfer the material work of the Interstate Commerce Commission, an independent department or bureau, a bureau that has never had any politics in it, that never was run politically, subject to an absolutely political department of this Government. The Department of Justice is a political department. It is filled to-day, as it has always been filled, by men who are supporters of the administration in power. It is a political department. Why should this transfer be made?[157]

Second, it was vigorously insisted that the powers of the commission were legislative in character. Mr. Peters of Massachusetts declared in the House that the findings of the commission were legislative and not judicial, and that to require the Attorney General to defend those findings on appeal was to give an executive officer control over the legislative acts of the commission.[158] Mr. Mann of Illinois spoke of the authority of the commission as a 'power . . . in the way of a legislative power which can not be conferred upon the courts.'[159] Senator Beveridge expressed the same idea somewhat more elaborately:

However, I desire to return to the question . . . as to the impropriety of the Interstate Commerce Commission appearing to defend its order. It is not a judicial tribunal. There is no parallel whatsoever between it and an inferior court which exercises only judicial functions. The Interstate Commerce Commission exercises only leg-

156. 45 Cong. Rec. 4241.
157. Ibid. 4832.

158. Ibid. 5521.
159. Ibid. 4573.

islative functions—not purely legislative, but administrative legislative functions. It does nothing more than Congress could do and would do if it could make itself familiar with all the details which are developed in these cases. Therefore there is no analogy whatsoever.[160]

Third, not only were the functions of the commission emphasized as legislative but the commission itself was again declared 'an arm of Congress' to be kept wholly free from executive control. The minority report of the House committee opposing the Mann-Elkins Act objected to the meddling by the Administration through the Attorney General with the 'arm of Congress,' as violating the constitutional doctrine of the separation of the three departments of government. Mr. Stevens of Minnesota elaborated this argument:

. . . What is the proper function of the Interstate Commerce Commission? Its proper function is to make effective our legislation relative to common carriers. It is an arm of Congress . . . When that commission acts its act is the law of the land, the law of Congress, one of our laws. Now, who does enforce our law? Do we do it or do our employees do it? The commission in making its order is one of the arms of Congress. But we have provided a great arm of the executive department of the Government to enforce our laws, of whatever character they may be. We have created the office of Attorney-General to enforce our laws, and we provide that the laws of the Interstate Commerce Commission shall be enforced just exactly the same as all other laws, as the gentleman from Iowa has stated, to be enforced by the executive branch of the Government.[161]

His position was supported in the Senate by Senator Cummins:

My objection is that, in the first place, the Department of Justice will be given an irresponsible and unappealable review upon the orders of the commission . . .

I am amazed that it is proposed by any reflecting person that a review of that kind shall be permitted in the administration of a law of this character. The Interstate Commerce Commission is but a committee of Congress. It has no judicial functions whatever that are not exercised day after day by the committees of Congress. Would you permit some other department of the Government, would you permit the Attorney-General to say whether an act of

160. Ibid. 6393.   161. Ibid. 5521.

Congress—because that is what an order of the Interstate Commerce Commission is—to say whether an act of Congress shall be defended or not defended? [162]

Senator Borah declared:

> It may be said that it is unseemly to have a tribunal, which has made an order, defend its own order. In view of the nature of the tribunal which makes the order, the kind of jurisdiction it exercises, I do not think that that objection applies. It is a board created for the purpose of carrying into effect the act of Congress, and as a board it makes an order, and not as a tribunal or a part of the judiciary system. But whether it is seemly or not, we must concede that it has worked so far satisfactorily, and that there has been no demand for a change, and no reason for a change assigned among those who are interested most in this kind of litigation.[163]

The conception of the Interstate Commerce Commission as an agency intimately bound to Congress was sharply crystallized during these debates. Representative Madden's statement that the commission 'is a mere bureau of the executive branch' [164] was like a voice crying in the wilderness.

f. *The commission as a planning agency*

The 1910 debates paid no attention to the commission as a planning agency. It was urged as an argument against the establishment of the commerce court that the commission as a body had not recommended it. This argument, however, was weakened by the fact that several individual members of the commission publicly sponsored the court. This included Chairman Knapp, who later became presiding judge of the court. Senator Newlands sharply criticized the creation of the Railway Securities Commission set up to investigate the problem of the control of railroad capitalization.[165] He felt that the Interstate Commerce Commission itself should conduct such an inquiry and present its recommendations to Congress. The point was not otherwise debated and the commission's responsibilities in the field of planning attracted no general attention.

162. Ibid. 3350.
163. Ibid. 6396.
164. Ibid. 4939.
165. Ibid. 8371.

5. THE ABOLITION OF THE COMMERCE COURT

To round out the story of the Mann-Elkins Act we shall complete the brief and inglorious history of the Commerce Court, although it adds nothing new to the story of the Interstate Commerce Commission. The court was set up in 1910. Mr. Knapp, the chairman of the Interstate Commerce Commission, resigned his position to become its presiding judge. The court had no conspicuous friends except President Taft and Attorney General Wickersham. It had not been launched in response to any public demand, and it entered upon its work in an atmosphere of suspicion and hostility.

Criticism of the court set in at once and increased in vigor as the court proceeded with its job. There were four main counts in the indictment against it. First, the court restrained most of the orders issued by the commission. It appeared to assume that its purpose was to curb the commission, and this created the impression that it was biased in favor of the railroads. Secondly, the court proceeded to try over again the cases already tried by the commission. Until sharply rebuked by the Supreme Court it tried virtually every case *de novo* on appeal. Third, it still took a long time to dispose of a railroad case and the speeding up of litigation which had been promised did not seem to occur. Finally, the Commerce Court decisions were reversed by the Supreme Court in ten of the twelve cases which went up on appeal. This unsuccessful record seemed to justify the taunt of Representative Sims of Tennessee that the boasted court of experts had turned out to be 'expert in error.' [166]

The court was defended mainly by the President and the Attorney General. They declared that a speeding up of litigation had occurred and that the time required for the handling of a railroad case had been reduced from a period ranging from nine months to two and a half years, to a period of from six to eight months. When the court was set up thirty-six cases had immediately been transferred to its docket, a much heavier burden than had ever before been imposed upon a new tribunal. Secondly, the reversals of the Commerce Court by the Supreme Court were not relatively larger in number than re-

166. 50 Cong. Rec. 4536.

versals of the circuit courts, and reversals were inevitable while the court's jurisdiction was being judicially determined. It was true that the Commerce Court had exceeded its jurisdiction, but the Supreme Court had put a stop to this usurpation. Finally, it was impossible to judge the merits of the issue in so brief a time. The court should be continued until a larger body of experience had been built up. It may be noted that President Wilson asked for an additional appropriation for the court, but he did not commit himself otherwise on the controversy over its continuance.

The legislative history of the abolition of the court is as follows: The Democrats captured the House of Representatives in the election of 1910. In December 1911 Mr. Sims of Tennessee introduced a bill in the House to abolish the court.[167] Hearings upon it were held by the House Committee on Interstate and Foreign Commerce. Attorney General Wickersham appeared and defended the court, but the committee reported in favor of its abolition. In 1912 a rider was attached to one of the major appropriation bills providing for the abolition of the court. This bill was reported favorably by the House committee, though a minority report was presented in which the Commerce Court was defended and a plea was made for an extension of its life. The bill passed the House. In the meantime Senator Poindexter introduced a bill in the Senate to abolish the court.[168] This was replaced by the House appropriation bill. The Senate Committee on Interstate Commerce reported in favor of continuing the court. The Senate, however, passed the appropriation bill with its death clause on August 9, 1912. On August 15, President Taft sent a veto message vigorously stating the arguments in defense of the court, and the bill failed to pass over his veto. It may be noted parenthetically that a Presidential campaign was in progress and that the Progressive Party's platform declared: 'in order that the power of the Interstate Commerce Commission to protect the people may not be impaired or destroyed, we demand the abolition of the Commerce Court.' The day after the President's veto was sustained another bill with a rider abolishing the Commerce Court was reported out of committee in the

167. H.R. 14129, 62d Cong., 2d sess. (1911).
168. S. 3297, 62d Cong., 2d sess. (1911).

House. It passed both houses, but was promptly vetoed by President Taft on August 21. Although the House mustered enough votes to override the veto, the Senate did not. Meanwhile, one of the members of the Commerce Court, Judge Archbald, was undergoing an impeachment trial on charges against his judicial rectitude both before and after his appointment to the new court. He was convicted, removed from office, and permanently disqualified on January 13, 1913. While members of Congress were in the main wise enough to separate the Archbald impeachment from the broader issue of the Commerce Court's continuance, there can be no question that this exposure of judicial misconduct emphasized in the public mind the danger and undesirability of the new tribunal. The Wilson Administration took office in March 1913, and a special session of Congress was called in April. Several bills proposing the abolition of the Commerce Court were introduced, but finally a rider abolishing the court was attached to the deficiency appropriation bill. The bill passed the House on September 9, the Senate on October 4, went to conference and passed both houses on October 14, and was signed by the President on October 22. Thus the Commerce Court ended its career.

F. The Commission under War-Time Control of Railroads

The war created a condition of national emergency. During this period the position of the Interstate Commerce Commission was somewhat anomalous; but the problems of railroad control and management which arose were not all temporary, nor did they all stem from the war itself. The nation's experience in dealing with those problems was of great importance, but not greater than were the psychological effects of such war-time control. War-time experience left an impress upon the railroad industry, upon government policy, and upon public opinion that made possible enlargements of the powers of the Interstate Commerce Commission at the close of the war which, without that experience, would have been impossible for many years to come.

1. BACKGROUND OF THE ACT OF 1918—INTERVENING LEGISLATIVE CHANGES

A number of legislative changes affecting the commission took place between the Mann-Elkins Act of 1910 and the Federal Control Act of 1918. In 1911 Congress passed the Locomotive Boiler Inspection Act,[169] which greatly increased the commission's power to enforce safety requirements. In 1912 the Panama Canal Act [170] was passed, forbidding ownership by railroads of competing ships using the canal, and charging the commission with the enforcement of this prohibition as well as with the handling of various problems involving the co-ordination of the activities of rail and water carriers. In 1913, as we have already seen, Congress abolished the Commerce Court and turned back its jurisdiction to the district courts and the circuit courts of appeal. Also in 1913 the Valuation Act [171] was passed. The valuation of railroad property had been a matter of vital importance ever since the Supreme Court, in *Smyth* v. *Ames*,[172] had declared that due process of law demands railroad rates that will bring the carriers 'a fair rate on a fair valuation of their property.' The Valuation Act gave the commission the colossal task of valuing all of the railroads, a task to be done under numerous and burdensome procedural requirements written into the statute. In 1914 the Clayton Antitrust Act [173] imposed upon the commission the duty of enforcing the Act upon carriers subject to control of the Interstate Commerce Act, and also the enforcement against the railroads of the provision forbidding stock acquisitions between corporations engaged in commerce when the effect was to lessen competition. In December 1915 President Wilson in a message to Congress suggested a 'commission of inquiry' to investigate the entire transportation problem.[174] In response to this request a joint committee of the House and Senate was

169. Act of Feb. 17, 1911, 36 Stat. at L. 913. For a useful summary of the safety appliance acts from 1893 to 1930 see *supra*, note 16, op. cit. p. 348, note 174.
170. Act of Aug. 24, 1912, 37 Stat. at L. 560.
171. Act of Mar. 1, 1913, 37 Stat. at L. 701.
172. 169 U.S. 466 (1898).
173. Act of Oct. 15, 1914, 38 Stat. at L. 730.
174. 53 Cong. Rec. 99.

set up under the chairmanship of Senator Newlands. This committee conducted hearings down to the time when the government took over the operation of the railroads.

In the meantime the World War was in full swing and American entrance into it seemed increasingly imminent. The Army Appropriations Act of 1916 [175] contained a section that authorized the President to assume complete control of all systems of transportation in time of war. This country entered the War in April 1917. In less than two weeks the Railroads' War Board was organized by a conference of all American railroad presidents. The board was a purely voluntary organization, created to undertake the co-ordination of railroad operations necessary for the meeting of military needs, and had no legal powers. In May 1917, to facilitate this work of co-ordination, the Esch Car Service Act [176] was passed, authorizing the Interstate Commerce Commission to establish reasonable car-service rules and to deal with service emergencies. On August 9, responding to requests made by the commission in 1915 and 1916, Congress increased the membership of the Interstate Commerce Commission from seven to nine and authorized the commission to divide itself into as many divisions of not less than three members as might be necessary.[177] These divisions were given full legal power to act, subject to review by the entire commission. This equipped the commission to handle its rapidly increasing tasks more efficiently.

For nine months after American entrance into the War the Railroads' War Board dealt with commendable effectiveness with the transportation problems arising from the War. In a special report [178] filed December 5, 1917, the Interstate Commerce Commission emphasized that unified operation of the railroads was an imperative necessity. This could be achieved either by government control or by private control under government supervision, and the commission, with one member dissenting, favored private control. As the winter progressed, however, conditions became acute; and on December 26 the President by proclamation took over the railroads and

175. Act of Aug. 29, 1916, 39 Stat. at L. 645.
176. Act of May 29, 1917, 40 Stat. at L. 101.
177. Act of Aug. 9, 1917, 40 Stat. at L. 270.
178. Printed in 32d Ann. Rept. of the I.C.C. (1918), 4 ff.

appointed Mr. McAdoo as Director General to manage them. This unified control of the railroads through a director general did not subordinate the commission to the executive. There was no thought of abolishing or suspending the commission, however clear it was that there must be granted to some authority much more flexible emergency power to deal with railroad rates than that which the commission enjoyed under normal conditions. On January 4, 1918, the President recommended to Congress the enactment of the Federal Railroad Control Act to stabilize the basis of the new authority. Bills carrying out the recommendation were promptly introduced and were reported out of committee without the holding of hearings. The new law was passed March 21, 1918.[179]

2. PROVISIONS OF THE ACT OF 1918

The Act provided in detail for the payment of compensation to the carriers and set up procedure for fixing that compensation. It authorized the President to fix 'just and reasonable rates.' These rates were to be filed with the Interstate Commerce Commission. The commission was authorized to review them on complaint and its review was made final. The Act provided, however, that in such review the commission must take into account that the railroads were being operated under a unified system and not under conditions of competition, and must further take into account the President's representation that an increase in revenue was necessary to the effective operation of the roads.

3. TOPICS AND ISSUES IN THE DEBATES

The entire debate on the Federal Control Act was, of course, colored by the war emergency, and centered chiefly around three topics which we shall briefly review:

a. *The delegation of rate-making power to the President*

It was strongly contended in both houses that the power to fix railroad rates, being a legislative power, ought not to be

179. Act of Mar. 21, 1918, 40 Stat. at L. 451.

given to the President. To do so was both unconstitutional and undesirable. As Senator Kellogg put it:

. . . Nothing is further from the business of a purely executive office. In no nation of the world is the making of rates in the hands of a single executive officer of the Government. There is no more reason for this power being delegated to one official, without the right of appeal, in times of war than there is in times of peace.[180]

Mr. Gordon of Ohio asked in the House:

What is there about the country being in war that makes the President of the United States competent to exercise a legislative function? [181]

The effect upon the commission of such delegation to the President was pointed out. Mr. Madden of Illinois declared that it would convert the commission into a 'debating society,' while Mr. Robbins of Pennsylvania feared that the commission would be virtually destroyed. It was urged that the rate-making power was not a war power and that the President could adequately manage the roads under a unified system without it. Furthermore, the President would be incompetent to fix rates and would have to rely upon the expert services of some other agency. As Mr. Campbell of Kansas expressed it:

. . . You can not arrive at a just and reasonable rate with a hop, skip, and jump. Even the President of the United States or the Director General of Railways can not do that. No man, no bureau, commission, or other creation of the law is so well qualified to fix railway rates as the Interstate Commerce Commission. Its members were appointed for their fitness and for their ability with respect to this particular work. There never was a time when just and reasonable rates were more essential than now while we are undergoing this transition with the facilities of interstate commerce, and to impose the responsibilities upon the President of making rates is to impose upon him a thing that he can not do and do according to the law—make them just and reasonable. His rates would be a guess.[182]

Senator Cummins agreed that the President could not personally fix rates and cynically offered to name the railroad officials who would be called in to supply the expert advice necessary.

180. 56 Cong. Rec. 2026. 182. Ibid. 2705.
181. Ibid. 2339.

Mr. Greene of Iowa feared that if the commission lost its rate-making power even temporarily it would never get it back again.

These arguments, however, did not prevail against the insistent claim that the war emergency made imperative this grant of power to the President. As Senator Watson of Indiana put it:

> . . . The Congress can not run the railroads; the judiciary can not run the railroads; and while in a time of peace the authority to make rates should remain lodged in the legislative branch of the Government, yet in order to properly and certainly finance the operations of all the railroads, under the provisions of the pending bill, it seems to me that there is no escape from the conclusion that it must be done by the executive branch of Government alone.[183]

Mr. Platt of New York emphasized the necessity for a speedy exercise of rate-making power, arguing that the commission was too slow, that emergencies could not wait upon its deliberations. Several members declared that the President would have to deal with the wages of railway employees and other problems dependent upon railroad revenues, and this he would be unable to do unless he could also control the rates upon which those revenues depended. Mr. Doremus of Michigan expressed this as follows:

> Now, what will be the situation if this amendment prevails? The President will control the operating expenses during Federal control and the Interstate Commerce Commission will control the operating revenues. In other words, you put the Interstate Commerce Commission at the intake pipe and leave the President of the United States at the spigot. And they seek to justify this serious division of authority by eulogizing the Interstate Commerce Commission. No Member upon the floor of this House has a higher regard for the Interstate Commerce Commission than I have. I freely acknowledge all their virtues and all their accomplishments; but the trouble with our friends upon the other side is that they are talking in terms of peace when we are in the midst of war.[184]

The question has been recently discussed whether Congress can constitutionally delegate more power to an independent commission than to an executive officer.[185] It is interesting,

183. Ibid. 2263.
184. Ibid. 2721.

185. For discussion see *infra*, 434 ff.

therefore, to have that issue raised in the debates in 1918. The discussion on this point was as follows:

Mr. Lenroot. The gentleman has stated that in the majority bill a rate fixed by the President is final. I ask him, as a lawyer, whether Congress has any power to delegate to the President the power to fix rates finally?

Mr. Decker. I will answer the gentleman's question by asking him another. Is not the President of the United States a citizen? Is there any reason why we can not delegate the power to him as much as to five or six citizens on the Interstate Commerce Commission?

Mr. Lenroot. The Interstate Commerce Commission acts under the rule laid down, carrying out the law, and we have made their rates final except they go so far as confiscation of property. Under the power delegated to the President in this bill there is no such power conferred.

Mr. Decker. I do not think that the gentleman has read the bill carefully, because the bill provides that the rates must be just and reasonable. It does not mean that the President can fix any rate, but he is to use reason, justice, and fairness, and avoid all discrimination. I have heard it said here that under this power he can make Chicago a desert. He can make Chicago a desert under this power if he wanted to violate his oath of office, but no intelligent man would use such discrimination against Chicago as to make it a desert without knowing that he was doing something wrong.[186]

Mr. Lenroot . . . The committee report pleads that the President ought not to be overruled, that it would be 'most unseemly'— I think that is the language—to permit the Interstate Commerce Commission to overrule him.

I want to say a word about the powers of the President. The President of the United States has no power, under this law, or under the law delegating to him the power to take over the railroads, that he exercises by virtue of his office in the sense that it is delegating to him a power that we could not delegate to anybody else. We could delegate this power to any official of the United States, and in carrying out this act the President is exercising only a delegated power, and in exercising that delegated power he is no greater by being President of the United States than the Interstate Commerce Commission.[187]

186. 56 Cong. Rec. 2531.   187. Ibid. 2538.

b. *The commission's power to review Presidential rate making*

A number of congressmen believed that the President's power to fix rates should be final and not subject to review by the commission. Two reasons were given: first, that such final authority is necessary as a war measure; second, that it is necessary in order to protect the independence of the Interstate Commerce Commission. This second argument was strongly pressed. Mr. Norris of Nebraska feared that if the commission acted as a reviewing agency it could not remain genuinely independent, but would be under the thumb of the President.[188] Mr. Barkley of Kentucky urged that the commission ought not to be made a 'rubber stamp.' [189] Rather than make the commission in any degree subordinate to the President, it would be better to keep it out of the picture altogether.

In contrast to this view it was proposed to make the commission an advisory agency to aid the President in the rate-making function. It should have the power to pass upon the soundness of the rates fixed by the President, but no power to set them aside. This was the view of Mr. Sims of Tennessee, who declared:

But when the public interest so requires the President may initiate rates, filing them with the Interstate Commerce Commission, to take effect upon such notice as he shall direct. Such rates are to be 'fair, reasonable and just.' But to guard against even remote possibilities of error the section provides that upon complaint the Interstate Commerce Commission shall make investigation, grant full hearings 'concerning the fairness, justice, and reasonableness' of rates so ordered by the President, and 'make report of its findings and recommendations' to the President for such action as he shall deem required in the public interest.

It has been suggested that after such hearing the Interstate Commerce Commission should be given power to make orders, thus in effect overriding the President's war power to make rates on transportation systems in his possession and control because of war conditions. It would, in the opinion of our committee, be most unwise to authorize the Interstate Commerce Commission to overrule the President in the exercise of his war powers—indeed, of any other powers. It should not be overlooked that the President is responsible

188. Ibid. 2318.   189. Ibid. 2477.

for the financial results of operating these great carrier systems with gross revenues approximating $4,000,000,000.[190]

Appearing before the committee Mr. McAdoo had urged the same point:

Now, as to the rate-making power, I think the President undoubtedly has the power to control rates during the time of Federal possession, under the present law. I think, on the other hand, that that power ought not to be exercised—and I am sure it will not be exercised—except in such cases as may be necessary in the public interest. I think it would be very unwise for the Federal Government to undertake through the Director General of Railroads—who merely represents the President in this control—to pass upon all the rates in the country, either de novo or as questions may arise concerning them. I think that the agency of the Interstate Commerce Commission ought to be employed, and that it ought to hear these questions from time to time as the public interest requires, and that the views of the Interstate Commerce Commission or their judgment as to what ought to be done in the circumstances ought to prevail, and I think would undoubtedly be permitted to prevail, except in so far as it might be wise for the President to modify or to change them. In other words, I feel that the commission ought to act in an advisory capacity while the President is in control of the railroads, and that its advice and suggestions about rates will be of great value.[191]

In the end the commission was given authority to pass on the rates fixed by the President and that review was made final. This arrangement was defended as a necessary protection to the rights of the shippers. As Mr. Black of Texas put it:

. . . But while I am in favor of . . . quick action, still I also want to preserve the right to the shipper to appeal to the Interstate Commerce Commission, and leave that commission with full power to be the final arbiter as to the justness and fairness of rates, and power to suspend them if they are found to be not just and reasonable.[192]

c. Side lights on the nature of the commission—its powers and status

A proposal to transfer one of the commission's major responsibilities to the executive department was bound to elicit some

190. Ibid. 2337.
191. Ibid. 2360.
192. Ibid. 2641.

comment on the general nature of the commission's power and
its relation to the departments of government. There was much
emphasis on the legislative nature of the rate-making function.
Mr. Gordon of Ohio declared:

> Of course, the fixing of rates is a legislative function, and Congress, having other things to attend to, created this great tribunal, the Interstate Commerce Commission, and invested it with authority to hear and determine these questions.[193]

And this was more sharply emphasized by Mr. Black:

> . . . If I understand the situation at all the Interstate Commerce Commission is a creature of the Congress of the United States . . .
> I understand further that the matter of judging as to the reasonableness of rates is not an executive function. The President of the United States is an executive officer and vested with executive powers by the Constitution, and that same Constitution says that Congress shall have the power to regulate interstate commerce, and that is where Congress gets its power to prescribe just and reasonable rates, which it does through the Interstate Commerce Commission. The matter of making rates is a legislative function, and for very proper reasons it has been delegated to the Interstate Commerce Commission, and it is certainly an erroneous statement to say that the commission is a creature of the President.[194]

Mr. Black went on to protest vigorously against the theory
that the commission was in any sense the creature of the President:

> . . . The gentleman from Missouri (Mr. Borland) and the gentleman from Virginia (Mr. Montague) advanced the novel proposition that the Interstate Commerce Commission is the creature of the President, and that therefore to permit it to be the judge as to rates would be making the creature greater than the creator. Gentlemen, the Interstate Commerce Commission is not the creature of the President. It is an independent body, created by an act of Congress of the United States.[195]

Mr. Madden supported this view:

> Mr. Chairman, the Interstate Commerce Commission is not the creature of the President. It is an independent department of the Government. It is so held to be an independent department. It is

193. Ibid. 2543.   195. Ibid. 2640.
194. Ibid. 2709.

not subject to the orders of the President and ought not to be subject to his orders.[196]

The judicial character of the commission and its work was also stressed. Mr. Townsend of Michigan referred to the commission as 'the people's tribunal, the tribunal that has stood between the people and the railroads.' [197] In arguing for the commission's power to review Presidential rates Mr. Black said:

. . . Why not a judicial body like the Interstate Commerce Commission? It is not an administrative body. It is more in the nature of a judicial body, with power to adjust equities between the shipper and the carrier. It does not operate railroads. It does not initiate rates. It irons out the differences which are bound to arise in the operation of the roads whether that operation shall be by the railroads or by a Director General appointed by the President of the United States.[198]

Mr. Dillon of South Dakota referred to the commission as 'a court to which the people may go,' and declared, 'I have failed to hear a single reason advanced why this court should now be disbanded and placed in the dump heap.' [199]

G. THE TRANSPORTATION ACT OF 1920—A CONSTRUCTIVE RAILROAD POLICY—THE COMMISSION ASSUMES BROAD MANAGERIAL SUPERVISION

The Transportation Act of 1920 [200] was a vitally important statute both in respect to the substantive powers of regulation which it created, and in respect to the changed responsibilities of the Interstate Commerce Commission. The experience of war-time control had left an indelible impression. Government operation had been unpopular, but there were few indeed who failed to realize that we should never be able to return to the old regime. It may be said that the Act of 1920 embodied our first constructive railroad policy. It represented a change from the old policy of restriction and discipline to that of a positive governmental responsibility to see that an efficient and self-sustaining transportation system should prevail. The Act was

196. Ibid. 2641.
197. Ibid. 2321.
198. Ibid. 2641.

199. Ibid. 2711.
200. Act of Feb. 28, 1920, 41 Stat. at L. 456.

based upon the most thoroughgoing and intelligent examination of the railroad problem, in all of its aspects, that had ever taken place.

1. BACKGROUND AND LEGISLATIVE HISTORY OF THE ACT OF 1920

We have seen [201] that in 1915 President Wilson had called for a careful study of the entire transportation problem and that in response to his request the Newlands committee, a joint committee of the two houses, had been set up. This committee conducted hearings from November 1916 to December 1917, when it abandoned its inquiry because of the advent of federal control. Its attention was not focused upon emergency problems but upon the broad transportation problem under normal conditions. In its thirteen months of activity it spread upon the record the views of a large number of experts upon railroad matters and its hearings were printed as an appendix to the hearings of the Senate committee which in 1919 was considering the bill that became the Transportation Act of 1920.[202] Thus the work of the Newlands committee forms an important chapter of the legislative history of that Act.

President Wilson's annual message of 1918 [203] dealt with the railroad problem. He presented no plan but declared that the nation clearly could not return to the old conditions of pre-war days. Almost simultaneously the Interstate Commerce Commission in its annual report [204] emphasized that important changes of policy and enlargements of powers were inevitable. On December 11, 1918, Director General McAdoo sent a letter to the chairmen of the Senate and House committees on interstate commerce proposing a five-year extension of government control of railroads as a transitional and experimental period.[205] This proposal precipitated the active consideration of the railroad problem.

During 1919 the House Committee on Interstate and Foreign

201. *Supra,* 106.
202. Hearings before the Senate Committee on Interstate Commerce on Extension of Tenure of Government Control of Railroads, 65th Cong., 3d sess. (1919), Appendix.
203. 57 Cong. Rec. 5.
204. 32d Ann. Rept. of the I.C.C. (1918).
205. Official United States Bulletin, Dec. 12, 1918.

Commerce, under the chairmanship of Mr. Esch of Wisconsin, held extensive hearings on the entire problem. The Senate committee, with Senator Cummins as chairman, held somewhat shorter hearings. Public interest in the railroads was at fever heat. Practically everyone had some solution to offer. The Congressional committees listened patiently to a large number of proposals. Of special interest and importance were the plans presented by the Association of Railway Executives, the National Association of Owners of Railroad Securities, the Investors Protective Association, the National Transportation Conference called by the United States Chamber of Commerce, and, finally, the Railroad Brotherhoods who presented the famous 'Plumb Plan.' On November 17 the House passed the Esch bill [206] which had emerged from these long deliberations, a bill that in its general features formed the substance of the Act of 1920. On December 20 the Senate substituted and passed the Cummins bill.[207] This bill had two novel features, a provision for the federal incorporation of all railroads and the establishment of a transportation board in addition to the Interstate Commerce Commission. This latter proposal we shall examine more closely at another point.[208] On December 24 President Wilson issued a proclamation announcing the return of the railroads to private operation on March 1, 1920. The divergent House and Senate bills went to conference, and it proved very difficult to effect a compromise. This was, however, finally done and the conference report was presented on February 18, 1920. Bitter debate ensued in both houses, but the imminence of the termination of federal control made delay impossible. The bill passed the House on February 21, passed the Senate on February 23, and was signed by the President on February 28. The next day at midnight the railroads were turned back to their owners in accordance with the Presidential proclamation and under the provisions of the new statute.

206. H.R. 10453, 66th Cong., 2d sess. (1919).
207. The amended bill S. 3288 replaced S. 2906, 66th Cong., 1st sess. (1919).
208. *Infra*, 119 f., 124 ff.

The Transportation Act of 1920 was a very comprehensive statute, and treated a number of problems with which the Interstate Commerce Commission was not directly concerned. We need discuss neither the provisions which dealt elaborately with the transfer of the railroads back to their owners, nor the clauses affecting labor, one of which established the Railroad Labor Board. The Act did enlarge the power and responsibility of the commission in four important ways:

First, it relaxed previous restrictions upon pooling, permitted railroads to acquire other railroads with commission approval, and instructed the commission 'to prepare and adopt a plan for the consolidation of the railway properties of the continental United States into a limited number of systems.' Secondly, it gave to the commission authority over railroad security issues as a means of guaranteeing a sound financial structure, and it required a certificate of public convenience and necessity from the commission for the construction or abandonment of a road. Thirdly, it drastically modified the rate-making power. It imposed on the commission the affirmative duty to fix railroad rates which would bring in a fair return upon the entire railroad investment of the country, and set up the famous 'recapture clause' designed to help get the weaker railroads on their feet. The commission was given power to establish minimum rates and to prevent injurious discriminations by the states against interstate commerce. Finally, authority to supervise car service, given to the commission temporarily by the Esch Act of 1917,[209] was elaborated and made permanent. This included the power to require adequate service, to prevent abuses in respect to it, and to exercise wide powers in emergencies. The commission was not structurally changed, but its membership was increased from nine to eleven.

We need not here review the long and vigorous debates on the recapture clause and other issues of railroad economics.

209. *Supra*, 107.

Important discussions, however, centered around the proposals persuasively put forward to change the Interstate Commerce Commission by dividing it up, by subtracting some of its important powers, and by setting up additional agencies to help administer the nation's new railroad policy. We may tabulate these briefly and indicate their chief sponsors.

a. *Proposals for reorganizing the national system of railway regulation*

Some of the proposals either did not directly affect the commission or would have made it into a wholly different kind of institution. The famous 'Plumb Plan' sponsored by the Railroad Brotherhoods called for government ownership of railroads and their operation under private lease. The so-called 'Amster Plan' provided for the federal incorporation of all railroads in one giant company to be supervised by the Interstate Commerce Commission. The 'Warfield Plan' undertook to guarantee a 6 per cent return on railroad investments; provided for six regional commerce commissions; and provided for the formation of a corporation managed by nine interstate commerce commissioners and eight representatives of the railroads, to serve as a clearing house for railroad operation. Passing these without further comment, we may mention the following proposals, which directly affected the commission and which received more serious consideration.

A federal railroad commission to supplement the Interstate Commerce Commission and to take over much of its executive and administrative work was proposed by the Railway Executives before the Newlands committee in 1916.[210]

A department of transportation under a Cabinet Secretary was urged by the Railway Executives in 1919.[211] This department would take over the administrative and executive tasks already in the hands of the commission and also the important managerial duties that Congress was clearly about to create.

A transportation board to supplement the Interstate Commerce Commission was more widely sponsored. This board would be independent in the sense of not being part of an exec-

---

210. *Supra*, note 202, op. cit. Appendix, vol. II, 104 f.
211. Ibid. 309 f.

utive department, and it would perform the administrative and managerial duties just mentioned. This proposal was made by the National Transportation Conference, a widely representative group called together by the United States Chamber of Commerce to consider the entire problem.[212] It was supported by the Railway Executives as a second choice if they were unable to get a department of transportation. A referendum held by the Chamber of Commerce gave overwhelming endorsement to the transportation board plan. The Senate Committee on Interstate Commerce was converted to the idea, and it was incorporated in Senator Cummins's bill as it finally passed the Senate.

The National Association of Railroad and Utility Commissioners favored a transportation board having purely advisory powers and charged with the duty of investigating railroad conditions and recommending policies to the Interstate Commerce Commission.[213] This received little consideration.

b. *The need for a separate planning agency*

The proposals just described rested upon common assumptions and were supported by arguments very similar in nature. One of these assumptions was that the effective planning of a national transportation policy must be handled by some agency other than the Interstate Commerce Commission. The Railway Executives, in defending in 1916 their proposal for a federal railroad commission, charged the Interstate Commerce Commission with failure to understand the necessity for broad planning and with inability to consider the transportation problem as a whole. They argued that, swamped with individual cases which it must handle, the commission was inherently unable to take a broad view of the whole situation. The proposed railroad commission would assume this important task of planning, with which an overburdened Interstate Commerce Commission was unable to cope. One of the major duties of the secretary of transportation, as head of the proposed department of transportation, was to organize this broad planning function. In the

212. Hearings before the House Committee on Interstate and Foreign Commerce on H.R. 4378, 66th Cong., 1st sess. (1919), vol. I, 190 f.
213. Ibid. vol. II, 1593.

words of Mr. T. D. Cuyler, chairman of the Pennsylvania Railroad:

> . . . He should be charged with the responsibility of recommending from time to time to the President such measures and policies as in his opinion would promote the interests of the public and the adequacy of the transportation service.[214]

As the discussions of the proposed transportation board proceeded, it became clear that one of its important responsibilities would be in the field of planning. It was to function as a sort of super-budget board, blocking out the policies necessary for the business interests of the railroad system and the welfare of the country, while the Interstate Commerce Commission was to adjust railroad rates to the terms of this proposed budget or plan. The report of the Chamber of Commerce emphasized this point:

> The development of a unified national system of transportation is an executive task that can be performed only by creating a board primarily administrative in purpose and organization. The Interstate Commerce Commission, in the regulation of rates and in the performance of the other duties with which it is charged, will have as much work as it can successfully perform.[215]

It seemed to be generally agreed that the Interstate Commerce Commission could not be expected to meet the planning needs which were felt to exist. Mr. Alba B. Johnson testifying before the House committee sharply criticized the commission for its failure at this point. He said:

> I now wish to give you another impression. This second impression was one of incredulous amazement that any group of eight men having to do with transportation in the United States could have lived and worked through these last few years and come before you without apparently the faintest realization that the country is confronted with a railroad problem requiring heroic measures.[216]

To this Commissioner Clark, representing the commission, replied that he

> . . . appeared on behalf of an administrative tribunal, possessing only delegated powers and charged with the administration of cer-

214. *Supra,* note 202, op. cit. 309.   216. Ibid. vol. II, 1536.
215. *Supra,* note 212, op. cit. vol. I, 1107.

tain acts of Congress. We have never thought that it was our mission to outline certain acts of Congress.[217]

c. *The merger of powers in the commission*

As new powers of railroad regulation were being created, it was vigorously argued, as in earlier debates, that conflicting and incompatible duties must not be conferred upon the Interstate Commerce Commission. This idea lay back of every proposal to take from the commission its administrative and executive powers. The Railway Executives in 1916 emphasized the violation of the separation of powers which they felt was inherent in the commission's authority. They said:

. . . The Interstate Commerce Commission is likewise clothed with different functions which are inconsistent and which violate the principle that the legislative, executive and judicial departments shall be kept separate and distinct . . .

. . . The foundation of our liberties is the separation of what are termed inconsistent functions of government. You have one judicial department; you have one executive department which is not judicial and not legislative; you have one legislative department which is not judicial and which is not executive. The ideal of free government is that those functions shall be kept distinct from one another. It was thought that if a legislator should be a judge there would be no use for the judge, because he would sustain his act as legislator, and so with these other functions; in order to be useful each department must be protected from invasion by the other. And yet we find that wholesome government principle is violated in the present organization of the Interstate Commerce Commission. They are judges; they are, in a measure, legislators; and they are administrators of the system of regulation.[218]

The constitutional argument, however, had by this time become purely academic, as no court had lent it any support. Much more cogent was the plea that the commission's administrative and prosecuting duties robbed it of the neutrality necessary for the impartial handling of its judicial tasks. This was emphasized repeatedly. Mr. Lovett, president of the Union Pacific, put it thus:

217. Ibid. vol. III, 2858.
218. *Supra,* note 202, op. cit. Appendix, vol. II, 104 f.

. . . One of the most substantial and insistent complaints of railroad owners and executives is that the performance of these executive duties of detection and prosecution, and the state of mind to which such point of view leads, tend naturally and inevitably to unfit the commissioners to act impartially in determining controversial matters which the law commits to them for decision.[219]

Speaking for the Railway Executives, Mr. Thom voiced the railroads' fear that they could never secure adequate appreciation of the operating needs of the carriers, the need for expansions and promotions, and other managerial problems, from a body like the Interstate Commerce Commission set up to handle the quasi-judicial duties of rate regulation and discipline.[220] Furthermore, the vitally important administrative and managerial duties which Congress was about to give to the commission would subject that body to intense political pressure. Its past freedom from such pressure was due to the fact that it had closely confined itself to quasi-judicial functions. It was further charged that if the commission was given the job of developing a national railroad system, conflicts within the commission about the relation of this policy to the commission's regulatory duties would be bound to ensue. As Mr. Alba B. Johnson pointed out:

Does it take the eye of a prophet to see what would happen within a commission made up partly of builders and partly of judges? At the first important difference of judgment over the amount of earnings necessary in the public interest the tribunal would be rent in twain and in a few hours two factions in the country would begin to struggle for control.[221]

And finally it was urged that the same men could not handle effectively two sorts of work so different in character. Neither job would be well done. As Mr. Johnson put it:

. . . What is proposed is to transform the commissioners from judges into men of action.

. . . But if you could and did transform these judges into men of action, what would become of the machinery of justice which it has taken us 32 years to construct and develop? [222]

219. *Supra,* note 212, op. cit. vol. II, 1315. 221. Ibid. 1534.
220. Ibid. 1208. 222. Ibid. 1532.

d. *Should there be a separate agency for administrative and managerial work?*

A vigorous drive was made, mainly by the railroads, to have created some kind of separate agency, a commission, a department, or a board, on which could be placed the administrative and managerial burdens which the government under the proposed statute was about to assume. These various proposals were defended on the following grounds:

In the first place, the Interstate Commerce Commission was already badly overworked. It had more tasks to perform than it could efficiently handle. The Senate committee in reporting out the Cummins bill providing for a transportation board declared:

Every member of the Senate knows that the Interstate Commerce Commission is the most overworked body of men in the Government of the United States; its members are able and industrious, and they labor continuously from the beginning to the end of the year. Nevertheless they cannot keep pace with the demands already made upon them, and, oftentimes, justice delayed is justice denied. The bill the committee has presented increases tremendously the work which some body of men must do if its provisions are promptly carried into effect. It was apparent to the committee that it must adopt one of two alternatives: It must either recommend a very considerable enlargement of the commission, with such division into sections as would permit independent action; or it must recommend the creation of a distinct body. It chose the latter alternative. In determining the division of work, power, and responsibility as between two bodies, the committee has traced a clear, obvious line. It has not been able, always, to observe the exact distinction; but, in the main, it has succeeded in doing so.[223]

In the second place, the burdens of the commission would be greatly increased by the new tasks being created. A transportation board was needed to take over this new work. As Senator Cummins expressed it in the Senate:

. . . The transportation board, on the other hand, is intended to act—if I may use the term, although I hesitate to use it—as a Government general manager of the railways of the country. I do not

223. S. Rept. 304, 66th Cong., 1st sess. (1919), Part 1. 20.

mean a general manager in the sense that it is to interfere with the ordinary movement of trains, but it is a general manager in the sense that it is watching for the public what should be added to our transportation facilities and opportunities as well.[224]

In the third place, the new and important administrative managerial functions could be efficiently and expeditiously performed only by a separate agency. The job of judging was one thing, the job of administrative management another. The Interstate Commerce Commission was equipped by tradition, by temperament, and by the requirements of law to act judicially or quasi-judicially, but it could never handle the important new functions under consideration. Speaking for the Railroad Executives Mr. Thom declared:

> My argument is that if we are to succeed as a business enterprise, the machinery which controls us must be suitable for prompt and adaptable action; it must be able to act with as near an approximation to what a business man would do in the control of his own business as the exigencies of the public interest will permit.
>
> Now, we have, I think, in the commission form of government and regulation, lost sight of that essential requirement of business conditions. We have organized the bodies of regulation on the basis of deliberation and on the basis that no business step can be taken until the end of deliberation, be it six months or be it a year.[225]

Mr. Lovett said:

> It must be apparent that these duties relating to the quality and character of the service rendered by the railroads, to the application of safety appliances and the maintenance of the same, to the condition of engines and other equipment and to the investigation, detection, and prosecution of violations of the law, and regulations with respect to accident reports, etc., could be very much more promptly and effectively handled in an executive department of the Government than by a semijudicial tribunal that can act only in conference. But the greatest advantage would be the time it would give the commission for the performance of its more important duties, of passing upon rates and determining questions which only such a body can properly determine, and also in relieving that commission of the petty prosecuting activities which tend to unfit its members for their more important duties.[226]

224. 59 Cong. Rec. 287.
225. *Supra*, note 202, op. cit. 504 f.
226. *Supra*, note 212, op. cit. vol. II, 1316.

These arguments were not left unanswered. The Interstate Commerce Commission through its representatives asserted that with proper internal reorganization it could handle successfully the new job. It emphasized, however, the importance of that reorganization. Commissioner Clark declared:

. . . The Commission has varied, important and rather multifarious duties. In my opinion the commission can successfully deal with the duties now resting upon it and those proposed to be assigned to it only by a thorough organization similar to that which would be created by Federal or private corporations having varied and important activities. It will be necessary to organize bureaus or subdivisions of the commission to take charge of the administration of certain acts or provisions of law, the commission in the first place interpreting the law and laying down the rule of policy to be followed, and retaining the right to make any changes in the rules so laid down, or to deal with important fundamental questions that might arise. It is physically impossible for one man to master and keep up with the details of the administration of the law affecting regulations of rates, fares, and charges, the valuation law, and the proposed new duties under the car service section, and the supervision of security issues. I believe that such an organization under the commission could be effected and be made efficient and effective. I do not doubt that the same end could in substance be reached under a logical division of duties and powers as between the commission and a board of transportation. Which plan shall be followed is largely a matter of policy to be determined by Congress, but as I indicated in my previous appearance before the committee, the commission is of opinion that one body with appropriate bureaus and subdivisions is better.[227]

It was urged further that a separate agency dealing with railroad policy and exercising administrative and managerial duties would tend to become an essentially political body, without the status of judicial aloofness and subjected to terrific pressures. Conflicts between the commission and the proposed transportation board seemed to be inherent in the very terms of their rather vaguely established jurisdictions. The commission itself, furthermore, would be seriously weakened in authority and prestige by what was regarded as a subordination of it to the new board.

227. Ibid. vol. III, 2896.

Finally, the House Committee on Interstate and Foreign Commerce bluntly declared that it would be a practical impossibility to draw a workable division line between the functions of such a board and those of the Interstate Commerce Commission. The committee declared that the task of administering the nation's railroad policy in all of its aspects ought to be left in the same hands. The proposed transportation board could not for many years acquire as thorough knowledge of the railroad problems as that already possessed by the commission. The administrative duties now assigned to the commission were being soundly administered, and had in no way interfered with the proper handling of the commission's judicial work. On the contrary:

> . . . The commission has been aided in the performance of its judicial functions by reason of the intimate knowledge its members have acquired as to practical problems of railroad administration arising out of the administration of these several acts. In short, your committee fears that the creation of a transportation board, no matter how clearly its duties may be differentiated from those that are to be left to the Interstate Commerce Commission, will result in a division of authority and hence in a divided responsibility.[228]

e. *Regional commissions*

It was urged during the debates that railroad regulation should be in some measure decentralized geographically by creating a number of regional commissions with authority to conduct hearings and to issue preliminary orders which would be subject to review by the Interstate Commerce Commission. This proposal came from the shippers and reflected the feeling that local interests had not been adequately recognized in some of the commission's proceedings. The advantages claimed for regional commissions were these: They would increase the efficiency of the Interstate Commerce Commission by relieving it of the task of conducting its own hearings. Regional commissions having greater knowledge of the facts could conduct these hearings more thoroughly and efficiently. Regulation would be brought 'closer home to the people,' and more exhaustive examination could be given to cases which the full commission had

228. H. Rept. 456 to accompany H.R. 10453, 66th Cong., 1st sess. (1919), 4.

been obliged to skimp under pressure of time. Finally, regional commissions located permanently in different parts of the country would work more amicably and effectively with state commissions. The Interstate Commerce Commission opposed this form of decentralization. If decentralization was desirable it would be better to create branches of the Interstate Commerce Commission, so that the regulatory machinery would remain integrated. The argument against regional commissions was summed up by the House committee as follows:

> . . . This phase of the problem was given very full consideration in the hearings and by the committee, with the result that the committee believed that it was better to leave the administration of the existing law and of the pending bill, should it become law, solely in the hands of the Interstate Commerce Commission. While such subordinate agencies might relieve the commission of some of its work, decisions would result which lacked uniformity. There might be as much diversity of decisions as there has been on the part of district courts with reference to war-time prohibition. Such diversity of decisions begets uncertainty, and uncertainty—especially in rate matters—is highly detrimental to the shipping interests and to the general public. Moreover, no time will be saved in the adjudication of rate cases by the creation of these subordinate agencies. The amount involved can not be the limitation, as in the case of the United States district courts, because of the fact that a rate case in which but a small amount of money is involved may involve the application of a principle of widest application. This would mean that appeals would be necessarily taken from the subordinate agency to the commission here at Washington resulting in greater delay than if no subordinate agency had passed upon the question.[229]

f. *Internal reorganization of the commission*

The drive to divide the job of railroad regulation between the Interstate Commerce Commission and a transportation board took no serious account of the alternative possibility of creating an internal division of labor within the commission itself. Such an internal reorganization was not, however, entirely ignored. Mr. Thom, speaking for the Railway Executives, admitted that 'the commission itself might perhaps be reorganized and its duties divided,' [230] but felt that this would not ade-

229. Ibid. 7.   230. *Supra,* note 202, op. cit. 503.

quately solve the problem. On the other hand, the opponents of the proposed transportation board urged that the commission could be so strengthened and reorganized as to render any new agency unnecessary. As we have just seen, Commissioner Clark, in asserting that the commission could cope with any new responsibilities Congress might give it, stressed the fact that internal readjustments would be necessary if the job were to be well done.

g. *The nature of the commission and its functions*

In the debates and discussions we have been analyzing there was a tendency to emphasize the judicial character of the commission's work and to refer to the commission as a court or tribunal. In 1906, to meet the charge that legislative or judicial powers were being delegated to it, the administrative or executive character of the commission was strongly stressed. When in 1910 there was fear of subordinating the commission to an executive department under the provision requiring the Attorney General to defend commission orders before the Commerce Court, emphasis was laid upon the legislative character of the commission and the fact that it was an 'arm of Congress.' In 1920, with vast administrative and managerial responsibilities about to be conferred upon it, the judicial nature of the commission was emphasized. As Mr. Johnson expressed it:

This, mark you, is a judicial body. It adjudicates citizens' rights. It has made peace in the United States where once there was conflict, and it is relied upon to continue the calm and even-handed administration of justice.[231]

And much of the railroads' argument for a department of transportation or a transportation board was based on the theory that administrative and executive duties ought not to be imposed upon judges.

231. *Supra,* note 212, op. cit. vol. II, 1534.

H. The Emergency Transportation Act of 1933—The Federal Co-ordinator of Transportation

The passage of the Act of 1920 minus any provision for a separate transportation board meant the final defeat of the drive to separate the administrative functions of the Interstate Commerce Commission from its quasi-judicial functions. The proposal seemed permanently shelved. Furthermore, the commission promptly took on the new and extensive duties imposed by the Act of 1920 and has carried the additional burden effectively. The Act of 1920 remains the basis for our present system of railway regulation and no substantial changes were proposed or made until the emergency legislation of 1933.

1. BACKGROUND OF THE EMERGENCY TRANSPORTATION ACT OF 1933

After the passage of the Act of 1920, railroad regulation moved along smoothly. The roads entered upon a period of substantial prosperity which continued until about 1929. The normal routine of the commission was upset during this period by one event which greatly increased its labors—the passage by Congress in 1925 of the Hoch-Smith Resolution.[232] This resolution was an attempt to instruct the commission so to juggle the rate structure as to secure lower rates for agricultural products. The attempt was far from successful.

The depression hit the railroads seriously, and the commission was faced with acute problems of railroad rate adjustments and modifications of service. The credit structure of the roads was seriously impaired. The recapture clause from which so much had been hoped in 1920 proved to be unworkable. No large amounts were 'recaptured' out of excess earnings and none of the funds so recaptured were loaned. The passage in 1932 of the Reconstruction Finance Corporation Act[233] provided some emergency relief on the credit side. The amendment to the Bankruptcy Act[234] passed in 1933 gave further aid to

232. Jan. 30, 1925, 43 Stat. at L. 801.
233. Act of Jan. 22, 1932, 47 Stat. at L. 5.
234. Act of Mar. 3, 1933, 47 Stat. at L. 1467.

railroads in financial difficulties, and the National Industrial Recovery Act [235] contained sections applicable to the railroads. Shrewd observers agreed, however, that if the railroads were to weather the storm some flexibility must be injected into their regulation and substantial co-ordination must be effected to eliminate wasteful duplication of effort and competition. To meet these needs the Emergency Railroad Transportation Act of 1933 [236] was passed.

2. LEGISLATIVE HISTORY OF THE ACT OF 1933

The legislative history of the Act of 1933 was very brief. Shortly after Secretary of Commerce Roper took office, railroad representatives presented to him a proposal for the reorganization of the railroads and for certain amendments to the Act. Mr. Roper invited three members of the Department of Commerce to meet with the railroad men. This group set up a three-man committee composed of Commissioner Eastman, the counsel to the House Committee on Interstate and Foreign Commerce, and the chief of the Transportation Division of the Bureau of Foreign and Domestic Commerce; these were to continue the study of the problem. At this juncture the Railway Executives produced a bill embodying the railroads' proposals. This bill called for regional co-ordinating committees to eliminate competitive wastes, and for relaxation of the prohibitions of the Antitrust Act. It further provided for a co-ordinator of transportation to initiate and supervise the work of the committees. The Department of Commerce committee revised this bill and presented it to the President. A White House conference on the bill was attended by the committee and by representatives of the railroads. After further discussions and revisions the President sent the bill to Congress, accompanied by a special message, on May 4, 1933.[237] Brief hearings were conducted by the Senate Committee on Interstate Commerce. There were brief debates in both houses but like most of the other early New Deal legislation the bill rolled smoothly along and became law on June 16, 1933.

235. Act of June 16, 1933, 48 Stat. at L. 195.
236. Act of June 16, 1933, 48 Stat. at L. 211.
237. 77 Cong. Rec. 2860.

3. SUMMARY OF THE PROVISIONS OF THE ACT OF 1933

The Act of 1933 fell into two major divisions. The first comprised certain emergency provisions intended to be temporary. The most important of these created a federal Co-ordinator of Transportation. This co-ordinator was to be appointed by the President or designated by him from amongst the members of the Interstate Commerce Commission. He was empowered to divide the railroads of the country into three groups—eastern, southern, and western. For each group there was to be a regional co-ordinating committee of five members selected by the railroads and two special members chosen by a method approved by the co-ordinator. The co-ordinator was to promote action by the railroads to reduce duplication of services and facilities, and to permit the joint use of terminals and trackage. He had broad power to promote actions for the elimination of railroad wastes in general. He was to make a study of the entire transportation problem and develop plans for its permanent improvement.

The second part of the Act comprised various permanent amendments to the Interstate Commerce Act. The recapture clause was repealed. No friend arose to defend it. The Act extended the existing power of the commission to permit or reject railroad consolidations and mergers by applying it especially to unifications effected through holding companies and the like. Finally the commission was given authority to delegate substantial powers to its employees and to single members of the commission.

4. TOPICS AND ISSUES IN HEARINGS AND DEBATES

The debates on the Act of 1933 centered first around the establishment of the office of Co-ordinator of Transportation and his relation to the commission; and second around the internal reorganization of the commission itself.

a. *The co-ordinator and his duties*

In his message submitting the transportation bill to Congress, the President explained the reason for setting up a Coordinator of Transportation in these words:

Our broad problem is so to coordinate all agencies of transportation as to maintain adequate service. I am not yet ready to submit to the Congress a comprehensive plan for permanent legislation.

. . . As a temporary emergency measure, I suggest the creation of a Federal coordinator of transportation, who, working with groups of railroads, will be able to encourage, promote, or require action on the part of carriers in order to avoid duplication of service, prevent waste, and encourage financial reorganizations. Such a coordinator should also, in carrying out this policy, render useful service in maintaining railroad employment at a fair wage.[238]

Commissioner Eastman elaborated before the Senate Committee on Interstate Commerce the functions of the co-ordinator. His statement is as follows:

It will be seen from the summary of the provisions of the act that the coordinator is in no sense to be a czar of the railroads. He is to be an administrative officer of the Government whose principal duty shall be to aid and promote and, if necessary, require the cooperation on the part of the carriers which it is believed the emergency demands and which it is difficult, if not impossible, for those companies with their jealousies and intense rivalries and individual interests and present legal inhibitions to accomplish without outside, disinterested help and the aid of the Government. The Coordinator is given power, appropriate to the emergency, to act without the long delays of emergency procedure. On the other hand, in view of the fact that the orders of the coordinator may override the prohibitions and restraints of many existing laws, State or Federal, the bill recognizes the need for an opportunity of review, after public hearings, by a public body experienced in these matters and knowing the reasons for the laws.[239]

Mr. Eastman emphasized the important duty of the co-ordinator to make recommendations for the general improvement of the national transportation system and, it may be added, Mr.

238. Ibid.
239. Hearings before the Senate Committee on Interstate Commerce on S. 1580, 73d Cong., 1st sess. (1933), 31.

Eastman continued to regard this planning function as the most important duty of the co-ordinator. Criticisms of the proposal were neither numerous nor impressive. Senator Borah felt that the commission itself could do everything the co-ordinator could do, and he objected to the co-ordinator's power to suspend the application of the antitrust laws to railroads.[240] Review of all of the co-ordinator's orders by the commission did not seem to him to be adequate protection. Representative James M. Beck of Pennsylvania disliked the whole arrangement, declaring, 'it is a very debatable question whether the Interstate Commerce Commission has not done far more harm to the railroads than it has done good in its operations of 45 years.' He asserted that the co-ordinator would, in fact, be a dictator equaled only in power by the dictators administering respectively the AAA and the NRA. 'And now the dictator of the railroads, will, like Pompey, Crassus, and Caesar, divide the entire industrial field of America between them and exercise dictatorial powers not unlike the great triumvirate of ancient Rome.'[241]

b. *The relation of the co-ordinator to the commission*

There was little discussion of the relation of the co-ordinator to the commission. It was clear that he was to have no final powers but that all of his orders were subject to review by the commission on appeal. Furthermore, if he were chosen from the commission itself, the Act disqualified him from sitting on appeal in any case originating before him.

c. *Internal changes in the commission*

The Act of 1920 authorized changes in the internal organization of the commission which were of great importance to it. These, however, did not attract outside attention. In 1917 the commission had been given a limited power to delegate authority to divisions composed of not less than three commissioners with review by the entire commission.[242] While this afforded a measure of relief it did not solve the problem. The commission

240. 77 Cong. Rec. 4254.   242. Act of Aug. 9, 1917, 40 Stat. at L. 270.
241. Ibid. 4946.

felt keenly the need of delegating to its staff final action in many routine matters. In its annual reports in 1928, 1929, and 1930 it asked Congress to authorize such delegations under definite restrictions. These were, first, that investigations undertaken on the commission's own motion, and therefore presumably of major importance, should not be delegated to subordinates. Secondly, contested cases involving testimony at public hearings should not be delegated except with the express consent of the parties. And finally, any party affected by such delegated powers should have the right to petition for a rehearing, either by a section of the commission or by the full commission.

In 1933 Commissioner Eastman presented to the House committee the commission's request for power to delegate its authority. His statement in behalf of the proposal is as follows:

Sound principles of organization demand that those at the top be able to concentrate their attention upon the larger and more important questions of policy and practice, and that their time be freed, so far as possible, from the consideration of the smaller and less important matters of detail.

A further, and to my mind serious, effect of the continual drive of this routine work is that it is difficult for the commissioners to find time to study the essential statistics of railroad operation, to grasp the trend of events, and to ponder in quiet over the really big questions of policy and principle. There is, of course, in the last analysis no more important work than that which the Commission can do.[243]

Mr. Eastman went on to explain why he believed that an internal reorganization of the commission's structure and procedure was vastly preferable to the proposal to transfer the commission's administrative duties to a separate agency. His argument on this point merits quotation at length.

Without going into details, one idea which persists in certain quarters is that the commission should be freed from its administrative duties and confined to those which are judicial. Apparently it is the thought that the administrative duties should either be eliminated or handled by some other public body. I find it very difficult to draw such a line of distinction between our duties. As a matter of law, the great bulk of our duties are neither administrative nor

243. Hearings before the House Committee on Interstate and Foreign Commerce on H.R. 7432, 72d Cong., 2d sess. (1933), 7, 9.

judicial but instead are legislative. That has several times been declared by the Supreme Court. The commission is not a court nor an executive department but an agency of Congress, created to do work, very largely, which would otherwise devolve upon Congress. About the only chiefly judicial work which we do, so far as I am aware, is the awarding of damages for past violations of the law which we administer, such as the charging of unreasonable rates in the past.

Of course, most of our legislative work involves the weighing of evidence offered by opposing parties, just as you have to weigh evidence on matters before you. But this is by no means confined to rate cases; it is equally true of every contested proceeding which we hear, whether it involves rates or securities or service or safety devices, or new construction or any other matter with which we deal. Nor is it true that the commission was ever intended by Congress to be a mere passive tribunal for the decision or arbitration of issues presented by opposing parties. The original act gave the commission the power to initiate investigations not only upon complaint but upon its own motion. It was intended that the commission should be an expert and active agency, with full powers of investigation into railroad affairs and with authority to produce of its own account such evidence as it might conceive the decision of a given case to require. It was recognized that the general public is in no position to present evidence relative to matters which are peculiarly within the railroad's own knowledge and which can only be ascertained through power to examine their books and records.

Finally, it is not true that controversies between shippers and carriers with respect to rates are the only railroad controversies which are affected with a public interest. As the interstate commission act now recognizes, there are many other controversies between carriers and investors, between carriers and their employees, between carriers and the general public, and between carriers themselves which are equally affected with a public interest. Good administration requires that the handling of such matters, which are interrelated, should be coordinated so far as practicable in the hands of a single public body. The commission uses all of its bureaus in the conduct of its work generally. Service agents, for example, have proved helpful in rate cases, as well as accountants and valuation engineers. I could give many illustrations of this sort of thing. If a division were to be made, I would not know where to draw the line between administrative duties on the one hand and judicial or quasi-judicial duties on the other hand. Nor do I believe that an attempt to draw such a line would serve any useful purpose. On the contrary, it would impair efficiency and effectiveness and increase expenses.[244]

These arguments proved persuasive, and without opposition the commission was given the authority it asked for. It may also be added that in the brief debates in 1933 no new light was thrown upon the nature of the commission's powers or its relations to the other branches of government.

5. THE LEGISLATIVE RECOMMENDATIONS OF CO-ORDINATOR EASTMAN

Commissioner Joseph B. Eastman was the logical man to be Co-ordinator of Transportation, and he was promptly appointed by President Roosevelt. He took seriously the task imposed upon him of recommending legislative changes and the planning of a more effective national transportation system. The thoughtful and cogently supported proposals presented in his four annual reports form a part of the recent legislative history of the Interstate Commerce Commission, even though some of them were not adopted. We may therefore summarize them here.

The first brief report of the co-ordinator was of a purely preliminary nature.[245] It discussed the question, Is there need for a radical or major change in the organization, conduct, and regulation of the railroad industry which can be accomplished by federal legislation? No legislation was, however, proposed.

The second report [246] recommended three bills. The first proposed national regulation of motor carriers engaged in interstate commerce, and with minor changes this bill became the Motor Carrier Act of 1935.[247] The second bill provided for the federal regulation of water carriers by the Interstate Commerce Commission. This authority was not at once granted to the Interstate Commerce Commission, but to the Maritime Commission by the Merchant Marine Act of 1936. The Transportation Act of 1940, however, took the power to regulate domestic water

244. Ibid. 11 f.
245. S. Doc. 119, 73d Cong., 2d sess. (1934).
246. S. Doc. 152, 73d Cong., 2d sess. (1934). Bills are S. 1629, S. 1632, S. 1635.
247. Act of Aug. 9, 1935, 49 Stat. at L. 543; *infra*, 142.

rates from the Maritime Commission and gave it to the Interstate Commerce Commission. A third bill proposed certain minor changes in the Interstate Commerce Act with which we are not concerned.

The co-ordinator's third report [248] launched out into more controversial waters. The earlier proposals were repeated, and changes in the Bankruptcy Act as it affected railroads were proposed. Turning to more general problems Mr. Eastman urged that if the Interstate Commerce Commission was to take over the regulation of all forms of transportation it must be better equipped to carry on the job. He presented three weaknesses in its organization. First, final authority on all important matters still rested in the full commission; and as this was too large in number for effective action, for many purposes final authority should be given to smaller groups. Second, the chairman of the commission carried the full working load of a commissioner and was therefore unable to exercise any administrative supervision. The chairmanship, moreover, rotated from year to year so that there was no certainty of getting or keeping the best man for the post. In the third place, reform in the procedure by which the commission worked could be secured only by action of the entire body rather than by a responsible administrative chairman. These were serious defects and to meet them the co-ordinator made definite and elaborate proposals.

In the first place, the chairman of the commission should be designated by the President and should serve his full term in that capacity. He should be made an administrative officer with responsibility for the efficient handling of commission business. In the second place, permanent divisions should be set up to handle special parts of the commission's work. These should deal with finance, railroad matters, water and pipe lines, motor carriers, and aviation. Special divisions should be set up *ad hoc* to deal with other problems. These divisions would vary in membership from three to five, and it was later proposed that their membership should rotate, which would require an increase in the membership of the commission. These divisions would have final authority to deal with problems lying within their jurisdiction. In the third place, there should be a control

248. H. Doc. 89, 74th Cong., 1st sess. (1935).

board consisting of the chairman of the commission and the chairmen of the several divisions, to supervise the administrative activities of the chairman of the commission. It should secure the specialization and co-ordination necessary in the field of regulation and, working with the co-ordinator, it should deal with all legislative matters. Mr. Eastman summed up the advantages of these three plans as follows:

> . . . It would give the Commission, what it does not now have, a permanent executive officer relieved from many routine duties and with the specific duty of promoting the expeditious and efficient conduct of its business and the improvement of procedure . . .
>
> It would provide for specialization in the regulation of the different types of carriers; but at the same time make provisions for the coordination of regulation through a Control Board, in order to avoid conflicting or inconsistent policies . . .
>
> No matter would be determined by a body of more than 5 members, and the usual number would be 3, thus avoiding the time-consuming deliberations of a larger body.[249]

In the fourth place, the Co-ordinator of Transportation should be retained as a permanent planning agency. Mr. Eastman felt strongly that the planning function could not be successfully carried on by a separate department of transportation or by any political body. The commission itself was too busy to plan, and planning was too important to be farmed out to subordinates. Planning must be carried on by someone associated with the commission but not overburdened by participation in its regulatory work. The need would be met by making permanent the office of Co-ordinator of Transportation.

The co-ordinator, however, did not carry with him his colleagues on the commission. The commission sent his report to Congress, but sent also its own vigorous objections to his proposals for its reorganization. These objections were as follows: It was premature to reorganize the commission until Congress decided whether to make fresh delegations of power. No new members were necessary to carry the existing load. The commission should be given wide authority to reorganize itself rather than be reorganized by the rigid statutory arrangements proposed by the co-ordinator. The control board would really be

249. Ibid. 23.

the commission, while the rest of the members would become little more than examiners. A permanent chairmanship would not be desirable, but if it were the commission already had power to keep its chairman in office. The centralization of administrative authority in a single officer was objectionable. No action was taken by Congress on Mr. Eastman's proposals.

The fourth report [250] of the co-ordinator repeated the recommendations previously made and answered the objections urged by the commission. Mr. Eastman stood his ground on all major points, insisting that statutory reorganization was necessary because the commission would not reorganize itself. The commission again repeated its objections to Mr. Eastman's plan, holding that new members were not needed and urging in place of his proposals the creation of a series of appellate divisions to which certain classes of commission business might be taken.

In February 1935 the Senate Committee on Interstate Commerce under the chairmanship of Senator Wheeler held hearings on Mr. Eastman's reorganization bill, and Mr. Eastman and Chairman McManamy both testified. Mr. Eastman repeated his charge that a body of eleven men 'partakes somewhat of the nature of a town meeting. It is inevitably unwieldy and slow in many of its movements, and it invites debate and divergence of opinion.' [251] He reiterated that the commission had no real executive head and required a permanent chairman to act as administrative director, subject at all times to the supervision of the control board. He contended that a regulating body could not plan.

. . . It is difficult for them to find time for general research into fundamental questions or for thought along broad lines. A regulating commission is not a court but it is like one in many ways.

If the Government is to deal wisely with transportation, however, it must be able to look ahead, prevent evils from developing, if possible, and plan for the future. A tribunal for the settlement of controversies is necessary, but some public agency should be locating the fundamental problems, both present and prospective, and giving study and creative thought to them.[252]

250. H. Doc. 394, 74th Cong., 2d sess. (1936).
251. Hearings before the Senate Committee on Interstate Commerce on Bills to Amend the Interstate Commerce Act (S. 1629, S. 1632, and S. 1635), 74th Cong., 1st sess. (1935), 104.
252. Ibid. 111.

To carry on this important function a permanent co-ordinator was needed.

Chairman McManamy replied that flexibility of organization was of vital importance to the efficiency of the commission. He elaborated his objections to a permanent chairmanship, and the general tenor of his testimony suggests that he regarded the task of long-range planning by the government to be substantially less important than did Mr. Eastman. No legislation grew out of the hearings. The office of co-ordinator continued year by year, but Congress allowed it to expire by limitation in June 1936 and Mr. Eastman resumed his former place on the commission.

It was not until three years later that anything was done in the way of reorganizing the commission. A commission order effective July 1, 1939, reduced the number of divisions in the commission to five and gave to each carefully defined jurisdiction. Each division was authorized to assign to individual members thereof any matter referred to the division, except investigations initiated by the commission or contested proceedings involving public hearings in which the parties do not consent to such delegation. The assignment to individual commissioners of the supervision of the various commission bureaus was continued. There was much more extensive delegation of work to individual members, subject always to review either by a division or by the entire commission. The annual rotation of the chairmanship was replaced by a three-year term, and the chairman was given the duty of seeing that the work of the commission was done promptly and efficiently. Mr. Eastman became the first three-year chairman in July 1939.[253]

I. Recent Legislation

We may mention briefly four statutes passed by Congress since the Act of 1933. None of these changed the structure or status of the Interstate Commerce Commission, but each affected its jurisdiction and power. The Federal Communications Act of 1934 [254] relieved the commission of all jurisdiction over communications by telephone and telegraph and gave it

253. 53d Ann. Rept. of the I.C.C. (1939), 1-5.
254. Act of June 19, 1934, 48 Stat. at L. 1064.

to the newly created Federal Communications Commission. The Interstate Commerce Commission had never fully exercised its authority over the telephone and telegraph companies and was wholly willing to have the additional burden taken away.

We have already mentioned the Motor Carrier Act of 1935 [255] based essentially upon the bill proposed by Co-ordinator Eastman. This was a very important statute. It imposed upon the commission the enormous task of setting up effective federal regulation of motor carriers engaged in interstate commerce. Not since the Hepburn Act of 1906 had the range of the commission's authority been so strikingly increased. In 1936 Congress passed the Merchant Marine Act [256] setting up the United States Maritime Commission. By so doing it repudiated the proposal made by Mr. Eastman that the regulation of water carriers be turned over to the Interstate Commerce Commission in order to secure a unified control of the nation's entire transportation system. The new commission, which we shall discuss in greater detail,[257] was given power to administer the new federal policy of ship subsidies, and assumed also what little federal regulatory power had previously existed over shipping companies. The Act authorized the President after an interval of two years to transfer to the Interstate Commerce Commission the limited regulatory power over shipping rates and service. The President did not, however, exercise this authority. It seemed unwise to transfer jurisdiction over water carriers by Executive order. After some delay it was decided to proceed by legislation. The President appointed special committees which during 1938 and 1939 explored anew the transportation problem and made proposals. After lengthy hearings by Congressional committees and much debate, Congress finally passed the Transportation Act of 1940.[258]

This statute placed inland and coastwise waterways under the Interstate Commerce Commission, but left foreign shipping in the hands of the Maritime Commission. As a result of this separate control over the two classes of water transportation

255. Act of Aug. 9, 1935, 49 Stat. at L. 543.
256. Act of June 29, 1936, 49 Stat. at L. 1985.
257. *Infra*, 267 ff.
258. Act of September 18, 1940.

the Interstate Commerce Commission is now able to impose on domestic water carriers much more drastic and comprehensive regulation than it had seemed feasible to impose on all water carriers when these had, under the earlier Act, included ocean shipping lines. These domestic water carriers are now subject to control roughly similar to that which governs the nation's railroads. Thus at last all the main classes of transportation by which interstate commerce is carried on, except air carriers, have been placed under a single regulatory authority, the Interstate Commerce Commission.

The Act of 1940, however, dealt with much more than water carriers. In its opening paragraph Congress announced a 'National Transportation Policy,' embodying among other things the impartial and balanced development of transportation by rail, road, and water, the promotion of safe and efficient service, reasonable rates, sound economic conditions for the carriers, fair wages and labor conditions, and co-operation with the states. The Act codified various amendments to the Interstate Commerce Act. It created a board of investigation and research of three members, appointed by the President and the Senate at salaries of $10,000 and empowered to command information. This board was instructed to investigate the relative place of the railroads, motor carriers, and water carriers in an adequately balanced national transportation policy, the extent to which the three types of carriers have received public financial support, the forms of taxation to which they are subjected, and any other matters relevant to the effectuation of the national transportation policy stated in the statute. The board is to make a preliminary report in 1941, and annual and final reports. It expires in two years unless continued for two more years by the President.

J. Recent Unofficial Proposals for Reorganization of the Interstate Commerce Commission

Before closing this history of the Interstate Commerce Commission we may mention two interesting proposals coming from unofficial sources and dealing with problems previously discussed, but still unsolved.

In March 1934 a transportation conference held at the

Union League Club at Chicago made public its report, which was as follows: Experience showed that the administrative commission was the ideal mechanism for government regulation, even though such a commission combined duties which were legislative, executive, and judicial. The Interstate Commerce Commission, however, was sadly overburdened and important changes were needed to secure the efficiency that is so imperative. There must be set up a completely unified system of regulation of the national transportation system. This unified regulation should be confided to the Interstate Commerce Commission as the best possible agency for handling the task. The commission must, however, be given relief in order to carry on its functions effectively. It should be relieved of what the conference described as 'the function of transportation promotion,' a function vitally necessary to the proper development and co-ordination of transport facilities. This task of promotion ought not to be handled by a quasi-judicial regulatory agency. It should be carried on by a single-headed organization completely free from regulatory responsibilities. Both regulation and promotion, however, must be kept free from political influence and therefore neither the Interstate Commerce Commission nor the proposed transportation promotion agency should be part of any executive department of the government. Here again the long-standing demand for a separate agency to plan and co-ordinate became articulate.[259]

In 1933, to meet the desperate situation arising out of the depression, the holders of railroad securities set up a special committee to investigate and propose measures of relief. This committee was composed of ex-President Coolidge, Alfred E. Smith, Bernard Baruch, Clark Howell, and Alex Legge. This committee, in a report which Alfred E. Smith was unwilling to sign,[260] attacked the merging of legislative, judicial, and executive powers in the hands of the commission, and recommended that the commission be so reorganized as to segregate internally these functions. The report stated that the quasi-judicial task of regulation suffered as a result of this combination of authority, and rendered the commission quite incapable of effective planning. It was therefore of vital importance to

259. *Report of Transportation Conference of 1933-1934,* 47-52.
260. *Report of the National Transportation Committee* (1933).

set up separate planning machinery through which the broad problems affecting the railroad industry could be adequately appreciated and dealt with.

Of some interest is the supplementary memorandum filed by Alfred E. Smith. Mr. Smith was convinced that the Interstate Commerce Commission had outlived its usefulness. He said:

> . . . I find, however, little in recent history to justify the continuance of the Interstate Commerce Commission as now organized. This implies no criticism of its members. They have attempted to function under an obsolete and unworkable law, and in the face of conditions which call for intelligent planning and leadership as distinguished from endless debate on details . . . I believe that too much emphasis has been placed on the judicial functions of the Interstate Commerce Commission, especially on valuation and rate making, and too little on the planning and administration.

Referring to the complications and difficulties which had arisen in connection with railroad valuation, Mr. Smith continued:

> . . . Suppose that just a little common sense had been substituted for all this scientific hash, this maze of regulation and red tape? I favor the abolition of the Interstate Commerce Commission and the creation in its place of a new department of transportation headed by one man, or a one man bureau head in the Department of Commerce determining policies with the approval of the Secretary of Commerce. What we need is a new transportation system, not endless hearings on a system that does not work.[261]

261. Ibid. 41 f.

IV

THE GROWTH OF THE COMMISSION MOVEMENT

I. THE FEDERAL RESERVE BOARD

A. THE FEDERAL RESERVE ACT OF 1913

THE second independent regulatory commission was the Federal Reserve Board set up in 1913. It was established to meet a very different problem from that assigned to the Interstate Commerce Commission, but a problem equally important. In composition, duties, and procedure the two bodies bore only a very superficial resemblance to each other, but one thing they had in common—they were both independent of the executive branch. Each was created in order that government control of a great economic problem could be made effective. The Federal Reserve Board, however, was essentially a managerial agency actually sharing in the direction of banking operations, exercising no quasi-judicial duties, and settling no disputes.

1. BACKGROUND OF THE FEDERAL RESERVE ACT

Prior to the Federal Reserve Act of 1913 [1] the United States had been carrying on under an antiquated and inadequate banking system. This system was built on the National Banking Act of 1863 with some later modifications. The banking and currency system of the country was a national disgrace. Periodically calamities in the form of bankers' panics emphasized the existence of what Carter Glass called 'the Siamese

1. Act of Dec. 23, 1913, 38 Stat. at L. 251.

twins of disorder . . . an inelastic currency and a fictitious reserve system.'[2] Bank reserves tended to flow to the financial centers where they were lent as call money to those operating on the securities exchange. The panic of 1907 sharply emphasized the need for reform. Out of the wreckage emerged the Vreeland-Aldrich Act of 1908,[3] passed as an emergency measure. This permitted national banks to issue 'emergency bank notes' on a more liberal security basis than before, but in limited amounts and under heavy taxation. More important still, it set up the National Monetary Commission composed of nine senators and nine members of the House, 'to inquire into and report to Congress at the earliest date practicable what changes are necessary or desirable in the monetary system of the United States or in the laws relating to banking and currency.'

The National Monetary Commission under the chairmanship of Senator Aldrich studied the problems assigned to it from 1908 until 1912. It accumulated a vast amount of information relating to foreign and domestic banking and monetary problems. It brought together a very extensive library. It ultimately submitted to Congress a report in forty-odd volumes,[4] accompanied by a bill for the complete reorganization of the American banking system. This bill, known as the Aldrich bill,[5] was introduced in the Senate by Senator Burton and referred to the Committee on Finance. It proposed to pool all bank reserves in one central system to be called the National Reserve Association. This was to be a corporation with capital subscribed by the member banks. Any national or state banks or trust companies could join. Subscribing banks located in contiguous territory were to be grouped into local associations. These, in turn, were to be organized into fifteen district associations, each one of which was to have a branch of the central association. Through its district branches, which were autonomous only in the exercise of the right to rediscount, the National Reserve Association exercised the principal banking functions of holding cash and reserves, discount and rediscount, transfers of balance, and note issue.

2. Carter Glass, *An Adventure in Constructive Finance* (1927), 60.
3. Act of May 30, 1908, 35 Stat. at L. 546.
4. S. Doc. 243, 62d Cong., 1st sess. (1911).
5. S. 4431, 62d Cong., 2d sess. (1912).

The Aldrich bill was popularly regarded as proposing a central bank, and to any scheme of central banking the Democrats, who had captured control of the House in 1910, were implacably opposed. The bill therefore was not actively considered in Congress, but throughout the long fight culminating in the Federal Reserve Act its influence was important. It loomed in the offing as a possible alternative, and represented a rallying point for the Republican opposition to the bill which finally passed. In his message to Congress on December 6, 1912, President Taft urged adoption of the Aldrich bill with modifications.

2. STEPS IN THE LEGISLATIVE HISTORY OF THE ACT

The Federal Reserve Act was passed after one of the most bitter and dramatic fights ever waged to enact an important federal statute. The story begins in the 62d Congress in 1912. In that year the House ordered an investigation of the 'money trust' by its banking and currency committee. Simultaneously it was decided to attempt reform of the banking legislation, and the House committee accordingly divided itself into two sections to handle these widely different tasks. The chairman of the committee, Mr. Pujo, took over the 'money trust' investigation and with Mr. Samuel Untermyer as counsel put on a very spectacular show. The subcommittee on banking reform under the chairmanship of Carter Glass of Virginia undertook to devise a reserve banking scheme. The Democratic platform of 1912 contained the statement: 'We oppose the so-called Aldrich bill or the establishment of a central bank.' The Glass committee accordingly did not seriously consider the Aldrich bill, but at the same time it felt free to use any parts of it or any of the materials collected by the National Monetary Commission that suited its needs. It began active work on a bill in the spring of 1912, but Congress adjourned in August with the work of the committee unfinished. In November the Democrats elected Woodrow Wilson as President, and a powerful majority in both houses of Congress.

During the short session of the expiring Congress the Glass subcommittee went forward with its task. Glass and Parker

Willis, the technical adviser to the committee, conferred with the President-elect during the winter months and Wilson made important suggestions which later formed the basis for the Act. During January and February the subcommittee held hearings but they did not disclose the nature of the bill which they were working upon. They had already arrived at the point of favoring a regional reserve system with a central board but were not as yet willing to expose the new plan to the opposition attack.

The Glass subcommittee expired on March 4, 1913. President Wilson summoned a special session of Congress on April 7 and forced it to remain in session until December 1 when the regular session of Congress convened; nevertheless work on the banking bill was delayed. The House Committee on Banking and Currency was not organized until early in June. Rumor has it that the banking interests in New York tried to bring about the abrogation of the seniority rule, which would make Glass chairman of the House committee, in order to secure a chairman favorable to the Aldrich bill. If this is true, President Wilson's influence was sufficient to prevent it, and Carter Glass became chairman of the House committee in June. Simultaneously Senator Owen of Oklahoma became chairman of the Senate Committee on Banking and Currency. Conferences were held at the White House at which the views of the President were made plain, and the influence of Wilson was dominant throughout. It is doubtful whether a majority of the House Democrats was really friendly to the federal reserve bill [6] that had been whipped into shape. A bitter fight ensued, and finally it was necessary to invoke the disciplinary action of a party caucus to bring Democratic support into line. Mr. Glass led this fight, and finally under caucus pressure the bill went to the full Committee on Banking and Currency, which on September 10 reported it to the House. After a five-day debate it passed the House on September 18 by a vote of 287 to 85. Only three Democrats voted against the bill; 48 Republicans voted for it and 82 against it.

The banking interests and other opponents of the Glass bill tried every possible means to prevent Senate action during the special session, but President Wilson refused to consent to an

6. H.R. 7837, 63d Cong., 1st sess. (1913).

adjournment without such action. The Senate Committee on Banking and Currency held extensive hearings, largely attended by the bankers. Tremendous pressure was directed against the bill. After long delay the Senate committee reported the bill without recommendation and a Senate debate ensued. A Senate caucus was held after which the House bill, somewhat altered, passed the Senate on December 19 by a vote of 54 to 34. Three Republicans voted for the bill and no Democrats voted against it. House and Senate differences were ironed out in conference; the conference report passed both houses on December 22, and the bill was signed on December 23.

3. SUMMARY OF THE ACT OF 1913

The Federal Reserve Act created a regional Federal Reserve System built up around twelve federal reserve banks, and placed this system under the general direction of a Federal Reserve Board.

Federal reserve banks were set up in twelve cities. These were bankers' banks, created mainly to hold bank reserves. Each had nine directors divided into three classes. Three represented the banks and were chosen by them; three were chosen by the banks to represent the commercial, industrial, and financial interests of the district; three were chosen by the Federal Reserve Board and one of these was to be chairman.

A Federal Reserve Board was set up, composed of the Secretary of the Treasury, who was to act as chairman, the Comptroller of the Currency, both ex officio, and five members appointed by the President to represent the financial, industrial, commercial, and geographical interests of the country. Two of the five had to be experienced in banking or finance. All appointive members held for ten-year staggered terms unless sooner removed for cause by the President, and from these the President designated a governor and vice-governor of the board; the governor was to be 'the active executive officer.'

The powers of the board were managerial and supervisory. They were managerial in respect to the fixing of the rediscount rate, the control of bank reserves, the issuance of bank notes, and other lesser matters. They were supervisory with respect to bank examinations and the power to remove directors and officers of reserve banks.

An advisory council was created composed of bankers who were selected from each reserve district by the banks. This council was to sit with the board, express its judgment upon matters of policy, and offer advice. It had, however, no legal powers.

4. TOPICS AND ISSUES IN HEARINGS AND DEBATES

The original issue in the struggle for banking reform lay between some form of central bank and a regional reserve system. This battle was lost, however, in the election of 1912, which placed in power a party firmly opposed to any central banking scheme; we need not, therefore, go into the merits of the controversy. On the Federal Reserve Act itself and especially on the provisions relating to the Federal Reserve Board there was discussion and controversy, which we may analyze.

a. *Nature of the federal reserve board's task—a supervisory and managerial job*

Those setting up the projected federal reserve board were aware that they were giving to it a new kind of regulatory power. The board's task was not one calling for hearings, arguments, trial examiners, and the settling of disputes between parties by quasi-judicial process. It was instead the control and management of banking policy and the directing of banking operations. The original Glass plan had provided a system of decentralized reserve banks with no central control over them. The Comptroller of the Currency was to supervise them as he had always supervised national banks. President Wilson, however, had insisted upon a central board as a 'capstone' of the whole system, and this had proved an entering wedge for a high degree of central control. Wilson wanted this board to do more than merely supervise the regional banks, but he insisted that it must exercise no direct banking functions. There was steady effort by certain Republican congressmen to give the board actual banking duties. As the bill took final shape it was clear that the federal reserve board was to exercise powers far beyond those of a bank examiner. Mr. Glass presented on behalf of the committee sixty-six duties [7] to be performed by the board. First, it was to have disciplinary control over the reserve banks and their officers, including the power to suspend and remove the latter, and under certain circumstances to liquidate the former. Secondly, it was to have full authority over bank-note issues. Thirdly, it would control the rediscount rate and could compel reserve banks to rediscount the paper of other reserve banks. Fourthly, it could readjust reserve requirements to meet the needs of the banking system. Broadly, it was to have power to see that a flexible bank-note currency was kept available and that the whole banking structure operated smoothly and securely. Parker Willis summed up the general character of the job assigned to the board as follows:

. . . This bill . . . keeps the control of the broad banking powers in the hands of the Government, while it leaves the actual transaction of banking operations to practical bankers in the district . . .

This bill has been criticized, I notice, in a good many quarters, as putting the Government into the banking business. It seems to me that it takes the Government out of the banking business. That is, it puts the funds of the Government into commercial use, and then lets the actual process of banking be carried on in these country districts by trained bankers, and it keeps Government supervision in the hands of Government officers . . .

It should be an organization for the exercise of large powers of supervision and control; while I think that the individual banks should be narrowly confined to business operations, going ahead on their own initiative, so far as that does not conflict with the general welfare. That strikes me as the distinguishing feature of this bill.[8]

b. *The board form for the control agency*

It was generally agreed that government authority over the banking system should be vested in a board rather than in a single officer. Mr. Glass originally proposed to leave this power in the hands of the Comptroller of the Currency, but this was before he had considered increasing the purely supervisory duties which that officer had long performed. President Wilson

7. H. Rept. 69, 63d Cong., 1st sess. (1913).
8. S. Doc. 232. vols. XV-XVII, 63d Cong., 1st sess. (1913), 3050 f.

had immediately and firmly insisted upon a board. As a matter of fact, the idea that federal control should be exercised by a board made it easier and safer to extend the range of that control. The bankers unanimously favored a board as a central control agency. The Aldrich bill, their pet proposal, had provided for one. Such a board was roughly similar to the boards of directors with which bankers were familiar. It seemed easier to protect a board from political control than to protect a single appointed official. And more important still, the board form of organization afforded an opportunity for banker representation, which the banking fraternity at the outset believed that they could secure. No one appears to have favored the concentration of banking control in a single officer.

c. *The independence of the board—The problem of ex-officio members*

The problem of the independence of the Federal Reserve Board was much more difficult and complicated than the problem of the independence of the Interstate Commerce Commission. This distinction was fully recognized by the Congressional leaders engaged in defining the board's powers and status. They gave to the new federal agency broad powers affecting the entire banking and currency system. Certain of these powers could not effectively be exercised in complete isolation from the executive branch of the government, particularly the Treasury. In fact, one of the problems relating to the Federal Reserve Board which has never been clearly settled is how far it is wise to associate it with and possibly subordinate it to Treasury policy, and how far it ought to enjoy the independence which we associate with the quasi-judicial regulatory bodies. The problem was not overlooked in the debates on the Act of 1913.

It is significant that bipartisanship was not required in the selection of the appointive members of the board. In explaining his bill in the House in September 1913, Mr. Glass proposed a federal reserve board of three ex-officio members and with appointive members chosen under the bipartisan rule.[9]

9. 50 Cong. Rec. 4644.

This bipartisan requirement was dropped out of the bill shortly afterwards, and later efforts to restore it failed. In the Senate, Senator Weeks emphasized that members of the board ought to be men experienced in banking and finance and chosen without reference to party affiliations.[10] At no time did any Senate bill contain the bipartisan requirement. It seems likely that the vigorous and successful demands for representation on the board of special groups and of special regions overshadowed the normal fear that partisan domination would result unless specifically forbidden. It may be noted that there has never been a bipartisan requirement affecting the Federal Reserve Board and there is no such requirement in the present Act.

The placing of the Secretary of the Treasury and the Comptroller of the Currency on the projected board as ex-officio members was a frank recognition of the vital interest which the executive branch of the government had in the board's domination of policies affecting currency and credit. How far could a federal reserve board wisely be made independent of the Treasury, and to what extent would the presence on the board of these executive officers undermine its independence?

There was sharp criticism of this ex-officio arrangement. The tasks which the board would have to perform were intricate and exacting. If properly done they would require the full time of highly competent persons. They could not be handled successfully by federal officials already burdened with the heavy load of other executive responsibilities. This point was clearly stated by Mr. Vanderlip before the Senate committee:

. . . I believe it is bad to have ex officio members on that board and to have ex officio members whose duties are already sufficient to engross their time fully. This will be a very important board; it will be a man's size job to be a member of this board. He ought to be devoting all his time to it. He ought to have experience. The board should have continuity. If you put Cabinet officers on that board they will of necessity go out with each change of administration, and may go much more frequently than that. They are fully engrossed, if they are properly looking after their other duties, and they can not, I believe, perform in a creditable manner the duties of this Federal reserve board.[11]

10. 51 Cong. Rec. 279.   11. *Supra,* note 8, op. cit. 1980.

It was urged even more strongly that the ex-officio membership would result in political control of the board by the administration in power. The Secretary of the Treasury and the Comptroller of the Currency are political officers. They represent the Administration. The Republicans protested that the proposed arrangement gave the President power to dominate completely the personnel of the board and consequently its policies. This control would center largely, of course, around the Secretary of the Treasury, and Mr. Mondell voiced his objections as follows:

> . . . Last, but not least, but, in fact greatest of all, the President appoints the Secretary of the Treasury, who is chairman of the board, supervisor of the manager, and director of the vice chairman the Comptroller of the Currency. In fact, the Secretary of the Treasury is the Pooh-Bah of the Glass system. He comes very near being the whole show.[12]

Various bankers also objected to what they feared would amount to partisan domination of the banking system. They declared that the federal reserve board should stand on 'the same high plane that the Supreme Court of the United States stands on or that the Interstate Commerce Commission stands on'[13] and they felt that this could not be attained under the system of ex-officio members.

These arguments did not prevail, although little effort was made to answer them on their merits. There was an underlying assumption that a certain degree of 'political' control was imperative if the proposed federal reserve board was to enjoy the broad powers to be conferred upon it. There was a disposition to minimize the partisan character which the board might take on as a result of ex-officio membership, and there was even a willingness to defend openly the theory that the banking and currency system of the country ought not to be wholly free from the control of the political party in power.

d. *The struggle for banker representation on the board*

The bankers throughout the country assumed that they would be given representation on any governmental board that

12. 50 Cong. Rec. 4690.
13. Mr. A. F. Dawson, president of an Iowa bank, *supra,* note 8, op. cit. 2097.

might be created for the management or control of banking. The Aldrich bill embodying the recommendations of the Monetary Commission had provided that thirty-nine of the forty-six directors of the central reserve association should be bankers, as well as five of the nine members of the executive committee. In fact, one of the most vulnerable points about this program was that it established banker control rather than government control. It may be noted also that the first draft of the Glass bill gave the bankers thirty out of the thirty-six board members.

The reasons urged in favor of banker representation were persuasive. The bankers had a tremendously heavy capital investment involved, and they very naturally desired to have substantial influence in determining the policies affecting that investment. Furthermore, the problems involved were essentially technical problems. They would demand the expert knowledge of experienced persons, and that pointed directly to men drawn from the banking world. It was also pointed out that only by placing on the board men drawn from the banking group would it be possible to prevent that organization from being swamped with political appointees or other unqualified persons. The bankers did not claim the privilege of selecting members of the proposed federal reserve board, but merely the privilege of nominating a group of men from whom the President might choose banker representatives. The position of the bankers on this point was clearly put by Representative Dyer of Kansas:

It has been recommended that the board be increased from 7 to 11, the four additional members to be selected from a list of nominees; each reserve bank in the 12 sections of the country to name one candidate eligible for membership on the reserve board; submit same to the President of the United States; and out of the 12 he to select the additional four members. If the Government fears to name four men from the nominees thus selected, why should not the bankers and business men be afraid to turn over this corporation with cash assets of more than $500,000,000, and which will absolutely control the destiny of the Nation's finances, to a politically appointed board, even though they be appointees of the President of the United States? The stockholders of the Central Banks of France, Germany, England, and Canada are trusted with the management of the respective banks. Why, therefore, can not our stock-holder banks have 4 out of 11 directors? [14]

The general belief that the banking group would be given representation was rudely shattered by the adamant opposition of President Wilson. It has been rumored that Mr. Bryan, suspicious of all bankers, was bitterly opposed to any form of banker control and won the President over to his position. Be that as it may, there is no question that President Wilson, single-handed, stopped the drive for banker representation. Mr. Glass gives us the dramatic story of the White House interview in which the issue was settled and settled finally. A delegation of bankers had come to Washington to press their point, conducted by Mr. Glass, who, along with Mr. McAdoo, strongly sympathized with the bankers' position. They went to the President's office and stated their case. After they had done so at great length, the President inquired quietly, 'Will one of you gentlemen tell me in what civilized country of the earth there are important government boards of control on which private interests are represented?' Silence ensued, and the President inquired further, 'Which of you gentlemen thinks the railroads should select members of the Interstate Commerce Commission?' As Mr. Glass put it, 'There could be no convincing reply to either question, so the discussion turned to other points of the currency bill; and, notwithstanding a desperate effort made in the Senate to give the banks minority representation on the reserve board, the proposition did not prevail.' [15]

The President's position was not without support in Congress. Senator Pomerene did not wish to impose any special qualifications upon members of the federal reserve board and objected to their being chosen to represent any special interest.[16] The President should be as free in making his selections as he is in nominating members to the Supreme Court. It was emphasized in the debates that in the European countries having central banks no representation on the controlling board had been given to the bankers themselves. Several congressmen argued that the absence of banker representation was one of the substantial merits of the proposed plan. While the hope of

14. 50 Cong. Rec. 4680.   16. *Supra*, note 8, op. cit. 1044.
15. Carter Glass, op. cit. 115.

the bankers to secure representation died slowly, it did finally die and there has been no later effort to revive the issue.

e. *Group and regional representation on board—* *Qualifications of members*

In view of the wide powers to be given the new board it was natural that groups and sections to which the control of credit was a matter of vital importance should seek to secure representation on the board itself. The qualifications of board members stated in the Act represent a final compromise of these competing claims.

In the first place, there was a definite drive to secure representation for agriculture. The original Glass bill had made the Secretary of Agriculture an ex-officio member of the board, but this provision was later dropped out. Many felt that the Secretary of Agriculture was too busy to render useful service as a member of the board and that his presence upon it would not give adequate representation to agricultural interests. This view was stated by Mr. Manahan of Minnesota:

. . . One member of the board appointed should, of course, represent the great industry of agriculture, which has never had the protection and help it deserves in the matter of banking facilities. Instead of being represented by one man, half of whose time is devoted to Cabinet duties and the other half to banking duties, agriculture is entitled as the most important industry of the country to the best service of two of its strongest representatives, one to devote his entire time as a Cabinet official and adviser of the President and the other as a member of the Federal reserve board to devote his entire time to the great subject of banking and currency as it affects the agricultural interests of the Nation.[17]

Agriculture did not secure representation until 1922.

In the second place, an effort was made to give the geographical sections of the country representation on the board. This was in part an expression of the rather common distrust which the western areas had of eastern financial domination. Representative Murray of Oklahoma stated the argument for sectional representation:

17. 50 Cong. Rec. 5019.

It is admitted by Mr. Glass and the proponents of this bill that it will all depend on this board of seven, and I tell you that they must not only be honest and competent, but they must represent every section of this country. This board, if selected east of Washington, would know little and care less about the agricultural and other interests in the Western and Southern States. Our commercial paper is entirely different. In Oklahoma about the only prime commercial paper is that based upon cattle and agricultural products, particularly cotton. Therefore I introduced an amendment in the caucus providing that not more than one of these four appointed by the President shall be selected from the same regional reserve district. That amendment was adopted.[18]

In the third place, it was strongly urged that the board should be composed of persons 'experienced in banking,' and an attempt was made to put into the act specific requirements in these terms. This seems on casual glance to be entirely appropriate. It was pointed out by Mr. Glass, however, that the board was intended to be a governmental institution, that it had no banking functions as such, that its primary responsibilities were to see that the banking interests of the people as a whole were adequately represented. He felt accordingly that it would be unfortunate to confine its members to the men drawn from the banking fraternity.[19] The Secretary of the Treasury and the Comptroller of the Currency, both to be ex-officio members of the board, were more than likely to be practical bankers, and he feared that the board would have too many bankers on it rather than too few. The effort to require indirectly that members of the board be bankers was regarded with the same suspicion in Administration circles as the early effort to secure direct banker representation. As the bill finally passed it required only two of the five appointed members to be 'experienced in banking or finance.' It provided that only one member should be chosen from each federal reserve district, and that the others should be chosen with due regard to 'different commercial, industrial, and geographical divisions of the country.'

18. Ibid. 5021.   19. Ibid. 4645.

f. *The advisory council*

Mr. Glass states that in the White House conference in June 1913, between the President and representative bankers of the country, the President stated his desire to have a federal advisory council created. This advisory council was to be a compensation to the banking interests for the denial of banker representation on the board itself, and was to be made up exclusively of bankers. It was to sit at stated times with the board in an advisory capacity. It was to be composed of one member from each federal reserve district, chosen by the reserve bank of the district. It was to have authority to confer with the federal reserve board on general business conditions, to make oral or written representations concerning matters subject to the board's control, and more specifically it could call for information and make recommendations concerning the rediscount rate, rediscount business, note issues, open market operations, and similar matters. The advisory council, however, was something more than a mere sop to the disappointed bankers. Mr. Glass regarded it as a highly valuable device through which

the X ray of publicity is turned full upon the operations of this Federal reserve board. There can be nothing sinister about its transactions. Meeting with it at least four times a year, and perhaps oftener, will be a bankers' advisory council representing every regional reserve district in the system. This council will have access to the records of the board and is authorized to give advice and offer suggestions concerning its general policy. How could we have exercised greater caution in safeguarding the public interest? [20]

Senator Owen, chairman of the Senate Committee on Banking and Currency, pointed out an added advantage of the advisory council in giving 'the Federal reserve board the intimate knowledge of the conditions of business in each and every section of the country where there is established a Federal reserve bank.' [21]

The bankers at the outset were far from pleased with the arrangement. Still hoping for direct representation on the board, they attached little significance to the advisory council. The American Bankers Association voted to oppose the crea-

20. Ibid. 4646.　　　　21. Ibid. 5998.

tion of the council and throw its influence behind direct representation. The United States Chamber of Commerce, however, approved the council. When it became apparent that the bankers were not going to secure direct representation, they made strenuous efforts to increase the power of the advisory council. It was proposed that the advisory council should establish an executive office in Washington with a board staff and that at least two members of the council should attend all meetings of the board, but without votes. This plan was not adopted and the council was given the status of a purely advisory body.

B. 'DIRT FARMER' REPRESENTATION ON THE BOARD— ACT OF 1922 [22]

The original proposal to put the Secretary of Agriculture on the Federal Reserve Board failed, and the farmers were left without direct representation. The power of the board over credit policy was, of course, very great and that credit policy impinged sharply upon the agricultural interests at a time when agriculture the country over was suffering severely. The farm bloc in Congress began in 1921 a drive for direct agricultural representation on the Federal Reserve Board, representation, furthermore, through a full-time appointed member rather than through the ex-officio service of a busy Cabinet officer. Senator Smith of South Carolina accordingly introduced an amendment to the Banking Act to read in part as follows: 'Of the five members thus appointed by the President at least two shall be persons experienced in banking or finance and one shall be a person experienced in and whose business and occupation is farming.' Explaining his amendment Senator Smith declared, 'Everyone knows that we are trying, in a way, to laymanize this board.' [23] Mr. Wallace, the Secretary of Agriculture, favored the principle of agricultural representation. At a hearing before the House Committee on Banking and Currency he said, 'It seems to me that the membership of a board, which in time, if not now, will, through the exercise of its administration of the great credit machinery of the country,

22. Act of June 3, 1922, 42 Stat. at L. 620.
23. 62 Cong. Rec. 505, 521.

have a very direct influence upon policies and business in general, should be a cross section of our industrial life, including agriculture.' [24] The proposal was vigorously supported by agricultural spokesmen in both houses. Common justice, it was said, required that the farmer have the protection which such representation would give. Senator Heflin pressed this point with eloquence:

> . . . To-day the Federal Reserve Board holds its foot upon the neck of the grain industry, the cattle industry, and the cotton industry and other industries of the United States, while Wall Street and Chicago look on and applaud. I am in favor of putting in the law this provision now before the Senate which requires the President to appoint a practical farmer as a member of the Federal Reserve Board as soon as another vacancy occurs. The business of agriculture is entitled to this recognition. We demand it. Justice and fair play justify us in demanding it.
>
> When the cattle industry and the cotton industry and the grain industry are in distress and need financial aid and have to call on the Federal reserve banking system, we want a real farmer on the Federal Reserve Board to look after those interests.[25]

He was vigorously supported by Senator Fletcher:

> That is the situation—not a farmer on the Farm Loan Board; not a farmer on the board of directors of a single Federal land bank, chosen by farmers. Think of it. The farmer has no voice in the choosing of the directors of the banks which he himself owns. Did you ever hear of such a situation as that? Is it not time that some people came here and put their heads together, representing the people of this country, and made an honest effort to see that the farmers of this country shall not be neglected and discriminated against in this humiliating and shameful way? Call it 'agricultural bloc' if you like; I would rather be a member of an agricultural bloc than of an aggregation of blockheads. The farmers of this country are not going to stand for that sort of treatment. They do not know what is going on until it is pointed out to them, but when they do know it you may look for something to happen.[26]

Many who saw little practical advantage in adding a 'dirt farmer' to the board felt the advantage that the psychological

---

24. Hearings before the House Committee on Banking and Currency on S. 2263, 67th Cong., 2d sess. (1922), 23.

25. 62 Cong. Rec. 517.

26. Ibid. 584.

effect of such a change would have in giving the farmer greater confidence in the Federal Reserve Board.

The proposal, however, met substantial opposition not only from the financial interests of the country but also from many friends of the farmer as well. Senator Norris objected on principle to setting up specific qualifications of this sort for membership on any governmental agency. He said:

I have never had much use for provisions of law which try to define the kind of a man who shall be put on a board by the appointing power. Very often when we enact laws we provide for a division between parties of the membership of boards. To my mind that is fundamentally wrong. If we enact a law which provides that a board consisting of five shall not have more than three of any one party on it we are fundamentally wrong. In the first place, assuming that a President or other appointing power wanted to carry the bill out in good faith, it limits him to such an extent that he is very often compelled to cast aside the men best fitted for the positions . . .

So, if in a law, you say to the President, 'You must appoint a man on this board who is a farmer,' he can pick a man who is a farmer who has no sympathy with farmers, who has no feeling whatever for agriculture, who would be the worst reactionary he could possibly get; yet he would technically comply with the law.[27]

He was supported by Senator Edge, who emphasized the undesirability of limiting the President's freedom of choice in the making of major appointments.[28] Senator McLean said the proposal was a device to 'stack' the Federal Reserve Board and insisted that the board, like the Supreme Court of the United States, ought never to be 'stacked.' [29] Besides these objections grounded on rather general principles, it was urged that the 'dirt farmer' requirement would be ineffective because it could be so easily evaded. Just what does it mean to require a member of the board to be 'a person whose business and occupation is farming'? Senator McLean declared, 'all that the worst pirate in Wall Street need do to qualify under the Senator's amendment is to buy a 10-acre farm and a cow and a few chickens.' [30] Senator Glass, who favored substituting the Secretary of Agriculture for the Comptroller of the Currency on the Federal

27. Ibid. 1198.
28. Ibid. 519.
29. Ibid. 524.
30. Ibid. 522.

Reserve Board, doubted the effectiveness of the 'dirt farmer' requirement. He said:

Frankly, however, I find myself in agreement with the Senator from Nebraska (Mr. Norris), who in his opening remarks said, in effect, that anyone who is simple enough to suppose that this proposed legislation is going to create a revolution in the policies of the Federal reserve banking system—that putting on a farmer is going to bring the millennium to the agricultural interests of the country—will find himself sadly deceived.[31]

Further attack on the 'dirt farmer' proposal took the form of a sort of *reductio ad absurdum*. This was illustrated by the amendment proposed by Senator Edge to add to the Federal Reserve Board two more members, one 'a person experienced in and whose business and occupation is manufacturing,' and the other 'a person experienced in and whose business and occupation is that of an official of organized labor.' Senator Edge declared:

Mr. President, needless for me to say, I do not favor the principle embodied in these amendments. This fact, I trust, I have already made clear. However, if any class is to be especially recognized, I think it only consistent to permit those who do approve of this policy to have the opportunity of going on record for or against the recognition of other important business or organized interests.[32]

Representative Loudon of New York, perhaps from different motives, introduced a similar amendment in the House for the addition of a labor representative to the board.[33]

A compromise was finally reached. The specific requirement that there be a dirt farmer was omitted, but an additional board member was created and the Act was amended to read as follows: 'In selecting the six appointive members of the Federal Reserve Board . . . the President shall have due regard to a fair representation of the financial, agricultural, industrial, and commercial interests, and geographical divisions of the country.'

31. Ibid. 1250.
32. Ibid. 525.

33. Ibid. 7520.

C. THE BANKING ACT OF 1933

Before discussing the Banking Act of 1933,[34] we may mention the campaign led by Senator Glass in January of that year to amend the Federal Reserve Act by removing the Secretary of the Treasury from the Federal Reserve Board. This was the culmination of a growing feeling of dissatisfaction with the influence and power of the Secretary in banking matters. Many prominent bankers had felt that the Administration exercised too great control through the Secretary, but Senator Glass was the most powerful supporter of the proposed change.[35] His views on this point commanded respect, for he not only was the father of the Federal Reserve System but he had been Secretary of the Treasury during the last days of the Wilson Administration. Speaking from his experience as Secretary, he declared that that official had altogether too much power in the banking field. He was able easily to dominate the policy of the board. He controlled two votes on the board, since the Comptroller of the Currency could be relied upon to follow his lead. Glass said that it had never been intended that the board should be used as an agency for 'stabilizing the market,' and he deplored the extent to which the President was able to dominate the policies of the board and the extent to which the board had become an adjunct of the Treasury. This position was strongly supported in the Senate. Senator Lewis felt that the Federal Reserve Board ought not to be drawn into active relations with the Treasury.[36] This alliance would create either a bureaucracy in which the Secretary dominated the board, or a bureaucracy in which the Secretary was dominated by the board. Either was objectionable. Senator Barclay went further and urged that all ex-officio members be removed from the board.[37] He objected to the influence which these officers exercised over the board. Almost the only opponent of the proposed change in the Senate was Senator Huey Long. He argued that the only way to keep the Federal Reserve Board under the control of the representatives of the people was to have on it a number of persons appointed by reason of their broad politi-

34. Act of June 16, 1933, 48 Stat. at L. 162.   36. Ibid. 2266.
35. 76 Cong. Rec. 1938 ff.   37. Ibid. 2275 ff.

cal interests. If the Secretary of the Treasury tended to dominate the board, there was all the more reason for keeping him
there since in that way the board was held effectively responsible. Senator Long stated this point as follows:

> It is said that it is desired to take him off because he dominates
> the board. That is all the more reason why he ought to be kept on
> the board. The responsibility ought to be charged to the adminis-
> tration in power. The people ought to understand it. The Senators
> ought to have somebody they can go to. Mr. President, we ought to
> be able to go to the Secretary of the Treasury to complain; we
> ought to be able to call him here. When the Secretary of the Treas-
> ury is dissociated from the Federal Reserve Board, then the Federal
> Reserve Board will constantly 'pass the buck' and say, 'it is the
> Treasury Department that is responsible,' and the Treasury Depart-
> ment will 'pass the buck' back and say that it is the Federal Reserve
> Board this is responsible.[38]

Senator Long further added that the proposal came too late.
Secretaries Mellon and Mills were gone. Why make a change
now that a liberal and democratic Secretary was about to take
office? The Glass amendment passed the Senate January 24,
1933, by a vote of 54 to 9, but no action was taken in the
House, and the attention of both houses was soon riveted on
new banking legislation of more comprehensive scope.

In the 71st Congress the Senate Committee on Banking and
Currency under the chairmanship of Senator Glass had been
instructed to inquire into the Federal Reserve System and to
recommend legislation. The Glass committee reported in the
spring of 1933 and laid before Congress recommendations [39]
which without much change became the Act of June 16, 1933.
The main provisions of the new Act were as follows: The term
of office of the six appointive members of the Federal Reserve
Board was increased from ten to twelve years to permit a vacancy to occur every two years. The board was given greater
control over its own internal management policies. The governor of the board was to preside when the Secretary of the
Treasury was not present and the board was allowed to manage
its own disbursements. In spite of Senator Glass's desire to remove the Secretary of the Treasury from the board, this pro-

38. Ibid. 2276.   39. S. 1631, 73d Cong., 1st sess. (1933).

posal was not included in the new Act. Senator Glass explained the omission as follows:

> That statement of the reasons why we eliminated the Secretary of the Treasury from the Board in the bill passed by the Senate 54 to 9 will cause Senators to wonder why we did not persist in that action . . . It was the unanimous judgment of your subcommittee that that official should be eliminated. We had not one single dissent from that view in the general committee. That provision of the previous bill is not included in this bill only by reason of the fact that the Secretary of the Treasury seemed to regard it as a personal affront to him and as a curtailment of his power which ought not to be made at this particular time. Therefore, we have omitted that provision of the bill. There may be a proposal to restore it, in which event I could not conscientiously oppose.[40]

Wholly through inadvertence the new bill omitted the clause limiting the power of the President to remove members of the board for cause. Senator Glass two years later declared that he 'must have been asleep when that was eliminated from the Act.' [41] There was no discussion on the point and the omission was not noticed. On the constructive side, the new statute created the Federal Open Market Committee. This committee was to have twelve members selected by the twelve reserve banks, and was to carry on open market transactions under rules laid down by the Federal Reserve Board. This substantially increased the board's power over the general financial policy of the country. The statute created the Federal Deposit Insurance Corporation, but since this did not actively concern the Federal Reserve Board or impinge upon its activities we need not consider it here. The Act broadened and more sharply defined the conditions of membership in the Federal Reserve System, limited speculative activities by member banks and their officers, and gave the Federal Reserve Board broad powers over the relations of member banks with foreign banks or bankers. The debates on the Glass report and the subsequent bill threw little light upon the powers and status of the Federal Reserve Board.

40. 77 Cong. Rec. 3725.
41. Hearings before a subcommittee of the Senate Committee on Banking and Currency on S. 1715 and H.R. 7617, 74th Cong., 1st sess. (1935), 398.

D. The Banking Act of 1935—Increased Powers of Management and Policy Control—Centralization

1. BACKGROUND OF THE ACT AND STEPS IN ITS LEGISLATIVE HISTORY

The Banking Act of 1935 [42] was a part of the New Deal. The Administration was seeking to establish a 'balanced economy,' and it needed more effective control over banking activities as a monetary instrument for the accomplishment of the general objectives of the whole program. The Act contained important provisions which need not concern us here, since they do not concern the Federal Reserve Board or its activities. The sections of the Act which relate to the Federal Reserve System were drafted by a committee of the Federal Reserve Board composed of Governor Eccles and four subordinates who were the heads of divisions in the board's administrative staff. The exact status of the new bill [43] and the degree of its sponsorship by the Administration is not clear. Senator Glass denied that it was an Administration bill. He declared in the Senate in July that the President had never read a word of it, that the Secretary of the Treasury had said that he had not read it, and that the•President in writing to the Senate Committee on Banking and Currency had stated that he had no objections to substantial revisions in the bill. The record indicates that the committee that drafted the bill did not consult with the governors of the federal reserve banks or with the American Bankers Association, nor did they seek the approval of the Federal Reserve Board as a body. The important changes which the bill included insured its careful consideration. Elaborate hearings were held by committees in both houses and there were extensive debates in both houses. The House passed the bill without major changes; the Senate, however, insisted upon limiting the President's proposed control over the Federal Reserve Board and the control of the board over regional banks. The House and Senate bills went to conference in August, and the conference committee report was agreed to by

42. Act of Aug. 23, 1935, 49 Stat. at L. 684.
43. H. 7617, 74th Cong., 1st sess. (1935).

both houses on August 19. The bill became law on August 23, 1935.

2. PROVISIONS OF THE ACT

The provisions of the Banking Act of 1935 that are relevant to this study fall into two groups. In the first place, changes were made in the organization of the Federal Reserve Board. The Secretary of the Treasury and the Comptroller of the Currency were removed from the board. Thus the long fight led by Senator Glass was finally won. The name of the board was changed to the Board of Governors of the Federal Reserve System and the terms of its members were increased to fourteen years. The chairman and vice-chairman of the Board of Governors were to be named by the President for four-year terms and were to be the executive officers of the board. The provision that the President might remove members of the board for cause, the provision inadvertently dropped out in 1933, was restored. In the second place, the Open Market Committee was reorganized and a central control over its operations was set up. The Administration and its friends felt that serious calamity could have been averted during the early stages of the depression had there been responsible control of those charged with the direction of open market operations. The Open Market Committee under the Act of 1935 consists of the members of the Board of Governors and five representatives of the federal reserve banks. The Board of Governors still makes the rules and regulations governing open market operations. By this important change the board assumed important responsibility in this field of financial control.

3. TOPICS AND ISSUES IN HEARINGS AND DEBATES

a. *The increased managerial and policy-making powers of the Federal Reserve Board—The Open Market Committee reorganization*

There was no concealment of the purposes of the proposed banking bill. It aimed to centralize control over banking and monetary policy, and it recognized the intimate connection between the two. It assumed that these important policies necessarily fitted into the program of any administration that might be in power. Mr. Eccles was perfectly frank on this point. He emphasized that the monetary system was inextricably tied in with banking. Congress could not possibly deal with one without substantial effects upon the other, and the Administration must be responsible for monetary policy. He said:

> It seems to me that an administration is charged, when it goes into power, with the economic and social problems of the Nation. Politics are nothing more or less than dealing with economic and social problems. It seems to be that it would be extremely difficult for any administration to be able to succeed and intelligently deal with them entirely apart from the money system. There must be a liaison between the administration and the money system—a responsive relationship. That does not necessarily mean political control in the sense that it is often thought of.[44]

> I cannot see how it is possible for Congress to operate a money system except through a body such as the Federal Reserve Board, or some other board that they may create for the purposes of carrying out the wishes of Congress, as provided in legislation which Congress passed.[45]

> . . . The change has arisen out of a growing recognition of the fact that monetary control must not be confined to control of currency because, to an ever increasing extent, the bank check has taken the place of currency. In this country fully nine-tenths of all payments are made by check rather than in cash. Control over the supply of money, therefore, involves under existing conditions a control over the volume of bank deposits and bank credit.[46]

The proposal to subordinate the Open Market Committee to the Federal Reserve Board was strongly defended on the ground that there was an intimate connection between the open market policies of the banks and the government's general monetary policy, and that it was impossible to separate these open market operations from the general conduct of banking affairs. The open market operations of the banks had greatly aided the government in financing the World War by strengthening the bond market, and the obvious necessity for

44. Hearings before the House Committee on Banking and Currency on H.R. 5357, 74th Cong., 1st sess. (1935), 191.
45. Ibid. 416.
46. *Supra,* note 41, op. cit. 283.

the supervision of these operations had culminated in the creation of the Open Market Committee in the Act of 1933. Mr. Eccles pointed out, however, that under that Act there was divided responsibility. The Federal Reserve Board and the Open Market Committee were operating in the same field, one sometimes obstructing the other. There was a clear need of responsibility and of unified control, and this control should come from the government and not from the banks.

It was denied that banking and monetary control ought to be tied together. Parker Willis, before the Senate committee, protested against making the banking system an adjunct of monetary policy. He declared:

. . . The function of the bank mechanism is that of keeping banking sound and safe and of keeping it at all times in position to perform its financial functions. It is not its duty to unstabilize or to stabilize production, trade, prices, and employment.

And we have at the present time a very serious difference of opinion among qualified authorities as to just how much it can do in any of those directions. It is ordered here, as if that were an unmistakable, unquestioned monetary power to do something which in my opinion it cannot do. And of course as to bringing the Reserve Board into areas about which it knows nothing and as to which no banking board is in position to act, you almost insure failure.[47]

It was urged that to place in the hands of a government board full authority over open market operations would subject open market policy to the control of the administration in power and permit the banking system to be used to aid a cheap-money policy. The president of the First National Bank of Chicago expressed his fear that the board would be able to 'force Government obligations on Federal Reserve banks which the investing public was unwilling to take.'[48] The bankers were clearly aware of the close connection between banking policy and monetary policy, but they believed that open market policy should be controlled by the banking interests rather than by political interests tied in with the Administration. Finally, Senator Glass objected that the centralized control set up violated the principle of regionalism on which the Federal Reserve

47. Ibid. 877.   48. Ibid. 376.

System had been established.[49] As finally passed the Act gave to the bankers some influence in the control of open market operations, but placed squarely upon the Board of Governors responsibility for the whole program involved.

b. *The independence of the Board of Governors of the Federal Reserve System*

The proposals in the Eccles bill by which the Board of Governors of the Federal Reserve System was to be given important policy-determining functions raised sharply the whole issue of the character and degree of the board's independence. This problem was very different from the question of the independence of a quasi-judicial body. The duties of the board, especially the new ones, were inextricably tied in with the monetary and credit policies of the Administration. To give the board the independence of a quasi-judicial body was to ignore the impact of its policy-determining powers upon the whole monetary program of the government. At the same time, the activities and policies of the board ought not to be governed by partisan considerations. There must be protection against exploitation of the board for partisan purposes. The problem of the board's independence took the form of a dilemma. Complete independence threatened confusion and obstruction in the field of policy; complete partisan control threatened exploitation of the public interest. The discussions moved back and forth from one of these positions to the other without producing any workable suggestions for securing the proper degree of independence.

The bankers urged that the Federal Reserve Board should have an absolute independence like that of the courts, with complete divorce from politics. Parker Willis mentioned the attempt of President Coolidge in 1924 to influence the rediscount policy of the Federal Reserve Board, and declared that it was essential that the board be wholly free from this type of political pressure.[50] A committee of the American Bankers Association stated that the Federal Reserve Board should be 'a body of such independence and prestige that it might be de-

49. Ibid. 371.   50. Ibid. 875.

scribed as the "Supreme Court of Finance and Banking." ' [51]
Professor Kemmerer of Princeton told the Senate committee
that 'the position of Governor of the Federal Reserve Board
should be as nonpolitical as that of the Chief Justice of the
United States Supreme Court.' [52] Mr. Owen D. Young deplored
the probable effect of the bill in enlarging Presidential control
over the policies of the Federal Reserve Board.[53] While recognizing that the board must always be subject to Congress in the
sense that Congress must formulate the nation's general policies
in this field, he felt that it was highly dangerous to subject the
board to the control of the executive branch.

On the other side of the picture it was argued that the political impact of the board's work could not be ignored. The
board's policies inevitably effect the public interest, and in a
responsible democracy these policies must be subject to politically responsible control. Even though it was important to
make the board as free as possible from partisan control, it was
even more important to make it independent of banking influences. Mr. Adolph C. Miller, a member of the Federal Reserve
Board, described the pressure on the board from the banking
interests.[54] He alleged that in 1929 the board had been virtually prevented from pursuing credit policies that it regarded as
sound, by the combined influence of the Secretary of the Treasury and the New York Federal Reserve Bank. Clearly, governmental control would be better than irresponsible banker
control.

The first and most important change affecting the independence of the Federal Reserve Board was the removal from it of
the Secretary of the Treasury and the Comptroller of the
Currency. We have seen that Senator Glass had long sponsored
this change and that in 1933 the Senate had voted in favor of
it.[55] In the debate on the Eccles bill Senator Glass again presented the arguments in favor of this change, emphasizing them
from his own experience as Secretary of the Treasury. The case
for the removal of the two ex-officio members of the board was
strengthened by the provisions which increased the board's
power over monetary policy. Professor Kemmerer pointed out

51. Ibid. 519.
52. Ibid. 331.
53. Ibid. 398.
54. Ibid. 730 ff.
55. *Supra,* 165 ff.

that the President, through the Secretary and the Comptroller of the Currency, would be able to use the board as an implement for carrying out unsound monetary policies, and would be under constant political pressure to do so.[56] Mr. Miller declared that the board would be merely 'an executive department.'[57] Mr. Owen D. Young told the Senate committee that he objected in theory to having the Secretary and the Comptroller of the Currency on the board, but that since the Secretary was bound to dominate the money market anyway, there was probably a practical advantage in keeping him on the board.[58] The American Bankers Association favored the removal of the two officers from membership, and declared that the President's power to appoint the governor of the Federal Reserve Board would enable him to secure unity of policy between the board and the Administration.

If the President lost a measure of authority over the Federal Reserve Board by the removal of the ex-officio members, he gained the authority to designate the governor of the board and to remove him from the governorship at pleasure. Mr. Eccles explained this grant of power as follows:

GOVERNOR ECCLES. That is right. He should have, it seems to me, the right of appointing the Governor to serve at his pleasure. I think that is in the interest of the Federal Reserve System. I think it is very necessary that there be a very close relationship and liaison between the banking system and the administration in power; and I think that the Governor of the Federal Reserve Board is the channel through which the relationship should develop, in the interest of the banking business.

MR. HOLLISTER. Can you not conceive of a situation where political exigencies might be in direct conflict with wise banking policy and wise credit policy?

GOVERNOR ECCLES. All I can say is that, if you have such exigencies—war is a case in point and depression is a case in point—then I think it would be very unfortunate if the administration was unable to carry out its program.[59]

The American Bankers Association approved of this grant of power to the President and suggested that the term of office of

56. *Supra,* note 41, op. cit. 338.   58. Ibid. 838 ff.
57. Ibid. 731.   59. *Supra,* note 44, op. cit. 363.

the governor should coincide with that of the President.[60] The United States Chamber of Commerce, however, protested that Presidential authority over the board would be dangerously increased by this control of the chairmanship.[61] Mr. Eccles pointed out that under the existing law the President had in practice exercised substantially this power and that the new proposal was therefore nothing revolutionary.[62]

An unsuccessful effort was made to abolish the representation of special interests on the Federal Reserve Board and to eliminate the principle of geographical or district representation. Mr. Eccles urged this change on the ground 'that the functions and duties of the Federal Reserve Board are such as to make it a body representing the Nation, rather than any group or combination of groups.'[63] Dr. E. A. Goldenweiser, chief of the Statistical Division of the board, supported the proposal. He said:

> . . . It seems to me that that substitution is a very good one, because it states the qualifications of the members of the Federal Reserve Board in terms of the principal function which they have to perform, and because it does away with the idea that the board should consist of representatives of different groups of the population, this man representing agriculture, this man banking, this man trade, and so on. It is better that each member of the Reserve Board, as a matter of law, should feel that he represents the country as a whole, and the interests of the country as a whole, and his job on the Board is to be engaged in the formulation of national credit and monetary policies.[64]

Senator Fletcher supported the proposal.[65] He said that the requirement of particular qualifications for board membership was wrong in principle and that no such policy had been applied to the Interstate Commerce Commission or the Federal Trade Commission. The idea of interest representation on the board was, however, too strongly entrenched to be dislodged and the proposal failed.

There was some discussion of the advisability of stiffening the proposal with regard to the removal from office of members of the board. This was part of the general drive to strengthen

60. Ibid. 515.
61. *Supra,* note 41, op. cit. 604.
62. *Supra,* note 44, op. cit. 189.
63. Ibid.
64. Ibid. 434.
65. 79 Cong. Rec. 11916 ff.

the independence of the board from Presidential control. Mr. Eccles objected to any such change. It was suggested that the removal provision be made identical with that in the Federal Trade Commission Act. At this time Mr. Humphrey had been removed from the Federal Trade Commission but the validity of his removal had not been decided by the Supreme Court. It seemed wiser to postpone any change with regard to the removal of members of the Federal Reserve Board until the Court had disposed of the Humphrey case. As we have seen, the clause in the original Act of 1913 restricting Presidential removal had been inadvertently omitted from the Act of 1933. This was restored in the Act of 1935, but without change.

An attempt was made to require bipartisanship in the membership in the Federal Reserve Board. There had never been such a requirement, although the matter had been discussed at various times. In the Senate, amendments were offered to the Eccles bill to provide that 'not more than four of the members of the board shall be members of the same political party, and in making appointments members of different political parties shall be appointed alternately as nearly as may be practicable.' [66] The amendment did not pass the Senate. No substantial body of opinion either in Congress or outside appeared to favor the injection of party lines into the picture.

Finally, there should be mentioned a proposal by Mr. Eccles designed to attract a higher type of man to membership on the board. This was to be accomplished by increasing the salaries of board members to $15,000 a year and by providing an adequate pension arrangement for retiring members. The salary provision was passed, but the pension arrangement was dropped out of the bill in the House and was not restored during the Senate debates. The pension was justified by Mr. Eccles on the ground that members of the board who serve a full term of fourteen years are ineligible to reappointment.[67] A man so long withdrawn from active participation in the banking business might find it difficult to re-establish himself, and the knowledge of this fact might make unavailable men who ought to be drawn into service on the board.

66. Ibid. 11841.   67. *Supra,* note 44, op. cit. 190 ff.

The Eccles bill contained provisions [68] which enlarged the authority of the Federal Reserve Board over the federal reserve banks. This centralization was bitterly opposed, particularly by Senator Glass,[69] a strong defender of the regional system, and the proposal failed. The bill permitted the board to delegate its functions to panels or divisions, a proposal patterned after the authority given the Interstate Commerce Commission. There was some discussion of this but the plan was not adopted.

Finally it may be useful to record Mr. Eccles's opinion of the relation of the Federal Reserve Board to Congress. His statement is as follows:

. . . The need for public control of the function of supplying the medium of exchange to the people of the United States, both by issuing currency and by regulating the volume of bank deposits, seems to me to be almost a noncontroversial matter. It is in direct recognition of the constitutional requirement that Congress shall coin money and regulate the value thereof. In delegating this power Congress has chosen, and, in my opinion, always will choose, to delegate it, not to private interests but to a Government body like the Federal Reserve Board, created by Congress to serve as its own agency in discharging its responsibility for monetary control.[70]

II. THE FEDERAL TRADE COMMISSION

A. BACKGROUND OF THE FEDERAL TRADE COMMISSION ACT

THE federal government struck its first blow at industrial monopoly with the Sherman Act of 1890. This was a disciplinary measure designed to forbid and punish. In its legislative history was no suggestion that its enforcement be given to an independent administrative agency patterned after the three-year-old Interstate Commerce Commission. The prohibitions of the Act were made absolute, and the Department of Justice and the courts were charged with its execution. The Sherman Act proved a disappointment, though we need not review here the reasons for this. By the turn of the century it had come to be widely felt that the simple machinery of criminal trials and

68. For Eccles's statement see *supra,* note 44, op. cit. 181 ff.
69. 79 Cong. Rec. 11826 ff.
70. *Supra,* note 41, op. cit. 280 f.

injunctions was proving inadequate to cope with the complicated problems of monopoly and unfair competition. Out of
this groping for more effective administrative apparatus
emerged the movement for a federal trade commission. The
progress of this movement may be sketched as follows:

A concrete beginning was made in 1903 when the Bureau
of Corporations was created in the Department of Commerce
and Labor. This had been recommended in the report of the
Industrial Commission of 1902. The bureau was an investigating agency set up to render expert aid in the study of the entire
corporation problem and particularly in the uncovering of
business activities and forms of organization which were in
violation of the Sherman Act. It was in an executive department and was clearly an adjunct to the executive branch. It
proved itself a useful organization and did a highly creditable
job. It was not, however, a regulatory body; it had power
merely to secure facts and make them public.

Underlying the whole trade commission movement lay a
steadily growing antagonism to trusts and monopolies, and a
growing belief that they were increasing in number and
power. Two of Mr. Bryan's Presidential campaigns had been
dominated by vigorous attacks on the trusts as the by-products
of Republican policy. President Roosevelt's program of 'trust
busting' had accomplished some results, had attracted much
attention, but had failed to strike at the root of the problem.
One of Roosevelt's major contributions was his classification of
'good trusts' and 'bad trusts' with the accompanying suggestion
that not all business combinations ought to incur the penalties
of the law. Despite all this activity, however, the impression
grew that the Department of Justice was not really adequate
to deal with the enormous business combinations then operating, that the Attorney General's office had sometimes played
favorites in its policies of antitrust prosecution, and that the
courts themselves were not rendering wholehearted aid to a
rigorous enforcement of the law.

In 1911 the Supreme Court handed down its notable decisions in the Standard Oil [1] and American Tobacco Company [2]
cases in which it announced the doctrine that the Sherman Act

1. *Standard Oil Co.* v. *United States*, 221 U.S. 1 (1911).
2. *United States* v. *American Tobacco Co.*, 221 U.S. 106 (1911).

does not prohibit all combinations in restraint of trade but only such as are unreasonable. These cases translated into legal terminology Roosevelt's classification of 'good trusts' and 'bad trusts' already mentioned. They served notice, furthermore, that the Court would in each case have to determine whether the business conduct under complaint amounted to an unreasonable restraint of trade or whether it could be regarded as reasonable. The Court's announcement of its so-called 'rule of reason' had an immediate and far-reaching effect. As a stimulus to legislative action it was perhaps as influential in the trade commission movement as the Wabash case [3] had been in stimulating action on the Interstate Commerce Act of 1887. The decisions announcing the 'rule of reason' were followed not merely by bitter criticism of the Court itself, but by widespread demand for Congressional action which would clarify and sharpen the provisions of the Sherman Act. We find emerging a rather general agreement amongst widely differing groups and classes that some sort of administrative commission would prove the effective means of dealing with the complicated and difficult problems relating to trusts and monopolies. But these different groups and interests, while favoring a commission, favored it for widely varying reasons, and proposed for it widely varying powers. These may be summarized:

In the first place, businessmen themselves tended to agree that a trade commission ought to be created. This attitude on their part was rather like the original enthusiasm which businessmen felt for the NRA. Several factors led them to favor a commission. They were at a low ebb in the business cycle. The depressed economic conditions had resulted in cutthroat competition, very destructive to sound business but difficult to abandon once it had been begun. This competition was carried on by unfair trade practices which the better elements in the business world disliked. In addition, businessmen were living under a fear of illegality and of uncertainty as to the exact limits of legitimate business conduct. They did not know where they stood. The decisions of the Court in the Standard Oil case and the American Tobacco Company case had confused rather than clarified their position. The honest businessman, trying to

3. *Wabash, St. L. & P.R.* v. *Illinois,* 118 U.S. 557 (1886). See *supra,* 38, 44.

keep within the limitations of the law, could not know what those limitations were until a court decision told him that he had passed them and punished him for so doing. An administrative commission to advise and aid businessmen in interpreting the law and in clarifying the limitations of legality would be highly desirable. The businessman would be willing to submit to a certain amount of regulation in order to secure this clarification of his rights and status. A still stronger motive for supporting a commission lay in the belief that such a body might be given authority to pass in advance upon forms of business organization and methods of business conduct. Many prominent industrialists favored an administrative agency which could thus stamp proposed business conduct with a guaranty of legality. Many forms of business activity falling technically within the prohibitions of the Sherman Act were believed to be fundamentally sound. A commission which could deal with these on their merits and approve some while rejecting others would aid business development and at the same time eliminate objectionable evils.

A second group favoring a trade commission comprised those who were relentless enemies of monopoly and who believed that unfair trade practices produced monopoly. They favored a much more powerful trade commission than did the industrialists. Their position was this: The enforcement of the Sherman Act had been vacillating and unsatisfactory, and there was clear need for administrative aid in its enforcement. There was needed an expert, continuing, and impartial agency to ferret out violations of the law and aid in their prosecution. Such a commission could be given the duty of determining in concrete cases what were 'unfair trade practices.' Under the doctrine of the Standard Oil case this job was left with the Court itself; whereas the task of defining unfair trade practices or unreasonable restraints of trade is essentially legislative, and should be performed either by Congress or by an agency of Congress. Such a commission could render further important service in working out the details of the decrees under which trusts and combinations were dissolved by the courts. The job of dissolving the Standard Oil Company and the American Tobacco Company had been badly bungled. Some aid had been rendered by the Bureau of Corporations, but no one was satisfied with the results or with the procedure. A permanent, expert commission would have been able to aid the Court in the performance of this difficult task. It could, furthermore, keep track of the results of such dissolutions. It could find out whether a dissolved trust had been dissolved effectively and whether it stayed dissolved, a function which the Department of Justice was ill-equipped to carry on. Finally, such a trade commission could secure even more information with regard to trust and corporation activities than had been secured by the Bureau of Corporations. It could be given some authority, perhaps, to standardize business accounting, and to make public the facts about business organizations necessary to keep them effectively in order. In short, the enemies of monopoly felt that a trade commission would be an indispensable aid in stiffening, clarifying, and enforcing public control of trusts and business combinations.

The third group urging a federal trade commission comprised those who believed that corporations engaged in interstate commerce should be either licensed or incorporated under federal law. To many this seemed the only effective means of exercising federal control. But if all such corporations were to be federally licensed or incorporated, it would be absolutely necessary to establish a commission to administer the law. Such a body would work out the detailed provisions under which licenses or charters should be granted and would serve as the supervisory agency to assure compliance with the conditions thus laid down.

Thus this threefold drive in the direction of a trade commission was in no sense a unified movement. Businessmen, desiring a mild and benignly helpful administrative body to aid them in the solution of their problems, had nothing but antagonism for the powerful commission advocated by the enemies of trusts and big business, and it was not long before there were sharp disagreements on the desirability of the particular proposals which were brought under discussion in Congress.

B. Steps in the History of the Act

The earliest and most influential sponsor of the federal trade commission idea was Senator Francis T. Newlands from Nevada. He had advocated a trade commission for many years and had often asserted that had such a commission been set up in 1890 to aid in the enforcement of the Sherman Act vastly better results would have been attained. On January 11, 1911, in speaking on the Tariff Commission, he outlined before the Senate his ideas as to such a commission.[4] On May 15, when the Supreme Court's decision in the Standard Oil case was handed down, Newlands renewed his demand for a commission, using the newly announced 'rule of reason' as the basis for that demand.[5] On July 5, 1911, he introduced in the Senate a bill[6] providing for an interstate trade commission. On July 26, 1911, the Senate directed its Committee on Interstate Commerce to inquire into the advisability of new legislation on the trust problem.[7] This committee took under advisement the bill that Newlands had introduced, but on August 21 he introduced a substitute bill[8] which provided the basis for much of the committee's inquiry.

While the Senate committee was proceeding with its investigation, the Presidential campaign of 1912 came on. No party could escape making some statement, however vague, upon a problem which was so sharply in the minds of everyone. The Democratic platform did not specifically propose a trade commission, but it did not rule out the possibility of such an agency. It declared: 'We favor the declaration by law of the conditions upon which corporations shall be permitted to engage in interstate trade,' and it went on to demand the rigorous enforcement of the antitrust legislation.[9] The Progressive platform advocated a trade commission in the following words:

. . . We urge the establishment of a strong Federal administrative commission of high standing, which shall maintain permanent active supervision over industrial corporations engaged in inter-State commerce, or such of them as are of public importance, doing for them what the Government now does for the National banks, and what is now done for the railroads by the Inter-State Commerce Commission.[10]

4. 46 Cong. Rec. 768 f.
5. 47 Cong. Rec. 1206 ff.
6. S. 2941, 62d Cong., 1st sess. (1911).
7. S. Res. 98, 62d Cong., 1st sess. (1911).
8. Also S. 2941, 62d Cong., 1st sess. (1911).
9. K. H. Porter, *National Party Platforms* (1924), 322.
10. Ibid. 341.

The Republican platform advocated a classification of the antitrust laws and also proposed a federal trade commission in these words:

In the enforcement and administration of Federal Laws governing interstate commerce and enterprises impressed with a public use engaged therein, there is much that may be committed to a Federal trade commission, thus placing in the hands of an administrative board many of the functions now necessarily exercised by the courts. This will promote promptness in the administration of the law and avoid delays and technicalities incident to court procedure.[11]

In February 1913, just before the incoming of the Wilson Administration, the Senate Committee on Interstate Commerce brought in its report through Senator Cummins. The committee advocated additional antitrust legislation and stated that

it will be very desirable to accompany such legislation with a measure establishing a commission for the better administration of the law and to aid in its enforcement. It may be fairly said that there is need of such a commission, even though the present statute is not supplemented in any manner; but it is apparent that if the new legislation is enacted the need of a commission will become more imperative.[12]

The duties that such a commission would perform were outlined by the committee: first, extensive activities in the field of investigation; second, the administration of some system of licensing corporations engaged in interstate commerce; and third, the rendering of expert aid to the courts and to the Department of Justice in the dissolution of trusts and other unlawful combinations.

At this juncture President Wilson moved into action. He had been for years an implacable enemy of trusts and monopolies. As governor of New Jersey he had driven through the state legislature the famous 'Seven Sisters Acts,' comprising as drastic state antitrust prohibitions as existed anywhere in the country. After his inauguration, the President persuaded Joseph E. Davies, one of his campaign managers and a close friend, to accept the post of Commissioner of Corporations and to aid in that capacity in laying the foundations for an improved antitrust policy. Mr. Davies has generously given the writer the

11. Ibid. 354.   12. S. Rept. 1326, 62d Cong., 3d sess. (1913), 12.

following account of the part played by the Bureau of Corporations under his direction in focusing the President's attention upon the idea of a trade commission:

President Wilson then suggested that I accept the post of Commissioner of Corporations . . . The Bureau of Corporations, he suggested, could be of great assistance to him in that connection; and he requested that under my direction the Bureau should immediately make an intensive study of all phases of the problem and provide him with a digest of the material and the facts available and give to him the benefit of concrete recommendations for the purpose of remedial legislation in connection with the problem of regulation of monopolies and the prevention of restraints of trade in interstate commerce.

When I assumed the post of Commissioner of Corporations in 1913, the Acting Commissioner was Dr. Francis Walker, an exceptionally able man and a widely known economist with much experience as chief economist of the Bureau of Corporations . . .

With the able assistance of Dr. Walker and these men, during the summer and autumn of 1913 I outlined, projected and directed the preparation of a brief on the facts and prepared conclusions therefrom for the President . . . The brief also contained the conclusions of the Commissioner of Corporations with reference to the situation, and concrete recommendations as to a legislative program in connection with the problem.

These recommendations were, briefly, that the antitrust laws should be amended and supplemented; first, by substantive amendments prohibiting certain practices such as price discrimination, exclusive contracts, and interlocking stock ownerships and interlocking directorships as to which, when standing alone, there was doubt as to whether they could be reached under the provisions of the Sherman Law; and, second, by the creation of a quasi-judicial administrative agency, an Interstate Trade Commission, which would be clothed not only with the investigatory power of the Bureau of Corporations but also with power to prevent unfair methods of competition—the 'seeds of monopoly'—before they had 'flowered' into a complete restraint of trade or into monopoly. It was designed to be a practical instrumentality, freed from some of the law's delays, to apply the remedy to the wrong, speedily and equitably. It was also contemplated that it should constitute a clearing-house for facts, and in its organization provide a body of legal, economic and business experience that would establish and gradually build up a body of rules by which honest business-men could be guided and measurably informed as to 'what business *could* do as well as what it could not do.' This memorandum or 'brief' developed into rather an extensive document. It was, however, completed in time to send to President Wilson at Pass Christian where he was spending his Christmas holidays, in time for his consideration prior to his message to Congress. Both concurrently with and after the preparation of this brief, I had numerous conferences with the President, outlining to him the progress of the work and the direction in which our thought was going. At the same time, with his approval, and in fact under his direction, I had many conferences with Senator Newlands of Nevada, who was the then Chairman of the Interstate Commerce Committee of the Senate, and with Congressman Charles Carlin, who was Chairman of the Judiciary Committee of the House of Representatives, and to whose Committees, respectively, it was anticipated that the President's proposals in his message to Congress would be referred. Practically all of the recommendations of the memorandum-brief were covered in the President's message to Congress. This brief was subsequently elaborated on and developed into the published report, 'Trust Laws and Unfair Competition,' (March 15, 1915), and was issued by me as Commissioner of Corporations. The information assembled was made available to the appropriate Committees of the 63rd Congress.[13]

On January 20, 1914, President Wilson read to Congress his message proposing a strengthening of the antitrust laws and the creation of a trade commission. His policy comprised two planks: First, there must be certainty in the law regulating business and industry. 'Nothing hampers business like uncertainty.' The antitrust laws must be given teeth and it must be made clear exactly what they forbid. Unlawful conduct must be 'explicitly and item by item forbidden by statute in such terms as will practically eliminate uncertainty.' Congress, in short, must itself define exactly what it means by unfair competitive trade practices. Second, a trade commission should inform, advise, and guide the businessman. But the President specifically ruled out any possibility that the commission might legalize in advance doubtful business practices. He said:

The opinion of the country would instantly approve of such a commission. It would not wish to see it empowered to make terms with monopoly or in any sort to assume control of business, as if the Government made itself responsible. It demands such a commission only as an indispensable instrument of information and publicity,

13. Letter of Mr. Davies to the writer, July 10, 1939.

as a clearing house for the facts by which both the public mind and the managers of great business undertakings should be guided, and as an instrumentality for doing justice to business where the processes of the courts or the natural forces of correction outside the courts are inadequate to adjust the remedy to the wrong in a way that will meet all the equities and circumstances of the case.[14]

The commission should also aid the courts in the working out of decrees of dissolution. The President did not at this point propose that the trade commission should have quasi-judicial or regulatory powers.

The House and Senate took prompt action upon the President's proposals. Representative Clayton introduced a bill [15] in the House, which was referred to the House Committee on Interstate and Foreign Commerce. Senator Newlands introduced a similar bill [16] in the Senate, which went to the Senate Committee on Interstate Commerce. The House committee reported out a bill providing for a federal trade commission without regulatory or quasi-judicial power. Its functions were to aid the Department of Justice by conducting investigations and to aid the courts in the working out of dissolution decrees. Those demanding more drastic legislation pointed out that the new commission would merely be the old Bureau of Corporations made independent. The House bill passed on June 5, 1914, and went to the Senate.

The Senate committee had before it the Newlands bill, which also provided for a weak commission with no regulatory powers. When the House bill was passed the Senate committee substituted that bill for the Newlands bill and went on with its hearings. At this point, however, the President underwent a definite change of front. The original proposal was that the new antitrust laws should define in specific detail just which unfair trade practices were to be unlawful; but this proposal had struck a snag. Such precise definition had proved impracticable; and the President, in consultation with Congressional leaders, had concluded that it would be necessary to formulate a broadly worded prohibition against 'unfair competitive trade practices' and to give to the proposed trade commission the quasi-judicial

14. 51 Cong. Rec. 1963.
15. H.R. 12120, 63d Cong., 2d sess. (1914).
16. S. 4160, 63d Cong., 2d sess. (1914).

job of applying this prohibition in concrete cases. The Senate committee, with some reluctance, adopted the President's proposal and reported a bill which made the trade commission a quasi-judicial regulatory agency, and this passed the Senate on August 5. The House refused to accept the Senate bill, and a conference committee was appointed which reported back a substitute bill in the form of the present Trade Commission Act. This passed the Senate on September 8, passed the House on September 10 with no dissenting vote, and was signed by the President on September 26, 1914.

C. Summary of the Federal Trade Commission Act

The Federal Trade Commission Act [17] may be briefly summarized under five headings:

1. A Federal Trade Commission of five was provided for. The members were to be appointed by the President with the advice and consent of the Senate, hold office for seven years, receive salaries of $10,000, and be removable by the President for inefficiency, neglect of duty, or malfeasance in office. The Bureau of Corporations was abolished and its duties transferred to the commission.

2. Unfair methods of competition were declared unlawful and the commission was empowered to issue cease and desist orders against them subject to court review.

3. The commission was made the agency for the enforcement of the provisions of the Clayton Act defining and prohibiting certain specific kinds of unlawful trade practices. Upon discovering violations of these provisions, the commission was to issue cease and desist orders against them subject to court review.

4. The commission was empowered to carry on investigations of business misconduct at the direction of the President or either house of Congress, and, more broadly, to compile information as to business and corporate practices.

5. It was authorized to aid in the working out of decrees dissolving trusts or unlawful business combinations and to supervise the enforcement of such decrees.

17. Act of Sept. 26, 1914, 38 Stat. at L. 717.

D. Topics and Issues in Hearings and Debates

In studying the legislative history of the Trade Commission Act one must keep in mind that the proposal went into Congress in the form of a bill to create a weak, advisory commission. It came out in the form of a statute setting up a strong commission endowed with quasi-judicial regulatory powers. Arguments and discussions relating to the proposed trade commission in its earlier form do not, naturally, indicate Congressional points of view upon the commission as finally established.

1. REASONS FOR CREATING AN INDEPENDENT COMMISSION

In dealing with the question of the independence of the Federal Trade Commission it is unnecessary to discuss why a commission was created rather than a single officer, or why a commission, if created, was to be independent rather than placed in a department. The two ideas, a commission and independence for the commission, were inextricably bound together. At no point was it proposed that a commission ought to be set up unless it be independent or that an independent officer should be created rather than a commission. The issue narrowed itself to the competing claims of the independent commission as against a subdivision of an executive department. The reasons that led to the creation of an independent commission may be presented as follows:

A controlling force moving legislative leaders to create the independent Federal Trade Commission was the model of the Interstate Commerce Commission. It is true that the Federal Reserve Board was also in existence, or at least had been created by statute, but it had not been organized and had as yet no body of successful experience to commend it. The Interstate Commerce Commission, however, had been in existence since 1887 and commanded widespread respect. It exerted a tremendous influence upon legislative thinking. Senator Newlands, the father of the trade commission idea, as early as 1911 had proposed a body similar to the Interstate Commerce Commission. Speaking in the Senate on his 1914 trade commission bill, he declared,

We have found in the Interstate Commerce Commission a non-partisan organization, which moves absolutely free from the influence either of Congress or of the President, an independent organization, charged with the enforcement of the interstate commerce act and commencing that enforcement at the same time that the Attorney General started in upon the enforcement of the Sherman antitrust law. We find, however, by way of contrast that almost every transportation question has been settled, whilst we are just upon the threshold of the adjustment of the trust question . . .[18]

Mr. Covington of Maryland, speaking in the House, not only desired a commission similar to the Interstate Commerce Commission but went on to explain that

the great value to the American people of the Interstate Commerce Commission has been largely because of its independent power and authority. The dignity of the proposed commission and the respect in which its performance of its duties will be held by the people will also be largely because of its independent power and authority. Therefore the bill removes entirely from the control of the President and the Secretary of Commerce the investigations conducted and the information acquired by the commission under the authority heretofore exercised by the Bureau of Corporations or the Commissioner of Corporations.[19]

Most of the witnesses appearing before committees of Congress in support of a trade commission referred to the Interstate Commerce Commission as a model, and in the report of the House committee that body is referred to upon practically every page.

In the second place, independence was demanded for the new trade commission as a means of correcting what many believed to be the partisan and pressure-controlled administration of the antitrust laws by the Department of Justice. Even those who were willing to say a friendly word for the Attorney General and his efforts to enforce the Sherman Act could not ignore the fact that he is a policy-determining officer, one of the President's political advisers, and inevitably subject to pressures tending to make difficult an even and impartial enforcement of the law. Senator Newlands drew attention to the fact that President Roosevelt's Attorney General had brought suit to dissolve the New York, New Haven, and Hartford combination, that this suit had been dismissed by President Taft's Attorney General,

18. 51 Cong. Rec. 11235.   19. Ibid. 8842.

and had been renewed by the Attorney General under President Wilson.[20] The drive for a trade commission was strengthened by the growing dissatisfaction with the government's enforcement of existing antitrust legislation. Rigorous and impartial law enforcement could be expected from an independent agency.

In the third place, any federal laws to regulate business ought to be enforced in a definitely nonpartisan manner. This type of regulation might expand and, if so, there was all the more reason for setting a precedent for nonpartisan and independent administration. As Senator Morgan expressed it:

. . . Whatever we do in regulating business should be removed as far as possible from political influence.

It will be far safer to place this power in the hands of a great independent commission that will go on while administrations may change. That is one reason why I believe in having all these matters placed, so far as they can be, in the hands of a commission, taking these business matters out of politics.[21]

The quasi-judicial nature of the proposed trade commission's work constituted a fourth argument for its independence. Senator Newlands had from the beginning regarded this as a basic reason for creating an independent body. He had expressed this view in 1911,[22] and in 1914 he repeated it:

The first question is: Shall an interstate trade commission of some kind be organized? I imagine that there can hardly be any difference of opinion on the point that there should be an administrative tribunal of high character, nonpartisan, or, rather, bipartisan, and independent of any department of the Government. I assume also that there should be a commission rather than one executive official, because there are powers of judgment and powers of discretion to be exercised. The organization should be quasi-judicial in character. We want traditions; . . . we want a body of administrative law built up. This can not be well done by the single occupant of an office, subject to constant changes in its incumbency and subject to higher executive authority. Such work must be done by a board or commission of dignity, permanence, and ability, independent of executive authority except in its selection, and independent in character.[23]

20. Ibid. 12623.
21. Ibid. 8857.

22. 47 Cong. Rec. 2444.
23. 51 Cong. Rec. 11092.

Later on in the course of the Senate debate he emphasized this point again:

> Then there is the power to punish by contempt for disobedience to the mandate of the law, which is much more effective than the criminal prosecution of individuals, bringing them before grand juries and petit juries and submitting all these questions to the varying influence, passions, and prejudices of the hour. I believe that in this way a complete system of administrative law can be built up much more securely than by the eccentric action of grand juries and trial juries.[24]

It was emphasized repeatedly that the quasi-judicial duty given to the commission would relieve the courts of a legislative task of interpreting and applying the vague concept of 'unfair competitive trade practices,' and it was generally agreed that this power could more safely be vested in an administrative agency than in the courts. The agreement, however, was not unanimous. Senators Borah[25] and Pomerene[26] both declared flatly that if this legislative power was to be delegated they preferred to see it go to the courts of law where it would be exercised in accordance with fair and established procedure rather than to a commission whose nature and methods were not yet clearly developed. Senator Sutherland objected on constitutional grounds to giving quasi-judicial power to a commission which he consistently described as 'a legislative commission.'[27] His argument on this point is developed at length at a later point.[28]

A fifth reason for making the trade commission independent was the desire to secure a body of experts competent to deal with highly complicated and technical problems. The members of the commission, as Senator Newlands put it, should be 'not simply experts in law, but experts in industry and trade,'[29] and the Senate committee in its report submitting the bill stated:

> . . . The work of this commission will be of a most exacting and difficult character, demanding persons who have experience in the problems to be met—that is, a proper knowledge of both the public requirements and the practical affairs of industry. It is manifestly desirable that the terms of the commissioners shall be long enough to give them an opportunity to acquire the expertness in dealing

24. Ibid. 12031.
25. Ibid. 11600 ff.
26. Ibid. 12874 ff.

27. Ibid. 12651 ff.
28. *Infra*, 210 f., 445 f.
29. 51 Cong. Rec. 12031.

with these special questions concerning industry that comes from experience.[30]

Stability and continuity of service were bound to be important elements in the make-up of the proposed commission. These could be secured only if that body was independent of direct political control. The uncertainties arising from the fluctuations in policy in the Attorney General's office with reference to the enforcement of the antitrust law had been a major reason for the proposal to set up a commission. The men in office charged with law enforcement this year would be gone next year, and the business world had nothing stable or reliable to tie to. With an independent body whose members held for substantial and overlapping terms of office, continuity of policy and stability of administrative method could be built up. In no other way could there be secured the 'continuous, consecutive, consistent administration of the antitrust law.' [31]

Finally, an independent commission having the qualities of nonpartisanship, expertness, and stability would command public confidence. This confidence, particularly upon the part of the business world, was felt to be of vital importance. Sound policy with respect to business regulation could hardly emerge in an atmosphere of suspicion and distrust. It was imperative to create an agency which would earn the respect and confidence of those with whom it had to deal, and independence was essential if this was to be done.

The independence urged for the proposed federal trade commission was not, however, unanimously viewed as a blessing. There were serious protests against what some regarded as the dangerous policy of placing the administration of an important statute in the hands of a body independent of responsible control. The view that the commission's independence violated the principles of democratic government was urged by Senator Borah:

I do not believe you can take a commission and separate it from the rest of the world so that it will not feel the influence and the power that affect other men. I have no criticism for the Interstate Commerce Commission, but that question has not been tested yet to its full; not by any means. You can not judge an institution of that

---

30. Ibid. 11089.   31. Ibid. 12623.

kind except in the sweep of the years, and I, as one, am not willing to take the currency question, the industrial business of this country, and the transportation business, and place all of those things entirely away from the electorate, entirely away from the recall of the people, with a bureau which is answerable in no respect to the people. In the end it will result in their moving to a very large extent in one groove and the people in another groove. I am not willing that the most tremendous affairs of government shall be wholly separated from the recall which the people have at stated periods with reference to the election of their officers.[32]

Other members of Congress shared this view. Senator Townsend referred to the new commission as one 'which is responsible to no power outside of its own will.'[33] Senator Clapp declared: 'We are creating one more body to confuse the public as to who is responsible for the nonenforcement of the law,'[34] and he charged that it would fall prey to the subversive influences of the business world. This fear was shared by Senator Works, who doubted whether the commission could withstand the pressures which would be brought to bear upon it by 'the powerful combinations of wealth.' He said:

. . . Can we expect such a commission to withstand their influence? They work in mysterious ways. They know what they want. They know how to get it. They lead and influence honest men as successfully as they corrupt and bribe dishonest ones. It is a perilous thing to give over to a mere commission such enormous powers for good or evil.[35]

Having summarized the reasons that led Congress to make the Federal Trade Commission independent, we may ask what lawmakers meant concretely when they talked about an independent commission? In the first place, it seems clear that Congress intended the new commission to be free from the pressure and control of the President. The Bureau of Corporations and the Department of Justice were both subject to Presidential direction. Their enforcement of the antitrust laws was bitterly criticized. Whatever the new commission was to be, it was to be different from these agencies; there was no intention of making it subject to Presidential control. In the course of the debate in the Senate the question was asked how the provision permit-

32. Ibid. 11235.
33. Ibid. 11871.
34. Ibid. 13050.
35. Ibid. 12276.

ting the President of the United States to direct the proposed
trade commission to make an investigation happened to get into
the bill. This, it was suggested, seemed inconsistent with the
theory of complete independence from direct Presidential control. Mr. Cummins, the Progressive Senator from Iowa, replied
as follows:

Mr. President, as I said yesterday, I do not think the commission
should act upon the suggestion of the President, and I did what
little I could to eliminate that provision from the bill while it
was under consideration by the committee. I think the whole sub-
section might well be stricken out. It does not add to the strength
of the bill and probably serves no useful purpose. The truth is, and
I am not betraying any confidence because I am not saying anything
that anyone ever told me, I am simply giving expression to my own
belief, the administration desires that part of the bill. It undoubtedly thinks that this commission should be called into activities
upon the suggestion of the President or the Attorney General. I do
not think so, but I have not believed that the presence of that provision was sufficiently important to change my general view of the
proposed legislation . . .

. . . I have always thought that a trade commission, as the Interstate Commerce Commission is, should be an independent tribunal
attached to no department of the Government, owing allegiance to
no officer of the Government. I think it should be clothed with adequate power of investigation. I think that it should be free to prosecute an investigation whenever it believes that it would serve the
public welfare to do so, and if in the course of the investigation
a violation of the antitrust law or any other law of the United States
relating to this subject is developed, I think it ought to report the
result of its investigation to the Attorney General, whose duty it is
to prosecute offenders; but I have never thought that we should put
into the law a provision that would enable either the President or
Attorney General to command its activities.

The objection to it—and I am now repeating the objection to it
that I made before the committee—the objection to it is that, as the
Senator from Idaho (Mr. Borah) said the other day, there have been
times when the antitrust law has been made the instrument, as is
alleged, of promoting political fortunes. The President is a political
officer; the Attorney General is a political officer connected with the
policy of the administration and of the country. The trade commission should not be affected by those influences; and it is my judgment . . . that it will accomplish more—it will establish itself more

firmly in the confidence of the people if it acts upon its own motion or acts upon a petition properly brought before it under certain provisions of the bill.[36]

In the second place, Congress thought about the independence of the proposed federal trade commission in terms of bipartisanship quite as much as in terms of freedom from Presidential control. They had before them, of course, the model of the Interstate Commerce Commission. Since appointments to the commission must be made by the President, they felt that the only way to prevent a completely partisan domination of the commission was to require a neutralizing number of members from the other party. It seems to have been assumed, a bit naïvely, that this bipartisan complexion would guarantee a resulting nonpartisanship, an assumption which later events proved false. It is clear, however, that this was regarded as a vital point, and it was discussed both in the committee reports and in the debates.

It is interesting to observe that Mr. Justice Sutherland in commenting upon the independence of the Federal Trade Commission in the Humphrey case was guilty of 'grasshopper exegesis' in building up his argument that Congress intended to leave the commission free from Presidential control. Referring to the Senate report presenting the bill which later became law he says:

The report declares that one advantage which the commission possessed over the Bureau of Corporations (an executive subdivision in the Department of Commerce which was abolished by the act) lay in the fact of its independence, and that it was essential that the commission should not be open to the suspicion of partisan directions.[37]

What the committee report actually says is:

One of the chief advantages of the proposed commission over the Bureau of Corporations lies in the fact that it will have greater prestige and independence, and its decisions, coming from a board of several persons, will be more readily accepted as impartial and well considered. For this reason also it is essential that it should not be open to the suspicion of partisan direction, and this bill provides,

36. Ibid. 11529 f.   37. 295 U.S. 602, 625 (1935).

therefore, that not more than three members of the commission shall belong to any one political party.[38]

Thus the committee's statement that bipartisanship is necessary to avoid partisan direction is made to serve as an argument in favor of freedom from Presidential control, which was what Mr. Justice Sutherland was defending.

In the third place, in the discussions on the nature of the independence of the proposed federal trade commission there was no comment in Congress or its committees on the power to remove members of the commission. This seems to have impressed no one as important. Senator Newlands, one of the most ardent defenders of an independent commission, in introducing the Senate bill in January 1914, omitted entirely any clause relating to the removal of members of the commission. So far as we can tell he did not regard the removal power as relevant to the general problem of independence. The bill as finally passed provided that the members of the commission might be removed by the President for misconduct, inefficiency, or malfeasance in office. This is the formula which appears in the Interstate Commerce Act with regard to the Interstate Commerce Commission and was apparently borrowed from that statute without discussion.

2. RELATION OF THE COMMISSION TO THE PRESIDENT AND TO EXECUTIVE POWER

What did Congress intend to be the relation between the proposed trade commission and the President? Did it regard the commission as an adjunct of the executive department? Did it intend to confer upon it powers which would normally be regarded as executive? What authority did it wish the President to have over the commission? In trying to find the answers to these questions it must be remembered that much of the Congressional discussion of the trade commission bill took place before the drastic change which gave the commission quasi-judicial duties and the authority to issue cease and desist orders. The President's original proposal and the bills introduced in both houses as a result called for the establishment of a weak

38. 51 Cong. Rec. 11089.

commission. At this stage the whole drive was to secure a more efficient and impartial enforcement of antitrust laws, which were themselves to be sharpened and clarified. Nearly everyone, therefore, who discussed the matter during this early period regarded the commission as an executive agency charged with executive and administrative duties. In 1911 Attorney General Wickersham had advocated an administrative commission of this kind:

> The Federal Department of Justice is not organized or equipped to maintain constant supervision and control over business organizations. It deals only with cases of violations of law. The activities of an administrative board or commission would be directed to preventing such violations and in aiding business men to maintain a continued status of harmony with the requirements of law.[39]

Senator Cummins emphasized the service which the commission was to render to the Department of Justice:

> What we propose to do here is not to arrest the enforcement of the antitrust law, not to weaken its remedies, not to allow any criminal under its provisions to escape, but to add to the Department of Justice an investigating tribunal of high character, of great experience well equipped to bring to the attention of the Attorney General those instances which may have escaped the inquiries carried on in that department, and thus secure through the Department of Justice a more efficient enforcement of that law.[40]

Mr. Brandeis, appearing before the House Committee on Interstate and Foreign Commerce in February 1914, had insisted:

> . . . We need the inspector and the policeman even more than we need the prosecuting attorney, and we need for the enforcement of the Sherman law and regulation of competition an administrative board with broad powers.[41]

President Wilson himself, at a press conference in January 1914, had stated that the commission was merely to supplement existing law-enforcement agencies. He graphically described the difference in the procedure of the trade commission and that

39. Ibid. 11094. Speech given at Duluth July 19, 1911.
40. Ibid. 11529.
41. Hearings before the House Committee on Interstate and Foreign Commerce on H.R. 12120 to Create an Interstate Trade Commission, 63d Cong., 2d sess. (1914), 4.

of the Department of Justice. He said that if the Department of Justice 'smells a rat' it starts to look for it, while the trade commission 'will be smelling around all the time.' When the trade commission thinks it is on the trail of a rat, it will call the attention of the Department of Justice to the trail.[42]

To what extent was the Congressional view of the commission's relation to the President changed as a result of giving the commission drastic regulatory power? Was this powerful quasi-judicial commission still to be looked upon as an agent of the executive branch? While this problem did not bother many members of Congress, those who considered it found no common answer. Senator Cummins, speaking in the Senate in July, declared:

> There is, in my opinion, this important difference between the trade commission that we are here establishing and the Interstate Commerce Commission. The Interstate Commerce Commission, in fixing rates, is a supplement to the Congress, because it is a legislative function to fix rates for public transportation, and therefore the Interstate Commerce Commission is a legislative-administrative tribunal combined. The trade commission that we here proposed to establish is purely an executive or administrative tribunal. It exercises no legislative functions whatever. I have looked upon it simply as an arm of the Government to help carry into effect the rule which we announce as the one that ought to control and govern the industry of the country.[43]

Senator Sutherland, however, sharply disagreed with this view. Throughout the entire debate he consistently referred to the proposed federal trade commission as a 'legislative' commission, similar in its nature and its power to the Interstate Commerce Commission; and much of his elaborate constitutional attack upon it, as we shall see later,[44] was based on the theory that other powers could not be given to a legislative commission. The precise nature of the quasi-judicial task conferred upon the commission was never clearly analyzed and no consensus of opinion on it emerged. Nor was there any adequate discussion of the President's authority, if any, over the commission and its activities. Senator Fletcher commented upon

42. *The New York Times,* Jan. 27, 1914, p. 7, col. 2.
43. 51 Cong. Rec. 12742.
44. *Infra,* 210 f., 445 f.

the President's power to remove members of the commission for cause, and declared that this was a wholesome and necessary check upon the commission. He thought it a more effective mode of control than the proposal that Congress discipline the commission, if necessary, by withholding its appropriations.[45] Senator Weeks, on the other hand, felt that the President's power to appoint and remove commissioners gave him undue influence over the commission and that this would be used for partisan advantage.[46] Senator Cummins, as we have seen,[47] felt that the President should not have power to direct the commission to make investigations. In his judgment it should be entirely free from Presidential direction. From this rather hit-or-miss discussion we may infer that those members of Congress who discussed the matter did not contemplate a trade commission operating under Presidential control. They could not agree on whether the quasi-judicial functions assigned to it were executive or legislative in character, and the question of what inferences regarding the range of Presidential supervision over the commission might be drawn from the character of its job was one upon which they expressed no opinions.

3. RELATION OF THE TRADE COMMISSION TO CONGRESS

The relation of the proposed federal trade commission to Congress elicited less discussion than did its relation to either the President or the courts. It was recognized that the commission would aid Congress by providing it with information on the complex problems connected with the regulation of business. This would enable Congress to legislate more intelligently than it otherwise could. The importance of this service was thus summed up in the report of the House committee:

It must be remembered that this commission enters a new field of governmental activity. The history of the Interstate Commerce Commission is conclusive evidence that the best legislation regarding many of the problems to come before the interstate-trade commission will be produced from time to time as the result of the reports of the commission after exhaustive inquiries and investigations. No one can foretell the extent to which the complex interstate business

45. 51 Cong. Rec. 11237.
46. Ibid. 12621 ff.
47. *Supra,* 194 f.

of a great country like the United States may require, alike for the benefit of the business man and the protection of the public, new legislation in the form of Federal regulations, but such legislation should always come by a sound process of evolution . . . It is largely the experience of the independent Commission itself that will afford Congress the accurate information necessary to give to the country from time to time the additional legislation which may be needed.[48]

While everyone favored having the commission give Congress expert advice, some feared at the outset that it might be given no other effective powers. The Progressives charged, 'The only purpose which the Democratic interstate trade commission will serve is that of news gathering for the courts and for Congress.' [49] It was urged that the commission needed teeth in order to render effective service.

It was believed by some that Congress must assume responsibility for the proper functioning of the trade commission. Testifying before the House committee, Mr. Brandeis proposed that the commission could be kept under the control of Congress by means of the appropriation power.[50] He appears to have had in mind something in the nature of a detailed budget covering commission activities, with the accompanying Congressional power to alter that budget and thereby control the direction of the commission's work. The same sort of disciplinary action was mentioned by Senator Cummins:

. . . If a commission goes wrong, it can be legislated out of existence. It is subject, in a way, to the temper of the people, and certainly subject to the power of Congress . . .

. . . We always have our hands on the commission, not to influence its action in a particular case but, if it proves unfaithful, to dispose of it by legislation.[51]

Other senators, however, regarded this type of Congressional control as neither effective nor desirable. Senator Fletcher, as we have seen, believed that the President's power to remove commissioners for inefficiency or misconduct was a preferable device for control; while Senator Reed felt that Congressional

48. H. Rept. 533, 63d Cong., 2d sess. (1914), 8.
49. Rep. Hinebaugh, Ill., 51 Cong. Rec. 8861.
50. *Supra,* note 41, op. cit. 10 f.
51. 51 Cong. Rec. 11236.

control through appropriations would be ineffective and that the only effective control lay in thoroughgoing court review of commission action.[52]

The question whether the trade commission would be a 'legislative' body and in any sense a direct agent of Congress did not arouse the interest of the lawmakers. Senator Sutherland, as we have seen, referred to the commission as a legislative commission, but he was the only one who did. He held that quasi-judicial power could not validly be given to such a legislative commission but he leaves us completely in the dark on what he thought about the effect on the status of the commission of the quasi-judicial power which was finally given to it.

4. RELATION OF THE COMMISSION TO THE COURTS

One of the arguments for a trade commission endowed with quasi-judicial power was that it would be able to relieve the regular courts of the task of legislating, by taking over the difficult task of interpreting in concrete cases what was meant by the vague term 'unfair competitive trade practices.' This, it was said, was essentially a legislative power. The commission could thus relieve the courts of a function which they were not well equipped to assume. This view, however, was disputed, and several senators charged that the courts were being stripped of their proper powers by the creation of a commission. If anyone was to be left with the job of giving meaning to such a term as 'unfair competitive trade practices,' it should be a judicial body which could be relied upon to reach its conclusions in accordance with fair procedure.

A major debate took place on the question whether the commission's finding of fact should be made reviewable by the courts. The lawmakers of 1914 did not realize the futility of this discussion or foresee that the answer was to lie not with them but with the courts themselves, which proceeded to convert practically every question of fact involved in a trade commission hearing into a question of law. Most of those who considered the matter carefully believed that the commission's findings of fact should be final. The commission was to be composed

52. Ibid. 13048 ff.

of experts; it was to have facilities for investigation not easily available to courts of law; why therefore create a body of administrative experts to find facts and then have those findings of facts overridden? Senator Cummins urged that it would ruin the commission and its usefulness if the statute permitted too broad a court review. To do so 'destroys entirely the value of the order of the commission.' He emphasized 'the disadvantage of permitting a court to review or retry every case brought and determined by the commission . . . I would not be in favor of establishing this commission if that is the rule to be applied.' [53] He said on another occasion,

> I believe the order of the commission . . . should be given precisely the same effect, when brought under review by a court, as is given under the interstate commerce law to an order of the Interstate Commerce Commission fixing a railroad rate; that the court ought not to review the merits of the order entered by the commission, but that it should be able to review the jurisdiction of the commission. [54]

Replying to a question, Senator Cummins declared that he was willing to give the trade commission 'the power to determine absolutely, and without appeal or review upon appeal, the question of unfair competition in any given case.' [55] He added that in helping to draft this legislation 'I tried to make it so that the courts would not have the power to review the discretion and the judgment exercised or the facts passed upon by the trade commission.' [56] This position was supported by others. Senator White declared that complete judicial review would 'render the commission absolutely useless; it will embarrass the situation and make more difficult and more tedious and tortuous the route to the end of the litigation.' [57] President Charles R. Van Hise of Wisconsin told the House committee that the commission's findings of fact must be final; otherwise the persons subject to the act would not disclose all of the evidence before the commission, with the result that the findings and determinations of the commission would be correspondingly discounted on appeal. [58]

This view was, however, sharply disputed by those who felt

53. Ibid. 13050.
54. Ibid. 11451.
55. Ibid. 11105.
56. Ibid. 12215.
57. Ibid. 13107.
58. *Supra,* note 41, op. cit. 345 ff.

that safety lay only in full judicial review. Their position was stated in various ways. It was suggested that if the courts could not review findings of fact they would be virtually obligated to give effect to commission orders. This assumed, inaccurately, that the courts would not enjoy the normal judicial discretion to determine whether the commission order should or should not be enforced. The argument was stated by Senator Sterling as follows:

> . . . Under the plain language of this act the court is the auxiliary to the commission, and the court has as much judicial power as the sheriff or the clerk of a court would have, its business being simply to enforce the order of the commission, and that is all. Its powers here are ministerial, not judicial.[59]

Senator Thomas declared that the bill

> invests the courts merely with authority to issue mandatory injunctions upon the request of the commission, if its order shall be disregarded by the corporation against which it may be aimed.[60]

This, he said, leaves 'judicial power' to the commission, where it does not belong, and imposes a 'ministerial duty' upon the courts. It was also urged that full court review of findings of fact was necessary in order to correct arbitrary action by the commission. This was stated by Senator Reed as follows:

> . . . Surely we are going too far in setting up a board of this kind with unlimited powers, and then denying the citizens any court review, for that is in effect the purpose of the Senator's amendment. A court review which permits a reversal only when there is no evidence whatever for the board to act upon is a court review that will amount to little, for I can not imagine a case coming under this board's eye as to which somebody could not be found who would insist that the practice under investigation was perfectly fair or, on the other hand, someone could not be found to furnish evidence that it was unfair.[61]

The final argument for judicial review of findings of fact was based on constitutional grounds. This was most fully developed by Senator Sutherland, who was more emphatic and thorough in presenting constitutional objections than anyone else. He

---

59. 51 Cong. Rec. 12215.   61. Ibid. 13049.
60. Ibid. 11181.

made the interesting suggestion that the trade commission in making its findings of fact would be serving as a referee. The report of a referee is necessarily subject to the scrutiny of the court to which it is made, and in the same way the commission's findings of fact should be subject to court review.

. . . In that view of it, and to that extent, this trade commission is nothing more than a referee—a referee of all the courts in the country—to ascertain the facts; but now, having ascertained them and having issued its order, the vice of the original section 5 was that the courts were given no authority to try the original case, to hear the evidence, to determine where the weight of it lies, and themselves to enter the judgment.

He further stated:

. . . We have conferred absolute judicial power upon the commission, so far as the facts are concerned, because we deny the right to the courts to review the facts, which, as I have already said, is as much of the essence of judicial power as the right to determine what is the law.[62]

5. PROBLEM OF PERSONNEL

The problems relating to the personnel of the new trade commission were discussed but casually, and what was said did not go to the root of the matter. The model of the Interstate Commerce Commission was followed and little thought was given to the question of whether some variation from that model ought to be considered. The new commission was to be composed of men chosen from both political parties. The principle of bipartisanship was well established and its application in this situation was not criticized or seriously discussed. The hope was frequently expressed that the members of the new commission would be 'experts.' The friends of the commission stressed the desirability of this, and they meant by 'experts' men particularly familiar with business and industry rather than lawyers; as Senator Newlands put it, 'not simply experts in law, but experts in industry and trade.'[63] Those opposing the commission looked with suspicion upon experts of this variety. Their opinion, voiced by Senator Sutherland, was that the important

62. Ibid. 13056.   63. Ibid. 12031.

decisions confided to the commission ought to be made by men trained in the law.

It is interesting to observe that the Trade Commission Act provided for no special qualifications for members of the commission. Nor does it state any disqualifications. Railroad men had been excluded by law from the Interstate Commerce Commission, because it was felt that they could not maintain complete impartiality. There was no similar exclusion of businessmen from the trade commission. The only positive requirement was that the members give full time to their duties and not engage in any other business.

6. DESIRABILITY AND CONSTITUTIONALITY OF THE QUASI-JUDICIAL POWER CONFERRED ON THE COMMISSION

Some of the most illuminating discussions in Congress turned on the desirability and constitutional propriety of giving to the commission its important quasi-judicial duties. That this was in a very real sense a breaking of new ground was fully recognized. While the Interstate Commerce Commission enjoyed rate-making powers exercised under quasi-judicial procedure, neither it nor the newly created Federal Reserve Board had been given the drastic disciplinary and regulatory authority here established. This was an important experiment and every phase of it was carefully canvassed.

We turn first to the discussions on the desirability of delegating quasi-judicial power, an issue which involved in part the further question of the character of the quasi-judicial power to be delegated. The statute forbade 'unfair methods of competition in commerce,' or, more briefly, 'unfair competition'; and this legislative 'standard' was to be applied to concrete cases by the quasi-judicial activity of the commission. Was 'unfair competition' a standard definite enough to make it safe and desirable to give the commission the power to interpret it? The sponsors of the bill insisted that the commission would not have unrestricted discretion in interpreting unfair competition, since unfair competition was a term known to the common law and the courts in numerous cases had construed its meaning. It was quite as definite as the standard 'just and reasonable rate' which guided the rate decisions of the Interstate Commerce Commission, or as the term 'restraint of trade' found in the Sherman Act. At the same time the friends of the trade commission bill did not intend the commission to be strictly limited, in interpreting unfair competition, to the common law meaning established by the courts. They desired a standard general enough to meet changing economic conditions. The effort of Congress to define precisely all activities that could be classified as unfair competition had failed. What was needed was a reasonably definite and yet comprehensive term, the meaning of which in specific situations could be worked out by an independent body functioning through quasi-judicial procedure. Thus there could be built up through the decisions of the commission a body of administrative law, a law the content of which would be based upon the findings of concrete experience.

The opponents of the commission urged that the standard set was vague and indefinite and that the commission in applying the test of unfair competition would be exercising drastic powers affecting business in accordance with no clearly defined standard. Senator Sutherland, while admitting that the term had a meaning in common law, pointed out quite accurately that the commission would not confine itself to that common law meaning.[64] Senator Borah argued that the power to be given to the commission was essentially legislative and that if anybody was to supply the concrete content of such a legislative standard as unfair competition, it should be the courts and not an irresponsible commission.[65] The same view was expressed by Senator Pomerene who said: 'If we can define it, as a Congress, I shall be glad to have it defined. If we can not define it, I want the courts to define it. I do not want it to be left to the single judgment of the commission itself.'[66] The debate on this point is well summarized by Gerard Henderson as follows:

. . . Indeed, the debates themselves suggest, what seems obvious from the text of the Act, that it was the Congressional intention to confer on the Commission, subject to court review, the duty of giving a detailed content to the general principle embodied in the phrase, and to employ, in fulfilling this duty, not only the rules and precedents established by the courts at common law and under pre-

64. Ibid. 11178.   66. Ibid. 12874.
65. Ibid. 11600.

vious statutes, but the technique of reasoning by analogy and upon principle, with which jurists are familiar.

. . . [Section 5] stated a general ethical and economic principle, and relied upon the course of administration and judicial decision to give it content.[67]

We may note at this point a contribution to the discussion which came from outside Congress itself. This was the appearance, during the debates on the trade commission bill, of ex-President Taft's little book, *The Anti-trust Act and the Supreme Court*. Mr. Taft rallied to the defense of the Supreme Court's bitterly criticized decisions in the Standard Oil and American Tobacco Company cases in which the 'rule of reason' had been announced in the interpretation of the Sherman Act. He declared that the Supreme Court, far from assuming legislative power as Mr. Justice Harlan had charged in his dissenting opinion, had merely done what Congress had intended it to do; namely, given to the common law term 'restraint of trade' its established common law meaning. This, he said, was a proper judicial function. Mr. Taft accordingly objected to any 'clarifying amendments' to the Sherman Act, since these would confuse and obstruct the proper judicial interpretation of the common law restrictions embodied in the Act. At the same time he felt that Congress ought not to use in a federal statute the term 'unfair methods of competition.' This would give the courts power which they ought not to possess. 'It is submitting, not to their legal, but to their economic and business judgment questions for decision that are really legislative in character.' Commenting briefly upon the pending trade commission bill he said:

I regret to say that this is the tendency of the pending bills in Congress, in which it is proposed to leave first to an executive board and then to the courts to declare and forbid what in their judgment is unfair competition. If this means more than what is included in unreasonable restraints of trade at common law . . . by the anti-trust law, it would seem to be conferring legislative power.[68]

While Mr. Taft's prestige was by no means at its peak at this time, there is no doubt that he voiced with force and clarity the

67. Gerard C. Henderson, *The Federal Trade Commission* (1924), 36.
68. Wm. H. Taft, *The Anti-trust Act and the Supreme Court* (1914), 116.

views of a large conservative group, especially in the legal profession.

A final argument against the desirability of delegating quasi-judicial power to the commission was that it would give to a single body an undesirable mixture of powers. More specifically it would give to the commission the power to prosecute and the power to judge. This objection was stated before the Senate committee by a representative of the United States Chamber of Commerce in these words:

I think . . . that the granting of such power to the Interstate Commerce Commission, or the granting of such power to the trade commission, would be most disastrous to the usefulness of these commissions that you could possibly conceive. Both of these commissions are quasi-judicial bodies. They reach conclusions upon investigation and report the facts, and any practice which would constitute them in the eyes of the public prosecutors—both judge and advocate—would, I think, impair their usefulness to an extent that it is impossible to exaggerate. They would lose the reputation which they have, or ought to have, for impartial consideration and decision, the same as any judge who was empowered to proceed to enforce his own decree or action in his own name or under his own supervision. I think it would be very serious.[69]

Senator Reed put it in this way:

Why, Mr. President, think of saying in this land of the free—and there is still a presumption that it is a land of the free—that five men can sit down in a room and say: 'We think, Mr. Jones, that what you are doing with your property is not fair. We have no rule to guide us. We have no law to blaze the way. Nobody has told us what is unfair. Congress has enacted no statute; the courts have registered no precedents; but we do not think your method of doing business is fair; anyhow it does not meet with our approval, and therefore you shall not do it.' Will anyone pretend that such a decree is due process of law? [70]

Senator Works expressed the same view:

. . . So we have in this one small commission an inquisitorial body with power to force information of every phase of a company's business, a legislative body to determine and declare what is unfair

69. C. F. Mathewson, Hearings on Interstate Trade before the Senate Committee on Interstate Commerce, 63d Cong., 2d sess. (1914), vol. 1, 87.

70. 51 Cong. Rec. 11113.

competition, and a court to try and convict the company for a violation of the law it has created and enjoin it from carrying on its
business in the way it has been doing.[71]

Perhaps the most vigorous statement of this criticism was that
made by Senator Lippitt:

I think it is also a great source of danger that in addition to the
commission being first charged with these detective duties it is also
empowered to act in a judicial capacity, for the commissioners will
come to the judgment seat in many cases with the case prejudged.
As it is the evidence their own representatives have collected which
is the basis of their decisions, they must have every disposition to
uphold its integrity, and in this respect they are given a broader
power than any court in the land. The case the judge decides is one
in whose make-up he has had no part. It is brought before him by
the parties interested, and if the Government is one of them it is
the United States attorney who is responsible for the correctness of
the charges upon which the case rests and the evidence presented is
of his selection. No pride of consistency, so far as the judge is concerned, is involved in the proceedings at all. Just the opposite will
be the situation in many of the cases that this commission is called
upon to decide, for before the accused can be brought before them
and their side of the case heard, the commission must have already
decided that the evidence is entitled to some standing. Under these
circumstances, it would not be human nature, however great the
desire of the commission to be just might be, for them to be impartial, and when you add to that the fact that the continuance of the
salaries upon which they live depends upon at least some of the
charges being sustained, how can it be possible for such a tribunal
to be entirely without prejudice? It is contrary to all the principles
and theories upon which our American system of justice has been
founded. Entire confidence in the disinterestedness of the court is
the basis of the trust with which the American people submit their
differences to its decision. To introduce this other element at all
seems to me a most dangerous innovation, even if it were applied
to the simple things about which men differ, but when such a tribunal is to pass upon the intricate and technical operations of general business, such a condition is fatal to fairness and justice.[72]

A vague constitutional argument was directed against the
delegation of quasi-judicial power to the commission, and since
other constitutional objections to the bill related more or less

71. Ibid. 12277.   72. Ibid. 13212 f.

closely to this point we may appropriately review here the whole constitutional discussion. The main argument against the constitutionality of the trade commission bill, in fact the only substantial argument, was made by Senator Sutherland. This has peculiar interest, not so much because of the intrinsic character of the argument itself as because it was Senator Sutherland who, as Mr. Justice Sutherland, was to write twenty years later the Supreme Court's important decision in the Humphrey case dealing with the constitutional status of the Federal Trade Commission.[73] We are thus able to study the development of Senator Sutherland's thinking upon this important point. What he thought in 1914 was very different from what he said in 1935.[74]

We have already seen that Senator Sutherland and he alone consistently referred to the proposed federal trade commission throughout the debates as a legislative commission.[75] He regarded it as an agency set up solely as an aid to or adjunct of Congress. It was a sort of sub-Congress, an inferior body exercising on a lower level powers akin to those of Congress itself. He believed that Congress could constitutionally give to the commission only the power which Congress itself could directly exercise. He recognized the propriety of allowing the Interstate Commerce Commission to fix railroad rates by quasi-judicial process, because the fixing of rates is a legislative power; and while it could not be given to a court of law it might properly be given to a body which is an agent of Congress. But to give to the trade commission the power to interpret and enforce the prohibition against 'unfair methods of competition' was to give it a job which Congress itself could not constitutionally perform. To issue a cease and desist order against business conduct which the commission found to be 'unfair competition' was essentially a judicial process. Senator Sutherland declared that it amounted to the issuance of an injunction by a legislative body.

. . . Certainly if we would define what should constitute larceny and declare that larceny was unlawful, we could not devolve the power to forbid larceny or punish larceny upon a commission. It would have to remain with the courts.

. . . My contention is that we have no right to confer this power

73. 295 U.S. 602 (1935).   75. *Supra*, 198.
74. For fuller discussion see *infra*, 455 ff.

at all upon the administrative body; that it is a judicial power and belongs to the courts; that Congress itself can not exercise it. Suppose, for example, that Congress instead of undertaking to devolve this power upon an administrative body were itself to make an investigation of some particular case where it is claimed that unfair competition existed and Congress was to come to the conclusion that there existed unfair competition, does the Senator from Illinois think that Congress could issue an injunction against the continuance of that practice? [76]

In vain did Senator Cummins and Senator Lewis point out [77] that the trade commission was not to issue an injunction or execute judicial process, but was merely to make by quasi-judicial procedure a finding of facts the legal consequences of which depended under the statute upon later judicial action in the federal courts. Senator Sutherland remained unconvinced, and insisted that judicial power was being unconstitutionally delegated to the commission.

He further urged that for the legislative standard 'unfair competition' to be applied by the commission to concrete cases involved an inescapable constitutional dilemma. If the commission in interpreting this term was to be free to exercise discretion rather than follow the rigid lines of established common law interpretation, then they were actually making the law under an unconstitutional delegation of legislative power; if, on the other hand, the commission was to be limited to the common law meaning of the term 'unfair competition,' then it was performing a judicial task and judicial power had been unconstitutionally conferred on the commission.

. . . I do not insist that the words 'unfair competition' are not words well known to the law, but I insist that if the words in the bill are to be interpreted in their legal sense, then they confer judicial power. If they are not to be construed in their legal sense, as the Senator from Nevada (Mr. Newlands) seems to contend they are not to be construed, but are to be given some popular meaning beyond that, then I insist that they are not sufficiently definite to furnish a standard.[78]

Senator Sutherland further urged, as we have seen,[79] that the powers of the courts also were unconstitutionally infringed by

76. 51 Cong. Rec. 12651 f.
77. Ibid. 12651 ff.
78. Ibid. 12874.
79. *Supra,* 203 f.

the provisions of the bill making final the commission's findings of fact. He believed that this limited the power of the courts by obligating them to enforce commission orders. Several other senators shared this view. The argument overlooked the fact that the authority given to the courts to enforce or set aside commission orders was to be exercised in the full enjoyment of judicial discretion, a discretion which implies the judicial right not to be bound by erroneous commission determinations.

Senator Sutherland directed constitutional attack also against the inquisitorial powers to be given the commission. The wide authority to be conferred upon the commission to investigate business conduct was alleged arbitrarily to invade private rights and impliedly to sanction unreasonable searches and seizures. It did not help matters in Senator Sutherland's mind that a similar power had long been enjoyed by the Bureau of Corporations. That power had not been exercised by the bureau and so no issue had arisen, but he believed the granting of inquisitorial powers equally unconstitutional in both cases.[80]

Finally it was urged, though not by Senator Sutherland, that the merger of powers in the proposed federal trade commission was an unconstitutional violation of the doctrine of the separation of powers. This argument was put by Senator Shields of Tennessee:

Mr. President, I believe that the powers of all three of the coordinate branches of the Government are proposed to be delegated to and vested in this commission. The commission is authorized to declare what constitutes unfair competition or unfair methods of competition, thus exercising legislative powers in creating offenses, both civil and criminal, and it also has the power to repeal such legislation by altering or vacating any order it may make in any particular case. The worst part of this legislative power, however, is that the commission is authorized to give it a retrospective effect; in other words, the commission may, after the act is done or committed for the first time, declare that such an act constitutes unfair competition and a violation of law.

The commission is given judicial power by the authority to call the offender before it, to hear proof, and determine his guilt or innocence. Executive power is conferred by the authority to bring suit

80. 51 Cong. Rec. 12806.

in the district courts of the country to enforce such orders as it may make. It is difficult for me to conceive a more pronounced and unlawful confusion and delegation of the powers of the three coordinate branches of our Government than is here attempted to be done.[81]

E. THE FEDERAL TRADE COMMISSION SINCE 1914

It is no part of our purpose to present a history of the Federal Trade Commission and its work. Such a story would involve us deeply in the concrete problems of business regulation. There is value, however, in trying to appraise the attitude of Congress toward the commission after it became a going concern. We shall therefore summarize briefly the statutory changes affecting the commission, together with various proposals relating to its organization and functions which failed of passage. Such a survey can be merely selective and not exhaustive, confining itself to the high spots in the commission's history.

1. LEGISLATIVE CHANGES AFFECTING FEDERAL TRADE COMMISSION

We may summarize briefly the major legislative changes which have affected either the powers of the Federal Trade Commission or its relations. These will be presented in the order in which they took place.

a. *The Webb-Pomerene Act of* 1918

In 1918 the Webb-Pomerene Export Trade Act [82] was passed, following in general recommendations which the Federal Trade Commission made to Congress. The statute was intended to encourage and stimulate our export trade by relieving those engaged in it from some of the restrictions of the antitrust laws. This relaxation of the laws was carefully limited, and the jurisdiction of the Federal Trade Commission was extended to 'unfair methods of competition used in export trade against competitors engaged in export trade.' The commission was authorized to proceed through its customary procedure against 'an association or any agreement made . . . by such association

---

81. Ibid. 13057.   82. Act of April 10, 1918, 40 Stat. at L. 516.

. . . in restraint of trade.' This statute merely gave the commission a new job; it in no way changed its status or relations.

b. *The Packers and Stockyards Act of* 1921

The Packers and Stockyards Act of 1921 [83] is of especial interest in a study of the Federal Trade Commission, first, because it resulted from one of the commission's most spectacular investigations, and second, because it is the most conspicuous case in which Congress after careful study has given an important quasi-judicial assignment to an executive department rather than to an existing independent commission able and willing to receive it.

The meat-packing industry, popularly known as the 'beef trust,' had been under fire since the turn of the century. In the public mind it was one of the worst monopolies, ruthlessly exploiting the farmer on the one hand and the consumer on the other. It had been 'investigated' by a number of Congressional committees, and the Department of Justice had made unsuccessful efforts to dissolve it under the Sherman Act. In February 1917 President Wilson directed the Federal Trade Commission to investigate the high prices of foods. In partial compliance with this order the commission in 1918 made its Report on the Meat-Packing Industry,[84] indicting the packers for monopolistic practices and proposing drastic measures for reform.

The report, made during war time, proposed that the federal government acquire ownership of stockyards and of refrigerator and stock cars, and take over operation in the public interest of branch houses, cold storage plants, and warehouses. These were the facilities through which monopoly was made effective. These proposals aroused bitter controversy. The resentment of the packing industry and much of the rest of the business world was extreme. The commission, it was said, had conducted its investigations with gross unfairness and had urged conclusions not supported by the evidence. Every possible effort was made to discredit the commission and its recommendations.

As the War came to an end it became obvious that no proposals of government ownership would be seriously considered.

83. Act of August 15, 1921, 42 Stat. at L. 159.
84. H. Doc. 1297, 65th Cong., 2d sess. (1918).

Regulation of the packing industry was, however, admittedly imperative, and four different plans were proposed for administering such regulation. These were: (a) by the Secretary of Agriculture; (b) by an independent commission; (c) by the Secretary of Agriculture and the Interstate Commerce Commission; (d) by the Federal Trade Commission and the Interstate Commerce Commission. The last two proposals called for regulation of the packers and of the stockyards by separate agencies. The Act of 1921 set up unified regulation of packers and stockyards and gave the task to the Secretary of Agriculture. The power conferred was closely similar to that given to the Federal Trade Commission and also included certain rate-making powers.

The considerations which led Congress to place the enforcement of the new statute in the hands of the Secretary of Agriculture were certainly not any abstract principles of public administration. It seemed wholly logical to give the task to the Federal Trade Commission, which had been created to do exactly this kind of work. The commission, however, was so bitterly hated and feared by the packers, and was viewed with such suspicion in respectably conservative quarters for its shocking proposal of government ownership, that it was politically out of the question to place the new job in its hands. The two proposals for a bifurcated system that would regulate the packers and the stockyards separately gave way to the demand for unified regulation. Finally the Secretary of Agriculture, Mr. Henry C. Wallace, persuasively argued that his department could easily take over the new regulatory job, inasmuch as the Bureau of Animal Industry and the Pure Food and Drug Inspectors division had field forces working in the packing houses and in constant touch with the industry at many points. They could take on the new functions with a minimum of expense and duplication of effort. This plan pleased the farmers, who looked upon the department as their special friend and protector. The idea of creating a brand new independent commission to administer the Act did not gain much support.

c. *The Securities Act of* 1933

In 1933 Congress passed the Securities Act,[85] forbidding the use of interstate commerce or the mails to advertise or sell securities not registered under the provisions of the law. The Federal Trade Commission was given the administration of this Act and the securities in question were to be registered with it. The commission added some sixty-five members to its staff to handle this heavy and important task. When, however, in 1934 Congress so extended the scope of the Act as to bring under federal control not merely securities but the exchanges upon which they are sold, it decided, after much debate and sharp disagreement between the House and Senate, to place the administration of the new Securities and Exchange Act[86] in an independent commission created for that purpose. The legislative history of this movement will be dealt with when we consider the Securities and Exchange Commission.

d. *The Robinson-Patman Act of* 1936

In 1936 a new job was imposed upon the Federal Trade Commission by the Robinson-Patman Antidiscrimination Act.[87] This statute forbids certain types of price discrimination practiced for the purpose of destroying competition. While the legislative standard by which the commission's duties under the new Act are defined is even more vague than that in the original Trade Commission Act, the commission's procedure in the enforcement of the new statute is that of the customary cease and desist order.

e. *The Miller-Tydings Act of* 1937

Congress in 1937 passed the Miller-Tydings Act,[88] legalizing certain carefully defined types of price-tying contracts and declaring them not to be unfair methods of competition under

85. Act of May 27, 1933, 48 Stat. at L. 74.
86. Act of June 6, 1934, 48 Stat. at L. 881.
87. Act of June 19, 1936, 49 Stat. at L. 1526.
88. Act of Aug. 17, 1937, 50 Stat. at L. 673.

the Trade Commission Act. The statute restricts rather than enlarges the responsibilities of the Federal Trade Commission.

f. *The Wheeler-Lea Act of* 1938

None of the foregoing statutes directly amended the Federal Trade Commission Act or changed the commission itself or its procedure. They merely added or withdrew areas of regulatory control. The Wheeler-Lea Act [89] passed in March 1938 substantially amended the basic Act of 1914. It not only enlarged the powers of the commission but it made certain procedural changes which strengthened its powers of enforcement. These changes may be summarized as follows: First, unfair or deceptive acts or practices in commerce were declared to be unlawful and were brought within the commission's reach. This change had long been urged by the commission itself. It will be recalled that the original Trade Commission Act extended only to unfair methods of competition. Second, the commission's cease and desist orders were made final within sixty days unless appealed from. Third, the Act fixed the time when orders of the commission from which appeals had been taken should become final. Fourth, civil penalties up to $5,000 were imposed for violations of cease and desist orders which had become final. Fifth, the Act made unlawful the dissemination of false advertising of foods, drugs, devices, or cosmetics, and defined these terms.

2. CONGRESSIONAL CONSIDERATION OF TRADE COMMISSION PROBLEMS AND ACTIVITIES

We may turn now to a consideration of Congressional discussions of the Federal Trade Commission in an attempt to discover what Congress has from time to time thought of the agency which it set up in 1914. These relate to various phases of the commission's work.

89. Act of Mar. 21, 1938, 52 Stat. at L. 111.

a. *Investigations by the Federal Trade Commission*

In its investigatory work the commission is subject by the terms of the statute to multiple control and responsibility. The investigations which the commission may undertake on its own initiative are rather general in character. By other provisions, however, the commission is required to investigate alleged violations by corporations of the antitrust laws when directed to do so by the President or by either house of Congress. It is further obliged to conduct certain inquiries on behalf of the Attorney General. Obviously Congress can at any time by statute require the commission to conduct an investigation not authorized by any of these provisions. The annual report of the commission for 1938 indicated that the commission since its establishment had conducted more than one hundred general investigations. Twenty-three were ordered by the President. The others were undertaken either on the commission's initiative or in compliance with resolutions of the Senate or the House.

This system of multiple responsibility and control has led naturally to conflict of opinion and criticism. Members of Congress interested in particular investigations have often been sharply critical of the commission for not pushing these inquiries more promptly or more vigorously. Resolutions have appeared in the Senate or the House directing the commission to report why action has not been taken in accordance with some prior mandate. On the other hand, those who believe that business should not be pried into and harassed have objected to some of the investigations and have attacked the commission for excessive zeal. The power of the President to order the commission to undertake costly investigations has raised difficult budgetary questions. If the President orders an investigation, must the commission finance it from its regular budget, is Congress obligated to underwrite it by a special appropriation, or should the President supply the money from his contingent fund or seek through the Bureau of the Budget a special appropriation? These questions have often been acute, and the way in which they have been handled has not clarified the theory of responsibility under which the commission carries on its work.

The problem of financing investigations has not, however, been the major problem which Congress has dealt with in this connection. Certain investigations have had political repercussions of tremendous importance. The authority to investigate the mammoth business concerns of the country is a power loaded with political dynamite. It is bound to arouse the bitter antagonism of those being investigated and to set in motion powerful political pressures. At the same time these investigations have been insistently demanded by those seeking a drastic enforcement of the antitrust laws. The kind of controversy which can arise from these conflicting pressures is illustrated by the meat-packers investigation already discussed.[90] This was a searching and thorough-going inquiry. It was conducted, moreover, with the aid of an attorney for the commission, Mr. Francis J. Heney, who had a definite flair for the spectacular and whose press releases made stirring reading. The commission's report brought a serious indictment against the packing industry and included in its recommendations the government ownership of some parts of the business. The report, as we have seen, was received by the conservative press with a violent outburst of denunciation. The Chamber of Commerce of the United States sent to the President an excoriating attack upon the commission and its report with the request that he fill existing vacancies on the commission with men who would radically change the commission's policy.

Difficulties arose regarding the precise scope of the commission's power of investigation. The statute limits this power by providing that it may extend to 'any corporation alleged to be violating the antitrust Acts.' From time to time the House or Senate has lost sight of this limitation and ordered the commission to undertake much broader investigations. This has placed the commission in an awkward position, and in one or two cases the Attorney General or the courts came to its rescue and re-emphasized the limited nature of its investigatory power. There has been some demand for broadening this power, but Congress continues to feel that it is better to state the particular objects for which the power may be exercised. It is feared that a general power to investigate might be abused.

90. *Supra,* 214 f.

In connection with commission investigations we see in action Congressional control of an independent agency through the power of appropriation. The presentation of the commission's budget to the appropriations committees of Congress has frequently stirred up discussion on the utility of the work being done. Motions to eliminate the entire appropriation and thereby abolish the commission have sometimes been made, while reductions in the amounts requested have occasionally been adopted. Congress has used the power of appropriation not only as a general club over the commission's head but also as a means of keeping the commission from undertaking investigations deemed either undesirable or in excess of the commission's power. Beginning about 1925, appropriation bills carried riders forbidding the use of appropriated funds for general economic investigations and restricting investigations to corporations alleged to be violating antitrust legislation.

b. *Trade practice conferences and agreements*

Another phase of the commission's work which has attracted a good deal of Congressional attention has been its development of trade practice conferences and agreements. It will be remembered that in 1914 the business interests of the country rather generally hoped that Congress would create an administrative agency with authority to give advance approval to various methods of business conduct. No such power was given to the Federal Trade Commission. It was feared that if an administrative agency were permitted to underwrite business practices the antitrust laws might be violated with impunity. In 1919 the commission embarked upon a new policy, that of calling trade practice conferences composed of the representatives of an industry and of acting as informal adviser in the formulation of agreements which would eliminate injurious competitive conduct and establish helpful rules for the carrying on of the business. The commission had no delegated authority to do this; but since its activities were wholly informal and since none of its advice carried any legal sanction, the new policy did not appear to be unlawful. This development was viewed with alarm by those members of Congress who feared any attempt to relax at any point the rigid provisions of the antitrust laws. Mr.

Patman of Texas charged that the trade practice conference work violated the spirit of the antitrust laws and exceeded the powers of the commission. He declared:

> Never in the history of our country before has a Government board so grossly and flagrantly abused the power intrusted to it. It is organizing trusts and monopolies when its duties are to destroy trusts and monopolies.[91]
>
> The President of the United States and his Cabinet have approved a policy adopted by the Federal Trade Commission and the Department of Justice which means the destruction of independent business . . . The President and his Cabinet, I am informed from a reliable source, put their stamp of approval, not only upon what the Federal Trade Commission and the Department of Justice have done in the past but what they expect to do in the future.[92]

To the same effect Representative Fulmer quoted from an earlier statement of the Attorney General as follows:

> The trouble about industry coming and requesting that they be allowed to put into execution certain trade-practice rules is when they go back and put them into practice they nudge a little here and they nudge a little there and then when we call their hand they come back with the statement: 'We have your indorsement.'[93]

The commission, however, went forward with its trade practice conference work and steadily won support for it. Businessmen endorsed it with enthusiasm and general opinion has come to regard it as one of the most constructive and valuable phases of commission activity. Congress has resisted all efforts to compel the commission to abandon this policy, and there have been attempts to secure statutory authorization for it and make trade practice agreements legally enforceable. In 1932 Senator Nye introduced a bill[94] for making all trade practice conference rules enforceable after they had been adopted by a majority of the industry and approved by the commission or the courts. This proposal was carefully considered. At the same time Senator Walsh of Massachusetts introduced a bill[95] which legalized trade practice conferences and authorized the Federal Trade Commission to give advance approval to co-operative contracts

91. 72 Cong. Rec. 6100.
92. Ibid. 8636.
93. 75 Cong. Rec. 7819.

94. S. 2626, 72d Cong., 1st sess. (1932).
95. S. 3256, 72d Cong., 1st sess. (1932).

for the curtailment of production and for other acts to avoid ruinous competition. Similar legislation was introduced and defended at length in the House by Mr. Jenkins of Ohio in 1935.[96] However, none of these bills passed. There is a clear distinction between the informal activities of the commission in connection with trade practice conferences and the proposed policy of legalizing trade practice rules. The present function of the commission is purely advisory. The commission can extend no immunities nor guarantee any protection against the rigid enforcement of existing federal laws. If Congress were to legalize the trade practice agreements they would become somewhat similar to the codes of fair competition set up under the National Industrial Recovery Act. Their formulation would be an important sublegislative activity, and intricate problems affecting the determination of policy and the enforcement of responsibility would be pushed to the front.

c. The President's relations with the Federal Trade Commission—The question of independence

It would be useful to know exactly the Congressional theory of the relations between the Federal Trade Commission and the President. This is probably impossible. Congress has never worked out any clear idea upon this point and such views as it has expressed have varied with changing circumstances. No issue has arisen which has made it necessary for Congress to clarify its thinking upon this problem. But from the Congressional debates and discussions since 1915 relating to the commission, we may piece together certain indications of what Congress has from time to time thought about the independence of the Federal Trade Commission and the degree of control and responsibility over it which the President enjoys.

Before doing this, however, we may allude briefly to the President's own attitude on the matter, especially the attitude of President Wilson. This is of interest not only for its own sake but because during the formative years of the commission Congress was inclined to take its cue from the President and be guided by his judgment. It will be recalled that President Wilson secured the inclusion in the Federal Trade Commission Act

96. 79 Cong. Rec. 8880 ff.

of the clause authorizing the President to direct the commission to make certain investigations.[97] He proceeded to use this power vigorously and many of the commission's most important investigations were made upon his direction. There is some evidence that Wilson himself believed that he had a rather more general power of directing commission activity. In a letter to the commission in February 1917 ordering the investigation of the meat-packing industry, he added the following paragraph:

> I am aware that the commission has additional authority in this field, through the power conferred upon it to prevent certain persons, partnerships, or corporations from using unfair methods of competition in commerce. I presume that you may see fit to exercise that authority, upon your own initiative, without direction from me.[98]

Wilson's whole thinking with regard to problems of this sort was colored by the war emergency. Upon America's entrance into the War, vast discretionary powers were delegated to the President, and Congress and the President seem to have regarded all federal agencies as available implements for the carrying out of war policies. Many of the major investigations which the President ordered related to war situations and were financed from funds outside the commission's budget. When the proposal to confer upon the President the right to fix the price of coal was being discussed, it was urged that the Federal Trade Commission should serve as the President's agent in the actual setting of these prices.[99]

In regard to the Congressional attitude toward this relation, it is clear that Congress considered the Federal Trade Commission as an adjunct of the Department of Justice in certain important aspects of its work. The statute authorized the President or either house of Congress to direct the commission to make investigations of corporations alleged to be violating the anti-trust laws. Obviously the purpose of these investigations was to produce evidence upon which the Department of Justice might proceed. While, in some cases these investigations resulted in new laws, more often they merely placed in the hands of the Attorney General evidence upon which he might move against

97. *Supra*, 194.   99. 55 Cong. Rec. 5360.
98. 56 Cong. Rec. 11063.

those engaging in illegal practices. In short, the commission was very definitely an agent of the executive branch and was recognized by Congress as being so.

That many members of Congress assumed that the Federal Trade Commission was subject to some degree of Presidential direction appears from a discussion in the Senate in February 1925. The following resolution was introduced:

Resolved, That the Federal Trade Commission be, and it is hereby, directed to forthwith transmit to the Senate a copy of its report on its investigation in 1923 and 1924 of the price of crude oil, gasoline, and other petroleum products and other data pertaining to the operations of the oil companies and refineries.[100]

A number of senators led by Senator Moses sought to amend the resolution in such a way as to direct the President to submit to the Senate the Trade Commission's report 'if not incompatible with the public interest.'[101] This was on the ground that action by the Department of Justice in the premises was apparently contemplated. There ensued an interesting debate whether the President had any responsibility in the matter at all. Senator Walsh of Montana declared that the Federal Trade Commission was an independent establishment and that it was a serious mistake to treat it as though it were in any sense subordinate to the President. He said:

Mr. President, the amendment proposed by the Senator from New Hampshire presents a rather important question, namely, whether the President of the United States can control the action of the Federal Trade Commission. I trust that idea will not be accepted by the Senate. I trust it will be understood that the Federal Trade Commission and the Interstate Commerce Commission and other bodies of like character discharging quasi judicial duties will not be regarded as under the domination of the President of the United States as are the various departments of the Government. My understanding about the matter is, that the President of the United States has no control whatever over the Federal Trade Commission or any of its acts. He has no authority to direct the Federal Trade Commission in any particular. If we want information from any of those bodies we must go to those bodies for the information.[102]

100. S. Res. 341, 66 Cong. Rec. 4018.   102. Ibid.
101. 66 Cong. Rec. 4635.

Senator Moses replied, 'The Senate should not be dealing directly with independent executive establishments; . . . the natural avenue of communication is through the President, who has to take the responsibility for a matter of this sort.'[103] Senator Norris declared that the Senate might properly deal directly with the Federal Trade Commission but that the commission itself should not have final decision on whether the disclosure of the information in its report would be in the public interest. Advice on that matter could properly be sought from the President or the Attorney General. To this Mr. Moses replied, 'Why should we set up a pipe line between the White House and the Federal Trade Commission? Let us deal directly with the White House.'[104] Throughout the discussions there is an undercurrent of implication that the commission's relations with the President cannot properly be ignored by the Senate. The commission did, however, transmit to the Senate the report asked for in the resolution quoted above.

The debates indicate that Congress has become aware of the President's power to control the policy of the Federal Trade Commission through its personnel. This control is bound up in the power of appointment and removal. We have seen that when the commission presented its highly controversial report upon the meat-packing industry in 1918 the Chamber of Commerce of the United States instead of protesting to Congress went directly to the President with its demand that the policy of the commission be modified by the appointment of two suitable men to existing vacancies. It does not seem to have been questioned that the President might properly utilize his appointing power to revolutionize commission policy. This whole question became more acute as a result of commission developments under the Humphrey regime between 1925 and 1933. The appointment of Mr. Humphrey by President Coolidge made him the directing head of a Republican majority of three on the commission, which proceeded to change radically the commission's policy and soften the rigor with which the commission enforced the statutes placed within its jurisdiction.[105]

103. Ibid. 4683.
104. Ibid. 4684.
105. Colonel William H. England, chief economist of the commission, in a letter to the writer, states: 'The period of Commissioner Humphrey's greatest

The policy followed under the Humphrey regime was acceptable to both President Coolidge and President Hoover. It was bitterly attacked, however, by the Democratic and Farmer-Labor minorities. In January 1933, Mr. Patman of Texas, denouncing what he regarded as Trade Commission collusion with trusts and monopolies, expressed the hope that when President Roosevelt took office he would 'certainly change the policy of the Federal Trade Commission, and put it back to its true original function or intent.' [106] Throughout the discussions of this whole period there runs an underlying assumption that the commission's policy, if not actually directed from the White House, at least conforms to the President's wishes, that the President cannot escape responsibility for the commission's policy, and that an incoming President objecting to such policy should change it, if not by the actual issuance of orders to the commission, at least by the making of suitable appointments. President Roosevelt's removal of Mr. Humphrey on the ground that Humphrey's policy with regard to the work of the commission was not in harmony with the President's policy evoked no protest in either house of Congress and practically no comment. The President was apparently doing in this situation what Congress assumed that he would and should do.

d. *Trade court proposal*

In 1932 Senator Nye introduced three bills affecting the Federal Trade Commission and its work. One [107] of these prohibited price discriminations and the practice of selling below costs. A second,[108] already referred to, legalized trade practice agreements. The third [109] provided for the establishment of a federal trade court. This court was to consist of a chief justice and eleven associate justices to be appointed by the President with the consent of the Senate and to hold office during good behavior. The chief justice was to be designated by the President.

influence did not extend beyond 1927 or 1928. Neither Commissioners VanFleet, Hunt, or Meyers, all of whom were Republicans, followed Commissioner Humphrey at all times; in fact, certain of them usually opposed his policies.'

106. 76 Cong. Rec. 1831.

107. S. 2628, 72d Cong., 1st sess. (1932).

108. S. 2626. *Supra*, 221.

109. S. 2627.

The court was to have a branch in each of the ten judicial circuits. Each judge was to be a resident within the circuit. The salaries of the judges were to be fixed at $12,500. The branch courts were to have jurisdiction over all suits arising under the antitrust acts and the Federal Trade Commission Act and this jurisdiction was to be exclusive and final except that it should be subject to review by the appellate division of the federal trade court. The branch court was to enforce, set aside, or modify orders of the Federal Trade Commission. The relation between the appellate division of the federal trade court and the branch courts was to be the same as that between existing circuit and district courts. Review of the judgments of the appellate division by the Supreme Court was to be by writ of certiorari.

This interesting proposal was overshadowed by the other proposals which accompanied it. In the hearings on the three bills attention was largely confined to the proposal to legalize trade practice agreements. Most of the witnesses before the Senate committee were vigorously backing the trade practice bill and seemed willing to accept the trade court bill as a means of getting the other when they mentioned it at all. Senator Nye in presenting the bill to the committee said:

> The . . . measure, S. 2627, providing for the creation of a Federal Trade Court . . . is designed to complement the bill to which I have just referred (S. 2626). The need for the expeditious consideration of questions arising under these 3 acts requires no comment . . . The plea is frequently made that the judges of our Federal courts are sadly overworked and with a constantly increasing demand upon their services matters of the highest importance are necessarily delayed for long periods of time before they can come to final decision. It is my hope and expectation that the creation of a new tribunal such as contemplated in this measure would, in the first place, provide a court which would be expert in the subject of business law and would, further, be in a position to interpret the law in the light of rapidly changing economic conditions, such as is not now possible.[110]

The Trade Commission itself, however, opposed the establishment of the federal trade court on the ground that there was

110. Hearings before a subcommittee of the Senate Committee on the Judiciary, 72d Cong., 1st sess. (1932), 6 f.

no need for it. Robert Healy, chief counsel of the commission, wrote to Senator Norris as follows:

I cannot see the slightest reason for establishing a Federal trade court. I do not believe that the Federal courts of the country are being clogged or overburdened with cases arising under the antitrust statutes. I cannot see any necessity for creating all this additional expense. This commission has pending in the various circuit courts of appeal not over 10 cases . . . So far as our observation goes the circuit courts of appeal are having no difficulties, so far as time is concerned, in disposing of the various cases before their courts to which the commission is a party.[111]

The trade court proposal was in essence a plan for the setting up of an administrative court modeled to some extent along the lines of the ill-fated Commerce Court of 1910. It was to provide a specialized tribunal for the handling of that branch of judicial business which affects the Federal Trade Commission and which arises under the antitrust laws and which is now handled by the district and circuit courts of appeals. The proposed tribunal would have had no jurisdiction not already existing in the regular constitutional courts.

III. THE UNITED STATES SHIPPING BOARD AND THE UNITED STATES MARITIME COMMISSION

A. THE SHIPPING BOARD ACT OF 1916

1. BACKGROUND OF THE SHIPPING BOARD ACT OF 1916

THE Shipping Board Act of 1916 [1] was an attempt to halt the long and steady decline of the American merchant marine. Prior to the Civil War, during the era of the famous clipper ships, this country enjoyed if not supremacy on the sea at least a status somewhere approaching equality. In 1861 American shipping in the foreign trade reached the all-time peak of 2,496,894 tons. By 1910 it had sunk to 782,517. Only 8.7 per cent of American foreign commerce was being carried in American ships.[2]

There were various causes for this decline in American ship-

111. Ibid. 275 f.
1. Act of Sept. 7, 1916, 39 Stat. at L. 728.
2. *Merchant Marine Statistics* (1932), 29 f.

ping. The ravages upon northern shipping during the Civil War destroyed many vessels which were never replaced. As steel ships came to replace wooden ships, English shipyards were able to build them more cheaply than could American shipyards, owing partly to higher American wages and partly to our high tariff policy. But our navigation laws required ships flying the American flag to be built in American shipyards, in spite of these differences in production costs. This inescapable competitive disadvantage retarded the growth of an American merchant marine.

We were as a nation aware of this decline of American shipping and its unfortunate consequences, but there was no agreement on how the problem could be met. All during the '70's and '80's there was much controversy about what policy should be followed to improve our merchant marine. Shipowners urged the policy of 'free ships,' which meant the privilege of buying ships in the cheapest market and sailing them under the American flag. The shipbuilders, on the other hand, were adamant against free ships, insisted upon retaining the navigation laws requiring American ships to be built in American shipyards, and urged that the differential in construction costs be covered by subsidies paid by the government. This controversy in varying forms continued down to the outbreak of the World War. The Democratic Party in general favored the free ship policy. The Republicans, though by no means united, favored government subsidies, either direct or indirect, and though the party as a whole never backed a direct subsidy program, it did support mail subsidies and other forms of bounties. During the '70's and '80's we tried some of these indirect subsidies, particularly mail subsidies; but the whole program turned out to be honeycombed with corruption and the subsidy policy was fairly thoroughly discredited in the public eye.

Between 1890 and 1910 a fairly steady drive was carried on to commit the government to a direct subsidy policy. Shipowners and shipbuilders buried the hatchet and joined in seeking to secure direct government aid for the shipping industry. Shipowners realized that the free ship campaign would never succeed. The strength of the subsidy drive rose and fell. It gained force as a result of Blaine's influential support, which led to a subsidy act in 1891; and it waned under Cleveland's Demo-

cratic Administration. It was sponsored by Senators Hanna,
Payne, and Frye in the late '90's, and Senate support was lined
up behind a program of heavy subsidies; but the argument that
such a subsidy would be an additional gift to the Steel Trust
was so convincing that it prevented the enactment of the bill.
In 1903 President Roosevelt urged the appointment of a merchant marine commission to study the entire problem. The
commission reported a proposal for a ship bounty measure,
which after considerable discussion was defeated in 1905 and
again in 1907. Senator Gallinger rallied the subsidy forces behind a bill in the Senate in 1910 and 1911, but the final defeat
of the Gallinger bill apparently convinced the subsidy group
that they were fighting a lost cause.

When the Democratic Party came into power in 1912 it
looked at the shipping problem from a new point of view. The
drive was launched for regulation rather than aid. Attempts
were made to eliminate in the shipping industry the gross
abuses under which free competition had been sacrificed. An
experiment with free ship legislation, a traditional Democratic
policy, proved a failure. To allow American capitalists to buy
ships in the cheapest market accomplished nothing, when the
risks in the shipping business were so great that capital was not
willing to buy ships in any market. The competitive status of
American shipping was made more precarious by the La Follette Seamen's Act of 1915,[3] which improved conditions of labor
on American vessels but required American shipowners to employ in the main American seamen. In 1915 the future of the
American merchant marine looked anything but rosy.

The outbreak of the World War revolutionized the status of
American shipping as it revolutionized nearly everything else.
At first there was panic and almost complete demoralization.
Ships did not sail for fear of capture. Foreign commerce was
at a temporary standstill and the shipping industry was para-
lyzed. The belligerent powers commandeered their own merchant ships for war purposes. The vastly increased demand
upon this country for products to be shipped abroad made un-
precedented demands upon our shipping facilities. There ensued a period of amazing prosperity for those shipowners who

3. Act of Mar. 4, 1915, 38 Stat. at L. 1164.

were still able to operate. Shipping rates in some cases rose to 700 per cent of their former level. But we did not have the ships, and it was vigorously urged that the government should undertake to acquire ships to meet the growing and profitable demand. The Secretary of the Treasury, Mr. McAdoo, proposed that the government appropriate $50,000,000 for the purchase of ships to add to our merchant marine, and this proposal became absorbed into and overshadowed the parallel drive in Congress for the more effective regulation of American shipping in the interests of reasonable rates and fair competition. A bill appeared in Congress in 1914 [4] proposing a shipping board with power to regulate shipping and with authority to create a corporation to purchase, charter, or build $50,000,000 worth of ships. This bill did not at first succeed, but with Administration support and a growing conviction that some such legislation was necessary, it reappeared in 1916 and was passed.

2. STEPS IN THE LEGISLATIVE HISTORY OF THE ACT OF 1916

The legislative history of the Shipping Board Act of 1916 runs as follows: Representative Alexander of Missouri at the request of the President introduced the shipping board bill [5] in the House early in 1916. It provided for a shipping board to be composed of two Cabinet members and three members appointed by the President. This board was to have power to investigate the whole merchant marine problem and make legislative recommendations to Congress; to exercise regulatory powers over shipping rates and unfair competitive methods; to purchase, charter, or construct vessels; to charter, lease, or sell vessels to American citizens for operation; and to create a corporation to carry out these managerial functions. Extensive hearings on this bill were held by the House Committee on Merchant Marine and Fisheries in February and March. Just as the bill was to be reported out, Mr. Alexander, the chairman of the committee, brought in a substitute bill [6] to replace it. This substitute increased the number of independent members on the board to five, forbade various unlawful competitive prac-

4. H.R. 18518, 63d Cong., 2d sess. (1914).
5. H.R. 10500, 64th Cong., 1st sess. (1916).
6. H.R. 15455, 64th Cong., 1st sess. (1916).

tices by water carriers, increased the board's authority to fix rates, and enlarged its authority to enforce its powers. It made, however, no important changes in the ship purchase program. The House committee reported the bill out in May and urged its adoption.[7] A minority of the committee filed a report supporting the creation of a shipping board but opposing the government ownership or operation of ships. The bill was debated in the House for several days and passed on May 20, 1916, by a vote of 209 to 161, a vote running largely along party lines.

Upon reaching the Senate the bill was referred to a subcommittee of the Committee on Interstate Commerce and was reported out [8] on July 19, 1916, after fairly extensive hearings had been held. The Senate committee struck out the provision for ex-officio or Cabinet members on the board and as a further protection to the shipping industry added certain restrictions relating to the purchase of ships and their possible operation by the government. Considerable debate took place in the Senate early in August, and the bill passed on August 18 by a vote of 38 to 21, 36 senators not voting. The House concurred in the Senate amendments on August 30, 1916, and the bill became law on September 7, 1916.

3. PROVISIONS OF THE ACT OF 1916

The Act of 1916 merged two programs with respect to shipping that have intrinsically nothing whatever to do with each other, and it created a common agency for carrying out both of them. The Act fell into two divisions. In the first place, it created a Shipping Board of five members with staggered six-year terms and with the customary bipartisan limitation. They were to be chosen upon the basis of fitness for the duties of the office and of fair representation of the geographical divisions of the country. They were removable by the President for inefficiency, neglect of duty, or malfeasance in office. The board was to elect its own chairman from its members.

In the second place, the Shipping Board was given powers which fell into two distinct categories. The first of these comprised the powers necessary to carry out the ship purchase pro-

7. H. Rept. 659, 64th Cong., 1st sess. (1916).
8. S. Rept. 689, 64th Cong., 1st sess. (1916).

gram. The board was to purchase, lease, or construct with Presidential approval and in American shipyards vessels suitable for naval auxiliaries. It was to charter, lease, or sell these vessels to American citizens upon terms and under conditions prescribed by the board and approved by the President. It was authorized to create a corporation under the laws of the District of Columbia to carry out these powers. This corporation could have a capital stock of $50,000,000, and this stock could be sold with the approval of the President. Having acquired these ships, the board was authorized to attempt their sale to private persons after due notice. If unable to sell the ships it was to report that fact to the President, who should thereupon issue an order stating that conditions prevailed which justified the operation of these ships by a corporation formed under the provisions of the Act. The second set of duties related to regulation. All shipping companies were required to file with the board all agreements on rates and charges, and the board was empowered to disapprove or cancel those which were unjustly discriminatory, unfair, or injurious to commerce, and to approve the others. Shipowners were required to file with the board, open to public inspection, maximum rates, fares, and so on, and these could lawfully be exceeded only with the board's approval. The board could replace rates found to be injurious or unreasonable by those which were not. It could require reports relating to the shipping business. It was given compulsory power to secure information, and orders issued by it were to receive the same treatment in the courts as orders of the Interstate Commerce Commission. Finally, the board was to investigate, in this country and abroad, relative costs of shipbuilding, ship operation, and marine insurance, and lay this information before Congress.

4. ISSUES AND TOPICS IN HEARINGS AND DEBATES

Congressional discussions of the shipping bill dealt more with the economic aspects of shipping policy than with the methods of administering that policy, and we are not here concerned with these economic issues. The level of the discussion was influenced by the emergency conditions in which it took place and the need for securing prompt action. The new policy of government ownership of ships was not embraced by the shipping interests or by businessmen generally. It was not popular with those who had been clamoring for subsidies, and much effort was exerted to devise ways and means by which government ownership of ships should be so restricted, and governmental operation made so difficult, that there would be a resulting advantage to the shipping industry. Nor was the policy of government regulation fully accepted. In fact this aspect of the proposed law was fought more bitterly than any other. It was urged that regulation would further handicap American shipping in competition with foreign shipping. It was pointed out that Congress could regulate only American ships, since any attempt to go beyond this would produce international complications. All of these problems were threshed out at great length.

a. *Should a shipping board be created?*

There was almost unanimous agreement that some kind of shipping board ought to be created. There was no agreement whatever on what such a board ought to do, and ideas concerning its proper functions ranged all the way from simple investigation to the substantial and far-reaching powers embodied in the Act. It is interesting to note that no one seemed to favor giving regulatory powers over the shipping industry to the Interstate Commerce Commission, a proposal which later [9] commanded a good deal of support. Mr. Alexander, chairman of the House committee, stated that this suggestion had not been seriously considered 'because the commission is already overworked.' [10]

b. *Ex-officio members on the board*

The sharpest controversy relating to the proposed board arose over the proposal to make two Cabinet officers ex-officio members. There was no such plausible reason for creating this kind of tie-in with the Administration as had led to the placing of the Secretary of the Treasury and the Comptroller of the Currency on the Federal Reserve Board. Commenting upon this

9. *Infra*, 269 f., 273 f.   10. 53 Cong. Rec. 8078.

parallel, Senator Weeks observed: 'My judgment is that one of the weakest phases of the Federal-reserve law is the provision inserted in the bill by the insistence of the administration that the Secretary of the Treasury and the Comptroller of the Currency should be members of the Federal Reserve Board.' [11] The demand for ex-officio representation on the board came mainly from the Administration. It was urged that the Secretary of the Navy should be a member because of his interest in the ships to be acquired as naval auxiliaries, and the Secretary of Commerce because the Steamboat Inspection Service and the Bureau of Navigation are both in the Department of Commerce. The debate on this whole issue was very one-sided and there was no convincing defense of the ex-officio membership proposal. Chairman Alexander of the House committee, whose bill contained the provision, indicated his lack of conviction in the matter by his willingness to accept an amendment by which the Cabinet members on the board were excluded from participation in the board's regulatory functions, and remained there merely to participate in the administration of the ship purchase program.

On the other hand, the argument against ex-officio membership was cogently developed. Shipping interests and businessmen generally wanted a 'nonpartisan' board, a euphemistic way of describing a bipartisan board. To place two Cabinet Secretaries on the board would tend to make it a political organization, and even if the board itself remained free from political influence the public generally would think it was politically controlled. In the House debate Mr. Hadley of Washington said:

. . . We ought to have one [shipping board] that will not be in any way shadowed with the suspicion of political control in the minds of the people of the country. I do not believe you can divorce that thought from the public mind if you constitute the board so that the voting power preponderates politically, as you provide in this case.[12]

Senator Jones expressed the same idea:

Mr. President, I think that the majority have made a very wise amendment in striking from this board the Secretary of the Navy and the Secretary of Commerce. If we are going to have a shipping

11. Ibid. 12557.   12. Ibid. 8279.

board, it ought to be one entirely free from politics; as free as it possibly can be. It ought to be entirely free of having as a part of its membership a purely political officer. It would be just as much out of place to have the Secretary of War a member of the Interstate Commerce Commission as to have any departmental officer on this board. The committee and the caucus did very wisely, I think, in cutting this provision out of the bill, and I hope that will be insisted upon when the bill goes to conference. The people will certainly have much more confidence in the impartiality of this board if there is not a Cabinet officer on it than if it has Cabinet officers in its membership.[13]

It was pointed out by both Mr. Hadley and Mr. Fess that Cabinet-officer membership would virtually nullify the bipartisan division on the board since, under normal circumstances, it would allow a President during one term to name five out of seven members for political purposes if he wished to do so.[14] Senator Weeks pointed out that Cabinet officers were an integral part of the political organization of the Administration. He said:

. . . Then, necessarily, the members of the administration are parts of a political organization, and it is impossible when a Secretary of the Treasury or a Secretary of Commerce or any other member of a Cabinet is a member of a board that that fact shall not have some influence on the activities of the board. Such boards like the shipping board, if they are going to be of any value at all, must be entirely removed from the immediate political influence which happens to be in control of the Government.[15]

It was urged that the political complexion which the board would acquire as a result of ex-officio membership was incompatible with the proper performance of its quasi-judicial duties. Mr. Mann of Illinois declared that it was dangerous to give regulatory or quasi-judicial work to partisan appointees.[16] Mr. Hadley criticized an arrangement which permitted the Cabinet members on the board to sit in judgment upon some of the interests of their own departments.[17] It was rather generally urged that the ex-officio members on the board would make it an entirely different body from the Interstate Commerce Com-

13. Ibid. 12447.   16. Ibid. 8078.
14. Ibid. 8285.   17. Ibid. 8279.
15. Ibid. 12557.

mission and that there was no more justification for such ex-officio members in one case than in the other.

It was felt that the presence of two Cabinet Secretaries on the board would dangerously increase Presidential authority over it. Mr. Towner of Iowa said that 'it is impossible for members of the Cabinet to sit in any board and not act as political representative of the administration.' [18] Mr. Fess of Ohio elaborated the same point and referred to the dominating control which he alleged that President Wilson had been able to establish over the Federal Reserve Board.[19]

It was pointed out that Cabinet Secretaries change with changing administrations and often more frequently. This would make it impossible for the board to establish and maintain continuity and certainty in policy and administration, and capital would be likely to avoid the risks incident to regulation by a board with a rapidly fluctuating membership. In view of the constant turnover in the personnel of the Shipping Board during the following fifteen years, without any ex-officio members, there is a certain irony in the seriousness with which this point was made.

A very persuasive argument against ex-officio membership was that Cabinet Secretaries would not have time to participate in the actual work of the board. The tasks to be given to the board were of appalling size and complexity. The regulatory functions of the board demanded, as in the case of the Interstate Commerce Commission and the Federal Trade Commission, the day-by-day attendance of the members in the hearing and deciding of cases. No Cabinet Secretary could spare so much time, and certainly he should not be allowed to help decide a case in which he did not sit. It was this objection which led Mr. Alexander of Missouri, whose bill included ex-officio Cabinet members, to propose that the Cabinet members should not share in the regulatory work of the board at all.[20] It was not surprising that the ex-officio membership clause was eliminated in the Senate and no serious attempt was made to restore it.

18. Ibid. 8282.   20. Ibid. 8280.
19. Ibid. 8285.

c. Qualifications of board members

The discussion of the qualifications which should be required for membership on the proposed board was similar to that regarding the make-up of the Federal Reserve Board, though much less extensive. Businessmen urged that the board be composed of men experienced in shipping. No objection to this was expressed, but many doubted whether a statutory requirement would ensure the selection of specially trained people. Mr. Alexander said that limitations of this kind upon the President's power of appointment had not been particularly effective.[21] The Act as finally passed merely provided that members should 'be appointed with due regard to their fitness for the efficient discharge of the duties imposed on them by this Act.' In view of later developments it is a little surprising that no attempt was made to secure the direct representation on the board of geographical areas. Perhaps these sectional interests were not at this time fully aware of the implications of the Act. In any event the statute provided merely that members be appointed with due regard 'to a fair representation of the geographical divisions of the country.'

d. Merging of regulatory and managerial powers

Only a few members of Congress drew attention to the conflict of interests involved in the board's duties by which the same agency was to regulate shipping and to own and perhaps to operate ships. The point seemed to make little impression. Criticism of this combination of duties was chiefly directed against its economic consequences rather than against any alleged violation of the principle of sound governmental organization. Senator Weeks, however, was seriously disturbed by this situation. He declared:

That would be the case if we owned one railroad and put it in the hands of the Interstate Commerce Commission to operate in competition with privately operated roads. They would feel a pressure which would compel the reduction of rates on the Government

21. Hearings before the House Committee on Merchant Marine and Fisheries on H.R. 10500, 64th Cong., 1st sess. (1916), 470 f.

line and which would probably affect the rates made for privately owned lines, so that all such investments would be unprofitable.

The same result will obtain in the case of shipping, if we buy ships and operate them under the control of a board, the board at the same time controlling the operations of privately owned ships directly in competition with them. We are going to have the result of a dual operation, a conflicting operation, and one in which the Government's investments are going to bring a less and less return as the pressure for lower rates continues.[22]

And Senator Cummins, who believed the whole ship purchase program to be unconstitutional, said:

I would be opposed to the regulation of such commerce in this bill, even if there were no other reason than the one I have given; but there is another reason, and it is fundamental, and no matter how the bill might be amended, it would compel me to vote against it. The Government is attempting to do two contradictory things in this proposed law. It is, first, endeavoring to regulate water commerce by undertaking the commerce itself, by acquiring ships with the right to operate them under certain conditions, or to charter them to others, attaching such restrictions and limitations as it may see fit to attach for their operation. That is one way we are attempting to regulate water commerce in this measure. Not content with that, we immediately proceed to regulate all ships through a system of declarations concerning what they may do or what they may not do, and conferring power upon the shipping board to enforce such regulations.[23]

e. *The relation of the board to the President*

The hearings and debates throw little light upon the President's relation to the proposed board. The Administration itself, as we have seen, felt that it had interests in the board's work which required the presence on it of the Secretaries of the Navy and of Commerce; and Secretary of Commerce Redfield before the House committee spoke of the proposed shipping board as 'under the constant guardianship of the Executive and of Congress.' [24] There were numerous vague references in the debates to the 'independence' of the proposed board without any attempt to define that independence; and it was

22. 53 Cong. Rec. 12558.
23. Ibid. 12797.

24. *Supra*, note 21, op. cit. 132.

often stated that in its regulatory work at least the board would be similar to the Interstate Commerce Commission. There was no discussion of the removal clause, obviously borrowed from the Interstate Commerce Act, providing that members of the shipping board should be removed by the President for inefficiency, neglect of duty, or malfeasance in office. It should be borne in mind that at this time the only relevant judicial interpretation of the President's removal power was to be found in the Shurtleff case,[25] in which the Court had held that the statement in a statute of specific causes for removal did not limit the President's removal power to those causes or preclude supplementary discretionary removals.

It is exceedingly interesting to observe that in the original bill and in the final Act the new board, whatever 'independence' it was supposed to have, was obliged to perform its more important managerial duties under the direction of or with the approval of the President. It was to acquire ships as naval auxiliaries with his approval. It was to sell or lease these ships to private citizens upon conditions which he approved. With his approval it was to sell stock in the corporation set up to carry out the ship purchase program, and if the board was unable to sell its ships it was to report to the President, who was to determine finally its inability to do so and order operation of the ships by a corporation set up under the Act. Thus it is impossible to allege that the Shipping Board was created to be an 'arm of Congress' wholly free from Presidential control.

B. THE MERCHANT MARINE ACT OF 1920

1. BACKGROUND OF THE ACT OF 1920

a. *The war emergency and the 'bridge to France'*

In spite of the zeal of the Administration to secure the passage of the Shipping Board Act, it was not until March 15, 1917, just before our entrance into the War, that the President completed the organization of the Shipping Board. In April this board, designed to exercise a limited regulatory power over peace-time shipping and to build forty or fifty auxiliary vessels as the nucleus of an American merchant marine, found itself

25. *Shurtleff* v. *United States*, 189 U.S. 311 (1903).

faced with the stupendous task of building 'the bridge to France.' Ten days after war was declared, the Emergency Fleet Corporation was set up to take over direction of the shipbuilding program. Congress promptly passed a law authorizing the acquisition of enemy ships interned in American ports.[26] On June 15, 1917, the President was authorized to requisition shipyards and ships at his discretion,[27] a power which he promptly delegated to the Shipping Board. This authorization was accompanied at the outset by an appropriation of $750,000,000 in contrast to the $50,000,000 originally planned. This was later increased to $2,884,000,000 and the figure finally passed $3,250,-000,000. This was more than twice the value of the world's entire seagoing commercial fleet before the War. The task assumed by the Shipping Board through the agency of the Fleet Corporation was the largest single task undertaken by the government during the War. The effect of this upon the other duties of the board was, of course, virtually to extinguish them. In its first annual report the Shipping Board stated:

The function of the Board, as contemplated by the Shipping Act, is essentially one of regulation, but since the entry of the United States into the war, and particularly since the delegation by the President of his powers under the urgent deficiencies appropriation act of June 15, 1917, the regulatory functions of the Board, as heretofore noted, have been subordinated to the exigencies of construction and operation.[28]

And it stated also: 'The Board in the exercise of these newly delegated powers acts solely as the agent of the President.' [29]

b. *Administrative confusion and mismanagement*

No more cogent argument can be found against the delegation of complex managerial duties to a board working under conditions of divided responsibility than the record of the United States Shipping Board and the Emergency Fleet Corporation. This record presents a sorry story of conflict of policy, divided control, and inadequate supervision. To begin with,

26. Act of May 12, 1917, 40 Stat. at L. 75.
27. Act of June 15, 1917, 40 Stat. at L. 182.
28. First Ann. Rept. of the U. S. Shipping Board (1917), 22.
29. Ibid. 6.

the board and the corporation had serious difficulties with personnel. There was rapid turnover in the membership of the board and in the staff of the corporation. This was due partly to the difficulty in securing the men desired, and partly to the resignations of men dissatisfied with the administrative set-up under which they had to work. The President persuaded General Goethals, the builder of the Panama Canal, to become general manager of the Emergency Fleet Corporation. Mr. William Denman was chairman of the Shipping Board. Conflict and misunderstanding between these two high officials finally forced the President to demand the resignations of both. It was perhaps natural for the manager of the Emergency Fleet Corporation to assume something approaching dictatorial powers in the hope of getting immediate and substantial results, and he chafed under the supervision which the Shipping Board, in the proper assumption of its own responsibilities, felt it necessary to exercise. The fact is, of course, that the administrative arrangements were wholly unsuitable to the performance of the task in hand.

The Shipping Board decided to acquire the vessels needed for war purposes by letting contracts to private builders rather than by having the government build them. There was bitter dispute over this, into the merits of which we need not go. It is clear, however, that the contract system proved slow, laborious, and costly, and presented a constant temptation to waste and corruption. A shipbuilding program was plotted for the acquisition of 18,000,000 tons dead weight of ships, and less than one-sixth of this was delivered before the end of the War.

The terrific pressure for immediate results led to a failure to maintain the normal checks upon financial operations which should surround any well-directed business operation.

Paper work and records, checking and investigation, were reduced to a minimum. Not until conditions had become so serious that the Treasury was threatening to withhold the grant of funds was a workable accounting system established. But it was then so far behind that it failed to achieve a current record by the time the war was over. Neither the members of the Board and the Corporation nor their staff knew where the Board's funds were, who was spending them and what they were spent for. It was not surprising that this situation was taken advantage of by the 'get-rich-quick' philosophy of the period. When Congressional investigating committees got busy—and they soon did—they were able to fill page after page with examples of padded contracts, excess charges and outright defalcations. Many of them went undetected by the Shipping Board members, who acted in good faith but had no time to make inquiries.[30]

Congressional discussions of the yearly appropriations for the support of the shipbuilding program revealed sharply the difficulty of getting any coherent information out of the Shipping Board or the Fleet Corporation regarding the details of its business management. All of this, of course, provided ammunition for the use of those who were basically opposed to government ownership and operation.

c. *The political reaction of 1918—Republican gains in Congress*

The Congressional election of 1918 registered a sharp reaction against the Wilson Administration. It was a forerunner of the 'return to normalcy' of 1920. It returned to power in both houses of Congress the group most bitterly opposed to government ownership and operation of shipping or anything else. With the end of the War there came the same pressure to force the government out of the shipping business as brought about the return of the railroads to private operation. But the problems involved were strikingly different. It was relatively simple to hand the railroads back to their owners. It was not at all simple for the government to unload a vast fleet of ships which had never been privately owned. Coupled with this drive against government ownership was the sharp reaction against the centralized emergency war-time powers of the President.

2. STEPS IN THE LEGISLATIVE HISTORY OF THE MERCHANT MARINE ACT OF 1920

During 1919 several bills appeared in the House to amend the Act of 1916 and to repeal war legislation. That introduced by Mr. Greene of Massachusetts was most thoroughly consid-

30. From an unpublished memorandum prepared for this study by John F. Miller.

ered.[31] By its provisions a mass of emergency war legislation and executive orders was to be repealed and the President's power over shipping transferred to the Shipping Board. The board was directed to sell its ships to American citizens 'in order that the merchant vessels now owned or controlled by the United States may be returned to or placed under private ownership and operation.' The Greene bill after scant debate passed the House on November 8, 1919, by a vote of 240 to 8. The Senate was now controlled by the Republicans and the bill went to the Senate Committee on Commerce, of which Senator Wesley Jones of Washington was chairman. Long hearings were held at which the shipping lobby was particularly active in presenting its claims and policies. It found willing ears, for the committee itself believed that the time was ripe for legislation designed to promote that private ownership of a substantial merchant marine which had been thwarted for so long. The committee drastically recast the Greene bill to strengthen it along these lines. In spite of its major importance it was debated in the Senate briefly and without any serious discussion of its major provisions, and with merely minor changes it passed the Senate without record vote on May 21, 1920. The rush for adjournment so that members might engage in the important political campaign already under way prevented the bill from receiving anything like the intelligent consideration it deserved. There was some opposition in the House to the drastic changes made by the Senate, but the bill came back from conference with most of the Senate provisions intact. A second reference to a conference committee produced little in the way of change. The bill passed the Senate on June 4 by a 40 to 11 vote, with 45 senators not voting, and on the same day passed the House by a vote of 145 to 120 with 158 members not voting. It was approved by the President on June 5, 1920.

3. PROVISIONS OF THE ACT OF 1920

The Merchant Marine Act of 1920 [32] may be summarized as follows: First, it announced the policy of Congress to maintain a fully adequate merchant marine in private hands, and it

31. H.R. 10378, 66th Cong., 1st sess. (1919).
32. Act of June 5, 1920, 41 Stat. at L. 988.

charged the Shipping Board with the duty of adhering to this general policy in the execution of its various functions. Second, it repealed a mass of war legislation affecting shipping, transferred emergency powers from the President to the Shipping Board, and with some minor exceptions ended the government construction and purchase of ships. Third, important powers were conferred upon the Shipping Board instituting various discriminations against foreign ships in favor of American ships. Fourth, it conferred upon the board broad discretion to sell and to operate the American fleet on such terms as the board 'might deem wise for the promotion and maintenance of an efficient merchant marine.' Preference was to be given to American citizens in the sale of vessels, and the board was authorized to maintain or establish trade routes upon which it might itself operate ships or sell or charter such vessels to private persons for operation. Fifth, the board retained all previous regulatory powers and some of these were extended. Sixth, the organization of the board was changed. It was increased to seven and the representation of definite geographical divisions was required in the appointment of its members. The President was to designate the chairman of the board although the board itself was to name a vice-chairman. There was no change in the clause authorizing the President to remove members of the board for inefficiency, neglect of duty, or malfeasance in office.

4. ISSUES AND TOPICS IN HEARINGS AND DEBATES

The Act of 1920 was much less adequately discussed than was that of 1916. Much of the discussion it did receive centered around the crucial problem of government ownership and operation of the fleet, and there was much comment on the vastness of the government's investment and the heavy losses which had been incurred. There was very little consideration of the important administrative problems involved, but we may summarize what there was.

a. *Separation of managerial from regulatory functions*

The question whether to continue the arrangement by which the Shipping Board exercised regulatory powers over the merchant marine and at the same time owned and managed a substantial part of it escaped consideration in the Congressional debates. It was discussed, however, by a number of witnesses before the Senate and House committees, and several proposals were made to place these functions into separate hands. Mr. Martin J. Gillen, an 'organization expert' who had been special assistant to the chairman of the Shipping Board, urged that the Fleet Corporation be completely separated from the Shipping Board and given the duty of liquidating the merchant fleet. The Shipping Board should retain the management of such part of the fleet as remained in the government's hands, should exercise regulatory power, and should help formulate our general merchant marine policy.[33] The segregation here suggested is clearly not the separation of regulation from administration, but merely the isolation of the task of selling out the government's interests in the fleet. Other witnesses, however, urged a sharp separation of the regulatory power over shipping from the management and operation of government ships. John B. Payne, chairman of the Shipping Board, was questioned at some length by Senator Jones on this point, but he declared that the existing arrangement was reasonably satisfactory and that the matter of organization was not after all one of much importance.[34] His only concrete suggestion was to reduce the Shipping Board's membership to three. Senator Jones himself was anxious to have all executive functions relating to shipping turned over to the Fleet Corporation. The corporation should be headed by a board of nine men appointed and removable by the President, and should be empowered to employ a highly paid general manager.[35] None of these suggestions found their way into the Act of 1920.

b. *Board organization for managerial duties*

There were a few who urged that a board was inherently incapable of handling efficiently a complicated administrative job.

33. Hearings before the House Select Committee on Shipping Board Operations, 66th Cong., 2d sess. (1920), Part 6, 2359, Part 8, 3197.

34. Hearings before the Senate Committee on Commerce on the Establishment of an American Merchant Marine, 66th Cong., 1st-2d sess. (1919-20), 1880 f.

35. Ibid. 1881. See his bill S. 3356, 66th Cong., 1st sess. (1919).

Mr. Munson of the Munson Lines made the radical suggestion that the Shipping Board should be replaced by an executive department headed by a Cabinet Secretary.[36] This would give centralized responsibility and a close correlation of shipping policy with the policy of the Administration. William Denman, former chairman of the Shipping Board, while not taking so radical a position, criticized board organization for the purpose of operating ships,[37] and Mr. Payne, then Secretary of the Interior, voiced the same opinion. He said:

. . . More than almost any job in this country, the running of a shipping business is an executive job. It is not the job for a commission. And if you have got to decide how a ship shall be allocated by seven men, two from the Pacific, two from the Atlantic, one from the interior, one from the Gulf, you won't do it. Can't do it. You have got to have somebody sitting at the ticker-go! [38]

c. *The organization of the Shipping Board*

The changes finally made in the organization of the Shipping Board received little consideration. The increase in the size of the board was effected without argument or explanation. Senator Jones justified the requirement of regional representation on the board by the stock argument that since the various sections of the country had an interest in our merchant marine policy, they ought to be specifically represented.[39] No one presented the other side of the case. There was desultory comment on the problem of board personnel. It was agreed that excellent men ought to be appointed to the board and that this had not always been done. No one proposed any formula for meeting this situation, although it was suggested that higher salaries might attract better men. Mr. Payne urged before the Senate committee the appointment by the President of a permanent chairman for the board:

. . . My only suggestion would be that there ought to be a permanent chairman appointed as such. Now, the only point about that is that whoever is President would be more careful in the selec-

36. Ibid. 747.
37. *Supra,* note 33, op. cit. Part 8, 3218.
38. Ibid. Part 14, 5199.
39. *Supra,* note 34, op. cit. 1915.

tion of the chairman. Where you have a board of five and the board select their own chairman, the rule of mediocrity necessarily prevails, because every man expects to be chairman. I do not criticize it. I am only talking of results.

. . . I would make a permanent chairman, to be appointed as such, just as the Chief Justice of the Supreme Court is appointed to be the Chief Justice . . . That of itself, by the very fact that he is to be chairman, calls upon the President to . . . select a commanding personality.[40]

d. *Planning by the Shipping Board*

Congress hoped in setting up the Shipping Board to secure from it adequate aid in shaping national policy affecting our merchant marine. The board was to be a planning agency making recommendations to Congress upon the basis of its familiarity with the whole shipping problem. Repeated resolutions in the Senate and the House called upon the board for advice and recommendation of this kind. As time went on it became increasingly clear that this planning service could not be rendered by an agency loaded down with the vast administrative responsibilities carried by the Shipping Board. The board's failure to function effectively as a planning agency was repeatedly criticized in Congress, and Senator Jones urged as a major reason for relieving the Shipping Board of its executive duties that the board would then be able to give Congress the help that it needed in the field of planning.[41]

e. *Relations of the Shipping Board to the President and to Congress*

The discussions of the Act of 1920 throw little light upon Congressional ideas as to the relation of the Shipping Board to Congress and to the President. During the War the board, like nearly everything else, was regarded as an agent of the President in the exercise of his vast war powers. The Act put an end to that and freed the board from direct Presidential control, but there was no discussion of the theory underlying the change. It is interesting to note, however, that Congress felt

40. Ibid. 1881 and 1915.   41. Ibid. 595 f.

somewhat uneasy over the broad delegations of power to the independent Shipping Board and its agent, the Fleet Corporation. This uneasiness was expressed from time to time in Senate or House resolutions asking the Shipping Board to delay some projected sale or the letting of some projected contract until the legislative body could secure more information and express its approval or disapproval. This indicates the inherent difficulty of effective legislative control of a managerial agency endowed with the complex responsibilities given to the Shipping Board.

C. THE DRIVE FOR SEGREGATION OF REGULATORY FROM OPERATING FUNCTIONS—1920 TO 1928

Without following in detail the hectic fortunes of the Shipping Board under the Act of 1920, we may survey the vigorous drive made during this period to segregate the operating functions of the board, carried on through the Fleet Corporation, from its regulatory and advisory functions. The story includes the effort made by the President to dominate the Shipping Board and its policies, and the bitter controversy over the proposed segregation of the board's functions. These two elements in the picture are important, though neither was successful.

1. SHIPPING BOARD DEVELOPMENTS DURING THE PERIOD

The new Shipping Board provided for by the Act of 1920 was not immediately set up. Nominations to the board made by President Wilson immediately after the passage of the Act were not confirmed by the Senate before adjournment, and Wilson's later recess appointments expired on March 4, 1921. Admiral Benson, who had been named as chairman of the board by Wilson and who was a federal officer anyway, held over under an agreement with President Harding until the new members could be appointed. This was finally accomplished on June 13, 1921. The new chairman of the board was Albert D. Lasker, a former advertising man. Harding, who had long been interested in merchant marine problems, undertook to dominate the policies of the Shipping Board through his close friendship with Lasker and through direct contacts with the board itself. Harding was a vigorous advocate of direct subsidies for American shipping and for more than a year he and Lasker carried on a vigorous drive to secure subsidy legislation. A subsidy bill finally passed the House in November 1922, but in spite of two Presidential messages and the calling of a special session the Administration was unable to secure its final enactment.

If the President's policies were to control the operations of the fleet, it was obvious that the Fleet Corporation must be given greater autonomy than was provided by the statute. Accordingly, on September 30, 1921, the Shipping Board, under Presidential pressure, passed a resolution making the Emergency Fleet Corporation a practically independent administrative and operating agency. This resolution declared that in the opinion of the board

the executive and personnel organization of the Emergency Fleet Corporation has been completed to such a standard of efficiency as to make it desirable that the United States Shipping Board should exercise through the United States Shipping Board Emergency Fleet Corporation various administrative powers and functions, thus making it possible for the United States Shipping Board to devote its attention to the study and determination of the broad and constructive questions of policy relating to the maintenance, development and encouragement of the American Merchant Marine, under the powers and duties imposed upon the United States Shipping Board by law.[42]

Accordingly, the chairman of the Shipping Board withdrew as president of the corporation and the members of the board withdrew as trustees. A list of the specific functions assigned to the Fleet Corporation was placed in the resolution. However, this segregation rested upon a somewhat unstable basis, for the board required the president and the trustees of the Fleet Corporation to deposit with them at the time of their appointment undated resignations. By this device the board retained power to recover complete control over the corporation at a moment's notice.

In August 1923 Mr. Coolidge became President, and at his request the board appointed Admiral Palmer president of the

42. Quoted in Hearings before the House Select Committee to Inquire into the . . . Shipping Board and . . . Emergency Fleet Corporation Pursuant to H. Res. 186, 68th Cong., 1st sess. (1924), Exhibits to Testimony, Part 7, 160.

Fleet Corporation, and the resolution of 1921 was so amended as to give the corporation control over its personnel and the settlement of claims. Almost simultaneously certain events set in motion the long and vigorous drive for the complete removal of the operating duties of the Fleet Corporation from the control of the Shipping Board. Serious friction arose between Admiral Palmer and the board. The board accused Palmer of exceeding his authority and of refusal to obey its orders and directions; Palmer replied that the efficient management of the fleet was obstructed by interference on the part of the Shipping Board contrary to the understanding under which he had assumed the presidency of the corporation. President Coolidge threw his support to Palmer. So bitter did the fight become that in March 1924 the House set up a select committee 'to inquire into the operations, policies and affairs of the United States Shipping Board and the United States Emergency Fleet Corporation.' This committee conducted an exhaustive investigation.[43] It produced five volumes of testimony and six volumes of supporting data. The witnesses were mainly officials of either the board or the corporation. The general public was not drawn in. The committee dealt mainly with matters of fleet operation rather than the problem of administrative organization. All of the witnesses wished to improve the relations between the board and the corporation, but only Admiral Palmer proposed to make the corporation wholly independent of the board. The committee submitted its report to the House of Representatives in December 1925.[44] It was divided four to three, and the minority filed a vigorous report of its own.

In the meantime the President was trying to effect the separation of the Fleet Corporation from the Shipping Board. He had urged this briefly in his annual message in December 1924,[45] and he repeated the recommendation with greater fervor in the annual message of 1925.[46] This additional fervor is explained in terms of a fight between the President and the Shipping Board in the summer and fall of 1925 over the

43. Ibid.
44. H. Rept. 2, 69th Cong., 1st sess. (1925).
45. 66 Cong. Rec. 54, *infra,* 260.
46. 67 Cong. Rec. 462, *infra,* 261,

board's determination to remove Admiral Palmer from the presidency of the Fleet Corporation, a result which could be readily enough accomplished by filing his undated letter of resignation. Palmer was, in fact, removed in this way on October 6, 1925. The central figure in the controversy between the board and the President was Bert E. Haney, a Democratic member of the board, originally appointed by President Harding. Haney's term expired and President Coolidge, obligated by the statutory requirement of bipartisanship to appoint a Democrat, gave Haney a recess appointment in June 1925. Haney and the President had some conversation at the time of the appointment, the exact nature of which became a matter of dispute later on. Haney had never approved of Palmer's management of the fleet, and upon securing what seemed to him to be fresh evidence of Palmer's disregard of the public interest he started an active campaign in the board to have Palmer removed. The President thereupon telegraphed to Haney on August 27, 1925, as follows:

> It having come to my attention that you are proposing to remove Admiral Palmer contrary to the understanding I had with you when I reappointed you, your resignation . . . is requested.[47]

Haney denied any such understanding as that referred to by the President, pointed out that the President must have known of his hostility toward Palmer, and flatly refused to resign.[48] A few weeks later the chairman of the Shipping Board, T. V. O'Connor, at the direction of the board wrote to the President bluntly stating that while the board at the President's request had given the Fleet Corporation a good deal of independence, the board now proposed, after study of the whole situation, 'to resume full and exclusive control of the Emergency Fleet Corporation.' [49] Here was open defiance of the President's wishes, and it obviously strengthened his determination to free the corporation from the domination of the board.

The President's position found support in other quarters. In his message of 1925 he referred to an elaborate report on

47. 67 Cong. Rec. 1944.
48. Ibid. Letter of Aug. 28. *The New York Times* of Sept. 2 in an editorial said: 'The spectacle of a member of the board refusing to resign when asked to do so by the President and questioning his veracity . . . is not pleasant.'
49. 67 Cong. Rec. 1949.

the subject by Henry G. Dalton, an experienced administrator, whom he had asked to investigate the whole problem. The Dalton report [50] strongly urged segregation. Meanwhile an interdepartmental committee, appointed in March 1924 by the President, under the chairmanship of Secretary Hoover filed a report also urging the segregation of the functions of the Shipping Board.[51] In 1925 the United States Chamber of Commerce held a National Merchant Marine Conference, which filed a report approving in substance the proposal for segregation made by the interdepartmental committee.[52] In December 1925, three bills were introduced into the House providing for the separation of the Fleet Corporation from the Shipping Board; hearings on them were held by the House Committee on Merchant Marine and Fisheries, and strong Administration influence was placed behind the most comprehensive of them.[53] The committee remained unconverted, however, and the bills were not reported out.

2. THE PRESIDENTIAL DRIVE FOR DOMINATION OF THE SHIPPING BOARD

Since the Shipping Board was set up as an independent agency, it is of interest to explore the extent to which and the methods by which the President, during the period under consideration, attempted to control it. The President's methods were three in number. In the first place, Presidential influence was made effective through the chairman of the board who was appointed by the President. Under the Act of 1916 the board selected its own chairman; under the Act of 1920 the chairman was chosen by the President. There is no question that the President's influence was greatly increased in this way. Admiral Benson testified to this effect before the select committee of the House in 1924. He said:

. . . It was, of course, well understood and well known that the relations between the President and the chairman were intimate and

50. H. Doc. 118, 69th Cong., 1st sess. (1925).
51. Hearings before the House Committee on Merchant Marine and Fisheries on H.R. 5369, H.R. 5395, H.R. 8052, 69th Cong., 1st sess. (1926), 174.
52. Ibid. 71 ff. See *infra*, 259 ff.
53. Ibid. The Administration supported H.R. 8052.

constant, and the board naturally felt that whatever the chairman brought to the board, he was expressing the policies of the President in what the administration wanted. In addition to that, the board more than once, or if not the whole board, members of the board, were called into consultation by the President and he showed his direct and personal interest in trying to develop the situation, and the board felt that the President was, in so far as circumstances would permit, sympathetic with the board in carrying out the policies, etc.[54]

The latter part of the Admiral's testimony describes also a second method by which the President sought to dominate the board, namely, direct contact with its members and the open exercise of the President's personal influence upon them. The President's influence appears to have been very strong. Testifying before the House committee in 1926, Malcolm M. Stewart, manager of the foreign trade department of the Cincinnati Chamber of Commerce, stated:

. . . It is not secret that the White House tried to control the Shipping Board. I have copies of letters that the President wrote to the board, one of them, anyhow, where he says, 'This is what I understood you were going to do, and this is exactly what I want done.' [55]

The President, as we have seen,[56] was able to induce the board to pass its resolution of 1921 greatly increasing the autonomy of the Fleet Corporation and allowing a large measure of Presidential control over corporation personnel.

In the third place, the President assumed throughout that he could remove members of the Shipping Board for failure to co-operate with his policies. Chairman Lasker told a group of newspapermen

that the President had advised him that, if any member of that Shipping Board did not go along in harmony with Chairman Lasker in his policies, he—Lasker—should notify the President, and he would discharge such member of the Shipping Board; that the only reason that he appointed any of them, except Mr. Lasker, was because the law required it.[57]

54. *Supra,* note 42, op. cit. Part v, 3765.
55. *Supra,* note 51, op. cit. 288.
56. *Supra,* 250.
57. Statement by Rep. Davis, Tenn., 63 Cong. Rec. 136.

The controversy between President Coolidge and Mr. Haney shows that the President felt himself fully justified in demanding Haney's resignation. It may be noted that the President did not remove Haney upon the latter's refusal to resign, and this may perhaps throw some doubt upon the President's conviction as to his legal power. *The New York Times* of October 11, 1925, stated that the President had asked Attorney General Sargent for an opinion as to the President's power to discipline the Shipping Board, but there is no formal opinion of the Attorney General upon this subject. Perhaps the President felt that he had lost his fight in behalf of Admiral Palmer anyhow, and in any event Haney's recess appointment would expire automatically if he did nothing further about it. It seems clear, however, that both Harding and Coolidge believed that they could properly use the removal power as a means of dominating Shipping Board policy. It may be noted further that neither of these threats of Presidential removal brought out any Congressional protest grounded on constitutional principles. Coolidge was sharply criticized for his action in the Haney case, but his critics did not suggest that he did not have the power to do what he had set out to do. That he did have such power seems to have been assumed by Senator Hitchcock, who charged the board with trying to wreck government ownership and operation of ships and who declared it to be the duty of the President 'to install a Shipping Board composed of men who will carry out the purposes of the Jones Act of 1920.' [58]

Congress, however, did not peacefully acquiesce in the President's attempt to control the board. The Act of 1920 had stripped the President of his emergency war powers, and throughout the period under consideration there was steady and vigorous minority criticism of the President's efforts to dominate the Shipping Board. While this came mainly from the Democratic side, it represented more than the normal opposition to a policy of the dominant party. Senator Ransdell of Louisiana declared that the Shipping Board was a creature of Congress and was responsible not to the President but to Congress.[59] Senator McDuffie of Alabama insisted that Congress rather than the President should decide how much authority

---

58. 64 Cong. Rec. 4742.   59. Ibid. 599.

should be delegated by the Shipping Board to the Fleet Corporation.[60] Senator Dill of Washington made a long and bitter attack upon the President's action in the Haney affair. He spread upon the record all of the facts and documents relating to the matter and stated the issue between Congress and the President as follows:

> . . . There is a question, as I see the situation, that is more vital and far more important than the question of the qualifications of the personnel of the Shipping Board or of the President of the Fleet Corporation, and the question—or at least one phase of it—is this: 'May the Chief Executive of the Nation control, by understandings or otherwise, the action and conduct of the Shipping Board or other organizations created by Congress for proper governmental purposes? And may such control be had, or the actions and conduct of such agencies established by Congress be influenced by understandings between the Chief Executive and the members of such agencies, in advance of their appointment or prior to their confirmation by the Senate?' Indeed, the question involved is, 'Shall governmental agencies created by Congress to carry out governmental purposes, with duties and policies prescribed by Congress, be controlled by the Chief Executive, and the judgment and discretion of the individuals charged by Congress to execute the law be influenced, circumscribed, or limited by the Chief Executive, or shall the members of such boards so created be permitted to exercise their judgment and the discretion which the law gives to them?'
> . . . How many other members have been appointed to the Shipping Board or to other boards and commissions which the President desires to influence or control after secret understandings?
> . . . The very fact that the President himself says there was such an understanding in the case of this member of the Shipping Board reveals a situation which becomes extremely objectionable and extremely dangerous, as I see it, to the independence of such commissions.[61]

He was supported by Senator Norris, who declared:

> . . . To my mind it is not so much that the President feels that he is entitled to control the workings of the board, although I do not believe that that is the spirit of the law at all; but the particular case illustrates something that it seems to me is much more dangerous than that—that he was controlling it by a secret understanding with its members that the country knew nothing about.[62]

60. 66 Cong. Rec. 2674.　　　　　62. Ibid.
61. 67 Cong. Rec. 1946.

Senator Fletcher expressed the same point of view and stated his opinion of the purpose and status of the independent commissions:

This shows that the purpose of Congress was to keep in office a continuing board, not to go out when the President went out, not under the control and dictation of the President at all, but a board selected with due regard to their fitness for the efficient discharge of the duties imposed upon them . . .

They were not to be rubber stamps of the Executive at all. There is no purpose in the world in making this territorial distribution of representation on the board if the President can reach an understanding with each member or appoint members of the board to do certain things. There is no purpose in the world in having their terms expire at different times, there is no purpose in the world in making them bipartisan, if they are simply to carry out the orders and directions of the Executive. The whole object of the act is set aside if any such idea is to prevail that the Executive shall lay down policies and shall see that those policies are carried out by dictation with reference to the use and disposition of the ships, the Shipping Board, and with reference to the Fleet Corporation or its president, or any other method is to prevail that overrules the purpose of Congress as clearly set out in the act.[63]

Senator King joined in the attack by criticizing President Harding's policy in dominating the Shipping Board through Chairman Lasker, a policy which he declared had reduced the other members of the board to figureheads.[64] Senator Edge of New Jersey declared that the 'independent agencies of the Government should be absolutely free from Executive domination, much less control.' [65]

Whatever Congress may have thought about Presidential control of the Shipping Board, it was forced by very practical considerations to realize the definite limitations under which any Congressional control could be made effective. Repeated efforts by the appropriations committees and other committees of Congress to secure accurate and adequate information with regard to the vast government interests confided to the Shipping Board were met in some cases by delay, in some cases by evasion, and in some cases by what amounted to flat refusal.

63. Ibid. 1947 f.   65. Ibid. 1954.
64. Ibid. 1949.

Representative Davis of Tennessee declared that the board had declined to give certain information asked for by a committee of the House and had justified refusal on the ground that 'it was not in the interest of public policy.' [66] Such an attitude upon the part of an independent agency presumed to be responsible to Congress provides food for much interesting speculation. Senator La Follette vigorously attacked the board for refusing to give information to Congress on request:

MR. LA FOLLETTE [of Wisconsin].   . . . Congress up to the present time has been denied full and definite information concerning the cause of those losses or the ships or lines upon which they have occurred. The Shipping Board—and I undertake to say that this information will startle Senators who are within the sound of my voice—flatly refused that information to Congress, as I read the record . . .

MR. DIAL [of South Carolina]. It occurs to me that if the Shipping Board had kept books they could have furnished the information sought.

MR. LA FOLLETTE. An examination of the testimony I think will convince anybody that the information could have been furnished, but it was not the purpose of the Shipping Board to uncover the facts. That has been the attitude of that Shipping Board ever since it has been in office; but more of that will, I think, appear later in the debate on this bill.

After an attempt to deceive the committee into the belief that the Shipping Board did not have the figures in question, a summary was finally produced before the committee giving the aggregate but not the detailed figures, and the detailed figures were flatly refused . . .

The fact is that the Congress is being asked to legislate upon a subject it knows nothing about and upon which it has been denied the very information necessary to enable it to act intelligently. [67]

That Congress wanted the President to have some responsibility in Shipping Board affairs is shown by the interesting provision in the Appropriation Act of February 11, 1927, [68] and in two subsequent acts which were identical. [69] A $10,000,000 appropriation was made to enable the Fleet Corporation to operate ships or lines of ships taken back from purchasers for

66. 63 Cong. Rec. 146.
67. 64 Cong. Rec. 514 f.
68. 44 Stat. at L. 1069 at 1082.
69. Act of May 16, 1928, 45 Stat. at L. 573 at 586; Act of Feb. 20, 1929, 45 Stat. at L. 1230 at 1244.

certain reasons; but the proviso was added that 'no expenditure shall be made for the purposes of this paragraph from this sum without the prior approval of the President of the United States.' Presidential and not Shipping Board approval is required. The proviso seems to imply the inevitability and desirability of Presidential supervision of fleet operations.

3. THE ISSUE OF SEGREGATION OF FUNCTIONS

A fairly substantial body of opinion favored the segregation of the functions vested in the Shipping Board and accepted the basic principle that the quasi-judicial job of regulation should be separated from the complicated administrative task of operating the fleet. Several plans for such segregation were proposed.

First, it was proposed to keep the Shipping Board as a regulatory and advisory body, and to place the Fleet Corporation under the direct control of the President. This should be done by vesting the ownership of the corporation stock in the President, thereby giving him authority to appoint the president of the corporation and the trustees. This was the plan urged by Admiral Palmer,[70] proposed by President Coolidge in his two annual messages,[71] and recommended in the Dalton report[72] and in the minority report of the select House committee.[73] A second proposal left the Shipping Board an independent, quasi-judicial body but transferred the Fleet Corporation bodily to the Department of Commerce. This plan was proposed in the Senate by Senators King, McKellar, and Walsh. A third proposal provided for a triple segregation of Shipping Board functions. The Shipping Board, reduced to three members, would remain an independent quasi-judicial body. The Fleet Corporation, either under Presidential control as a corporation or in the status of a new Cabinet department, would continue the administrative and operating functions as handled by the Fleet Corporation. All promotional and investigational duties would go to the Department of Commerce. This plan was proposed by the interdepartmental committee of which Secretary

70. *Supra*, 251.
71. *Supra*, 251, *infra*, 260 f.
72. *Supra*, 253.
73. *Supra*, note 44, op. cit. 58.

Hoover was chairman, was at once favored by the United States Chamber of Commerce, and was incorporated in those bills introduced in the 69th Congress which received the most serious consideration.[74] A fourth plan was almost identical with the last, but proposed the abolition of the Shipping Board and the transfer of its regulatory duties to the Interstate Commerce Commission.[75] These proposals do not differ in basic principle. While calling for different varieties of administrative structure, each demands the sharp separation of the quasi-judicial regulatory job from the administrative task of fleet operation.

a. *Arguments for segregation*

The arguments supporting the proposed segregation of Shipping Board functions may be summarized as follows:

In the first place, the board form of organization is ill-adapted to the operation of a vast business. Such a task demands a single-headed organization with direct responsibility. This was the first and perhaps basic argument of all those who urged that the management of the fleet be segregated from the regulatory responsibilities of the Shipping Board. The minority report of the House select committee stated:

> Your committee members joining in these views also believe that a board of seven men, representing various sections of the United States, and both political parties, with all members having equal authority, is not a proper organization for the efficient handling of a great business enterprise . . . We do not believe that such a board of joint and of divided responsibilities is properly constituted to pass upon the details of such a vast business as the shipping operations of the United States.[76]

President Coolidge in his message in 1924 declared:

> . . . It has been demonstrated time and again that this form of organization results in indecision, division of opinion and administrative functions, which make a wholly inadequate foundation for the conduct of a great business enterprise.[77]

74. *Supra,* 253.
75. An alternative plan proposed by the U. S. Chamber of Commerce; *supra,* 253.
76. *Supra,* note 44, op. cit. 56.
77. 66 Cong. Rec. 54, *supra,* 251.

And in his message in 1925, he added:

I do not advocate the elimination of regional considerations, but it has become apparent that without centralized executive action the management of this great business, like the management of any other great business, will flounder in incapacity and languish under a division of council. A plain and unmistakable reassertion of this principle of unified control, which I have always been advised was the intention of the Congress to apply, is necessary to increase the efficiency of our merchant fleet.[78]

The report of the United States Chamber of Commerce on the National Merchant Marine Conference in 1925 declared:

A board of seven men may sit in judgment upon the acts of those who are entrusted with administrative responsibility and they may regulate the services and charges of carriers or corporations engaged in transportation, but such a board is not the logical agency for the effective administration of difficult executive tasks.[79]

In 1921 Senator Borah vigorously urged one-man responsibility for the administration of fleet operations. He said:

. . . One of the faults of the shipping business so far as it is concerned in the present discussion, in my judgment, is the fact that we have a Shipping Board instead of a single individual upon whom absolute responsibility could be fixed and where we could have unity of action.

. . . We have a Shipping Board of seven members, and we are paying each of them $12,000 a year—that is, $84,000—not for efficiency, not for quick action, not for responsibility, not for unity of action, but to complicate the situation, to delay, to divide responsibility, and to leave the matter in a much worse condition than it would be if we had a single individual at $12,000 a year . . .

As I have said before, Mr. President, it is almost impossible for the Congress of the United States to decline to create offices, and to abolish an office is practically impossible. I realize that. This is not the only commission we have—we have a number. And I want to suggest from the floor to Gen. Dawes, who is now engaged in a great economy campaign, that if he will run through the commissions we have and trim out these commissions and cut them down to where they ought to be, where they are performing executive duties, where they have not any judicial or quasi-judicial functions to perform, he will not only render a service to the Government in the matter of

78. 67 Cong. Rec. 462, *supra*, 251.   79. *Supra*, note 51, op. cit. 107.

economy but he will render a service to the Government in the matter of getting real service from the men who run it.[80]

The same point of view was expressed by Senator Edge in the 69th Congress. He declared:

Personally, if there is sufficient public business—and perhaps there is—for the Shipping Board to be continued as an independent agency of the Government for the regulation of rates and other proper responsibilities, I shall be entirely satisfied to see such a board continued. In that event and for those responsibilities the board should be a judicial board and independent of the President. From the standpoint of the operation of going business, however, I am convinced that the going business of the Government or of a private corporation or individual is of such character that it can not be administered satisfactorily or successfully by a board. I believe such a responsibility in the case of the Government is of the same type, only in a greater degree, as the going business of any other department of the Government, where, through a Cabinet officer or the head of a department, the President's policy is naturally or should be reflected.[81]

Perhaps the most persuasive and elaborate statement of the argument was that made by Secretary Hoover before the House committee in 1926. He said:

The Shipping Board was originally conceived largely for regulation of discriminations and other bad practices in ocean traffic. It was established on a bipartisan and later on a regional basis. Then it was loaded with the most gigantic administrative task ever undertaken by a government—that is the construction and management of $3,000,000,000 worth of shipping. The whole board has, from the necessity of its creation, had equal or independent responsibilities from the nominal administrative head. We have had some seven or eight heads to the organization in its nine years of administrative life. No commercial organization would have survived such changes. I do not believe this form of organization was ever adapted to the task.

The necessarily divided minds of the best board in the world has always resulted in failure in executive work. Every member must have a four-way independent responsibility. He is responsible for every act of the board to the country as a whole, to his particular constituency, to his political party and finally to Congress. There is only one responsibility that he does not have and that is to the

80. 61 Cong. Rec. 5407 f.   81. 67 Cong. Rec. 1955.

President of the United States who, at least under the spirit of the Constitution, should be vested with all administrative authority. Every member of the board, if he had been left alone, could probably have made a success of the merchant marine before now. However, such a set-up of joint and divided responsibility if it comprised the most consummate genius in the world is the negation of possible success in business management and even of the very plan of our Government—that is, that there should be single-headed responsibility in executive and administrative functions.

Just as there should be single-headed responsibility in executive and administrative functions, I believed there should be joint responsibility of several men in all Government functions of a semi-judicial or regulatory order. All these latter functions are deliberative in type whereas most of the functions of business administration require rapidity of decision and singleness of direction.

In the way the Shipping Board has grown up it is to-day in effect solely responsible to Congress and as a matter of fact has repudiated the authority of the President. I do not believe that Congress ever conceived it was undertaking direct responsibility for the administration of the operation of ships, but this is the result to-day. It is one reason why we have made no more progress with our merchant marine than we have.[82]

It was argued in the second place that the division of control and responsibility between the Shipping Board and the Fleet Corporation produced conflict and confusion. In the theory of the law the Fleet Corporation was the servant of the Shipping Board and completely subject to its control, but the board had never been able to make that control thoroughly effective and the conflict between the two bodies contributed to the general mismanagement of the whole enterprise. Admiral Palmer had testified strongly on this point and had urged that single and undivided control of the fleet was essential.[83] Many congressmen felt that no satisfactory results could be expected as long as the friction between the board and the corporation continued, and that it would continue until the two agencies were completely separated.

In the third place it was vigorously urged that since the government itself had entered the shipping business as a competitor, it was highly unfair to private shipping interests to

82. *Supra,* note 51, op. cit. 13 f.
83. *Supra,* note 42, op. cit. Part v, 3920 ff.

have the same governmental authority regulate the industry on the one hand and operate vessels in competition on the other. The minority report of the select committee of the House stressed this point:

> The fundamental objection to giving to the board authority to operate our ships is that the board is primarily a judicial and regulatory body with jurisdiction over all vessels of the United States, whether privately owned or belonging to the government. It is not open to debate that it is wrong in principle for a body with responsibilities of this character over *all* vessels to be directly concerned in the operation of *some* of them.[84]

A fourth argument was urged by Secretary Hoover in the passage quoted. In his view the management of important administrative operations without direct responsibility to the President violates at least the spirit of the Constitution. This is very interesting and appears to put Mr. Hoover on record as doubting the constitutional propriety of conferring upon an independent agency administrative and executive powers.

In the fifth place, not only are boards in general unfitted to manage business enterprises but specifically the Shipping Board was charged with the management of a business about which its members knew little or nothing. They did not have the expert knowledge essential to successful administration. The minority report of the select committee emphasized this:

> . . . It constitutes no reflection upon the present members of the board nor upon their qualification as members of the board, as it was originally conceived to direct attention to the fact that not a single member prior to his appointment had ever had experience in the operation of merchant ships. What justification can there be for turning over to men inexperienced in such respect the responsibility for carrying on so vast, so complicated, and so technical a business as the shipping operations of the United States in world trade.[85]

A sixth argument for segregation stressed the necessity of freeing the Shipping Board from administrative and operating responsibilities so that it might devote its energies to the important task of planning. The Shipping Board's resolution of 1921 justified conferring a measure of administrative autonomy

84. *Supra,* note 44, op. cit. 56.   85. Ibid.

on the Fleet Corporation on this ground.[86] The board would let the corporation operate the fleet so that it might devote itself to problems of policy.

Finally, Senator Jones of Washington defended taking from the Shipping Board the management of the fleet in order to remove that management from immediate range of Congressional interference. The Shipping Board is responsible to Congress; the temptation is strong for Congress to intervene in administrative matters; the results of this upon efficient administration are thoroughly bad. Senator Jones declared:

. . . Mr. President, the bane of Government ownership and operation is the interference of Congress in the administration of the affairs of any governmentally owned proposition. What is one of the great criticisms of this bill? It is that it gives too much power and too much discretion to the Shipping Board, and yet the Panama Railroad Steamship Co. has had absolute and unlimited discretion, and has fixed the salaries of all of its employees; yet we haggle here in the Senate over the salaries of men in the Shipping Board, making provision that no more than so many shall get more than so much, no matter what the needs and requirements may be, and, as I have said, passing resolutions every day disrupting the organization, passing resolutions which mean an expense of thousands of dollars in the preparation of data which comes here printed, and which nobody ever looks at. Talk about running Government business in that kind of way! It can not be done. But if we would give them the power and the discretion which has been given and allowed to the Panama Canal Railroad Steamship Co. there would be some hope of success, I admit.[87]

b. *Arguments against segregation*

Those who opposed the segregation of Shipping Board functions and favored the *status quo* mustered an effective defense of their position and managed to win out in the end. They argued first that the government's interest in the merchant marine was too vast to be safely left in the hands of a single man. As the select committee of the House put it, 'We are not in sympathy with the proposal that this vast and important business should be turned over to any one man, no matter who

86. *Supra,* 250.   87. 64 Cong. Rec. 3321.

that man may be.'[88] Representative Cooper of Wisconsin, whose vote on the select committee made a majority against segregation, urged the danger of centralized executive control. He declared:

> Mr. Chairman, the more I think of this, the more I am reminded that Thomas Jefferson said that 'the Republic of the United States is, in large part, founded upon distrust of men in places of executive power.'[89]

It was pointed out in the second place that many problems connected with the operation of the fleet intimately affected the broad policies governing the whole American merchant marine. These broad policies demanded the careful consideration of a deliberative board. It was not urged that the Shipping Board should itself operate the fleet, but that it must retain effective control of those who do. The select committee of the House declared that the Shipping Board must be independent of executive domination even though the regulatory powers of the board were 'theoretical and ethereal.' The report stated:

> We believe that the ships should be operated by other officials than the Shipping Board, and that such officials should be given a free hand in the administrative features and details of operation. However, we believe that such officials should be appointed by and answerable to the Shipping Board for the execution of the general policies determined by the board.
>
> We likewise believe that the Shipping Board should determine the general policies, prices, and terms for the sale, charter, or operation of our ships.[90]

The rest of the argument against segregation and the executive control of the fleet ran along very familiar lines. Regional interests had to be placated, and that could be effectively managed only through a board upon which geographical regions could be represented. A bipartisan board was necessary to prevent the abuses resulting from partisan domination and partisan patronage. Executive control would jeopardize continuity of policy. The management of the fleet should not be subject to the danger of a complete political turnover in personnel and in policy every four years. Finally, the large eastern ship-

88. *Supra,* note 44, op. cit. 28.   90. *Supra,* note 44, op. cit. 19.
89. 62 Cong. Rec. 1872.

ping interests would find it easier to secure preferences and concessions contrary to the public interest from executive officials than from an independent shipping board. This fear was strong in the minds of those representing the western shipping interests. They felt that their best chances of securing equitable treatment lay in having their own regional representatives in positions of authority.

In spite of the plausibility of their case, in spite of the distinction of those who urged it and the vigor and adroitness with which it was presented, those seeking to separate the quasi-judicial regulatory functions of the Shipping Board from the administrative tasks of the fleet operation failed to win their point. The House bills were never reported out of committee and no legislation was passed.

D. The United States Maritime Commission of 1936

1. THE BACKGROUND OF THE ACT OF 1936

In 1928 the shipping interests, with the encouragement of the Republican Administration, launched a successful drive for ship subsidies. The statute which passed [91] was in fact purely a subsidy measure. It did not change the organization of the Shipping Board or the Fleet Corporation. It increased the construction loan fund and liberalized the terms of repayment. It provided for postal subventions. The Postmaster General certified the mail routes and the Shipping Board specified the types of vessels required. Contracts were made by the Postmaster General. The results of the Subsidy Act of 1928 were extremely unsatisfactory. The Act failed to stimulate the investment of any capital in the shipping industry and the net results in building up our merchant marine were negligible. The temptation to dishonesty and mismanagement in the allotting of subsidies proved too strong to be resisted. A Congressional committee under the chairmanship of Senator Black made a thorough investigation of the administration of the mail subsidies.[92] The facts uncovered constituted one of the sorriest stories in the history of American maladministration. Under

91. Act of May 22, 1928, 45 Stat. at L. 689.
92. S. Rept. 898, 74th Cong., 1st sess. (1935).

the statute all mail contracts were to be let after competitive bidding. It was found that of forty-three such contracts, forty-two had been let without competitive bidding. The disclosures by the Black committee led to immediate and drastic action. The Independent Offices Appropriation Act of 1934 [93] cancelled all ocean mail contracts.

Before the mail subsidy fiasco had worked itself out, certain organizational changes were made in the Shipping Board. By the Economy Act of 1932 [94] the Shipping Board was reduced from seven to three members, and the terms of its members were reduced to three years. In June 1933 President Roosevelt, acting under the authority of the Economy Act of 1932 as amended in 1933,[95] issued his famous executive order No. 6166 making numerous changes in the structure and status of administrative agencies. By a section of this order the Shipping Board and the Fleet Corporation were both transferred to the Department of Commerce, where they were merged into the United States Shipping Board Bureau. The President's order read:

The functions of the United States Shipping Board, including those over and in respect to the United States Shipping Board Merchant Fleet Corporation, are transferred to the Department of Commerce, and the United States Shipping Board is abolished.

The United States Shipping Board Bureau was set up in the Department of Commerce on August 10, 1933.

2. STEPS IN THE LEGISLATIVE HISTORY OF THE ACT OF 1936

In June 1934, the Secretary of Commerce at the request of the President appointed an interdepartmental committee on shipping policy to conduct the fullest possible investigation and to recommend legislation. Largely upon the basis of the interdepartmental committee's report,[96] President Roosevelt on March 4, 1935, recommended to Congress new legislation with

93. Act of June 16, 1933, 48 Stat. at L. 283.
94. Act of June 30, 1932, 47 Stat. at L. 382, at 408.
95. Act of Mar. 3, 1933, 47 Stat. at L. 1489; Act of Mar. 20, 1933, 48 Stat. at L. 8.
96. Report of the Interdepartmental Committee on Shipping Policy, printed in Hearings before the House Committee on Merchant Marine and Fisheries on H.R. 7521, 74th Cong., 1st sess. (1935), Appendix, Part 3.

respect to our merchant marine.[97] He made two major proposals: First, he advocated direct subsidies to aid in the construction and operation of ships, since government loans and mail subsidies had failed to accomplish the development of an adequate merchant marine. Thus after twenty years of consistent opposition to ship subsidies the Democratic Party was committed by the President to the most far-reaching subsidy policy ever proposed. Secondly, the President recommended the reorganization of the administrative machinery necessary to deal with shipping problems. He urged that the regulatory and quasi-legislative duties of the Shipping Board Bureau be transferred to the Interstate Commerce Commission, while the Department of Commerce should retain the administrative functions. The President's proposal was as follows:

Legislation providing for adequate aid to the American merchant marine should include not only adequate appropriation for such purposes and appropriate safeguards for its expenditure, but a reorganization of the machinery for its administration. The quasi-judicial and quasi-legislative duties of the present Shipping Board Bureau of the Department of Commerce should be transferred for the present to the Interstate Commerce Commission. Purely administrative functions, however, such as information and planning, ship inspection, and the maintenance of aids to navigation, should, of course, remain in the Department of Commerce.[98]

Congress promptly began the task of drafting legislation along the lines suggested. Senator Copeland and Representative Bland worked out together a bill [99] which was introduced into both houses and, after hearings in the House and Senate, was resubmitted. The later Copeland-Bland bill [100] provided for a United States maritime authority of five members under a chairman appointed by the President, to which all of the quasi-judicial and quasi-legislative duties of the Shipping Board Bureau were to be transferred. The Department of Commerce was to retain only clearly administrative tasks, such as ship inspection and the like. The authority was to administer operating and construction subsidies and was authorized also to build

97. 79 Cong. Rec. 2859 f.
98. Ibid. 2860.
99. S. 2582 and H.R. 7521, 74th Cong., 1st sess. (1935).
100. H.R. 8555, 74th Cong., 1st sess. (1935).

ships and sell them under certain statutory conditions. Existing regulatory powers were augmented by giving the new authority the power to fix reasonable maximum and minimum rates in foreign shipping. To co-ordinate rail and water traffic the bill created a joint transportation board composed of the Secretary of Commerce and two members representing the maritime authority. This board was to study problems of co-ordination and make recommendations to the Interstate Commerce Commission and the maritime authority.

Representative Moran introduced in the House a bill [101] creating a United States merchant marine corporation controlled by five directors chosen by the President and Senate and charged with full responsibility over the merchant fleet. It also created a United States maritime commission of three members to exercise the regulatory powers of the Shipping Board Bureau and to have control over employment conditions even to the extent of fixing minimum wage scales. More seriously considered than the Moran bill was that proposed by Mr. Eastman, the Federal Co-ordinator of Transportation.[102] Mr. Eastman's proposal placed the regulation of shipping rates and practices in the hands of the Interstate Commerce Commission. Extensive hearings were held on the Eastman proposal. After the Bland •bill passed the House, Senators Gibson and Guffey working with Senator Copeland offered amendments. The amended bill, further modified in conference, became the Act of 1936.

3. PROVISIONS OF THE ACT OF 1936

The Merchant Marine Act of 1936 [103] created a United States Maritime Commission of five members appointed by the President with the advice and consent of the Senate. The President names the chairman of the commission. The six-year terms of office are staggered. The membership must be bipartisan and the President's power to remove members is restricted. There are no specific qualifications for membership but the statute

101. H.R. 7981, 74th Cong., 1st sess. (1935).
102. S. 1632, 74th Cong., 1st sess. (1935).
103. Act of June 29, 1936, 49 Stat. at L. 1985.

directs the President to appoint persons who have fitness for the task assigned to them.

To the new Maritime Commission was transferred all the property and interests of the United States Shipping Board Bureau and the United States Fleet Corporation, and the corporation was dissolved. All of the functions of the Shipping Board Bureau were transferred to the new agency, but after two years the President might by executive order transfer to the Interstate Commerce Commission all regulatory duties and responsibilities previously vested in the bureau.

The powers of the Maritime Commission include the regulatory powers that previously existed, broad powers of investigation, and the authority, previously vested in the Postmaster General, to let ocean mail contracts. The statute authorizes an elaborate system of construction and operating subsidies which the new commission is to administer. Under certain circumstances the commission may build ships which may be leased under charters drawn and administered by the commission.

4. ISSUE AND TOPICS IN HEARINGS AND DEBATES

a. *The segregation of functions*

The chief issue regarding the organization of the new commission was that of the segregation of functions. Again, as in the discussions in the '20's, there was no clear agreement on how the functions relating to our merchant marine should be distributed. By the President's executive order of June 1933, all of the functions of the Shipping Board and of the Fleet Corporation had been dumped upon the Department of Commerce. This, however, was a temporary expedient. The President in his message of 1935 [104] had proposed to keep the administrative functions relating to shipping in the Department of Commerce and to transfer the quasi-judicial and the quasi-legislative job to the Interstate Commerce Commission. The interdepartmental committee [105] had followed the same general line of division except that they had proposed to give the quasi-judicial and the quasi-legislative tasks to a new inde-

104. *Supra,* 269.   105. *Supra,* note 96, op. cit. 1128 f.

pendent agency rather than to the Interstate Commerce Commission. The Black committee devised a wholly different type of segregation.[106] They proposed to transfer the quasi-judicial duties to the Interstate Commerce Commission and to give the quasi-legislative and administrative tasks to a new independent commission. Certain of the shipping interests desired the separation of the quasi-judicial job of regulation from the quasi-legislative task of allotting ship subsidies. They did not care whether the regulatory tasks went to the Interstate Commerce Commission or to a new commission, but they urged that the administration of subsidies should go to the Department of Commerce. There was general agreement amongst those who offered opinions at this time that the quasi-judicial and the purely administrative functions relating to shipping should be separated. The chief disagreement was whether policy determination and the administration of subsidies should be joined with the job of regulation or with the more purely administrative functions. The provision permitting the President after two years to transfer the regulatory authority of the Maritime Commission to the Interstate Commerce Commission was quite frankly a compromise to satisfy those who were still demanding some kind of segregation.

On the merits of the controversy over segregation the debates and hearings of 1935 and 1936 contributed nothing new. Emphasis was placed upon the undesirability of giving the power to regulate the shipping industry to the same body which was to administer the government's own business interests in the shipping field. It was felt that impartial regulation could not be expected from this arrangement. As a matter of fact no one spoke up during the discussions to defend the placing of all functions in the hands of a single independent authority. But in the end the Senate Committee on Interstate Commerce discarded without argument the whole notion of segregation. It declared:

It is stated that the Maritime Authority should not possess both administrative and regulatory powers. There is no precedent in the existing Federal laws for this contention. Every independent governmental commission created prior to and during the present administration possesses and exercises both administrative and regula-

106. *Supra,* note 92, op. cit. 45.

tory powers. The development of an adequate merchant marine is as distinctive a problem as that involved in the regulation of communications, securities exchanges, and so forth.[107]

b. *Organization of the commission*

There was little discussion of the composition of the new commission. The original House bill had provided for regional representation, and the stock arguments in defense of regionalism were presented. It was urged in reply that regional representation on the old board had led to log-rolling, and the requirement was dropped out. The requirement that the members of the commission should be appointed because of their fitness for the work assigned to them had, of course, no practical significance. The normal restriction upon the President's power of removal was written into the Act without debate. An amendment in the House to add to the causes for which members of the Maritime Commission might be removed 'the receipt of any gratuity or other valuable thing' was not adopted.

c. *The Interstate Commerce Commission to regulate shipping*

The proposal made by Mr. Eastman [108] and supported by the President and by the Black committee, that regulatory powers over shipping should go to the Interstate Commerce Commission, was discussed at some length. It was apparent, however, that it would not be adopted. While some of the shipping interests were indifferent whether they were regulated by the Interstate Commerce Commission or by some other independent commission, it was the general opinion in the industry and in Congress that the Interstate Commerce Commission was 'railroad minded,' that it was not familiar with shipping problems, that it was already overburdened with work, and that therefore it would be unwise to confer upon it new regulatory duties in the foreign commerce field. Eastman's proposal had grown out of his oft-expressed belief that national control over transportation in this country was in essence a single problem, that it could be handled effectively only by centralized author-

107. S. Rept. 1721, 74th Cong., 2d sess. (1936), 4.
108. *Supra,* 270.

ity, and that the Interstate Commerce Commission was the most appropriate agency for exercising that control. Congress did not regard the new Merchant Marine Act as a step toward the co-ordination of transportation control, and the Interstate Commerce Commission was left out of the picture unless the President after two years decided to transfer to it the regulatory functions conferred.

d. *Rate-making power over shipping*

The Copeland-Bland bill increased the regulatory powers of the proposed maritime commission by authorizing it to establish maximum and minimum shipping rates. The power to fix maximum rates was bitterly opposed by the shipping interests, who claimed that such regulation would put them at a serious competitive disadvantage. They wanted minimum rates, however, to protect American shipping from the competition of foreign tramp steamers. It was urged that to fix foreign shipping rates would lead foreign governments to retaliate in ways disadvantageous to American shipping interests and to American importers. Perhaps the decisive factor in eliminating the more drastic rate-making power from the final Act was the receipt by the Senate committee of advice from Secretary of State Hull pointing out that the proposed power might seriously embarrass the negotiation and maintenance of trade agreements with other nations.[109] In his opinion unilateral regulation would be a mistake. The Merchant Marine Act of 1936 therefore in no way enlarged the regulatory duties which had been exercised by the Shipping Board and the Shipping Board Bureau.

e. *Labor relations*

Finally an attempt was made to give to the new commission authority over labor relations. Demands that this be done were made by seamen's organizations. The result was the inclusion in the Act of a provision that on subsidized ships the Maritime Commission should investigate employment and wage conditions and incorporate in subsidy contracts 'minimum manning scales and the minimum wage scales, and reasonable working

109. Letter to Sen. Wheeler, May 16, 1935.

conditions for all officers and crews employed on all types of vessels receiving operating differential subsidy.' The commission was to hear complaints against the wages and conditions that it had established and it was thus made the final authority for the administration of labor relations.

5. THE TRANSPORTATION ACT OF 1940

As we have already seen [110] the Transportation Act of 1940 took from the Maritime Commission all jurisdiction over domestic waterways and gave it to the Interstate Commerce Commission. Thus was the long fight won to get the control of all the major systems of interstate transportation into the hands of the same regulatory agency. The new statute left the Maritime Commission otherwise unchanged.

IV. THE FEDERAL POWER COMMISSION

A. THE INTERDEPARTMENTAL EX-OFFICIO POWER COMMISSION OF 1920

1. BACKGROUND OF FEDERAL WATER POWER ACT OF 1920

THE problem of power control in this country has proved difficult and complicated. This has been partly owing to difficulties inherent in the nature of the field of control, but perhaps even more to jurisdictional problems. There has been conflict between the states and the federal government regarding the precise line that divides their respective fields of authority over navigable rivers and power lines. We have finally worked out such a federal-state division line, but during the process there was much dispute and uncertainty. Jurisdictional conflicts arose also among the three federal departments upon which haphazard legislative enactments had conferred authority over various phases of the power problem. The War Department had broad authority. Its permission was required for the building of any structures that would impair navigation in any of the navigable waters of the United States.[1] An Act of 1901 [2]

---

110. *Supra*, 142.
1. Act of Sept. 19, 1890, 26 Stat. at L. 454.
2. Act of Feb. 15, 1901, 31 Stat. at L. 970.

gave the Department of the Interior the right 'to permit the use of rights of way through the public lands, forest, and other reservations of the United States.' Rules governing the issuance of these permits were made by the Secretary of the Interior, and such permits were revocable by the Secretary at discretion. The Department of Agriculture controlled the national forests and the important problem of the relation of forest cover to stream flow, which had a direct effect upon water power development. The results of this division of power and responsibility were exceedingly unsatisfactory. Conflicts of policy with regard to the development of power projects grew up between the three departments; furthermore, the policies of the departments tended to fluctuate with each change of Administration. The discretion conferred upon the Secretaries of the three departments and particularly the discretionary power of the Secretary of the Interior to revoke permits made investment risks in power developments on public lands very great. Private capital anxious to develop power sites was reluctant to embark upon major projects because of the uncertain status of its legal rights. Hydroelectric development was slowed up by the complications and uncertainties here described.

President Theodore Roosevelt was keenly interested in the proper development of the nation's resources. He saw the need for co-ordinated control over the power resources of the country and in 1907 he appointed the Inland Waterways Commission to study the entire problem. In 1908 this commission reported,[3] urging 'some administrative machinery for coordinating the work of the various departments.' The President transmitted this report to Congress and recommended the co-ordination of administrative agencies dealing with power, protection against monopoly, the establishment of fees from licenses, and a time limit upon power privileges granted to private interests.[4] Also in 1908 President Roosevelt vetoed the Rainy River bill as making an improvident power grant,[5] and in 1909 vetoed the James River bill.[6] The first of these bills was passed over his veto, but his various messages tended to

3. S. Doc. 325, 60th Cong., 1st sess. (1908).
4. Ibid. iii ff.
5. H.R. 15444, 60th Cong., 1st sess. (1908); veto message, 42 Cong. Rec. 4698.
6. H.R. 17707, 60th Cong., 2d sess. (1909); veto message, 43 Cong. Rec. 978.

clarify in the minds of Congress some of the issues of power control, and resulted in the enactment on June 23, 1910, of a statute limiting to fifty years all grants of rights of way on public lands.[7] The statute, however, did not change the administration of power control.

This confused situation continued through the Administration of President Taft. The opinion steadily grew that a single federal agency was necessary to handle this important problem, although there was always a powerful undercurrent of opposition to any federal authority which would restrict private enterprise or place costly limitations around the granting of power rights to private interests. The pressure of war finally brought action. Confronted by the necessity of pushing industrial production to the maximum, the government was faced with a possible shortage of coal. The emergency might be met by an adequate supply of hydroelectric power, but there was no adequate supply, and the deficiency was generally agreed to be due to the unsatisfactory administration of water power grants. It was the drive to win the war which finally leveled the barriers of departmental jurisdiction and ironed out interdepartmental jealousies. The result after much delay was the Federal Water Power Act of 1920.[8]

2. STEPS IN THE LEGISLATIVE HISTORY OF THE ACT OF 1920

Between 1910 and 1920 a stream of bills found their way into Congress, calling for better federal regulation of power resources. It was generally agreed that something should be done but it was difficult to secure agreement upon any single plan. The three departments concerned were reluctant to give up the jurisdiction which they had and which seemed to them necessary for the proper management of departmental interests.

In 1914 a bill which had the backing of the Secretary of the Interior was introduced [9] in the House. It authorized the Secretary of the Interior to issue power leases for terms of fifty years, with the approval of the Secretaries of War and Agriculture if they were concerned. These leases were to provide

7. Act of June 23, 1910, 36 Stat. at L. 593.
8. Act of June 10, 1920, 41 Stat. at L. 1063.
9. H.R. 14893, 63d Cong., 2d sess. (1914).

the reasonable and continuous development of power projects. They could be revoked by court action only, but they were subject to recapture by the government at the end of fifty years upon the payment of due compensation. House and Senate committees held elaborate hearings upon this bill. The numerous witnesses from the power industry found it hard to determine their position. They favored the simplification of administrative procedure involved in the proposal, but they objected to the wide discretion vested in the Secretary of the Interior. The industry was still hoping to get leases of federal power sites without any regulation at all, and was not able to agree upon any alternative plan. In the House hearings, O. C. Merrill, Chief Engineer of the Forest Service and later the first executive secretary of the Power Commission, proposed the creation of an independent water power commission built along the lines of the Interstate Commerce Commission.[10] This proposal, however, was neither supported nor discussed. The bill passed the House but not the Senate and it was never revived.

The Rivers and Harbors Act of 1917 [11] created a Waterways Commission of seven members appointed by the President, with salaries of $7,500 each. Its functions were general in scope, but it had no regulatory or mandatory powers. An appropriation of $100,000 was made to finance its work. A few months earlier Franklin K. Lane, the Secretary of the Interior, had started a move for an interdepartmental power commission. He enlisted the support of President Wilson and the President invited the Secretaries of the Interior, War, and Agriculture to serve as a committee to draft a bill that would deal with water power on the public domain, in the national forests, and on navigable waters. The three Secretaries produced a bill which with some changes became the Water Power Act of 1920. In December 1917, President Wilson summoned the Congressional committees to the White House and gave them what Mr. Esch of Wisconsin later referred to as the 'sanctified draft' [12] of the water power bill. It was promptly introduced in

10. Hearings before the House Committee on the Public Lands on H.R. 14893, 63d Cong., 2d sess. (1914), 415.
11. Act of Aug. 8, 1917, 40 Stat. at L. 250.
12. 56 Cong. Rec. 9667.

the House as an Administration bill.[13] Bent upon securing the enactment of this bill, the President never appointed the members of the Waterways Commission authorized by the Rivers and Harbors Act of August 1917.

The power commission bill had long and difficult sledding. At the request of the President and under special rule, the House created a special Committee on Water Power to consider the numerous water power bills then before it and combine them in one comprehensive bill. This committee was composed of eighteen members: six drawn from the Committee on Agriculture, six from the Committee on the Public Lands, and six from the Committee on Interstate and Foreign Commerce. In the preceding December the Senate had passed a bill [14] relating to power development on navigable rivers, and to expedite the passage of one comprehensive measure this Senate bill was amended to include the substance of several bills, notably the Administration bill creating a power commission. Elaborate hearings were held by this special committee on the radically amended Senate bill; it was reported out in June, and after lengthy debate in the House was passed on September 5, 1918. The Senate sent the bill to a conference committee, but in spite of urgent pressure no report came from the conference committee before Congress adjourned on November 21, 1918. No conference report was presented during the succeeding short session of Congress, and the bill accordingly died.

When the next session of Congress convened, the same bill [15] was introduced by Mr. Esch in the House on May 26, 1919. It was referred to the Committee on Water Power, which reported it out on June 24. It was debated from June 27 to July 1, when it was passed and sent to the Senate, where it was referred to the Committee on Commerce on July 8. It was reported out favorably on September 12 and placed on the Senate calendar, but no action was taken before Congress adjourned in November. In the following short session of Congress the bill, after brief debate, passed the Senate on January 15, 1920. It again went to conference, from which it was re-

13. H.R. 8716, 65th Cong., 2d sess. (1918), 56 Cong. Rec. 890.
14. S. 1419, 65th Cong., 1st sess. (1917).
15. H.R. 3184, 66th Cong., 1st sess. (1919).

ported out at the end of April. It passed the House on May 4, 1920, by a vote of 259 to 30. On May 28 it passed the Senate by a vote of 45 to 21, with 30 not voting, and was signed on June 10.

3. PROVISIONS OF THE ACT

The Act of 1920 set up a Water Power Commission composed of the Secretaries of War, Interior, and Agriculture. Two of these were to constitute a quorum and the President was to designate the chairman. The commission was to appoint an executive secretary at a salary of $5,000 and might request the President to detail an officer of the United States Engineering Corps for commission work. The work of the commission was to be performed by and through the Departments of War, Interior, and Agriculture and their engineering, technical, and clerical staffs. It was given the following powers: to investigate fully the utilization of water power resources; to license water power developments by private interests upon public lands; to determine the net investment made by such licensees as a basis upon which the government might recapture at the end of the fifty-year period; to prescribe rules and regulations governing the accounts kept by licensees and to fix the annual charges to be paid by these licensees to defray the cost of administering the Act; to hold hearings upon the granting of licenses and preliminary permits; to fix interstate power rates and to regulate the security issues of interstate power companies. The Act repealed the provision of 1917 creating the Waterways Commission, which had never been set up.

4. TOPICS AND ISSUES IN HEARINGS AND DEBATES

The committee hearings and debates upon the Water Power Act were colored by the sense of pressure felt by everyone to find a prompt solution to a seriously urgent problem. The proposal made by the interdepartmental committee was experimental and seemed reasonably conservative. While there were differences of opinion about the best type of agency for the handling of the power problem, there was willingness to compromise in order to secure action.

There was sharp controversy over the establishment of an

ex-officio commission composed exclusively of Cabinet members. No one knew from experience how such an administrative agency would work, since the scheme had never been tried before. The general argument in favor of the ex-officio commission was that it would not be a new agency but merely an arrangement under which existing agencies would work together on a common problem. This was the view taken by Secretary Lane and elaborated in the debates in the House. By this device the joint judgment of the three Secretaries could be brought to bear upon the problems involved and this was necessary to their satisfactory handling. Senator Jones of Washington, while not personally favoring the ex-officio commission, summarized in the Senate the argument in favor of it:

> . . . This commission . . . would promote unity of action, together with economy of operation, through segregating all authority in this board, whose members would bring to its aid the personnel and vast machinery of the three great governmental departments over which they preside. Personally, I doubt very much the wisdom of the establishment of this commission composed of Cabinet officers, but I am sure it is the best we can get and so I am willing to accept it in order to get legislation.[16]

There were many who felt that an independent commission roughly similar to the Interstate Commerce Commission would be vastly better than an ex-officio commission. It was urged that Cabinet officers could not give adequate time to the work of the commission, and that to vest authority in them would give to the President a dangerous control over the whole power situation. Furthermore, Cabinet members are admitted partisans who hold office for relatively short terms, so that the commission could not hope to maintain continuity of policy. Mr. Esch had constitutional doubts about the ex-officio commission:

> The Interstate Commerce Commission is a branch of Congress and exercises as such a legislative function, and you are here giving to three Cabinet officers, a part of the executive, legislative functions.
>
> The bill seeks to confer this power on three Secretaries as to rates, and rate-making is a legislative function. Why not give it to the body which Congress has created to determine rates? Why give

16. 59 Cong. Rec. 244.

it to three officers belonging to the Executive branch of the Government? [17]

Senator Norris, while reluctantly supporting the bill, urged the necessity for a permanent full-time commission:

The bill provides for a commission of Cabinet officers. I think it ought to be a permanent body of men who would become experts in that line after they have been in office a while, removed entirely from political control, taken entirely out of politics, and not confined to Members of the Cabinet, who, as everybody knows, change with every administration, and a good many times during an administration, and new men are put in who do not know anything about the business.[18]

It remained, however, for the unhappy experience of the ensuing ten years to sharpen the arguments against the ex-officio commission and in favor of the full-time independent commission.

Mr. Walsh of Massachusetts proposed that the members of the power commission should be drawn from the membership of the Interstate Commerce Commission, which was already familiar with rate making and similar problems of regulation; if necessary the Interstate Commerce Commission could be enlarged.[19] This suggestion did not receive much support. It was urged in reply by Mr. Esch of Wisconsin that the three Departments of War, Agriculture, and Interior were vitally interested in power problems and ought to be represented on the power commission, while the Interstate Commerce Commission was wholly unfamiliar with those problems; furthermore, only by the ex-officio scheme could the expert staffs of the three departments concerned be effectively utilized without extra expenditure.[20]

There was some discussion of the status of the executive secretary provided for in the bill. It was argued that such an executive secretary would in the circumstances inevitably come to manage the affairs of the commission, a prophecy which proved correct, but it was an objection which carried small

17. Hearings before the House Committee on Water Power, 65th Cong., 2d sess. (1918), 101, 461.
18. 59 Cong. Rec. 246.
19. 58 Cong. Rec. 2018 f.
20. Ibid. 2019.

weight at the time. Others contended that the executive secretary ought to have substantial power and prestige and should be paid a high salary. In reply it was said that if he were made a powerful officer the Cabinet Secretaries on the commission would be tempted to relegate to him important decisions which the full commission ought to handle.

The debates on the whole were not very searching. There was general agreement that an experiment was being tried, that the proposal embodied in the bill would probably need revision in the light of experience, but that prompt action was desirable and the present bill presented a workable compromise.

B. THE INDEPENDENT FEDERAL POWER COMMISSION OF 1930

1. BACKGROUND—THE BREAKDOWN OF THE INTERDEPARTMENTAL COMMISSION

It was probably necessary to learn from actual experience that an ex-officio commission such as that set up in 1920 could not work successfully. In the next ten years this lesson was thoroughly learned. It is true that at the very outset the new organization functioned fairly smoothly, even though its efforts were inadequate to meet the important problems assigned to it. Its administrative work was ably directed by O. C. Merrill, formerly Chief Engineer of the Forest Service and an accounting expert on hydroelectric power problems. The competence of Mr. Merrill as executive secretary could not, however, make up for the basic defects in the administrative structure which had been created.

The vital problem of commission personnel was never adequately solved. The executive secretary was the only administrative officer paid by the commission itself. All other commission officers and employees were loaned by the Departments of War, Interior, and Agriculture. In 1928, thirty-three persons were thus being loaned. While this was at best not an ideal arrangement, it was rendered less satisfactory by the fact that officers and employees thus detailed to the Power Commission had to be paid from the budgets of the departments from which they came without any increase in the departmental appropriations to cover the loss of their services. As early as January 1921, Mr. Esch of Wisconsin declared in the House that it was obvious that the Power Commission was not going to get from the three departments the co-operation which had been expected.[21] It was urged in defense of these personnel arrangements that the commission was merely handling in a centralized way the same jobs which the three departments had previously handled piecemeal. This, however, was not true. The Act of 1920 had provided for the granting of fifty-year licenses for power development projects, and a very large number of applications for these licenses were promptly filed. By January 1921, 134 such applications were in the hands of the commission, and the task of making the preliminary surveys necessary to pass upon them was a new and a very substantial burden, far beyond the capacity of the commission's limited staff.

The commission tried almost steadily from 1920 through 1928 to persuade Congress to give it an independent staff. Shortly after it was set up, it sponsored in Congress a bill which would allow it to appoint its own central staff instead of being dependent upon the departments. Secretary of War Baker strongly supported this recommendation, but there were no results. The statute provided that licensees should pay substantial fees to cover the cost of administering the Water Power Act. The commission was steadily receiving in such fees a good deal more money than it would have cost to put it on an independent footing, and in 1927 the Senate passed a bill to allow the use of these fees to pay the commission's staff. It was impossible, however, to win the House to this point of view. The commission had been set up upon the basic idea that a new and independent agency of power control was undesirable. Mr. Snell of New York pointed out that to give the commission an independent staff would change the entire policy with regard to the administration of the Act by making it an independent bureau.[22] It was also objected that such a change would greatly increase the power and importance of the executive secretary, who, it was pointed out, was the person most active in urging the change. Mr. Rayburn of Texas declared: 'We might as well face the proposition that this is a bill to get the camel's nose under the tent.'[23] In 1928 Congress extended some relief[24] by

21. 60 Cong. Rec. 902.
22. 69 Cong. Rec. 5072.
23. Ibid. 5076.
24. Act of May 16, 1928, 45 Stat. at L. 573.

authorizing the Power Commission to pay its own personnel, a personnel still detailed from the three departments, thereby relieving the departmental budgets and insuring more effective co-operation. The following year the amount of money allocated to this purpose was substantially increased, but this belated action came too late to forestall the drastic reorganization of the commission. Granted that the ex-officio commission might have worked more satisfactorily than it did, the fact was clear that for eight years it had failed to accomplish the initial purposes of Congress and was consequently destined to be replaced by a wholly different type of organization.

We may summarize briefly the major indictments against the commission during the ten-year period under review: In the first place, the commission was inadequate for the job assigned to it. Starved in funds and in personnel, it made no serious attempt to grapple with the three major tasks inherent in any program of federal power control: the supervising of accounting, the valuation of power project investments, and the regulation of power rates. Bogged down under a volume of business which it could not adequately handle, the commission was able to produce results only after long delays; and while this in some ways suited the power interests, who were anxious to ward off regulatory action, it prevented the prompt and efficient administration of power policy. In the second place, the Secretaries of War, Agriculture, and the Interior were too busy to give much time to the work of the commission, and as a result the executive secretary tended to become the real commission. Much depended, therefore, upon the character of the secretary. The results of that arrangement might not be seriously objectionable if the secretary were strong and competent; they would be calamitous if the secretary were a weak man and under the influence of the power industry. In the third place, friction grew up in the staff of the commission. The executive secretary who succeeded O. C. Merrill in 1929 was at loggerheads with the chief accountant and the solicitor, and the commission seemed unable to iron out these difficulties. As a result of these liabilities the commission developed a reputation for inefficiency and for failure to protect the government's interests adequately against the aggressions of the power industry.

2. STEPS IN THE LEGISLATIVE HISTORY OF THE ACT OF 1930

In his message of December 3, 1929, President Hoover proposed the establishment of a full-time independent power commission. He stated:

The Federal Power Commission is now comprised of three Cabinet officers, and the duties involved in the competent conduct of the growing responsibilities of this commission far exceed the time and attention which these officials can properly afford from other important duties. I recommend that authority be given for appointment of full-time commissioners to replace them.[25]

The Senate Committee on Interstate Commerce under the chairmanship of Senator Couzens was directed to investigate 'the transmission of power by wire,' [26] and it plunged into this task with thoroughness and energy. On February 18, 1930, Senator Couzens introduced a bill [27] for the creation of an independent full-time commission. This was referred to the Senate Committee on Interstate Commerce, was reported out favorably on April 11, and passed the Senate on May 12. The House Committee on Interstate and Foreign Commerce had been considering a somewhat similar bill of its own which had been introduced in January 1930, and upon which hearings had been held.[28] The Couzens bill was referred to this committee in the House on May 16. The House committee reported the bill, which was debated briefly and passed the House on June 9. Senate and House differences were ironed out in conference; the conference report passed the Senate and the House on June 16 and June 19 respectively, and the bill was signed on June 23, 1930.

3. CHIEF PROVISIONS OF THE ACT OF 1930

The Water Power Act of 1930 [29] had but one purpose, to reorganize the Power Commission. It did not change the duties assigned to the commission by the Act of 1920. Section 4 of the new statute provided:

25. 72 Cong. Rec. 25.
26. S. Res. 80, 71st Cong., 1st sess. (1929), 71 Cong. Rec. 2161.
27. S. 3619, 71st Cong., 2d sess. (1930).
28. H.R. 11408, 71st Cong., 2d sess. (1930).
29. Act of June 23, 1930, 46 Stat. at L. 797.

This Act shall be held to reorganize the Federal Power Commission created by the Federal Water Power Act, and said Federal Water Power Act shall remain in full force and effect, as herein amended, and no regulations, actions, investigations, or other proceedings under the Federal Water Power Act existing or pending at the time of the approval of this Act shall abate or otherwise be affected by reasons of the provisions of this Act.

But the organization of the commission was completely changed. The ex-officio members were eliminated. The new commission was to consist of five members appointed by the President with the advice and consent of the Senate, for five-year staggered terms. One of these commissioners was to be designated by the President as chairman 'and shall be the principal executive officer of the commission.' But it was further provided that 'after the expiration of the original term of the commissioner so designated as chairman by the President, chairmen shall be elected by the commission itself, each chairman when so elected to act as such until the expiration of his term of office.' A vice-chairman was also to be chosen by the members of the commission. Not more than three of the commissioners could be members of the same political party. Persons employed by or financially interested in power companies were disqualified, and the commissioners were to give full time. The salary was fixed at $10,000.

The commission was given its own staff. The statute provided for a secretary, a chief engineer, general counsel, solicitor, and chief accountant. Subject to civil service laws the commission might appoint 'such other officers and employees as are necessary in the execution of its functions.' These regulations applied to the central organization in Washington. It could, however, request the President to detail one or more army engineers or officers to serve the commission in its field work. Similarly engineers might be detailed from the Departments of the Interior and of Agriculture.

4. TOPICS AND ISSUES IN HEARINGS AND DEBATES

a. *Ex-officio* versus *full-time independent commission*

In the hearings and debates on the Act of 1930 the argument for a full-time independent commission was thoroughly developed in a rather one-sided debate. Few members of Congress and few outside witnesses had either inclination or courage to defend the existing commission or to urge its continuance. That it must be replaced by a commission roughly similar to the other independent regulatory agencies was generally assumed. Much of the discussion centered around the shortcomings of the ex-officio arrangement, and it was now possible to talk in terms of concrete experience. It had been demonstrated that the Cabinet Secretaries comprising the commission did not have time to handle its work. Testifying before the Senate committee, William V. King, chief accountant of the commission from its beginning, stated that during the nine years of its existence the commission had held ninety-nine meetings, an average of eleven per year, and that these had been usually about thirty minutes in length—an expenditure of five and a half hours per year of the time of the commissioners.[30] Engrossed with their other Cabinet duties, the commissioners had not had time to conduct hearings as a body, or to inquire into and settle staff difficulties. They had had neither the time nor the background to formulate power policies. They had not had time to deal with questions of valuation, a task too important to be handled by subordinates. All this was freely admitted by the Secretaries themselves. As Secretary of War Weeks stated bluntly: 'There are not hours enough in the day to enable me to do my legitimate duties as Secretary of War.' [31] The result was that responsibility was placed on men who found it impossible to assume it and who thereby became, as Representative Celler of New York put it, 'out-and-out figureheads.'

. . . With all due respect to them, Congress might just as well have put the King of England, Mussolini, and Albert Einstein on the commission as far as any spontaneous, decisive action originating with the commissioners is concerned.[32]

It was shrewdly pointed out that one of the reasons for the commission's neglect of some of its statutory duties was that the commission itself, unable to grasp the problems and do the actual work, was unwilling to assume major responsibilities in

30. Hearings before the Senate Committee on Interstate Commerce Pursuant to S. Res. 80, 71st Cong., 2d sess. (1930), 41.
31. 65 Cong. Rec. 5383.   32. 72 Cong. Rec. 8199.

the premises. This was clearly put by Mr. Parker in the House debate:

They are way behind in all of their work for the reason that a big proposition of this kind cannot be looked after by subordinates. When that is done, who is responsible? The Secretaries themselves are responsible, and they do not want to assume responsibility for things about which they know nothing. Therefore, the commission has not worked. That was testified to, with all humility, by the Secretaries who appeared before our committee.[33]

It was further pointed out that this difficulty could not be met merely by increasing the administrative staff, since that did not meet the problem of responsible direction. Mr. James F. Lawson, acting chief counsel of the commission, declared before the Senate committee:

. . . Any attempt to relieve the heads of the departments of the burden of the work, without relieving them of the power of decision, will fail. If they are going to decide they must dig into the case to find what is the right thing to do. Since they can not have time to dig into all the important cases, the result, if more subordinates are introduced into the driving mechanism, will simply be more delay.[34]

While the old Power Commission had never got around to regulating interstate power rates, it was insisted that such rate making was necessary and could be safely handled only by a bipartisan and quasi-judicial board. Furthermore, the important tasks of power control demanded a permanence of personnel and continuity of policy which could never be secured under an ex-officio commission. That it had not been secured was evident from the statement Mr. Lawson made regarding the turnover in the commission since 1920:

. . . The Federal Power Commission has been in existence not quite 10 years. During that period, twice with a clean sweep, the personnel has been changed five times, there having been five different Secretaries of War, five different Secretaries of the Interior, and four different Secretaries of Agriculture. The ravages of death can not be provided against and the vicissitudes of politics are sometimes not to be deplored. It is to be deplored, however, that the membership of a commission having the enforcement of such a

33. Ibid. 10333. 34. *Supra*, note 30, op. cit. 358.

policy can not be selected with particular reference to the character of the work to be done, and remain long enough to secure expertness in the principles to be applied and familiarity with the forces operating for and against public interest.[35]

It was also emphasized that the problems of power control were too technical to be handled by laymen, but required persons with some technical training. It was readily admitted that the Secretaries of War, Agriculture, and the Interior had no close familiarity with power problems.

In the 1930 debate the constitutional argument was again presented that the legislative task of rate making, which might properly be given to the Interstate Commerce Commission since that body was a 'branch of Congress,' could not validly be given to a commission composed of three of the major executive officers of the federal government. This was developed by Mr. Huddleston of Alabama before the House committee.[36] The Secretaries constituting the commission were part of the executive branch and responsible to the President, but in regulating power rates they would be performing a function for which they would be responsible not to the President but to Congress. This was an anomalous situation which ought to be corrected.

The argument thus built up for a full-time independent commission was met but feebly. It was, however, reiterated in the House that it was undesirable to create another large independent agency which would inevitably expand and spend large sums of money, especially since such an agency would duplicate work now being done adequately through the Departments of War, Interior, and Agriculture.

b. *The status of the executive secretary*

The status of the executive secretary of the commission was discussed at length. It was recognized that the executive secretary was really the Power Commission, and experience had shown no way of preventing his being so. The commissioners were entirely dependent upon his judgment and discretion;

35. Ibid. 357.
36. Hearings before the House Committee on Interstate and Foreign Commerce on H.R. 11408, 71st Cong., 2d sess. (1930), 39 ff.

they had no body of information upon the basis of which to question or overrule him. It had become much more valuable therefore to those seeking licenses or concessions to have a friendly understanding with the executive secretary than to have any amount of opportunity to argue before the full commission. Under the most favorable circumstances this situation was objectionable. But the circumstances had not always been favorable, and Senator Norris of Nebraska and Senator Walsh of Montana openly charged that the executive secretary was a tool of the big power companies.[37] There had been open friction between the executive secretary and other members of the commission's staff, a friction alleged to be due to the overriding by the secretary of the efforts of the chief accountant and solicitor to guard the government's interests against the aggression of the power interests.

c. *Personnel of the commission*

The debates and hearings spread upon the record the unsatisfactory status of the commission's personnel. Members of the commission themselves admitted that the public interest in power developments was not being adequately protected because of the inadequacy of the commission's staff. Furthermore, some of the commission's duties were so technical as to be beyond the capacity of the personnel of the three departments upon which the commission had to depend. Chief Accountant King declared that there were no accountants in the three departments sufficiently familiar with power problems to be useful to the commission.[38] As a result the work of the commission fell steadily behind.

d. *Relation of the commission to the President*

There was a certain reluctance to sever completely the connection between the Departments of War, Interior, and Agriculture and the management of power interests—a lingering feeling that these departments had somehow a vested interest which they ought to be allowed to protect. The interesting

37. 72 Cong. Rec. 4937 f. and 6944 ff.   38. Ibid. 3894.

proposal was therefore made and discussed several times in the hearings that the Power Commission be composed not of Cabinet Secretaries but of special assistant secretaries.[39] These assistant secretaries could devote their entire time to the work of the commission but at the same time would be responsible to their respective departments. The proposal received scant support. It was pointed out that it solved no basic problems. It did not eliminate the awkward results of interdepartmental control. The commission would still be responsible to the executive departments and the work would still be carried on by men of lesser calibre than the job deserved. The Secretaries themselves objected to the proposal, probably realizing that they could not escape ultimate responsibility under any such arrangement.

e. *Segregation of functions*

There was brief mention of the possibility of segregating the regulatory functions of the proposed power commission from its administrative work. Secretary Wilbur and Senator Dill discussed this [40] before the Senate committee and agreed that it might be desirable to leave to the executive departments the responsibility for the granting of licenses, while delegating the rate-making power to an independent commission. The problem seems not to have been regarded as important and nothing further was said or done about it.

f. *Status and nature of independent commissions*

During the hearings and debates several influential members of Congress aired their views regarding independent regulatory commissions in general. Senator Dill expressed himself both before the Senate committee and in the Senate debate:

I want to call attention to this fact, that a commission such as the Interstate Commerce Commission and certain other commissions, is a sort of hybrid in this Government which is responsible to nobody directly. It is neither legislative, judicial, nor executive. It partakes of all of them, but is not responsible; whereas the Executive is close to the people, and the giving away of rights such as

39. *Supra*, note 30, op. cit. 298 ff.   40. Ibid.

water-power rights ought to be under the control of somebody who is responsible directly to the people.[41]

I need not discuss here the matter of responsibility to the people on the part of the commissions of the Government. They are a hybrid creation, in that their duties partake of the nature of the administrative, the judicial, and almost the legislative itself. They are responsible to nobody directly. Nobody is directly chargeable except themselves. The President names them and the Senate confirms them, and thereafter they hold office until the end of their terms. Their records are never submitted to the people of the country and nobody can be held directly responsible for what they do.[42]

Mr. Blanton in the House urged that to confer powers of control upon an independent commission would result in loss of effective responsibility:

Well, I want the three Secretaries to continue to be responsible to the people. They are now responsible to the President of the United States, and he is responsible to the people. If they do anything improper, the President has the right to remove them, but when these five commissioners are appointed they are in office for so many years, and they become independent and arrogant, and they do fix the salaries of at least four officers . . .

As long as the power is in the hands of the Secretary of Agriculture, the Secretary of the Interior, and the Secretary of War the people of the United States are safe, as they are responsible to the President, but whenever the power is taken out of their hands and put in the hands of this special commission, my colleagues, you are giving up power that you should keep in your own hands. It is power which you should control and which you should not give up by this bill.[43]

g. *Removal power of the President*

Finally, it is interesting to note that Congress had in mind the Supreme Court's decision in *Myers* v. *United States* [44] when it omitted from the Act of 1930 the customary provision restricting the President's power to remove members of the commission. This came up as follows in the House debate:

Mr. Cochran [of Missouri]. Will the gentleman explain to the House why the Interstate Commerce Committee struck out the following language of the Senate bill?—Any commissioner may be

41. Ibid. 301.

42. 74 Cong. Rec. 1252.

43. 72 Cong. Rec. 10333.

44. 272 U.S. 52 (1926).

removed by the President for inefficiency, neglect of duty, or malfeasance in office, but for no other cause.

MR. PARKER [of New York]. Because he already has that power and it has been so decided by the Supreme Court. He can remove any public official at any time for malfeasance in office.

MR. COCHRAN. How about inefficiency and neglect of duty?

MR. PARKER. He has that power.[45]

C. THE POWER COMMISSION SINCE 1930

There have been no important changes in the organization of the Federal Power Commission since 1930, but there have been one or two interesting developments with regard to its personnel and some increases in its power.

1. CONTROVERSY OVER DISMISSAL OF KING AND RUSSELL—SENATE *versus* PRESIDENT

The first act of the new Power Commission after its members were appointed by President Hoover embroiled it in a bitter controversy with the Senate. President Hoover named as members of the commission George Otis Smith as chairman, Claude L. Draper, Marcel Garsaud, Ralph Williamson, and Frank McNinch. The day after their confirmation by the Senate the commission dismissed from office the chief accountant, William V. King, and the solicitor, Charles R. Russell. These two men had been in conflict with Mr. Bonner, the executive secretary, for a long time. Mr. Bonner was also removed from office but he was transferred to a post in one of the executive departments. The dismissal of King and Russell, generally regarded as the staunch defenders of the public interest against the encroachments of the big power companies, was viewed by the leaders in the Senate with astonishment and anger. Senators Wheeler, Norris, and Walsh led the assault.[46] Senator Wheeler declared that the President should at once remove from office the commissioners who had been guilty of this act in defiance of the public interest.[47] Senator Black inquired whether there was any legal barrier against the removal of the commissioners

45. 72 Cong. Rec. 10332.
46. 74 Cong. Rec. 1445, 1597 ff.
47. Ibid. 1598.

for such a reason and was told that there was none.[48] When the President did not act, Senator Wheeler urged that Congress should get rid of the commissioners by withholding appropriations for their salaries, and was joined in this opinion by Senator Johnson.[49] The Senate passed a resolution requesting the President to return to the Senate the nominations of the commissioners in order to permit reconsideration. The President bluntly refused to do this, having been advised by Attorney General Mitchell that the appointments were legally complete and that the Senate had no further power with respect to them. The President defended his position on legal grounds and also declared that the removal of the three officers was fully justified since the new commission ought to have full authority to choose its own staff. Upon the refusal of the President to return the nominations, the Senate reconsidered its action upon the nomination of George Otis Smith, the newly appointed chairman, and rejected it. Smith declined to recognize the legality of this action and continued to hold his office. The Senate thereupon appropriated money to institute a *quo warranto* action against Smith, alleging that the office was vacant. In *United States* v. *Smith* [50] the Supreme Court decided against the claims of the Senate and the controversy died out. Mr. King was ultimately reinstated. The incident was perhaps of no major importance. It settled an interesting constitutional point and it had the unfortunate effect of making the Power Commission appear, temporarily at least, unfriendly to those who were attempting to protect the government's vital interests in power resources.

2. REORGANIZATION OF PERSONNEL UNDER ROOSEVELT

The Act of 1930 omitted any restriction upon the President's power to remove the members of the Power Commission since Congress assumed that it could not validly restrict that power. The Act also provided that the President should name the first chairman of the commission but that thereafter the members of the commission should elect the chairman. In July 1933,

48. Ibid. 1599.
49. Ibid. 1931.
50. 286 U.S. 6 (1932). All relevant documents are printed in the opinion.

George Otis Smith, the chairman appointed by President Hoover, resigned his chairmanship, explaining that he was thereby acquiescing 'in the desire of President Roosevelt to have a man of his own selection.' [51] In spite of the clear statutory authority of the commission to select Smith's successor, the President on July 18 wrote to the commission, 'In view of the resignation of George Otis Smith as chairman of the Federal Power Commission, I hereby designate Hon. Frank R. McNinch as chairman and request the immediate concurrence of the commission.' [52] This letter indicates that the President realized that he must secure the concurrence of the commission in his selection of Mr. McNinch as chairman, but it also indicates an expectation that he would secure that concurrence by asking for it. We may assume that he was aware that his power of removal could be used to accomplish his ends. On October 31 Mr. Smith resigned from the commission. It was reported and not denied that the President had requested his resignation in order to make the commission 'fully responsive to the desires of the President and an effective instrument with which to forward his power policies.' [53] Thus the President was able to reorganize the commission for the more effective promotion of his own plans.

3. THE FEDERAL POWER ACT OF 1935—(THE HOLDING COMPANY ACT) [54]

We are not here concerned with the provisions of the Acts of 1935 dealing with power holding companies. These substantially broadened the scope of federal regulation. They imposed upon the Power Commission new duties of importance but not duties essentially different in kind from those which other regulatory agencies had long enjoyed. The new laws also brought the Power Commission into active contact with other departments and agencies which exercised authority in the same field. These changes, however, did not change the organization of

51. *The New York Times,* July 20, 1935, p. 27.

52. 14th Ann. Rept. of the Federal Power Commission, 68.

53. I have drawn here on the unpublished dissertation of L. V. Plum, Princeton University, *The Federal Power Commission;* I have used Dr. Plum's monograph extensively in this chapter.

54. Act of Aug. 26, 1935, 49 Stat. at L. 803.

the commission, or its fundamental relations to Congress or the President.

V. THE FEDERAL RADIO COMMISSION AND THE FEDERAL COMMUNICATIONS COMMISSION

A. THE RADIO ACT OF 1927—THE ONE-YEAR COMMISSION

1. THE BACKGROUND OF RADIO LEGISLATION

THE development of federal regulation of radio communication and the radio industry has been in certain ways unique. In this case an important industry was clamoring to be regulated for its own protection, although without any agreement on the form or method of regulation. Here an imperative physical necessity for radio control emerged long before any settled policies could be worked out, and to meet it Congress used more frankly and openly the method of trial and error than in any other similar situation, and placed greater reliance upon the regulatory agency to evolve and formulate basic plans and policies.

Early legislation in the field of radio was not regulatory in character. One of the first practical uses of radio was for communication from ship to shore, and in 1910 Congress passed a statute requiring in the interests of safety that every vessel carrying fifty or more passengers be equipped with wireless apparatus.[1] The Act was administered by the Bureau of Navigation in the Department of Commerce and Labor.

By this time the general use of wireless had increased until further regulation was necessary. Radio interference became an important factor, especially as it affected the radio work of the Army, Navy, and Coast Guard, and a bill drawn by them with the aid of the solicitor of the Department of Commerce and Labor was introduced in 1910. The bill required a license from the Secretary of Commerce and Labor for both sending and receiving apparatus. Its original draft authorized the Secretary to draft the rules and regulations for the issuance of these licenses, but opposition to the delegation of such important power to the Secretary led to the incorporation of these rules

1. Act of June 24, 1910, 36 Stat. at L. 629.

and regulations in the Act itself, and left the Secretary with no discretion with regard to licensing. All radio operators and stations were required to be licensed. The provision requiring licenses on receiving sets was eliminated, but the other provisions remained and this Act, passed in 1912,[2] remained the basic radio statute until the Act of 1927. Final impetus for the passage of the Act of 1912 came from two sources. The first was the *Titanic* disaster, which focused public attention upon radio protection for ships; the second was the government's desire to participate in the London Radio Telegraph Conference. The United States had delayed ratifying the International Radio Telegraph Convention of 1906 (Berlin) until 1912, and it was under an obligation to give effect to the Berlin Convention.

Radio problems continued, however, to increase in number and importance. In February 1922, Secretary of Commerce Hoover called the first of a series of annual radio conferences attended by representatives from all branches of the industry. These annual conferences were important. They provided an opportunity for those interested in radio problems to become articulate, and they made Secretary Hoover a leader with respect to radio problems. The first conference urged a higher degree of government control and proposed legislation; and in succeeding years the activities of the Secretary of Commerce in regard to radio regulations were shaped in the main by the proposals and policies discussed at these conferences.

The constructive efforts of Mr. Hoover and others, especially Stephen Davis, solicitor of the Department of Commerce, were brought to an abrupt end by a series of adverse court decisions culminating in 1923 in the ruling [3] of the Court of Appeals of the District of Columbia that the Secretary of Commerce under existing statutes had no authority to refuse a license to a wireless station. His duty under the Act was purely ministerial. Secretary Hoover had been proceeding on the assumption that his power to license carried with it by implication the power to withhold a license and to assign to licensees privileges on the air which were protected by law. In 1926 this decision was followed by a federal district court in *United States* v. *Zenith*

2. Act of Aug. 13, 1912, 37 Stat. at L. 302.
3. *Hoover, Sec. of Commerce* v. *Intercity Radio Co. Inc.,* 286 Fed. 1003 (1923).

Radio Corporation,[4] and this case held further that the Secretary of Commerce had no power under the statute to make any regulations affecting radio licenses. These decisions, together with the announcement by the Department of Commerce on July 9, 1926, that it would thereafter act only as a registration bureau, resulted in almost complete chaos in the radio field. 'A mad scramble to get on the air ensued and a broadcast of bedlam resulted. The demand for government regulation was now imperative since the very existence of the industry was threatened.'[5]

2. STEPS IN THE LEGISLATIVE HISTORY OF THE RADIO ACT OF 1927

The White-Dill Radio Act of 1927[6] traces its direct ancestry back to a bill introduced by Representative White of Maine in January 1923,[7] although others were introduced as early as 1920. It was drafted by the first radio conference, through its legislative committee. Its provisions made it plain that the radio industry wished Secretary Hoover to administer whatever radio regulation might be set up, for it gave important powers to the Secretary of Commerce. He was to classify stations and operators, prescribe the nature of the service rendered by each class, assign wave lengths, license stations 'in the public interest,' grant or withhold permits for the building of new stations, and finally, refuse a license to any company which in his judgment was monopolizing or seeking to monopolize radio communication. It would be hard to find a case of the delegation of more drastic authority to an executive officer. Associated with the Secretary was to be an advisory committee of twelve members. Six of these were to be chosen, one each, by the Secretaries of State, War, Navy, Agriculture, Commerce, and the Postmaster General; the other six were to be persons familiar with radio communication and were to be chosen by the Secretary of Commerce. To this advisory committee the Secretary could refer in his discretion any matter relating to administration; also changes in laws, regulations, or treaties regarding radio; and scientific problems requiring further study.

4. 12 Fed. (2d) 616 (1926).
5. E. P. Herring, *Public Administration and the Public Interest* (1936), 160.
6. Act of Feb. 23, 1927, 44 Stat. at L. 1162.
7. H.R. 13773, 67th Cong., 4th sess. (1923).

The House Committee on Merchant Marine and Fisheries held hearings on this bill early in 1923. It was on the whole favorably received. It had Administration support and the radio industry in the main approved it. It was reported favorably to the House and debated. There was some criticism that the powers of the Secretary of Commerce were too broad, and that there was no adequate protection against monopoly and no regulation of rates. It passed the House but was not acted upon in the Senate.

In the next Congress, in February 1924, the White bill [8] was again introduced and in March further hearings on it were held by the same House committee. In April 1924 the Senate passed a bill [9] merely reaffirming that the use of the ether was the possession of the people of the United States and providing for control by the President in time of war or national emergency; the committee took the White bill and reported it to the House in May as an amendment to this Senate bill. The House never considered the bill and in the following January it was sent back to the committee. The bill was felt to be fatally defective in one respect. It authorized the Secretary of Commerce to refuse a station license to companies which in his judgment were attempting to monopolize the industry. It was felt that this power could not safely be given to an executive officer. Secretary Hoover himself vigorously objected [10] to this grant of authority at the first hearings on the White bill and withdrew his support from it when the provision was finally left in. The radio lobby naturally opposed it, and the bill was not reported out of the committee.

At the Fourth National Radio Conference in November 1925 Secretary Hoover made an important address urging legislation.[11] He emphasized that there were two basic radio problems to be met. The first was the problem of traffic control in radio, and this he believed was a one-man job. The second was the problem of allocating radio traffic channels, and this he felt was a semi-judicial task which ought to be handled by a board.

8. H.R. 7357, 68th Cong., 1st sess. (1924).

9. S. 2930, 68th Cong., 1st sess. (1924).

10. Hearings before the House Committee on Merchant Marine and Fisheries on H.R. 7357, 68th Cong., 1st sess. (1924), 11.

11. Printed in Hearings before the Senate Committee on Interstate Commerce on S. 1 and S. 1754, 69th Cong., 1st sess. (1926), 50 ff.

The legislative committee of the conference proposed that the Secretary of Commerce be placed in charge of the traffic control phase of the problem. In December 1925 Mr. White accordingly introduced a bill [12] upon which hearings were held in the House committee, and on March 3, 1926, he introduced a new bill [13] which contained important modifications. The objectionable monopoly provision was replaced by an authorization to the Secretary to refuse licenses to those who had been convicted in court of a violation of the antitrust laws. The advisory committee was replaced by a radio commission of five members appointed for four-year terms and drawn from both parties and from five geographical regions. This commission was to deal with such matters as the Secretary might refer to it, but the new bill provided also that every decision or order of the Secretary relating to radio could be appealed to the commission by anyone feeling aggrieved. Secretary Hoover had urgently pressed for this, objecting to the provision in the earlier White bill which had permitted appeals only through the Secretary.[14] In the new bill the Secretary was to have no authority over the final decision of the commission, but the decisions both of the Secretary and of the commission could be appealed to the Court of Appeals of the District of Columbia. Within two days this bill was reported out favorably by the committee with the exception of Ewin L. Davis of Tennessee, who filed a minority report criticizing the bill for not adequately suppressing monopoly, and urging the establishment of a full-time independent commission to handle the job of radio control. The bill was debated in the House and passed on March 15 by a vote of 218 to 123, 89 not voting. It went the following day to the Senate Committee on Interstate Commerce, where it promptly struck a snag. The Senate committee under the chairmanship of Senator Dill was unanimous in its belief that a full-time independent regulatory commission should be established, and had under consideration a bill to that effect.[15] The Senate committee amended the House bill

12. H.R. 5589, 69th Cong., 1st sess. (1925).
13. H.R. 9971, 69th Cong., 1st sess. (1926).
14. Hearings before the House Committee on Merchant Marine and Fisheries on H.R. 5589, 69th Cong., 1st sess. (1926), 11 f.
15. S. 1754, 69th Cong., 1st sess. (1926).

by striking out all after the enacting clause and inserting the
Senate bill. In this form the bill was reported out [16] on May 8,
and passed the Senate on July 2. A conference was called but
Congress was eager to adjourn, and as the disagreement between the Senate and House seemed fundamental, the conference committee decided that it was impossible to effect a
compromise in the brief time available. It reported the situation back to the two houses and recommended the passage of
an interim resolution regarding licenses and property rights.
Congress passed the resolution and adjourned. Congress convened in December, and on January 29, 1927, the conferees
presented a bill which was a compromise between the positions taken in the Senate and the House. The House passed
the conference report on January 29, the Senate on February
18, and the bill became law February 23, 1927.

3. PROVISIONS OF THE ACT OF 1927

The Radio Act of 1927 was an interesting experiment in the
field of administrative regulation in the relations created between the new commission and the Secretary of Commerce. Its
provisions may be summarized as follows:

First, the Act created a Federal Radio Commission of five
members with six-year staggered terms, appointed by the President with the advice and consent of the Senate. The first chairman was to be named by the President and thereafter the commission itself was to elect its chairman. It was required that
the commissioners be citizens, reside in one of five geographical zones at the time of appointment, and have no financial
interests in the radio industry. The commission was to be bipartisan. The salary for the first year was to be $10,000. The
commission was given broad administrative and quasi-judicial
powers. It was to classify radio stations and prescribe the nature of their services, assign frequencies and wave lengths, determine locations of classes of stations, regulate the kind of
apparatus used, establish regulations to prevent interference,
establish areas or zones to be served by any station, hold hearings, and summon witnesses for the purpose of making investi-

16. S. Rept. 772, 69th Cong., 1st sess. (1926).

gations relevant to its duties. It had also certain appellate functions. Applications for station licenses, renewals, or changes were to be referred by the Secretary of Commerce to the commission for definite action. The Secretary might refer to the commission any matter upon which he desired its judgment. From any decision or regulation of the Secretary an appeal could be taken to the commission by anyone aggrieved thereby. The review on appeal was to be *de novo* and was to be final save for appeal to the Court of Appeals of the District of Columbia. Review by the court was on both law and facts, but was confined to the record made by the licensing authority.

Second, certain purely administrative powers were left in the hands of the Secretary of Commerce. He was to receive all applications for station licenses although he could not act upon them. He was to license and fix the qualifications of station operators and suspend such licenses for cause. He was to inspect transmitting equipment, designate the call letters of stations, and conduct investigations designed to uncover violations of the Act or the terms of licenses.

Third, this division of labor was to continue for one year only. The Secretary of Commerce was then to take over all the powers and duties of the Radio Commission except its power to revoke licenses and its appellate powers, and the commission itself was to become merely an appellate body. Applications for station licenses, their renewal or modification, must be referred to the commission in case of dispute or conflict. The Secretary could still refer to the commission for decision such matters as he might care to handle in this way. The commission ceased to be a full-time body at the end of the year and the compensation of its members was thereafter on a *per diem* basis.

4. TOPICS AND ISSUES IN HEARINGS AND DEBATES

a. *Departmental* versus *commission control*

There was sharp dispute concerning the kind of authority that was to administer radio regulation. Should this important job be given to the Secretary of Commerce or to a new full-time independent commission? A strong case was presented for allowing the Department of Commerce to continue and extend its control over the radio industry. Those who urged this were less articulate than those who favored a commission, but their case was greatly strengthened by the confidence which the industry and everyone else felt in Secretary Hoover, who had assumed a position of leadership in radio matters. It was clear that much of the work involved in radio regulation was administrative in nature, and with regard to it direct responsibility and quickness of action were imperative. There was also strong objection to the creation of another commission. Mr. Larsen of Georgia charged in the House that these commissions had proved costly and unnecessary; that the Interstate Commerce Commission had authority to control interstate communication rates but had never done anything about it. He pointed out that it is impossible to abolish a commission once it has been set up, even though it is no longer needed; that there was not enough work to keep a full-time radio commission busy and that it would become an idle 'swivel-chair brigade.' He said, 'Our national commission octopus is already too large; his legs are too long. I am in favor of lopping them off instead of trying to grow more.' [17] In the Senate Senator Bingham of Connecticut objected to the creation of another one of those 'three-in-one commissions,' which he regarded as a menace to the basic doctrine of the separation of powers.[18]

The argument for a full-time independent radio commission ran along the following familiar lines: First, the job to be done lay beyond the competence of any one man. With all respect to Secretary Hoover, he would be unable to deal personally with radio problems but would have to farm them out to subordinates. Second, it would be unsafe to give this important task to one man. All the changes were rung on this point. Departmental control would be autocratic. As Senator Watson declared:

. . . If it is to be in any department it places in the head of that department autocratic power over this tremendous agency, the greatest that could ever be conceived by the mind of man for the creation of public opinion and the formulation of public thought.[19]

17. 67 Cong. Rec. 5579.   19. Ibid. 12357.
18. Ibid. 12498.

Senator Dill was similarly disturbed. He feared that one-man control of radio might endanger the freedom of speech and absence of censorship which were of such vital importance. Only in a bipartisan commission could these important interests be fully protected.[20] The Senate Committee on Interstate Commerce in its report declared:

The exercise of this power is fraught with such great possibilities that it should not be entrusted to any one man nor to any administrative department of the Government. This regulatory power should be as free from political influence or arbitrary control as possible. A commission which would meet only occasionally would gain only a cursory and incomplete knowledge of radio problems. It would necessarily be largely dependent on the administrative authority, namely, the Secretary of Commerce, for expert knowledge it would require.[21]

It was also pointed out that the important quasi-judicial tasks involved in radio regulation would not be impartially handled by one man. Third, it was urged that full-time administrators devoting their entire energy to the job could handle it more effectively than anyone else. Senator Dill declared that what was wanted was an 'authoritative body on the great problems of radio,' [22] a group of men who would have radio as a sole interest. These men should be men of broad vision who could bring to the problems of regulation a fresh point of view. It was unnecessary and undesirable that they be experts, for they would have at their disposal at all times the technical knowledge of experts. Finally it was already being suggested that an independent commission was necessary to regulate not merely radio but the telegraph and telephone industries as well. This foreshadowed the later drive for a communications commission.

b. *Should radio control be given to the I.C.C.?*

It had been proposed before the House committee in 1912 that the control of radio should go to the Interstate Commerce Commission, which under a statute passed in 1910 [23] already

20. Ibid. 12356.
21. *Supra,* note 16, op. cit. 2.
22. 67 Cong. Rec. 12356.
23. Mann-Elkins Act of June 18, 1910, 36 Stat. at L. 539.

had jurisdiction over communication by telegraph and telephone. Whatever plausibility this suggestion originally had had disappeared by 1927. It was pointed out by Representative Davis of Tennessee in his minority report [24] and by Senator Dill [25] that the Interstate Commerce Commission had ignored the problems of telephone and telegraph regulation, that it had no time and no expert knowledge with which to approach them. In view of this record there was little comment on the proposal to turn over to the overworked Interstate Commerce Commission the infinitely more complicated task of radio control. That commission would have to set up a new bureau and delegate the job to subordinates. It would be better to set the bureau up as an independent agency and it would cost no more to do so.

c. *Segregation of administrative from quasi-judicial functions*

The perennial question whether administrative and quasi-judicial tasks should be placed in the same hands was bound to arise in connection with radio control. Secretary Hoover repeatedly voiced his settled conviction that these types of authority ought not to be given to the same man or group of men. As we have seen, he vigorously objected when the original White radio bill proposed to confer upon the Secretary of Commerce the quasi-judicial power to deny a radio station license if in the Secretary's judgment the applicant was monopolizing or trying to monopolize the radio industry.[26] In his address before the Fourth National Radio Conference in 1925 he stated his views clearly:

It seems to me that we have in this development of governmental regulation two distinct problems. First is a question of traffic control. This must be a Federal responsibility. From an interference point of view, every word broadcast is an interstate word. Therefore, radio is a 100 percent interstate question and there is not an individual who has the most rudimentary knowledge of the art who does not realize that there must be a traffic policeman in the ether, or all services will be lost in complete chaos of interference. This is

24. H. Rept. 464, 69th Cong., 1st sess. (1926), 17 f. *Supra,* 301.
25. 67 Cong. Rec. 12356.
26. *Supra,* 300.

an administrative job, and for good administration must lie in a single responsibility.

The second question is the determination of who shall use the traffic channels and under what conditions. This is a very large discretionary and semi-judicial function which should not devolve entirely upon any single official and is, I believe, a matter in which each local community should have a large voice—should in some fashion participate in a determination of who should use the channels available for broadcasting.[27]

However, if the Secretary of Commerce was to be given quasi-judicial regulatory power over radio, Mr. Hoover believed that an appellate body should be set up to review the orders and decisions of the Secretary. While convinced that the administrator ought not to be given semi-judicial duties, Mr. Hoover was even more emphatic that administrative duties should not be given to quasi-judicial bodies. In his testimony before the House committee in 1926 he said:

. . . I have agreed that this whole matter required a great deal of thought in this aspect, that we have gone on for a great many years in creating commissions and endowing executive officials with large regulatory and semijudicial and semilegislative authority, without any proper comprehension of where the division line of these functions lay; that, obviously, questions of a semijudicial or semilegislative character, that develop under an assignment of authority by our Congress, should be in the hands of commissions and they should not be in the hands of administrative officials. On the other hand, we have gone on, parallel with the foolishness of assigning such functions to individuals, with the equally foolish assignment of administrative and executive functions to such boards, and we have some of the worst debacles in the Government from an administrative point of view in the country. In radio legislation, aside from this one question as to who may enjoy the radio privilege in a limited field, the functions are practically all of them of an administrative character.[28]

He did not, however, commit himself when asked whether he favored the establishment of an independent radio commission.

27. *Supra,* note 11, op. cit. 57.   28. *Supra,* note 14, op. cit. 14.

d. *The one-year arrangement*

The plan whereby the administration of radio control was to be given to the radio commission for a year, at the end of which time it was to be turned back to the Secretary of Commerce, was frankly a compromise between the views of the Senate and the House. Explaining it in the House, Mr. Scott of Michigan pointed out that the arrangement would allow Congress at the end of the year to decide how well the plan had worked and whether commission control should be continued.[29] Senator Dill, while favoring an independent full-time commission, stated that a radio commission by a year of administrative experience would be well enough educated to make an effective appellate body if and when its status was changed.[30] It was clear that the one-year provision was designed merely to make legislation possible. No one assumed that 'the major problems of regulation were being squarely met and solved.

e. *The designation of the chairman of the commission*

Some discussion arose with regard to the designation of the chairman of the commission, though none of this discussion went into the merits of the question or disclosed any appreciation of its importance. It was desirable to have the President name the first chairman so that someone would have authority to call the commission together and get its work started. There was objection to making this arrangement permanent, however, and it was pointed out in the House that the Interstate Commerce Commission and the Federal Trade Commission select their own chairmen. A compromise was reached whereby the President named the first chairman and thereafter the commission selected its chairman.

f. *Court review of commission action on licenses*

It was widely felt that the power to grant, revoke, or modify station licenses, a power to be exercised under the vague guid-

29. 68 Cong. Rec. 2564.   30. Ibid. 2869.

ing standard of the public interest, convenience, and necessity, was too vitally important to be exercised by any administrative body without judicial review of the most complete scope. Accordingly, the Court of Appeals of the District of Columbia was authorized to review the decisions of the proposed radio commission in license matters and to reach its own independent judgment regarding the soundness and justice of the commission's action. Senator Cummins warned the Senate that this review created constitutional difficulties,[31] since the constitutional courts could not review the discretionary orders of an administrative body without invalidly exercising non-judicial power. His warning was ignored; it was not until the decision of the Supreme Court in the General Electric Company case in 1930[32] that Congress learned that he was right.

g. *General views on the independent commission*

The debates on the Radio Act of 1927 offered an opportunity for the airing of Congressional views on the independent commission as a type of governmental agency. Mr. Lehlbach of New Jersey in the House charged that independent commissions in general were irresponsible and bureaucratic. He said:

... As a general principle, I am opposed to independent commissions in our Government and did not look with favor upon the creation of one for the regulation and control of radio.

Independent commissions not incorporated in one of the departments of the Government and subordinate to the head of that department were obviously not contemplated by the framers of the Constitution as having a place in the structure they created. In the three great coordinate divisions of the Government—the legislative, the judicial, and the executive—the framers intended that the executive, as well as the legislative, should be directly responsible to the people. They created the office of President for a stated term, the incumbent to be elected by the representatives of the people, with the resultant opportunity given to the people to sit in judgment upon his administration. When they created departments to carry on the various functions of administration, they placed at the head of each an officer of the President's selection and responsible to him.

31. 67 Cong. Rec. 12354 f.
32. *Federal Radio Commission* v. *General Electric Co.,* 281 U.S. 464 (1930). *Infra,* 313

Thus all the functions of administration are vested in agencies responsible ultimately to the President, who in turn is responsible to the people. The creation of independent commissions performing administrative functions and not subject to the guidance and control of the Chief Executive was an afterthought and not contemplated in the original structure of our Government. In most instances it has not been productive of beneficent results. For example: It is not an unreasonable suggestion that the maintenance, operation, and development of our merchant marine would have been carried on more efficiently and more economically if, instead of creating an independent United States Shipping Board, its functions had been vested in a bureau or division of the Department of Commerce . . .

These various independent commissions are, in fact, directly responsible to no one in the Government. They are subject neither to supervision or control. In theory they are responsible directly to Congress. Manifestly, a legislative body has no means of making any control effective save by the unsatisfactory methods of imposing limitations on appropriations and conducting sporadic investigations when grave abuses come to light. Such freedom from restraint by a commission, board, or bureau tends to develop bureaucracy in its worse form . . .

The Interstate Commerce Commission exercises functions so ramified, so far-reaching, and of such vital importance that it may well occupy a position subordinate to no department. However, here again it is fair to consider whether it would not be better to create in its stead a department of transportation and communication, with a Cabinet officer at its head and incorporated in the executive family, rather than leave it outside of the orderly scheme of government contemplated by the Constitution.

For these considerations I do not like the creation of an independent commission for the regulation of radio communications, even temporarily . . . If I could write this legislation, I would provide for an organization in the Department of Commerce responsible to the Secretary of Commerce and subject to his control. I would not even have an advisory commission to whom might be referred matters within the administrative functions of the department.[33]

33. 68 Cong. Rec. 2570.

B. THE YEAR-BY-YEAR COMMISSION—THE COMMISSION 1927-34

1. DEVELOPMENTS DURING PROBATIONARY PERIOD

a. *The Radio Commission's first year*

The Radio Commission got off to a bad start. It was obliged to begin its work under serious handicaps. Congress failed to pass the deficiency appropriation bill of 1927 and left the commission without any money. It had to borrow such staff as it could from other departments. During the year two of its members died and one resigned. The Senate had confirmed only three of the commissioners, and for the last four months of its year the commission had carried on with but four members, only one of whom had been confirmed. Under these circumstances it was not surprising that the commission proved inadequate to the crisis confronting the radio industry. It began its efforts by calling a four-day conference from which valuable suggestions were derived but of which the net results were meagre. At the end of the year it was obvious that order had not been restored, that only the worst cases of radio interference had been eliminated, and that the commission had fallen far short of accomplishing what had been expected of it. Particularly had it failed to reduce the number of stations.

b. *The Radio Acts of* 1928 *and* 1929

For two years Congress, chiefly out of inertia, continued the year-by-year status of the commission. As the end of the first year approached it was apparent that Congress must do something about the commission, for if it did nothing the duties of the commission would automatically be turned over to the Secretary of Commerce and the commission itself would become a purely appellate body. While no one was satisfied with the accomplishments of the first year, it was recognized that the commission had operated under serious difficulties and had not had a fair opportunity to show what it could do. The Senate had on its hands the confirmation of three members of the commission and one vacancy to be filled. Should these appointments be confirmed for the statutory period of six years or should some temporary policy regarding them be followed? To meet this situation a bill continuing the *status quo* for another year was introduced by Senator Watson [34] and referred to the Committee on Interstate Commerce, which reported it out favorably early in February 1928. The bill was frankly another compromise to meet an emergency; the commission retained its powers, the salaries of the commissioners remained at $10,000 and their term of office was not changed. The Senate, however, amended the bill so that the terms of all the commissioners would expire in February 1929, and passed it without roll call on February 6. On March 12 the House passed the bill with the amendment destined to cause so much trouble, requiring an equality of radio facilities between geographical zones according to population and between states within each zone according to population. The conference report, retaining both Senate and House amendments, passed the House on March 21, passed the Senate on March 24, and the bill became law on March 28.[35]

During the second year the commission made substantial improvements in radio control. It set up a policy of cleared channels for certain stations; it brought local interference under control; and it formulated definite policies with respect to the 'public interest, convenience, and necessity' provisions of the law. In the winter of 1928-9 Congress again discussed whether to continue the commission in its present form or to put into effect the changes provided for in the Act of 1927. But while the discussions in the committee hearings went very thoroughly into the issue, Congress again postponed making any final decision. In December 1928 Mr. White introduced in the House a bill for a continuance of the *status quo* for another year; it was reported out of committee in February, passed the House on February 19, passed the Senate on March 1, and was approved March 4, 1929.[36] As the result of a filibuster by Senator Copeland, this Act continued the commission only to December 31, 1929.

34. S. 2317, 70th Cong., 1st sess. (1928).
35. Act of Mar. 28, 1928, 45 Stat. at L. 373.
36. Act of Mar. 4, 1929, 45 Stat. at L. 1559.

c. *The Radio Act of December* 18, 1929

The forces of inertia continued to pull steadily toward the continuance of the Radio Commission on this temporary basis. But in his annual message of December 1929 President Hoover urged 'the reorganization of the Radio Commission into a permanent body from its temporary status.' [37] There had been a steadily growing drive for a single communications commission and legislation to that effect was being formulated; in order therefore to have freedom to act Congress in December 1929 put the Radio Commission on indefinite tenure. Early in December legislation was introduced which passed House and Senate almost without debate on December 16 and was signed two days later.[38] By this Act the ultimate future of the Radio Commission was not definitely settled, but the policy of year-by-year probation was abandoned. The Act provided that all powers vested in the Radio Commission by the Act of 1927 should 'continue to be vested in and exercised by the Commission until otherwise provided for by law,' and that the period during which members of the commission should receive $10,000 was 'hereby extended until such time as is otherwise provided for by law.' On February 21, 1930, the Senate confirmed nominations to the commission for the two- to six-year terms specified in the original Act instead of for one year only.

d. *The Act of July* 1, 1930

On May 19, 1930, the Supreme Court of the United States in the case of *Federal Radio Commission* v. *General Electric Company* [39] declined to review a decision of the Court of Appeals of the District of Columbia which had reviewed a discretionary order of the Federal Radio Commission. As Senator Cummins had predicted, the Court held that a constitutional court could not validly review the exercise of administrative discretion. Under the Act of 1927 the Court of Appeals of the District of Columbia was to review the orders of the commission, and was instructed to take new evidence under such con-

37. 72 Cong. Rec. 25.   39. *Supra*, 309 and note 32.
38. Act of Dec. 18, 1929, 46 Stat. at L. 50.

ditions as it might deem proper, and reach such decision upon the merits as seemed to it just and reasonable. This, said the Supreme Court, is not the exercise of judicial power, and these administrative findings may not be brought to the Supreme Court of the United States for ultimate review. Congress therefore passed a statute on July 1, 1930,[40] to correct this situation. The jurisdiction of the Court of Appeals of the District of Columbia to review decisions and orders of the Federal Radio Commission was limited to questions of law. Findings of fact made by the commission, if supported by evidence, were made final, and there was to be no review by the court of the exercise of purely administrative discretion. In short, the Radio Commission was given the same status with respect to the review of its decisions by the courts as the other regulatory commissions. In 1933 in *Federal Radio Commission* v. *Nelson Brothers Bond and Mortgage Company*[41] the Supreme Court held that the earlier defect had been corrected and it accepted for review appeals brought under the provisions of the new statute.

2. TOPICS AND ISSUES IN HEARINGS AND DEBATES ON THE CONTINUANCE OF THE COMMISSION

During this period of chaos and uncertainty radio policy was being dealt with by trial and error and by inertia. Sharp differences of opinion existed as to what ought to be done. There were at least four fairly clear possibilities. First, the arrangement provided by the Act of 1927 and designed to continue for one year only could be made permanent. Second, the plan intended by the Act of 1927 to go into effect after one year could be put into operation. This would give to the Secretary of Commerce full regulatory powers both administrative and quasi-judicial and keep the Radio Commission as an appellate body. Third, the commission could be abolished entirely and the whole job of radio regulation be turned over to the Department of Commerce. Fourth, a permanent full-time independent commission could be set up and the Department of Commerce relieved of all radio responsibility.

40. Act of July 1, 1930, 46 Stat. at L. 844.
41. 289 U.S. 266 (1933).

From 1927 to 1930 the issue seemed to be drawn between the first two possibilities listed. There were very few advocates of exclusive executive administration of radio regulation, and those who favored a full-time independent commission did not push their claims vigorously. They were willing to allow the existing commission further opportunity to prove itself; there was a growing conviction that ultimately the question of the creation of a commission to regulate all forms of communication would arise, and that the present arrangement might well be continued until that larger issue had to be met.

The wisdom of continuing the Radio Commission as created by the Act of 1927 seems to have been more or less taken for granted. Legislative inertia pulled strongly in this direction, as well as the realization that the broad problem of the regulation of all forms of communication lay just around the corner. The defense of the existing arrangement ran along the following lines: The commission had been set up to aid in planning a national radio policy and had not had time to complete that work. Senator Dill laid emphasis on this point.[42] Although he preferred a full-time independent commission, he was willing to continue the commission on a yearly basis but with short terms for the commissioners, since he felt that Congress during this experimental period should retain the power to get rid of commissioners who proved unsatisfactory.[43] It was pointed out further that the licensing of radio stations was a judicial or semi-judicial and not an administrative task, and that it ought therefore not to be given to the Secretary of Commerce. It was also suggested that to convert the commission into a purely appellate body as originally provided in the Act of 1927 would seriously interrupt the work of radio regulation, since the Department of Commerce was not equipped to take over the duties of the commission. Finally, it was predicted that all of the orders and decisions of the Secretary of Commerce would be appealed to the commission if it were set up as an appellate body, and therefore the commission might better make the decisions in the first place.

Though obviously in defense of a lost cause, the argument for placing radio regulation in the Department of Commerce

42. 70 Cong. Rec. 3748 f.   43. 69 Cong. Rec. 2533; 72 Cong. Rec. 714.

was cogently presented in the House and Senate hearings on the bills from which emerged the Act of March 4, 1929. The principal spokesman for this position was Commissioner O. H. Caldwell, whose experience on the commission and ability as a technical expert lent weight to his argument. He and other witnesses presented six reasons in support of their position:

First, the Radio Commission had not handled its job successfully. Mr. Caldwell said that the work of the commission had from the beginning been a matter of compromise:

> All radio men, Senator, are agreed on certain principles of allocation, about cleared channels, powers of stations—in other words the method of laying down to the American people the maximum of radio service, but the work of the Radio Commission has always been a compromise. And the pity of it is that it has always been a compromise away from what is sound scientifically. In many affairs of life I believe in men getting around a table and reaching a compromise. But when the physician gives his opinion in a case and gives his diagnosis, it is the height of absurdity to call in men who do not understand medicine or surgery and attempt to compromise with the physician's expert opinion.[44]

He asserted that the Radio Bureau in the Department of Commerce was a more efficient administrative agency than the commission could possibly be, and refuted the argument that the department was not equipped to handle the mass of technical work involved:

> Some questions have been asked as to just what the radio division of the Department of Commerce is. That radio division at present consists of 135 people, in comparison with the Radio Commission's present staff of 82 people. The staff of the radio division of the Department of Commerce includes 65 trained radio men, who are competent radio experts, scattered over the country. The Radio Commission at this time has only four trained radio men outside of the two officers who have been loaned it by the Army and Navy.
> . . . Those men supervise the operation of all of the radio stations of the country, including the ships, the land stations, the broadcasting stations, and 16,000 amateurs.[45]

44. Hearings before the Senate Committee on Interstate Commerce on S. 4937, 70th Cong., 2d sess. (1929), 145.
45. Ibid. 145 f.

Second, in the interests of fair play the tasks of administering a regulatory statute ought not to be given to the quasi-judicial body which must determine whether the regulation has been fairly administered. Under the existing arrangement the commission sat in review on its own original acts and findings and judged controversies to which it was one of the parties. It should be relieved of all administrative work if it was to perform satisfactorily its judicial work. Manton Davis, general counsel of the Radio Corporation of America, in testifying before the Senate committee in 1929 urged the segregation of administrative from judicial work on this ground:

. . . In my judgment, Senator, radio decisions must of necessity divide themselves up into administrative decisions and quasi judicial decisions. You, in your wisdom, when you enacted the law, provided that the Radio Commission should, during the period of one year while there were some fundamental principles being laid down, exercise both administrative and the quasi judicial functions. Now, for the reasons that I have pointed out, in my mind the administrative functions are coming along so fast that if you in your wisdom permit the brush to be cleared by the hundreds and hundreds of administrative decisions to be taken in the administrative way that your legislation first provided, and leave the commission free to handle the larger and the controversial, quasi judicial matters as you originally wrote the law, that we who are engaged in the radio business and are earnestly desirous that it shall move and not stand still, will find ourselves better served, that the people of the United States will be better served, and the Radio Commission will be able to do a job more satisfactory to itself.[46]

This was definitely the view of Mr. Caldwell:

. . . The commission should be left free to perform its important appellate and judicial duties of reviewing the controversies and the controversial cases without being overloaded with all of this administrative detail with which it is being cluttered up at the present time.[47]

Third, one-man control was necessary to efficient administration. The problems of radio were technical in the extreme and beyond the capacity of a commission. No commission

46. Ibid. 83 f.   47. Ibid. 150.

could hope to administer with real efficiency and a commission organized on the basis of regional representation was in this respect the worst of all. Representative Celler of New York attacked the commission on this ground:

> . . . You know you cannot ride two horses going in a different direction at the same time. Well, even more so you cannot ride five horses going at the same time in five different directions.
> . . . You have seen fit—contrary to my wishes, at least—to look upon radio as a sort of pie to be divided into five equal parts. You may as well try to divide the rainbow into five equal parts as to try to divide the radio spectrum into five different parts.[48]

While the Secretary of Commerce would have to delegate large powers to his subordinates were he given this unified responsibility, it was urged that it is easier to delegate power safely and efficiently in an executive department than in a commission.

Fourth, it was alleged that the job which the commission had been set up to do was very largely done. Some of the basic problems of radio regulation had been solved, and there was no longer need for a commission to serve as a deliberative body for the formulation of radio policy.

Fifth, a commission was not a suitable body to administer the regulation of an expanding industry based upon a swiftly evolving art. The problems calling for determination were too complicated and arose too rapidly to lie within the competence of a commission. Manton Davis pointed out that the Interstate Commerce Commission was set up long after the formative period in the railroad industry had passed, and gave it as his opinion that had the Interstate Commerce Commission been forced to deal with railroad development from its inception it would have proved inadequate to the task.[49] This argument is interesting, since it implies that a commission is a less effective agency through which to carry on an experimental and exploratory program of regulation than is a centralized administrative unit.

Finally, it was alleged, and some members of the commission agreed, that political pressure could work more easily upon the commission than it could upon the Secretary of Commerce,

48. 70 Cong. Rec. 3775.   49. *Supra,* note 44, op. cit. 88.

and that the diffusion of responsibility amongst five men made that pressure more dangerous. As Mr. Caldwell put it:

> The pressure upon the supervising authority of radio is such that I believe it will always be at a disadvantage unless that could be carried back to some man in whom the country has unquestioned confidence. I feel that five commissioners will always be at a disadvantage under such an arrangement.[50]

In the hearings Commissioner Caldwell elaborated his fundamental belief that the administrative work should reside in a department and appellate semi-judicial functions should lie separate, preferably in a board or commission:

> . . . In the principle of organization of government such organization should be through the established forms of the constitutional government. That has been my view from the beginning. My experience in the past two years, and particularly the past year, on the commission has, however, crystallized and reinforced my views as to the difficulty of operating an administrative problem through a commission . . .
>
> I am referring only to the administrative function of the commission. I have expressed thorough approval of the appellate function.
>
> . . . Certainly my experience of the past two years has shown the value of having an expert appellate body. I feel that it is of the greatest importance that the body which passes in review on a radio controversy should have enough of the background of the subject so that it can pass on the questions skillfully and expertly . . .
>
> Certainly the review of such controversies and the adjustment of such controversies can be settled more fairly and more wisely by a commission of five men than by any one man.[51]

> . . . I think in the law itself there is one fundamental difficulty . . .
>
> The commission sits in judgment on an applicant who is appealing against its own decision. Complete fairness of decision and the true purpose of the commission as an appellate body, I believe, can only be attained when the commission does not have to sit in judgment in these cases where it is itself one of the contenders, or to pass judgment upon appeals from its own acts or allocations. For simple consistency certainly the administrative function should be wholly separated from the appellate function.[52]

50. Hearings before the House Committee on Merchant Marine and Fisheries on H.R. 15430, 70th Cong., 2d sess. (1929), 334.

51. Ibid. 445 f.   52. *Supra,* note 44, op. cit. 151.

C. FEDERAL COMMUNICATIONS ACT OF 1934

1. BACKGROUND OF THE ACT

It will be recalled that in 1910 Congress gave the Interstate Commerce Commission jurisdiction over interstate telephone and telegraph communication. During and after the hearings on the proposed radio bills, the proposal was made to set up a commission which should exercise unified control over all facilities for interstate communication. Mr. Ewin L. Davis of Tennessee made this proposal in his minority report to the House as early as 1926,[53] but no serious discussion took place at that time. For a period of years the crucial and inescapable problem was that of radio control, and Congress seemed disposed to tackle first things first.

In 1929 a bill [54] was introduced in the Senate calling for the creation of a communications commission to regulate 'all common carriers engaged in the transportation of intelligence by wire or wireless.' It was to consist of five members chosen from five zones. It was essentially the Radio Act of 1927, but it transferred to the commission all powers with respect to radio vested in the Secretary of Commerce as well as the power over telegraph and telephone companies enjoyed by the Interstate Commerce Commission. Hearings on the bill were conducted by the Senate Committee on Interstate Commerce, which made some changes in the bill but did not report it out, not because the committee opposed it on its merits but because it was regarded as premature.

In 1933 President Roosevelt requested Secretary of Commerce Roper to set up an interdepartmental committee to make a thorough study of the whole problem of the regulation of communications. Associated with this committee were the chairmen of the Senate and House committees on interstate commerce. On January 23, 1934, the interdepartmental committee filed its report with the President.[55] This report drew attention to the existing division of authority over wire and

53. *Supra,* 306.
54. S. 6, 71st Cong., 1st sess. (1929).
55. Senate Committee Print, Study of Communications by an Interdepartmental Committee, 73d Cong., 2d sess. (1934).

radio communications. That authority was distributed amongst the Radio Commission, the Department of Commerce, the Postmaster General, the Interstate Commerce Commission, and the President. There was neither unified control nor centralized responsibility. The committee recommended that all regulation of communications be handled by a single body. It expressed no clear preference between an independent commission and administration by a department as the agency for this control, but it stated that if the control of communications was given to an executive department, a board of appeals should be set up for the purpose of review. It strongly urged the establishment of an advisory council for the planning of policy in the field.

The President immediately sent the report of the interdepartmental committee to Congress accompanied by a special message.[56] In this message he urged the creation of a communications commission to exercise unified control over the entire field. To it should be transferred the powers now vested in the Radio Commission and those of the Interstate Commerce Commission with regard to telephone and telegraph. The commission should have full powers to make investigations and to recommend legislation.

A bill[57] incorporating the President's proposal was introduced in the House. It did not change the substantive regulation of the radio industry, but it consolidated the control of radio, telephone, and telegraph in a single body. In the Senate a much more drastic and novel bill[58] was introduced, proposing in fact an entirely new radio law. It fixed by statute the mileage separation between high-powered stations; it reduced the licensing period for radio licenses; it permitted the commission to impose fines of $1,000 per day on station owners for certain offenses; it permitted the revocation of station licenses without a hearing; and it limited sharply the right of appeal. Hearings were conducted on the bill; it was modified and reported out on April 19,[59] was debated in the Senate, amended, and passed without roll call on May 15.

56. S. Doc. 144, 73d Cong., 2d sess. (1934).
57. H.R. 8301, 73d Cong., 2d sess. (1934).
58. S. 2910, 73d Cong., 2d sess. (1934).
59. As S. 3285.

The amended Senate bill went to the House Committee on Interstate and Foreign Commerce on May 21. It was reported out on June 1, again amended, and after short debate passed without roll call on June 2. It went to a conference committee which further modified the drastic proposals of the Senate. The conference report passed both houses on June 9, and the bill became law June 19, 1934.[60]

2. PROVISIONS OF THE FEDERAL COMMUNICATIONS ACT OF 1934

a. *The commission*

The new Federal Communications Commission was composed of seven members appointed by the President with the advice and consent of the Senate for seven-year staggered terms. The chairman was to be designated by the President. The disqualification of those in any way associated with the radio industry was more rigid than in the Act of 1927. The requirement of regional representation was eliminated, but the commission was to be set up on the customary bipartisan basis. The salaries remained at $10,000 and provision was made for a fairly elaborate administrative staff.

b. *Reports and investigations*

The Act reflected anew the hope of Congress that it could secure some help from the commission in the field of radio policy planning. The commission was to report annually and to engage actively in the collection of data upon the whole problem of the regulation of radio and wire communications. In addition, the statute directed the commission to submit to Congress on February 1, 1935, a special report incorporating 'such amendments to this act as it deems desirable in the public interest.'

c. *Powers of the commission*

The powers of the commission fell into two general categories which need not be elaborated. First, the commission took over the regulatory power over telephone and telegraph for-

60. Act of June 19, 1934, 48 Stat. at L. 1064.

merly quiescent in the Interstate Commerce Commission. It was given the power to fix just and reasonable rates, to forbid discriminations, to outlaw interlocking directorates, to fix the valuation of properties engaged in the industry, to issue certificates of necessity and convenience for the establishment of new lines, and to specify forms of accounts. A second group of provisions dealt with radio. These were set out in detail and all of them were to be exercised 'as public convenience, interest, or necessity requires.' Stations were to be licensed under a long list of rules set forth, licenses were to be revoked for cause, and renewals were to be limited. The provisions relating to radio regulation were almost identical with those in the Act of 1927.

d. *Divisions of the commission*

The commission was authorized to divide itself into not more than three divisions of three members each. Each division was to choose its own chairman. There were elaborate provisions relating to the delegation of power to these divisions as well as similar delegations to employees or boards of employees.

3. TOPICS AND ISSUES IN HEARINGS AND DEBATES

The hearings and debates on the establishment of the communications commission threshed little new straw, but many familiar arguments were brought forward. Senator Pittman urged that the protection of private rights required that the judicial aspects of radio regulation be sharply segregated from the administrative aspects:

. . . If the functions of this commission are to be primarily judicial, then there are objections to mixing in a judicial body administrative functions other than to carry out orders. For instance, we do not like to have one body be collector of evidence, the prosecutor, the judge that sentences, and the sheriff that hangs. That is contrary to our form of government. I have in mind right there the elimination of the Department of Commerce on the question of the inspection and gathering of evidence; if this body's chief function is to be judicial in character, then it would seem that we should have some other body to seek the evidence, prepare it, and submit it, that body probably being the Department of Commerce.[61]

General Harbord, president of the Radio Corporation of America, urged a similar segregation for somewhat different reasons:

> . . . My feeling about the commission . . . is the double character of the commission, the combination of legislative and judicial functions in a body of men who are not very immediately responsible to Congress and certainly not to the Executive.
> I regard commissions . . . as we ordinarily have them, as a device for the evasion of responsibility, and I feel that the communications of this country are worthy of a Cabinet position . . . I think that the lawmaking body might easily, as other countries do, set up a ministry for communications—a Cabinet officer whose responsibility is directly fixed.[62]

On the question of relieving the Interstate Commerce Commission of its responsibilities with regard to telephone and telegraph there was little debate. Commissioner Eastman supported the change. He said:

> In my opinion—and I think this opinion is shared by other members of the commission—the telephone, telegraph and cable are more closely connected with radio than with the railroads. And while I have given no great amount of study to the question, I am inclined to believe that the supervision of communications companies by one commission would be preferred to the present method of divided control.[63]

There was some difference of opinion regarding the method of creating divisions within the commission itself. The Senate bill created them by statute while the House bill authorized the commission to work out the details of its own subdivisions.

The most interesting discussion related to ways and means of providing for adequate long-range planning in the radio field. It seemed desirable to get such results as were possible from the commission itself, and that body was accordingly directed to study the broad aspects of the field of control and

61. Hearings before the Senate Committee on Interstate Commerce on S. 6, 71st Cong., 1st sess. (1929), 183.
62. Ibid. 1328.
63. Ibid. 1581.

to give to Congress the benefit of its advice. It was widely felt, however, that this would not be adequate; that an administrative commission would not be able to meet the insistent demand for broad policy planning; and therefore the commission would need special machinery for this particular job. Captain S. C. Hooper, who was the minority member of the interdepartmental committee, proposed an advisory council from which broad planning as well as consideration of departmental interests might be expected.

Inasmuch as there is a very close relationship, insofar as availability of facilities is concerned, between the departments of the Government operating their communication systems, such as the Army, Navy, Coast Guard, and the Airways Division, and the organizations, both domestic and international, which operate public service communications systems, it would seem advisable to establish a national communication advisory council consisting of representatives appointed by the President from the various interested Government departments including the Department of State. This National Advisory Council, together with the civil body responsible for the administration of civil communications, would be charged with the formulation of policies primarily. Where these policies involved, either directly or indirectly, the interests of nongovernment communications organizations holding license under the Government, or directly involved the interest of the public, the civil communications administration and the advisory council should be constituted as a communications committee of the whole to hold public hearings at which any person who could qualify as an interested party would be permitted to appear and give evidence as well as arguments.[64]

Later on this proposal was urged in the hearings before the House committee, but received, on the whole, small consideration. To serve a somewhat similar end Representative Scott of California introduced on August 23, 1935, a special resolution [65] for the creation of a broadcasting research commission to study not merely the technical aspects of the radio industry but the broad lines of policy in accordance with which it ought to be regulated. He formulated his proposal as follows:

64. *Supra,* note 55, op. cit. 10.
65. H. Res. 370, 74th Cong., 1st sess. (1935); 79 Cong. Rec. 14400 f.

It is believed that the Communications Commission does not desire and is in no position and is not qualified to undertake the investigation specified in the resolution. The members of that Commission are engaged in the performance of administrative and other duties in connection with the regulation of electrical communications as a whole which require full-time attention and it would be unreasonable to expect them to take the time necessary for the intensive investigation described in the proposed resolution . . .

It should be noted that the proposed broadcasting research commission would be a temporary body, appointed by and responsible to the president, the chairman, who would, presumably, give full-time attention to the work. The object of proposing a commission of this type is to make available for the investigation the services of persons who could and would not ordinarily accept appointment on a Federal commission. It is believed that distinguished and disinterested citizens would be attracted by the opportunity of taking part in a nonpartisan attempt to formulate a sound and permanent policy regarding broadcasting.

In the fall of 1934 the Communications Commission held hearings in Washington on a proposal to set aside a fixed percentage of facilities for educational programs and stations. At these hearings the industry, represented by network companies and the National Association of Broadcasters, presented a consolidated and effective case against the specific proposal before the Commission and against any departure from the status quo, while the outside groups presented half-baked irreconcilable proposals that had no effect whatever on the Commission, and the Commission decided to recommend disapproval of the proposal. The Commission has now called a conference on May 15 for the purpose of considering means of further cooperation between educational interests and the industry, and it is expected that the industry will again appear with a well-organized case to oppose the proposals of the so-called 'pressure groups.' It is believed that this method of meeting the claims and proposals of persons and groups not associated with the industry and not satisfied with broadcasting will continue to produce confusion and disappointment, that piecemeal revision of the act or regulations will prove to be unsatisfactory.

It is for these reasons that we advocate the appointment of the broadcasting research commission to investigate the industry and the proposals of outside groups and to lay down a policy and program for the future.

V

THE NEW DEAL REGULATORY COMMISSIONS

I. THE SECURITIES AND EXCHANGE COMMISSION

A. THE SECURITIES ACT OF 1933 AND THE FEDERAL TRADE COMMISSION

1. THE BACKGROUND OF THE ACT

THE attack upon the more obvious abuses in connection with the sale of securities began in the states. In 1909 Governor Hughes of New York appointed a committee to investigate the problem. It recommended legislation regulating stock exchange transactions, but no action was taken. In 1911 Kansas blazed the trail by passing the so-called 'blue-sky law.' This action was followed rapidly by the other states, and at present practically all have laws of this type. Some of these license the sale of securities; others are mainly penal statutes which undertake to punish fraud. Active federal interest in this general problem dates from 1913. In that year the Pujo committee,[1] set up by the House to investigate the nation's financial system, extended its inquiry to stock exchange manipulation and brought in a bill [2] proposing federal regulation of stock exchanges. No action was taken upon this recommendation. The government's interest in the matter was increased by the difficulties it encountered during the War from the sale by speculators of bonds which paid exceedingly high interest rates in competition with Lib-

---

1. *Supra*, 148.   2. H.R. 1593, 62d Cong., 3d sess. (1913).

erty bonds which did not. These operators took Liberty bonds in payment, and when they were placed on the market their value was depressed. A bill [3] backed by the Treasury was introduced in the House to deal with this unwelcome competition. At the same time the Federal Trade Commission was urged to use its authority to meet the situation. The commission considered the matter and proposed new legislation [4] of its own. Hearings were held in the House on the Treasury bill, but a strong lobby of investment bankers opposed it and the House Judiciary Committee killed it.

This did not, however, kill Congressional interest in the problem itself. With each succeeding Congress from the war period on, the flood of bills proposing stock exchange regulation increased, until in the 72d Congress there were six Senate bills and eleven House bills. With a few exceptions no action was taken on any of these bills by any committee, but .they represent a persistent drive which at last culminated in legislation. The Democratic national platform of 1932 contained a plank vigorously demanding protection of the investing public.

2. STEPS IN THE LEGISLATIVE HISTORY OF THE SECURITIES ACT OF 1933

On March 29, 1933, President Roosevelt presented to Congress a brief message [5] urging legislation 'for Federal supervision of traffic in investment securities in interstate commerce.' He emphasized that there must be no government approval either express or implied of any securities issue. There must, however, be full publicity and information regarding security issues, and this information must be a matter of public record. Responsibility must be placed upon the seller of securities to insure their compliance with law and their freedom from fraud. The old adage 'Let the buyer beware' must be supplemented by the slogan 'Let the seller also beware.' Protection to the public in these matters should be secured with the least possible interference with honest busi-

3. H.R. 15922, 65th Cong., 3d sess. (1919).
4. Ann. Rept. Fed. Trade Comm., 47 f.
5. 77 Cong. Rec. 937 and 954.

ness. Senator Ashurst introduced a bill [6] embodying the President's recommendations, which was first referred to the Senate Committee on the Judiciary but immediately transferred to the Committee on Banking and Currency. This committee proceeded to hold elaborate hearings and presented a bill [7] which, with the addition of the Senate amendment creating the Corporation of Foreign Security Holders, became substantially the Securities Act of 1933. It was reported out of committee on April 27, amended, and passed the Senate on May 8.

The House Committee on Interstate and Foreign Commerce under the chairmanship of Mr. Rayburn of Texas had meanwhile been working along parallel lines. It perfected a bill in April which was also the product of joint consultation. Mr. Rayburn acknowledged the assistance given by members of the Federal Trade Commission, both past and present, representatives of the Department of Commerce, and Messrs. Frankfurter, Landis, and Cohen. The bill [8] was introduced in the House on May 3, referred to the Committee on Interstate and Foreign Commerce, and reported back by them the following day. Under special order it was debated and passed on May 5 and sent to the Senate. There was no dispute on the bill. To get it to conference and thus hasten its passage, the Senate passed the House bill by striking out all clauses after the enacting clause and substituting its own bill. On May 22 the conference committee reported; the House passed the conference report on the same day; the Senate passed it the following day; and the President signed the bill on May 27.

3. THE PROVISIONS OF THE ACT

The Securities Act of 1933 [9] was in reality a federal blue-sky law. It sought to protect the buyer of securities and to impose both civil and criminal responsibility on the seller. It dealt, however, with new offers of securities, rather than with securities which were outstanding. Its provisions may be put into

6. S. 875, 73d Cong., 1st sess. (1933).

7. S. 875, 73d Cong., 1st sess. (1933). This later became the Senate amendment to H.R. 5480, *infra*.

8. H.R. 5480, 73d Cong., 1st sess. (1933).

9. Act of May 27, 1933, 48 Stat. at L. 74.

five groups: (1) Certain classes of securities were exempt from the operation of the Act. These included government securities and those of banks and railroads that were otherwise subject to regulation. (2) All securities offered to the public must be registered with the Federal Trade Commission. This requirement was enforced by denying the use of the mails and all facilities of interstate commerce in connection with security issues or sales unless the securities were thus registered. Registration was granted only upon the filing with the Federal Trade Commission of searching information regarding the issuer of the security and the security itself. There were provisions for making certain essential facts public for the benefit of prospective buyers. (3) Civil and criminal penalties were established for untrue statements or the omission of required information. (4) The Federal Trade Commission was given authority to enforce the Act with the aid of the Department of Justice and the courts. (5) A Corporation of Foreign Security Holders to conserve and advance the interests of the holders of foreign securities which had been defaulted was to be created upon the declaration of the President. The President has never, however, taken this action.

4. TOPICS AND ISSUES IN HEARINGS AND DEBATES

The hearings and debates on the Act of 1933 threw little light on the commission problem, as there was no searching discussion. For a number of reasons Congress was ready to proceed quickly and without much debate. There was little partisan opposition. The Republicans themselves were in favor of some regulatory legislation affecting the sale of securities, and it was not quite respectable to oppose openly a program so universally applauded. The calendar of Congress was crowded with much more important legislation. The prestige of the President was tremendous and Congress was still following White House direction without much disposition to question or object. Finally, the legislation itself had been most carefully drawn by very competent advisers.

The Federal Trade Commission was charged with the enforcement of the Act. A majority of the state blue-sky laws were enforced by single officials rather than by boards or commissions, but it was generally assumed in Congress that a commission should administer the Securities Act, since the statute delegated important rule-making duties and other broad discretionary powers. The President was apparently willing to see the new job go to the Federal Trade Commission. He was in the process of reorganizing that body; he had made one new appointment on May 26; he had removed Mr. Humphrey during the summer; and by the first of June 1934 he had appointed all five members of the Federal Trade Commission. He had not yet been told by the Supreme Court [10] that he was without authority to remove these officers except for cause.

What serious debate there was on the Securities Act turned on the issues relating to the actual scope and content of the regulatory powers which the Federal Trade Commission was to exercise. There was no discussion of the problems of administrative organization. In fact the provision of the statute most warmly debated was the one most irrelevant to our present inquiry, that which aimed to set up the Corporation of Foreign Security Holders.

B. The Securities Exchange Act of 1934 and the New Commission

1. BACKGROUND OF THE ACT AND PROPOSALS FOR STOCK EXCHANGE CONTROL

It was obvious at the time of its enactment that the Securities Act of 1933 was only an entering wedge, a part of a larger program. As we have seen, the Democratic platform of 1932 had pledged the party to the 'regulation to the full extent of federal power of exchange trading in securities,' and this meant something more than simply the registration of securities sold. On March 2, 1932, the Senate instructed its Committee on Banking and Currency to carry on an investigation of stock exchanges and their activities. This committee retained Mr. Ferdinand Pecora to direct its investigation. In April 1933 and again in June this committee was authorized to enlarge the scope and depth of its inquiry, and by the time the Securities Exchange Act of 1934 was enacted, it had

10. *Humphrey's Executor* v. *United States*, 295 U.S. 602 (1935).

printed twenty-one volumes of hearings. As these investigations progressed, four major proposals emerged which forced themselves upon the consideration of the committees of Congress dealing with this important problem. Two of these came from governmental sources and two from outside sources. President Roosevelt on February 9, 1934, sent a special message [11] to Congress calling for the regulation of stock exchanges.

a. *Report of the Roper Interdepartmental Committee*

An interdepartmental committee created by Secretary Roper [12] to investigate this whole problem presented a program for stock exchange control. [13] This plan called for regulation through the licensing power and through supervision by a federal stock exchange authority. The exchanges were to be licensed to operate under rules and regulations adopted by the exchanges in compliance with requirements set by the authority. Should an exchange refuse to adopt proper rules, it became liable to the loss or suspension of its license, to a fine, or to the requirement that it change its personnel. The stock exchange authority was to be given very broad discretionary powers. A representative of the stock exchanges was to be a member of the authority. If the Federal Trade Commission rather than the authority should be charged with the enforcement of the act, two new members were to be added to make a separate division. The regulatory power created by the bill operated upon the exchanges, not upon individual brokers or dealers.

b. *The Fletcher Plan*

Senator Fletcher, the chairman of the Senate Committee on Banking and Currency, sponsored another plan. This plan originated with a group consisting of James M. Landis, [14]

11. S. Doc. 132, 73d Cong., 2d sess. (1934).

12. The members were John Dickinson, A. A. Berle, A. H. Dean, J. M. Landis, and H. J. Richardson.

13. Senate Committee Print, Stock Exchange Regulation, 73d Cong., 2d sess. (1934).

14. Then a member of the Federal Trade Commission in charge of the administration of the Securities Act.

Benjamin M. Cohen, Thomas Corcoran, and Ferdinand Pecora.
Lawyers connected with the stock exchanges were also consulted. They produced a bill [15] which was actively considered
in both House and Senate committee hearings. The Fletcher
plan provided for registration as the means of regulating stock
exchanges. It defined in detail a long list of forbidden practices. The Federal Trade Commission was to enforce the act
and its disciplinary power was to extend not merely to the stock
exchanges and their members but to corporations, traders, and
brokers by means of rules, regulations, and direct orders. This
proposal was the most drastic of any which received consideration.

c. *The Whitney Plan*

The witnesses appearing before the Congressional committees from the stock exchanges asserted that they favored federal regulation. They undoubtedly realized that regulation
was inevitable. They demanded, however, that the stock exchanges should be given in large part the power to regulate
themselves. They were probably influenced not merely by a
natural desire to escape drastic control, but also by the technique exemplified in the Federal Reserve System and in the
NRA code authorities, the technique of self-discipline under
supervision. Mr. Richard Whitney, then president of the New
York Stock Exchange, presented a plan [16] which carried the
approval of all the exchanges. It provided for a stock exchange
authority of a highly mixed character. Two members were to
be appointed by the President, two were to be Cabinet officers,
preferably the Secretaries of the Treasury and of Commerce,
one was to be appointed by the Open Market Committee of
the Federal Reserve System, and two were to represent the
stock exchanges. One of these last was to be named by the New
York Stock Exchange, the other by the exchanges outside of
New York. This authority was to control the amounts of margins which members of exchanges must require and maintain
on customers' accounts. It was to have adequate power to require stock exchanges to adopt rules and regulations 'prevent-

15. H.R. 7852 and S. 2693, 73d Cong., 2d sess. (1934).
16. Printed in Hearings before the Senate Committee on Banking and Currency on S. Res. 84, 56, and 97, 73d Cong., 2d sess. (1934), Part xv, 6641 f.

ing not only dishonest practices but also all practices which unfairly influence the price of securities or unduly stimulate speculation.' There was appended a long list of these practices. Finally the authority was to investigate the situation presented by the same person being a broker and a dealer, to adopt rules about it if necessary, as well as rules with respect to short selling.

d. *Twentieth Century Fund Proposal*

The Twentieth Century Fund had underwritten an investigation of its own.[17] Its proposals were similar to those of the Roper committee in placing upon the exchanges the duty of administering the policy of the act; in other words, the fulcrum of regulation was to be the exchange rather than the individual. On the other hand, the plan was similar to the Fletcher proposal in incorporating in the statute itself .the minimum requirements and prohibitions instead of delegating the formulation of detailed regulations to the administrative authority. The plan called for a 'regulatory authority' but did not specify whether it should be a single officer or a commission, or be dependent on or independent of other administrative agencies.

2. STEPS IN THE LEGISLATIVE HISTORY OF THE ACT OF 1934

The Senate and House committees, confronted with these varied and impressive proposals, conducted elaborate hearings. The House Committee on Interstate and Foreign Commerce held hearings from February 14 to March 24, 1934, canvassed the various plans, and listened to many witnesses. As its deliberations proceeded the committee evolved a milder substitute for the Fletcher proposal, a bill which made the Federal Trade Commission the regulatory body to enforce its provisions. This measure[18] was introduced by Mr. Rayburn on April 25, referred back to committee, reported out on April 30, and debated from April 30 to May 4, on which day it passed the House.

17. Twentieth Century Fund, Inc., *Stock Market Control* (1934).
18. H.R. 9323, 73d Cong., 2d sess. (1934).

The Senate Committee on Banking and Currency conducted hearings from February 26 to March 16. Its bill,[19] thrice revised and calling for the creation of a new securities and exchange commission, was introduced by Senator Fletcher on April 30. It was referred to the committee and reported back on the same day. It was debated from May 7 to May 11, when it passed the Senate under the number of the House bill which had gone to the Senate committee on May 4.

The differences between the two measures made a conference necessary, and both houses made substantial concessions in order to reach agreement. The House agreed to the creation of a new independent securities and exchange commission instead of using the Federal Trade Commission for the enforcement of the act. The Senate agreed to the House provision vesting the control of margins in the Federal Reserve Board rather than in the new commission. It agreed to the House salary schedule of $10,000 for commissioners and the House provision that the commission be supported by a regular budget rather than by fees collected from those subject to regulation. The conference report was brought in on May 30, passed the Senate on the same day, and passed the House on June 1. The Act was signed by the President on June 6, 1934.

3. THE PROVISIONS OF THE ACT OF 1934

The provisions of the Securities Exchange Act [20] were as follows: First, a Securities and Exchange Commission was set up composed of five members appointed by the President and the Senate, holding office for five-year staggered terms, receiving $10,000 salaries. There was the customary bipartisan rule as to membership. There was no restriction upon the President's removal power. Second, the Act established or distributed three types of power. It transferred to the new commission the power over the registration of securities which the Act of 1933 had conferred on the Federal Trade Commission. It provided for the policing of the stock exchanges through an elaborate system of registration and control. It did not adopt the principle of self-regulation by the exchanges nor did it try to

19. S. 3420, 73d Cong., 2d sess. (1934).
20. Act of June 6, 1934, 48 Stat. at L. 881.

define in detail the substance of all of its prohibitions and regulatory rules. The commission was allowed fairly broad discretion in the formulation of rules and regulations but was limited to rules and regulations issued in the enforcement of the statutory provisions. Finally, the regulation of margin requirements was placed in the Board of Governors of the Federal Reserve System.

4. TOPICS AND ISSUES IN HEARINGS AND DEBATES

a. *The range of discretion delegated to the commission*

There was sharp dispute on the point which most intimately affected those who were to be subject to regulation. How far and how deeply should federal regulatory power extend? How broad should be the discretion of the regulatory body? How vague were to be the standards under which the proposed commission was to act? We have indicated roughly the divergent points of view on this issue in presenting the four major plans which had emerged during the discussions. The stock exchanges wanted the privilege of self-regulation under supervision. They preferred to have 'broad' powers conferred upon the commission rather than 'deep' ones. Their position was explained by Mr. Whitney:

> . . . Instead of having a fixed rule of law, which can only be changed by an act of Congress and cannot be changed if Congress is not in session—instead of having a fixed rule of law, we advocate the power being put in a commission to make these rules and regulations, which, if they are wrong, they can immediately change. If they are right, then these rules and regulations will stay in effect.
>
> But we are fearful of the danger that may result of placing such rules and regulations with which we, as the authorities of the exchange, do not agree, into a law which cannot be changed . . . except by Congress—and in the meantime disaster, chaos, and panic may result, and the only person who is hurt is the public.[21]

The Roper committee, while defending a lesser degree of self-regulation by the exchanges, urged also that very broad discretion be given the commission to make rules and regulations. They said in their report:

21. Hearings before the House Committee on Interstate and Foreign Commerce on H.R. 7852 and H.R. 8720, 73d Cong., 2d sess. (1934), 726.

Your committee has considered as an alternative suggestion that the proposed enactment cover in its detailed provisions all known unfair, inequitable and unsocial practices by express provisions with a minimum discretionary power of regulation by the governmental body responsible for enforcement.

While it is possible to fix by law certain basic standards as a guide to conduct in the matter of regulation of exchanges, these must be limited to minimum requirements. The point specifically is that while certain provisions might be included in any regulations, such provisions should not be the only power of correction left open to an administrative agency, but it should have broad discretion to operate directly on various abuses as the future may prove them to exist. It is not proposed that the Government so dominate exchanges as to deprive them of initiative and responsibility, but it is proposed to provide authority to move quickly and to the point when the necessity arises.[22]

John Dickinson, Assistant Secretary of Commerce, who was their principal spokesman, told the House committee:

The Roper Committee report went on the theory that if governmental regulation attempts to do too much directly and to control and intervene directly in the first instance over the whole field which it covers, it is in danger of breaking down under its own weight and proving ineffective. In the report of the Roper committee, therefore, the action of the Government through the proposed stock exchange authority—which incidentally was to have no other duties than to be a stock exchange authority and was to be free to devote its entire time to the task of exchange regulation—nevertheless the functions, the regulatory functions of this governmental agency were held in reserve and were employed only to supplement and supervise what in the first instance was self-regulation of the exchanges.

No doubt the exchanges will frequently fail to do a good job of regulating their members, but even so, it seemed to the Roper committee during their deliberations likely that Government regulation was likely to be more effective and less unwieldy if it was applied to the exchanges in an effort to make them do their own job and to come down on them like a ton of bricks if they did not do their job of direct regulation and [than] attempt to perform it from the very beginning and in the first instance by governmental policing methods . . .

Now, of course, it may be said cynically—and I think that there is

22. *Supra,* note 13, op. cit. 5 ff.

a good deal in it, and of course we have to recognize the weakness of human nature—it may be said that the idea of self-regulation is just a device to avoid regulation and so in some instances it no doubt is; but self-regulation in the first instance, with the Government holding its power in reserve to see that that self-regulation is exercised, is after all a necessary recourse in view of the mere physical limitations in time and in personnel, which operate on the direct exercise of the powers of government as the task of regulation becomes more and more extensive over a wider and wider field . . .

I conceive the effective performance of such a task as consisting primarily in the guidance and supervision of the disciplinary activities of the exchanges themselves . . .

If an exchange fails adequately to enforce its rules, its dereliction, in view of the relatively small number of exchanges that the Federal authority would have to oversee, would be relatively easy to discover and disciplinary action could be applied promptly by the Federal agency to the extent, if necessary, of placing all of the members of that exchange under Federal licenses, for the time being, and keeping them there until conditions on that exchange were improved.[23]

As the bill moved on its way through Congress the broad discretion which it vested in the regulatory authority was sharply attacked. Senator Steiwer declared:

. . . The bill is unusual in that it not only clothes the commission with the right to make rules and regulations but it continues the power of the commission to change and alter and amend those rules and regulations . . . There is no provision in the bill requiring the rules and regulations to become effective at some future date. They may, in the judgment of the commission, become effective forthwith. There is no requirement in this bill that the rules and regulations shall be published at any particular time, or that any other effort shall be made to confer notice upon those who might be affected by the rules and regulations . . .

In almost every case the nature of the denunciation, that is, the statement of the crime, is in terms of rules and regulations.

. . . Therefore the crimes which are created by this bill are crimes which we do not know today . . . and yet . . . we are called upon to give our approval to section 30, including section 30 (b), which penalizes violations of rules and regulations.[24]

The Fletcher plan provided for the detailed definition of forbidden practices and for a commission empowered to

23. *Supra,* note 21, op. cit. 513 ff.   24. 78 Cong. Rec. 8280.

deal directly with individual offenders. The powers of the commission must be both extensive and specific. Without such powers the commission would be helpless. Mr. Corcoran told the Senate committee:

> Really to say that the Congress should put a commission without very large powers in charge of the regulation of stock exchanges, would be like advising that one put a baby into a cage with a tiger to regulate the tiger. For a commission must have full powers or the stock exchanges and the forces allied with the stock exchanges, which are supposedly being regulated, will actually regulate the regulators.[25]

He further insisted that there must be an adequately clear statutory standard to guide the commission in the exercise of its discretion, a standard which he referred to as 'the bright line' of administrative regulation. This he described as follows:

> If you give an administrative commission complete discretion, without any bright line [which] may be regarded as at least a norm, the commission cannot stand up against the applicant [who] asks for a liberalized ruling. It will be the brokers who have a very heavy interest in commissions volume that will always be before the Trade Commission, or any other administrative body that is administering this law. They will be always wanting to put margins lower.
>
> Unless you give the administrative body a bright line behind which it can say, 'Congress told us this is where to stop,' the administrative body is going to be in a hard way all of the time.[26]

This specific and drastic control was attacked by the representatives of the stock exchanges; Mr. Whitney declared that it was not regulation but outright control; [27] and the representatives of the Twentieth Century Fund described it as 'dictatorship.' [28] What finally emerged was, of course, a compromise. The Act as passed legislated specifically about as far as was possible but left a substantial residue of rule-making discretion in the hands of the commission.

25. *Supra*, note 16, op. cit. 6466 f.   27. Ibid. 227.
26. *Supra*, note 21, op. cit. 105.   28. *Supra*, note 16, op. cit. 6938.

b. *Stock exchange representation on the commission*

The question whether representatives from an industry to be regulated should be appointed to a regulating body was not a new question. As we have seen, the issue had been raised and settled in the process of establishing the Federal Reserve Board.[29] Mr. Whitney, representing the stock exchanges, proposed that two members of the regulating authority be chosen by the exchanges themselves, on the ground that it was necessary to secure people familiar with the technical aspects of the business to be controlled. In the Roper committee plan it was proposed, and repeatedly defended by Mr. Dickinson, that at least one person on the governing board should be 'skilled by experience in exchange work.' [30] The committee declared that it was desirable 'that a representative of the stock exchanges should be drawn into the administrative agency'; not that the exchanges were to select this representative, but 'one of the members of the commission or authority should be required by law to be a man thoroughly experienced in stock-exchange practices.' However, no one on the commission or authority should continue to be active in market transactions, but must dissociate himself completely from stock exchange activity.[31]

It was impossible, however, to build up much support for the idea of stock exchange representation. The chairman of the House committee declared that such representatives on a regulatory body would lack influence because they would be inevitably regarded as special pleaders.[32] In the report of the House committee there is an admirable summary of the whole argument against representation of special interests:

Insofar as 'experts' are concerned, it is a commonplace of administrative statesmanship that boards of men who are experts in details rarely agree among themselves, and in their very expertness with the trees seldom perceive the woods of broad public policy. The well-learned lesson of democratic government with 'experts' is that they should be kept on tap but not on top.

Insofar as making up a permanent Government regulatory body from representatives of special vested interests is concerned, it has

29. *Supra,* 155 ff.
30. *Supra,* note 21, op. cit. 515.
31. *Supra,* note 13, op. cit. 5 ff.
32. *Supra,* note 21, op. cit. 393.

long ago been learned that no harmony of policy can result from a regulatory body packed with advocates of warring interests, and that the inevitable result of placing on a regulatory authority able advocates who have at heart the definite interest of a particular class which will profit by the least possible regulation is stultification of the regulation.[33]

It is probable that the attitude of the average congressman was accurately stated by Senator Fletcher when he inquired, 'What is the use of having a regulatory body controlled by those to be regulated?' [34]

c. *Federal Trade Commission* v. *new independent commission*

There was complete agreement on all sides that the new law should be administered by a commission or board. No voice was raised in behalf of placing stock exchange regulation in the hands of an executive department or officer. Should this commission be the Federal Trade Commission, or a new and independent securities and exchange commission? In favor of using the Federal Trade Commission was the group which supported the Fletcher proposal, the House Committee on Interstate and Foreign Commerce, and later the House itself, and a number of members of the Senate, notably Senators Norris and Costigan. Senator Costigan, in fact, made perhaps the most cogent argument put forth on this side of the question.[35] The proponents of a new commission were the Senate Committee on Banking and Currency, and the Senate, Mr. Richard Whitney and the stock exchanges, and most of those favoring the Roper plan. The Roper plan itself suggested both alternatives, but indicated a preference for a new commission. Mr. Dickinson strongly disapproved of the Federal Trade Commission as a regulatory body for this purpose.

The argument presented for using the Federal Trade Commission may be summarized under six points: First, the Federal Trade Commission had a high reputation for efficiency and impartiality and had established sound traditions in the management of its work. While this statement did not draw universal assent, it contained much force, so much indeed that

33. H. Rept. 1383, 73d Cong., 2d sess. (1934), 16.   35. Ibid. 8397 ff.
34. 78 Cong. Rec. 8162.

Mr. Rayburn of Texas and Mr. Mapes of Michigan in the House debate intimated that the stock exchanges objected to the Federal Trade Commission as a regulatory body for the enforcement of the new law because they were anxious to escape effective regulation.[36] Second, the Federal Trade Commission had already expanded its staff to handle its work under the Securities Act, had acquired much relevant data and experience, and was already dealing effectively with a large segment of the problem under consideration. In the interests of economy and efficiency it would be better to build on this going concern, capitalizing its experience and its traditions, rather than to start from scratch and set up a new agency. Third, the Federal Trade Commission could take over immediately the administration of the new law. It was stated that a delay of at least six months would result if the new regulatory task were given to a new agency which must build a staff and acquire familiarity with the difficult problems assigned to it. Fourth, it was undesirable to create a new independent agency if this could be avoided. There were already too many agencies, and the Federal Trade Commission could adequately handle the job which Congress had created. Senator Norris voiced this objection and referred to the successful work of the Trade Commission in administering the Securities Act.[37] In the House Mr. Mapes ventured the not very accurate prophecy that the administration of the new law would not be a very large job and that not much new machinery would be necessary.[38] Fifth, the Federal Trade Commission would be more aggressive in the enforcement of the new law than would a new body. Persuasive support of this argument lay in the eagerness of the stock exchanges to stay out from under Federal Trade Commission control. There was always a hope that a new organization would be less drastic and ruthless than many businessmen felt the Federal Trade Commission to be. Sixth, if the Federal Trade Commission administered the Securities and Exchange Act it would be necessary to establish within the commission a panel or section devoting its time exclusively to this important work. It would then be possible to allow appeals to be taken from the orders or decisions of

36. Ibid. 8109 f.   38. Ibid. 7924.
37. Ibid. 8499 ff.

this section to the full commission. This system of administrative appeals was felt to be highly desirable. This was stated by Mr. Mapes:

Furthermore, there is one provision in this bill which I think makes it very desirable to clothe the Federal Trade Commission with authority to administer it. The bill provides that the commission shall be divided up into divisions. To one division will be assigned the duty of administering this act. Then the bill provides that anybody who feels aggrieved at any order of the Commission made under this act, or of any division of the Commission, can appeal to the full Commission. That appeal will be passed upon not by the two or three men who are principally concerned with the administration of this particular act but by the other members of the Commission as well. They may have a clearer, a more general, and saner view because of their other work. I think that is a consideration of no small importance . . .[39]

The argument for the establishment of a new commission also fell under six heads. First, the new regulatory job was exceedingly heavy, much heavier than could be well handled by a section of the Federal Trade Commission. This has turned out to be true, and no one at present would disagree that if the Securities and Exchange Act was now being administered by a division of the Federal Trade Commission we should have a case of the tail wagging the dog. This point was emphasized by those who were impressed with the complex and exacting character of the task created by the new law. Second, not only was the job heavy, but it was highly specialized, and not only was it highly specialized, but it was irrelevant to the main tasks for which the Federal Trade Commission is responsible. The only way in which the Trade Commission could hope to handle it effectively would be by creating what would in essence be a subcommission; certainly the Trade Commission itself could not as a body add the enforcement of the new law to its already burdensome list of responsibilities. Third, certain psychological advantages would result from the establishment of a new body. A new and separate agency would enjoy a prestige and influence which would not attach to a mere subdivision of an older regulatory body. Senator Barkley summarized opin-

39. Ibid.

ion on this point of view, saying that if the Federal Trade Commission had to administer the bill

> it would have to be done under a subordinate bureau under the Federal Trade Commission; that it would be a sort of lean-to under the Commission's original activities; while if a separate commission were appointed public attention would always be focused upon that separate commission. It was the theory also that the President could pick five men just as well qualified to administer the law separately as he could pick three additional men to be appointed to the Federal Trade Commission as a sort of subcommittee of the Federal Trade Commission to administer the law.
>
> . . . The committee felt that a separate commission, whose duties would be centralized around the stock market and stock securities, would be in a better position to serve the public than a branch of the Federal Trade Commission.[40]

Fourth, it was felt that businessmen generally feared the Federal Trade Commission and viewed its activities with hostility. The stock exchanges shared this point of view. If the Trade Commission were to administer the new law, it would mean that stock exchange regulation would be carried on in an atmosphere of suspicion and hostility which might not surround a new agency. Mr. Whitney expressed the fear of the stock exchange community toward the Trade Commission in the following statement before the Senate committee:

> If this proposal is carried out, the Federal Trade Commission can, through its control of so many of the varied phases of the financial and economic life of the country, restrict the operation of and even destroy corporations that incur its displeasure. The Federal Trade Commission does not have to convict a corporation of any particular illegal transaction, but can regulate it out of existence by control of credit, restrictions on new financing, removal of its securities from exchanges, and so forth, without in any way justifying its motives or the soundness of its judgment.[41]

It may be added that the Federal Trade Commission had many enemies in Congress who were by no means anxious to see its powers and responsibilities enlarged. Fifth, the establishment of a new commission was, of course, the only effective way of making possible direct stock exchange representation on the regulatory body. This objective, so dear to the hearts

40. Ibid. 8162.   41. *Supra,* note 16, op. cit. 6916.

of stock exchange groups, undoubtedly helps to explain their desire for a brand new agency. Finally, it would be easier to consolidate in a single agency devoted to the purpose the various activities which impinge upon the financial and credit structure of the country. A securities and exchange commission could be given comprehensive control over a wide range of matters clearly irrelevant to the major tasks of the Federal Trade Commission. Without exception those who favored a new commission assumed that the administration of the Securities Act of 1933 would be transferred to the new body rather than left in the hands of the Federal Trade Commission.

II. THE NATIONAL LABOR RELATIONS BOARD

A. Background of the National Labor Relations Act

THE Wagner Act of 1935 [1] is the first genuinely regulatory federal statute dealing with relations between labor and capital. In two particulars it is unique amongst statutes that set up federal regulatory agencies. In the first place it extends the government's disciplinary power to one of the most bitterly controversial fields of modern life—the field of labor relations. Antagonisms and prejudices run deeper here than almost anywhere else. Secondly, the Act lies in a field in which there has been a longer period of experience and a more varied range of experimentation than had preceded the setting up of any other regulatory agency. This experience had been accumulating in two distinct areas. For nearly fifty years the government had been exercising influence if not authority in railway labor disputes, and since the World War it had been making tentative moves in the more general field of labor disputes affecting interstate commerce. We cannot set out in detail the results of the government's trial and error operations in these two fields, but no picture of the National Labor Relations Board would be adequate which did not set it against the background of these earlier efforts of the government to secure industrial peace. We shall summarize, therefore, very briefly the development of federal labor policy in the two fields mentioned,

1. Act of July 5, 1935, 49 Stat. at L. 449.

emphasizing the results of experimentation with varying administrative structures and procedures.

1. RAILWAY LABOR BOARDS—MEDIATION AND ARBITRATION

a. *The Arbitration Act of October 1, 1888*

The first federal statute dealing with labor relations, passed in 1888,[2] dealt solely with railway labor. It provided for voluntary arbitration by a board of three arbitrators, one appointed by each party to the dispute and a chairman selected by the two appointed. There was no provision for the enforcement of awards. The President was to appoint a temporary commission to investigate the causes of any railway labor dispute. This was to consist of the United States Commissioner of Labor as chairman and two other members appointed by the President. No arbitrations took place under the Act, but an investigating commission was set up to investigate the Pullman strike of 1894. It had no influence on the strike but it brought in a report[3] recommending the creation of a permanent commission of three members to have a regulatory power over railway labor relations similar to that of the Interstate Commerce Commission over rates.

b. *The Erdman Act of June 1, 1898*

The Erdman Act of 1898[4] inaugurated the policy of government mediation and conciliation in railway labor disputes. It created an agency for this purpose composed of the United States Commissioner of Labor and the chairman of the Interstate Commerce Commission. On the request of either party to a dispute threatening the interruption of interstate commerce by rail, this agency was required to make contact with the parties and use its best efforts to settle the issue amicably. The investigation provisions of the Act of 1888 were discontinued, but the arbitration provisions were retained and strengthened. The two commissioners were instructed to at-

2. Act of October 1, 1888, 25 Stat. at L. 501.
3. United States Strike Commission, *Report on the Chicago Strike of June-July*, 1894 (1895).
4. Act of June 1, 1898, 30 Stat. at L. 424.

tempt to secure the arbitration of disputes in case mediation failed, and to appoint a neutral chairman for arbitration purposes if necessary. Awards of arbitration reached under this procedure were made final and enforceable. The Act was more limited in scope than the Act of 1888, since it applied only to employees engaged in the operation of trains.

The Erdman Act was not used until 1906, but during the next seven years sixty-one cases were settled under it. It was successful up to a certain point, but it was inadequate to deal with the entire problem and it had two fundamental weaknesses. In the first place, the Commissioner of Labor and the chairman of the Interstate Commerce Commission found themselves obliged to devote their entire time to the administration of the Act. It came to be obvious that the job required the full time of a larger board. Secondly, the Act had been drawn to deal with disputes affecting a single railroad. The two-man board was too small to handle disputes between the railroad brotherhoods and groups of railroads.

c. *The Newlands Act of 1913*

As labor disputes affecting railways tended to increase, a drive was made to strengthen the Erdman Act. The National Civil Federation, of which Seth Low was chairman, took the initiative; but railway labor, the carriers, and the two commissioners under the Act all co-operated. The resulting Newlands Act of 1913 [5] created a full-time Commissioner of Mediation and Conciliation, with an assistant, and a Board of Mediation and Conciliation consisting of the commissioner and two other officers of the government appointed by the President. The Act retained the provision for voluntary boards of arbitration, but these boards could now consist of either three or six, as the parties might stipulate.

From earlier experience emerged the conclusion that the Board of Mediation and Conciliation must be a completely independent body. The representatives of labor were the most vigorous in pressing this point of view.[6] The board must be

5. Act of July 15, 1913, 38 Stat. at L. 103.
6. A. B. Garretson, pres. Railway Conductors, *Hearings before the Senate Committee on Interstate Commerce on S. 2517*, 63d Cong., 1st sess. (1913), 47 f.

free from all suspicion of bias or political pressure. It must not, therefore, be composed of representatives of employers and employees, nor should it be set up as a bureau in a government department. Only Secretary of Labor Wilson disagreed; [7] he felt that the agency should be a part of the Department of Labor, since major functions of mediation had been assigned to the department by law.

This statute in its turn worked smoothly at first but finally proved inadequate. Labor became acutely dissatisfied. Public arbitrators did not understand the technical facts involved in many disputes and the results of arbitration were not satisfactory. The board handled seventy-one controversies, of which fifty-two were settled by mediation, six by mediation and arbitration, and the rest in various other ways. The final collapse of the Act was owing to failure to settle the nation-wide dispute which finally culminated in the passage in 1916 of the Adamson Act.[8] This really amounted to the liquidation of the Newlands Act, and resort to its provisions practically ceased. Then American entrance into the World War sharply altered the entire picture.

d. *War-time labor control in railroad industry*

Under government operation of the railroads the Director General replaced the carriers in dealing with labor. A Division of Labor was set up by the railroad administration to administer labor relations. An advisory board on railroad wages and working conditions was also created to hear and investigate matters presented by employers or employees. This board advised the Director General, who had power to make agreements on wages and working conditions. Railway boards of adjustment were created to settle disputes concerning the interpretation of these agreements. It was fully recognized, however, that this was an anomalous and temporary situation.

7. Ibid. 68 f.
8. Act of Sept. 3, 5, 1916, 39 Stat. at L. 721.

e. *United States Railroad Labor Board of* 1920

The Transportation Act of 1920 [9] returned the railroads to private management. Title III of this Act dealt with railroad labor; its pertinent provisions were the following: All railroad labor disputes were to be considered first in conference between representatives of carriers and of labor, and an effort was to be made to settle them. If they could not be settled in this manner they were to go to the Railroad Labor Board for 'hearing and decision.' This board was appointed by the President and consisted of three groups of three members each, representing labor, management, and the public. It was not authorized to mediate or adjust disputes, but was to reach decisions on the merits. Boards of adjustment were permissible under the Act but were not required.

The legislative history of this section of the Act of 1920 indicates that it was an orphan child. No hearings were held upon it, and neither labor nor the railroads were consulted. The Director General was consulted but later disclaimed any share in shaping the policy of the Act.[10] It seems to have been the product of the conference committee of the two houses. It was viewed with hostility by everyone affected by its provisions.

The Railroad Labor Board had a brief and unhappy history. Its accomplishments were far from impressive. Its powers were said to represent a 'compromise between compulsion and persuasion.' It could not arbitrate; it could not mediate; but it made a somewhat futile effort to do something of both. It was composed of partisans drawn from both sides, with neutrals holding the balance of power. The three representatives of the public proved to be highly obnoxious to labor. There were long delays in securing action. The board lost the confidence both of the carriers and of labor and finally the labor group flatly refused to have anything to do with it. In *Pennsylvania Railroad Co. v. U. S. Railroad Labor Board*,[11] the Court held that the board had no power to enforce its decisions in any labor dispute. The only sanctions it could rely upon were the

9. Act of Feb. 28, 1920, 41 Stat. at L. 456.
10. Walker D. Hines, Hearings before a subcommittee of the Senate Committee on Interstate Commerce on S. 2646, 68th Cong., 1st sess. (1924), 184 ff.
11. 261 U.S. 72 (1923).

sanctions of public opinion, and it had by this time lost the support of public opinion.

f. *Railway Labor Act of May 20, 1926—Board of Mediation*

In his message [12] to Congress in 1923 President Coolidge stressed the need for amending the labor provisions of the Act of 1920. In the next year the railroad brotherhoods prepared a bill [13] for this purpose, which was submitted to the Senate Committee on Commerce and on which hearings were held. There was sharp opposition from the carriers, from the Railroad Labor Board, and from various company unions. The bill was reported out with substantial changes in 1926. Finally representatives of the railroads and of the brotherhoods joined together to work out a mutually satisfactory bill. This was based on the 1924 bill but included changes which met the objections of the carriers. This bill,[14] which became the Railway Labor Act of 1926,[15] provided that all disputes should be considered in conference by the representatives of employers and employees. Boards of adjustment were to be established by agreement for the settlement of grievances. A Board of Mediation was created consisting of five members appointed by the President with the consent of the Senate. This board was to mediate disputes; if mediation failed, it was to attempt to bring about arbitration. If arbitration was resorted to, the awards were made enforceable. If all these efforts failed, the Board of Mediation was to report to the President, who was empowered to create an emergency board to investigate and report on the dispute. It may be noted that the Board of Mediation had no compulsory powers. It could decide nothing. Furthermore, like the board created under the Newlands Act, it was composed of full-time representatives of the public rather than representatives of interest groups.

12. H. Doc. 1, 68th Cong., 1st sess. (1923), 6.
13. S. 2646, 68th Cong., 1st sess. (1924).
14. S. 2306, 69th Cong., 1st sess. (1926).
15. Act of May 20, 1926, 44 Stat. at L. 577.

g. *Amendments of 1934—National Mediation Board*

The Act of 1926 and the activities of the Board of Mediation gave general satisfaction. Substantial compliance with the spirit and provisions of the Act continued well into the depression. Its breakdown occurred in the case of bankrupt railroads of which there came to be a good many. Receivers appointed for these roads by the federal courts did not feel bound by the provisions of the Act of 1926. They interfered with collective bargaining, and they sometimes imposed upon labor the obnoxious yellow-dog contracts. The Railroad Reorganization Act of 1933 [16] put a stop to this. It forbade any receiver of a railroad to change labor conditions save under the provisions of the Act of 1926. It forbade yellow-dog contracts, all interference with collective bargaining, and all coercion of employees. A few months later the Emergency Railroad Transportation Act of 1933, [17] amongst its other provisions, extended the labor provisions of the Railroad Reorganization Act to all railroads, whether bankrupt or not.

As the Emergency Transportation Act was about to expire, labor naturally desired to make permanent its labor provisions. In 1934 important amendments [18] were accordingly made to the Railway Labor Act of 1926. These were as follows: A much-needed National Adjustment Board was created, but the earlier regional or system boards were still permissible. The Board of Mediation had its name changed to the National Mediation Board. It remained an independent agency but was reduced to three members, since the National Adjustment Board was to take over much of its previous burden of minor cases. The National Mediation Board was authorized to settle representation disputes without intervention by the carriers. Such intervention had presented a difficult problem. The new provision eliminated the employer completely from the procedure by which the authorized representatives of labor were to be designated. The Act clarified somewhat further the right

16. Act of Mar. 3, 1933, 47 Stat. at L. 1467.
17. Act of June 16, 1933, 48 Stat. at L. 211.
18. Act of June 13, 1934, 48 Stat. at L. 954.

of labor to organize and bargain collectively, and provided penalties for interference with this right by carriers.

No serious controversy arose over these amendments. There was some discussion of the propriety of giving the board independent power to act in representation cases. Mr. Winslow, the chairman of the Board of Mediation, believed that the board could not safely be given any compulsory powers, since such powers were incompatible with the successful conduct of mediation proceedings.[19]

2. GENERAL LABOR BOARDS—ANTECEDENTS OF NLRB

Congress was much slower in extending its regulatory authority to the field of general labor than it was in dealing with railway labor problems. In fact, such federal influence as had been called into play in this broader field had been mainly that of the President in various efforts at conciliation. No regulatory machinery of any kind had been set up by law. The World War, however, provided a reason for federal intervention here as in many other fields.

a. *The War labor boards*

When the United States entered the World War it became clear that the government was dependent as never before upon an uninterrupted labor supply. It was imperative that there be a complete moratorium on labor disputes. At the outset there was great confusion and complete decentralization in the government's relations with labor. Each department and agency that employed labor or was dependent upon it was left to handle its own problems. After certain preliminary explorations and some sorry experience with an unsystematized labor policy, President Wilson set up by proclamation on April 8, 1918, the National War Labor Board.[20]

This board was given two main functions: the first, to mediate and conciliate labor disputes which might threaten produc-

19. Hearings before the Senate Committee on Interstate Commerce on S. 3266, 73d Cong., 2d sess. (1934), 134 f.

20. E. Berman, *Labor Disputes and the President of the United States* (1924), 139.

tion; second, to act as a court of appeals for the various labor adjustment agencies set up in industries. It was composed of twelve members. Five were chosen by the employers' associations, five by the American Federation of Labor, and two 'public' representatives were chosen by these two groups. The board was allowed to use the machinery in the Department of Labor for mediation and conciliation. There was a high degree of flexibility in its organization and in its procedure, and it kept constantly adjusting itself to new situations and new needs. It found, for example, that it was necessary to develop a corps of examiners to aid it in conducting its hearings. The board operated for seven months during the War. Its success was impressive, particularly since it had no statutory basis and no powers to enforce its findings. It operated both as a mediating and arbitral board and as a quasi-judicial body. It came to an end on May 31, 1919, having disposed of 1,245 cases.

A different agency was necessary to deal with other phases of the labor problem, and accordingly the War Labor Policies Board was created.[21] It was under the chairmanship of Felix Frankfurter and was made up of representatives from all of the departments and major agencies which dealt with labor. Its function was to evolve a labor code dealing with wages, hours of labor, and general employment policies of the various war agencies, and to co-ordinate such policies. The execution of these policies, however, was left to the various departments. The board functioned effectively during the period of the War. It may be noted that Franklin D. Roosevelt served on the War Labor Policies Board as a representative of the Navy Department and thus had a share in these early federal efforts in the field of labor regulation.

b. *Early New Deal labor boards*

The period from the close of the War to 1933 was an exceedingly difficult one for organized labor. Labor unions had very uphill work. Many major industries were entirely ununionized and collective bargaining was not very successful. Improvement in the status of labor, particularly the encour-

21. May 13, 1918, by the Department of Labor.

agement and protection of collective bargaining, was one of the challenging problems confronting the Roosevelt Administration in 1933.

The National Labor Board. The National Industrial Recovery Act [22] contained the now famous Section 7a—labor's 'Magna Charta.' This guaranteed the right of labor to organize and bargain collectively without interference. It outlawed yellow-dog contracts and it required that employers comply with maximum hours, minimum rates of pay, and other conditions of employment approved or prescribed by the President. Section 7a was taken over bodily into the President's Re-Employment Agreement,[23] but neither NIRA nor PRA set up any machinery for the enforcement of these labor provisions, although in some cases local compliance boards made some efforts in this direction.

The need for an enforcement agency became acute, and on August 5, 1933, the President issued a press release setting up a National Labor Board.[24] The status of this board was regularized by an executive order of December 16, 1933, and the board was strengthened by executive orders of February 1 and 23, 1934. The board was made up of three representatives of labor, three of industry, and an impartial chairman. Later there were five representatives of each group instead of three, and two vice-chairmen were added. The functions of the board were as follows: it was to secure the enforcement of Section 7a and the President's Re-Employment Agreement; to set up regional labor boards and to hear appeals from such boards; to conduct elections for the selection of labor representatives; to report all interference with such elections and all violations of Section 7a to the Attorney General; and to attempt through mediation, conciliation, and arbitration to bring about the settlement of all labor disputes threatening the industrial peace of the country.

The National Labor Board worked with reasonable success during the early period of enthusiasm following the setting up of the NRA. It soon became apparent, however, that it suffered from fundamental weaknesses and defects. That its

22. Act of June 16, 1933, 48 Stat. at. L. 195.
23. Leverett S. Lyon (ed.), *The National Recovery Administration* (1935), 11.
24. *The New York Times*, Aug. 5, 1933, p. 2, col. 2.

membership represented labor and capital may have made it
a suitable agency for arbitration, but it rendered it ineffective
as a regulatory body. It had no independent power to enforce
its orders. If it discovered illegal labor practices it could do
one of two things, or perhaps both: it could report the matter
to the NRA authorities who, if they agreed with the National
Labor Board, could remove the Blue Eagle from the guilty
employers; or the board could report the situation to the
Department of Justice and hope to see legal action started.
Friction developed between the National Labor Board and the
NRA authorities with respect to a number of important labor
policies and this seriously weakened the board.

The National Labor Relations Board of 1934. The National
Labor Board did not meet the vital problems in the labor field
and some drastic change was clearly needed. In March 1934
Senator Wagner introduced his first labor disputes bill,[25] but
no Congressional action ensued. At the end of the session the
President sent to Congress the draft of what finally passed as
Public Resolution 44,[26] a stopgap proposal aimed to strengthen
existing machinery dealing with the labor situation. This resolution authorized the President to appoint labor boards with
power to hold elections of labor representatives for purposes
of collective bargaining, and to take testimony under oath and
to issue orders regarding such elections. The board was to investigate issues, facts, practices, or activities of employers or
employees in any controversy arising under Section 7a, or burdening or obstructing, or threatening to burden or obstruct,
the full flow of interstate commerce. There was, however, no
code of unfair labor practices.

Under this resolution the President, by an executive order
of June 29, 1934, created the National Labor Relations Board
and abolished the National Labor Board. The new board consisted of three members selected by the President. The principle of group representation was abandoned and three full-time
persons were chosen to represent the public interest.

The board was set up 'in connection with the Department
of Labor.' It was required to use the mediators, conciliators,
and statistical experts of the department. It was required to

25. S. 2926, 73d Cong., 2d sess. (1934).
26. Act of June 19, 1934, 48 Stat. at L. 1183.

assist the Secretary of Labor in the work of the department and to report monthly to the President through the Secretary. In appointing and retaining officers and employees and in incurring financial obligations, the board, under an executive order of November 15, 1934, was obliged to secure the approval of the Secretary of Labor. The Secretary, however, had no power to review the findings or orders of the board.

The powers of the board were as follows: it was to investigate the activities of employers, to conduct elections, to hold hearings on complaints brought under Section 7a, to set up rules and regulations for collective bargaining, and to act as a board of arbitration on request. It was an improvement over its predecessor but it, in turn, suffered from fundamental defects and worked in the face of serious obstacles. When it was set up it had been generally assumed that it was to be a sort of 'Supreme Court' of labor, a body to which all labor problems would ultimately be brought. It never occupied this key position, however, because of the creation and retention of a number of special labor boards set up for special industries. Among these were the National Longshoremen's Board, the National Steel Labor Policy Board, the Petroleum Labor Policy Board, and a collection of NRA code boards. The board was further hampered by the constant conflict with the NRA authorities on matters of policy. It was dependent upon the NRA for enforcement of its orders and in crucial cases the President tended to back the NRA rather than the board. The enforcement of its findings through the Department of Justice was unsatisfactory. The process was long drawn out and since the board had no power to subpoena witnesses it was unable to build up a record adequate for judicial review. When the Department of Justice took one of its cases it handled it *de novo* with the consequent duplication of effort and loss of time. The board was weakened with respect to its most important function by the judicial review of its election orders. The chief purpose of Resolution 44 was to aid collective bargaining by giving the Labor Board effective control over the election of labor representatives; but, by appealing to the courts from the board's election orders, employers were able to prevent or delay effective enforcement. Enforcement of the board's orders through removal of the Blue Eagle was dependent upon the uncertain support of the NRA, and as time went on the penalty itself came to be less dreaded by the industries. It was clear that out of this confusion of authority there must eventually be sought a clean-cut and centralized power to deal with the labor problem.

B. Steps in the Legislative History of the Wagner Act

1. WAGNER LABOR DISPUTES BILL OF MARCH 1, 1934

Senator Wagner's labor disputes bill has already been mentioned.[27] Its principal provisions were as follows:

First, a national labor board was to be appointed by the President and the Senate, consisting of two labor representatives, two representatives of the employers, and three from the public. The three public members were to have five-year terms on full time; the others were to be appointed annually and paid by the day. The chairman was to be named by the President from the public group.

Second, a number of unfair labor practices were defined and forbidden.

Third, the board's jurisdiction over such practices included the issuance of complaints, the holding of hearings, and the making of orders. It could apply to the courts for the enforcement of its orders as does the Federal Trade Commission. Its findings of fact were to be conclusive. There was to be judicial review of its orders but the courts were forbidden to enjoin it from taking action or holding hearings under any complaint.

Fourth, the board was to act as a board of arbitration upon request and arbitral awards were made enforceable in the courts.

Fifth, it was given power to hold elections of labor representatives by secret ballot.

Sixth, it could subpoena witnesses and by resort to the courts compel obedience.

Seventh, the bill created a United States conciliatory service in the Department of Labor under a director of conciliation appointed by the Secretary of Labor. In this body was placed the power to mediate and conciliate labor disputes. There had,

27. *Supra,* 355.

of course, been a conciliation service in the department for many years.

Hearings were conducted on the Wagner bill by the Senate Committee on Education and Labor, which reported it out in amended form.[28] The committee's changes may be summarized thus: First, a national industrial adjustment board was set up 'in the Department of Labor,' to be composed of three members representing the public and holding office for five-year, overlapping terms. The President was to designate the chairman. There were to be in addition six representatives each of labor and industry, appointed by the President and the Senate, as a panel from which the chairman was to select members of the board from time to time. The board was to select its own staff but was at liberty to request services from the Department of Labor. Second, unfair labor practices were defined and forbidden. Third, the board was to proceed against such practices 'whenever the Secretary of Labor shall notify the board that there is reasonable cause to believe that any person has engaged in or is engaging in any such unfair labor practice.' The committee's report was not brought to a vote.

2. THE WAGNER-CONNERY LABOR RELATIONS BILL

On February 21, 1935, Senator Wagner introduced another labor relations bill and its counterpart was introduced in the House.[29] The Wagner bill went to the Senate Committee on Education and Labor, which reported it out on March 2, and after a two-day debate it passed the Senate on May 16 by a vote of 63 to 12. Upon reaching the House it went to the Committee on Labor, of which Mr. Connery was chairman. The committee reported it out with amendments on May 21, but at the request of Chairman Connery it was sent back to the committee on June 5 and on June 10 was reported out again with further amendments and made a special order in the House on June 19. It was there debated under a three-hour time limit and with much criticism of the so-called 'gag rule.' It passed the House without roll call. The Senate disagreed with the changes made in the House and the bill went to conference.

28. S. Rept. 1184, 73d Cong., 2d sess. (1934); S. 2926.
29. S. 1958, H.R. 6288, 74th Cong., 1st sess. (1935).

The conference report passed both houses on June 27 and the bill was signed by the President on July 5.

C. PROVISIONS OF THE NATIONAL LABOR RELATIONS ACT

In speaking of the Labor Relations Act,[30] Secretary Perkins stated [31] that it had three major purposes: It aimed to incorporate Section 7a of the National Industrial Recovery Act into permanent law. It set up a labor relations board to conduct the elections of labor representatives and to prevent unfair labor practices. And it established machinery for enforcement.

These purposes were embodied in the following provisions of the statute: First, the declared policy of the Act was to prevent or settle labor disputes which disrupted interstate commerce. Second, a National Labor Relations Board was created. It had three members appointed by the President with the advice and consent of the Senate, holding office for five-year staggered terms. There was no requirement of bipartisanship. The President designated the chairman. The members could be removed by the President for neglect of duty or malfeasance in office after notice and hearing. Third, the right of collective bargaining was guaranteed. Fourth, unfair labor practices by employers were defined and forbidden. Fifth, the board was empowered to settle questions of representation of labor for bargaining purposes. Sixth, the board's procedure and the machinery for enforcing its orders were modeled on that of the Federal Trade Commission.

D. TOPICS AND ISSUES IN HEARINGS AND DEBATES

Industry opposed the Labor Relations Act in its entirety. It was not, however, interested in the specific administrative features and its representatives did not discuss them. Those favoring the Act were sharply divided on certain issues relating to its structure and status.

30. Act of July 5, 1935, 49 Stat. at L. 449.
31. Hearings before the House Committee on Labor on H.R. 6288, 74th Cong., 1st sess. (1935), 277.

1. DEPARTMENTAL *versus* INDEPENDENT COMMISSION

There was no dispute about making the National Labor Relations Board an independent body. No one proposed that the Act should be administered by a departmental bureau or by a single administrator. There was, however, disagreement about the relation which the board was to bear to the Department of Labor. Should the proposed labor relations board be completely independent, like the Federal Trade Commission, or should it be an independent board in the Department of Labor? The National Labor Relations Board created by executive order in 1934 [32] had been thus placed in the Department of Labor, and its status in the department was explained clearly by Miss Perkins.[33] The board was to be absolutely independent as to its decisions and orders. These were not to be subject to review either by the President or by the Secretary of Labor. The board was expected to exercise only quasi-judicial duties. At the same time the board's budget was to be handled by the Department of Labor and the Secretary of Labor was to approve appointments to its staff. The board was expected to use the facilities of the Department of Labor. This same status was proposed but not adopted for the Social Security Board,[34] and was finally given to the Bituminous Coal Commission when it was set up in 1935.[35] It is the status which was proposed for the judicial sections of the independent commissions in the plan of the President's Committee on Administrative Management.[36] The Interstate Commerce Commission of 1887 was similarly in the Department of the Interior.[37]

There was substantial support for giving the board this status of independence 'in the Department of Labor.' Secretary Perkins was the strongest advocate of the plan, and she succeeded in converting to her position Chairman Connery of the House Committee on Labor. The Senate Committee on Education and Labor had favored the arrangement in reporting

32. *Supra*, 355.

33. Hearings before the Senate Committee on Education and Labor on S. 2926, 73d Cong., 2d sess. (1934), 24 ff.; *infra*, note 38, op. cit. 60 ff.; *supra*, note 31, op. cit. 280 ff.

34. But passed by the Senate.   36. Report with Special Studies, 39-42.
35. *Infra*, 379 ff.   37. *Supra*, 62.

the amended Wagner bill in 1934. President Roosevelt apparently favored the plan, since he had given this status to the board set up by executive order in 1934. He did not, however, press the issue during the debates in 1935. Finally, the arrangement was strongly urged by representatives of organized labor speaking through William Green [38] and expressing the opinions of John L. Lewis and John L. Frey.

Opposing the location of the Labor Relations Board in the Department of Labor and urging complete independence for it were Senator Wagner,[39] who won over the Senate committee to his point of view; Francis Biddle,[40] chairman of the existing National Labor Relations Board; H. A. Millis,[41] also a member of the board; Professor Lloyd Garrison,[42] a former member; and Representative Marcantonio of New York of the House Committee on Labor, who filed a powerful and probably effective minority report on this point.[43]

The arguments supporting the placing of the Labor Relations Board in the Department of Labor were most persuasively presented by Secretary Perkins in her testimony before the two committees of Congress.[44] These arguments ran as follows: First, it would avoid creating a new independent agency of which we already have too many. Second, the board would have greater prestige if associated with the Department of Labor than if it were left outside. Third, it would be easier to bring about an effective integration of all labor activities if they were all housed under one roof. Fourth, it would be easier to avoid the duplication of services. Experience showed that independent agencies were reluctant to utilize facilities existing in other departments of the government. Fifth, if independent, the board would tend to infringe upon the conciliation work of the department, since independent agencies usually tried to enlarge their own jurisdiction. Sixth, the approval by the Secretary of Labor of staff appointments to the board would tend to bring the general administration of the board's work into line with the prevailing practices in the executive

38. Hearings before the Senate Committee on Education and Labor on S. 1958, 74th Cong., 1st sess. (1935), 114 ff., 196 f.; *supra*, note 31, op. cit. 207 ff.
39. *Supra*, note 31, op. cit. 21.
40. *Supra*, note 38, Senate Hearings, 85 ff.
41. Ibid. 177 f. 43. H. Rept. 1147, 74th Cong., 1st sess. (1935), 26 ff.
42. Ibid. 131 ff. 44. *Supra*, note 33.

departments. Seventh, by giving management of the board's budget to the department it would relieve a quasi-judicial body of the political burden of arguing its case before Congressional committees. Eighth, if the board was wholly independent the public would be confused about the lines of jurisdiction and the division of labor between it and the department. Ninth, if placed in the department the board would have a direct channel of communication to the President through a Cabinet officer. This was important, since the board would occupy a regular place in the policies of the Administration and could most effectively work through the good offices of a Cabinet Secretary. Tenth, labor boards occupying a similar status existed in New York and elsewhere and the arrangement had worked well.

Miss Perkins's arguments were supplemented by those of William Green representing the American Federation of Labor, whose plea ran more along sentimental lines. He agreed that the board must be absolutely independent in its decisions and orders, but he urged that it be placed in the Department of Labor because that department was the friend of labor. He said:

> You know labor is a bit sentimental, because it feels that the Department of Labor is set up for labor. We appealed to Congress for the creation of a Labor Department for years and years. Congress responded, the Labor Department is there, and we have a peculiar interest in that Department.[45]
>
> It is difficult to explain, perhaps, but nevertheless it is true, that the laboring people throughout the country look to the Department of Labor as their Department. They feel that it was particularly created for the purpose of promoting and advancing their economic, social, and industrial welfare.[46]

Mr. Green said that to have a labor relations board outside the Department of Labor would detract from the prestige and usefulness of the department itself.

The arguments for a completely independent status for the new board were nowhere more cogently presented than in the minority report filed by Representative Marcantonio of New York, accompanying the House committee report.[47] They ran

45. *Supra,* note 38, Senate Hearings, op. cit. 115.   47. *Supra,* note 43.
46. *Supra,* note 31, op. cit. 207.

roughly as follows: First, complete independence was necessary to insure complete impartiality. The very fact urged by Mr. Green that the Department of Labor is 'the friend of labor' was itself an argument for independence. The board was to be essentially judicial in its character and if placed in the department there would be a strong tendency to make it conform in its decisions to the general policies of the department. Second, equally important was the appearance of impartiality; the board must not only be impartial but the public must believe it to be impartial. Everyone knew the Department of Labor to be 'pro labor,' since it was set up in labor's interest; if, therefore, the board was in the department it would be suspected of sharing the bias of the department. Third, precedent pointed to the status of independence. Most of the important quasi-judicial jobs had been given to completely independent agencies; whereas Secretary Perkins's argument, logically extended, would place all independent commissions in executive departments. Fourth, the board was to be an agent of Congress, not of the President. This point was urged late in the discussion and after the Supreme Court's decision in the Humphrey case.[48] Fifth, Cabinet officers already had more work than they could do effectively, and the Secretary of Labor would be unable to supervise efficiently the affairs of the board. Sixth, it was imperative that the quasi-judicial tasks assigned to the labor board be kept sharply separate from the tasks of conciliation and mediation, and this could be most effectively done by creating wholly separate agencies. Seventh, it would be easier to secure impartial and able men to serve on a completely independent board. Eighth, the board needed the prestige which would be gained by independence. Ninth, the independence of the board would be ultimately undermined by departmental control of its budget. Tenth, it was not enough to give the board independence of decision; it must also have independent control of the early stages through which labor cases pass. Many disputes might never reach the board for adjudication. Judicial independence would not be adequate, therefore, in cases which never reached the board. Eleventh, conciliation and mediation were bound to be con-

48. *Humphrey's Executor* v. *United States*, 295 U.S. 602 (1935).

fused with adjudication if both were carried on in the same department, because each was used at a different stage in the progress of labor disputes.

The friends of complete independence won their fight. We have seen that the Senate committee of 1934 had been willing to put the labor relations board into the Department of Labor. Senator Wagner appears to have converted the committee to the view that the board should be set up as an independent agency in the Department of Labor. The House committee under Chairman Connery had been won over by Miss Perkins to the opposite point of view, but Representative Marcantonio by filing his minority report appears to have convinced the House, and it supported his position and that of Senator Wagner. In conference committee, after the Humphrey decision, the phrase 'independent agency in the Executive Department' was dropped out. Why, asked the conference, in the light of the Court's decision, should the statute declare an independent board to be 'in the executive branch'? [49]

2. THE MERGER OF POWERS IN THE BOARD

Relatively minor attention was paid to the alleged merger in the proposed labor relations board of administrative and quasi-judicial power. The point was emphasized by one or two witnesses representing industry. Mr. Emery, general counsel of the National Association of Manufacturers, referred to the proposed board as the 'pooh-bah of Federal administrative and executive authority.' [50] Industry wanted a highly judicialized board, a sort of labor court, and was anxious to eliminate the board's discretionary power and thus draw the teeth from the act. Representative Blanton attacked the combination of powers given to the board and alleged that it was made judge, jury, bailiff, prosecutor, and executioner.[51] Other witnesses, including Milton Handler,[52] general counsel to the existing Labor Relations Board, and Francis Biddle,[53] its chairman, defended the

49. H. Rept. 1371, 74th Cong., 1st sess. (1935), 4.
50. *Supra,* note 38, Senate Hearings, op. cit. 847.
51. 79 Cong. Rec. 9700 ff.
52. *Supra,* note 33, Senate Hearings (1934), op. cit. 36 f.
53. *Supra,* note 31, op. cit. 176.

mixture of powers as necessary to the efficient administration of the law and supported by precedent.

3. SEPARATION OF CONCILIATION FROM ADJUDICATION

Congress learned from its early experience with labor boards that an agency suitable to regulate and adjudicate could not also carry on effectively the tasks of conciliation and mediation. This was recognized by the friends of the Wagner-Connery bill. Senator Wagner had this in mind when he proposed in his 1934 bill a separate conciliation service in the Department of Labor. Secretary Perkins was well aware of the problem involved; and argued that for the very reason that the board must be kept sharply away from the tasks of conciliation and mediation, it ought to be placed in the department for purposes of adequate integration.[54] Dr. William Leiserson, the chairman of the Petroleum Labor Policy Board, pointed out the difficulty of an absolutely sharp separation of conciliation from adjudication and declared that the labor relations board could not be entirely cut off from all mediation functions.[55] It was generally agreed, however, that this separation should be as sharp as possible and this position was stated in the report of the Senate Committee on Education and Labor as follows:

It is of special import that the National Labor Relations Board is not empowered to engage in conciliation of wage and hour disputes insofar as that activity can be carried on by the Department of Labor. Duplication of services is thus avoided, and in addition the Board is left free to engage in quasi-judicial work that is essentially different from conciliation or mediation of wage and hour controversies. And of course the binding effect of the provisions of this bill forbidding unfair labor practices are not subjects for mediation or conciliation.

The committee does not believe that the Board should serve as an arbitration agency. Such work, like conciliation, might impair its standing as an interpreter of the law. In addition, there is at present no dearth of arbitration agencies in this country.[56]

54. *Supra*, note 33, Senate Hearings (1934), op. cit. 21.
55. Ibid. 235 f.
56. S. Rept. 573, 74th Cong., 1st sess. (1935), 8.

4. GROUP REPRESENTATION ON THE BOARD

Experience had also thrown light on the problem of group representation on a regulatory labor board. The first Wagner bill [57] had provided for a board upon which industry and labor had representation, and Secretary Perkins had lent her support to this plan.[58] Mr. William Green, naturally enough, urged that there should be representation of labor on the board.[59] The representatives of industry, however, anxious to secure a highly judicialized tribunal, were strongly opposed to interest representation. Various compromise proposals were discussed but in the end the National Labor Relations Board was set up without group representation and even without the customary requirement of political bipartisanship.

5. REMOVAL OF BOARD MEMBERS AND THE HUMPHREY CASE

When the Wagner-Connery bill was introduced it contained no provision relating to the removal of members of the board and this point was wholly ignored during the early stages of the history of the bill. The Supreme Court's decision on May 27 on the Humphrey case [60] stating that Congress could validly restrict the President's power to remove members of the independent regulatory commissions, had an immediate influence upon Congressional thinking. The decision strengthened the hand of those who were urging for the labor relations board a status of complete independence, and it undoubtedly was responsible for the incorporation into the Act of an amendment providing that members of the board should be removable by the President for neglect of duty or malfeasance in office, but only after notice and public hearing.

57. S. 2926, *supra*, 357.
58. *Supra*, note 33, Senate Hearings (1934), op. cit. 23.
59. *Supra*, note 31, op. cit. 207 ff.
60. *Humphrey's Executor* v. *United States*, 295 U.S. 602 (1935).

E. Proposals to Change the National Labor Relations Board

It was probably inevitable that a steady and bitter attack should be made on the National Labor Relations Board and all its doings. The Wagner Act itself was so obnoxious to most employers that nothing could have made its administration popular with business. Until the Supreme Court's decision in 1937,[61] opponents of the Act clung to the hope that it would be held unconstitutional. When these hopes were blasted they embarked on a drive for legislative amendment. Standing committees of both the House and Senate conducted elaborate and reasonably impartial hearings with a view to proposing changes. In 1939 the House created a special committee of five under the chairmanship of Representative Smith, one of the board's bitter opponents, to undertake a more aggressive investigation and make recommendations. At the same time a number of individual senators and representatives were studying the whole problem and eventually introduced bills to modify the Wagner Act and reorganize the board.

None of the proposals has so far been adopted, and we need not deal with them in detail. Their principal features may be summarized as follows: First, several bills, including that of the Smith committee, contained devices for separating the board's functions of 'prosecution' under the Wagner Act from the functions of adjudication; these are analyzed more fully in a later chapter.[62] Second, two of the bills required the board 'so far as practicable' to use the same rules of evidence as a United States District Court. Third, changes in the membership of the board were proposed. These included making it bipartisan, giving labor and employers representation on it, enlarging it, and reorganizing it by the 'ripper' proposal of the Smith committee to abolish the present board and put another in its place. Fourth, judicial review of the board was extended to its findings of fact.

It is not impossible that the National Labor Relations Board is destined to serve as a guinea pig upon which various experi-

61. *N.L.R.B.* v. *Jones & Laughlin Steel Corp.*, 301 U.S. 1 (1937).
62. *Infra*, 714 f.

ments in the field of administrative and quasi-judicial organization and procedure will be carried on. In the meantime the board has taken measures to improve its own internal administrative management to insure the maximum degree of impartiality and efficiency.

III. THE NATIONAL BITUMINOUS COAL COMMISSION

A. THE COAL COMMISSION OF 1935

1. BACKGROUND OF ACT OF 1935

a. *Conditions and problems in the soft coal industry calling for regulation*

THE soft coal industry in this country has been in a fundamentally unhealthy condition for a number of decades. It has been and is one of our 'sickest industries.' There are certain peculiarities of the industry which have contributed to this result. In the first place, it is highly individualistic. Soft coal mines are widely scattered both geographically and in point of ownership. There are numerous small units and marginal mines. It has proved almost impossible to organize the business of producing soft coal; the conditions are such that cutthroat competition tends to be normal, and every form of unfair competitive practice is resorted to. In the second place, in no other industry does the labor factor play so important a part. Some five hundred thousand workers are employed in the industry and over two million persons are dependent upon it. From 60 to 65 per cent of the cost of production is the price paid out in wages. It has been truly said that when you sell coal you are selling labor. Consequently, there is in the industry a hair-trigger sensitiveness of the employer-employee equilibrium to fluctuations in price. The miners have found it easier to organize than have the producers, and strikes have been more extensive and prolonged than in most other industries. In general the labor problems are of fundamental importance. A third peculiarity is that the consumers of coal are normally in a stronger strategic position than the producers. The largest consumers of soft coal are the railroads and the steel industry.

They are much better organized than the coal companies, and they have sometimes been able to force coal prices down below the actual costs of production.

As a result of these factors together with others, the soft coal industry since the World War has been facing very difficult problems. Normally, there is a steady surplus capacity in soft coal mines. This surplus capacity dates at least as far back as 1899, and has been due to competitive overdevelopment during high-price periods. Along with this has come a reduction in actual demand for coal due to the increasing competition of other fuels, such as gas and oil, and of the convertible energy of water power. During the long strikes in the industry, such as that of 1922, consumers of coal were led to experiment with substitutes and some of them never gave them up. There have also been technological developments which have resulted in great economies in the use of coal and a resulting reduction in demand. Finally, the industry has suffered along with all others from the general business stagnation of recent years.

b. *Previous federal action affecting the soft coal industry*

It had long been felt that the only solution of the problems confronting the soft coal industry lay in some form of federal action, but there had been no agreement on what this action should be and there had been doubts regarding its constitutional propriety, since the coal industry had not been held to be a 'business affected with a public interest.' [1] As far back as 1913 representatives of the coal industry appealed to the committees of Congress considering the Federal Trade Commission Act to set up a separate commission to stabilize the coal industry and to eliminate unfair competitive practices. Between 1913 and 1919, nineteen investigations of the industry were conducted either by committees of Congress or by special bodies. Some of these dealt with the labor aspects of the problem; the later ones, however, dealt with the effects of destructive competition.

The government regulated the soft coal industry during the

1. *Cf.* the forthcoming book by R. H. Baker on *The National Bituminous Coal Commission* in the Johns Hopkins University Studies in Historical and Political Science.

War. Under the Lever Act [2] the price of coal was regulated, and its distribution was directed by the Fuel Administration. Some of the provisions of these regulatory measures were again invoked by the government during the disastrous coal strikes of 1919, 1920, and 1922, when emergency conditions paralleling those of the War prevailed. As a result of the strike of 1922, a United States Coal Commission was set up to investigate the whole problem. In its report of 1923 [3] it urged the continuance of fact-finding machinery and proposed the federal licensing of those who shipped coal in interstate commerce.

In 1928-9, hearings were held by the Senate Committee on Interstate Commerce on a bill [4] to regulate the bituminous coal industry. This proposed a commission to license all producers engaged in interstate commerce. Such licensed producers could lawfully form marketing pools and engage in co-operative selling under the supervision of the commission. The commission could fix maximum prices which might be agreed upon by such pools. The right of collective bargaining was guaranteed. No legislative action, however, was taken on this bill.

In October 1931, a meeting was held in New York of all producers, sales agents, and attorneys from the soft coal industry. A voluntary regional sales agency, known as Appalachian Coals, Inc., was established to regularize the marketing of coal in the area involved. Doubts about the legality of this organization under the antitrust laws delayed the spread of the plan, but the Supreme Court upheld it in the case of *Appalachian Coals, Inc.* v. *United States.*[5]

In 1932 the so-called Davis-Kelly bill [6] was introduced in the Senate and hearings were held by the Senate Committee on Interstate Commerce. This bill called for an independent bituminous coal commission to license all coal companies engaged in interstate commerce. Such licenses were to comply with rules made by the commission to assure collective bar-

2. Act of Aug. 10, 1917, 40 Stat. at L. 276.
3. S. Doc. 195, 68th Cong., 2d sess. (1925).
4. S. 4490, 70th Cong., 2d sess. (1928).
5. 288 U.S. 344 (1933).
6. S. 2935, 72d Cong., 1st sess. (1932).

gaining and to control marketing pools. During the hearings on this bill, Representative Lewis brought in a bill [7] based largely on the British Coal Mines Act of 1930. Both bills were under consideration when the NRA was set up in 1933 and were accordingly dropped.

One of the first codes of fair competition to be established under the National Industrial Recovery Act was the Bituminous Coal Code, and it was one of the most successful. The industry appeared to be ripe for some form of self-regulation, and the code was embraced with considerable enthusiasm. Prices rose, wages rose, hours of labor were reduced, and trade practices were regulated. Collective bargaining was guaranteed and the United Mine Workers of America lost no time in organizing the industry. The success of the code was, however, relatively short-lived. There were administrative difficulties due to the lack of adequate staff. It was found difficult to stabilize prices or to co-ordinate the prices set up in different areas. The co-operative spirit waned and cutthroat competition began to creep back in. It was much more difficult to maintain minimum prices than it had been to maintain maximum prices during the War. It began to appear that the industry was not capable of the self-discipline necessary to stabilize itself, and that more effective and direct federal control was necessary if a return to chaos was to be avoided. When the National Industrial Recovery Act was invalidated by the Supreme Court in May 1935,[8] all efforts to retain or enforce the coal code were abandoned.

2. STEPS IN THE LEGISLATIVE HISTORY OF THE GUFFEY ACT
OF 1935

In May 1934, officers of the United Mine Workers began consultations with a committee of operators of the National Coal Association set up under the code to see if a mutually satisfactory bill could be worked out for submission to Congress. This joint committee worked for five months but was unable to reach an agreement. The joint report of the international officers of the United Mine Workers to the 34th Con-

7. H.R. 9924, 72d Cong., 1st sess. (1932).
8. *Schechter* v. *United States*, 295 U.S. 495 (1935).

stitutional Convention summarized the net results of this effort:

> After some fourteen months' operation of the Recovery Code, sensing the reluctance of officials to enforce it and yielding to the pressure of large consumers, price chiselers began to appear and multiply in the nation's markets, and the need for more effective legislation became clear.
>
> In the summer of 1934, a joint legislative committee of representative operators and officials of your organization was formed to promote such legislation. After numerous sessions it became manifest that the committee as such could not agree owing to the divergent views of many of the operators. The discussions, however, continued, and the offices of the United Mine Workers were made an open forum for operators, mine workers, wholesalers, retailers and representatives of consumers. The results were submitted to certain members of Congress and in January 1935 Senator Guffey in the Senate and Congressman Snyder in the House introduced the bill, since known as the Guffey-Snyder Bill.[9]

The Guffey-Snyder bill,[10] introduced in January 1935, was drafted mainly by Henry Warrum, general counsel of the United Mine Workers. It was modeled largely upon the Lewis bill of 1932,[11] which in turn had followed the British Coal Mines Act of 1930. Shortly after its introduction, Representative Lewis and Senator Hayden reintroduced the Lewis bill.

The provisions of the original Guffey-Snyder bill throw light upon the way in which thinking upon this important problem developed. These provisions were as follows: (a) The production and distribution of coal is 'affected with a public interest.' (b) A national bituminous coal commission was to be created in the Department of the Interior. Three of its five members were to be dissociated from the coal mines or oil industries, one was to represent coal producers, and one the miners. (c) A bituminous coal labor board of three members, appointed by the President, was to be set up in the Department of Labor. (d) A code of fair competition was to be established. A tax of 25 per cent on the sale price of coal was to be levied, and 99 per cent of this tax was to be returned to those who signed the

9. Proceedings of the 34th Constitutional Convention of the United Mine Workers of America (1936), vol. 1, 26 f.

10. S. 1417 and H.R. 4661, 74th Cong., 1st sess. (1935).

11. *Supra,* 371.

code. (e) Twenty-four districts were to be established. In each was to be set up a board of six: five members selected by the producers voting on a tonnage basis; the other member chosen by the organization of employees representing the preponderant number of employees in the industry—which meant, of course, the United Mine Workers. (f) A national coal-producers board was to be created, composed of representatives appointed by the district boards. This board was to allot tonnage quotas to each district upon the basis of estimates provided by the district boards of the amount that could be disposed of. The district boards in turn were to assign proportions of the quota to the individual mines in the district. (g) Maximum and minimum prices of coal were to be fixed by the district boards, subject to the approval of the commission. (h) The Secretary of the Interior was to set up a national coal reserve by purchasing coal lands on approval of the commission. This was to check the wasteful and excessive production of coal. No lands in the reserve were to be mined or leased without permission of the commission. Three hundred million dollars was to be appropriated for this purpose.

The bill was referred to the Senate Committee on Interstate Commerce. Hearings were held by a subcommittee in February and March of 1935. As modified by the subcommittee the bill was introduced again on April 2 by Senator Guffey, referred to the Committee on Interstate Commerce, and reported back on April 11. No action on this bill was taken and it was later replaced by the bill which, in the meantime, had passed the House. In the House the revised Guffey-Snyder bill [12] had gone for hearings to a subcommittee of the Committee on Ways and Means. During these hearings vigorous opposition was presented, partly on general economic grounds and partly on constitutional grounds. The constitutional doubts were enormously increased by the Supreme Court's decision in the Schechter case in May 1935.[13] It looked for a time as though the subcommittee would fail to report the bill favorably. In the course of its deliberations, President Roosevelt sent his famous letter of August 16 urging the committee to report the bill and declaring, 'I hope your committee will not permit

12. H.R. 8479, 74th Cong., 1st sess. (1935).
13. *Supra,* 371.

doubts as to constitutionality, however reasonable, to block the suggested legislation.' [14] The subcommittee lined up four to three against the bill but reported it to the full committee without recommendation. Of the twenty-five members of the Committee on Ways and Means, fourteen opposed the bill. The committee finally reported it out by a vote of 12 to 11, with two members not voting. The bill had been modified in the committee to conform to the Schechter decision and also to incorporate certain compromises which had been reached at the so-called Shoreham Conference at which representatives of producers and labor had been able to adjust some of their differences. The committee's bill,[15] as thus amended, was introduced by Representative Snyder on August 13, referred to the Committee on Ways and Means, and reported back the following day. It was made a special order on August 16, was debated, amended, and passed on August 19 by a vote of 195 to 168.

On August 19 the House bill went to the Senate, where it was substituted for the Senate bill. Debate began in the Senate on August 20. The bill was amended and passed by the Senate on August 22 by a vote of 45 to 37. The House disagreed with the Senate amendments and a conference was agreed to. The conference report passed both houses on August 23. The vote in the House was 186 to 150; in the Senate no roll call was taken. The bill was signed by the President on August 30.

3. PROVISIONS OF THE BITUMINOUS COAL CONSERVATION ACT OF 1935

As finally passed, the Act [16] lacked two important provisions found in the original bill. The provisions for the establishment of quotas, modeled presumably upon the British Act of 1930, and for the creation of a bituminous coal reserve were eliminated. The Act contained the following provisions: (a) It was to continue in force for four years. (b) It created the National Bituminous Coal Commission in the Department of

14. 79 Cong. Rec. 13449.
15. H.R. 9100, 74th Cong., 1st sess. (1935).
16. Act of Aug. 30, 1935, 49 Stat. at L. 991.

the Interior to report annually to the Secretary of the Interior. There were five members appointed by the President with the consent of the Senate for four-year terms. All members were to be disinterested and there were no representatives of labor or industry. The commission was to fix maximum prices if the interests of the consuming public required it. It was to hold hearings on complaints of unfair trade practices, a list of which, borrowed from the coal code, was incorporated in the Act, and it was to issue orders restraining them. It was to make studies and investigations looking to the increase of the use of coal, safety in mines, and the rehabilitation of displaced miners. It was to study the problem of production control (since the quota provisions had been dropped) and report to Congress through the Secretary of the Interior by January 6, 1936. It was to appear before the Interstate Commerce Commission in any cases on freight rates on bituminous coal. (c) A new provision created a Consumers' Counsel, also in the Department of the Interior, to report annually to the Secretary. This officer, appointed by the President and the Senate, was to appear in the interests of consumers in any hearing before the commission, to conduct any independent investigation to enable him to represent the consumers, and to call on the commission for information for this purpose. (d) A Bituminous Coal Labor Board of three members was set up 'assigned to the Department of Labor'; it was appointed by the President and Senate, and consisted of a representative each of labor and the producers, and a disinterested chairman. It was authorized to adjudicate disputes regarding collective bargaining and interference therewith, to order and, if necessary, conduct elections of representatives of labor, and to order code members to deal with representatives of labor in collective bargaining. It could offer to mediate disputes and upon the written request of the parties it could arbitrate them. Wage agreements negotiated through collective bargaining with two-thirds of the tonnage producers of any district were to constitute the minimum wages for the district and were filed with the Coal Labor Board. (e) Twenty-three districts were created for nine minimum price areas. (f) In each district was created a District Board, composed of from three to seventeen members holding two-year terms. One member was to be selected by the labor organization representing the preponderant number of employees in the district (not in the industry as in the original bill), one-half of the others was to be chosen by a majority of the producers, and the other half by the producers voting on a tonnage basis. The district boards were to fix minimum prices in the districts, subject to revision by the commission. The boards were also to send to the commission statistics showing actual production costs. (g) A tax of 15 per cent was laid on the sale price of coal at the mine and a 90 per cent drawback was allowed to those who signed and observed the coal code.

4. TOPICS AND ISSUES IN HEARINGS AND DEBATES

The debates on the Guffey bill reflected to some degree the heavy pressure brought to bear by the United Mine Workers as well as by the President. They reflected sharp differences in basic economic philosophy and they covered extensively the constitutional issues. But there was no thorough discussion of the administrative aspects of the new legislation and many of its unique and interesting features received no comment at all. The topics related to the present field of inquiry were as follows:

a. *Self-regulation* versus *government regulation*

The bill represented an interesting experiment in the field of industrial self-regulation, an experiment without precedent in the field of federal control. In so far as they could agree on anything, the producers favored self-regulation rather than direct government regulation. Only thus, they urged, could there be sufficient flexibility to meet the complex and changing problems of the industry. Part of this self-regulation was to operate under immunities from antitrust prohibitions. It was strongly urged by industrialists who opposed the bill that no new commission be created but that the Federal Trade Commission be made into a judicialized policy-determining body with authority to grant immunity under the antitrust laws to certain trade associations in the industry.[17] Representatives of the American Bar Association appeared before the Senate subcommittee to protest against having the district boards chosen by the producers and the labor unions. They argued that these boards should be government officials appointed by direct government authority. To invest unofficial bodies such as these with legal powers was a dangerous and unconstitutional innovation. When the Supreme Court invalidated the Guffey Act[18] the following year it specifically mentioned that legislative power had been invalidly delegated to non-official bodies. The Act as passed was a compromise between self-regulation and government regulation; but as the debates on the bill progressed the changes made all tended to stiffen governmental control at the expense of self-regulation.

b. *Interest representation on the commission*

The original bill had sought to enlist the services of both labor and the producers in the regulatory process. Labor itself, speaking through the officials of the United Mine Workers, was eager to have direct labor representation on the coal commission, although they did not insist upon any fixed quota. Henry Warrum[19] and John L. Lewis both urged this. Lewis distrusted persons appointed as 'disinterested,' and declared that they were seldom sympathetic to the labor point of view.[20] The producers apparently did not feel the need for direct representation. They were willing to have all the members of the commission 'disinterested'; they said that the commission was similar in its functions to the Interstate Commerce Commission and its members should have similar qualifications.[21] The operators who desired direct representation could not agree on the basis on which it should be worked out.[22] The chief opposition to interest representation came from the large

17. Hearings before a subcommittee of the House Committee on Ways and Means on H.R. 8479, 74th Cong., 1st sess. (1935), 493 f.
18. *Carter* v. *Carter Coal Company*, 298 U.S. 238 (1936).
19. *Supra*, note 17, op. cit. 68.
20. Hearings before a subcommittee of the Senate Committee on Interstate Commerce on S. 1417, 74th Cong., 1st sess. (1935), 609 f.
21. Ibid. 431.
22. Ibid. 611 ff.

consumers of bituminous coal, such as the railroads and the steel industry. They feared, and perhaps reasonably, that a coal commission representing the miners and the producers would be tempted to raise wages and prices unreasonably and leave the consuming public to pay the bill.[23]

c. *Consumer protection through the Consumers' Counsel*

It was felt that the consuming public, which had often paid through the nose before, was not adequately protected from price exploitation merely by having the coal commission composed of disinterested persons. Something more was needed, and this was provided through the establishment of the independent officer known as the Consumers' Counsel, an officer completely independent of the commission and actively guarding at all times the interests of the consumer.

d. *Merger of powers*

The familiar argument that incompatible powers were merged in the proposed commission was presented, but the issue was not discussed at any length. Mr. Louis Caldwell, a distinguished lawyer long interested in this problem, presented a brief [24] before the House committee, criticizing the new commission on the ground that it merged prosecuting and judicial functions and charging also that judicial power was given to the commission in violation of the Constitution.

e. *Civil service requirements*

The original Guffey bill exempted all employees of the coal commission and the coal labor board from civil service requirements. This brought sharp attack in the Senate from Senator Walsh [25] of Massachusetts and Senator Norris [26] of Nebraska. They asserted that the commission must be protected from the undermining influence of patronage mongers.

23. Ibid. 169.
24. Statement in Opposition to the Minimum-Price-Fixing Features of the Guffey-Snyder Bill, June 25, 1935.
25. 79 Cong. Rec. 14076.
26. Ibid. 14077.

Finally, after some discussion, the staffs of the commission, the labor board, and the Consumers' Counsel were put under civil service requirements.

f. *Bipartisanship*

The Senate amended the Guffey bill to establish the customary rule of bipartisanship with respect to the membership of the commission. No debate took place on this point and the amendment was dropped out during the deliberations of the conference committee. Neither house sought to reinstate it.

g. *Location of the commission and the Consumers' Counsel in the Department of the Interior*

The Davis-Kelly and Lewis bills of 1932 had proposed a wholly independent bituminous coal commission. The Guffey-Snyder bill as proposed and finally passed placed the Bituminous Coal Commission and the Consumers' Counsel 'in the Department of the Interior.' This gave to these bodies an entirely unique status. No other independent regulatory commission was thus located inside one of the regular executive departments. The status thus created was somewhat similar to that proposed by the President's Committee on Administrative Management for the judicial sections to be created out of the independent regulatory commissions.[27] In the case of the Coal Commission, however, there was no suggestion of separating the administrative from the judicial functions of the agency. It is an interesting fact that there was no discussion either before Congressional committees or in Congress of this unique arrangement. There was no explanation of why the arrangement was made, or what the practical implications of it were supposed to be. As established, the relation between the commission and counsel and the department was as follows: The budget of the commission and the counsel, and in some cases their supplies, were cleared through the Department of the Interior, and the annual reports to Congress also passed through the office of the Secretary of the Interior. The Secre-

27. Report with Special Studies, 39-42.

tary, however, had no authority over the personnel of either agency or over any phase of the administration of the Act. Certainly he had no power to pass upon or revise any of the commission's orders or decisions. After some experience under the arrangement, Secretary Ickes testified before a subcommittee of the House Committee on Appropriations regarding the actual relations between the Coal Commission and his own department. He said:

. . . The Coal Commission is not within our jurisdiction at all. We have nothing to do with it. We clear their budget, but that is about all. We make no appointments for them, and we have nothing to do with the policies. I would like to say a word on that point. This does not go to the question of the Budget so much as to the question of general legislative policies.

In the President's reorganization plan he brought out the fact that there are a good many independent agencies set up from time to time in the Government which are not under any department, and it has been indicated that there should be some measure of control of them . . .

I said to Senator Guffey at the time of his first bill that I did not believe in responsibility without power. They placed it in the Interior Department, but that does not mean that we have a particle of control over it. It had as well be outside, so far as we are concerned. I do not know of anything going on in the Coal Commission, except what I read in the newspapers.[28]

Mr. Henry Warrum, who had helped draft the 1935 Act, told a subcommittee of the Committee on Ways and Means that the Coal Commission 'in one sense of the word got nothing but a roof over their heads in the Interior Department.' [29] But he did not elaborate this.

A competent student of the whole problem summed up the relation between the commission and the department in the following words:

. . . The Commission was completely independent of the Department of the Interior. That department exercised no control over Commission personnel or over the administration of the act. The annual reports of the 1935 Commission were printed in the annual

28. House Hearings on the Interior Department Appropriation Bill for 1939, 75th Cong., 3d sess. (1938), Part 1, 23 f.
29. *Supra,* note 17, op. cit. 84.

reports of the Department of the Interior. The annual reports of the 1937 Commission were printed separately and were merely sent to the office of the Secretary of the Interior for forwarding to Congress. The budget, and, in some cases, supplies were channeled through the Department of the Interior. The presumption is that the budget officer of that Department could have recommended reductions, but he never did so since the Commission was regarded as 'independent.' Actually the Commission dealt with the Budget Bureau directly, even though going through the formality of presenting its estimates through the Interior Department, and the Budget Bureau exercised a far greater control than the Interior Department in not allowing some of the budget estimates of the Commission. Although the relationship of the Commission to the Department of the Interior, as provided in the Coal Act, is not without precedent, it is difficult to see what is accomplished by such an arrangement.[30]

In the summer of 1936, Chairman Hosford of the Coal Commission commented to the writer upon the commission's status in the Department of the Interior. He suggested that the Guffey Act was mainly a conservation act, and that the position of the commission in the department may have been owing to a desire to place all conservation activities in a single department. The operators in general preferred to see it independent. Labor was willing to have it in the department but demanded for it an independent status within the department, because some of the officers of the United Mine Workers distrusted the Bureau of Mines, and did not wish to have the new Coal Commission placed on a basis of equality with it. Mr. Hosford said that the commission had been wholly free from interference of any kind from the department. Budgetary control by the department had been a help rather than a hindrance, and he described the department's relation as that of a protector, 'like a big brother.' He felt that independence with respect to its major tasks was desirable during the commission's formative period, since it permitted quick action and freedom from red tape. He thought that after the experimental period had passed it might be wise to give the commission bureau status within the department.

30. Baker, op. cit. 104 f. of manuscript.

B. THE COAL COMMISSION OF 1937

1. BACKGROUND—INVALIDITY OF THE ACT OF 1935

Everything seemed to conspire to get the 1935 Coal Commission and Guffey Act off to a bad start. The bill passed Congress after the passage of the regular appropriation bill for 1936. Money for creating the new commission would thus have to be provided in the deficiency appropriation bill. A filibuster in the Senate, however, prevented the passage of this bill, which carried an item of $200,000 for the administration of the Act. The commission was therefore obliged to borrow supplies, office space, and personnel. Most of these were contributed by the Department of the Interior under an arrangement whereby the commission was to repay when it received its own funds. Some of the staff was taken over from the defunct NRA. The commission retained a skeleton form until the passage in January 1936 of an adequate appropriation. The Consumers' Counsel had begun operating with a borrowed staff of four persons. Besides being left without money, the commission encountered great difficulties in getting the district boards to co-ordinate bituminous coal prices amongst the various districts. Some of the boards set up to fix these prices were accused of not wanting to reach an agreement. The troubles of the Coal Labor Board were equally serious. It confronted a tremendous labor problem with inadequate funds and no employees except a few borrowed from the Department of Labor. It therefore found itself unable to cope with the task effectively.

Within twenty-four hours after the passage of the Guffey-Snyder Act, President Carter of the Carter Coal Company began court action to enjoin the enforcement of the statute. Although this was thrown out as being prematurely brought, it was later brought again. By the end of 1935 over eighty suits were pending, either attacking the validity of the entire statute or seeking to enjoin the collection of the tax. In May 1936 the Supreme Court, in a 6-to-3 decision, invalidated the labor sections of the Guffey Act and held that the price-fixing provisions were so closely connected with them as to render the entire statute void. This was the case of *Carter* v. *Carter Coal Company*.[31]

The Carter case reduced the commission to a skeleton; it was left with no important substantive job. Two days after the Carter decision Senator Guffey introduced a coal bill which was substantially like the Act of 1935 minus the labor provisions. Representative Vinson introduced it in the House. The Senate committee held hearings but the House committee did not. The bill passed the House but Senate action was prevented by the threat of a filibuster by Senator Holt of West Virginia at the end of the 74th Congress, and the bill died.

2. STEPS IN THE HISTORY OF THE GUFFEY-VINSON ACT OF 1937

On January 6, 1937, Senator Guffey reintroduced his bill, and Representative Vinson again introduced essentially the same measure in the House.[32] These were essentially the bills introduced in 1936. Senator Guffey had made the reintroduction of the measure the subject of a campaign pledge as well as a definite promise to the United Mine Workers. Hearings on the bill were held by a subcommittee of the Senate Committee on Interstate Commerce but these hearings were narrowly limited. A few congressmen appeared but only three outsiders came. Most of the hearing was given over to the testimony of Chairman Hosford of the Coal Commission. The Senate committee brought in a brief report, as did the Ways and Means Committee of the House, although the latter held no hearings. Debate in each house was very brief and there was minority criticism of the failure of the two committees to hold adequate public hearings. The bill passed the House on March 11. No record vote was taken but a motion to recommit was defeated by a vote of 39 to 340. The bill passed the Senate on April 5 by a vote of 58 to 15. The bill went to conference and the conference report passed the Senate on April 9 and the House on April 12, without record vote in either case. It was signed by the President on April 26, 1937.[33]

31. 298 U.S. 238 (1936).   33. Act of April 26, 1937, 50 Stat. at L. 72.
32. S. 1 and H.R. 4985, 75th Cong., 1st sess. (1937).

3. MAJOR CHANGES IN THE LAW

While much of the Act of 1935 was retained, it was imperative to make some changes and it seemed desirable to make others. These may be summarized as follows:

First, the declaration of policy in the Act, which had been criticized by the Court in the Carter case, was changed. The new Act declared that the regulation of prices and unfair practices in the bituminous coal industry was necessary to the promotion of interstate commerce and to the removal of burdens and obstructions therefrom.

Second, the National Bituminous Coal Commission was increased to seven members: two experienced bituminous coal mine workers, two experienced producers, and the other three disinterested. None could have any financial interest in any phase of the business.

Third, the taxing arrangements were changed. A tax was laid of 1¢ per ton and an additional tax of 19½ per cent of the fair market value of coal at the time of sale was levied on non-code producers.

Fourth, minimum prices and marketing regulations instead of being adopted by district boards of twenty-three producing areas subject to review by the commission were now to be adopted by the commission on recommendation of the district boards.

Fifth, the labor provisions of the 1935 statute were omitted. There was, however, a declaration of policy that labor had the right to organize and engage in collective bargaining, and the government was forbidden to purchase coal not produced in accordance with this policy.

Sixth, the provisions regarding price fixing and unfair trade practices were applied to intrastate commerce when such commerce unjustly discriminated against interstate commerce.

Seventh, the Consumers' Counsel remained in the Department of the Interior but reported directly to Congress instead of through the Secretary.

Eighth, civil service requirements were substantially relaxed.

Ninth, a new and more specific separability clause was inserted.

4. TOPICS AND ISSUES IN HEARINGS AND DEBATES

No very extensive or illuminating discussions or debates took place on the 1937 Act. We may comment briefly, however, upon a few of the issues which had to be faced and the points of view which emerged with respect to them:

a. *Constitutional problems*

It is not relevant to this study to deal with the constitutional problems involved in drafting the new statute. The committees of Congress approached this problem seriously, for they had no desire to write again a statute which would be held void. John Dickinson, who had defended the 1935 Act in the Supreme Court, aided in drafting the new bill. Solicitor General Reed was summoned before the Committee on Ways and Means to express an opinion on the constitutional issue. While there was no report of his testimony, Representative Vinson intimated that he had taken a favorable view of the proposed legislation.[34] The chairman of the House committee asked the Attorney General for an opinion on the constitutionality of the bill only to be told that in accordance with law and long-established precedents, the Attorney General could not give Congress constitutional advice on pending legislation.[35]

b. *Interest representation on the Bituminous Coal Commission*

Under the Act of 1935 the commission was composed of five disinterested persons. In approaching the new statute, labor demanded definite representation on the commission in order to provide that protection for its interests which had been struck down by the Supreme Court when it invalidated the labor sections of the earlier Act. The position of labor on this point was presented by John L. Lewis before the Senate Committee on Interstate Commerce. In the hearing on the 1936 bill he said:

Now, as the quid pro quo of supporting this bill, the United Mine Workers agree that the bill should provide for representation

34. 81 Cong. Rec. 2031.   35. Ibid. 2040.

of the workers, as such, by two members on the Commission. Why? Merely because the right to fix the price levels of the industry, carries with it the rights to fix the wage structure and the living standards of the workers in this industry. And we think our people have more right to be heard in the courts of last resort, as affecting this industry, before those prices are fixed. That is the reason we want two representatives of labor on this enlarged commission of seven.[36]

Mr. Lewis was prepared to force this demand even if direct representation for labor was felt to require as a logical corollary the direct representation of producers. He was supported by Mr. Charles O'Neill, chairman of the legislative committee of coal operators. Mr. O'Neill said:

This is my attitude about that, Senator: The old act provided certain protections and set up certain principles, granting to the labor employed in the coal mines certain rights under the law. Those provisions were struck down by the Supreme Court. And the result of it is that in this bill there is no room for proper provisions for the protection of labor. Consequently, the theory back of suggesting an increased membership for the Commission, and the placing of representatives of industry upon it, was to give labor some representation on the Commission—where the prices that would be fixed were indirectly going to control labor's wages—so that labor would have some voice, somewhere along the line, in the official fixing of the prices which finally meant their wage scale. And that is the only way we knew how to obtain a voice for labor on that . . .

I suppose it was a natural corollary that the producers should be represented. I do not know whether the producers would insist upon that or not. In my judgment I do think that labor ought to be recognized somehow in the bill.[37]

This representation of specific interests on the commission was attacked by Senator Borah, who feared that a combination of the two groups of representatives might fix prices so high that the consumer would be exploited. He urged that a majority, at least, of the commission ought to represent the public.[38]

---

36. Hearings before the Senate Committee on Interstate Commerce on S. 4668, 74th Cong., 2d sess. (1936), 213.

37. Ibid. 210 f.

38. 80 Cong. Rec. 10079.

c. *Price fixing by government agency* versus *unofficial agency*

There had been sharp attack on the provisions of the Act of 1935 under which the district boards had fixed minimum prices and set up marketing regulations subject to the approval or modification of the commission. The American Bar Association had objected to this on the ground that governmental authority was being farmed out to unofficial agencies.[39] The Supreme Court, in the Carter case, had referred to the arrangement with disapproval, though it had not been made the direct basis of the Court's decision.[40] The Act of 1937 transferred to the commission the power to adopt minimum price and market regulations upon the proposal of the district boards. Actually there was no practical difference between the two provisions, but there was a substantial difference in legal theory which won the ultimate approval of the American Bar Association representatives for the new Act. The commission was given the further authority to remove members of the district boards for cause.

d. *Status of the commission in the Department of the Interior*

Again there was no discussion or explanation of the unique status of the Coal Commission and the Consumers' Counsel in the Department of the Interior. At the request of the Consumers' Counsel he was allowed to report directly to Congress but he still remained in the department. The only allusion to the matter was made by Representative Dingell in the House. He did not clearly understand the relation as it existed. He said:

Mr. Chairman, I was not altogether willing to go along on the question of whether or not this commission should be under the Secretary of the Interior. I thought possibly it would have been wise to make of this an independent commission, responsible directly to Congress, but I agreed to submerge my ideas in the matter, provided

39. Hearings before a subcommittee of the Senate Committee on Interstate Commerce on S. 1, 75th Cong., 1st sess. (1937), 63.
40. *Carter* v. *Carter Coal Company,* 298 U.S. 238 (1936) at 311.

the consumers' interests were carefully considered and fully protected.[41]

Mr. A. H. Feller has made the suggestion that the commission
was kept in the department 'perhaps because it was felt that
the prior situation of the commission should not be changed
pending Congressional action on the President's message of
January 12, 1937, which recommended that all independent
agencies be placed "in" executive departments.' [42]

e. *Civil service exemptions*

The Coal Commission had tried to secure relaxation of the
civil service requirements imposed by the Act of 1935. Chairman Hosford declared that the commission was badly hampered in setting up its staff and in securing properly experienced people.[43] The new Act made these relaxations exceedingly generous. They were so substantial, in fact, that they resulted in a situation which came a little later on to verge upon
the scandalous and which gave rise to severe criticism and ultimate reorganization of the commission.

C. ABOLITION OF THE BITUMINOUS COAL COMMISSION

On May 9, 1939, President Roosevelt submitted to Congress
Reorganization Plan No. II, under the Reorganization Act
passed a month earlier. By a provision of this plan the National Bituminous Coal Commission was abolished and its
functions transferred to the Department of the Interior,[44]
where it has since been set up as the Bituminous Coal Division. The office of Consumers' Counsel was also abolished and
the duties given to the Solicitor of the Department of the
Interior. In making the change the President observed:

. . . Thus the task of conserving the bituminous-coal resources of
the country may be carried on directly by the head of the Department principally responsible for the conservation of fuel and other

41. 81 Cong. Rec. 2055.
42. A. H. Feller, 'Prospectus for the Further Study of Federal Administrative
Law,' *Yale Law Journal* (1938), vol. XLVII, p. 654, note 41.
43. *Supra*, note 39, op. cit. 247 f.
44. 84 Cong. Rec. 5285.

mineral supplies. The Congress placed this Commission in the Department of the Interior, but experience has shown that direct administration will be cheaper, better, and more effective than through the cumbersome medium of an unnecessary commission.[45]

Under the statute reorganization plans submitted by the President take effect unless within sixty calendar days the two houses of Congress pass a concurrent resolution of disapproval. An effort was made to secure the Congressional disallowance of Plan No. ii, which embodied many changes besides that affecting the Bituminous Coal Commission. The effort failed when the Senate rejected without debate a resolution of disapproval. In the Senate discussion of the resolution, Senator Holt inquired: 'Were any tears shed over the demise of the Bituminous Coal Commission?' And Senator Byrnes replied: 'I know of none.' [46] Thus the National Bituminous Coal Commission passed out of the picture, apparently unlamented.

IV. THE CIVIL AERONAUTICS AUTHORITY

A. Background of Federal Regulation of Civil Aeronautics

THE development of aviation has been speedy and dramatic, and has presented correspondingly pressing and difficult problems. Orville Wright's historic flight of 120 feet was made on December 17, 1903; five years later Wright sold to the United States Army its first airplane. In 1911 the first mail was carried by air between two Long Island towns. By the outbreak of the World War, European nations were outstripping this country in the technical development of aviation and on March 3, 1915, President Wilson approved an Act[1] creating the National Advisory Committee for Aeronautics. This committee of unpaid members was given the duty of supervising, directing, and conducting fundamental scientific research and experiment in aeronautics. It continues to carry on highly important scientific work in the field assigned to it. On May 15, 1918, the first regular air mail service in this country was

45. H. Doc. 288, 76 Cong., 1st sess. (1939), 3.
46. 84 Cong. Rec. 5502.
1. Act of Mar. 3, 1915, 38 Stat. at L. 928.

established between Washington and New York. The mail was carried by Army fliers who continued to render this service until 1926.

1. THE MOVEMENT FOR THE REGULATION OF CIVIL AERONAUTICS [2]

It soon became clear that government regulation at certain points was essential to the safe and proper development of aviation. The problem of safety was the first to command attention. In 1922 and 1923 Senator Wadsworth of New York introduced two bills setting up a bureau of civil aeronautics in the Department of Commerce to establish federal safety regulations in the field of civil aviation. These passed the Senate but not the House. In the absence of federal action, the states kept hammering away at the edges of the problem, and by 1925 nineteen states had laws regulating varying phases of it. In 1921, however, the Commissioners on Uniform State Laws had put on record their judgment that only federal legislation could adequately cope with the problem.[3]

In 1924 Colonel William Mitchell startled the country by his sensational charges against the Army and Navy air forces, and the private interests which he alleged they were serving. To investigate the Mitchell charges the House of Representatives set up a select committee under the chairmanship of Mr. Lampert to inquire into the operations of the United States air service. This committee conducted hearings from October 1924 to March 1925 and brought in an elaborate report[4] in which it recommended a unified military air service and the regulation of civil aeronautics by the Department of Commerce.

President Coolidge appointed in the fall of 1925 a committee of distinguished citizens under the chairmanship of Dwight Morrow to conduct a similar and independent investigation. This committee sat for some four weeks. Its report[5] exonerated the Army and Navy of any maladministration, urged the keep-

2. Cf. Charles S. Rhyne, *The Civil Aeronautics Act* (1939).
3. *Handbook of the National Conference of Commissioners on Uniform State Laws* (1921), 289.
4. H. Rept. 1653, Inquiry into Operations of the United States Air Services, 68th Cong., 2d sess. (1925).
5. Report of President's Aircraft Board, Nov. 30, 1925.

ing separate of the Army and Navy air forces, but agreed with the Lampert committee's recommendation that air commerce be regulated by the Department of Commerce. The reports of these two committees gave impetus to the movement for legislation which had been gathering strength in Congress and which resulted in the passage of the Air Commerce Act of May 20, 1926.[6]

The Act of 1926 did not provide for any economic regulation. Its sponsors did not desire federal action which might in any way impede the growth of a new industry. The Act did, however, give the Secretary of Commerce broad legislative and administrative powers to provide for air safety. Under these provisions all aircraft moving in interstate commerce had to register with the department and be rated, and without satisfactory rating such aircraft could not be used. Pilots were similarly examined and rated, and could fly in interstate commerce only under departmental licenses. On the request of any airport, the department was to rate its air navigation facilities. Finally, the department was to draft and enforce air traffic rules. These important powers were delegated by Secretary Hoover to a new branch for aeronautics set up in the department under an assistant secretary. In 1934 certain amendments [7] enlarged the government's power to investigate accidents in civil aviation. The Act of 1926 thus amended remained the only federal regulation of civil aviation until 1938.

2. THE AIR MAIL PROBLEM AND ITS INFLUENCE ON THE MOVEMENT FOR REGULATION

The first federal law dealing with air mail was the Air Mail Act of February 2, 1925,[8] which gave to the Postmaster General the authority to let contracts under specified conditions to private companies for the carrying of mail. The payment offered for the carriage of air mail proved an inadequate inducement to private capital and developments were very slow. The Act of 1925 was amended slightly in 1926 and in 1928. On April 29, 1930, Congress passed the Watres Act,[9] which

6. 44 Stat. at L. 568.
7. Act of June 19, 1934, 48 Stat. at L. 1113.
8. 43 Stat. at L. 805.   9. 46 Stat. at L. 259.

gave to the Postmaster General broad powers of economic regulation over air mail carriers. Under the policy of the Act payment for the carriage of air mail was to serve as a subsidy to
encourage and support civil aviation, and within the limits of
the appropriations made available the Postmaster General had
practically unlimited control over the air routes which might
be flown and the compensation to be paid. Congress, in short,
gave to the Postmaster General a blank check with which to do
business with the aviation companies, and the results of this
were more depressing than surprising. There were obvious
favoritism and mismanagement in the administration of the
Act, and in February 1933 the Black committee was set up in
the Senate to investigate both the methods whereby air mail
and ocean mail contracts had been acquired and the financial
practices of the beneficiaries of federal subsidies. The Black
committee did not immediately conduct public hearings but
proceeded by other methods to uncover the facts. Its final report [10] a year later presented unmistakable evidence of collusive bidding for air mail contracts and other objectionable
practices.

On February 9, 1934, Postmaster General Farley issued an
order,[11] effective in ten days, canceling all domestic air mail
contracts. Farley's action was based on information secured by
the Black committee as well as on that which he had himself
acquired. He explained that the contracts had been collusive
and contrary to law and that some of them had been extended
illegally by his predecessor. The efforts of the carriers to enjoin
the cancellation by court action failed. The President then
directed the Army to take over the carrying of the mail, and
the unfortunate results of this brought matters to a crisis. The
Army operation of the mail service resulted in sixty-six accidents and the killing of twelve pilots in less than three months.
It was obvious that the Army was not equipped to render this
important service.

The acute situation thus created resulted in swamping Congress with bills. Over forty were introduced in one month
during the second session of the 73d Congress (1934). President Roosevelt wrote to Senators Black and McKellar out-

10. S. Doc. 51, 74th Cong., 1st sess. (1935).
11. *The New York Times*, Feb. 10, 1934, p. 1, col. 2.

lining his views on appropriate legislation, and after a good deal of haggling and difficulty the Air Mail Act of June 12, 1934,[12] was passed. This was frankly designed to meet the temporary emergency which had arisen. It turned back the task of carrying the mail to private carriers but it subjected them to the authority of three different branches of the federal government. The Post Office was to award the air mail contracts and establish routes and schedules; the Interstate Commerce Commission was to fix the rates of compensation by quasi-judicial process; the Bureau of Air Commerce was to license pilots and planes. The Act also created a Federal Aviation Commission of five members appointed by the President 'to report to Congress not later than February 1, 1935, its recommendations of a broad policy covering all phases of aviation and the relation of the United States thereto.' This commission was promptly set up under the chairmanship of Clark Howell. While the Act of 1934 authorized this broad investigation it did not itself provide for the regulation of any non-air mail carriers.

B. THE DRIVE FOR FEDERAL REGULATION—THE ACT OF 1938

On March 26, 1934, Senator McCarran, a member of the Black committee, introduced a bill [13] providing for the economic regulation of civil commercial aviation to be enforced by an independent commission. This was offered as a substitute for the air mail bill but was not passed. On January 30, 1935, the Federal Aviation Commission brought in its report.[14] It had done its work thoroughly and well. It presented 102 recommendations relating to all aspects of the regulation of aviation. On the administrative side it recommended that: 'There should be created an air commerce commission, its members appointed by the President by and with the consent of the Senate for long terms . . . subject to merger by executive order at any time with any other body of a similar nature having similar functions.' The Federal Aviation Commission examined a proposal to give the Interstate Commerce Commission the power to regulate aviation and emphatically rejected it.

12. 48 Stat. at L. 933.
13. S. 3187, 73d Cong., 2d sess. (1934).
14. S. Doc. 15, 74th Cong., 1st sess. (1935).

On January 31 President Roosevelt sent the commission's report to Congress, accompanied by a message[15] in which he endorsed virtually all of the commission's recommendations save one. He disagreed with the proposal to set up an independent regulatory commission and urged that the task of regulation should be given to the Interstate Commerce Commission. Viewing the commission's proposal as a temporary one he said: 'Therefore in the interim before a permanent consolidated agency is created or designated over transportation as a whole, a division of the Interstate Commerce Commission can well serve the needs of air transportation.' On June 7, 1935, the President renewed his suggestion to Congress that the Interstate Commerce Commission be empowered to take over the regulation of aviation.[16]

On June 10, 1935, Senator McCarran introduced a bill[17] to carry out the President's recommendations. He was willing to support the President's proposal although 'never abandoning my thought or idea that it should be an independent commission.'[18] The McCarran bill followed the lines of the Eastman bills[19] then before Congress. Mr. Eastman, as Co-ordinator of Transportation, was promoting a program looking toward the centralized control of all transportation facilities. His water carrier bill and motor carrier bill were aimed to effect such centralization under the jurisdiction of the Interstate Commerce Commission. The McCarran bill placed air carrier regulation in the same position. Hearings were held on the McCarran bill by a subcommittee of the Senate Committee on Interstate Commerce, of which Senator Donahey was chairman. Many witnesses appeared including some of the most distinguished figures in the field of aviation. Mr. Eastman told the committee that the Interstate Commerce Commission should be given the authority proposed and said that the commission could competently handle the job.[20] The bill was

15. Ibid. iii f.
16. H. Doc. 221, 74th Cong., 1st sess. (1935).
17. S. 3027, 74th Cong., 1st sess. (1935).
18. Hearings before a subcommittee of the Senate Committee on Interstate Commerce on S. 3659, 75th Cong., 3d sess. (1938), 6.
19. *Supra*, 137 f.
20. Hearings before a subcommittee of the Senate Committee on Interstate Commerce on S. 3027, 74th Cong., 1st sess. (1935), 107.

vigorously opposed by the Post Office Department and the Department of Commerce. At the conclusion of the hearings the bill was rewritten and reintroduced in the Senate,[21] but while it was debated it did not come to a vote before the end of the 74th Congress.

When the 75th Congress opened in January 1937, Senator McCarran promptly introduced his air carrier bill in two sections, and companion bills were introduced in the House.[22] Senate and House committees held lengthy hearings and brought in favorable reports. But again no legislative action ensued. While there were other superficial reasons to explain this, the real reason lay in the conflicting pressures brought to bear by certain government departments. The situation had settled into a long stalemate between the Post Office and the Interstate Commerce Commission. Referring to this in a House debate the following year, Mr. Mapes of Michigan said:

. . . After these two bills got on the calendars of the House and the Senate a monkey wrench was thrown into the machinery somewhere, and no action was ever taken on either of them. The truth is that some of the departments opposed those bills because they proposed to transfer some of the jurisdiction now being exercised by them over air commerce to the Interstate Commerce Commission.[23]

At this point effective leadership seemed imperative; and at the suggestion of the Secretary of Commerce the President took a hand and created an interdepartmental committee on aviation. This committee was to review all pending proposals for air carrier regulation, attempt to iron out the difficulties involved, and bring in workable recommendations. It was composed of assistant secretaries or other high officials from the six executive departments which had an interest in aviation: State, War, Navy, Commerce, Post Office, and the Treasury. Why the Interstate Commerce Commission was left out in the cold did not appear upon the surface, but a year later Representative Withrow in the House debate on the civil aeronautics bill made this comment:

. . . It seems rather peculiar that the Interstate Commerce Commission was not represented on that interdepartmental committee,

21. S. 3420, 74th Cong., 1st sess. (1935).
22. S. 2 and S. 1760; H.R. 5234 and H.R. 4652; 75th Cong., 1st sess. (1937).
23. 83 Cong. Rec. 6403.

but representatives of the I.C.C. were permitted only to testify before that committee and their testimony is not available either to the House Committee on Interstate and Foreign Commerce or to the House itself. To me, this interdepartmental committee may be likened to a sewing circle. If you do not attend the sewing circle you get your feathers plucked. Believe me, in this particular instance they certainly plucked the I.C.C.[24]

1. THE INTERDEPARTMENTAL COMMITTEE AND ITS BILL

The Interdepartmental Committee on Civil Aviation was appointed in August 1937 and held hearings from October until early December. It called numerous witnesses and accumulated much testimony. The record of its proceedings was never published, although it was preserved in typewritten form, and there was later criticism in Congress that this body of material had not been made more readily available to Congressional committees. The committee proceeded to draft a bill which was described as a composite of all the bills of the last four or five years. This bill provided for the unified regulation of aviation both with respect to economic matters and safety. It proposed a civil aeronautics board of three members appointed by the President with the consent of the Senate. The chairman, appointed by the President, was to be the executive officer of the board. The President's power to remove members of the board was unrestricted. Finally, it was provided that 'the exercise or performance of any other power or duty of the Board which is not subject to review by courts of law shall be subject to the general direction of the President . . .' This bill was sent to the President who placed it in the hands of Senator McCarran and Representative Lea on January 4, 1938.

2. ACTION IN THE HOUSE—THE LEA BILL

Mr. Lea, chairman of the House Committee on Interstate and Foreign Commerce, had a keen interest in aviation legislation and he promptly invited the assistance of the interdepartmental committee. The committee assigned for this purpose Mr. Clinton M. Hester, who had been an alternate to

24. Ibid. 6505.

the representative from the Treasury on the interdepartmental committee and had also been chairman of its subcommittee for drafting; it also designated Mr. S. G. Tipton and Mr. F. D. Fagg, who was Director of the Bureau of Air Commerce. For about two months these gentlemen worked with Mr. Lea on the draft of an aviation bill. Four different drafts were made before one was secured which Mr. Lea was prepared to introduce and sponsor. One of these, it may be noted, was a draft embodying the general plan for commission organization suggested by the Brownlow committee,[25] which had prepared the proposals on which the President's reorganization program was based.

As a result of these efforts Mr. Lea, on March 4, 1938, introduced a bill [26] which was referred to the Committee on Interstate and Foreign Commerce. The Lea bill provided for unified economic and safety regulation of the aviation industry. It set up a civil aeronautics authority similar to that proposed by the interdepartmental committee, but with five members instead of three. It retained the provision giving the President direction over the powers and duties of the authority not subject to review by courts of law. It set up an air safety board 'within the authority' of five members to be appointed by the authority to investigate and report upon accidents. On March 8 President Roosevelt in a press conference referred to this bill with approval and expressed the hope that it would be passed.

Hearings were held on the Lea bill from March 10 to April 1, and it was then referred to a subcommittee of the Committee on Interstate and Foreign Commerce, which proceeded to give it careful study. Mr. Lea was chairman of this subcommittee. There had been objection in the full committee to the section in the bill providing for Presidential supervision of the functions of the authority not subject to review by the courts. Out of the further study of this provision came the proposal for the establishment within the authority of a separate administrator, a proposal which is attributed to Mr. Bulwinkle,[27] although Mr. Hester and Mr. Wadsworth of New York were also working along the same lines.

25. President's Committee on Administrative Management, Report with Special Studies, 39-42, 203-43.

26. H.R. 9738, 75th Cong., 3d sess. (1938). 27. 83 Cong. Rec. 8868.

On April 28 the amended bill was reported out by the Committee on Interstate and Foreign Commerce. A minority report was presented urging that the Interstate Commerce Commission be given regulatory authority over aviation. This bill contained three major administrative provisions: It created a civil aeronautics authority of three members, appointed by the President and Senate for six-year staggered terms, and removable by the President only for stated causes. It established within the authority an administrator and a safety board, to be appointed by the President and the Senate. These officers had no fixed terms and were left removable by the President at his discretion. On May 6 the bill was made a special order on the House calendar and on May 18 it was debated and passed.

3. SENATE ACTION—THE McCARRAN BILL

In January 1938 the President sent for Senator McCarran, gave him the draft of the interdepartmental committee bill, and told him that the original McCarran proposal in 1934 to establish an independent agency for the regulation of aviation was sound. On March 11 Senator McCarran introduced a bill [28] which provided for an independent commission to exercise full power over the economic and safety aspects of aviation. He described it as 'a new agency . . . of the type Congress usually establishes to carry out under prescribed standards the duties which Congress itself is unable to perform.' [29] It was to be responsible to Congress and not to the President.

It might here be stated that from January to June, when the civil aeronautics bill was passed, there took place in the House and Senate a friendly—if sometimes acrimoniously friendly—battle to get an aviation bill passed under Senator McCarran's name which nevertheless contained provisions to which Senator McCarran was opposed. The senator had been for so many years the exponent of an independent commission for aviation, a type of control in which the others substantially agreed, that there was a disinclination on the part of everyone to steal his thunder and pass the bill under another aegis because they differed with him on the matter of centering respon-

28. S. 3659, 75th Cong., 3d sess. (1938).
29. *Supra,* note 18, op. cit. 9.

sibility for the commission in the President rather than in Congress. This was, however, a vital difference, since aviation is so closely allied to national defense; and it was a difference to which Senator McCarran was bitterly opposed.

On March 30, therefore, Senator Truman and Senator Copeland each introduced almost identical bills, both of which differed from the McCarran bill particularly with respect to the scope of Presidential authority. Senator Truman's bill [30] was referred to the subcommittee of the Committee on Interstate Commerce, of which he was chairman; Senator Copeland's bill [31] was referred to the Committee on Commerce, of which Senator Copeland was chairman. Senator Copeland's interest in aviation dated back to the inquiry conducted by his committee into the crash in which Senator Bronson Cutting was killed in the spring of 1935.

The Copeland bill provided for an independent aviation authority of five members appointed by the President and the Senate; the personnel was to be bipartisan and the members were to hold office for six-year staggered terms. The President was to name the chairman who was to be the executive officer of the authority. There was no restriction upon the President's power to remove members of the authority. The President was given definite supervision over overseas and foreign air carriers and other closely allied matters. Brief hearings on the Copeland bill were held on April 5 by the Senate Committee on Commerce of which Senator Copeland was chairman. On April 6 and 7, a subcommittee of the Senate Committee on Interstate Commerce, of which subcommittee Senator Truman was chairman, conducted hearings on Senator McCarran's bill and Senator Truman's substitute bill. In the course of these hearings Mr. Hester testified [32] that the Administration favored the Truman substitute rather than the original McCarran bill. Truman tried to secure substantial changes in the McCarran bill to make it conform to the provisions of the Truman bill and still make it acceptable to Senator McCarran, but the fundamental difference could not readily be bridged. For the time being things appeared to be badly tied up.

30. Offered as a substitute in the nature of an amendment to S. 3659.
31. S. 3760, 75th Cong., 3d sess. (1938).
32. *Supra,* note 18, op. cit. 15.

On April 14 Senator McCarran introduced a new bill[33] which was referred to Senator Copeland's committee, and five days later introduced the same bill[34] so that it could be referred to the Truman subcommittee. Senator McCarran, in the course of the Senate debate in May, explained his course of procedure as follows:

Following the introduction of these measures, I undertook the preparation of a further draft designed to follow the outlines of the measures of the Senator from Missouri (Mr. Truman) and the Senator from New York (Mr. Copeland), and, insofar as possible, the substance of the latter without undue sacrifice of the principles and provisions of Senate bill 3659 [the original McCarran bill]. This draft was introduced by me on April 14, 1938 as Senate bill 3845, which was referred to the Committee on Commerce, and on April 19, 1938 was introduced as Senate bill 3864 and referred to the Committee on Interstate Commerce. This draft retained in modified form the provisions of the measures of the Senator from Missouri and the Senator from New York for Presidential approval or disapproval of certain action of the authority, specifically restricting that situation to overseas and foreign air transportation, and providing the manner in which such matters should be submitted to the President.[35]

On April 20 the Senate Committee on Commerce reported out the new McCarran bill with some amendments, and it was debated from May 7 to May 16; there was especially bitter controversy concerning the removal power of the President over the aeronautics authority. The McCarran bill restricted this removal power to the causes stated in the statute. Senator Truman introduced an amendment to eliminate these restrictions on the President's removal power, urging this change on constitutional grounds.[36] Senator McCarran violently opposed the Truman amendment, and threatened to vote against the bill and also to have his name removed from it if the amendment were incorporated.[37] In spite of his opposition the amendment passed the Senate and the amended bill passed on May 16.

33. S. 3845, 75th Cong., 3d sess. (1938).
34. S. 3864, 75th Cong., 3d sess. (1938).
35. 83 Cong. Rec. 6636.
36. Ibid. 6430 and 6724 f.
37. Ibid. 6854.

4. FINAL ACTION

The amended Lea bill, as we have seen, passed the House on May 18. As soon as this action was taken, Mr. Lea asked unanimous consent to take from the Speaker's table the Mc-Carran bill which had passed the Senate two days before, to strike out all after the enacting clause, and to substitute for it the provisions of the Lea bill. This was agreed to. He then asked unanimous consent to vacate the proceedings by which the Lea bill had just been passed and to lay that bill on the table, and this was also agreed to. In consequence the House passed its own bill with the Senate number attached to it. On May 23 the Senate debated the House amendments and on May 26 asked for a conference. The conference committee adopted most of the provisions of the House bill, but acceded to the Senate desire for a five- rather than a three-man authority. The conference report passed the House on June 11 and the Senate on June 13. The bill, still with McCarran's name attached to it, was signed by the President on June 23.

C. PROVISIONS OF THE ACT OF 1938

The Civil Aeronautics Authority Act of 1938 [38] may be summarized as follows: A Civil Aeronautics Authority was created composed of five members appointed by the President and the Senate for six-year staggered terms. They are removable by the President only for cause. They must be citizens, must have no pecuniary interest in the industry, and are to be appointed with due regard to fitness. Not more than three members may come from one political party. The President designates the chairman annually as well as a vice-chairman.

The powers of the authority fall into three categories. The first are powers of economic regulation. The authority issues certificates of necessity and convenience to air carriers and may suspend or revoke them. Rates charged must be reasonable and publicly posted and the authority may change them if they are found to be unreasonable. The authority fixes compensation for air mail service. It has supervision over the business

38. Act of June 23, 1938, 52 Stat. at L. 973.

practices of air carriers, prevents the use of unfair methods of competition, and approves consolidations, mergers, and pools. Interlocking corporate relations are forbidden except as the authority may approve. Secondly, the authority administers safety regulations. Its powers are similar to those of the Bureau of Air Commerce under the earlier statutes. It licenses pilots and aircraft; it establishes air traffic rules, and regulations as to maximum hours; and it rates air facilities and training schools. It employs inspectors for the enforcement of these provisions. Finally, it has certain general authority. It co-operates with state aeronautic agencies; it reports on and publishes the results of its own work together with useful information collected by the Administrator or the Air Safety Board; it recommends to Congress annually or more often legislative changes. It was specifically instructed to report at the end of the first year what further federal regulation was desirable in the field of foreign and overseas air service.

An Administrator is set up 'in the Authority.' He is appointed by the President and the Senate. He must be a citizen having no pecuniary interest in the industry. He is removable by the President at pleasure and is thus wholly independent of the authority, although he may be directed by the authority to perform certain functions on its behalf. This office was set up to take care of the 'executive functions' involved in aviation regulation. These were summarized by the Administrator in 1938 as follows:

> These functions involve the construction, operation and maintenance of airway and lights and other signals along the highway and the air ports, the enforcement of the air traffic rules, the conducting of development and planning work, the promotion of air commerce and similar activities.[39]

There is created and established within the authority an Air Safety Board. This consists of three members appointed by the President and the Senate for six-year staggered terms. One member must be an active airline pilot. The board elects its own chairman annually. The President may remove the board at pleasure. It chooses its own personnel and is completely independent of the authority. Its duties are to investi-

39. C. M. Hester broadcast July 18, 1938, Air Commerce Bulletin, vol. x, 34.

gate and report on air accidents and their causes, and to make recommendations to the authority which will aid in preventing such accidents.

D. Topics and Issues in Hearings and Debates

The legislative history of the Civil Aeronautics Act is unique in that most of the major controversies arose on matters of administrative organization. Everyone agreed that economic and safety regulation was imperative and that it should follow the traditional lines of other public utility regulation. There was, however, sharp disagreement as to what governmental body should administer these regulatory powers and how that body should be organized.

There were several reasons why these administrative problems received the attention which they did. In the first place, many of the difficulties which the new legislation aimed to correct had resulted from the administrative confusion which characterized the early handling of the problem. Authority over aviation had been scattered among numerous governmental agencies with no serious effort at co-ordination. In the second place, the Roosevelt Administration was interested in problems of administration. This was evidenced by the early proposals of the Co-ordinator of Transportation looking toward the unification of transportation control,[40] and by the elaborate program for administrative reorganization embodied not only in the report of the Brownlow committee [41] but in the parallel recommendations of Senator Byrd's committee.[42] In the third place, whether fortuitously or not, the air legislation was drafted with the aid of experts whose attention was focused on administrative problems and who were versed in the principles of administration. Finally, the Supreme Court's decision in the Humphrey case [43] in 1935 had thrown into confusion the previous ideas with respect to the status of regulatory agencies. No one was quite sure just what the implications

40. *Supra,* 137 f.
41. *Supra,* note 25.
42. S. Rept. 1275, 75th Cong., 1st sess. (1937).
43. *Humphrey's Executor* v. *United States,* 295 U.S. 602 (1935). For discussion see *infra,* 455 ff.

of the Humphrey decision were, with the result that more attention was given to questions of administrative organization than might otherwise have been the case.

1. A NEW COMMISSION *versus* THE INTERSTATE COMMERCE COMMISSION

Should aviation be regulated by the Interstate Commerce Commission or by a new independent agency created for the purpose? We may trace the development of Congressional and Presidential thinking on this question. In 1934 and 1935 Senator McCarran's first bill [44] and the proposal of the Federal Aviation Commission [45] both called for a new independent commission. It should be noted, however, that the regulatory commission proposed at this time was to deal only with commercial aviation and leave to the Department of Commerce the important field of private flying. In 1935 and 1936 there was a shift to the point of view that the Interstate Commerce Commission should be utilized to regulate aviation. Co-ordinator Eastman was carrying on his drive for a unified administration of the federal regulation of all transportation, a program embodied partially in his water carrier and motor carrier bills.[46] The President was disposed to support this program and Senator McCarran, anxious to secure the best results possible, fell in line behind the proposal to utilize the Interstate Commerce Commission. Here again the regulation proposed was commercial and did not include the entire field of flying. In 1937 and 1938 there was a shift back to the position that a new independent agency should be created. President Roosevelt himself was probably responsible for this change and we may speculate as to the reasons which influenced him. In the first place, he had not been getting on very happily with some of the major independent commissions. In the hearings before the House Committee on Interstate and Foreign Commerce on the Lea bill, Representative Wadsworth said: 'I think I am not far wrong in saying that there has been friction between the executive branch of the government and some of these independent commissions, and the friction revolves around the exercise

44. *Supra,* 393.   46. *Supra,* 137 f., 394.
45. Ibid.

of executive functions by a quasi-judicial commission.' [47] Mr. Hester replied: 'That is right.' In the second place, the program sponsored by Co-ordinator Eastman for the centralized federal regulation of all transportation by the Interstate Commerce Commission had broken down. The office of Co-ordinator had not been continued.[48] Mr. Eastman's bill calling for water carrier regulation by the Interstate Commerce Commission had not passed, but instead the Merchant Marine Act of 1936 [49] had set up a wholly independent Maritime Commission. Furthermore, the House in 1938 had gone to the point of repealing the section in the Merchant Marine Act which authorized the President, after two years, to transfer by executive order the regulatory powers of the Maritime Commission to the Interstate Commerce Commission.[50] In the third place, the President was unquestionably influenced by the administrative proposals made by the Brownlow committee,[51] some of which were later embodied in the reorganization bill. Finally, the President, perhaps owing to these other factors, had been leaning toward a rather drastic reorganization of the Interstate Commerce Commission. His ideas on this point had been embodied in his message of April 11, 1938, dealing with the question of relief and railroads. He said:

From the point of view of business efficiency, such as a private corporation would ask, it would seem to be the part of common sense to place all executive functions relating to all transportation in one Federal department—such as the Department of Commerce, the Department of the Interior, or some other old or new department. At the same time all quasi-judicial and quasi-legislative matters relating to all transportation could probably be placed under an independent commission—a reorganized Interstate Commerce Commission.[52]

Other factors also explained the zeal for a new commission. The interdepartmental committee had recommended a new agency; [53] for the jealousy with respect to aviation control which had grown up within the government prior to the ap-

47. Hearings before the House Committee on Interstate and Foreign Commerce on H.R. 9738, 75th Cong., 3d sess. (1938), 149.

48. *Supra*, 141.
49. *Supra*, 142, 267 ff.
50. *Supra*, 271 f.

51. *Supra*, note 25.
52. 83 Cong. Rec. 5235.
53. *Supra*, 396.

pointment of the interdepartmental committee, and which had made that committee necessary, was so strong as to make it very unlikely that the Interstate Commerce Commission as then organized would be given the new job of regulation. Finally, the program for the regulation of aviation had come to demand the location of all authority over all aspects of aviation, including non-commercial flying, in one body, a program which would impose upon the regulating agency much broader powers than those which had earlier been thought of as readily transferable to the Interstate Commerce Commission.

The arguments in favor of using the Interstate Commerce Commission for the regulation of aviation were neither new nor startling. They ran as follows: In the first place, that commission was fully equipped to be the central and unified authority in which all federal regulation of transportation should be placed. This had been the position taken by President Roosevelt in his message of January 31, 1935, already mentioned. He had said:

> . . . At a later date I shall ask the Congress for general legislation centralizing the supervision of air and water and highway transportation with adjustments of our present methods of organization in order to meet new and additional responsibilities.
>
> . . . I believe that we should avoid the multiplication of separate regulatory agencies in the field of transportation. Therefore in the interim before a permanent consolidated agency is created or designated over transportation as a whole, a division of the Interstate Commerce Commission can well serve the needs of air transportation. In the granting of powers and duties by the Congress orderly government calls for the administration of executive functions by those administrative departments or agencies which have functioned satisfactorily in the past and, on the other hand, calls for the vesting of judicial functions in agencies already accustomed to such powers. It is this principle that should be followed in all of the various aspects of transportation legislation.[54]

This position had been taken by Commissioner Eastman in various hearings before Congressional committees,[55] was supported by Professor Emory R. Johnson in his volume on

54. *Supra*, note 14, op. cit. iii f.
55. H. Rept. 2254, Part II, Minority Report to accompany H.R. 9738, 75th Cong., 3d sess. (1938), 3.

government regulation of transportation,[56] and was strongly urged by the minority of the Committee on Interstate and Foreign Commerce in protesting against the Lea bill in May 1938.[57] In the second place, the Interstate Commerce Commission was a known quantity, long established, experienced and stabilized. Congress could be sure exactly what kind of administration it would get from the commission. A witness before the Senate Committee on Interstate Commerce in April 1938 expressed this view as follows:

. . . We believe there is a great advantage in having air transportation regulated by an experienced body, such as the Interstate Commerce Commission, where the rules and practices are known and the effects can be reasonably predicted.

Any new agency must necessarily be an unknown quantity until it has gone through a character-building period during which time practically all of its rules, procedure, practices, and so forth, must be worked out by trial and error, and after many years they will probably be on the same footing with an agency such as the Interstate Commerce Commission insofar as actual results are concerned. In other words, a new agency will have to go through a long period before it becomes stabilized in the same way and to the same extent as the Interstate Commerce Commission practices are stabilized today.[58]

Along the same line Representative Mapes of Michigan, in the hearings on the Lea bill, observed:

We have not been very successful during the last 3 or 4 years in setting up efficient commissions. We had an illustration yesterday of some trouble in the T. V. A., and we have had trouble with the Coal Commission. Why not let the established institutions handle this work? Why not enlarge their powers a little and let them do these things and avoid the trouble these new commissions have caused? [59]

Finally, emphasis was placed upon the additional expense which would inevitably result from the setting up of a new organization.

The arguments for creating a new aeronautics authority were substantial. In the first place, everyone agreed that the

56. *Government Regulation of Transportation* (1938), 659.
57. *Supra*, note 55, op. cit.
58. *Supra*, note 18, op. cit. 49.   59. *Supra*, note 47, op. cit. 143.

Interstate Commerce Commission was already heavily burdened. Its duties had recently been increased by the Motor Carrier Act.[60] It could not hope to act with speed and efficiency. The Bureau of Air Commerce in the Department of Commerce had some 2,500 employees, and the job of assimilating this vast personnel and these complicated responsibilities into its overcrowded organization and routine would be beyond the capacity of the commission, efficient as it was. The Federal Aviation Commission had stated this argument clearly. It had said:

> . . . The need for such a commission to deal with certain problems of aviation seems to us clear. The work that it would have to do is so specialized and so extensive that we make strong recommendation that it should be either a separate and wholly independent body or a quasi-independent division of an over-all commission or group of commissions dealing with all phases of transportation.
>
> . . . There would seem to us to be great danger that through the placing of an additional burden upon an already heavily loaded agency delay might be caused where promptness and certainty of action are of the utmost importance, and that in the formative stage of a new regulatory doctrine there might be an inevitable feeling for analogies with other forms of transportation where such analogies may be superficially attractive but valid only in a very limited degree and actually misleading beyond that point.[61]

In the second place, the old argument was trotted out that the Interstate Commerce Commission would be 'railroad minded' and not 'air minded.' It was in part this suspicion with regard to the commission's complete impartiality which had led to the creation of the Maritime Commission rather than the passage of Mr. Eastman's water carrier bill.

In the third place, and this was the most compelling argument of all, it was urged that the commission could not take over the centralized unified control of aviation in all its aspects as was being proposed, and yet the job ought not to be divided. It was one thing to give to the commission the quasi-judicial job of regulating the economic phases of the air carrier industry; it was quite different to dump on the commission in addition the responsibility for safety regulation and for the growing problems of non-commercial flying. Many of the functions

60. *Supra,* 142.   61. *Supra,* note 14, op. cit. 53, 244.

proposed for the new aeronautics authority were from the standpoint of the orthodox regulatory commission unique and difficult. This argument was effectively put by Mr. E. S. Gorell, president of the Air Transport Association of America, in his testimony before the Senate committee in April 1938.

In the first place—and this point is most important of all—the only possible way that there can be a centralization of jurisdiction over the different phases of aeronautics is through the creation of a new body. It is agreed by the Departments of State, Treasury, War, Navy, Post Office, and Commerce that there is no other way to accomplish this end. It is quite safe to say, I believe, that the Interstate Commerce Commission itself would regard as undesirable any effort to saddle upon it the regulation of the ordinary private flyer, or the installation and operation of navigation aids, or the direction of technical aeronautical development work, or the other matters relating to safety, and so forth, which under the pending bill, would be vested in a new authority. Thus, to centralize jurisdiction, there must be a new body.[62]

Even the Interstate Commerce Commission itself tended to shy away from these new responsibilities. Three members of the commission admitted that the new job of unified regulation of aviation could not be taken on without drastic reorganization of the commission.[63]

Finally, it was strongly urged that it would be unconstitutional to impose upon an independent quasi-judicial commission the extensive executive duties falling within the field of aviation control. Mr. Hester, testifying before the House committee on the Lea bill, bluntly declared that these executive duties could not validly be placed beyond reach of Presidential control. He said:

This change in the administrative agency was considered advisable also because a large proportion of the functions to be exercised under this legislation will be executive in character. Other important functions, such as the issuance of certificates and permits for overseas and foreign air transportation, will affect international relations and national defense. Therefore, it was believed essential that these functions be exercised under the direction of the President, in whom the Constitution vests such functions, rather than by

62. *Supra,* note 18, op. cit. 34.   63. 83 Cong. Rec. 6407 f.

an agency completely independent of the President as is the Interstate Commerce Commission.

In order to give the President his constitutional authority over the executive functions and those affecting international relations and national defense, and at the same time to preserve the independence of the Authority in proper cases, the Authority would exercise its executive functions through its chairman subject to the general direction of the President, and, except with respect to overseas and foreign air transportation, would exercise its quasi-legislative and so-called quasi-judicial functions independently of the executive branch of the Government.[64]

Mr. Hester pushed his argument even further in the following colloquy:

MR. MAPES. Do you think that the Supreme Court would take away the functions which you consider executive, that the Interstate Commerce Commission is exercising?

MR. HESTER. Well, the Supreme Court does not do that, of course. Congress would have to do it.

MR. MAPES. The Supreme Court could say that it is outside the constitutional power.

MR. HESTER. That is right. I think that the Supreme Court would say insofar as the Interstate Commerce Commission exercising those functions is concerned, that it is under the control of the Chief Executive and that it is his duty to take care that those particular laws be faithfully executed.[65]

2. THE PROBLEM OF ESTABLISHING PRESIDENTIAL RESPONSIBILITY FOR EXECUTIVE TASKS IN THE REGULATION OF AVIATION

If the task of regulating aviation necessarily includes important executive functions as well as quasi-judicial functions, is there any way to maintain proper Presidential supervision over the former and equally desirable independence for the latter? This came to be one of the central issues connected with the aviation bills. This was not a question of trying to segregate executive from quasi-judicial functions by assigning them to wholly separate agencies. No one proposed that sort of segregation. There had been too much piecemeal control and divided responsibility, and those closely familiar with aviation

64. *Supra,* note 47, op. cit. 38.   65. Ibid. 51.

problems were quick to declare that a sharp separation of executive from regulatory duties was not only undesirable but impossible. Mr. Fagg, Director of the Bureau of Civil Aeronautics, in response to questions by Representative Wadsworth of New York, declared that there was an inextricable interweaving of the two kinds of functions and concluded with the remark:

. . . Here, after a long and painstaking study of a very highly technical subject matter—quite unlike rail, water, or bus transportation—we propose for your consideration the sacrifice of logic to experience, in the interest of what we believe to be a common good.[66]

It was generally agreed that a large amount of executive work would inevitably have to be given to the proposed aeronautics authority. Mr. Hester suggested that fully 90 per cent of the work of the authority would be executive in character [67] and it was, of course, a matter of record that the Bureau of Civil Aeronautics had carried a substantial burden of executive work for many years.

It was recognized that a constitutional problem existed here. The sponsors of the new legislation assumed that they could not constitutionally give important executive duties to a body which was wholly independent of Presidential direction. This was the firm conviction of Representative Lea and of Senator Truman, both of whom justified their legislative proposals as means of meeting this constitutional difficulty. Mr. Lea said:

It is the belief of the committee that we have written a bill in harmony with the Humphrey decision. We limit the power of the President to remove the members of the authority. We leave him unlimited authority to remove the members of the safety board and the administrator, because those officers are manifestly executive officers, concerning whom the President has the right of removal.[68]

The Congressional leaders believed, in short, that the Supreme Court in the Humphrey case [69] had been willing to hold the Federal Trade Commission immune from Presidential domination *because* the Federal Trade Commission did not exercise any purely executive duties. With the problem thus shaped, we may summarize the various methods which emerged in the

---

66. Ibid. 151.
67. Ibid. 49.
68. 83 Cong. Rec. 8867.
69. *Supra,* 403.

numerous legislative proposals for meeting this interesting and difficult problem. It should be stated before discussing these administrative devices that Senator McCarran had no use for any of them. He was unimpressed by the alleged constitutional difficulties and insisted that the entire task of aviation control could and should be vested in an independent agency completely free from all Presidential supervision.

One device to retain Presidential control of executive functions relating to aviation was that embodied in the Truman and Copeland bills.[70] It called for a separate commission with an executive chairman to be appointed by the President, whose removal power over the whole authority was unrestricted. Through this chairman would funnel the executive work of the agency. The theory was that the executive work would be handled by a chairman chosen by the President for that purpose, and that while the President through the removal power would have the opportunity to direct or review the authority's executive work, he would refrain from any interference with its quasi-judicial work.

A second possible solution lay in the principles embodied in the Brownlow committee report.[71] Mr. Hester, who had been helping the Brownlow committee as legislative draftsman, worked out an organization chart showing how the plan could be applied to the aviation problem. Full initial responsibility and control was vested in the Director of the Bureau of Air Commerce in the Department of Commerce, but appeal from all decisions of the director on quasi-legislative or quasi-judicial questions would go to a board of air commerce appeals set up independently but within the department. From the decisions of this board appeals would go to the courts. Mr. Hester tried to arouse Mr. Lea's interest in this plan but without success. This came out in the hearings on the Lea bill:

MR. HESTER. I am glad you raised that question, Congressman, because this has been described as the Brownlow plan. This is far-removed from the Brownlow plan. If it were the Brownlow plan you would take the regulatory commission and place it in an executive department. You would then divide the work into sections. One would be an administrative section and one would be a judicial section. The judicial section would exercise no executive func-

70. *Supra,* 399. 71. *Supra,* note 25, op. cit.

tion whatever. It would sit as an administrative court. The administrative section on the other hand would be headed by one man who would exercise all of the functions under the head of the department.

He would do all of the investigating; he would do all of the prosecuting; he would prepare all of the complaints, and the judicial section, which would be composed of five or seven men, or whatever happened to be the number decided upon, would sit as an administrative court and appeals would go directly to the court.

MR. MAPES. Did you attempt to carry out the ideas of the Brownlow Committee in setting up this new Authority?

MR. HESTER. In fairness to Mr. Lea and the committee, I must say when we came up here, within the interdepartmental draft, we did have a provision in it that to a certain extent related to the Brownlow Committee report; but Mr. Lea was unwilling to accept the provision and so we took it out of the Department of Commerce and it is a completely independent establishment, both with respect to its executive authority and its administrative work.[72]

The device most extensively discussed for meeting this problem was that embodied in the interdepartmental committee draft [73] and in the first Lea bill.[74] Under this arrangement the aeronautics authority was left removable by the President at pleasure, and his general directing authority was defined in the following provision: 'The exercise and performance of the powers and duties of the Authority which are not subject to review by courts of law shall be subject to the general direction of the President.' This provision was in the Lea bill at the time of the hearings before the House Committee on Interstate and Foreign Commerce. Mr. Hester, who had a good deal to do with drafting the proposal, was on the stand for several days.[75] He explained that this provision was not the Brownlow plan although it was probably somewhat influenced by it. He was immediately challenged to state which powers and duties of the authority were subject to review by courts of law. He admitted frankly that he could make no clean-cut tabulation. Replying to his questioner he said: 'We would be very glad to have some light on that subject from you, Mr. Congressman.

72. *Supra,* note 47, op. cit. 51 f.
73. *Supra,* 396.
74. H.R. 5174, 74th Cong., 1st sess. (1935).
75. *Supra,* note 47, op. cit. 36 ff., 133 ff., 403 ff., 433 ff.

We had considerable difficulty with it ourselves.' [76] His position was that this line between executive functions not subject to review by the courts and the quasi-judicial functions which were would have to be worked out by the courts. He declared that the promotional work of the authority was obviously executive, but that this was not all of its executive work. He pointed out that there were precedents for embodying such a distinction in legislation and called attention to the fact that the Economy Act of 1932 'contains a provision which authorizes the President to segregate regulatory functions from those of an executive character.' It was impossible to clarify the clause, and the net result of the discussion is summed up in a colloquy between Mr. Hester and Mr. Wadsworth:

MR. WADSWORTH. And here we are again mixing the two.

MR. HESTER. No; we are not. We are to a certain extent separating that under this bill in this separate establishment. You have the quasi legislative or so-called quasi judicial functions exercised entirely independent of the President and independent of the executive branch of the Government. The agency will sit as an administrative court in exercising those functions.

MR. WADSWORTH. That is your purpose?

MR. HESTER. That is right.

MR. WADSWORTH. But, I doubt if you can define it in the English language in this bill so that it will be absolutely ironclad in drawing that line of demarcation.

MR. HESTER. The courts are the ones to draw that, of course.

MR. WADSWORTH. Then we will have to wait for the courts to decide it.

MR. HESTER. I do not think we will have much difficulty, because of the fact that executive decisions as a general rule are not subject to review by the courts. There must be a question of law involved. You always have a question of law involved in connection with the making of rates and the issuance of certificates of convenience and necessity; but in determining whether or not you would build air navigation facilities, there is no question of law involved. [77]

Mr. Hester further contributed his views as to the status of the proposed authority and its location in the federal system:

MR. BOREN. Mr. Hester, this bill clearly places the new Authority in the executive branch of the Government, does it not?

MR. HESTER. No; only with respect to the executive work.

76. Ibid. 53.   77. Ibid. 145.

MR. BOREN. And the other work it has will be in the judicial branch of the Government?

MR. HESTER. No; it will be a legislative agency, independent of the executive branch.

MR. BOREN. Under the Humphrey decision, the Federal Trade Commission is made an orphan child, so far as the three constitutional branches of the Government are concerned?

MR. HESTER. That is correct.[78]

The plan finally adopted for meeting the problem under discussion was, as we have seen, worked out by a subcommittee of the House Committee on Interstate and Foreign Commerce and was never discussed or debated in any thorough fashion. The plan created within the Civil Aeronautics Authority two executive or administrative agencies, the Administrator and the Air Safety Board, which are independent of the authority, subject to discretionary removal by the President, and charged with specific duties. The authority itself is left independent of Presidential control, since its members may be removed only for stated causes, but it has authority to work through the Administrator and to delegate to him portions of its own jurisdiction.

E. THE RETURN OF THE CIVIL AERONAUTICS AUTHORITY TO THE DEPARTMENT OF COMMERCE

The Civil Aeronautics Authority did not long remain an independent agency. On April 11, 1940, the President presented to Congress Reorganization Plan No. IV, under the Reorganization Act of 1939, and this put the authority back into the Department of Commerce; the agency remained independent with respect to its quasi-judicial and quasi-legislative functions.

This move should not have been wholly unexpected. In the discussions on the civil aeronautics bills it had been suggested that the independent authority should be a temporary agency set up to meet an immediately acute problem. The President had outlined a program for the far-reaching reorganization of the Interstate Commerce Commission to deal with all forms of interstate transportation, and in 1939 Mr. Lea introduced his

78. Ibid. 57.

Omnibus Transportation bill [79] which embodied this broad program and in so doing placed air transportation under the commission. The recent shift of aviation's regulatory agency may perhaps be the first step in a general program for a single transportation agency to regulate all forms of carriers.

By the President's plan the Civil Aeronautics Authority and its functions, the Administrator and his functions, and the functions of the Air Safety Board were transferred to the Department of Commerce. The functions of the Air Safety Board and of the Civil Aeronautics Authority were consolidated in a new Civil Aeronautics Board. The Administrator of Civil Aeronautics, who is under the direction of the Secretary of Commerce, together with the Civil Aeronautics Board constitute the Civil Aeronautics Administration.

There was bitter opposition to this change and a vigorous effort was made to block it. All the usual arguments for the independence of a quasi-judicial body were restated. The excellent achievement of the independent authority and of the Air Safety Board were extolled. The unhappy early record of the Department of Commerce in the field of aviation control was recalled.

The President's statement of his reasons for making the change was very brief. He merely remarked that it was part of a program for the improvement of the organization of the executive department by reducing the number of administrative agencies and simplifying the task of executive management. Those supporting the plan denied that it would result in loss of efficiency or in political pressure upon the regulatory officers.

In September 1940 an advisory group of twenty leading figures in the varied phases of civil aviation was named to assist the Civil Aeronautics Administration of the Department of Commerce in the solution of current problems and the planning of future development.

79. H.R. 2531, 76 Cong., 1st sess. (1939).

VI

THE CONSTITUTIONAL STATUS OF THE INDEPENDENT REGULATORY COMMISSIONS[1]

THERE is an old Hindu fable, put into humorous verse by John G. Saxe, about the six men of Indostan 'to learning much inclined, who went to see the Elephant (though all of them were blind).' Each in his groping touched a different part of the beast's anatomy; and the six loudly announced in turn that the elephant was like a wall, a spear, a snake, a tree, a fan, and a rope.

And so these men of Indostan
Disputed loud and long,
Each in his own opinion
Exceeding stiff and strong
Though each was partly in the right
And all were in the wrong.

The technique of the six blind men in classifying the elephant appears to have been followed by many who, at various times, have discussed the constitutional nature and status of the independent regulatory commissions. In legislative hearings and debates, in lawyers' briefs, and in court decisions there has been a readiness to state with dogmatic precision in which of the three departments of government the commissions belong, which of the three powers of government they exercise, and other similarly definite facts about their legal nature and rela-

1. This chapter is condensed from an article of the same title which appeared in the *Cornell Law Quarterly*, vol. XXIV (December 1938, February 1939), 13 ff., 163 ff.

tions. Thus one may collect at random the following labels applied to the Interstate Commerce Commission, not, it is true, by blind men, but by men whose attention was closely riveted on some particular phase of the commission's work or procedure:

This Commission is in essence a judicial tribunal. (Commissioner Prouty, 1907.) [2]

The Commission is not a court. It is an administrative body. (Chairman Knapp, 1902.) [3]

The commission is not a part of the executive branch of this Government; but is really the arm of Congress. (Report of House Committee on Interstate and Foreign Commerce, 1912.) [4]

The Interstate Commerce Commission at the present time is an executive body. (Commissioner Prouty, 1905.) [5]

The Interstate Commerce Commission is a purely administrative body. (Supreme Court of the United States, 1912.) [6]

The function exercised by the Commission is wholly legislative. (Supreme Court of the United States, 1927.) [7]

The very able lawyers who, as members of the House of Representatives and the Senate, framed the Interstate Commerce Act of 1887, carefully avoided conferring on the Interstate Commerce Commission any kind of power except only executive power. (Senator Joseph B. Foraker, 1906.) [8]

Each of these quotations has in it an element of truth, but no one of them contains all the truth. Each resulted from the impact of some problem or circumstance which centered attention upon part, but not all, of the commission's work and relations. They are probably not so inconsistent as they appear; but it is rather remarkable that no serious attempt has thus far been

2. Quoted in Hearings before the Senate Committee on Interstate Commerce, 65th Cong., 3d sess. (1919), 309 f.
3. Hearings before the House Committee on Interstate and Foreign Commerce, 57th Cong., 1st sess. (1902), 269.
4. H. Rept. 472, 62d Cong., 2d sess. (1912), 6.
5. Hearings before the Senate Committee on Interstate Commerce Pursuant to Senate Resolution 288, 58th Cong., 3d sess. (1905), vol. IV, 2863.
6. *Interstate Commerce Commission* v. *Humboldt Steamship Co.*, 224 U.S. 474, 484 (1911).
7. *United States* v. *Berwind-White Coal Mining Co.*, 274 U.S. 564, 583 (1927).
8. 40 Cong. Rec. 3107 f.

made to deal thoroughly with the constitutional problems involved in the nature of the independent regulatory commissions and their relations to the three major departments of government. The Supreme Court of the United States has contributed only piecemeal analysis of the problem. It has been obliged to answer many specific questions regarding the commissions, but it has usually refrained from generalizations and has contributed no essays on constitutional law in which the commissions were broadly viewed. Its opinions bearing on the commissions are rationalizations of results which further sound national administration, rather than efforts to deal philosophically with the fundamental legal relations involved. For this we should be grateful and not critical. The regulatory commissions did not come into being full-blown; they have evolved by the process of trial and error. They have not remained static; they have taken on new forms and functions and relations. It would have been calamitous if the freedom of their growth and the flexibility of their structure and their relations with the departments of government had at an early date been frozen into a fixed pattern by judicial decisions based upon what could only have been a partial and inadequate view of the whole problem. There have been many valuable monographs and articles dealing with the legal and constitutional problems affecting the commissions and their work. They too have dug deeply in narrow areas. They have not attempted to cover the entire ground.

This chapter attempts to put in one place the main facts about the commissions in their legal character and relations, to appraise the place they occupy in our constitutional system, and to consider some of the constitutional problems relating to them which remain unsolved. The discussion falls into two major divisions. First, the commissions will be studied in the light of the constitutional doctrine of the separation of powers, and the impact of that doctrine upon their structure, functions, and relations. Second, we shall examine the constitutional and legal relations which the commissions bear to Congress, to the President, and to the courts.

I. THE INDEPENDENT REGULATORY COMMISSIONS AND THE DOCTRINE OF THE SEPARATION OF POWERS

ALTHOUGH legislators and administrators would at times like to forget it, the American constitutional system rests upon the doctrine of the separation of the three powers of government. The Constitution separates the three major powers of government, assigning each to its own department or division; thus it seeks to avert that threat to the liberties of the people which Montesquieu and his followers believed must result from a merger of the three powers, or any two of them, in the same hands. Furthermore, from the three so-called 'distributing clauses' [9] of the Constitution is derived the rule that no legislative, executive, or judicial power of the United States can be delegated to any government, department, officer, or agency other than that in which the Constitution vests it. It is further inferred that each of the three departments is fully protected in the exercise of its own peculiar powers from any interference or usurpation by any other department.

Viewed superficially the independent regulatory commissions appear to violate the doctrine of the separation of powers at every vital point. They seem to exercise simultaneously functions which are legislative, executive, and judicial, thus merging in the same hands powers which ought constitutionally to be separately administered. At the same time the legislative and judicial powers of the commissions appear to have been given to them in violation of the constitutional rule that Congress may not delegate its legislative power, or confer the judicial power of the United States upon any one except a duly constituted federal court. If we assume that under the Constitution there are but three major departments of the government, it is not easy to fit the independent commissions into one of these departments to the exclusion of the others. We may turn, therefore, to a closer analysis of some of these problems.

9. Art. I, § 1, cl. 1; Art. II, § 1, cl. 1; Art. III, § 1, cl. 1.

A. The Merger in the Commissions of Legislative, Executive, and Judicial Powers

Is there an unconstitutional merger in the independent regulatory commissions of legislative, executive, and judicial powers —powers which, under the doctrine of the separation of powers, must be kept separate? That such a merger of powers exists was one of the first charges to be hurled against the proposed interstate commerce commission in the Congressional debates in 1886.[10] In January 1941 a member of the Attorney General's Committee on Administrative Procedure stated:

> . . . I think it both correct and fair to say that the whole Committee recognizes the plain undesirability of commingling the function of investigation or advocacy with the function of decision.[11]

Criticism of the regulatory commissions on this score grows more persistent and more virulent rather than less.

It is natural that this charge of improper merging of powers in the commissions should be strongly urged, for the chief advantage to be gained from the threefold separation of powers is supposed to be the protection of individual liberty against the dangers resulting from the merging of legislative, executive, and judicial powers in the same hands. Montesquieu, the author of the classical statement of the doctrine, vigorously stressed this point:

> When the legislative and executive powers are united in the same person, or in the same body of magistrates, there can be no liberty, because apprehensions may arise lest the same monarch or senate should enact tyrannical laws, to execute them in a tyrannical manner. Again, there is no liberty, if the judiciary power be not separated from the legislative and executive. Were it joined with the legislative, the life and liberty of the subject would be exposed to arbitrary control; for the judge would be the legislator. Were it joined to the executive power, the judge might behave with violence and oppression. There would be an end of everything were the same man, or the same body, whether of the nobles or of the people, to exercise these three powers, that of enacting laws, that of

10. *Supra*, 58 ff.
11. S. Doc. 8, 77th Cong., 1st sess. (1941), 249.

executing the public resolutions, and of trying the causes of individuals.[12]

Madison in *The Federalist* declared more briefly but more sharply:

The accumulation of all powers, Legislative, Executive, and Judiciary, in the same hands, whether of one, a few or many, and whether hereditary, self-appointed, or elective, may justly be pronounced the very definition of tyranny.[13]

Dissenting in the Myers case, Mr. Justice Brandeis said:

The doctrine of the separation of powers was adopted by the Convention of 1787 not to promote efficiency but to preclude the exercise of arbitrary power. The purpose was not to avoid friction, but, by means of the inevitable friction incident to the distribution of the governmental powers among three departments, to save the people from autocracy.[14]

It is natural, therefore, that any governmental agency in which legislative, executive, and judicial powers appear to be merged in the same hands will be subject to the closest scrutiny to determine whether the basic doctrine of separation has in reality been violated.

It has been mentioned that the point was raised in the debates on the Interstate Commerce Act in 1886.[15] Mild as were the powers at first given to the Interstate Commerce Commission, Senator Morgan of Alabama charged that the statute combined very skillfully powers from all three departments,[16] while Mr. Oates in the House declared:

I believe that it is absolutely unconstitutional and void, because to my mind it is a blending of the legislative, the judicial, and perhaps, the executive powers of the Government in the same law.[17]

When Congress in 1902 was considering a bill enlarging the regulatory powers of the Interstate Commerce Commission, Mr. Walker D. Hines, then vice-president of the Louisville and Nashville Railroad, told a Senate committee that the commission 'is supervisor, detective, prosecutor, plaintiff, attorney, and

12. *The Spirit of the Laws* (1748), Book XI, ch. 6.
13. *The Federalist* (1788), No. 47.
14. *Myers* v. *United States*, 272 U.S. 52, 293 (1926).
15. *Supra*, 421.   16. 17 Cong. Rec. 4422.   17. 18 Cong. Rec. 848.

court. No tribunal charged with such functions can have the attributes which ought to characterize a judicial tribunal.' [18] In 1916, when it became apparent that even wider powers were likely to be given to the Interstate Commerce Commission, the Association of Railway Executives re-stated more elaborately the constitutional attack on the merger of powers in the hands of the commission.[19] The same constitutional attack was urged during the debates in Congress in 1914 against the alleged merger of powers in the Federal Trade Commission.[20] And every independent regulatory commission has been sharply attacked on this same ground.

The Supreme Court, however, has never held void any of the statutes by which alleged mergers of legislative, executive, and judicial powers are created, nor has it given any encouragement to those who attack the regulatory commissions on this constitutional ground. It appears to be wholly unimpressed by the objection, although this is not owing to unawareness of the situation at issue. In *Federal Trade Commission* v. *Klesner*, Mr. Justice Brandeis observed: 'While the Federal Trade Commission exercises under § 5 the functions of both prosecutor and judge, the scope of its authority is strictly limited.' [21] There is no indication that this combination of executive and judicial power caused any constitutional tremors in the mind of Mr. Justice Brandeis. The present judicial attitude is stated by a lower federal court in these words:

The spectacle of an administrative tribunal acting as both prosecutor and judge has been the subject of much comment, and efforts to do away with such practice have been studied for years. The Board of Tax Appeals is an outstanding example of one such successful effort. But it has never been held that such procedure denies constitutional right. On the contrary, many agencies have functioned for years, with the approval of the courts, which combine these roles. The Federal Trade Commission investigates charges of business immorality, files a charge in its own name as plaintiff, and then decides whether the proof sustains the charges it has preferred. The Interstate Commerce Commission and state Public Service Commissions may prefer complaints to be tried before themselves.

18. Hearings before the House Committee on Interstate and Foreign Commerce on Bill to Amend the Interstate Commerce Law, 57th Cong., 1st sess. (1902), 493.

19. *Supra*, 122.   20. *Supra*, 208 f.   21. 280 U.S. 19, 27 (1929).

If an administrative tribunal may on its own initiative investigate, file a complaint, and then try the charge so preferred, due process is not denied here because one or more members of the board aided in the investigation.[22]

By ignoring the whole question, the Supreme Court has left us without explaining authoritatively why the alleged merger of the three powers of government in a single regulatory body does *not* violate the doctrine of the separation of powers. It is possible, however, to suggest a number of cogent reasons for this omission.

First, the Court had upheld the constitutionality of the regulatory commission technique before this objection was seriously felt or presented. The state railroad commission, the prototype of the later federal commissions, received the Supreme Court's blessing in the Railroad Commission cases [23] in 1886. When the validity of the Interstate Commerce Act was attacked in *Interstate Commerce Commission* v. *Brimson* [24] in 1894, the Court held that judicial powers had not been unconstitutionally given to the Interstate Commerce Commission, and the broader point that legislative, executive, and judicial powers were invalidly merged was neither argued nor ruled upon. When in 1919 a lower court passed for the first time upon an order of the Federal Trade Commission, it sustained the statute with the comment that 'grants of similar authority to administrative officers and bodies have not been found repugnant to the Constitution'; [25] while the Supreme Court merely assumed the validity of the Federal Trade Commission Act without directly commenting on it.[26]

Second, the Supreme Court has always interpreted the doctrine of the separation of powers with great flexibility. The fact that the Constitution itself contains important deviations from a strict separation of powers, deviations necessary to the smooth running of the governmental machine, could hardly fail to impress on the Court that a rigid or mechanical application of the

22. *Brinkley* v. *Hassig*, 83 Fed. (2d) 351, 356 f. (C.C.A. 10th 1936).
23. 116 U.S. 307 (1886).
24. 154 U.S. 447 (1894).
25. *Sears, Roebuck and Co.* v. *Federal Trade Commission*, 258 Fed. 307, 311 (C.C.A. 7th 1919).
26. See C. McFarland, *Judicial Control of the Federal Trade Commission and Interstate Commerce Commission* (1933), 7 f. and cases cited.

doctrine is both unnecessary and unwise. As Frankfurter and Landis put it:

> Nor has it [the doctrine of separation of powers] been treated by the Supreme Court as a technical legal doctrine. From the beginning that Court has refused to draw abstract, analytical lines of separation and has recognized necessary areas of interaction.[27]

The powers of government which under the doctrine of the separation of powers must be kept separate are the legislative, executive, and judicial powers granted by the Constitution to Congress, to the President, and to the constitutional courts. These powers could not be invalidly merged in a regulatory commission unless, in turn, they had been granted to that commission. But the Supreme Court, as we shall shortly see, has steadily denied that either legislative or judicial power in the constitutional sense has been given to the commissions. If the commissions do not possess the legislative and judicial powers separated by the distributing clauses of the Constitution, then clearly those powers have not been unconstitutionally merged in creating the commissions. The powers exercised by the commissions may be mixed, but they are not the powers which it is constitutionally improper to mix.

Third, the courts did not wish to find the regulatory commissions unconstitutional, since they regarded them as necessary. As the Supreme Court became increasingly familiar with the commissions and with the problems with which they were dealing, it came to feel that the commission technique was essential to the successful handling of the difficult tasks involved in the government regulation of business. Strong governmental necessity could not be lightly ignored. As early as 1894 the Court, in the Brimson case, had pointed out that the regulatory commission was indispensable to the effective exercise of the commerce power. It said:

> An adjudication that Congress could not establish an administrative body with authority to investigate the subject of interstate commerce and with power to call witnesses before it, and to require the production of books, documents, and papers relating to that sub-

27. F. Frankfurter and J. M. Landis, 'Power of Congress over Procedure in Criminal Contempt in "Inferior" Federal Courts—A Study in Separation of Powers,' *Harvard Law Review*, vol. XXXVII (1924), 1010.

ject, would go far towards defeating the object for which the people of the United States placed commerce among the states under national control. All must recognize the fact that the full information necessary as a basis of intelligent legislation by Congress from time to time upon the subject of interstate commerce cannot be obtained, nor can the rules established for the regulation of such commerce be efficiently enforced, otherwise than through the instrumentality of an administrative body, representing the whole country, always watchful of the general interests, and charged with the duty not only of obtaining the required information, but of compelling by all lawful methods obedience to such rules.[28]

The district court made the same point more sharply in commenting on the Federal Trade Commission in the Sears, Roebuck case:

With the increasing complexity of human activities many situations arise where governmental control can be secured only by the 'board' or 'commission' form of legislation.[29]

It seems to be the settled disposition of the courts to regard the independent regulatory commissions as vitally necessary parts of the mechanism of modern government.

Fourth, from the very beginning, the work of the regulatory commissions, in all important particulars, has been held closely subject to judicial review. The courts have thus been able to set aside orders or decisions of the commissions which they regarded as *ultra vires,* unjust, or otherwise subversive of private rights. The alleged merger of powers thus becomes unimportant, since the Court is able to see that no substantial injustice results. If the major reason for keeping the powers of government separate is to prevent the exercise of arbitrary power, and if the exercise of arbitrary power is effectively prevented by judicial review, then the Court need not worry separately over the supposed merger of powers. Without this close judicial supervision of commission work, the constitutional objection we are discussing might have received more serious attention.

Finally, it has been easier and more satisfactory to the Court to exercise its constitutional scrutiny of the regulatory commissions within the flexible limits of the test of due process of

28. *Interstate Commerce Commission* v. *Brimson,* 154 U.S. 447, 474 (1894).
29. *Sears, Roebuck and Co.* v. *Federal Trade Commission,* 258 Fed. 307, 312 (C.C.A. 7th 1919).

law than to try to work with the vague doctrine of the separation of powers. Had the due process test not been available, the Court might possibly have invoked the separation theory; but it has not been necessary to do that, and it is obvious now that it will never be done. The Supreme Court has held that a violation of the doctrine of the separation of powers does not *per se* amount to a denial of due process of law.[30] It is possible, however, that a merger of powers might take such a form as to amount to a denial of due process. Should Congress create a regulatory agency in which legislative, executive, and judicial powers were fused in such a manner as to invite and effect arbitrary abridgement of private rights, we may assume that the Court would protect those rights by invoking the due process clause rather than the doctrine of the separation of powers. In short, if there was ever any vitality at all in the constitutional principle that the three powers of government may not validly be merged in the same hands, it has long since been assimilated to 'the much more flexible and practicable doctrine of due process.

B. Delegation of Powers to the Commissions

The most important corollary of the doctrine of the separation of powers is that the powers given to the three departments may not be delegated to other departments or agencies. If the legislative power is vested in Congress, then it logically follows that that power cannot be farmed out to anybody else. The doctrine of the non-delegability of legislative and judicial powers is the phase of the separation of powers theory which has most often engaged the attention of the Supreme Court. By what means have the powers given by Congress to the independent regulatory commissions been so rationalized as to avoid conflict with the constitutional prohibition against delegation? No grant of power to any commission has been held by the Court to violate the rule against delegation; and yet it is generally agreed that the commissions exercise legislative, administrative, and judicial powers. How has this paradoxical result been achieved?

30. *Dreyer* v. *Illinois*, 187 U.S. 71, 84 (1902).

1. HAVE LEGISLATIVE POWERS BEEN DELEGATED TO THE COMMISSIONS?

Has Congress delegated legislative power to the regulatory commissions? Viewed realistically, every commission appears to exercise legislative power in at least one way, and some of them in two. In the first place, every regulatory commission has the power to issue rules and regulations: the power of sub-legislation. These rules and regulations may be grouped and classified and labeled in various ways, but they are legislative in nature. No one who scans the voluminous regulations of the Interstate Commerce Commission in the field of safety appliance requirements or motor vehicle licensing can fail to realize that here is a body of legislation vastly more important than many of the formal statutes passed by Congress itself. This power to issue rules and regulations has been conferred by Congress from the foundation of our government upon executive and administrative officers. It is by no means confined to the regulatory commissions.

A second way in which legislative power is exercised by some of the regulatory commissions is more specialized and distinctive. Here Congress embodies in a statute a legislative 'standard' or principle which it believes should control business conduct or relations, and delegates to a regulatory commission the power to make that standard effective by the issuance of orders which apply the standard to concrete situations. It is this power which the Interstate Commerce Commission exercises in issuing a railroad rate order. Congress has declared by law that railroad rates shall be 'just and reasonable' and has given to the commission the job of determining in a concrete situation what a 'just and reasonable' rate is and of issuing an order establishing that rate. This rate-making function is legislative in character. The Supreme Court has so described it repeatedly.[31] State railroad and other public utility rates were originally fixed by legislation. There is no doubt of the constitutional power of Congress to embody in a statute each individual railroad rate now established by the Interstate Commerce Commission.

---

31. *United States* v. *Berwind-White Coal Mining Co.,* 274 U.S. 564, 583 (1933); *Morgan* v. *United States,* 298 U.S. 468, 479 (1936).

What has been the attitude of the courts toward these delegations of power? Briefly, it has taken shape in a settled judicial policy of upholding these delegations of power as necessary to the administration of government, but without sacrificing the constitutional theory that legislative powers cannot be delegated. This problem of eating its constitutional cake and having it too the Court has very adroitly solved by two rather different methods, which may be briefly described.

The first and earliest of these methods is to use labels or definitions which avoid the constitutional difficulties. Much may be accomplished in an argument if one is allowed to write his own definitions. If the power which it is necessary to delegate to regulatory agencies can be called something other than 'legislative power,' then the constitutional rule is left intact. This may be put in the form of a syllogism as follows:

> *Major premise:* Legislative power cannot be constitutionally delegated by Congress.
> *Minor premise:* It is essential that certain powers be delegated to administrative officers and regulatory commissions.
> *Conclusion:* Therefore the powers thus delegated are not legislative powers.

The logical hiatus in this reasoning is concealed by attaching a distinctive name to the powers thus delegated. And this is what the Court has done. In fact, it has used two names: first, 'administrative,' and second, 'quasi-legislative.'

The term 'administrative' was a useful term to apply to the sub-legislative powers given to administrative officers and commissions. It is not used in the Constitution itself, it is different from the word 'legislative,' and there is no authoritative definition of it. Thus in 1911 in the case of *United States* v. *Grimaud,* which upheld the power of the Secretary of Agriculture to issue regulations for grazing on public lands, Mr. Justice Lamar said:

> In the nature of things it was impracticable for Congress to provide general regulations for these various and varying details of management . . . In authorizing the Secretary of Agriculture to meet these local conditions, Congress was merely conferring administrative functions upon an agent, and not delegating to him legislative power.[32]

32. 220 U.S. 506, 516 (1911).

Perhaps even more useful to the Court has been the prefix 'quasi,' which can be attached to the terms 'legislative' and 'judicial.' Legislative power cannot constitutionally be delegated by Congress; but there is no prohibition against the delegation of 'quasi-legislative' powers. According to Mr. Justice Sutherland in the Humphrey case,[33] 'quasi-legislative' power is what the Federal Trade Commission enjoys, along with 'quasi-judicial' power. Congress, in short, has not invalidly delegated legislative power to the regulatory commissions because the power which it has delegated turns out to be 'quasi-legislative' and not legislative.

A second judicial attitude toward this problem discards this juggling of definitions and deals more directly with the realities involved. This second judicial theory may be put thus: Legislative power has not been delegated to the independent regulatory commissions within the meaning of the constitutional rule, if that power must be exercised by the commissions within the limits of a legislative policy or standard blocked out with reasonable clearness in the statute by which Congress granted the power. To put it in the words of Mr. Justice Sutherland (who used both techniques as occasion arose), '. . . Congress can not delegate any part of its legislative power except under the limitation of a prescribed standard . . .' [34]

The judicial and professional recognition that legislative power has been and must be delegated by Congress to other governmental agencies appears with increasing frequency. In his presidential address to the American Bar Association in 1916 Elihu Root asserted:

Before these agencies [the administrative tribunals], the old doctrine prohibiting the delegation of legislative powers has virtually retired from the field and given up the fight. There will be no withdrawal from these experiments. We shall go on; we shall expand them, whether we approve theoretically or not; because such agencies furnish protection to right, and obstacles to wrong-doing, which under our new social and industrial conditions cannot be practically accomplished by the old and simple procedure of legislatures and courts as in the last generation.[35]

33. *Humphrey's Executor* v. *United States*, 295 U.S. 602 (1935).
34. *United States* v. *Chicago, M. St. P. and P. R. Co.*, 282 U.S. 311, 324 (1931).
35. Ann. Rept. of the American Bar Association, vol. XLI (1916), 368 f.

In responding to the resolutions of the Attorney General upon the death of Chief Justice White, Chief Justice Taft, referring to White's decision holding that legislative power had not been delegated to the Interstate Commerce Commission, said:

> The Interstate Commerce Commission was authorized to exercise powers the conferring of which by Congress would have been, perhaps, thought in the earlier years of the Republic to violate the rule that no legislative power can be delegated. But the inevitable progress and exigencies of government and the utter inability of Congress to give the time and attention indispensable to the exercise of these powers in detail forced the modification of the rule.[36]

So generous, in fact, was the Court's treatment of what appeared to be delegations of legislative power to regulatory commissions and administrative officers that Professor E. S. Corwin was led to say in 1934 that 'Congress is enabled to delegate its powers whenever it is necessary and proper to do so in order to exercise them effectively.' [37] The requirement that legislative power, if delegated, must be delegated 'under the limitation of a prescribed standard' was still insisted upon by the Court, but the standards set up were in some cases so vague as to impose small restraint upon the discretion of those to whom the power was delegated.[38]

In two important cases, however, the Supreme Court proceeded to take up this slack and sharpen the meaning of its present rule regarding delegations of legislative power. In *Panama Refining Co. v. Ryan* [39] and in the Schechter case [40] the Court held void delegations of legislative power to the President on the ground that the National Industrial Recovery Act set up no clear standards or criteria to serve as limitations upon the President's uncontrolled discretion. The net result seems to be that while the standards limiting the delegations of legislative power may be vague, they may not be too vague, and they certainly must not be wholly lacking. A standard is too vague when it does not offer a guide which can be seen and

36. Proceedings on the Death of Chief Justice White, 257 U.S. xxv f. (1922).

37. E. S. Corwin, *The Twilight of the Supreme Court* (1934), 145.

38. *New York Central Securities Corporation* v. *United States*, 287 U.S. 12 (1932); *Federal Radio Commission* v. *General Electric Co.*, 281 U.S. 464 (1930).

39. 293 U.S. 388 (1935).

40. *Schechter* v. *United States*, 295 U.S. 495 (1935).

followed by those exercising the delegated power. Or, stated a bit differently, the standard must be clear enough to be visible to the naked eye of the Court, so that that tribunal can determine whether the officer or agency is following the standard instead of exercising uncontrolled discretion.

It thus appears that in dealing with the delegation of legislative power the Supreme Court has essentially paralleled, though without the corresponding labels, the situation which exists with regard to federal judicial power and has recognized the existence of two grades of legislative power, one which cannot constitutionally be delegated by Congress, and one which can. By Article III of the Constitution 'the judicial power of the United States' is given to the Supreme Court and the inferior federal courts created by Congress. This judicial power can be given only to the regularly constituted United States courts, and this principle has been enforced with absolute rigidity. Nevertheless, practical necessity has required from time to time that 'judicial power' be given to agencies which are not courts created under Article III. Congress could not effectively exercise its powers without making such grants. The Supreme Court solved the problem by holding that there are two categories of judicial power possible under the Constitution. There is 'the judicial power of the United States' which is granted by Article III and which can be granted only to the constitutional courts; and there is a less sacrosanct, garden variety of judicial power which Congress, in exercising its delegated powers, may give to 'legislative courts.' [41] Inherently the two kinds of power are the same, although they operate usually in different fields. In much the same way the courts have actually recognized two categories of federal legislative power. There is the legislative power which, for the sake of pursuing the analogy, may be labeled 'the legislative power of the United States,' the legislative discretion conferred by the Constitution upon Congress. This may not be delegated. But there is also a lesser variety of legislative power which Congress in the carrying out of its legislative responsibilities may delegate to independent regula-

41. This distinction between 'constitutional' and 'legislative' courts was carefully drawn by Marshall in *American Insurance Co.* v. *Canter,* 1 Peters 511, 546 (U.S. 1828); it is elaborated in the light of later decisions in W. G. Katz, 'Federal Legislative Courts,' *Harvard Law Review,* vol. XLIII (1930), 894.

tory commissions or to administrative officers. This second type of legislative power is, however, really 'sub-legislative' power, in the sense that it must be exercised within the limits of standards set up by Congress to block out at least the rough outlines of a primary legislative policy. Marshall, who was a confirmed constitutional pragmatist, virtually made this distinction in 1825 in the case of *Wayman* v. *Southard,*[42] although he made no attempt to find names for the two grades of legislative power. The courts have continued to use his distinction. Thus the neat and effective device whereby the courts sidestepped the problem presented by the non-grantability of 'the judicial power of the United States' provides an equally convenient solution to the problem of the non-delegability of legislative power. We have come close to adopting the theory without the names.

Finally, it seems probable that the rule against the delegation of legislative power, like the rule against the merger of the three powers of government in the same hands, will be assimilated into the constitutional guarantee of due process of law. The delegations of legislative power which the courts have held bad are those in which legislative power has been granted without the accompanying protection of an adequate guiding standard. There is a practical reason for this rule. It is for the protection of the rights of the citizen that democratic governments give broad law-making powers to a representative legislature, and not to a single officer or administrative agency. To permit such an officer or agency to exercise legislative power unrestrained by legislative standards is to subject the citizen to the danger of an arbitrary power against which he may have no effective protection. It is but a short step from this to the position that one whose rights have been impaired by the exercise of unrestrained legislative discretion in the hands of an administrative officer or agency is being deprived of liberty or property without due process of law. In short, the rule against the delegation of legislative power as it is now construed exists not for the purpose of keeping alive an abstract principle of political philosophy, but for the purpose of surrounding private rights with a protection just as readily available under the due process clause. In fact, the doctrine of the non-delegability of

42. 10 Wheaton 1 (1825).

legislative power could safely be scrapped as long as due process of law remains the effective constitutional guarantee it now is.

2. CAN MORE LEGISLATIVE POWER BE DELEGATED TO AN INDEPENDENT REGULATORY COMMISSION THAN TO AN EXECUTIVE OFFICER?

The interesting theory has recently been set forth that Congress may constitutionally grant more legislative and judicial power to an independent regulatory commission than to an executive officer. Or, to put it in another way, Congress could not validly delegate to an executive officer the kinds of power which have been given to the Interstate Commerce Commission and the Federal Trade Commission.

This is worthy of careful consideration. A clear statement of this doctrine appeared in the brief presented to the Supreme Court for the appellants in *Isbrandtsen-Moller Co.* v. *United States* [43] in 1937. The point arose in this way: The Economy Act of 1932 authorized the President to transfer or consolidate by executive order executive agencies or functions. President Roosevelt made extensive use of this power and, among other changes, transferred the United States Shipping Board to the Department of Commerce, where it became the United States Shipping Board Bureau. The appellant, a shipping company, attacked the validity of an order directed against it by the Shipping Board Bureau. It contended that the Economy Act did not intend to give the President power to transfer or alter the independent regulatory commissions, of which the Shipping Board was admittedly one; and that if it did intend to give such power it was, for that reason, unconstitutional, since the powers enjoyed by the Shipping Board could not validly be given to an executive officer such as the Secretary of Commerce. In the appellant's brief the argument is stated thus:

The functions of the United States Shipping Board were so broadly defined by Congress in the Shipping Act, 1916, and the Merchant Marine Act, 1920, and were of such a quasi-judicial and quasi-legislative character, that they obviously could not be performed properly or at all by an executive department or bureau, and it would have been a violation of the fundamental constitu-

43. 300 U.S. 139 (1937); the brief and argument were presented by Mr. James W. Ryan of New York.

tional doctrine of separation of powers if Congress had intended those functions to be delegated to or exercised by an executive department or bureau. Assuming that a slight degree of legislative power may be delegated to an executive department, or rather become effective after a hearing and finding by an executive department, surely there is a limit and that is when, as in the present case, the legislative and judicial power attempted to be delegated is so great and substantial, and so inconsistent with its exercise by an executive department, that the executive department would become predominantly a legislative or judicial body rather than an executive body, so far as the exercise of those functions was concerned.[44]

The Court decided the case without ruling on this point.

Some of the language used in the Schechter case is said to support this theory. In that case Chief Justice Hughes declared that legislative power was invalidly delegated to the President by the provisions of the National Industrial Recovery Act, which authorized him to promulgate codes of fair competition. The term 'fair competition' was too vague a standard to guide the President's legislative discretion. The Chief Justice referred with approval, by way of contrast, to the Federal Trade Commission's task in applying the legislative standard, 'unfair methods of competition,' and went on to say:

. . . What are 'unfair methods of competition' are thus to be determined in particular instances, upon evidence, in the light of particular competitive conditions and of what is found to be a specific and substantial public interest . . . To make this possible Congress set up a special procedure. A commission, a quasi-judicial body, was created. Provision was made for formal complaint, for notice and hearing, for appropriate findings of fact supported by adequate evidence, and for judicial review to give assurance that the action of the Commission is taken within its statutory authority . . .

In providing for codes, the National Industrial Recovery Act dispenses with this administrative procedure and with any administrative procedure of an analogous character.[45]

From this statement it is inferred that the delegation of power to the President in the National Industrial Recovery Act is bad

44. Brief for appellant, 48.
45. *Schechter* v. *United States,* 295 U.S. 495, 533 (1935).

because he is an executive officer, while the delegation of power to the Federal Trade Commission is good because it is an independent 'quasi-judicial' body.

This whole theory is unsound. There is no reason arising from the doctrine of the separation of powers why the same powers should not be delegated to an executive officer as to an independent commission. First, there is nothing in the doctrine of separation of powers itself which supports such a theory. The rule against delegation of legislative power limits the scope and nature of the power which Congress may turn over to some one else. It was never intended to restrict Congress in selecting the officer or agency to whom the power was to be given. If Congress can delegate the power at all, there is no restriction upon its choice of a grantee. This point is effectively presented in the brief for the government in the Isbrandtsen-Moller case:

. . . Appellant's position appears to be that, although the powers in question can properly be delegated, the Constitution permits Congress to delegate them only to a particular kind of officer or agency. This is a constitutional doctrine, novel in conception and startling in its consequences . . . If, as appellant suggests, Congress cannot delegate quasi-legislative or quasi-judicial power to an executive department or officer, it must, if it wishes to delegate such power at all, create a special commission or bureau for that purpose. Acceptance of this principle would lead inevitably to the creation of a kind of fourth grand division of the federal government consisting solely of these independent commissions or bureaus. This is a radical departure from traditional concepts of the nature of the federal government which finds no support in the language of the Constitution or in the decisions of this Court.[46]

Second, the Supreme Court has upheld delegations to executive officers of the same powers which the independent commissions enjoy. When Congress enacted the Packers and Stockyards Act of 1921, it debated at length whether to give the administration of the statute to the Federal Trade Commission or to the Secretary of Agriculture. It gave it to the Secretary. The powers conferred, including rate making and the suppression of unfair competitive practices, are essentially the same as those exercised by the Interstate Commerce Commission and the Fed-

46. Brief for the United States, 78 f.

eral Trade Commission. The constitutionality of this Act has been upheld by the Supreme Court.[47]

Finally, what this argument is groping after is a due process limitation relating to procedure, and not a separation of powers limitation at all. It may be that a delegation of quasi-legislative and quasi-judicial power to an executive officer may be so loosely stated as to be bad, while a differently stated delegation of the same power to a quasi-judicial commission would be good. The difference would lie, not in the nature of the grantee, but in the fairness of the procedure by which the granted power is to be exercised. This, it seems to me, is all that Chief Justice Hughes is driving at in the passage in the Schechter case already quoted. If the National Industrial Recovery Act had granted to the Federal Trade Commission *the same powers in the same terms* in which they were given to the President, the grant would have been equally bad. The grant to the President was unaccompanied by any procedural requirements to protect against arbitrary action those subject to the power granted, whereas the Federal Trade Commission is required to carry on its work in accordance with an already approved procedure, quasi-judicial in character. The legality of the procedure is the point at issue, not the kind of agency. In short, another separation of powers argument turns out, upon analysis, to be a due process argument.

3. GRANTS OF JUDICIAL POWER TO THE COMMISSIONS

The doctrine of the separation of powers forbids the giving to any one except the constitutional courts the judicial power granted by the Constitution. At the same time the independent regulatory commissions have powers which look suspiciously like judicial powers. And yet the courts have found here no violations of the doctrine of separation of powers. This result may be explained in a number of ways.

First, as already noted,[48] the Supreme Court has neatly solved the problem of any invalid grant of 'the judicial power of the United States' by recognizing that there is another brand of federal judicial power which is not the judicial power of the

47. *Stafford* v. *Wallace*, 258 U.S. 495 (1922).   48. *Supra*, 432 f.

United States within the meaning of Article III. The judicial power of the United States is vested in the constitutional courts created by Congress under Article III and can be given to no one else. Not only would it be unconstitutional to grant it to any other body; it would be impossible to do so. This is true because as soon as it is granted to any one other than a constitutional court the power becomes *ipso facto* not the judicial power of the United States but the other sort of federal judicial power, the kind that can be granted to what are called 'legislative courts.' Congress has never sought to confer any portion of 'the judicial power of the United States' upon any independent regulatory agency.

Second, it would not violate the doctrine of the separation of powers for Congress to give federal judicial power to a regulatory commission, so long as it is not 'the judicial power of the United States,' but it would violate the due process clause. To make a delegation of 'judicial power' valid Congress must transform the regulatory agency into the kind of body constitutionally capable of receiving and exercising judicial power. The inherent attributes of a court cannot be given to a non-judicial body, especially an administrative body. The final adjudication of private rights, the independent power to compel testimony, cannot without violating due process be delegated to agencies like the Interstate Commerce Commission [49] which also enjoy wide ranges of legislative and administrative discretion. Not all the lines of distinction between administrative tribunals such as the independent regulatory commissions and the legislative courts have been sharply drawn in court decisions, but in so far as those distinctions are constitutional in nature they are pricked out in terms of due process of law and not the separation of powers.

Third, the functions of a judicial nature which have been given to the independent commissions are conveniently labeled

49. In *Interstate Commerce Commission* v. *Brimson*, 154 U.S. 447, 485 (1894), Mr. Justice Harlan said: 'The inquiry whether a witness before the Commission is bound to answer a particular question propounded to him, or to produce books, papers, etc., in his possession and called for by that body, is one that cannot be committed to a subordinate administrative or executive tribunal for final determination. Such a body could not, under our system of government, and consistently with due process of law, be invested with authority to compel obedience to its orders by a judgment of fine or imprisonment.'

'quasi-judicial.' That effectively meets any attack based on a supposed violation of the separation of powers. There can be no objection to the grant of quasi-judicial powers. Bodies which receive them become, to that extent, quasi-judicial bodies. When the term quasi-judicial is used, and the Supreme Court has added it to its vocabulary, it serves to describe such a function as that exercised by the Federal Trade Commission in issuing a cease and desist order against an unfair trade practice. Here the task of determining that a particular practice is an unfair competitive trade practice, and that such a practice has been indulged in, is combined, in the form of a restraining order, with the judicial application of the results to the persons concerned. The application of a legislative standard to concrete cases involving the rights of parties and of the public is a quasi-judicial function. And this is perhaps the most important work of the independent regulatory commissions; certainly it is the task which most clearly justifies their separate and independent existence. But in granting this quasi-judicial power there is no violation of the doctrine of the separation of powers.

Finally, Congress may properly require regulatory bodies, whether commissions or officers, to perform sub-legislative or administrative tasks by a procedure substantially judicial in character. The courts insist that the fixing of a rate is a legislative function.[50] Congress could itself establish railroad rates by the same procedure by which it passes any other statute. But when this rate-making power was given to the Interstate Commerce Commission, Congress required that it be exercised in accordance with a semi-judicial procedure. And the courts would require such procedure under due process of law even if Congress did not require it by statute. But here there is no grant of judicial power. The power is legislative; it is only the method of exercising it which is judicial.

We may conclude, then, that the doctrine of the separation of powers has not been invoked, and will not be invoked, to prevent the delegation to the independent commissions of substantial legislative and judicial powers. The doctrine of non-delegation never had much vitality, and it has lost through the use of labels and other devices of convenience most of what little it had. But this will not result in the serious impairment

50. *Supra,* 428.

of individual rights or in the exercise of arbitrary power. These will continue to be unconstitutional as deprivations of life, liberty, or property without due process of law.

C. Does the Separation of Powers Require That the Independent Commissions Be 'in' Some One of the Three Departments?

Does the doctrine of the separation of powers require that every federal governmental agency be located *in* one of the three departments, legislative, executive, or judicial, or be definitively classified as a legislative, executive, or judicial agency? If so, in which of the three departments do the independent regulatory commissions belong, and what legal consequences result from their being in one department rather than another? Is it possible that an agency may constitutionally be *in* more than one department at once, or in none of them? If these last alternatives are possible, do they necessarily result in the creation of a 'fourth department'? These problems deal with the 'organizational' location of the commissions and not with the nature of their powers. They are important questions because some judges and writers have assumed that every commission must be *in* some one department. They have tried to decide which department this is, although they have had difficulty in agreeing. They have then proceeded to infer, from this departmental domicile, important conclusions regarding the relations of Congress or of the President to the commissions.

First, does the doctrine of the separation of powers require that every agency of the federal government be definitely and completely *in* some one of the three departments? There is judicial dictum which leans toward an affirmative answer. In *Kilbourn* v. *Thompson,* decided in 1881, Mr. Justice Miller said:

It is believed to be one of the chief merits of the American system of written constitutional law, that all the powers entrusted to governments, whether state or national, are divided into the three grand departments of the executive, the legislative and the judicial. That the functions appropriate to each of these branches of government shall be vested in a separate body of public servants, and that the perfection of the system requires that the lines which separate and divide these departments shall be broadly and clearly defined.[51]

In *Springer* v. *Philippine Islands* the Court held that the Organic Act under which the islands were governed established a separation of the three powers of government identical with that implicit in the Constitution of the United States. Mr. Justice Sutherland said:

> Thus the Organic Act, following the rule established by the American Constitutions, both state and Federal, divides the government into three separate departments—the legislative, executive and judicial . . . And this separation and the consequent exclusive character of the powers conferred upon each of the three departments is basic and vital—not merely a matter of governmental mechanism.
>
> . . . Putting aside for the moment the question whether the duties devolved upon these members are vested by the Organic Act in the Governor-General, it is clear that they are not legislative in character, and still more clear that they are not judicial. The fact that they do not fall within the authority of either of these two constitutes logical ground for concluding that they do fall within that of the remaining one of the three among which the powers of government are divided.[52]

This had nothing to do with independent regulatory commissions, but it seems to suggest that the Constitution creates three departments, that these are mutually exclusive of each other, save as the Constitution provides otherwise, and that an agency must necessarily, therefore, be in one of the three. Applied concretely, this requires that the Interstate Commerce Commission be *in* one of the three departments. Obviously the commission is not *in* the judicial department. It must then be either *in* the legislative department or *in* the executive department, and there are those willing to support the claims of each department. The possibility of any middle ground is ruled out. In a word, the Constitution in dealing with the departments established a perfect trichotomy, and left no room for any confusing and annoying fringe around the edges.

This analysis seems unsound for several reasons: In the first place, the doctrine of the separation of powers does not require

51. 103 U.S. 168, 190 f. (1881).   52. 277 U.S. 189, 201 f. (1928).

that every governmental agency be snugly located wholly inside the boundary lines of a single department. It is true that most of them are so located and that the status of those which are not may seem anomalous. The three distributing clauses of the Constitution deal with governmental powers, legislative, executive, and judicial. It is *powers*, not *departments*, which are separated. The Constitution wisely left to Congress a broad discretion in establishing the governmental machinery by which these powers are to be exercised. No precise and definite rule has emerged by which to trace the boundary lines of the legislative and executive departments. The Constitution by alluding to the 'heads of departments' assumes that there are executive officers besides the President; but there has been no authoritative answer to the question whether the 'legislative department' includes more than Congress itself, or if so just how much. Now if the doctrine of the separation of powers had always been applied with such absolute rigidity that under no circumstances could the three powers of government be either *merged* or *delegated,* we could then draw clear and mutually exclusive departmental lines and determine without difficulty in just which of the three departments every agency belongs. But we have, with full judicial approval, scrapped the theory that the three powers of government cannot be merged in a single agency; and we have practically scrapped the doctrine of the non-delegability of powers. If the doctrine of the separation of powers, as presently construed, permits a single agency to exercise two or more of the three powers of government, and permits executive or administrative officers to exercise legislative power, then by what logical compulsion must we conclude that the doctrine of the separation of powers requires us to locate each of these multi-functional agencies in a single one of the three departments? It is much sounder to recognize that we have, and must have, federal governmental agencies which are not *in* one department to the exclusion of the others, but which so straddle at least two of the departments as to be in reality essential parts of each. This is the status of the independent regulatory commissions.

In the second place, Congress has not tried to place every federal agency inside a single department. It has proceeded upon the theory that in some cases this cannot and therefore need not be done. The truth of this may be tested by trying to name the departments in which certain important governmental agencies actually belong. One may begin with the legislative courts, such as the Court of Claims, the Customs Court, and the Court of Customs and Patent Appeals. In which of the three departments of government are these legislative courts located? They exercise judicial power. They do not, however, exercise 'the judicial power of the United States.' Each of these courts was set up to perform by judicial procedure a job which had before been carried on by executive officers. In the case of the Court of Claims the task had been handled both by executive and legislative officers, since claims against the government had before this been passed upon both by the Treasury Department and by Congress. Since these courts are not constitutional courts they cannot be in the judicial department in the constitutional sense. And yet Congress has made them so completely independent of Congress and of the President that they can hardly be in the legislative or executive departments. It is equally difficult to allocate the United States Board of Tax Appeals. This body was set up to replace the Committee on Appeals and Review in the Treasury Department. The statute creating the board declares it to be 'an independent agency in the executive branch of the government,' and the Supreme Court has said, 'The Board of Tax Appeals is not a court. It is an executive or administrative board . . .' [53] For all practical purposes, however, the Board of Tax Appeals is a legislative court. Its members are called and call themselves judges (their wives enjoying social precedence as the wives of federal judges!); and while they do not have life tenure, they have no responsibility to the President or to Congress, and cannot be directed or controlled by either. The declaration by Congress that the board is in the executive department has no relevance to the board's actual functions or relations.

In setting up two independent regulatory commissions, Congress attempted in a half-hearted way to put them in one of the executive departments. The Interstate Commerce Commission when established was required to send its annual report to the Secretary of the Interior, who was instructed to provide the

53. *Old Colony Trust Co.* v. *Commissioner of Internal Revenue,* 279 U.S. 716, 725 (1929).

commission with officers and supplies and to approve its expense vouchers and the appointment and salaries of its employees.[54] These provisions were repealed in 1889.[55] The Guffey Act of 1935 provided, 'There is hereby established in the Department of the Interior a National Bituminous Coal Commission,' and gave to the Secretary of the Interior control of the commission's budget and certain other administrative 'housekeeping' functions. This relation, continued by the Act of 1937, remained until the commission was made an integral division of the Department of the Interior by Presidential order in 1939.[56] But where would the Bituminous Coal Commission have been had it come out of the Department of the Interior? Would it have remained in the executive branch of the government, though not in any of the ten departments, or would it by some automatic process have slid over into the legislative branch? Congress has never told us where it thinks the other independent regulatory commissions are located and it is a reasonable inference that it does not regard the question as important.

In the third place, the task of allocating governmental agencies to a single department is completely futile. The important thing about an agency is the character of its job, not its geographical location in the governmental system. That location has no necessary bearing upon the powers, relations, or constitutional status of the agency. Suppose we agree that the Board of Tax Appeals is 'in the executive branch,' as Congress has said, or that the Interstate Commerce Commission is in the legislative branch. We have not thereby created any legal relation between the agency and the department. The position of the Secretary of Agriculture under the Packers and Stockyards Act makes it clear that a purely executive officer firmly established in the executive department may be given legislative powers and be an agent of Congress. The important thing is what the officer does and not where he is. There can be no objection to allocating all of the officers and agencies of government to particular departments more or less arbitrarily if we keep it clearly in mind that we are merely attaching labels. But

54. Act of Feb. 4, 1887, 24 Stat. at L. 379.
55. Act of March 2, 1889, 25 Stat. at L. 855.
56. *Supra,* 388 f.

if the designations have no practical consequences there can be no constitutional necessity for making them.

Nothing seems clearer from a study of this whole problem than the futility of trying to apply to the vitally important administrative development of the last fifty years any rigid concepts drawn from the doctrine of the separation of powers. This can be effectively illustrated by tracing the changes in the attitude on this point of Mr. Justice Sutherland, who had an almost dominating share in the judicial interpretation of these problems, and who may be said to have grown up with the problems as they emerged in varying forms. Mr. Justice Sutherland's thinking upon this problem seems to have run through the following phases: First, in 1914, when the Federal Trade Commission bill was being debated, Mr. Sutherland, then United States senator from Utah, bitterly opposed the bill on constitutional grounds. His position was this: Congress may properly create a Federal Trade Commission similar to the existing Interstate Commerce Commission and endowed with power to investigate unfair competitive trade practices and report its findings back to Congress for appropriate action. Such a commission Senator Sutherland referred to as a 'legislative' commission, and he so designated the Interstate Commerce Commission. It was legislative because the power delegated to it was a power which Congress itself could properly exercise if it had the time and energy. When it was proposed, however, to give to the Federal Trade Commission the power to issue a cease and desist order under the procedure set up in the present statute, Senator Sutherland protested that this was a violation of the doctrine of the separation of powers, since it conferred upon a legislative commission authority which was judicial in character. This power was in reality the power to issue an injunction; it was not a power which could be exercised directly by Congress itself, and it was not, therefore, a power that could be given to a legislative commission.[57] It may be added that this was the argument of a man who was firmly opposed to the passage of the Federal Trade Commission Act on grounds of general policy. It is clear, however, that Senator Sutherland had not in 1914 discovered the possibilities of the terms quasi-

57. 51 Cong. Rec. 12651; for Senator Sutherland's views in greater detail, see ibid. 11602 f., 12651 f., 12806 ff., 13056.

legislative and quasi-judicial as a descriptive label for the kind of job assigned to the Federal Trade Commission. He believed that a legislative commission can constitutionally be given only the kind of power which Congress itself could directly exercise. In other words, a genuinely regulatory commission would be a constitutional impossibility.

Second, Senator Sutherland became a Justice of the Supreme Court in 1922. In the important case of *Myers* v. *United States* [58] in 1926, he is found with the majority supporting Chief Justice Taft's conclusion that the President's power to remove federal officers appointed by him with the advice and consent of the Senate is an essential part of the inherent executive power granted to the President by Article II of the Constitution. Since Mr. Justice Sutherland concurred without qualification in this case, we may assume that he either agreed, or did not feel it important to register disagreement, with Chief Justice Taft's important dictum sweeping the members of the independent regulatory commissions into the scope of the President's illimitable power of removal.

Third, in 1928 Mr. Justice Sutherland wrote the opinion of the Court in *Springer* v. *Philippine Islands*,[59] in which he adhered to the orthodox doctrine of the separation of powers. He announced not only that doctrine but also the doctrine of the separation of departments. He indicated that if a particular office or agency of government is not *in* either the legislative or judicial departments, it must of necessity be in the executive department. He appeared to rule out the constitutional possibility that an agency may straddle the lines dividing the three departments in such a way as to be an integral part of more than one.

Fourth, in 1935 Mr. Justice Sutherland again spoke for the Court in *Humphrey's Executor* v. *United States*,[60] in which it was held that Congress could validly restrict the power of the President to remove members of the Federal Trade Commission. By this time he had either forgotten or discarded all of the ideas about the commission and its powers which he had voiced in the Senate in 1914. He also discarded the dictum of Chief Justice Taft in the Myers case, with which he had tacitly

58. 272 U.S. 52 (1926).
59. *Supra,* note 52.

60. 295 U.S. 602 (1935).

agreed. He stated in the Humphrey opinion that the Federal Trade Commission is 'wholly disconnected from the executive department,' that it is an agent both of Congress and of the courts, and that it exercises quasi-legislative and quasi-judicial power. Such executive power as it has is exercised incidentally and in addition to these other powers. While he does not say in so many words that the commission is *in* the legislative branch, it seems clear that that is what he means.

Fifth, in 1937 Mr. Justice Sutherland was on the bench during the oral argument in the Shipping Board case.[61] One who was present reported the following colloquy: Mr. James W. Ryan, counsel for the shipping company, was urging upon the Court the argument, earlier summarized, that the United States Shipping Board could not constitutionally be put by executive order or by act of Congress *in* the executive branch. The Shipping Board, he argued, was not an 'executive' agency and could not be an 'executive' agency because it was not *in* the executive branch of the government.

Justice Sutherland, who had been sitting back in his chair and asking occasional questions during the course of the argument, leaned forward quickly when he heard this.

'Did you say that the Shipping Board was not in the executive branch of the government?' He spoke as though he did not believe he had heard correctly, and several other Justices smiled condescendingly at counsel as though he were making a far-fetched proposition.

'Yes, your Honor,' Mr. Ryan replied.

'What makes you think that? Where do you find any legal basis for such a conclusion?' the Justice wished to know.

'Why, in your Honor's opinion in the Humphrey case, this Court held that the Federal Trade Commission and similar regulatory agencies were not in the executive branch of the government. The Shipping Board fell within the same general category as the Federal Trade Commission and the Interstate Commerce Commission.' Mr. Ryan then proceeded to read certain portions of that opinion.

'What branch of the Government do you think the Shipping Board was in, if it was not in the executive branch?' the Justice wanted to know.

61. *Isbrandtsen-Moller Co.* v. *United States*, 300 U.S. 139 (1936).

'In the legislative branch, your Honor.'

Justice Sutherland shook his head, as though he disagreed, and seemed to be thinking the question over as the discussion went on to other points. As we have seen, the Court decided the Shipping Board case upon grounds which made it unnecessary to answer these interesting and important constitutional questions, and with Mr. Justice Sutherland's retirement from the bench we shall probably never know if he believed an independent regulatory commission must of necessity be in one of the three departments, and if so whether it is in the legislative or the executive department.

The results of our analysis thus far may be summarized: First, the doctrine of the separation of powers does not prevent substantial delegations of legislative and judicial power to the independent regulatory commissions. Second, it does not prevent the merger in them of legislative, executive, and judicial powers. Third, it does not require that a commission be in any one of the three great branches of government, or be classified as a legislative, executive, or judicial agency. Perhaps these conclusions are negative in character; but there is value merely in laying constitutional ghosts. The commissions are hybrids; but they are not for that reason unconstitutional.

II. RELATIONS OF THE COMMISSIONS TO CONGRESS, TO THE PRESIDENT, AND TO THE COURTS

THERE remains the task of analyzing the constitutional relations of the independent regulatory commissions to each of the three branches of government. What kinds of control over them may Congress, the President, and the courts exercise? What limits are there upon the scope and methods of that control?

A. CONGRESS AND THE COMMISSIONS

1. POWER TO CREATE AND TO REGULATE FUNCTIONS AND PROCEDURE

Congress has the power to create independent regulatory agencies; and in creating an office or agency, independent or not, Congress may specify exactly the duties to be exercised and the procedure to be followed. But the power of Congress does not stop here. It may exercise a rather clumsy continuing control in three ways: First, it may pass statutes or resolutions directing the commissions to pursue certain policies or take certain actions in specific situations. A notable example of this was the Hoch-Smith resolution of 1925,[62] which directed the Interstate Commerce Commission in establishing a rate structure to consider the conditions in various industries and, specifically, to fix the lowest possible lawful rates on agricultural commodities. In 1922 Congress, under pressure from organizations of commercial travelers, required the commission to issue interchangeable mileage books at 'just and reasonable rates.'[63] The commission's order complying with this statute was held void by the Supreme Court but without prejudice to the power of Congress to pass statutes directing commission action.[64] In the main, however, Congress has confined itself to the giving or taking away of powers, and has not tried to direct a commission how to use its powers in particular situations. Unless these directions are so arbitrary as to deny due process of law, there is no constitutional objection to them, no matter how bad they may be on grounds of policy. The power exercised is the same as that by which the duties of the commission were originally defined. We may assume, however, although there is no judicial authority, that an attempt by Congress to control a commission's exercise of its quasi-judicial power in a specific case would be a violation of due process of law.

Second, Congress holds the purse strings. Approval or disapproval of a commission's work may be tangibly expressed in the Congressional treatment of its budget. That this power may be used by Congress to deal with concrete situations is shown by the rider attached to the Independent Offices Appropriation bill in 1925, forbidding the use by the Federal Trade Commission for certain investigations of business activity of any of the

62. Joint Resolution of January 30, 1925, 43 Stat. at L. 801. For comment, see I. L. Sharfman, *The Interstate Commerce Commission* (1931), vol. 1, 227 ff., and E. P. Herring, *Public Administration and the Public Interest* (1936), 196.

63. Act of August 18, 1922, 42 Stat. at L. 827; cf. I. L. Sharfman, op. cit. 226.

64. *United States* v. *New York Central Railroad,* 263 U.S. 603 (1924).

funds appropriated.[65] While Congress may abuse this power, there can be no doubt that it has it.

Third, Congress may exert control over a commission by legislating its members out of office. In 1930 Congress 'reorganized' the Federal Tariff Commission by terminating by law the terms of the commissioners in office.[66] A partial change in personnel was thus brought about through a new set of Presidential appointments. In the case of agencies whose members can be removed by the President for cause only, this is the only legal way to secure a complete change in personnel at one time.

2. COMMISSIONS AS 'ARMS OF CONGRESS'—DOES THIS DESCRIBE A LEGAL RELATION?

A common formula describes the independent regulatory commissions as 'arms of Congress'; Mr. Justice Sutherland was apparently expressing the same idea when he referred to the Federal Trade Commission as 'an agency of Congress.' [67] Those who use the term seem to imply that it describes a peculiarly close relation to Congress and a peculiar degree of independence from Presidential control.

We have already seen that the commissions are arms of Congress in the sense that they do things which Congress itself might do had it the time and expert knowledge.[68] The commissions make numerous fact-finding investigations upon the basis of which Congress may legislate. Some of them have rate-making powers, which are legislative in character and could be exercised directly by Congress.[69] There is no constitutional reason why Congress itself should not by special statute issue radio station licenses or grant ship subsidies instead of giving these tasks to the Federal Communications Commission and the United States Maritime Commission.

But the regulatory commissions have functions which could not constitutionally be performed by a legislative body. Congress may define by statute an 'unfair method of competition' or an 'unfair labor practice,' but it cannot issue a cease and

65. Act of March 3, 1925, 43 Stat. at L. 1203; see Herring, op. cit. 127.
66. Act of June 17, 1930, 46 Stat. at L. 590, 696.
67. *Humphrey's Executor* v. *United States*, 295 U.S. 602, 628, 620 (1935).
68. *Supra*, 428.   69. Ibid.

desist order forbidding an individual to continue such a practice. Congress cannot do the judicial work of the Interstate Commerce Commission in reparations cases. Nor can it perform the executive work of the same commission in enforcing the Safety Appliance Acts, or the managerial work of the Maritime Commission in the handling of construction and operating subsidies for shipping. It is clear that 'arms of Congress' do things which Congress cannot do.

Finally, no task has been given to an independent regulatory commission which could not, with equal constitutional propriety, be given to an executive officer. Quasi-legislative and quasi-judicial powers have long been assigned to executive officers; indeed, over forty regulatory statutes involving the use of such powers are administered in the Department of Agriculture alone.[70] Under the Packers and Stockyards Act the Secretary of Agriculture fixes rates and suppresses unfair competitive practices. Chief Justice Hughes declared in 1936 that the Secretary was performing a 'legislative' function, since he was acting as an 'agent of Congress.'[71] Presumably, then, he too is an 'arm of Congress.'

In short, in any common-sense meaning of the term, an arm of Congress is not a distinctive designation. Every officer and agency created by Congress to carry laws into effect is an arm of Congress. If we confine the term to the independent commissions we must remember that it is at best an artificial description of and not a reason for their independent status. We cannot prove the commissions independent of the executive by calling them arms of Congress, when we mean by arms of Congress agencies which are thus independent. The term may be a synonym; it is not an argument.

3. POWER OF CONGRESS TO CONFER ON COMMISSIONS THE STATUS
OF INDEPENDENCE

An important and difficult constitutional question concerning the relation of Congress to the commissions is that of the

70. These are set out in F. F. Blachly, *Working Papers on Administrative Adjudication*, printed for the Senate Committee on the Judiciary, 75th Cong., 3d sess. (1938).

71. *Morgan* v. *United States*, 298 U.S. 468, 479 (1936).

nature and extent of Congressional power to make the commissions independent. Independence here means freedom from the normal control exercised by the President over his subordinates, not independence in the geographical sense of being outside the ten executive departments. The power of Congress to confer this status of independence is of great practical importance, and the theories upon which it rests are the subject of sharp controversy.

In the first place, Congress may constitutionally set up agencies free from the discretionary control of the President. This was established in the Humphrey case,[72] which held that such independence had been given to the Federal Trade Commission. In exercising its authority 'to make all laws necessary and proper for carrying into execution' its delegated powers, Congress enjoys wide discretion to determine the structure and legal relations of the agencies set up to do its will. It may choose, within limits later to be discussed,[73] whether to assign a regulatory job to an executive agency or to a commission independent of normal executive control. The anomalous status of the Board of Tax Appeals [74] suggests a somewhat befuddled legislative purpose to do both at the same time. The board is declared to be 'in the executive branch,' but its members can be removed by the President only for cause. Congress may find it hard to decide what to do in these matters, but once it does decide, it has full constitutional power—subject to the limitations later discussed—to confer independence or not, as it wishes.

In the second place, Congress is not required to assign quasi-legislative or quasi-judicial jobs only to bodies which are independent.[75] It is not compelled to do so either by the doctrine of the separation of powers or by the requirements of due process of law. The idea that independence is ever constitutionally necessary is refuted by the fact that the Packers and Stockyards Act is administered by a Cabinet Secretary and that that Act has been held valid. It is true that the Supreme Court has made no secret of its approval of the independent regulatory commis-

---

72. *Humphrey's Executor* v. *United States*, 295 U.S. 602, 628, 630 (1935).
73. *Infra,* 459.
74. *Supra,* 443.
75. *Supra,* 451.

sion as an instrument for the exercise of regulatory powers.[76] It has even been suggested that the rigid procedural requirements imposed on the Secretary of Agriculture in the two Morgan cases [77] may drive the administration of the Packers and Stockyards Act into the hands of an independent commission by making it impossible for a Cabinet Secretary to comply with those requirements and do anything else. But Congress need not create an independent commission to do any particular job.

The third and really important question is whether there are constitutional limitations on the power of Congress to make agencies independent, and, if so, what they are. There is again sharp difference of opinion on these questions and there is no clear answer to them in the decisions of the Supreme Court.

It is clear that Congress may constitutionally give to an officer a practical sort of independence from Presidential control by specifying in elaborate detail the nature and scope of his duties and the methods to be followed in performing them. This may be pushed to the point of making his duties purely ministerial. Such officers are not thereby made independent in the sense of being beyond the reach of the President's discretionary power of removal, but the President cannot authorize or require them to deviate from their statutory duties. This was all worked out in a persuasive dictum by Mr. Justice Thompson in the Kendall case in 1838. He said:

> . . . It by no means follows [from the vesting of executive power in the President] that every officer in every branch of . . . [an executive] department is under the exclusive direction of the President . . .
>
> There are certain political duties imposed upon many officers in the executive department, the discharge of which is under the direction of the President. But it would be an alarming doctrine that Congress cannot impose upon any executive officer any duty they may think proper, which is not repugnant to any rights secured and protected by the Constitution; and in such cases, the duty and responsibility grow out of and are subject to the control of the law, and not to the direction of the President. And this is emphatically

76. See *Schechter* v. *United States*, 295 U.S. 495, 533 (1935).

77. *Morgan* v. *United States*, 298 U.S. 468 (1936); *Morgan* v. *United States*, 304 U.S. 1 (1938). For a penetrating comment on the practical implications of these cases see A. Feller, 'Prospectus for the Further Study of Federal Administrative Law,' *Yale Law Journal*, vol. XLVII (1938), 662 ff.

the case where the duty enjoined is of a mere ministerial character . . .

To contend, that the obligation imposed on the President to see the laws faithfully executed implies a power to forbid their execution, is a novel construction of the Constitution, and entirely inadmissible.[78]

The weight of opinion (there being no judicial decision in point) is that the President cannot validly review a quasi-judicial decision reached by one of his subordinates in pursuance of statutory authority. It is clear, however, that while the President cannot change the decision if he does not like it, he may remove the executive officer.[79] This may have the practical effect of giving the President his way in the first instance. Could Congress confer discretion in matters not quasi-judicial upon a subordinate executive officer and make his exercise of that discretion final? There is no judicial answer, but experience and logic support the view that the officer's discretion could not be thus placed beyond the President's reach. There is no doubt, however, that Congress may limit the discretion of officers and thereby narrow the range of Presidential direction. The independence which results is established to protect the job rather than the officer from Presidential control.

a. *The doctrine of the Myers and Humphrey cases*

From a practical point of view the only way in which Congress can make the regulatory commissions independent is by limiting the discretionary power of the President to remove their members from office. If he can remove them at pleasure, he can control them; if he cannot remove them, he cannot control them. The only judicial answers we have to the question how far Congress can go in restricting the President's removal power are to be found in *Myers* v. *United States* [80] and *Humphrey's Executor* v. *United States*.[81] The two cases were widely, elaborately, and ably discussed.[82]

78. *Kendall* v. *United States ex rel. Stokes,* 12 Peters 524, 610 ff. (U.S. 1838).
79. *Myers* v. *United States,* 272 U.S. 52, 135 (1926).
80. 272 U.S. 52 (1926).
81. 295 U.S. 602 (1935).
82. *Cf.* W. J. Donovan and R. R. Irvine, 'The President's Power to Remove Members of the Administrative Agencies,' *Cornell Law Quarterly,* vol. xxi (1936), 215 ff., and J. Hart, *Tenure of Office under the Constitution* (1930).

In the Myers case the Supreme Court held by a six-to-three vote that Congress could not constitutionally restrict the President's power to remove a first-class postmaster appointed by him with the advice and consent of the Senate. The attempted restriction was a requirement that the Senate concur in the removal of the officer. The Court's result was supported by two main arguments. One was historical and undertook to show that long-standing governmental practice had recognized an illimitable removal power in the President. The other argument rested on the theory that the President's power of discretionary removal is an inherent part of the executive power granted to the President by Article II of the Constitution, and is also implied from the constitutional mandate to 'take care that the laws be faithfully executed.' If the removal power comes from the Constitution directly, then it cannot be taken away or pruned down by Congress without violating the doctrine of the separation of powers. Chief Justice Taft had been President of the United States, and from the vantage point of this administrative experience indulged in some rather sweeping dicta in the Myers opinion. He asserted that Congress was without authority to restrict the President's removal power, not merely in the case of postmasters and similar executive officers, but even in the case of the quasi-judicial commissions.[83] It seems probable that in his opinion the only officers who could be placed by Congress beyond the reach of the President's discretionary removal were judicial officers—i.e. judges of territorial and legislative courts.[84]

In *Humphrey's Executor* v. *United States* [85] the Court unanimously discarded Chief Justice Taft's dictum in the Myers case and held that Congress could validly forbid the President to remove a member of the Federal Trade Commission except for the causes stated in the statute. Mr. Justice Sutherland declared that the question whether the President's power of removal can be limited by Congress depends 'upon the character of the office,' and the rule of the Myers case was held to apply only to 'purely executive officers.' He recognized that in respect of 'the character of the officer' there was a great difference be-

83. *Myers* v. *United States,* 272 U.S. 52, 135 (1926).
84. Ibid. at 154 ff.
85. 295 U.S. 602, 631 (1935).

tween a postmaster and a member of the Federal Trade Commission and he therefore added:

> To the extent that, between the decision in the Myers case, which sustains the unrestrictable power of the President to remove purely executive officers, and our present decision that such power does not extend to an office such as that here involved, there shall remain a field of doubt, we leave such cases as may fall within it for future consideration and determination as they may arise.[86]

The narrow holding of the Humphrey case is that Congress may validly protect members of the Federal Trade Commission from Presidential removal except for causes stated in the statute. The scope of the removal power depends upon the character of the office. What characteristics does the Federal Trade Commission have which distinguish it from a postmastership? According to Mr. Justice Sutherland there appear to be four. First, the commission 'occupies no place in the executive department . . . and exercises no part of the executive power vested by the Constitution in the President.' Second, it acts 'in part quasi-legislatively and in part quasi-judicially' in administering the legislative standard of 'unfair methods of competition.' Third, it is a 'legislative agency' in making investigations, and reports thereon to Congress. Fourth, it acts as 'an agency of the judiciary' in its 'master in chancery' relation to the courts. In contrast to this, a postmaster is a 'purely executive' officer and the Myers case therefore holds no more than that Congress cannot limit the President's power to remove an officer who is 'purely executive.'

The opinion is extremely unsatisfactory. It is loosely reasoned and employs terms which are not clearly defined. The proposition that the commission 'occupies no place in the executive department . . . and exercises no part of the executive power vested by the Constitution in the President' is unsupported and begs the major question at issue. The opinion does not indicate whether all four of the characteristics stated above are necessary in order to protect the commission from discretionary removal by the President. Would the fact that it acts 'quasi-legislatively and quasi-judicially' be enough, or must it also be an agency of Congress and the courts, or of either of them? When Mr. Jus-

86. Ibid. at 632.

tice Sutherland commented upon the nature of 'executive officers' and 'executive power' he fell into hopeless ambiguity.
He said:

. . . A postmaster is an executive officer restricted to the performance of executive functions. He is charged with no duty at all
related to either the legislative or judicial power. The actual decision in the Myers case finds support in the theory that such an officer is merely one of the units in the executive department and
hence inherently subject to the exclusive and illimitable power of
removal by the chief executive, whose subordinate and aid he is.[87]

This does not tell us whether the postmaster is an executive
officer because of the nature of his job or because he is one of
the 'units in the executive department.' If we assume that he is
an executive officer because he exercises executive power, what
do we mean by executive power? There is further confusion on
this point. The opinion states that the Federal Trade Commission 'exercises no part of the executive power vested by the
Constitution in the President.' Later, in speaking of the duties
of the Federal Trade Commission which are not quasi-legislative or quasi-judicial, it says: 'To the extent that it exercises
any executive function—as distinguished from executive power
in the constitutional sense—it does so' as an incident to its other
powers. This seems to suggest that there are two kinds of executive power—the constitutional variety given by Article II to
the President, and 'executive functions,' which are something
different. It is inferred that the exercise by an officer of 'executive functions' would not be incompatible with the status of
independence, while the exercise of executive power 'in the
constitutional sense' would be. But neither variety of executive
power is defined or explained.

The Humphrey decision left one important problem unsettled, since the issue was not involved. What is the status of the
removal power in respect to a commission which not only 'acts
quasi-legislatively and quasi-judicially' but also has important
executive powers? The problem in the Humphrey case was
simplified because the Federal Trade Commission has no substantial executive duties which are not an integral part of its
quasi-judicial work. The Interstate Commerce Commission,
however, carries on the executive task of enforcing the Safety

87. Ibid. at 627.

Appliance Acts, a task certainly not 'incidental' to the quasi-judicial job of rate making. The commission is obviously not purely executive in the sense in which the Humphrey opinion uses the term; neither is it purely quasi-legislative and quasi-judicial. This is true of most of the regulatory commissions and this means that their constitutional status was not determined by the Humphrey case.

One cannot predict just where the Supreme Court will place the line dividing agencies which may be protected from discretionary removal from those which may not. It is probable that the line will be a practical one, in the drawing of which the doctrine of the separation of powers will weigh less than considerations of policy. The following conclusions are ventured regarding the present status of the commissions in this respect.

First, the President's illimitable removal power is not confined by the Humphrey case to purely executive officers. To hold this would have been pure dictum. What Mr. Justice Sutherland does say is that the Myers decision, on its facts, could not go beyond upholding the President's power to remove a purely executive officer. He did not hold, and could not hold, that the power either stopped there or went further. To insist, indeed, that Congress can make independent all officers and agencies which are not purely executive would permit the virtual destruction of the President's effective control of the executive branch. Few officers and agencies perform duties which are purely executive, and Congress can easily deprive a purely executive officer of that status by giving him some quasi-legislative or quasi-judicial task. The sound rule is this: If the *major* or *primary* functions of an agency are executive in nature, the President retains full power of removal, even though the agency has in addition quasi-legislative and quasi-judicial powers which, taken by themselves, would justify a status of independence under the Humphrey rule.

Second, the Humphrey opinion makes the quasi-legislative and quasi-judicial work of the Federal Trade Commission the basic reason for giving the commissioners immunity from executive removal. Mr. Justice Sutherland used both the term 'quasi-legislative' and the term 'quasi-judicial' to describe the commission's task of administering the legislative standard of 'unfair methods of competition.' The function is more commonly called merely quasi-judicial. We may conclude that the constitutional justification for independence is the performance of quasi-judicial duties, and that Congress, in its discretion, may set up independent agencies for the purpose of doing such work.

Third, the writer believes that executive tasks cannot constitutionally be given to independent agencies unless they are clearly incidental to the quasi-judicial functions which justify independence. This seems to be clearly implied in the language of the Humphrey opinion [88] and to be required by the logic of the Myers decision. Quasi-judicial functions can be and are given to executive officers. Congress is not obliged to place quasi-judicial tasks in the hands of independent agencies. But the Constitution requires that executive functions be performed under direction of the President, and the Myers case holds that Congress may not withdraw them from that direction by limiting the President's power to remove the officers who perform them. It follows that Congress may not properly give to the independent commissions functions which, separately considered, could not validly be made the exclusive job of an independent agency. Any other rule permits the crippling of the President's executive power and loads the quasi-judicial independent bodies with constitutional contraband.

Congress has not followed this rule. It has not hesitated to give to the independent commissions any jobs which could be conveniently dumped upon them. The Interstate Commerce Commission has the executive task of enforcing the Safety Appliance Acts. No one claims that this work is quasi-judicial or that a separate independent body could be set up for its exclusive administration. The Maritime Commission has important managerial and executive duties in respect to construction, operating subsidies, and the leasing of government-owned vessels. It is believed that the giving of major executive duties to commissions which lie out of reach of the President's discretionary removal is unconstitutional. A decision to this effect would revive the President's removal power and abolish the

88. Mr. Justice Sutherland, as already mentioned, took pains to indicate that such executive functions as the Federal Trade Commission possesses are 'incidental to its quasi-legislative and quasi-judicial' duties. 295 U.S. 602, 628 (1935).

independence of the agencies. Congress could meet this situation by relieving the commissions of work which is not quasi-judicial or reasonably incidental to quasi-judicial work, and by giving the executive jobs to executive officers it would further sound administration.

b. *Can Congress make a commission completely independent by taking away the President's power to remove for cause?*

Congress has never created a completely independent regulatory commission. The independence of these commissions has consisted in immunity from the President's discretionary removal power; the President has always been given power to remove members for causes stated in the statute. Is it constitutionally necessary to do so? Could Congress validly give to the Interstate Commerce Commission the status which the Budget and Accounting Act gives to the Comptroller General and the Assistant Comptroller General? This status is described as follows:

. . . The Comptroller General or the Assistant Comptroller General may be removed at any time by joint resolution of Congress after notice and hearing, when, in the judgment of Congress, the Comptroller General or Assistant Comptroller General has become permanently incapacitated or has been inefficient, or guilty of neglect of duty, or of malfeasance in office, or of any felony or conduct involving moral turpitude, and for no other cause and in no other manner except by impeachment.[89]

89. 31 U.S.C. § 43 (1934). On June 4, 1920, President Wilson vetoed the Budget and Accounting bill because he believed these removal provisions were unconstitutional. He said:
The section referred to not only forbids the Executive to remove these officers but undertakes to empower the Congress by a concurrent resolution to remove an officer appointed by the President with the advice and consent of the Senate. I can find in the Constitution no warrant for the exercise of this power by the Congress. There is certainly no express authority conferred and I am unable to see that authority for the exercise of this power is implied in any express grant of power. On the contrary, I think its exercise is clearly negatived by section 2 of Article II. That section . . . provides that the Congress may by law vest the appointment of such inferior officers as they think proper in the President alone, in the courts of law, or in the heads of departments . . . Regarding as I do the power of removal from office as an essential incident to the appointing power, I can not escape the conclusion that the vesting of this power of removal in the Congress is unconstitutional and therefore I am unable to approve the bill.—H. Doc. 805, 66th Cong., 2d sess. (1920).

There is no judicial decision on this point. It can be plausibly argued that the President cannot be deprived of the power to remove for cause any officer not engaged in legislative or judicial work, since to do so would prevent him from taking 'care that the laws be faithfully executed.' Strong reasons of policy have led Congress to allow the President to remove members of the independent commissions for cause. The only alternatives are to legislate them out of office or to impeach them; but both these methods are cumbersome and neither provides an effective way of enforcing even minimum standards of efficiency and honesty. The opinion in the Humphrey case is careful to speak of the independence of the Federal Trade Commission in terms of freedom from the President's *discretionary* removal power, and assumes throughout that the power to remove for cause is a necessary and appropriate Presidential power.[90]

B. THE PRESIDENT AND THE COMMISSIONS

1. THE PRESIDENT'S POWER TO APPOINT COMMISSIONERS

The President has power to appoint members of the regulatory commissions. Such members are 'officers of the United States' within the meaning of the clause of Article II, which gives the President power with the advice and consent of the Senate to appoint ambassadors, judges, and so forth, 'and all other officers of the United States, whose appointments are not herein otherwise provided for, and which shall be established.' Congress may give to the President alone, to the heads of departments, or to the courts of law, the power to appoint 'such inferior officers as they think proper.'[91] Conceivably, then, an independent commission could be appointed by a Cabinet Secretary, though for practical reasons this is not likely to occur. But Congress itself cannot constitutionally appoint 'an officer of the United States.' The Supreme Court so held in *United States* v. *Ferreira* in 1852.[92]

May Congress validly specify by statute qualifications which officers must have, or disqualifications which they may not

90. *Infra*, 463 ff.
91. Art. II § 2.
92. 13 Howard 40, 51 (U.S. 1852).

have? In a letter to the Senate in 1822, President Monroe strongly contended that:

In filling original vacancies—that is, offices newly created—it is my opinion, as a general principle, that Congress has no right under the Constitution to impose any restraint by law on the power granted to the President so as to prevent his making a free selection of proper persons for these offices from the whole body of his fellow-citizens.[93]

Whatever plausibility this theory may have had, it has long since passed into the discard. It seems well established that Congress may specify qualifications and disqualifications for office so long as it does not violate the provision of Article VI that 'no religious test shall ever be required as a qualification to any office or public trust under the United States.' In creating the regulatory commissions Congress has set up tests which the President must reckon with in appointing their members.[94] The requirements commonly stated are those of partisanship, citizenship, residence in a geographical area, technical or expert fitness, and the like. Persons having a financial interest in the business or industry to be regulated are usually ineligible. In one case an officer who has served one term is made ineligible to another term.

Congress continues to set up these requirements; and those which are specific, such as the disqualification for financial interest, or the requirement of citizenship, could probably be enforced in the courts, although there is no case on this point.[95]

93. There was disagreement on this in Monroe's Cabinet. See the following statement by John Quincy Adams, then Secretary of State:
Received a notice from the President for a cabinet meeting at his house at 11 o'clock. President [Monroe] has concluded to send his message only to Senate. He [Monroe] proposed to nominate again Colonel Towson and Colonel Gadsden after they had been rejected by the Senate . . .
Crawford makes it a constitutional question whether Congress can limit the selection of persons to whom the President's right of nomination shall be confined for appointment to office; for instance, whether a law could confine the nomination of a judge or Attorney-General to persons learned in the law; commissioners of the navy to captains in the naval service, and the like. The President entertains the same opinion, and has expressed it in the message. Mr. Thompson, the Secretary of the Navy, maintained the contrary to which I also inclined.—Entry in diary dated April 12, 1822, *Memoirs of J. Q. Adams* (1874), vol. II, 488.

94. See chart at end of book.

95. It seems to be implied, however, in *United States* v. *Le Baron*, 19 Howard 73, 78 (U.S. 1856).

Some of the others, such as the requirement that a commissioner be appointed because of special fitness for the job, are to be regarded as pious admonitions rather than legally enforceable requirements.

These statutory qualifications still leave the President much latitude in making his appointments. President Coolidge attempted to employ the rather dubious practice of using the power to appoint a commissioner, or to withhold such appointment, as currency with which to purchase a discretionary removal power denied by statute. This was done by demanding as the price of an appointment to the Federal Tariff Commission an undated letter of resignation which the President was free to use at any time without public explanation if he wished to do so. The request was refused and the appointment was withheld.[96] Whatever the general propriety of such a course may be, there is no legal recourse against it.

2. THE PRESIDENT'S POWER TO REMOVE COMMISSIONERS

We have touched upon some aspects of the President's power to remove members of independent regulatory commissions in discussing the power of Congress to limit it; [97] but there are other aspects of the President's removal power which merit attention.

In the first place, the President has discretionary power to remove officers whom he appoints if there is no Congressional restriction upon that power. This was established in *Ex parte Hennen* in 1839.[98] The President's power to remove is implied from his power to appoint as well as from the grant of executive power in Article II, and therefore reaches, in the absence of statutory restriction, even officers not 'purely executive' within the rule of the Myers case. Therefore, if Congress wishes to protect a regulatory commission from the President's discretionary removal power, it must do so by positive legislation. In the case of several commissions—the Federal Power Commission, the Securities and Exchange Commission, and the

96. D. J. Lewis had been appointed to the Tariff Commission by President Wilson. The undated resignation was requested as a condition to his reappointment in 1925. See Herring, *supra*, note 62, op. cit. 96.

97. *Supra*, 454 ff.

98. 13 Peters 230 (U.S. 1839).

Federal Communications Commission—there is no limitation on the removal power and the President can, accordingly, dismiss any or all members of these commissions at his pleasure.[99]

The President is authorized to appoint the chairmen of some commissions. In no such case is there statutory limitation on his power to remove the chairman from his chairmanship, although in some cases he can remove him from his commissionership only for cause. The President may thus make changes in the chairmanship at his discretion. This power is important from the point of view of practical administration; it does not extend, however, to chairmen who are selected by the commissions themselves.

In the second place, the power to remove for specified causes is a much more powerful implement in the hands of the President than is commonly realized. In the Acts creating the regulatory commissions, the causes for which the President may remove members, where any are specified, are inefficiency, neglect of duty, incompetence, misconduct, or malfeasance in office. The Acts differ in this respect for no logical reason.[100] The Federal Reserve Act authorizes the President to remove members of the Federal Reserve Board 'for cause' without defining what 'cause' is.

The typical provision that members of the Interstate Commerce Commission may be removed by the President for 'inefficiency, neglect of duty, or malfeasance in office' gives the President, it is believed, the following authority over the commission: First, under penalty of removal, he may exact reasonable efficiency and absolute integrity. His authority should extend to collective as well as individual inefficiency. Incompetent administrative management, negligence or tardiness in the performance of duties, susceptibility to improper pressure, laxness in the enforcement of punitive statutes, usurpation of authority, dishonesty, or official misconduct would, any one of them, justify the removal of a single commissioner or any number of commissioners to whom responsibility for such derelictions could be brought home. In short, if the commission is

99. For criticism of this doctrine see A. Larson, 'Has the President an Inherent Power of Removal of his Non-executive Appointees?' *Tennessee Law Review*, vol. xvi (1940), 259 f.

100. See chart at end of book.

not doing its job competently and honestly, the President has full power to 'clean house,' to 'reorganize' the commission under the authority of the removal clause quoted above. Second, the President can force an independent regulatory commission to comply with executive orders of general application unless Congress clearly indicates that such orders should not apply. These executive orders relate to a multitude of matters which affect the general efficiency of the government. To put an extreme case, if Congress established an independent commission with no statutory direction as to the recruiting and tenure of its staff of employees, the President might by executive order under authority of the Civil Service Act extend the provisions of that Act to the commission's staff. If Congress did not wish such executive orders to be extended to the commission it could, of course, exempt it by statute. Otherwise, the refusal of the commission to obey the President's executive order would constitute neglect of duty or misconduct, which would justify the removal of the commissioners from office. Finally, an independent commission may be required by law to perform duties at the direction of the President. This is not common. The Federal Trade Commission Act, however, declares it to be the duty of the commission 'upon the direction of the President or either house of Congress to investigate and report the facts relating to any alleged violations of the anti-trust acts by any corporation.' Clearly a refusal by the commissioners to undertake an investigation at the direction of the President would justify their removal from office for 'neglect of duty.'

It is highly desirable that Congress give serious attention to the exact statement of the causes for which members of the independent commissions may be removed by the President. This Congress has never done. By a more careful and precise statement of causes for removal, Congress could define more sharply the President's authority, could with complete safety extend that authority into areas where it may at present be in doubt, and in this way could ensure a higher degree of administrative efficiency upon the part of the commissions without jeopardizing their independence in the performance of their quasi-judicial work.

Under what procedural limitations, if any, does the President exercise his removal power? It is clear that there are no such restrictions on discretionary removal; and this includes removal of members of those commissions in respect to which the removal power is not limited by statute. The President need not have any reasons for such removal; if he has reasons they need not be good ones; and he need not give the officer any opportunity to be heard or to answer charges. Neither explanation nor courtesy is required. When President John Adams removed his Secretary of State, Timothy Pickering, in 1800, he accomplished the job in a four-line note: 'Sir: Divers causes and considerations essential to the administration of the government, in my judgment requiring a change in the department of state, you are hereby discharged from any further service as Secretary of State. John Adams.' [101]

In several cases Congress has not only stated the causes for which a commissioner may be removed, but has also required notice and hearing. Thus, a member of the National Labor Relations Board 'may be removed by the President, upon notice and hearing, for neglect of duty or malfeasance in office, but for no other cause.' [102] It is clear that if Congress can constitutionally limit removal to stated causes it can prescribe a reasonable procedure to insure compliance with the limitation. It is unnecessary, however, for Congress to do this. The Supreme Court has indicated that notice and hearing are necessary in such cases even when not required by statute. This has also been the uniform holding of the state courts.[103] This requirement appears to be grounded in due process of law. In *Shurtleff* v. *United States* [104] the Court held that the President's removal of Shurtleff without giving him notice and hearing proved that the removal was not made for any of the causes of removal stated in the statute. The doctrine seems eminently sound. If the President removes an officer upon a charge of dishonesty, the officer seems clearly to be denied due process of law if he is not notified of the charge and given an opportunity to defend his character against it. Legitimate executive

101. O. Pickering and C. W. Upham, *Life and Times of Timothy Pickering* (1875), 488.

102. 29 U.S.C.A. § 153 (a) (Supp. 1938).

103. See F. J. Goodnow, *Principles of the Administrative Law of the United States* (1905), 313 and cases cited.

104. 189 U.S. 311 (1903).

discretion is not impaired by compelling the President to follow this fair procedure.

C. THE COMMISSIONS AND THE COURTS

1. THE COMMISSIONS AS AGENTS OF THE COURTS

In the Humphrey case, Mr. Justice Sutherland referred to
the Federal Trade Commission as 'an agency of the judiciary.' [105] He had in mind the section of the Federal Trade Commission Act which provides that, in suits brought under the
anti-trust laws, the courts may refer to the Federal Trade
Commission as a master in chancery the working out, under
procedure designated by the court, of appropriate decrees of
dissolution or otherwise. This provision loomed large in the
debates on the Federal Trade Commission bill. It was believed
that this 'master in chancery' function would be one of the
most important responsibilities of the proposed commission.
It was, in fact, a major argument for creating a commission.
It was widely felt that the task of 'dissolving' the Standard Oil
Company and the American Tobacco Company after the government had won its important suits against them in 1911 had
been badly bungled. The courts were not competent to deal
with these complex tasks and therefore the Federal Trade Commission, an independent and permanent body of 'experts,'
should be called in to aid the courts in the highly technical
work of formulating decrees of dissolution.

Perhaps the commission could have rendered important and
valuable service to the courts under this section, but it has not
been allowed to try. In one suit, the district court ordered a
plan of dissolution to be prepared by the respondent and filed
with the Federal Trade Commission, which, acting as a master
in chancery, was to submit a plan of dissolution to the court.
Intervening litigation prevented the commission from doing
this, and the final decree was formulated by another method.[106]
In two other instances matters were referred to the commission

105. *Humphrey's Executor* v. *United States,* 295 U.S. 602, 628 (1935).
106. *United States* v. *Corn Products Refining Co.,* 234 Fed. 964 (S.D.N.Y.
1916). For comment on the commission's activity and the final disposition of
the case see *Statutes and Decisions Pertaining to the Federal Trade Commission,
1914-1929* (1930), 791.

for investigation and report, one by a circuit court of appeals [107] and one under an agreement between the Attorney General and certain paper manufacturers.[108] These are the only cases in which the Federal Trade Commission has acted as 'master in chancery.' [109] No constitutional problems appear to be involved.

2. JUDICIAL REVIEW OF COMMISSIONS

We turn now to the important problem of the judicial review of the work of the independent regulatory commissions. To what extent is such review constitutionally required? By what methods is it exercised? What is its scope? Judicial review of the work of the commissions does not differ from review of the work of other administrative officers doing similar jobs.

a. *Constitutional necessity for judicial review*

Judicial review of the independent regulatory commissions is constitutionally necessary because the commissions are 'regulatory.' They impinge upon private conduct and the use of private property. In this respect they differ from the numerous agencies which lend on give away public money or dispense government privileges. An individual cannot demand on constitutional grounds a judicial scrutiny of the work of an agency which gives him or denies him something to which he has no right at all. But when the government, through an independent commission or otherwise, licenses a business, fixes rates or charges, polices business conduct in the interests of fair competition, or forbids 'unfair labor practices,' the due process clause of the Fifth Amendment guarantees basic fairness in substance and procedure. It requires further that there be an opportunity to present these questions of fairness to the courts for review. This•is sometimes spoken of as 'the rule of law,'

107. *Federal Trade Commission v. Balme*, 23 Fed. (2d) 615 (C.C.A. 2d 1928). See *Statutes and Decisions Pertaining to the Federal Trade Commission, 1914-1929* (1930), 676.

108. Under this agreement the commission was made an arbitrator to decide on a fair selling price for newsprint paper sold by the ten manufacturers in question. See *Ann. Rept. of the FTC for year ending June 30, 1918*, 4 f., 18.

109. I am indebted to Dr. Francis Walker, former Chief Economist of the Federal Trade Commission, for the information on this point.

the time-honored principle that a man is entitled to have his legal rights determined by a court. He is entitled, to use another venerable phrase, to his 'day in court' in which he may question any official conduct which he thinks impairs his legal rights. The rule of law (now assimilated to due process of law) does not require that the citizen's legal rights shall be dealt with only in the courts. Nor does it require that a court must do over again the work of the regulatory commission which fixes a rate or enjoins an unfair business practice. It does require that the courts at some point have the opportunity to determine whether the rights of parties have been fairly decided by agencies which have not exceeded their legal powers. In the Minnesota rate cases,[110] in 1890, the Supreme Court held that the question whether a rate established by a railroad commission was reasonable was a judicial question upon which due process of law required an opportunity for a court review. The courts have adhered to this doctrine and have applied it to the quasi-judicial work of all of the federal regulatory commissions.

b. *Methods of judicial review*

Professor Stason has conveniently classified the methods of judicial review of regulatory administrative action into three categories.[111] First, there is review provided for by statute. Second, review may be exercised by the common law procedures of *certiorari, mandamus,* and prohibition. Third, it may come about through collateral attack in actions for damages against officers or suits for injunctions to restrain unlawful official conduct. This analysis is general, and comprehends both state and federal judicial review. In the case of the federal commissions, procedure for judicial review is provided by statute.[112]

110. *Chicago, Milwaukee and St. Paul Railway* v. *Minnesota,* 134 U.S. 418 (1890).
111. E. B. Stason, *Cases and Other Materials on Administrative Tribunals* (1937), Ch. 9.
112. F. F. Blachly, *supra,* note 70, op. cit. *passim.*

c. Scope of judicial review

Assuming that some judicial review of the work of the regulatory commissions is required, what is the scope of that review?
Does any part of the work of a commission lie beyond the
scrutiny of the courts? Can a commission decide any matters
with finality? These are important problems both in constitutional law and in public administration. We may group our
analysis of them into two divisions and deal first with the judicial review of commission findings or decisions; and second,
with the judicial review of commission methods and procedure.

(1) *Judicial review of commission findings or conclusions.*
In the first place, the commissions make important decisions
in the field of policy. These involve the exercise of administrative discretion, and the courts will not review them on their
merits. In fact, the constitutional courts cannot review the
exercise of administrative discretion, since to do so would be
an exercise of non-judicial power in violation of the doctrine
of the separation of powers. When the Radio Commission was
created, it was authorized *inter alia* to grant broadcasting station
licenses and to renew them 'where public convenience, interest
or necessity will be served thereby.' An applicant for a license
or a renewal thereof could appeal to the Court of Appeals of
the District of Columbia if the commission ruled against him.
This court was authorized to take additional evidence if it
deemed it proper to do so and to 'hear, review and determine
the appeal upon said record and evidence, and [to] alter or
revise the decision appealed from and enter such judgment
as it may deem just.' [113] In *Federal Radio Commission* v. *General Electric Company* [114] the Supreme Court refused to review
a decision of the Court of Appeals of the District deciding an
appeal from the Radio Commission. The function of the commission in granting or renewing licenses was a 'purely administrative function' and 'the provision for appeals to the Court of
Appeals does no more than make that court a superior or
revising agency in the same field.' The Court of Appeals of the
District is a 'legislative court' to the extent that non-judicial

113. Act of February 23, 1927, 44 Stat. at L. 1162.
114. 281 U.S. 464 (1930).

duties may validly be imposed upon it; [115] but its non-judicial duties cannot be reviewed by the Supreme Court. Congress had therefore to limit the appeal from commission orders to questions of law in order to make possible their ultimate review in the Supreme Court.[116] Congress may, of course, provide for a review of commission findings of policy either by an appellate administrative body or by a legislative court, but administrative review is not to be confused with judicial review.

In the second place, conclusions of law made by a commission must be open to review by the courts. No administrative agency can decide finally a question of law. Any statutory attempt to permit this would deny due process of law. A commission must in the first instance interpret the statute under which it works; but that interpretation is always subject to judicial review. The questions of law on which the independent regulatory commissions rule are sometimes constitutional, sometimes statutory, sometimes a mixture of both. A notable case in which the Interstate Commerce Commission made a vitally important decision on a question of law, both constitutional and statutory, was the Shreveport case.[117] Acting under a statutory mandate to eliminate rate discriminations against interstate commerce, the commission ordered a Texas railroad to cease charging certain freight rates fixed by state authority and applicable to purely intrastate traffic. This was because these rates were so low that they resulted in serious discrimination against competing interstate traffic carried at higher rates deemed reasonable by the commission. In issuing this order the commission had to conclude first that the statute permitted it, and secondly that it did not exceed the constitutional power of Congress over interstate commerce by interfering with commerce which was admittedly intrastate. Clearly these questions of law could not be finally decided by the commission. They were appealed first to the Commerce Court and thence to the Supreme Court.

115. *O'Donoghue* v. *United States,* 289 U.S. 516 (1933). It is, however, in other respects a constitutional court.

116. By Act of July 1, 1930, 46 Stat. at L. 844, Congress limited the review by the Court of Appeals to 'questions of law' and provided that findings of fact if supported by substantial evidence should be conclusive. In *Federal Radio Commission* v. *Nelson Bros. Bond and Mortgage Co.,* 289 U.S. 266 (1933), the Supreme Court held that the reviewing of commission action by the Court of Appeals had thereby been made judicial in nature.

117. *Houston, E. and W. T. Ry.* v. *United States,* 234 U.S. 342 (1914).

Both tribunals sustained the commission. To allow a commission to determine questions of law with finality would permit it to determine its own jurisdiction and power and to impinge upon the legal rights of individuals without allowing them recourse to the courts in accordance with the 'rule of law.'

It is not always easy to draw the line between a question of law and a question of policy to be settled by administrative discretion. In close cases the courts have usually regarded the questions involved as questions of law. The Federal Trade Commission Act authorized the commission to discover and to suppress by cease and desist orders 'unfair methods of competition in commerce.' The members of Congress in general thought they were giving the commission power to develop an administrative law in this field by defining in the light of their expert knowledge and experience just what concrete acts constituted 'unfair methods of competition.' Some held a narrower view of the power given. The commission assumed that it had broad discretion to define unfair methods of competition and that in doing so it was acting for Congress, which had originally contemplated defining a long list of such practices in the statute. The Supreme Court, however, in the Gratz case [118] in 1920, put an end to this interpretation by announcing that 'the words, "unfair method of competition," are not defined by the statute . . . It is for the courts, not the Commission, ultimately to determine as a matter of law what they include.' Thus a question of policy was converted into a question of law.

In the third place, the independent regulatory commissions make almost countless findings of 'fact.' These are necessary in order that the commission may know when and how to exercise its regulatory powers. One of the most cogent reasons for setting up a commission is to provide an expert body of officers to 'find facts' in fields so extensive and so technical as to be beyond the capacity of Congress or the courts. The fact-finding responsibilities of the Interstate Commerce Commission are the chief justification for its staff of some 2,500 persons. These tasks could be assigned to the courts only at the risk of judicial paralysis. A difficult problem in the field of administrative law is that of determining how far administrative findings of fact may be made final—i.e. the extent to which due process of law

118. *Federal Trade Commission* v. *Gratz*, 253 U.S. 421 (1920).

requires judicial review of such findings. The difficulties are increased by the fact that the line between a question of law and a question of fact is often uncertain, and that in their legal significance not all 'facts' found by regulatory commissions are of the same variety.

There is, first, what is sometimes called a 'constitutional fact.' This is a fact which must be determined in order to decide a constitutional issue. The simplest example is the 'fact' of the value of railroad property upon which reasonable railroad rates must be based. To meet the test of due process of law a railroad rate must not be confiscatory. It is confiscatory if it does not permit the carrier to earn a 'fair return' upon a 'fair valuation' of the property used for the purposes of transportation.[119] What constitutes fair return is a question of law upon which the courts must have the last word. What is the fair valuation of the property of a railroad is a question of fact. But it is a fact the correct determination of which is essential to the protection of the respective rights of the carrier and the public. Accordingly, the courts have held that there must be judicial review of administrative findings of constitutional facts.[120] To allow the Interstate Commerce Commission to value railroad property with finality would deny due process of law.

There is a second category of 'jurisdictional facts.' These are facts upon the existence of which rests the commission's jurisdiction to act. They are illustrated by the case of *Crowell* v. *Benson.*[121] Leaving out of account certain unique and complicating factors, the case was this: The United States Employees' Compensation Commission has jurisdiction under the Longshoremen's Act[122] to award compensation for injuries arising within the limits of federal admiralty jurisdiction. It was disputed whether an injured workman was employed at the time of injury, and the commission decided that he was. The Court held that the fact of employment was a jurisdictional fact. If the man was employed the commission had jurisdiction; if he was not employed it did not. Accordingly, due process of law required a judicial review of the commission's finding of this

119. *Smyth* v. *Ames,* 169 U.S. 466 (1898).
120. *Ohio Valley Water Co.* v. *Ben Avon Borough,* 253 U.S. 287 (1920); *Prentis* v. *Atlantic Coast Line,* 211 U.S. 210, 228 (1908).
121. 285 U.S. 22 (1932).
122. Act of March 4, 1927, 44 Stat. at L. 1424.

fact. The Court went further and held that the Court must not only review the finding on the fact, but that it must try the issue of fact *de novo*. We may conclude that judicial review of commission findings of jurisdictional facts is required on constitutional grounds.[123]

Third, we may group together without specific label all other kinds of 'facts.' The Interstate Commerce Commission finds as a fact that a carrier has allowed a rebate to a shipper. The Federal Trade Commission finds that a manufacturer has made a price agreement which obstructs fair competition. These are mere facts, neither constitutional nor jurisdictional, and if they are determined by fair procedure and supported by evidence they are ordinarily beyond the reach of judicial review. The independent commissions carry on a steadily increasing volume of fact finding which is not subject to judicial review on the merits.

Judicial review of fact finding by the commissions has taken two forms. First, the courts, barring explicit statutory restriction, may try the issue of fact *de novo* on appeal. In the early days the courts looked with suspicion and jealousy upon the powers given to the regulatory commissions, and Congress was by no means sure of its authority to place any limits upon the judicial review of commission fact finding. Prior to the Hepburn Act of 1906, the laborious and expert 'findings' of the Interstate Commerce Commission counted for little or nothing in the judicial review of the commission's work. The courts did over again the commission's job, and the prestige of the commission was destroyed by the fact that there was no point or issue upon which its decision was final. Under the Hepburn Act a second mode of review gradually emerged; and by 1912 the Supreme Court was following the rule that orders of the commission would be set aside only for mistakes of law, arbitrary action, or lack of substantial evidence in support of fact determinations. At present there is no regulatory commission whose findings of fact are not treated as conclusive if supported by substantial evidence, and the courts will not themselves hear

123. The whole problem is discussed in J. Dickinson, '*Crowell* v. *Benson*; Judicial Review of Administrative Determination of Questions of "Constitutional Fact,"' *University of Pennsylvania Law Review*, vol. LXXX (1932), 1055. See also F. R. Black, 'The "Jurisdictional Fact" Theory and Administrative Finality,' *Cornell Law Quarterly*, vol. XXII (1937), 349, 515.

new evidence upon review. Congress has in most cases required by law that this measure of respect shall be accorded to the findings of the commissions; but even in the absence of statute the courts now follow this rule in order to avoid doing over again the commissions' most exacting work.

(2) *Judicial review of commission methods and procedure.* Judicial scrutiny extends not merely to the conclusions of the commissions but also to their methods of reaching those conclusions. Their procedure must, in the first place, meet the requirements of due process of law. Just what these are will vary somewhat with the nature of the power exercised or the rights regulated. There is always an essential minimum comprising notice and hearing and a variety of procedural steps deemed necessary to a fair and open determination of the rights involved. We need not discuss these elements in detail. A commission must, in the second place, follow all statutory mandates as to procedure. These may be elaborate and may go beyond the requirements of due process of law. In some cases Congress allows the commission to formulate its own rules of procedure. In all cases, however, the commission must follow whatever statutory directions there are, and the courts will review its procedure to make sure that it has done so. In the third place, where a commission is authorized by Congress to set up its own rules of procedure, it will be required by the courts to adhere to them until they are modified in the regular way. It will not be permitted to improvise other procedure. Such rules, issued under statutory authorization, acquire the force of law.[124] The commission can change the procedure, therefore, only by first changing the rules.

Judicial scrutiny of commission procedure goes beyond examination of minimum compliance with technical rules. It extends to the essential fairness of the entire proceeding. As it is possible to give a person a grossly unfair trial without deviating from any of the technical requirements of criminal procedure, so a regulatory commission may act unfairly and at the same time abide by every formal procedural requirement. Unfairness may take the form of the suppression of evidence, or

124. *United States ex rel. Denney* v. *Callahan*, 54 App. D.C. 61, 294 Fed. 992 (1924), holds that the rules of the Board of Education of the District of Columbia have the force of law and must, therefore, be followed by the board.

any mark of bias. The courts will set aside as a denial of due process of law a result reached through a procedure technically correct but nevertheless characterized by prejudice or unfairness.[125]

3. UNSOLVED PROBLEMS CONCERNING THE RANGE OF JUDICIAL CONTROL OF INDEPENDENT REGULATORY COMMISSIONS

The range of judicial control over the commissions is not governed by a set of fixed rules. A minimum of judicial supervision is required by the Constitution, but since this is defined by the courts themselves it is by no means immutable. Beyond this there are substantial elements of flexibility in the extent of judicial control. This has important effects upon the administrative process, and there is value in studying the factors which tend to enlarge or contract it.

The courts control in large measure the range of their supervisory authority by keeping flexible and in some cases vague the principles under which it is exercised. For example, the courts hold that findings of 'jurisdictional facts' must be reviewed. But close analysis discloses no precise line between jurisdictional facts and other facts which commissions must determine. In *Crowell v. Benson* [126] the fact of the employment relation was held to be jurisdictional. But most of the other facts which the commission determines can be looked upon as jurisdictional if the courts wish to regard them so.[127] Furthermore, we have seen that the courts pass judgment upon the essential fairness of the procedure used by a commission. If the court gains an impression of good faith and scrupulous adherence to sound procedural rules, it maintains an attitude of aloofness, confining its review to the constitutional or statutory minimum. But if the subtle evidences of fairness and impartiality are lacking and the court finds that evidence has been carelessly or prejudicially handled, it may extend its supervision to the point of virtually doing over again the administrative tasks. This was the Supreme Court's attitude toward the Fed-

125. *Chin Yow* v. *United States,* 208 U.S. 8 (1908); *Kwock Jan Fat* v. *White,* 253 U.S. 465 (1920).
126. 285 U.S. 22 (1932).
127. Mr. Justice Brandeis emphasized this in his dissenting opinion in *Crowell v. Benson,* 285 U.S. 22, 73 f. (1932).

eral Trade Commission during its earlier years, when the Court felt that the findings of the commission supporting its orders were not clear and fair deductions from the evidence but were rationalizations of conclusions reached when the complaints charging unfair competition were filed.[128] The courts have not been reluctant to exercise such control as they deem essential to the full protection of the rights of those affected by the regulatory process. Their point of view is expressed in the oft-quoted comment of Mr. Justice Harlan:

> . . . The courts have rarely, if ever, felt themselves so restrained by technical rules that they could not find some remedy, consistent with the law, for acts, whether done by the government or by individual persons, that violated . . . justice or were hostile to the . . . principles devised for the protection of the essential rights of property.[129]

The practical implications of this judicial attitude are clear. The courts will not stand by and see a job of regulation so bungled by a commission or administrative officer that private rights are inadequately protected. They will inject themselves into the picture and assume revisory and controlling power to the extent necessary to protect such rights. If we wish to confine to a minimum the participation of the courts in the administrative process, we must see that that process in the hands of the commissions is so perfected as to safeguard private rights without judicial intrusion. If the commissions earn judicial respect they will be given a wide range of immunity from judicial interference. If they do not command that respect they will be 'reviewed' practically to the point of being superseded by the courts.

Our constitutional findings may be summarized as follows:

First, the doctrine of the separation of powers, as judicially developed, does not prevent the creation of hybrid governmental agencies, (a) in which legislative, executive, and judicial powers are merged, (b) to which legislative powers are delegated and judicial powers granted, (c) which straddle the boundary lines of the three branches of government and which cannot be classified as clearly legislative, executive, or judicial.

128. G. C. Henderson, *The Federal Trade Commission* (1925), Ch. 3.
129. *Monongahela Bridge Co.* v. *United States,* 216 U.S. 177, 195 (1910).

Second, Congress may, but need not, place the performance of quasi-judicial and quasi-legislative functions beyond the reach of the President's executive control through his discretionary removal power.

Third, Congress cannot constitutionally withdraw from the President's executive control agencies to which it gives executive duties, duties which could not be made the exclusive work of an agency independent of Presidential control.

Fourth, the President retains considerable authority to 'take care that the laws be faithfully executed' in the power to remove for cause the members of agencies which have been protected against his discretionary removal.

Fifth, a minimum range of judicial supervision of the independent commissions is required by the Constitution. The courts extend this control when they feel that the protection of private rights demands it, but sound commission organization and procedure tend to keep it at the minimum.

VII

AMERICAN STATE EXPERIENCE WITH
REGULATORY COMMISSIONS

IT is not possible in the scope of this book to make any detailed study of the regulation of business in the American states. A monograph could be written upon each regulatory agency in each state. But without attempting this, it still seems desirable to include some conclusions from the more striking phases of state experience and to point out what appear to be the more established trends. It will be helpful to know whether the states have tended to follow the models set in our federal regulatory agencies; and it will be even more useful to know what new techniques and policies in the regulatory field have been wrought out in what Mr. Justice Holmes once referred to as the 'insulated chambers afforded by the several states.'

It is possible to include in this study at least a minimum comment upon state experience in the regulatory field based on a survey of the leading regulatory agencies in twelve selected states made by Professor James W. Fesler of the University of North Carolina. These states were chosen to include the major types of regulatory policy and technique. The states studied were California, Illinois, Massachusetts, Mississippi, New York, North Carolina, North Dakota, Ohio, Oregon, Pennsylvania, Texas, and Wisconsin. In each state Professor Fesler studied the agencies which regulate the following interests: the professions; public utilities; banks and investments; insurance; conditions of labor; boxing, wrestling, and horse racing; and control of liquor. The results of these studies are being published piecemeal. The following comments are based almost exclusively upon the material which Professor Fesler collected, much of which has not yet been printed.[1]

One could hardly expect state and federal experience in the regulatory field to run closely parallel. There are many points in common; but differences in approach, in policy, and in method are numerous and important, and these differences must be kept in mind if intelligent comparisons are to be made. They may be summarized as follows:

First, the administrative framework of the federal government is, in theory at least, an integrated hierarchy heading up in the President of the United States. Although independent agencies have multiplied in recent years, they are still exceptions to the rule, deviations from normal organizational theory. In contrast to this, state governments are in the main made up of many disconnected executive and administrative units bound together by no hierarchical principle and usually owing responsibility to no one except the electorate. Thus the state of Oklahoma has nearly a dozen and a half statewide administrative and executive officers elected by the people. The tradition, therefore, for setting up entirely separate and independent agencies has ordinarily been much stronger than any competing pressure to place these bodies under centralized executive control.

Second, it follows from what has just been said that in the states the status of independence, in the sense in which that term is being used in this study, is assigned promiscuously, and often illogically, to new units of government. There is, in short, little connection between the status of independence and the character of the job to be done. In the federal government, on the other hand, independence has usually been reserved for those bodies which carry on important regulatory functions. The sponsors of national agencies have had to assume a burden of proof in securing for them the status of independence— although it must be admitted that this burden of proof has not always been fully met, nor has independence always been granted for the same reasons.

Third, the federal commissions, with few exceptions, have

1. Cf. the following articles by Professor Fesler: 'Independence of State Regulatory Agencies,' *American Political Science Review*, vol. xxxiv (1940), 935 ff.; 'The Independence of State Utility Commissions,' *Journal of Politics*, vol. ii (1940), 367 ff. and vol. iii (1941), 42 ff.

large and well-organized staffs. This is, of course, chiefly the result of growth. The Interstate Commerce Commission, with its staff of over 2,500 persons, is larger than the entire government of some of the smaller states. State commissions, on the other hand, have usually been kept small. Their staffs often number only ten or twelve persons. This is more than a purely statistical difference. The size of the federal organizations not only permits, but often demands, different methods and internal arrangements, as well as greater differentiation in the assignment of functions.

Fourth, there are differences between Congress and the state legislatures which affect the problem under review. Congress sits more frequently and for longer periods. Many state legislatures meet only every other year for two or three months at a time. Presidential leadership over Congress is normally much more effective and continuous than any leadership which a state governor is likely to exercise over a state legislature. These are factors which may have a bearing upon the status which may be given to a body set up to exercise regulatory power. They are certainly factors which condition the relations which such agencies have with the legislature or the governor.

Fifth, federal regulatory commissioners are usually men of experience, often the ablest officers in the entire government; they are well paid, and they command the respect of Congress. There have been few exceptions. Such a generalization cannot be made, however, about the personnel of the average state regulatory agency. Here we find men of smaller capacity, frequently chosen for considerations of purest partisanship. These differences have an important influence in shaping the relations of the regulatory agencies to the other branches of government and in determining how far and in what ways their discretion ought to be limited.

A final difference lies in the degree of intimacy of contact between federal and state regulatory bodies and the ordinary citizen. Few of us have much to do with the Interstate Commerce Commission, the Federal Trade Commission, the Federal Reserve Board, or the other federal regulatory bodies. The individual is affected by what these agencies do, but he is not acutely aware of it. In the states, however, the regulatory agencies deal with many problems of intimate concern to the consumer. They fix the prices he pays for commodities and services, they regulate the conditions under which he works if he is an employee, the conditions under which he may enter and carry on a profession, and similar personal concerns. They make him ever conscious that the government is at his door. This results in forms of pressure upon the state regulatory bodies which differ in kind and intensity from those to which the federal commissions are subjected. These pressures may shape the character of the state agencies, the scope of their powers, and the methods which they are permitted to use.

Apart from these differences between the federal and state regulatory agencies, the state commissions differ sharply from each other in the kind of jobs they do, the broad policies they embody, and the methods they use. The regulatory tasks assigned to them range all the way from the regulation of a prize fight to the fixing of railroad rates. Some of these state bodies exercise police control of the narrowest sort, dealing with matters directly affecting public health, safety, or morals; others administer the most important forms of economic control. Some supervise forms of business which enjoy no assured protection from the state, such as the liquor business and racing; here the regulatory power sometimes approaches pure discretion. In contrast to this, other state commissions regulate traditionally entrenched interests which enjoy well-protected constitutional rights. There is wide range in the intrinsic importance of the regulatory tasks. Some affect few people and might not seriously be missed; others are clearly indispensable. In some cases those subject to regulation are well organized and articulate and can exert political pressure upon the policy and method of regulation; in other cases the 'regulatees' are few and scattered and enjoy no political influence.

With this background in mind we may summarize some of the conclusions which Professor Fesler's investigations appear to justify. We shall therefore take up, first, the problem of the independence of state regulatory agencies, second, the questions relating to the possible segregation of their functions, and finally, problems of organization and personnel.

I. THE INDEPENDENCE OF THE STATE REGULATORY AGENCIES

THE problem of the independence of state regulatory agencies is much more confusing than the parallel problem in the federal field. There are various ways of defining the term independence. It may mean nothing more than detachment from the normal hierarchical structure of the executive branch; or it may mean freedom from political control or the influence of special interest groups. There is general agreement that our federal independent commissions ought to be wholly impartial and treat with even-handed justice and neutrality the conflicting interests brought before them, even though there might be reasonable disagreement whether they should be independent of the executive branch; whereas concerning the state regulatory agencies, many of which deal with matters of intimate concern to our citizens, there is sharp difference of opinion whether these agencies ought to be impartial and wholly neutral. The independence of the federal commissions is a device to induce, if not to guarantee, an impartial quasi-judicial administration of regulatory power; but the meaning of independence is ambiguous as soon as we enter the state field and doubt the desirability of having regulatory agencies which are quasi-judicially impartial.

In regard to the state public utility commissions, perhaps the most important state regulatory bodies, there are three distinct views on the desirability of making them judicialized, impartial, and therefore independent agencies. The first view is that this detachment and independence is a denial of the main purpose for which the commissions were set up. They were created to give the consumer fearless and aggressive protection against the monopolistic oppression of the utilities. They were created to carry on a crusade and to assist the exploited. To allow them to assume the role of the impartial judge is to deprive the consumer of this much needed protection. A second view is that the utility commissions must be wholly impartial and must maintain a judicial attitude in resolving the conflicts of interest which arise between the utilities and the consuming public;

if they are to make decisions affecting the property rights of the companies, it is grossly unfair to have them biased by a special loyalty to the consumer. A third theory is that the function of the regulatory agency is not one of prosecution or adjudication, but merely one of fact finding. It is the duty of the commission to discover the facts with respect to public utility rates and services, how these relate to the legislative policies governing these matters, and what conclusions may thus be drawn and appropriately embodied in a decision or rule. Those holding this view feel that the commissions should enjoy independence in the sense of freedom from all possible outside pressures.

Each of these views can be defended with a good deal of cogency. It is quite clear, however, that each, if effectively implemented, may lead to a different policy with respect to the structure, the powers, the procedures, and the intergovernmental relations of the regulatory commission. We have, in short, something which approaches a dilemma. The consumer stands in need of aggressive protection for his interests and believes that the state utility commissions ought to give it to him. The utilities feel that they also are entitled to protection, at least to the exent of being regulated by an impartial quasi-judicial authority. Can these conflicting interests be reconciled, and if so, how? Numerous answers have been suggested and most of them point in the direction of some kind of division of labor or segregation of functions under which the tasks of protecting the consumer and performing the functions of a judge shall not rest upon the same shoulders. We shall comment on these proposals for segregation at a later point.[2]

To what extent are the state regulatory commissions independent of the governor's influence? It is not easy to generalize upon this point. Any answer must be hedged about with many reservations. In many American states important administrative agencies, including the regulatory commissions, occupy positions of essential equality with that of the governor. The governor is merely one of a number of more or less co-equal divisions of the executive branch. Where centralization has proceeded to the point of making the governor the head of an executive hierarchy, the relation of the regulatory agency to the

2. *Infra*, 487 ff.

governor does not differ sharply from the relation of the federal commissions to the President. There are some states in
which the governor appoints these agencies, removes their members at his discretion, and makes them, so far as he is able, a
part of his political machine. In these states he dominates
actually and potentially their policies and behavior. In other
cases the state constitutions go to considerable pains to see that
the governor has no actual authority over the regulatory commissions. In a few states he does not even appoint the members,
since they are chosen by popular election; and in many cases
the power of removal, which is the governor's only effective
instrument of control, is so closely limited as to give him no
real power over these bodies. Which of these situations prevails does not seem to depend upon any commonly recognized
principle, but must be explained in terms of the history of
state administrative development, or, in some cases, in terms
of pure chance. Certainly no policy or theory emerges here
which has any useful bearing upon the problem of the status
of the federal commissions.

Independence of state regulatory bodies from outside pressures has been a matter of concern in a number of states. This
is probably true because these pressures are perhaps more
numerous and powerful in the states than in the federal government, and the chances of their being effective to the detri-
ment of the public welfare are correspondingly greater. One
method of insulating the commissions from these pressures is
to have them popularly elected, and there are a number of
states in which this policy prevails. But such a policy made a
much stronger appeal to students of government thirty years
ago than it does now. Experience with the results of popular election under long-ballot conditions has forced a reluctant cynicism even upon many who have firmly believed that
the people ought by direct participation to manage the affairs
of government. There is little hope that the electorate of a
state can be brought to know or care enough about the issues
involved in the selection of the officers we are discussing to
make possible an intelligent and independent choice. Popular
election is most likely to result in the popular ratification of
prearranged party slates.

Another means of warding off sinister pressures on regulatory bodies is to have these bodies chosen by the courts. Theoretically this ought to assure complete objectivity and result in the selection of commissioners without reference to political or economic affiliations. Actually the objections to such a program are substantial. To draw the courts into the processes of state policy and administration is likely to result in serious repercussions upon the courts themselves, without any adequately compensating advantages to the other branches of government. There is no strong body of opinion supporting this proposal.

This leaves the states with essentially the same facilities that are available to the federal government to protect regulatory agencies from outside pressure. These do not go much beyond an effort to guarantee the high quality of commission personnel and to disqualify for membership on regulatory bodies persons whose business interests would be likely to render them biased.

A method that has been utilized in a number of states to protect regulatory commissions from political pressure has received little attention in the federal field. This is the policy of making the commissions independent of state legislative and gubernatorial control by giving them complete financial independence. This may be done by placing the whole cost of regulation upon the shoulders of those who are regulated. Either general or special assessments are levied upon the utilities, and the funds thus created make it unnecessary for the public utility commission to go back to the legislature for financial support. This plan commands considerable support. It has been used with apparent success in a number of cases in Great Britain, and many students of business regulation in this country regard it as sound and practicable. However, this proposal is also sharply criticized. It is urged that such a device either directly or indirectly limits the aggressiveness of the regulatory body and creates the danger that those subject to regulation will come to enjoy too much power in determining the policy and methods of control. Here, again, generalizations are unsafe, since these criticisms have far greater force when applied to some forms of regulation than to others.

We may conclude, then, that independence in state regulatory agencies is a different thing and has a different significance from the independence of the federal commissions. When Congress creates an independent agency, it thereby serves notice that it is creating something out of the ordinary. It indicates that it wishes it let alone. The creation of an independent state agency, on the other hand, may have no special significance. In the case of most federal agencies the status of independence is a major factor influencing the commission's attitude and policies. In the states it may be only a minor factor. But in state government and federal government alike, the problem of the independence of regulatory bodies is closely tied in with the equally difficult problem of segregation of commission functions and the problem of commission personnel.

II. SEGREGATION OF FUNCTIONS IN STATE REGULATORY COMMISSIONS

IN approaching the question whether there ought to be some segregation of the varying phases of the task of regulation, we find two separate issues involved. The first arises, as we have seen,[3] from the dual role assigned to the major state regulatory agencies, in that they are charged with the aggressive protection of consumer interests and also with the impartial adjudication of conflicting rights. This is the familiar issue of independence presented by the so-called prosecutor-judge merger, the evil genius of governmental regulation of business, common to state and nation. The states, however, have been more versatile in seeking a solution to this enigma than has the federal government. From the state experience studied by Professor Fesler, five fairly distinct methods of dealing with this prosecutor-judge combination have been evolved. These may be briefly mentioned:

One plan to segregate the regulatory functions is to remove from the regulatory commissions, and here we are speaking chiefly of the public utility commissions, the duty of protecting consumer interests. This duty is taken over by the municipalities in whose areas the utilities operate. These local governments serve as prosecutors of wrongdoing and protectors of the exploited, thus leaving to the public utility commission merely the role of adjudication. It is not necessary to try to appraise

3. *Supra,* 483 f.

this plan. Perhaps the strongest criticism of it is that it decentralizes the responsibility for the protection of the public interest by giving it to local government officials who may or may not rise adequately to the challenge.

A second proposal would divide the commissions into two separate but connected bodies, one of which would hear cases and issue quasi-judicial rules and orders, while the other would take over the tasks of consumer protection and other administrative duties. This proposal has been discussed but not actually adopted. It embodies the general principle of the plan presented by the Brownlow committee.[4]

A third device would create an internal segregation of duties within the staff of a closely unified commission. There would be a special prosecuting section to deal with the earlier phases of the regulatory task, and a separate review section which would take these cases, pass upon them, and give to the full commission objective advice. There are many ways in which the details of this internal rearrangement could be worked out.

A fourth plan would assign to the commission the task of protecting consumer interests even though this still left in the same hands both prosecuting and quasi-judicial duties, but it would establish a special administrative court to which all commission decisions and rulings might go.

Finally, the problem has been dealt with by creating a separate office of 'consumers' counsel' to take over the task of conducting prosecutions in the consumers' interest. This officer ferrets out and prosecutes exploitation carried on by the utilities. This leaves the commission free from any responsibility to assume the role of an advocate, while at the same time the adequate protection of all interests is provided for. This scheme has been tried in a number of states with highly satisfactory results. One of its obvious advantages is the psychological one of focusing attention upon the protection of consumer interests and at the same time dissociating in the public mind the prosecuting function from that of the quasi-judicial.

These various proposals need not be evaluated here. They are significant as evidence that the states are concerning themselves with the problem and that state experiments may be tried in the field of segregation which may add to our wisdom

4. *Infra,* 709 ff.

and experience. Yet state public utilities commissioners themselves appear to have little use for any of the plans for the segregation of commission functions. In 1937 a committee of the National Association of Railroad and Utilities Commissioners circulated to the membership of that body a questionnaire asking for an expression of opinion upon four proposals for such segregation [5] which conformed roughly to those outlined above. The results of the inquiry showed scant approval of any of these plans and a strong consensus of opinion that such attempts at segregation would be unworkable and produce no useful results.

The discussion of this problem in many states will remain purely academic for a long time to come because of the meager staffs with which many of the state commissions are provided. A body may be too small to be divisible, and this is true of some state commissions.

Another problem of segregation of functions, or division of labor, in the state regulatory agencies does not relate to the prosecutor-judge merger of powers but concerns the efficient management of the general administrative duties assigned to the commissions. What devices are most likely to assure efficient administrative management in disposing of the work of the commissions? Is the board as a unit to direct the entire volume of business? If not, what delegations of power or divisions of responsibility will produce the most efficient results? There has been some experimentation in this area. Some states have given attention to it, while in others the problem has been dealt with in a wholly inadvertent manner. The schemes which have been worked out for some segregation of administrative responsibility have usually been built up around the position and relationship of the commission chairman or some full-time executive officer. It is not feasible to try to review the diversified practices of even twelve states in this connection. The state of Wisconsin, however, has for many years been a pioneer in dealing with problems of business regulation and methods of public administration, and in its regulatory bodies has tried out a number of techniques to effect segregation of administrative responsibility. The more conspicuous of these

5. National Association of Railroad and Utilities Commissioners, *Report of the Committee on Progress on Public Utility Regulations* (1938).

devices may be mentioned to indicate how the problem may be approached.

By one scheme, Wisconsin has assigned regulatory duties to a single commissioner. The Commissioner of Insurance holds office for a four-year term and exercises legislative, administrative, and quasi-judicial power. There is, obviously, no segregation here. This method is analogous to the many situations in the federal government in which regulatory duties are given to executive officers.

A second Wisconsin method is to create a part-time commission with a part-time secretary or administrator to manage its administrative work. This scheme is clearly suitable for the handling of the relatively less important and burdensome jobs of regulation. It prevails in the State Athletic Commission and the State of Wisconsin Aeronautic Board. These part-time boards must, of course, have an office, but the administrative duties do not justify the employment of a well-paid and full-time executive.

In the third place, there are part-time commissions which carry on their administrative responsibilities with a full-time executive. In these cases there is a clear attempt to segregate administrative duties from the quasi-judicial and rule-making phases of regulation. The commission selects and may remove the executive officer. The plan is like that followed in organizing a number of the British regulatory and operating boards; it is also similar in principle to the commission-manager plan of city government. With some differences in structural details, this scheme is embodied in the State Conservation Commission, in the State Board of Health, and in the Department of Agriculture and Markets.

A fourth device used in Wisconsin is to create a full-time commission without any separate executive officer. This principle is followed in the State Banking Department, the Grain and Warehouse Commission, and the Wisconsin Labor Relations Board. Here the duties of regulation are fairly consistently sub-legislative and quasi-judicial in character. While there is a delegation of internal administrative duties, the members of the commission carry on its work as a body, meeting daily or with substantial regularity, without the overshadowing influence of any chairman or director set apart from the others.

Finally, Wisconsin uses the plan of creating a full-time regulatory commission with a full-time and well-paid executive officer. This arrangement exists in the Wisconsin Trade Practice Department, the Public Service Commission, and the Industrial Commission. The arrangement in the Public Service Commission is unique and interesting. The commission has three members appointed by the governor and senate for six-year overlapping terms. The commission appoints a director who receives a good salary and serves for an indefinite term. He may be removed by the commission 'at pleasure,' provided a public hearing is held, but the commission's decision to remove is final; and he is also removable by the governor for inefficiency or misconduct. He is thus under a dual responsibility for the competent and satisfactory handling of his office.

There are doubtless many variations of these five types of administrative organization; these are, however, sufficient to indicate that some effort is being made, in Wisconsin at least, to adjust the form of the regulatory commission to the differing tasks of regulation.

III. ORGANIZATION AND STRUCTURE

FROM what has been said in discussing the problems of commission independence and the segregation of commission functions, it is apparent that the American states have followed widely varied patterns in determining the structure and organization of the regulatory commissions. Some of this variety has been due to conscious experimentation and some of it to chance. It would be neither useful nor feasible to catalogue all these institutional variations, but some of the unique ones may be mentioned as well as some which may be safely called typical.

A. METHODS OF SELECTION

There is more opportunity for variety in the methods of selecting members of the state regulatory agencies than exists in the federal government, where the Constitution requires appointment by the President and the Senate. The federal example is, however, followed in a large majority of the states with respect to most of the state boards and commissions. The governor, either with or without confirmation by the council or senate, appoints the members of the commissions. As we have seen, the members of some state regulatory bodies are elected by popular vote in those states in which the sound principle of the short ballot has not yet taken hold. There are some cases in which these bodies are composed of ex-officio members drawn from the executive branch of the state government, but the experience with ex-officio commissions in the states runs parallel to federal experience with the same device. It has worked well in neither area. Busy state or federal officers cannot efficiently take on, and effectively administer, an important regulatory task; and the attempt to make them do so usually results in placing the major work of the commission in the hands of a secretary or other subordinate official who comes to exercise wide powers without effective responsibility. The consensus of opinion favors the policy of appointment of commission members by the governor with the consent of the state senate.

B. QUALIFICATIONS AND DISQUALIFICATIONS OF MEMBERS

State experience throws little light on the problem of what statutory qualifications, if any, should be required of the members of regulatory bodies. Statutory qualifications are almost completely lacking in the states, even for boards and commissions charged with the handling of highly technical tasks. Of the twelve states studied by Professor Fesler the state of Wisconsin alone sets up the special qualification of familiarity with railroad affairs for one member of its Public Service Commission. Yet even there this requirement has become practically meaningless, since the functions of the commission have so changed that state railroad matters are of relatively negligible importance. In seeking reasons for not requiring commission members to be experts, it could be suggested that there is no common agreement on just what kind of expertness is desirable, how to define it in a statute, or how to get it once it is defined. Many students of public administration reject entirely the idea that regulatory bodies ought to be made up of technical experts. They feel that the members should be broadly trained, well educated, and of wide experience. They should employ experts, but they need not be experts. It is probably true also that in many an American state the old-fashioned idea that one citizen is as good as another, that anyone is presumably competent to hold any public office, has had an influence in keeping special statutory qualifications for commission membership out of the picture. The result is that the qualifications of these officers lie in the discretion of the appointing authority. It should be noted that the requirement of bipartisanship, so commonly imposed upon the federal commissions, is followed only very occasionally by the states.

Nor is there is any novel state practice in the matter of statutory disqualifications. They are not very numerous, and the few that do exist follow the generally accepted principle of barring from membership on a regulatory board persons whose business or financial affiliations are such as to create a presumption of bias.

C. Representation of Group Interests

We have seen that in the federal government there has been a steady refusal to organize regulatory commissions upon the principle of definite representation of group interests. With regard to at least some of the state regulatory bodies, however, the problem of group representation remains an active issue. About half of the state labor boards have members drawn from labor, from the employers, and from the public. In spite of unhappy experience with the earlier federal labor boards thus constructed, there is a sharp difference of opinion among the state administrators on the wisdom of the arrangement.

There has been state experimentation with a somewhat analogous scheme. This requires the governor, in appointing the members of regulatory bodies, to choose them from panels of nominees presented either by interest groups or by outside organizations having no definite interests at stake. Four members of the Banking Commission in New York represent the banking interests and are nominated to the governor by a system of proportional representation in the banking fraternity. In Pennsylvania six members of the Banking Commission are chosen by the governor from a panel of fifteen named by the bankers of the state. Recently a legislative committee in Pennsylvania proposed that the Commissioner of Insurance be chosen by the governor from a list of names submitted by the insurance companies of the state. Although this proposal did not become law, the governor, thinking well of the idea, decided to give it a trial, and invited the companies to nominate a commissioner. They were unable, however, to agree, and took so long in reaching any conclusion that the governor in disgust ignored them and made his own appointment. A commission set up in New York in 1933 to study the control of alcoholic beverages had an interesting plan for the selection of the proposed liquor board. Three nominations each were to be made by the executive committee of the New York State Bar Association, the Council of the Medical Society of the State of New York, the Executive Committee of the Chamber of Commerce of the State of New York, and the Council of the New York State Federation of Labor. From these twelve nominees the governor was to select five commissioners, one of whom must be a woman. And the *reductio ad absurdum* of this general principle appears in the Wisconsin statute creating a three-man Grain and Warehouse Commission, the members to be chosen by the governor. No statutory qualifications are mentioned, but the governor is required to get recommendations from the governor of North Dakota, the governor of New York, and the Board of Trade of the City of Superior. This weird requirement appears to have had no discernible effect upon the personnel of the commission, which Professor Fesler describes as being pretty definitely political in character.

D. REMOVAL OF COMMISSIONERS

There are a great many more ways of getting state commissioners out of office than prevail in the case of federal commissioners. In some states there are no special provisions regarding the removal of these officers; their removal is therefore governed by whatever general provisions the state constitution contains. Where commissioners are popularly elected, they can of course be retired from office by the simple process of failure to re-elect them. They could be made subject to popular recall, but this system does not prevail in any of the states included in Professor Fesler's inquiry. In a few states the commissioners may be removed by the governor at his discretion. This arrangement is usually limited to commissions dealing with liquor regulation and the like rather than to those regulating major economic interests. North Dakota, for example, provides that the Liquor Control Board may be removed by the governor 'at any time and without cause.'

More common is the policy of vesting the power of removal in the governor with restrictions upon it similar to those limiting the President's power to remove independent commissioners. Removal is here limited to causes stated in the statute, usually misconduct or incompetence. Some states, such as New York and Wisconsin, set up careful procedural limitations upon the governor's removal power, and require the filing of charges and the holding of a public hearing. In some states the courts will determine in the last analysis whether the removal is in conformity with the law. In Oregon, however, it is provided that the governor may remove members of the Public Utilities Commission for cause after notice, hearing, the filing of charges, and the preparation of a record of all the proceedings, but there may be no review by the courts.

Removal of officers by impeachment, which is possible in some states, requires no comment. The brutal device of removing the members of a commission by so-called 'ripper' legislation, a law abolishing a commission and replacing it with another, has by no means been wholly discredited. It was employed in Pennsylvania in 1935 in the case of the Public Utilities Commission and in North Carolina in 1933. There is little to be said for it, except that it works.

The device of requiring legislative, or perhaps only senatorial, participation in the removal of an officer is unsatisfactory. It makes the removal power practically unworkable where legislatures hold only biennial sessions, and it results in stalemates between the governor and the legislature in particular cases.

E. Compensation of Members

State experience with the paying of their regulatory boards and commissions is not particularly illuminating. The salaries appear to range from $1,600 a year to $15,000, depending upon the size and wealth of the state, the intrinsic importance of the job, and other collateral matters. No useful generalizations are possible. Low salaries are likely to prevail in those states where political tradition still looks askance upon paying any public servant more than the average industrious citizen can earn by hard work. The salary level of the commissions follows the salary level of the state government as a whole, and usually no special attention is paid to the value or demands of a particular job.

F. Terms and Tenure of Commissioners

State commissioners generally hold office for statutory terms ranging from two to ten years. These terms do not appear to vary according to the kind of regulatory function. There is almost universal adherence to the principle of overlapping terms for the members of a commission, and in some states this is particularly desirable since the record of long-drawn-out delays in the handling of public utility cases makes a sudden and complete turnover in membership highly undesirable. Professor Fesler found that in some states the average tenure of commissioners was greater than the statutory term, indicating the prevalence of reappointment.

G. The Office of Chairman

The chairmen of the regulatory commissions in the states studied are appointed in most cases by the governor. The power of the governor over the commissions is thus either actually or potentially increased. The status of the chairman and his relations to the governor on the one hand and to the commission on the other have received little careful consideration. The chairman sometimes receives a higher salary than his colleagues. Frequently he has special executive or administrative duties, though this is not invariably true. There is often a separate executive officer or director in addition. In many situations, the chairman, if he possesses the ability and character, may make himself a dominating figure in the particular field of regulation.

H. COMMISSION STAFFS

The problems of staff differ a good deal in the state regulation area from those in the federal government. It has already been mentioned that, in the main, state commissions have small staffs. This limits to some extent what can be done with the commission in the way of segregation of functions or division of labor. Small staffs result in many cases from legislative desire to keep down the cost of state government; in some cases they are due to influences which do not desire too aggressive enforcement of state regulatory policy.

Civil service regulations exist in only a minority of the states, and the presence or absence of effective civil service rules has an intimate bearing upon the staff problems of the regulatory bodies. Pennsylvania has no civil service law; but in that state and certain others something has been achieved in the way of satisfactory personnel traditions without the aid of definite statutes. It is Professor Fesler's judgment that in the case of the public service commissions, at any rate, there has grown up a sound tradition in the matter of the tenure of the expert staffs. The turnover has not been great in this field, even in times of depression. Politics and low salaries are, of course, serious obstacles to sound personnel development, but in the larger and wealthier states something approaching a career service is growing up in the staffs of some of the major boards and commissions. The commissions are always subject to outside competition in retaining their staff experts. In some cases, however, public utility companies have entered into gentlemen's agreements not to raid the commissions, thereby eliminating one of the important difficulties with which federal administrative agencies are confronted. The state commissions lose their good men to the federal government and to other states perhaps more often than to private business.

Several conclusions may be drawn from this brief account of state experience with regulatory commissions. First, there is greater variety in the structure, procedures, and relations of the state commissions than in those of the federal commissions. Second, this greater variety has not been due usually to conscious experimentation; much of it has been haphazard and fortuitous rather than planned. Third, it seems probable that controlled experiments with regulatory commission problems are more likely to be carried on with useful results in the federal government than in the states. Interest in the federal commissions is much keener than in the state commissions, and abler people are studying these problems in Washington than in the states. The states seem destined to follow rather than to lead. Finally, the conclusion is necessary that in comparison with the vitally important problem of securing personnel of high calibre, the problems of structure and procedure of the state commissions seem minor. The latter have intrinsic importance and should not be neglected; yet with really able and honest men in control even very mediocre administrative machinery seems to run with relative smoothness. Without such men, no amount of modern streamlining gives sound and efficient administration.

VIII

BRITISH EXPERIENCE IN THE
REGULATION OF BUSINESS

THE following pages trace briefly the experience of the British government in handling the tasks of economic regulation which are analogous to those assigned to our independent regulatory commissions. The object of this summary is to discover whether British experience can aid us in the wise solution of our own problems of government regulation. Can we learn from British experience anything useful about the legitimate limits of government control, the structure of regulatory agencies and their methods of procedure, the principles of political responsibility affecting them, and the devices for recruiting suitable personnel? The reason for such a comparative study of different ways of doing the same thing is not that we could blindly copy British methods, even if we desired to do so. In this country it is a reasonable assumption that a governmental device or procedure which works well in New York would probably work well also in Ohio or California; but even the most superficial student of English and American government knows that the mere fact that a governmental method works well in England creates no presumption that it could be successfully transplanted to the United States. We should be alert, however, to appraise the methods used in England to attain the results we ourselves desire, in the hope that we may avoid British mistakes and capitalize British successes. This is the purpose and the point of view of the present study of English regulatory policy and method.

At the outset of such a comparative study it is at once clear that the areas of economic regulation are not the same in England as in the United States. We subject stock exchanges and the issuance of securities to drastic and detailed administrative control. There is no similar governmental control in England, and stock promoters are subject only to the severe English criminal laws punishing misrepresentation and fraud. There is nothing in England comparable to our Federal Reserve System with the rigorous control it exercises over American banking. And while the British Board of Trade has a narrow police control over those business practices that ignore the stop signs of the law, there is no British trade commission or any agency with the disciplinary power over business conduct exercised by the Federal Trade Commission. Nor does any British agency possess the broad and drastic powers of the National Labor Relations Board, although the principle of collective bargaining has been firmly established in England for many years.

On the other side of the picture, British collectivism has occupied a number of fields which we still leave to regulated private enterprise. Radio broadcasting in England is a government monopoly administered by the British Broadcasting Corporation and financed from taxes laid on receiving sets. The generation and wholesale distribution of electric power is likewise a government monopoly functioning through the 'Grid.' Very recently the British overseas airways were bought by the government and are now operated by it. Much more direct and drastic regulation of prices and production has been set up in England in the fields of agriculture, fisheries, and cotton spinning than we have set up even under our recent legislation affecting these and similar industries. Thus it is clear that there is nothing inherent in these various types of economic enterprise which inexorably requires that they be placed under government control. The appropriateness of such control grows out of the peculiar problems, traditions, and needs of each country. It will aid a clearer understanding of the significance of British experience in the regulatory field to appraise briefly the more important factors which have conditioned the scope and methods of control of economic enterprise.

I. THE BACKGROUND OF BRITISH REGULATION AND CONTROL

A. Factors Influencing the Field of Regulation

MANY of the factors which have tended to control the areas within which British economic regulation either penetrates or does not penetrate are essentially indigenous to England. In the first place, the doctrine of *laissez faire* had its origin and early growth with English economic and political theorists; and, since it was congenial to the entrepreneurs of a developing industrial economy, it made a lasting impression on the British mind. While it has been weakened by the advance of collectivism and regulatory policy, it still retains a strong hold on British thinking. The careful observer will note one clear manifestation of the continued vitality of the doctrine of *laissez faire* in what appears to be a sharp repugnance to the idea of drastic governmental regulation of a business or economic interest which is still left in the hands of its owners. British policy on this point seems to fluctuate between two sharply contrasted extremes. On the one hand there is the very limited and highly judicialized type of regulation illustrated by the control of the Railway Rates Tribunal over the privately owned British railways—a minimum exercise of governmental power. On the other hand there is the outright government ownership or leasing of important enterprises and their direct operation by the government, as in the British Broadcasting Corporation's monopoly of radio transmission, the Central Electricity Board's ownership and management of the Grid, and the ownership and operation of London's local transportation facilities by the London Passenger Transport Board. But in between these two widely differing forms of governmental control there is little or nothing. British policy looks askance at the degree of governmental control to which American railroads are subjected at the hands of the Interstate Commerce Commission, or which the Securities and Exchange Commission exerts over stock exchanges and investment houses. If a business or industry in England is to remain in private hands, there seems to be a sort of *laissez faire* tradition that keeps governmental regulation at the minimum; and when more drastic public control seems necessary, the government takes the enterprise over and runs it directly. American policy, on the other hand, leans toward maximum governmental regulation but shies away from collectivism.

A second factor restricting the growth of British regulation of business is one which is implicit in British character and in the relative maturity and conservatism of British business development. The British have an ingrained respect for vested interests and a regard for tradition and for ancient institutions. The idea that a new British fiscal policy might properly extend to the taking over by the government of the Bank of England, or even drastic governmental regulation of that venerable institution, would be a shock to the British public mind beyond anything we would feel under similar circumstances in this country. The further fact stands out that there has been in Great Britain much less unscrupulous exploitation of the public interest by 'big business' than in the United States. Government regulation of business in this country has too often been necessitated by glaring abuses and a callous disregard by private capital of its public responsibilities. England has not wholly escaped these evils; but they have not in the main been serious or prolonged enough to dominate government policy. English business enterprise has tended to be sound and conservative; and it would be foreign to the innate pragmatism of the Englishman to shape his governmental policy to meet possible evils which may never come.

A third factor pulling for conservatism in the British regulation of business has been the fact that vested economic interests in England enjoyed virtually unchallenged political supremacy much longer than in the United States. Only fairly recently has political power been acquired in England by any large group having economic interests sharply clashing with those of the large landowner and the capitalist. Only within recent years has British labor become politically articulate; while the agricultural industries have long been represented in the councils of the nation by the upper and middle aristocracies whose essential economic and political outlook was fundamentally the same as that of the British industrialist. There is nothing in English history analogous to the sharp clash of economic and political group interests such as emerged in the American Granger movement which started the drive for drastic railroad regulation in the United States.

On the other side of the picture are factors which have facilitated or stimulated the British regulation of economic enterprise. The most obvious of these, though not the most influential, is the absence in the British system of government of any constitutional restraints on governmental regulation. British government rests upon the central principle of Parliamentary supremacy. Judicial review is unknown. There is no higher or more binding law than a British statute, and no British court has any authority to scrutinize the validity of any statute or declare it invalid. When the question arises whether Parliament shall embark upon some policy of business regulation there is no need to worry whether the proposed control is 'constitutional' or not; it is merely necessary to decide whether it would be wise and successful. This contrasts sharply with the rigid legal limitations under which American regulatory policy developed. Prior to 1935 (marked by the Supreme Court's decision in the case of *Nebbia* v. *New York*) governmental control of prices or rates, together with the obligation of common service, could validly be imposed only upon those businesses which, in the judgment of the Court, were 'affected with a public interest.' Even with this test discarded in the Nebbia case, there is still the constitutional requirement that government regulation of business conform to what the Supreme Court regards as due process of law. It is fair to observe that the British and American positions in this matter have recently tended to approximate each other. In Britain, regulation of business conforms to sound standards of public policy (the only requirement in England), and this would very probably meet the test (required in America) of due process of law. The vital difference remains, however, that in England the determination rests finally with the legislature; in the United States it remains with the Supreme Court.

In the second place, the development of British regulatory and collectivist policy in regard to business has been encouraged by the equanimity, if not positive enthusiasm, with which the British public looks upon the spread of public ownership and control of economic enterprises. There is much more pub-

lic ownership in England than in this country; there appears to
be complete public satisfaction with it; and this has been true
from an early date. The reasons for this may be briefly stated:
First, embarking on a public ownership venture in England
did not involve taking an industry or a utility away from the
'haves' and giving it to the representatives of the 'have-nots' (a
clash of economic group interests frequently characterizing the
launching of a public ownership project in the United States);
it meant rather the transfer of title and control from the prior
owners to a government dominated by the owners' own economic group. Thus the change was not viewed as cataclysmic;
it did not represent an irresponsible popular drive against the
vested interests. Second, public ownership in England has usually been highly advantageous to the prior owners. They have
received just, if not more than just, compensation. Important
here was the early development of the fair and efficient Private
Bill procedure in the British Parliament. This guaranteed that
when private property interests in specific cases were menaced
by proposed legislative policy, as when a city asked permission
to take over its gas works, the procedure should be judicial,
should permit the threatened interests to be represented by
counsel, and should ensure a decision on the merits. England
has thus escaped the curse of 'special legislation' affecting private interests, which had so damaging an influence in early
American political history in undermining legislative integrity
and destroying public confidence in that integrity. Third, the
equanimity with which government regulation or ownership
of economic enterprise is viewed in England is due to the high
efficiency level and the high personal calibre of the British officials who operate government enterprises. English city councils
were established on a sound basis as early as 1835; by 1865 a
mature and efficient system of administrative management had
emerged in the local government field, so that when public
regulation, or later public ownership, became expedient, there
were already in existence well-organized and powerful governmental bodies which commanded public confidence. In this
country there is well-grounded fear that a publicly owned utility or a regulatory policy will fall into the hands of political
spoilsmen at the worst, or administrative amateurs at the best.
The fine traditions of the British Civil Service guaranteeing

the continuing tenure in office of trained experts stand as a protection against political exploitation and bungling in the administration of British policy. Further assurance of the efficient administration of regulatory or collectivist policy is the fundamental British principle of political responsibility. Cabinet responsibility to the House of Commons provides an opportunity to expose and correct administrative abuses on the national level, while the analogous committee system in local government enforces similar responsibility of municipal officers to the city council. We have in the United States no equally effective methods of holding our administrative officers accountable to the public will.

In the third place, British governmental regulation of business has been hastened and extended by the pressure of external relations and of war. The first World War wrought an important upheaval in many kinds of vested interests. It produced a powerful impulse toward social control. It brought the present regulation of British railways; it paved the way for the government's electricity policy embodied in the publicly owned Grid. War, or the threat of war, will almost always necessitate forms of control which would not be acceptable to the public mind in time of peace; but seldom does the passing of the war emergency restore the *status quo ante*. The United States abandoned federal operation of the railroads when the War ended; but war experience prepared the public mind for the Transportation Act of 1920, a far more drastic measure of public control than would have been tolerated in the pre-war period. So in England there was no complete 'return to normalcy,' but rather a fairly substantial carry-over into peace of the regulatory policies which war had necessitated. The present study takes no account of the effect of the second World War upon British governmental agencies.

B. Factors Influencing British Techniques of Economic Regulation

It appears that most of the more important factors which have determined the range of governmental regulation of business in England are indigenous to that country. Even more sharply unique are the factors which have shaped the administrative methods and techniques by which British regulation of business has been carried out. These may be usefully summarized at this point:

In the first place, as already mentioned, the principle of political responsibility and the devices for enforcing it are a vital and persistent factor in every phase of British government. The Ministry must retain the confidence and support of the majority in the House of Commons in order to remain in office. Arbitrary conduct or inefficiency upon the part of even a very humble officer or employee of the government may cause embarrassing questions to be asked in the House of Commons. A Cabinet Minister, or in an extreme case the entire Ministry, may be seriously 'on the spot' if suitable explanations of the cause of the protest cannot be presented or convincing assurances of reform given. No one can escape this accountability, and it would be hard to exaggerate the effect of it upon the morale and temper of the British official. British government is geared on the tradition and practice of the responsibility of every part of the government to Parliament.

There are two characteristically British devices which aid in enforcing the responsibility we have been discussing. The first is the Royal Commission. These are *ad hoc* bodies set up to conduct broad inquiries, to formulate plans and policies, to devise administrative techniques. While they may include from time to time some 'decorative' members who do not carry their own weight, in the main they are manned by distinguished and public-spirited persons of ability and experience. They make available to the government and the nation a statesmanlike appraisal of public policies in the more technical fields; this could hardly be secured from the bureaucrats of the civil service. Many of the members of these Royal Commissions could not be drawn permanently into the service of the government, but are willing to give their time and effort on specific jobs. The Royal Commissions have rendered invaluable aid both in exposing situations demanding reform and in making constructive proposals. The second device is the traditional control of administration in England by the Treasury. The steady and relentless check imposed by the authorities which control the funds affords a useful protection against administrative extravagance and inefficiency.

The second factor is the high calibre of British official personnel already mentioned. Many an alluring venture into some new area of governmental control which may tempt an American legislature takes on a speculative or even hazardous aspect when the difficult problem is faced of securing honest, impartial, and competent officers and employees to administer it. Personnel problems do not seriously influence such policy decisions in England. If Parliament decides to embark upon a program of business regulation or government ownership, it assumes, as it may safely do, that a nonpartisan and efficient staff will be provided to administer the program. Students of government the world over pay tribute to the superb tradition and high efficiency of the British Civil Service. In fact, students of government outside of England may perhaps view it with greater veneration than do some English observers who do not hesitate to describe the typical British civil servant as wound up hopelessly in official red tape and terrified by innovations. Yet the integrity, disinterestedness, and efficiency of these English public servants must command the admiration and envy of Americans still suffering under the abuses of the spoils system.

The high quality of English official personnel is not confined to the British Civil Service. There are brackets of public service in England above the civil service level. These include administrators, members of governing boards, and other officers exercising important powers and wide discretion. Many of these upper officials are recruited from the educated leisure class in England, men usually of substantial means and assured social standing who respond to the call for public service in accordance with a long-standing and honorable tradition. They command public confidence; they render valuable service with a disinterestedness and a breadth of vision not always found in the man who holds public office because he needs the salary. While some 'stuffed shirts' will be found in this group, the fact remains that in recruiting public servants from this class the English government is able to mobilize a larger degree of public-spirited and disinterested ability than is drawn into the service of the government in the United States. In this connection, the legal profession in England makes a notable contribution to public life.

A third factor which has shaped the techniques of British regulatory policies is the long-standing tradition which permits the farming out of governmental powers to private and voluntary associations or groups. Striking illustrations of this are found in the legal and medical professions. Admission to the bar and the discipline of members of the bar in England are not governmental prerogatives as in this country. They are controlled rather by the organized lawyers of the country through the agency of the Inns of Court. Similarly the medical profession, not the British government, licenses physicians to practise and enforces the disciplinary rules of the profession. In the United States we have a traditional prejudice against thus vesting private persons or organizations with governmental authority; and we also have constitutional restrictions against such delegations of power. In England, however, their system seems wholly acceptable in theory, and has, in the main, worked well in practice. As we shall see at a later point, virtually all the British marketing schemes, agricultural and otherwise, were organized along these lines. Drastic powers to fix prices and market quotas have been given to bodies chosen by the industry itself. A sort of 'guild' control has been established whereby particular businesses or, industries are given important compulsory powers of self-government. There is a general over-all governmental supervision of the whole scheme, and there is evidence of a trend away from guild control; but there can be no doubt that this policy of delegating governmental functions to private persons or interests has played an important part in the British regulation of business and industry.

C. Classification of British Agencies

Before embarking upon the following description and analysis of British agencies for the control of business and industry, a word may be said about the classification used and the method of treatment followed. This classification of agencies is the writer's own creation devised merely to make more lucid the present analysis of British experience. The categories set up are not always mutually exclusive, and there could be disagreement whether a particular agency belonged in the one of these categories or the other. My friend Professor Laski examined this classification and remarked without enthusiasm that it was probably as good as any, but that, of course, logical classification of these agencies is impossible because of the hit-or-miss way in which they have been set up and the lack of any logical consistency in their organization or functions. What has been done is to group British agencies into two major divisions: first, those which are *non-departmental* in the sense that they fall outside any of the normal executive hierarchies which are headed by Cabinet Ministers, and second, the *departmental* agencies, which are always regulatory, such as those located in the Board of Trade, the Ministry of Transport, the Ministry of Agriculture, and so on. The non-departmental agencies have been further divided into those which are *regulatory,* such as the Railway Rates Tribunal, and those which are *operating* or *service* agencies, such as the British Broadcasting Corporation or the Central Electricity Board. The non-departmental regulatory agencies have been further subdivided into (a) judicialized tribunals approximating administrative courts, such as the Railway and Canal Commission; (b) administrative tribunals exercising much wider policy-determining powers, such as the Electricity Commissioners or the Road Transport Authorities; and (c) the 'guild' authorities, agencies of industrial self-government, represented by the agricultural marketing boards.

In dealing with the British agencies a common pattern of treatment has been followed. A bit of historical background is given to show how need for government regulation arose and what controversies and compromises lay back of the present arrangements. Essential facts about the structure and personnel arrangements of each agency are briefly summarized. The scope, nature, and importance of the powers exercised are analyzed. Procedures for carrying on the regulatory function are examined. Attention is given to the important problem of the relations, formal or informal, which an agency has to other branches of the government, and to any attempts which seek to effect co-ordination of effort. Finally, an attempt is made to appraise the degree and nature of the independence enjoyed by the agency, or the extent to which it feels or escapes normal Ministerial control. The purpose of all this is, of course, to learn as much as we can about how the British government has gone about the job of regulating business and industry, and how relevant this British experience is to the problems of economic regulation which we face in the United States.

II. NON-DEPARTMENTAL AGENCIES EXERCISING REGULATORY POWER [1]

A. Quasi-judicial Tribunals—Administrative Courts

1. THE RAILWAY AND CANAL COMMISSION

a. *Background of British railway control* [2]

THE development of the railway industry in England brought problems as acute as those in this country, though somewhat different in nature. No restriction was placed upon the number of competing railways which might be built, and free competition ran riot. While the Board of Trade was authorized in 1840 to inspect and report on new proposals, it appeared to sanction anything asked for; with the result that 'in the four years 1844-47 there were chartered 637 separate roads with a total authorized length of about 9400 miles.' [3] While this competition was ruinous to many railways, it was accompanied also by the growth of agreements to exploit the shipper. A steady drift toward monopoly appeared. At the same time the dominant *laissez faire* philosophy of the day viewed with fear and aversion the thought of government regulation.

Statutory control was not lacking. It had, in fact, existed from the first. Railways had to be chartered and this was done by separate statutes; Parliament was inundated by floods of these bills. The power to inspect and report, which the Act of 1840 gave to the Board of Trade, was very similar to the assignment given later to the highly successful Massachusetts railroad commission; but the Board of Trade achieved no similar success. In 1844 and again in 1846 Parliament tried to reduce the burden arising from almost countless railway bills by creating statutory commissions to report to Parliament on proposed

---

1. Cf. W. A. Robson, *Justice and Administrative Law* (1928).
2. Cf. M. E. Dimock, *British Public Utilities and National Development* (1933), 63 ff.
3. A. T. Hadley, *Railroad Transportation* (1895), 167.

charters. The experiment failed. The commissions enjoyed no real power or responsibility and therefore commanded no confidence. The Act of 1844 provided for a revision of railway rates which netted dividends of over 10 per cent; it also provided for a compulsory 'Parliamentary train' each day at a penny a mile third class.

The menace of railway monopoly finally led to a Commission of Inquiry in 1853. Its report bore fruit in the Railway and Canal Traffic Regulation Act of 1854, which set up regulations to prevent discrimination in railway rates and unfair competition, and was enforceable by the ordinary courts of law. This statutory regulation failed miserably. The courts were confronted with technical problems of which they were ignorant; the costs of litigation under the statute were high; and the railways succeeded in preventing any effective enforcement. It became clear that the simple enactment of a law was not going to solve the problem, and further Parliamentary inquiry was set in motion through a committee set up in 1872.

Upon the report of this committee was based the Regulation of Railways Act of 1873, which created the famous Railway Commission—the first semi-administrative tribunal which England ever established for regulatory purposes. The committee of inquiry found that competition had essentially ceased in the matter of railway charges and concluded that a specialized body was needed to take over the job of law enforcement. The Railway Commission had three members, paid £3,000 each. One had to be a lawyer and one had to be connected with the railroad business. The commission's assignment was to break up rate discriminations and preferences and to guarantee facilities for through traffic by the enforcement of the Act of 1854. It had no executive power; it could not initiate actions or policies, but could only deal with complaints brought by aggrieved persons. It was in essence a specialized court whose members, it was hoped, would become expert and be able to deal effectively with railway problems beyond the capacity of the ordinary English judge. It was similar in a vague way, and in less ambitious form, to our own ill-fated Commerce Court of 1910.

The Railway Commission, 'a feeble step in the right direction,' proved wholly inadequate to deal with the increasingly pressing problems of railway control. Its failure was due to the lack of adequate power and to the existing chaos of railway statutes. Each railway had its own rate schedules, embodied in private acts, and bearing no relation to those of other roads. The committee of 1872 had rejected the idea of a general statutory revision of rate schedules. 'By 1886 railway law was contained in 1,880 Acts, modified by 1,300 amending Acts.' [4] To deal effectively with this confused mass was utterly impossible, as the history of the commission amply proved. As one observer said: 'It has power enough to annoy the railroads, and not power enough to help the public efficiently.' [5] The commission itself was dominated by the legal mind of its lawyer member and took a narrow view of its duty. The costs of litigation before it were almost prohibitive. Furthermore, the commission was helpless to protect from the vengeance of the railways the indiscreet shipper who complained of unfair treatment. The commission's essential failure was not fully realized and exposed until the report of the Parliamentary committee set up in 1881-2 to explore the need for new railway legislation. American observers, viewing the commission casually and arrested by the idea of an administrative regulatory tribunal, advertised the commission in the United States so favorably that it probably had substantial influence upon the movement which resulted in the creation of the Interstate Commerce Commission. It had, in short, a much better American reputation than it deserved.

b. *The Act of* 1888

The Railway and Canal Commission was created by statute in 1888. The time had come for more effective railway control and the Parliamentary committee of 1881-2 had brought in a severe indictment of the results of the Act of 1873. The new statute provided for a complete change of rate schedules and a scrapping of the old chaotic maze of individual rates. The Board of Trade was ordered to set up new maximum rates by Provisional Order, and these were ultimately put into effect. By an Act passed in 1894, any increase in rates beyond the maximum required the approval of the Railway and Canal Commission, which thus acquired important restrictive power

---

4. Dimock, op. cit. 71.   5. Hadley, op. cit. 173.

over the rate structure. By later statutes other powers were given to the commission; but in 1921, for reasons which will be explained later,[6] most of the commission's authority over railways was given to the new Railway Rates Tribunal.

c. *Structure and personnel*

The Railway and Canal Commission is simple in structure. It has three full-time members. The chairman is a judge of the High Court, appointed by the Lord Chancellor and assigned to the commission for a five-year term. The other two members are named by the Home Secretary and one must have had experience in the railway business. The terms of these two members are arranged at the time of appointment, but are not specified in the statute. Any member may be removed for incompetence or misconduct by the Lord Chancellor. A maximum salary of £3,000 is fixed by the statute; the actual salaries are determined, save in the case of the High Court judge, by the Home Secretary. The members are eligible to reappointment. They must dispose of any financial interest in the railway business before assuming office.

d. *Functions*

Since 1921 the Railway and Canal Commission is no longer an important agency in the field of railway control. It retains a long list of powers relating to railways which sound impressive and which under nineteenth-century conditions may have been important, but they are of very minor significance now. Of these the following are the most conspicuous: (a) The commission has jurisdiction to enforce the statutory requirement of 'all reasonable facilities for receiving, forwarding, and delivery of traffic.' Shippers who claim the lack of such adequate facilities may resort to the commission in hope of relief. By the Act of 1921 the commission was authorized to order a railway to provide 'reasonable railway services, facilities and conveniences' provided they did not cost over £100,000. The Act contained the joker, however, that such requirements could not

6. *Infra,* 517 f.

be enforced if the company could show that such expenditures would jeopardize the financial interests of existing stockholders. No order has ever been issued under the Act of 1921 and the commission does not have much business under the original provision. (b) The commission is authorized to prevent 'undue preferences in rates or service.' Important originally, this power has become negligible. Since the Act of 1921, discriminatory rates are impossible. Such undue preferences as may come to the attention of the commission usually relate to methods of packing goods for shipment, or to complaints of towns or villages that they are not receiving fair and adequate service. (c) It has power to review on appeal local tax assessments on railway property, and (d) to enforce the Cheap Trains Act of 1883 which requires a minimum number of low-fare trains per day. It has never had a case under this Act.

In addition to these powers or ghosts of former powers relating to railways the Railway and Canal Commission has a number of what may be called 'miscellaneously dumped' powers quite unconnected with any problems of transportation. Parliament has given these powers to the commission because it was more convenient to use a ready-made quasi-judicial tribunal for a new function than to set up a new agency, and perhaps also because the commission is not overworked. (a) Under the Coal Mines Act of 1930, discussed later,[7] the commission had to approve any compulsory scheme of reorganization. These compulsory schemes had to meet four statutory tests; and in the only case brought before the commission it interpreted these tests with a strictness which not only led to the rejection of the scheme but also made futile any further attempts to use the powers granted by the Act. The statute was later repealed and the commission relieved of its duty thereunder. (b) Much of the commission's business arises under an Act of 1923 giving it authority over the acquisition of mineral rights on private lands. A power of eminent domain is delegated to private operators under government control whereby they may acquire the right to purchase mineral rights on private lands. Such compulsory takings must first be approved by the Board of Trade and appeal from its rulings lies to the commission, which makes final decision. (c) The commission hears certain appeals from

7. *Infra,* 587.

rulings of the Metropolitan Water Board, determines the compensation which the Post Office must pay for running telephone or telegraph wires across private lands, and hears appeals from actions of licensees under the Petroleum Act of 1934. None of these odd jobs is big enough to justify a separate agency, but each calls for the occasional services of a not overworked tribunal accustomed to acting as a sort of administrative court.

e. *Procedure*

The Railway and Canal Commission is in reality a court of law and so regards itself. Its procedure is not quite as formal as that of an ordinary law court, but nearly so. That procedure follows roughly the rules of common law. The chairman of the commission, a High Court judge, has final authority to decide which questions arising before the commission are questions of law and to rule on those which are. The result is that he dominates the entire proceeding, completely overshadowing his lay colleagues. Cases are presented to the commission by counsel, who address the bench formally as 'My Lord.' Since the cases are usually technical, able lawyers are required and the resulting costs of litigation are high. This is true although the actual fees of the commission are nominal. The decisions of the commission on matters of fact are final; but appeal lies to the Court of Appeals on questions of law, save railway valuation decisions, which may go directly to the House of Lords. The commission is a court of record, and its decisions, with opinions in full, are printed in the law reports. It costs the government, salaries included, about £7,000 per year, which the Exchequer collects from the railways. The commission has no power to initiate any sort of action. It can act only when matters are brought to it by an aggrieved party.

f. *Relations with other agencies or departments*

As a court the commission has no active relations with any other branch of the government. No Ministry has any direct or even indirect contact with it, and certainly no power to influence its decisions. Parliament could by statute alter the commission or modify its powers just as it could in the case of any court, but it exercises no power over the commission as a going concern. The commission maintains no contacts with any of the other governmental agencies which deal with problems of transport. In fact, it leans over backward to avoid doing so. Its members admit that in many of its decisions it must be guided by its concepts of 'public interest'; but it allows itself small opportunity to discover what the 'public interest' is. It has no relations with the public. It makes no legislative recommendations to Parliament. It issues yearly a formal report, listing decided cases and commenting briefly on its work.

g. *Appraisal*

While not important enough to be the object of any widespread active animosity, the Railway and Canal Commission is not a popular body. This is owing in part to its complete aloofness and in part to the high degree of judicialization which results from the dominating influence of the High Court judge who is its chairman. The costs of bringing cases before the commission are felt to be prohibitive, except to the railways, which can well afford to pay, and therefore discriminatory against the poor shipper. The commission has displayed in its decisions a conservatism and a regard for vested interests which have not endeared it to the people generally. Its decision in the Coal Mines Reorganization Scheme case, referred to above,[8] left a bad flavor, for it was widely felt that the commission had rendered the statute ineffective by an over-restrictive interpretation. The belief is growing that the commission should be abolished; that the Railway Rates Tribunal should take over its railway powers and the other powers be distributed elsewhere. A committee of the House of Commons reported in 1932 that the total volume of business did not warrant continuance of the commission at a cost of £7,000.[9] It is felt that what is needed is not an expensive and highly formalized court, but a cheaper, more flexible, and more aggressive body with powers of initiating action.

8. *Supra*, 514.   9. Dimock, op. cit. 75.

2. THE RAILWAY RATES TRIBUNAL

a. *Background of the Railways Act of* 1921

The experience of the World War revolutionized governmental control of railroads both in the United States and in England. In this country it produced the Transportation Act of 1920; in England it produced the Railways Act of 1921, creating the Railway Rates Tribunal. The railway problem in England at the outbreak of the War was growing acute. Amalgamations were increasing but were under no adequate public control. There were still many separate companies, and the situation permitted all the wastes of competition with none of its advantages. During the World War the British government took over the railways and operated them under unified control. At the close of the War there was agreement upon one point, though perhaps only one: that the railways could not possibly be returned to the *status quo ante,* a multitude of private companies inadequately regulated. As in the United States, various proposals for the nationalization of the railways were brought forward. These came from the Labour Party and the Trade Unions. The Government in power rejected government ownership, and the Act of 1921 was a compromise which sought the advantages of unified control under private ownership. Sir Eric Geddes, the Minister of Transport, said in introducing the bill: 'I want to give the railways a reasonable amount of freedom in their management, and the community a proper amount of control.' [10]

The Act of 1921 did two main things: First, it effected the compulsory amalgamation of the old railway companies into four main groups, thus pretty completely stopping railway competition. These amalgamations were worked out under the supervision of an *ad hoc* Railway Amalgamation Tribunal. The four new consolidated companies remained in private ownership and control, and the old companies were liberally compensated for the losses sustained during the war period. Second, the Act created a new body, the Railway Rates Tribunal, to take over effective supervision of railway rates and to absorb most of the powers relating to railways previously exercised by

10. Parliamentary Debates (1921), vol. CXLII, 354.

the Railway and Canal Commission. No one suggested placing the new and drastic powers in the hands of the older agency. Rumor has it that at this juncture one of the members of the Railway and Canal Commission was incapacitated by senility. To place the administration of the new statute in its hands would have seemed grotesque. What was needed was an impartial tribunal, less highly judicialized, less aged, less formal, and more efficient and flexible.

b. *Structure and personnel*

The new rates tribunal is composed of three members appointed, through the Crown, by the Minister of Transport, the President of the Board of Trade, and the Lord Chancellor. The selection is actually made by the Minister of Transport. One member must be a lawyer, and he is chairman; one is experienced in railroad affairs; and one in commercial affairs. In practice, these members are selected after consultation with the interests they represent. The term of office is seven years, but as the members are re-eligible, and are removable only for incompetence or misconduct, the tenure is usually permanent. The members give their full time to their duties and divest themselves upon appointment of any railway or commercial interests or connections. They receive substantial salaries arranged with the Treasury at the time of appointment. The statute provides for the appointment of two panels of additional persons. One panel of thirty-five persons represents mainly trading, labor, agriculture, and passenger interests. The other panel of eleven represents the railway interests. Upon the request of any litigant before the tribunal, or upon the initiative of either the tribunal itself or the Minister of Transport, an additional member from each panel may be added to the tribunal. This is to provide assurance that fair consideration will be given to all interests involved in any case. The tribunal regards it as an evidence of confidence in itself that no such additional members have so far been asked for. If it were exercising its powers to supervise the rates and services of the London Passenger Transport Board, two members familiar with local transportation problems would be added; but this has never occurred. The tribunal has no staff of examiners, engineers, or accountants. The Minister of Transport pays its salaries and provides it with quarters and such service as it needs.

c. *Functions*

With a few minor exceptions the Railway Rates Tribunal is responsible for the establishment and supervision of all rates at which railway traffic is carried in England. This vitally important assignment is handled in the main through the exercise of three distinct grants of authority. These may be briefly explained:

(1) *The annual review of rates.* The statute provides for an annual automatic review by the tribunal of all railway rates. The Minister of Transport can in his discretion order this review omitted in any year, but he has never done so. The purpose of this annual review is bound up in the famous 'standard revenue' requirement of the Act of 1921. While those framing the Act sought a more elastic and efficient system of rate making, they were unwilling to sacrifice the interests of railway investors. Accordingly the Act provided that the tribunal should fix rates in such a way as will 'yield, with efficient and economical working and management, an annual net revenue (hereinafter referred to as "standard revenue") equivalent to the aggregate net revenues of the year 1913 of . . . the companies absorbed by the amalgamated company.' This has turned out to be a joker. The year 1913 was a year of great prosperity. Motor traffic was in its infancy and its competition had not begun to cut into railway revenue. At no time since 1921 have the English railways come anywhere near the 'standard revenue' of 1913. The best year was 1929, when earnings were only 15 per cent under this figure. Nor did the railways in spite of their lessened revenues feel like demanding of the tribunal the increases in rates which the statute authorized, since they realized that higher rates would drive away business and reduce net earnings. It was not until 1937 that they felt justified in asking, at the time of the annual review, a flat rate increase of 5 per cent, and this, after exhaustive hearings, the tribunal granted. It is amply clear that the 'standard revenue' requirement hamstrings the tribunal and prevents scientific rate making. Part of the tribunal's duty at the annual review, upon finding that

the roads are not earning the 'standard revenue,' is to determine whether this is owing to inefficiency and bad management. It has never found it to be so.

(2) *Exceptional rates.* An important part of the tribunal's business is concerned with its supervision and approval of 'exceptional rates.' These are not to be confused with 'undue preferences' or discriminations, which are rigidly banned. They are, rather, point-to-point rates established by special agreement between a railroad and a shipper to cover the transportation of a particular commodity. They are based on the standard rates (rates built up by applying standard schedules to twenty-one classes of traffic), but are usually much lower. These exceptional rate agreements must all be reported to the Minister of Transport. Those more than 40 per cent lower or 5 per cent higher than standard must go to the Railway Rates Tribunal for its approval. Some are as much as 70 per cent below standard. The tribunal in passing on them must be convinced that they will not injure other shippers, and will not impair the earning capacity of the railway. The tribunal handles these exceptional rates with great dispatch and in enormous bulk. Few of them are contested or present controversial questions, since the railways in practice do not apply for them unless they have a cast-iron case. More than a million of these rates have been approved since 1928. In a 'test week' in 1935 a check revealed that 83 per cent of the total traffic was carried under these rates, and that this traffic produced 86 per cent of British railway earnings. The reason for this is that the 'exceptional rate' is the railway's most effective method of meeting the competition of the motor carrier. Water competition is not serious; coastal traffic is not an important factor and the railways now own most of the canals.

(3) *Agreed charges.* Since 1933 'agreed charges' have been permitted by statute if approved by the Railway Rates Tribunal. This is another method of protecting the railways against the ruinous competition of the motor carrier. Agreed charges are not point-to-point rates. They are agreements between large concerns or associations of traders and the railways covering all of the traffic of such concerns or associations. They usually contain provisions barring the use of motor carriers if railway facilities are available. They are likely to be made with

very large concerns. The Woolworth Company, for example, has such an agreement for the shipment by rail of all of its goods in return for a flat payment to the railroad of 4 per cent of the retail price of the goods thus shipped. These agreed charges may be applied for either by the railways or by traders, but usually the railways apply. Shippers may appear before the tribunal to protest against agreed charges, but the motor carriers are not allowed to appear, although they usually are vitally affected. The Railway Rates Tribunal deals with agreed charges with very great care. They occupy most of its time.

Besides these three major functions the tribunal has a number of miscellaneous duties, all of them relating to transportation and railway matters. It passes upon applications for changes in the general classification of railway traffic. These are usually not contested and take little time. It has power to determine the reasonableness of the methods of packing fragile commodities for shipment by the railroads. It has a highly specialized duty in the matter of apportioning 'derating' rebates (special concessions to the railways in the matter of local taxation) between certain classes of traffic. This is, in reality, a system of providing a subsidy, mainly for the export trades, and especially for coal. Finally, the tribunal has extensive powers of supervision and review on appeal of the London Passenger Transport Board.[11] It must review the fares charged by the board on complaint of any local authority within the area, and any increases in fares beyond those fixed by statute must receive the tribunal's approval. It may, furthermore, order the board to make, or refrain from making, any changes in its services or facilities. It is no small tribute to the astuteness with which the London Passenger Transport Board has managed its affairs, and the high efficiency of its public relations department in handling complaints, that there is as yet no case in which an appeal has been made to the tribunal from the board's actions.

d. *Procedure*

The Railway Rates Tribunal is a court, though it is more of an administrative body and less of a court than the Railway and Canal Commission. It is a court of record. It may examine

11. *Infra,* 600 ff.

witnesses on oath, though it does not often do so. Its rules of procedure, within certain statutory limits, are fixed by the tribunal itself subject to the consent of the Minister of Transport, the Lord Chancellor, and the President of the Court of Sessions. The tribunal has avoided over-judicialization of its procedure, which has been kept fairly informal and flexible. While counsel may appear before it, and do so in important cases, as in the 5 per cent rate increase hearing in 1937, most of the tribunal's business is carried on without legal aid. Long-drawn-out hearings are discouraged, informal settlements between parties are encouraged, and much of the tribunal's time is taken up in approving arrangements which have been made before being presented. The lawyer-chairman of the tribunal does not overshadow the other members, as in the Railway and Canal Commission. All three members participate equally in the hearings, question witnesses, and appear to have equal influence. The chairman is addressed as 'Sir' rather than 'My Lord,' but when counsel appear before the tribunal they do so in the customary gowns and wigs. The tribunal's decisions on questions of fact are final, but there is appeal to the Court of Appeals on questions of law. It may render its decisions by a majority vote, but has thus far always been unanimous. The tribunal costs about £12,000 per year, and this is paid out of the Exchequer, but the government recoups most of it by a levy on railways. The cost of bringing a case before the tribunal has been kept surprisingly low.

e. *Relations with other agencies or departments*

The Railway Rates Tribunal is an independent body. It is neither controlled by nor responsible to the Minister of Transport, although it has certain statutory points of contact with him. The Act requires the Minister to give the tribunal 'such assistance as it may require,' but the tribunal appears to get the information it needs directly from the railways and does not call upon the Minister for aid. The Minister, on his part, may place before the tribunal 'such information as he thinks relevant.' He may also 'appear and be heard in any proceedings before the Tribunal.' He does send a representative to hold a 'watching brief' at the annual review of rates, but he makes no other effort to participate in the tribunal's proceedings. On one occasion the tribunal made a suggestion to the Minister concerning the effect of agricultural rate (tax) rebates on farmers, but the Minister did not act upon it. Thus the relations between the tribunal and the Minister appear to be perfunctory and unimportant.

Parliament exercises no control, direct or indirect, over the tribunal's decisions. The Minister of Transport may be asked questions relating to the tribunal, but in replying he merely agrees to secure the information asked for and disclaims all responsibility for the tribunal's activities. Questions regarding the tribunal and its work may arise at the time of voting money for its maintenance. The tribunal is, of course, subject at all times to the exercise of the sovereign power of Parliament, which may alter its organization or functions, or even abolish it altogether.

The tribunal maintains no relations or contacts with any other regulatory bodies—a fact which constitutes a serious defect. It has no advisory bodies associated with it, nor does it maintain any public relations office. It does, however, keep in close touch with associations of traders and with the railway interests.

f. *Appraisal and comment*

The Railway Rates Tribunal commands universal respect for impartiality and efficiency. It does admirably the job assigned to it. It is frequently referred to as a 'model administrative tribunal.' It is, however, a tribunal and not an administrative or planning agency. It has no substantial staff and no initiative. Criticisms directed against it relate almost entirely to the statutory limitations under which it works. In the first place, it is widely urged that the 'standard revenue' provisions of the Act of 1921 are unwise. The tribunal's hands are tied. It ought to be empowered to do a real job of rate making free from the obligation to protect arbitrarily the highly inflated railway investments. Secondly, it is urged that the tribunal does in reality exercise important policy-determining powers which affect the entire British transportation system, and that therefore it ought not to be entirely independent but should bear some measure of responsibility to the Government. It is urged in the third place that the tribunal should be given the power to initiate proceedings and conduct independent investigations. It should actively enforce statutory requirements, as does our Interstate Commerce Commission, instead of having to wait for cases to come before it on complaint. It should furthermore be given the power relating to railways (reasonable facilities jurisdiction) which still remains in the Railway and Canal Commission.

A final criticism is directed against the complete absence of any co-ordination between the tribunal's activities and those of other agencies in the same area. There was a clear illustration of this while the writer was in London during the summer of 1937. The Railway Rates Tribunal was holding hearings upon the application of the railways for a flat 5 per cent increase in rates. At the same time a voluntary arbitral tribunal under the chairmanship of Sir Arthur Salter was working out an adjustment of railway wages. While rates affect wages, and wages affect rates, each body proceeded on its way firmly disregarding the existence of the other. Perhaps effective co-ordination in this field can hardly be hoped for as long as the Railway Rates Tribunal is hamstrung by the standard revenue provision; but certainly it ought not to be ruled out as neither possible nor desirable. Nor is there intelligent co-ordination between the activities of the tribunal and the road transport authorities who control the destinies of the railways' strongest competitors. Not only do the two agencies have no connection with each other, but the road transport (motor carrier) interests are not allowed to appear before the Railway Rates Tribunal even in cases in which their interests are most vitally affected.

3. ROAD AND RAIL APPEAL TRIBUNAL

The Road and Rail Appeal Tribunal is a highly judicialized tribunal to which appeals are taken from the decisions and rulings of the area licensing authorities which regulate the road transport of goods—what in this country would be called motor trucking. It is admittedly backhanded to deal with an appellate body before discussing the agencies whose decisions it reviews; but this study concerns itself with administrative methods and relations rather than with economic policies of regulation, and the Road and Rail Appeal Tribunal has more in common with the Railway and Canal Commission and the Railway Rates Tribunal than with the road traffic licensing authorities. For purposes of clarity, the British term 'road transport' is roughly equivalent to the American term 'motor carrier traffic.'

a. *Background from which the tribunal came*

The first big step in the regulation of British road transport was the Road Traffic Act of 1930, which applied only to passenger vehicles. It created a number of Area Traffic Commissioners throughout the country for purposes of licensing and regulation. These were appointed by the Minister of Transport and appeals from their rulings went to him. This procedure was sharply criticized, first because it was felt that the Minister was not an unprejudiced reviewing authority, and second because at the outset the Minister declined to state the reasons for his decisions or to give written opinions. In 1933 Parliament passed the Road and Rail Traffic Act, which extended government control to the road transport of goods. The pressure of the goods transport interests resulted in the creation of a special appeal tribunal to handle appeals from the area licensing authorities in goods transport cases. A need was felt for an impartial, independent, quasi-judicial body. Appeals in passenger transport cases still went to the Minister as before.

b. *Structure and personnel*

The Road and Rail Appeal Tribunal, thus created, has three members. They are appointed by the Minister of Transport in consultation with the Lord Chancellor, the President of the Board of Trade, and the Secretary of State for Scotland. The chairman is a lawyer of standing; his term of office is ten years and he gives full time and receives a substantial salary. His two associates are part-time officials, neither lawyers nor experts, and serve for three years. Any of the three may be removed for incompetence or misconduct by the Minister in consultation with the Ministers who concurred in the initial appointments. Members of the House of Commons and those interested in the goods transport business are not eligible. The obvious purpose is to create a body in which the full-time lawyer-chairman dominates the part-time laymen.

c. *Powers and functions*

The substantive duties of the tribunal need not be described here. It hears appeals from the decisions of the area licensing authorities which administer the detailed and complicated regulations under which goods transport licenses are issued and licensees regulated. These we shall deal with later.[12] The powers granted over goods vehicles do not include the fixing of rates or charges, as is the case with passenger vehicle regulation.

d. *Procedure*

The tribunal determines its own rules of procedure with the consent of the Lord Chancellor, the President of the Court of Quarter Sessions, and the Minister of Transport. The procedure tends to be highly judicialized, although the rules of evidence are less strict than in the regular law courts. Cases are usually presented by barristers and the costs of appeals are high. One of the chief items of expense is the cost of typing the voluminous transcript of the record of proceedings before the area licensing authority. The tribunal regards itself as a court for the judicial interpretation of the statute. In reality its duties compel it to pass judgment upon important questions of policy. Its zeal for judicial impartiality is shown by its practice of not reading the transcript of the record of a case on appeal prior to the public hearing. It was felt that if the members read the record privately beforehand they might prejudge the case. The tribunal accordingly punishes itself by requiring the oral reading of the entire transcript. This sometimes takes four or five days. The tribunal, while not required by statute to do so, travels about to hear cases in order that costs to litigants away from London may be kept down.

The chairman dominates the work and proceedings of the tribunal. He instructs the members on points of law, prepares memoranda on cases for the use of the other members, handles the office and administrative work, and prepares the tribunal's

12. *Infra,* 548.

opinions. It was early decided to issue written opinions, and a volume of case law is therefore growing up. The chairman does his work with the aid of a clerical staff of five. The tribunal usually sits only every other week so that the chairman may have time for his arduous duties. The burden of work resting on the tribunal is very heavy. It is especially burdensome to the part-time members who, of course, have other responsibilities. It is hoped that the growth of a body of precedents interpreting the basic statute will tend to decrease the volume of business, and there are some signs that this is happening.

The tribunal is not required to accept as final the determinations of fact made by the area licensing authorities. These area officials have no power to subpoena witnesses and compel testimony. The Appeal Tribunal, of course, does. Actually, the tribunal treats with respect the findings of fact made by the area authorities. The decisions of the tribunal itself are final, and there is no appeal even on questions of law. The cost of the tribunal, salaries, and office expenses are paid out of the budget of the Minister of Transport, though some of this is recouped from fees collected.

e. *Relations with other agencies*

The tribunal maintains no official contacts with the Minister of Transport. The Minister has no means of influencing any decision of the tribunal or of laying before it his views on any matter of policy. He has no right to appear before it, or be represented, as he may before the Railway Rates Tribunal. There are some courtesy contacts maintained, but these do not go beyond the sending to the Minister by the chairman of the tribunal of copies of its decisions and its annual report.

Parliament may debate the tribunal on the budget estimates, but the Minister of Transport assumes no responsibility for it to the House of Commons and therefore there is, in fact, no Parliamentary control.

The tribunal has no relations with any of the other governmental agencies concerned with transport problems. As a judicial body it shrinks from contacts with private organizations or associations of either shippers or carriers. It tries, with substantial success, to occupy a position of complete isolation.

f. *Appraisal and comment*

Opinion regarding the tribunal is somewhat divided. No one denies that it has performed with scrupulous fairness and reasonable efficiency the task given to it as it has interpreted that task. There is feeling in many quarters, however, that the tribunal's work includes fairly major decisions in the field of transport policy, that such policy decisions are inescapably involved in the tribunal's interpretations of a none too explicit statute, and that such powers ought not to be given to a highly judicialized and politically irresponsible body. It is probable that more 'policy' is bound up in the tribunal's jurisdiction than was foreseen. There is further criticism that the tribunal is a formal, unapproachable body which it is very expensive to use.

It is interesting that criticism of the tribunal comes largely from the very interests which, in 1933, persuaded the Government to set it up—the goods transport interests. The reason for this change of view lies mainly in the fact that the Minister of Transport has since 1933 eliminated the main objections to the earlier system of appeals to the Minister in passenger transport licensing cases. These appeals are now handled with impartiality, and the practice is being followed of publishing opinions giving reasons for the Minister's decisions. The goods transport people now feel that they would prefer this improved procedure of appeals to the Minister of Transport to the more highly judicialized and costly appeals to the Road and Rail Appeal Tribunal. The tribunal's answer to this is that these interests do not really want the complete impartiality which they are now getting, but prefer a more flexible system under which they would be able to exert pressure in their own behalf. Without attempting to settle this issue, it does appear that there is a strong case for an appellate procedure which permits a quicker and more sensitive responsiveness to changes in goods transport policy than the Appeal Tribunal makes possible.

B. ADMINISTRATIVE TRIBUNALS

In labeling certain British regulatory agencies 'administrative tribunals' we do not suggest that they are widely different from the highly judicialized tribunals we have been discussing. The two have many common characteristics, and their distinguishing features represent differences of degree rather than of kind. The administrative tribunal is not a court and does not regard itself as one. Its procedure and methods are informal and flexible. It exercises a wide range of discretion in making decisions which turn on questions of policy. It is closely similar in many respects to our own independent regulatory commission. It is not in any sense an administrative court.

1. THE ELECTRICITY COMMISSIONERS

In discussing the Electricity Commissioners we are again dealing, as in the case of the Road and Rail Appeal Tribunal, with but one of two major agencies set up to control a single problem—the production and transmission of electricity. The second, the Central Electricity Board, will be discussed later.[13] It is the operating agency which, under the supervision of the Electricity Commissioners, owns and manages the Grid. It is not an administrative tribunal. The relations between the commissioners and the board will be made clear even though the two are dealt with in separate parts of this study.

a. *Background of British regulation of electricity* [14]

It was not until electrical science had perfected the electric light and made it generally practicable that there arose any need for government regulation of the electrical industry. The first step toward such regulation was the Electric Lighting Act of 1882, which was passed to deal with the increasing stream of applications for permission to generate and supply electricity for lighting purposes. The Act of 1882 gave the Board of Trade power to grant special licenses to any local authority, company, or person to supply electricity in specified areas. These licenses were subject to numerous conditions. The accounts of the

13. *Infra*, 574 ff.
14. Cf. Dimock, op. cit. 195 ff.; G. Haldane, 'The Central Electricity Board and other Electricity Authorities,' in W. A. Robson (ed.), *Public Enterprise* (1937), 105 ff.; T. O'Brien, *British Experiments in Public Ownership and Control* (1937), 29 ff.; L. Gordon, *The Public Corporation in Great Britain* (1938), 84 ff.

licensees were to be submitted to the inspection of the Board of Trade. There were regulations about the digging up of streets for the purpose of laying pipes. Compensation for damage to private persons was required. All consumers were to be treated equally, and compulsory service was guaranteed to all applying within the area. Prices could be limited, and regulations were to be set up to insure safety. The Board of Trade was to maintain inspection to discover violations of these conditions, and penalties were then enforceable by the courts. The whole arrangement, impressive enough on paper, proved in operation not to be very effective.

The policy of the Electricity Act of 1882 was heavily weighted in favor of local municipal electrical undertakings, which were definitely encouraged. This was natural, since the supplying of electricity was not yet a commercially profitable enterprise and there were, accordingly, no vested interests to be dislocated. The areas which single generating stations could supply were small and corresponded roughly with municipal areas. Electricity, in short, looked like another needed public utility, like water and gas, in the supplying of which municipal enterprise would be likely to succeed. Accordingly, important advantages were given to the local governmental units in the field of electricity supply. They were to be licensed in preference to any private company if they desired to be. The municipality was given the right after twenty-one years to purchase by compulsion on terms favorable to itself any privately owned electricity undertaking. Private companies were also subject to certain forms of control by the municipal authorities within whose borders they carried on their business.

The Act of 1882 retarded the normal development of a great industry. The conditions imposed upon the private entrepreneur, especially the threat of expropriation after twenty-one years, were such as to discourage capital. Municipal authorities were not very energetic in promoting electrical development. Many of them had municipal gas plants with which they wished no competition, and often a city council would secure an electricity franchise simply to forestall the setting up of a private company and then make no use of it. While some successful electricity enterprises were launched, the development on the whole was much slower than in other countries. The Act of

1882 saddled upon the country a parochial form of control over electricity supply and distribution. As a government committee of inquiry observed many years later:

. . . The outcome of the Act of 1882 was the establishment in succeeding years of a large number of undertakings, generally restricted in area to that of an individual local authority district. Such districts were, with a few exceptions, densely populated Boroughs and Urban Districts, leaving the more sparsely populated rural areas almost entirely unprovided for. These undertakings, limited to one local authority district, still form a preponderating part of the structure of electricity distribution today, and the parochial point of view which the policy of the early legislation tended to create, still persists . . .[15]

In 1888, under pressure from the new electricity supply companies, the minimum term of a company franchise or license was extended from twenty-one to forty-two years. At the same time competition was allowed between undertakings in the same area. Technical advances were being made in the industry, and alternating current was developed as an alternative to direct current. The two types of current still compete, since no effective measures for standardization have even yet been developed.

In 1898 a Parliamentary joint select committee recommended that power companies be set up to serve several areas instead of just one. This was so effectively opposed both by private interests and by local authorities that the Electric Lighting Act of 1899 increased rather than lessened the parochial character of electricity regulation. The Act forbade companies to consolidate without the consent of Parliament, and more important still it forbade any electricity enterprise, private or municipal, to supply power or lay lines outside its prescribed area without the consent of Parliament. This meant that an enterprise could not serve consumers in the surrounding 'fringe.'

By the turn of the century the electrical industry had progressed from merely supplying electric light to the vastly more important work of supplying electric power. This brought a flood of applications from private companies to supply power

15. Report of the Committee on Electricity Distribution (1936), 5.

to wide areas. A Parliamentary committee considered the whole problem and reported in favor of granting licenses along these broader lines. But the opposition of local authorities to the various power bills based on the committee's report resulted in hedging in the new electric power franchises with crippling restrictions. Among these were the following: Power companies could supply consumers with 'power' but not with light. They could supply power in bulk to such authorized undertakers as desired it, but could exercise their powers within the area of any existing authorized undertaker only with its consent, though such consent was not to be 'unreasonably withheld.' The establishment of these new power companies was important as a precedent, as a partial assault upon parochial control; but the companies never developed as vigorously as they might. The limitations were burdensome and capital was not easy to attract.

The first World War tremendously expanded the demand for power, and it emphasized as nothing else could have done the glaring inadequacies of the existing system of supply and distribution. There were over 600 separate undertakings generating electricity. They were producing on the average 5,000 horse power, though efficiency of operation required a minimum of at least 20,000 horse power. The areas of operation were uneconomical in size. Many of the plants were inefficiently managed, the price situation was bad, and the machinery for inspection and control was weak and inadequate. It was obvious that drastic reorganization of the industry could not be long delayed. A new Electric Power Supply Committee, known as the Williamson committee, was set up and in 1918 reported a proposal for such reorganization. Its basic plan called for the centering of the generation and main transmission of power in sixteen regional authorities. This amalgamation was to be effected by compulsory power vested in a central authority. A bill based on the Williamson committee report passed the House of Commons, but it was largely emasculated by the House of Lords, which struck out all compulsory powers of amalgamation and left no effective authority for national planning. In this form it became law.

This statute, the Electricity Supply Act of 1919, was, however, a beginning step toward the national regulation of the electric power industry. It created the Electricity Commissioners, a body of five members, to which were assigned two principal powers. First, it received most of the powers of license and regulation which had been exercised by the Board of Trade; these will be discussed at a later point.[16] Second, the Electricity Commissioners were to serve as a national planning agency to bring about needed amalgamations and reorganizations. The commissioners were placed under the new Ministry of Transport also created in 1919.

The results accomplished under the Act of 1919, while not negligible, fell far short of meeting the major problems clamoring for solution. The regulatory duties of the Electricity Commissioners were competently discharged, but they did not include effective control of prices or service. On the side of planning the new arrangement failed completely. Without power to compel amalgamations, practically none were effected. Persuasion proved wholly inadequate. The Electricity Commissioners found themselves without authority to bring about needed co-ordination in the industry. They could not compel the interconnection of existing systems, nor could they compel a small station operating at high cost to buy power in bulk from a larger and more efficient station.

b. *The Weir committee and the Act of* 1926

The demand for thoroughgoing reform became increasingly urgent. A new committee of inquiry was set up in 1925 under the chairmanship of Lord Weir. It took its assignment seriously and, furthermore, it had access to information and experience acquired by the Electricity Commissioners during the five years since 1919. Demand for drastic reorganization was coming from the British business world. Great Britain was lagging far behind her chief business competitors in the utilization of electric power. By 1924-5 the United States and Germany had electrified 73 per cent and 66 per cent of their industrial plants respectively, while Great Britain had electrified but 48 per cent of hers. Only half of the British generating stations could justify their existence on the basis of operating efficiency.

The Weir committee proposed drastic changes, and these

16. *Infra,* 535 f.

were embodied in the Electricity Supply Act of 1926. By this statute the entire system of generating electricity has been nationalized, concentrated in a small number of carefully placed stations with an interconnecting system of transmission lines, and placed in the hands of the Central Electricity Board. This board, which we shall study in detail later,[17] is separate and distinct from the Electricity Commissioners. It was felt that it should be quite free from political pressure and control. But the Electricity Commissioners, in addition to their existing regulatory powers, serve as an expert supervisory body under whose direction and control this operating board carries on its work. Thus the Electricity Commissioners occupy a somewhat anomalous position between the Minister of Transport to whom they are directly responsible, and the Central Electricity Board over which they exercise broad supervisory power.

c. *Structure and personnel*

The Electricity Commissioners are appointed by the Minister of Transport with the concurrence of the Board of Trade. There may not be more than five members; at present there are four. Two are appointed for fixed terms of from two to seven years, and are eligible to reappointment. The others serve during the pleasure of the Crown, which of course means permanent tenure. Three are full-time officers, the others part time. The three full-time officers are selected for practical commercial and scientific knowledge and wide business experience, including experience in the electrical industry; actually these three members have from the beginning been electrical engineers. Persons having any interest in any electricity undertaking are ineligible. The commissioners use technical assistance constantly, and employ a staff of their own which they appoint and to which civil service conditions apply. The staff salaries are, however, fixed by the Minister of Transport, who is responsible for the budget of the commissioners. The Electricity Commissioners are essentially an administrative body, exercising some quasi-judicial functions. They do not, however, claim 'judicial detachment' as do the tribunals we have been discussing. The cost of maintaining the Electricity Commissioners

17. *Infra,* 574 ff.

is met by a levy on the industry based on the amount of current sold. Any surplus collected is redistributed.

d. *Functions and powers*

The powers and duties of the Electricity Commissioners have been conferred by numerous statutes beginning with the basic Act of 1919. They fall into two major groups: quasi-judicial regulatory powers, and planning functions. These may be briefly summarized:

As we have seen, the Electricity Commissioners received by the Act of 1919 the regulatory powers over electricity undertakings previously vested in the Board of Trade, and these have been augmented from time to time since 1919. They are exercised under the general supervision of the Minister of Transport. (a) The commissioners are the licensing body to which all applications from would-be suppliers of electricity go. They conduct full inquiry on these applications and reach a decision. (b) They must approve all new generating stations, overhead transmission lines, or extensions of either. Proposals for these come from the Central Electricity Board. (c) They issue 'fringe orders,' allowing electricity authorities to supply electricity beyond their statutory areas. A city wishing to supply a suburb must secure such a fringe order. (d) A statute of 1922 provides for a review of electricity prices every three years on complaint of interested parties. The Minister of Transport usually refers these complaints to the Electricity Commissioners for action, though he is not bound by their decisions. (e) They receive and publish full financial and statistical reports from all electrical authorities. (f) They approve loans made by local authorities for electrical undertaking purposes. (g) They establish regulations to promote public safety and the efficient supply of current to consumers. (h) They may issue orders requiring changes in the type of current, in frequency and volume, and in equipment, in order to effect the 'standardization' so sorely needed in British electricity supply systems. Appeals from such standardization orders go to the Minister of Transport on grounds of unreasonable expense. Difficulties of enforcement have prevented any effective use of this important power. (i) The commissioners may authorize the creation of joint electricity authorities, but local jealousies have thus far prevented much progress along this line. (j) They have power to settle disputes between local electricity authorities. (k) Most of the electricity powers of the Minister of Transport are exercised 'through' or 'after consultation with' the commissioners. (l) Finally, the commissioners exercise general supervision over the Central Electricity Board. They must see that the plans and activities carried on under the authority of the board fall within the terms of the statutes. This is an important duty and occupies much time. The division of authority between these two important agencies is not entirely clear. The board must secure the consent of the commissioners in numerous matters. The commissioners, if hostile, could seriously cramp the board's freedom of action, but harmonious relations have thus far prevailed. The commissioners also serve as an arbitral body to settle disputes about compensation between the Central Electricity Board and the owners of generating stations, and disputes between the board and landowners whose property may be taken.

The planning functions of the Electricity Commissioners are of great importance, but they were acquired somewhat fortuitously. The original bill of 1926 provided that the Central Electricity Board should draw plans for national electricity generation and main transmission schemes, which should be submitted to the Electricity Commissioners for approval; this would have made the new Central Electricity Board both a planning and an operating body, leaving to the commissioners only regulatory and supervisory functions. For no clear reasons the House of Lords reversed this arrangement, and the Act of 1926 gave to the Electricity Commissioners the task of drafting the plans for national electricity schemes, and to the Central Electricity Board the administration of them. These planning functions include dividing the country into electricity 'zones,' the selection of stations for the generation of current, and the mapping out of the main transmission lines over the entire country. When these plans have been formulated by the commissioners into draft schemes, they are sent to the Central Electricity Board, which works out the necessary details. They are then published, and any persons or undertakings affected may claim the right to be heard.

These are the formal legal arrangements allocating the responsibility for national electricity planning. In actual practice, however, the writer is reliably informed,[18] the planning function has largely passed over to the Central Electricity Board. The plans are likely to be drawn by the engineers and the technical staff of the board, and submitted to the commissioners. While the legal formalities may be scrupulously observed, the actual work of planning has slipped over into the hands of the technical experts best equipped to handle it.

e. *Procedure*

Problems of procedure before the Electricity Commissioners have never loomed very large. In handling their numerous quasi-judicial functions they follow roughly the procedure of a tribunal. Parties are sometimes represented by counsel, but the commissioners are engineers and businessmen and not lawyers, and they do their work with efficient informality. While they have not escaped criticism, they do enjoy a reputation for scrupulous fairness and good judgment.

f. *Relations with other agencies or departments*

By statute the Electricity Commissioners are wholly under the direction of the Minister of Transport. This applies to matters of policy as well as to specific minor matters. The consent of the Minister is necessary to an electricity franchise; but the commissioners draft the orders to which the consent is given. The commissioners advise the Minister in certain matters, but he is not obliged to follow their advice. In certain cases, as in the matter of orders for the standardization of equipment, appeals lie from the commissioners to the Minister. Finally, the budget of the commissioners requires the Minister's approval.

In practice, the Electricity Commissioners enjoy virtually complete independence in their day-to-day work. The Minister exerts no influence on their decisions on technical or quasi-judicial matters. Perhaps the technical character of much of their work is in itself a protection against political interference. But their immunity from pressure goes beyond that, and re-

18. Conversation with Graeme Haldane in 1937.

sults from the clear disposition of the Minister to protect their independence and impartiality. There are, however, matters of broad policy affecting the government's control of electricity supply and distribution on which the Minister must assume direct responsibility and on which, therefore, he issues instructions to the commissioners. In all such matters they are a part of his department and subject to his direction. In short, the happy result seems to have been achieved of permitting the Electricity Commissioners to act with complete independence and impartiality in their day-to-day handling of cases, and especially in matters affecting private rights, and at the same time insuring their conformity to broad lines of national policy in the field.

The relation of the commissioners to Parliament is that of a departmental subdivision. The commissioners are responsible to the Minister and he is responsible for them to the House of Commons. All the customary procedures for enforcing this responsibility are available. In addition, certain orders of the commissioners, such as the granting of electricity supply powers, must be approved by a resolution of Parliament. This kind of business has its special place on the calendar of the House of Commons and is handled *pro forma* without Parliamentary consideration on the merits.

The relations between the Electricity Commissioners and the Central Electricity Board have been briefly sketched and will be mentioned again when the latter body is discussed. It is enough to indicate here that the Central Electricity Board is an executive operating agency whose duty it is to carry into execution plans for which the Electricity Commissioners are responsible. Its methods of doing so are subject at all points to appeal to the commissioners by the interests affected. The division of labor and responsibility seems a sound one. Graeme Haldane has described it thus to the writer: 'There is a technical operating board which in practice, though not in law, draws up technical plans and which is supervised by an outside agency having ultimate responsibility to the Minister. This combines the necessary freedom from political control of the day-to-day administration of a highly technical job with the machinery for guaranteeing that that job be carried out within the limits of the law and in general conformity to the government's broad policies.' There is no statutory or official arrangement for collaboration or mutual consultation between the commissioners and the board. Such collaboration does, however, go on constantly and the informal relations between the two bodies have been harmonious.

The commissioners are brought into frequent touch with public and private opinion. The electrical industries in England are well organized, and there are many associations representing the varied interests involved. The commissioners have contacts with these and keep in touch with different shades of opinion.

g. *Appraisal and comment*

The success of the Electricity Commissioners within the scope of their present jurisdiction is admitted on all sides. They are regarded as fair and efficient, and this high public regard is shown by the fact that all the proposals for enlarging the government's power over the electricity industry contemplate giving such new powers to the commissioners rather than to new agencies.

There is sharp public criticism of the fact that the Act of 1926 deals with only half the electricity problem. It established nationalization of the generation and main-line transmission of electricity; it left untouched the vital problems involved in the distribution and sale of electricity to the consumer. In this area chaos still prevails. The situation was graphically described in the report of the McGowan committee:

. . . According to the evidence which has been placed before us, there were, at the 31st March, 1934, no less than 635 separate authorised undertakers, comprising . . . the Central Electricity Board, 3 Joint Electricity Authorities, 5 Joint Boards, 373 Local Authorities, and 253 Companies and persons . . .

These vary in size from an undertaking having an area of supply of a few hundred acres and only selling a few thousand units per annum to an undertaking having an area of 5,000 square miles and selling upwards of 500 million units per annum.

. . . The present admitted lack of uniformity in systems of supply and voltages, tariffs and methods of charge, facilities for hire or hire-purchase of apparatus, assisted wiring, etc., is undoubtedly due primarily to the existence of such a large number of separate undertakings.

. . . In the case of distribution voltages, there are as many as 43 different declared voltages for low and medium pressure supplies ranging between 100 and 480 volts.

. . . The multiplicity of undertakings involves multiplicity of boundaries. The existence of different tariffs, different systems of supply and different facilities on opposite sides of those numerous boundaries (in many cases on opposite sides of the same street) is the main reason which has led to a public demand for greater uniformity.[19]

Several proposals have been brought forward to deal with these pressing problems. All aim at some measure of national control and amalgamation in the distribution of electricity. The Labour Party in 1932 proposed nationalization of the entire industry, thus giving the government a free hand to wipe out the last vestiges of the present parochial system of control. The McGowan committee, already mentioned, proposed that the Electricity Commissioners should appoint regional commissions endowed with compulsory powers to effect regional amalgamations. These regional schemes would be approved by the Electricity Commissioners, which would continue to serve as the one central supervisory authority over the entire industry.

In 1937 the Government brought in a bill based mainly upon the proposals of the McGowan committee. This bill proposed that a group of boards be set up in areas throughout the country to manage the local distribution of electricity; these to be, in substance, little central electricity boards, each operating within its own area. The supervision of these regional boards and the co-ordination of their programs was to be placed in the hands of the Electricity Commissioners. This scheme would have vastly enlarged the authority of the commissioners and changed in some measure the nature of their powers. The bill did not pass.

In October 1937, the King's speech contained a promise that 'a measure for improving the distribution of electricity will be laid before you.' In May 1939, the Minister of Transport, in response to a question, said in the House of Commons: 'The

19. Report of the Committee on Electricity Distribution (1936), 13 f.

reorganization of electricity distribution is regarded as a matter of major importance with which it is intended to deal as soon as circumstances permit.' Up to date, circumstances have apparently not permitted. It is now pointed out that unified and efficiently co-ordinated regional systems of electricity distribution would offer larger and more important targets to German bombers than do the existing little independent systems which, inefficient as they are, render their little communities relatively self-sufficient.

2. ROAD TRANSPORT AUTHORITIES

We have already discussed the Road and Rail Appeal Tribunal, the judicialized body which in matters affecting the road transport of goods (trucking) hears appeals from the officers who exercise the initial control. We now turn to the agencies which actually regulate the road transport both of passengers and of goods, an essentially administrative job.

a. *Background of road transport regulation in England*

The early growth of motor transportation in England was in no way unique. It passed through the same experimental stages of development as in this country. At the outset it made headway against unsympathetic and rigorous control. For many years it was illegal to drive any motor vehicle on any British highway, unless a man walked ahead of it carrying a large red flag. Until 1930 a twenty-mile speed limit prevailed nominally all over Great Britain; and the licensing of motor vehicles, such as it was, remained in the hands of the local authorities.

The first World War expanded motor transport in all its forms, and the return of peace brought two separate and acute problems. The first of these was cheap, unregulated bus competition on the public streets and highways, with its resulting dangers to life and property. During the rush hours in the large cities fleets of 'pirate' buses would operate, racing perilously with each other in a mad scramble for passengers, while during the quiet hours bus service would be woefully inadequate. It was clear that effective control was imperative. London began the solution of its problem with the concentration in 1912 of control over London's underground transport system in a combine headed by Lord Ashfield, who was later to become chairman of the London Passenger Transport Board.[20]

The second problem was the ruinous effect upon the British railways of the competition of trucks and buses. Railway receipts were falling for other reasons in the 1920's: the railways were burdened with many statutory requirements and the necessity of paying a return on heavy capitalization; they paid heavy taxes; they had to pay for the upkeep of their roadbeds and their costly rolling stock. They were, in short, quite unable to stand up permanently against the road transport industry.

A drive for government control was set in motion to meet these two problems, especially the problem of competition. In this drive the British railways were perhaps most influential. They had substantial political influence, and were much better organized than the motor transport operators who were, in the main, either individuals or small new companies. The drive for government control was aided by the trade unions, who knew that working conditions were bad in so new and disorganized an industry and hoped to improve them through government regulation. Aid was also lent by the better-organized road transport operators themselves, who wanted relief, from whatever source, from cutthroat competition. These pressures produced in 1929 a Royal Commission on Transport, which made a full investigation of the whole problem.

The first report of this commission dealt with the problems of passenger transport, and its recommendations were embodied in the Road Traffic Act of 1930. It was wholly natural to begin at this end of the problem, since it was the most pressing. Buses and other passenger vehicles were subject to numerous local license requirements, and to the regulations and decisions of local authorities who were guided by no uniform principles.

In 1933 the commission made a second report dealing with goods transport, and this report formed the basis of the Road and Rail Traffic Act of 1933. While the Acts of 1930 and 1933 follow the same principles, the administrative machinery set up by them differs sufficiently to justify separate treatment.

The development of road transport regulation aroused no

20. *Infra*, 600 ff.

party controversy. The Royal Commission on Transport was appointed by a Conservative Government. The first legislative step in the program was taken under the leadership of Herbert Morrison, Minister of Transport in a Labour Government. The program was completed under a 'Liberal-National' Minister of the National Government.

b. *Regulation of passenger transport*[21]*—The Area Traffic Commissioners*

i. *Structure and personnel*

Under the provisions found in the Road Traffic Act of 1930 England and Wales were divided into ten areas and Scotland into two. For each of these, the Minister of Transport names three traffic commissioners. One is chosen from a panel named by the county councils in the area; one from a panel named by the boroughs and urban districts; one, the chairman, is the free choice of the Minister. The chairman is a full-time officer chosen for a seven-year term but eligible to reappointment. The other two are part-time officers, serve for three years, and are re-eligible if their names remain on their respective panels. The Minister of Transport provides such staff and office facilities as are necessary, and the salaries of the commissioners and their staffs are fixed by him in consultation with the Treasury. The commissioners must have no financial interest in any road transport undertaking, and must be dismissed by the Minister if they acquire any. The full-time chairman, as was intended, dominates his colleagues. These are likely to be burdened with the duties of local government administration; they have little time to give; they are often irregular in attendance. The chairmen of the various areas meet together at intervals to discuss their common problems and this tends to accentuate their leadership over their colleagues. The commissioners carry on their duties 'under the direction' of the Minister; but the chairmen are usually men of ability and standing and are encouraged to act with independence.

21. Cf. D. N. Chester, *Public Control of Road Passenger Transport* (1936).

ii. *Powers and functions*

The powers of the Area Traffic Commissioners are associated with the granting and revoking of licenses for public service passenger vehicles, vehicles which carry passengers for hire, such as taxis and buses. These powers do not cover 'contract carriages,' which are hired as a whole for a particular occasion, or privately owned pleasure·cars. The granting of taxi and bus licenses is a vitally important function, since the conditions attached cover the whole field of possible regulation. The licenses, which are granted for one year at a time, fix the fares to be charged, time-tables to be followed, frequency of runs, routes, speed, and places where passengers may be picked up and set down.

Licensing policy is required by the statute to be governed by two main considerations, first, the problem of traffic congestion, and second, the problem of competition. In dealing with the first of these, the area commissioners before granting a new license must be satisfied that there is room on the roads and streets for new buses and that congestion of traffic will not result. More important is the second mandate, that new licenses must not produce undesirable competition. Existing services are to be protected against interlopers, and 'rush-hour' competition is not permitted to skim the cream off the profits to be derived from that heavy volume of business. Wasteful competition, in short, is ruled out and existing operators may appear before the Area Traffic Commissioners and oppose a new license by showing that they themselves can adequately provide any needed service. If they can show this, the new license will not be granted. The area licensing authority must also protect the British railways from the competition of the road transport industry. As we have seen, the railways were partly responsible for the passing of the Act. They are required by statute to run regular services all the year round, and they expect protection against cheaper fares and temporary 'peak-period' interlopers. Although road transport operators may not appear before the Railway Rates Tribunal to defend themselves against railway competition, the railways constantly use their right to appear before the Area Traffic Commissioners to protest against the licensing of new road transport facilities. To secure a license it is not enough for the motor operator 'to show that there are people desirous of traveling to a certain place to which the road service is inadequate; he must also show that the railways do not adequately cater for this need.' [22] The commissioners will also make sure that bus fares are not so low that railway business is adversely affected. Thus the whole licensing policy is heavily weighted for the benefit of vested railway interests. This has obvious advantages for the beneficiaries, but it is cogently urged that those advantages are not shared by the passenger who wishes to ride as cheaply and conveniently as he can.

The Area Traffic Commissioners have power to revoke road transport licenses for non-compliance with the conditions contained in them. They license all drivers and conductors on public service vehicles. The regulations governing the conduct of drivers are, however, made by the Minister of Transport. The Act of 1930 provides that wages and conditions of labor must be 'fair.' This is not easy to enforce, since there is no positive power in the commissioners to fix wages or determine working conditions. Labor complaints may be made to the commissioners, who may refer them to the Minister of Transport or to an industrial court for arbitration. The statute directs the commissioners to bring about the maximum coordination of all transportation facilities within the area; but since it confers no concrete powers to this end, it remains the expression of a pious hope.

iii. *Procedure*

The Area Traffic Commissioners are not a court, but a body of administrative officers. The statute requires that in handling applications for licenses a public hearing must be held at which objections may be presented. The procedure at these hearings is largely discretionary with the commissioners, and it is kept informal. Legalistic arguments are discouraged; but even here a good lawyer is a help and counsel are frequently employed. This may be hard on the small applicant who may find himself pitted against the highly paid barrister of a large railway corporation.

22. Ibid. 133.

The commissioners delegate some of their functions to a single member, usually the full-time chairman. Two are a quorum for a public hearing, but in case of disagreement there is a rehearing before all three. The issuance of operators' licenses is handled by established and informal routine. An appeal lies to the board of three commissioners if such a license is refused.

iv. *Appeals from the Area Traffic Commissioners*

If a driver or conductor is refused a license by the commissioners he may appeal to the Court of Quarter Sessions, whose decision is final.

Appeals from the decisions of the Area Traffic Commissioners on the licensing of vehicles may be taken within one month to tne Minister of Transport. The grounds of appeal must be in writing and notice given to interested parties. The Minister then appoints 'some one with legal experience,' but not a member of the department, to hold a public hearing. This representative of the Ministry has the transcript of the hearing before the commissioners. He does not try the case *de novo;* he allows fresh evidence only in exceptional cases; and he tries to determine whether the decision below was clearly wrong. He makes a complete report to the Minister, who then decides as he sees fit, though naturally he usually follows the recommendations laid before him. The Minister may order the commissioners to reverse action already taken, or he may affirm their decisions. His rulings do not bind the commissioners as permanent principles to be applied in all future cases, but there is a natural disposition to follow them. The decision of the Minister is now published with a written opinion giving the reasons for it. The earlier practice of announcing decisions without giving any reasons caused bitter complaint, and was partly responsible, as we have seen, for the creation of a separate appellate tribunal by the Act of 1933 for the handling of appeals in goods transport cases.

There is still disagreement about which method of appeal is best. The chief argument against appeals to the Minister and for a separate appeal tribunal is that the Minister will not be wholly unbiased in deciding the appeals. There is always a disposition on the part of the 'chief' to back up his subordinates. While the force of this objection has been largely met by the new procedure just described, it is still felt in some quarters that appeals ought to go to an 'independent tribunal.' The case for appeals to go to the Minister is that it is undesirable, if not calamitous, to let lawyers loose in this field; that to do so would breed delay, legalism, and a mass of case law unrelated to principle or policy. It is declared that in practice the Minister has handled cases impartially and has by no means 'rubber-stamped' the findings of the commissioners. From 1931 to 1934 the Minister did in fact reverse or modify the decisions of the commissioners in 39 per cent of the cases appealed. Furthermore, as an able student of the problem says:

. . . The strongest argument against such a tribunal [an independent tribunal] is the difficulty of reconciling conflicting policies. The Minister in making his decision must follow, consciously or unconsciously, a certain policy; even interpretation of statute law cannot avoid this. If his powers were transferred to another body, a policy would still be required, but there would be this difference: by reason of its power to make Orders on Appeal the tribunal's policy would override the Minister's policy whenever it differed. The Minister's control would be weakened and with it Parliamentary control, for no one would be responsible to Parliament for the tribunal's policy. This would be an unsatisfactory position and any attempts to remedy it could hardly result in more than some further unnecessary complication of the present licensing system.[23]

v. *Relations with other departments*

While the Area Traffic Commissioners are under the Ministry of Transport, the Minister does not interfere either by direct instruction or by indirect pressure with their decisions in individual cases. It has been cogently urged that such interference would be *ultra vires*. On two occasions the Minister sent to the commissioners statements of 'policy' in the nature of general instructions. The commissioners ignored these instructions and there have been no more. This does not mean, however, that the Minister is without influence or authority over the commissioners. He appoints them and presumably

23. Ibid. 81.

appoints persons who share his views. Through the system of appeals just described he may make his policies effective through decisions. The periodical meetings of the chairmen of the Area Traffic Commissioners occur in the office of the Minister. On these occasions information and points of view are exchanged, and harmonious relations are established and kept alive.

The commissioners have no direct contacts with Parliament. The Minister of Transport is responsible to Parliament for the general results of their work. He answers questions about them, but he makes it clear that their decisions, unless appealed, are beyond his reach. The commissioners have no formal relations with any other regulatory bodies in the transport field. There is still a complete absence of co-ordination of government effort in this area.

c. *Regulation of goods transport*

The regulation of goods transport in England dates from the Road and Rail Traffic Act of 1933, and forms the second part of the program of the Royal Commission on Transport, which, as we have seen,[24] had been working on the problem since 1929. The machinery set up for the administration of goods transport regulation is simple: the licensing authority is the chairman of the Area Traffic Commissioners sitting alone. There were perhaps two reasons for using this single officer rather than the whole body of Area Traffic Commissioners: First, in passenger transport licensing it was necessary for reasons of political expediency to give the local areas representation on the licensing authority, since these local areas previously exercised this power themselves; whereas goods vehicles had not been subject to local control. Second, it seemed unwise to burden the part-time Area Traffic Commissioners with new duties, since their duties under the Road Traffic Act of 1930 were very burdensome. There were obvious advantages, moreover, in using the experience and ability of the full-time chairman instead of setting up a new agency for the enforcement of the Act.

As goods transport licensing authority the chairman's sole task is to license all goods vehicles (trucks); he has no control

24. *Supra,* 542 f.

over rates, as do the Area Traffic Commissioners in the field of passenger fares. As goods vehicles serve several different purposes there are three types of license, labeled 'A,' 'B,' and 'C.' The A license must be held by a public carrier; the B license is held by one carrying his own goods as well as those of others (limited carrier's license); the C license covers the carriage of goods 'in connection with the trade or business' of the license holder. The C license is granted as a matter of routine if the applicant has not been guilty of gross violations of regulations and the vehicle is in sound condition; but the licensing authority has wide discretion in the granting of A and B licenses. He may refuse the license if, in his opinion, the new vehicle would be 'in excess of requirements,' due regard being paid to the 'public interest' and to the interest of those already providing transport facilities. Consideration is of course given to the record of the licensee in obeying the regulations and the conditions of his license.

Certain statutory principles govern the issuance of goods transport A and B licenses: First, a newcomer to the industry must show that the work he proposes to do could not be done by any existing facilities, whether motor vehicles or railways. This is a heavy burden of proof for the applicant to assume. The test is not whether there are shippers who would like to patronize him, but whether such shippers could use, whether they wished to or not, existing facilities either road or rail. The purpose of this is chiefly to protect the railways against motor truck competition. Second, all the regulations of the Minister of Transport in regard to equipment, size, weight, safety devices, and the like must be fully met. To see that this is done inspectors are appointed by the Minister. Third, licensees must keep an accurate record of trips and times. Fourth, road transport employers must pay fair wages and observe fair working conditions. The Act of 1933 set up a voluntary National Joint Conciliation Board to settle disputes in this field. It has not been successful, and a departmental committee has recently recommended compulsory enforcement of standards agreed upon.

The procedure before the goods transport licensing authority is like that before the Area Traffic Commissioners. The same man controls each. The only important difference is that the former is a single officer and the latter is a board of three.

The problem of co-ordination amongst regulatory bodies in the field of transport has been mentioned. No less than eight different agencies in the English government have jurisdiction over transportation. The Minister of Transport has relations with a number of these, but has no adequate power to co-ordinate their activities. Not only are these agencies independent of each other, but in some cases they are required by statute to follow different principles and policies. There are thoughtful people who believe that the only solution of the problem lies in the nationalization of all transport facilities.

In conclusion it may be observed that the Area Traffic Commissioners and the chairman as licensing authority are in many respects similar to the Electricity Commissioners. They are bodies under the ultimate direction of a responsible Minister, and perform independently important functions of regulation and control. There appears to be a satisfactory relation between policy determination and adjudication, and there have been no clashes on matters of policy between the Minister and these administrative agencies.

C. Guild Agencies—Industrial Self-Regulation under Government Supervision

1. THE AGRICULTURAL MARKETING BOARDS

a. *The guild principle in English economic regulation*

It has already been mentioned that British tradition and practice have long looked with favor upon giving important legal powers of self-regulation to organized groups. Self-regulation has always existed in the legal and medical professions, and has permeated many other fields in which regulation is necessary. It has become part of the British pattern of thought. In England it is unnecessary to worry about a constitutional doctrine of the separation of powers or its corollary, the doctrine that legislative and judicial powers may not be delegated. Therefore when need arises in Great Britain to subject to discipline or supervision interests which have previously been unrestricted, it is natural to explore first the possibility of setting up some system of self-regulation or self-discipline to be administered by representatives of the interests affected. For want of a better term we shall speak of this method of regulation as 'guild' control, since it is somewhat reminiscent of the type of authority exercised for so long by the mediæval guilds.

b. *Background of the Agricultural Marketing Acts* [25]

The almost uninterrupted slump in agricultural prosperity in England dates from an early period. The repeal of the Corn Laws in 1846 and the establishment of free trade took from British agriculture the artificial governmental protection previously enjoyed. By degrees, competition from abroad forced agricultural prices down, and this tendency has continued fairly steadily to the present time. Agriculture was temporarily stimulated during the first World War and benefited by emergency laws enacted to meet the national crisis. This legislation was repealed in 1921, and agricultural prices and wages were left to find their own level. The result was a sharp decline in the prices of farm products, which in turn reduced farm wages to so low a point that it was found necessary in 1924 to re-establish minimum wages by law. This helped the farm laborer, but increased the difficulties of the farmer.

In 1923 the Linlithgow committee was appointed to determine why there was so wide a difference between the low prices which the farmer received for his products and the high prices paid by the consumer. The committee reported that the machinery for marketing and distributing farm products was defective and that government action in that area was necessary, but no governmental action resulted from this report. There was a strong feeling that the farmers' co-operative movement already begun needed strengthening, and that farmers thus organized should be encouraged to provide relief without governmental intervention. For some ten years the government did nothing for the British farmer except to improve somewhat the credit facilities available to agriculture.

The world-wide depression which struck in 1929 fell upon an already depressed agricultural industry in Great Britain and

25. Cf. W. H. Jones, 'The Agricultural Marketing Boards,' in W. A. Robson (ed.), *Public Enterprise* (1937), 247 ff.

nearly ruined it. The Labour Government in power from 1929 to 1931 was not able to extend much aid to the farmer, since Labour support came chiefly from the cities; the Labour group in Parliament needed the support of the Liberals to retain their majority, and the Liberals were free traders. It was obvious, however, that something had to be done.

(1) *The Agricultural Marketing Act of* 1931. The Act of 1931 was the first step in a new program for the rehabilitation of British agriculture. It laid the foundation for the present system of marketing schemes. There already existed some associations of agricultural producers which had been able to influence prices and curb over-production. The new law was an enabling act which permitted organizations of producers of farm products 'to control their product effectively, as to price and volume, with statutory compulsion on possible recalcitrant producers, should a majority decide in favor of such a step.' This was in reality guild control, a farming out of legal regulatory powers to organized groups of private individuals. The government had no initiative in the matter, but had to wait until the organized producers of any agricultural product decided to exercise the powers granted by the statute. The Act of 1931 did not control the flow of agricultural imports, since the Labour and Conservative groups were hopelessly split on the issue of free trade versus tariff. Only one agricultural group, the producers of hops, organized under the Act of 1931.

(2) *The Agricultural Marketing Act of* 1933. The National Government which succeeded the Labour Government made important and needed changes in the earlier Act. The statute which it passed in 1933 set up restrictions upon agricultural imports, a measure vitally necessary to protect the British farmer, and allowed the government to set in motion the machinery for the setting up of marketing schemes, although it did not permit the imposition of such a scheme unless the producers affected agreed to it. It is unnecessary to set out in detail the operation of the Agricultural Marketing Act as it has been applied to the various producing groups in Great Britain, but it is desirable to sketch in broad terms the major features of this interesting type of guild control. These will now be summarized.

c. *Methods of setting up marketing boards*

A group of producers of a commodity, if they convince the Minister of Agriculture that they are 'substantially representative,' may prepare a 'scheme' and submit it to the Minister. This scheme must be given suitable publicity. The Minister hears objections and may order a public hearing under a competent and impartial person appointed by himself. He may modify the scheme, and he consults with the Board of Trade in relation to it. If he is convinced that the scheme will lead to the more efficient production or marketing of the product, he lays it before Parliament, which must pass a resolution approving it. The Minister then issues an order putting the scheme into effect. In doing so he is subject to the following conditions: All of the producers of the product must be registered and a poll of them taken. The scheme must be favored in this poll by two-thirds of the producers as well as by the producers of two-thirds of the product. If less than one-half of the producers vote, the Minister may declare the scheme void.

This method depends upon the initiative of the producers to get a scheme into operation. If the producers do not act, the Minister of Agriculture may appoint a 'reorganization commission' to inquire fully into the desirability of action in connection with any agricultural product. This commission has power to compel testimony and secure relevant information. If its findings justify it, it may draft a scheme and present it to the Minister. The Minister then presents the scheme to the producers concerned, hears objections to it, and then follows the same procedure as is outlined above. Thus there are two ways in which marketing schemes come into being.

d. *Structure and personnel*

Marketing schemes are administered by marketing boards. These boards vary substantially in the details of their organization. They range in size from eleven, in the case of the Pigs Board, to thirty-one, in the case of the Potato Board. They are all producers' boards, representative of and elected by the registered producers of the regulated commodity, who then co-opt a limited number of persons. One of the extra members is always a member of Parliament. The chairmen and vice-chairmen of the boards usually receive substantial salaries; the other members receive small salaries and often render only part-time service. The boards are required to appoint executive committees of not more than seven, but as these executive committees get no extra salary, the day-to-day administration of the boards' affairs centers in the chairmen and vice-chairmen (save in the Potato Board). The tenure of board members is usually for two or three years with the terms staggered to afford continuity.

e. *Powers and functions*

There is also considerable variation in the powers and duties performed by the several marketing boards. The following are the powers which a marketing board may possess and which most of them do possess: First, a board may buy all of the product over which it has control and may thereafter sell, grade, pack, store, advertise, and transport it. Second, it may compel producers to sell only to it or through an agency which it designates. Third, it may buy and either sell or lease to producers machinery necessary to produce, prepare for sale, or market the product. Fourth, it may fix the prices, terms, and persons to or through whom the product may be sold. No product over which it has jurisdiction may be sold by anyone but a registered producer. All the rules and orders of the board are binding upon all producers not specifically exempt. The marketing boards enjoy a good deal of discretion in regard to the powers they actually exercise, as well as to procedure.

f. *Procedure*

Since the marketing boards are usually large and unwieldy, a good deal of the actual business falls to an 'inner cabinet' of some kind, though final action must have the approval of the full board. Money may be raised or fines levied only by the entire board. The money to operate the marketing scheme is raised by levies on the registered producers. The actual procedure of any board is, as might be expected, informal.

The most interesting phase of the marketing scheme procedure is that set up for the specific protection of producers and consumers. The powers granted to the marketing boards are so far-reaching that special safeguards against their abuse were deemed necessary. There are two safeguards for consumers, who seriously need protection since the schemes are of, by, and for the producers.

The first of these safeguards takes the form of consumers' committees of which there are three, one for schemes covering Great Britain, one for England and Wales, and one for Scotland. The first two overlap and have the same chairman. Members are appointed by the Minister, who consults with the Board of Trade on one member, and with various co-operative societies on the others. The committees represent the consumers' interests. They inquire into the operation of the marketing schemes and report to the Minister upon acts or policies which they believe to be injurious to the consumers' interests. If the Minister believes these complaints to be serious enough, he refers them to a committee of investigation for further inquiry. The consumers' committees themselves have no power to compel testimony or the production of documents, and have been rendered fairly useless by their inability to get at essential facts.

The second safeguard for the consumer are the committees of investigation, of which again there are three. These have five members each, appointed by the Minister. They consider the complaints from the consumers' committees, referred to them by the Minister. They report on these matters to the Minister, but he is not obliged to follow their advice. If he decides to act he may do one of three things: (1) he may require the marketing board to correct the situation complained of; (2) after consulting with the Board of Trade he may lay an order before Parliament so amending the marketing scheme as to correct the matter; (3) by the same process he may revoke the scheme entirely. The committee of investigation may also consider complaints from producers when these are referred to it by the Minister.

If the producers find themselves in dispute with the marketing boards, the statute authorizes the Minister to appoint an arbitrator to iron out the difficulties, and this is in practice a very common and useful procedure.

g. *Relations of the marketing boards to the Minister of Agriculture*

The marketing boards are not appointed by the Minister of Agriculture. He has no direct connection with their establishment nor does he have any control over their day-to-day operations. None of the things which the boards do fall clearly under his supervision. It is necessary, however, to emphasize that the Minister does have important powers which condition the major activities of the boards, and that his permission is necessary before they may undertake certain activities. We shall summarize these forms of direct and indirect control by the Minister.

In the first place, indirect control by the Minister over the marketing boards might result from the investigations of the consumers' committees and the committees of investigation, but in practice these committees have been so feeble that nothing has resulted. Second, the Minister must approve the setting up of any development boards and appoint some of their members; development boards are created to co-ordinate two or more marketing schemes. Third, the Minister shares in the administration of the limitation and control of imports. This is primarily vested in the Board of Trade, which must, however, consult with the Minister of Agriculture and the Secretary of State for Scotland and Northern Ireland. Since the domestic marketing boards are dependent upon import restrictions, this is a real weapon in the hands of any Government that wishes to use it. It has not so far been used. Fourth, the Minister has power to alter the nature and composition of marketing boards. These changes may be initiated by the boards themselves through the procedure used in setting up the original scheme, or the Minister may by order extend or modify the powers of the board to permit it to function more effectively. While there are restrictions here, he enjoys some power to make changes without resorting to highly complicated procedure. Fifth, the Minister has power to revoke marketing schemes. This may be done on the initiative of the marketing boards, or upon demand of the registered producers as evidenced by a poll. In either case the Minister may order revocation. He may also order it on his own initiative by laying the matter before Parliament and securing its approval. Sixth, the Minister may amend a marketing scheme by acting upon the report of an agricultural marketing reorganization commission appointed by him. Such a commission consists of a chairman and four members. Outstanding men have been chosen for this service and, armed with full power to secure necessary information and compel testimony, they have conducted thorough and serious inquiries. They do not work under the supervision of the Minister, but they have usually co-operated with him, and their reports are likely to conform to his views.

h. *Relations with Parliament*

The Minister of Agriculture is responsible to Parliament for the general working of the agricultural marketing schemes. He presents the annual reports of the marketing boards to Parliament. He answers questions in the House of Commons on matters of broad policy, though not on matters of detail. Parliament has plenty of opportunity to debate the marketing boards and their work. These opportunities arise in connection with matters of finance and in the cases in which Parliament must give its approval to certain orders of the Minister concerning the boards. While there is no real continuous Parliamentary control, heavy pressure can be exerted on Parliament with regard to the boards, and this has more than once occurred.

i. *Relations with other bodies*

The Act of 1933 authorized the establishment of development boards. As already mentioned, these are joint bodies set up to bring about needed co-ordination between related commodity schemes. Thus the Bacon Development Board [26] was created to co-ordinate the activities of the Pigs Marketing Board and the Bacon Marketing Board. The marketing boards also maintain contacts with trade associations of various sorts. Thus there is close relation between the Hops Marketing Board and the Brewers' Society, which is the sole consumer of British

26. *Infra*, 561.

hops. Such contacts are of course an essential part of the normal routine of any effective marketing program, and are encouraged by the informality of the day-to-day procedure of the marketing boards.

2. THE APPLICATION OF THE MARKETING STATUTES

We cannot deal in detail with each of the marketing schemes set up under the Acts of 1931 and 1933. They all follow the same general pattern. The comments which follow aim to show the general scope of the entire marketing program, and to play up such unique characteristics or developments as experience with the separate schemes has brought to light.

a. *The Hops Marketing Board*

The hops marketing scheme was set up under the Act of 1931, and was amended and strengthened in 1934. The production and marketing of hops had been controlled during the World War by the government, and thereafter, not too effectively, by voluntary associations. There was sharp need to stabilize the market, since the yield of hops fluctuated yearly. The Hops Marketing Board consists of eighteen members, fourteen chosen from hops districts; the chairman is chosen by the board; the members are chosen annually and are eligible to re-election; salaries are determined at the annual meeting of the producers. The board has a complete grip upon the production and marketing of British hops. All producers are registered; the amount of hops which they produce is controlled by the board through production quotas; hops may be sold only through the board, and a price is guaranteed to producers over a five-year period, deficiencies being made up by levies upon merchants. The whole scheme operates as a fairly tight monopoly, and it is difficult for anyone to secure permission to start up as a new producer.

The marketing of hops is simplified by the fact that all the hops go to the British brewers, who are themselves well organized. Accordingly a permanent joint committee has been set up to co-ordinate the various interests involved. It consists of four representatives of the Brewers' Society, four from the Hops Marketing Board, and three chosen by the Minister of Agriculture. The whole scheme appears to have worked efficiently, and has escaped the public criticism directed against some of the other marketing schemes, since the only consumers' interests involved are those which are indirectly reflected in the price of beer. The ordinary consumer is probably unaware that he is affected at all.

b. *The Milk Marketing Board*

A milk marketing scheme went into effect in October 1933. It resulted from pressure from more than one direction. The price of milk received by the farmer had declined sharply between 1921 and 1932, and the big distributing combines favored some regulation as a protection against unrestricted competition. A poll of milk producers showed 96 per cent in favor of the scheme.

The Milk Marketing Board as set up is in no essential feature unique. It has seventeen members, twelve chosen by regional producers and five others. The terms of office are staggered to give continuity, and members are re-eligible. There is an executive committee of seven members, but it has proved of little importance. Day-to-day administration is handled by the chairman and vice-chairman, who receive salaries of £1,500 and £700 respectively. The powers of the board are extensive. All milk producers must be registered and may be prosecuted for selling milk if they are not. Registered producers may be punished by the board for violation of regulations. The board acts as an intermediary between milk producers and retailers, and is the only channel through which milk may be sold. It fixes the prices to be paid to the producers, and the price to be charged by wholesalers. Wholesale prices are fixed after consultation with representatives of the wholesalers. Unlike some of the other marketing schemes, the milk scheme makes no attempt to control production except through the control of prices. To stabilize prices to producers, the board maintains a pooling arrangement in each of the regions established by the Act, and an inter-regional compensation fund compensates the districts where prices are low. This stabilization actually operates to extract from the consumers of liquid milk a subsidy which is paid to the manufacturers and consumers of butter, cheese, and the like. The board has important powers of general regulation and promotion: it advertises milk products, engages in 'consumption steering' by such devices as cheap milk to school children, sells or rents apparatus to producers, licenses milk depots and factories, and exercises other similar functions. It receives funds from the government to pay certain types of subsidies, and it also makes levies on the producers for certain purposes. This financial dependence on Parliament has permitted broader debate and closer Parliamentary control than might otherwise have occurred, but these government subsidies are intended to be temporary.

There has been sharp and continuous criticism of the results obtained under the milk marketing scheme. This became so serious that the Minister of Agriculture appointed a Milk Reorganization Commission to investigate the entire industry and its problems and bring in a constructive report. This commission reported in 1936, making proposals so important as to warrant their careful analysis at a later point in this study.[27]

c. *Pigs and Bacon Boards*

The pigs and bacon marketing schemes were set up late in 1933 to deal with the critical condition of the bacon industry. Foreign competition was proving ruinous, and the disorganized state of the industry resulted in violent price fluctuations, instability in the supply of pigs, and general inefficiency.

The Bacon Marketing Board and the Pigs Marketing Board are essentially the same in structure and functions. The former has sixteen members, and the latter thirteen. The Pigs Board set up regional committees throughout Great Britain; these are in the main regulatory and have little to do with trading. The breeders of pigs and the curers of bacon are required to be registered. The two schemes are based fundamentally upon an estimate of the 'normal annual consumption' of bacon, and an import quota is established to keep within this limit. The Pigs Board has tried without much success to establish a production quota, and it has power to determine the price at which pigs are sold to the bacon curers, who are obliged to buy from

27. *Infra,* 566 ff.

the Pigs Board. The Bacon Board determines the kinds and grades of bacon to be produced and regulates the volume of production. The two boards between them settle upon the number of pigs to be produced and establish a 'standard contract price.'

It shortly became clear that the mechanism for co-ordinating pig breeding and bacon curing must not remain in the hands of two separate and autonomous bodies. The results of independent action were not satisfactory, and the patience of the public and of the producers themselves was exhausted. Accordingly in 1935 the Bacon Development Board was set up. This body has eleven members: three, including the chairman and vice-chairman, are appointed by the Minister, and four each by the Pigs and the Bacon Boards. The expenses are borne by the two boards.

The Bacon Development Board serves as a co-ordinator and arbitrator between the Pigs Board and the Bacon Board, though a producer, if aggrieved by its decisions, may still take the question to arbitration. The Bacon Development Board seeks to co-ordinate the capacity and location of bacon curing plants with the supply of pigs, since experience shows that there are not enough pigs produced. The general policy has been to refuse to license new curing plants, and ultimately to close down surplus plants by the withdrawal of licenses. The board may also carry on technical marketing research to advertise the industry, and may require certain minimum standards of hygiene and efficiency.

By 1936-7 it was apparent that all this machinery had failed to meet the needs of the situation, although some useful results had been achieved. The supply of pigs continued to be inadequate and unpredictable, since the producers were not prevented by any legal means from diverting their pigs into the unregulated pork market; and stabilization of the market proved to be impossible. In 1938, therefore, the Bacon Industry Act was passed to relieve the situation. It canceled the bacon development scheme of 1935, which created the Bacon Development Board, and set up a new Bacon Development Board on which the government has a larger, although still minority, representation. Of the thirteen members, five are appointed by the Minister of Agriculture; the remaining eight are nominated by the Pigs Board and the Bacon Board. The new board is very much more powerful than its predecessor. It acts, of course, in virtually all matters in consultation with the two marketing boards, but the latter are required to obey the written directions of the Development Board. Should they fail to do so, or should they act contrary to its policies, the Minister of Agriculture has power to transfer the functions involved to the Development Board, either upon the application of the board itself or of either marketing board, such order of transfer to be approved by Parliament. The Act provides for factory rationalization schemes to control the facilities for the production of bacon. These may be prepared by the Development Board, or by the Bacon Board. They are then submitted to the Minister and must be approved by Parliament. The Bacon Marketing Board assigns the quotas for bacon curing to the industry. Pigs for bacon are to be supplied to curers under long-term contracts at prices guaranteed by the government for three years, the price to cover everyone's cost and to give the economical producer a small margin of profit. The keynote of the entire scheme is stated to be efficiency, and it aims to make the industry self-supporting within a period of three years.

d. *The Potato Marketing Board*

The potato marketing scheme was set up in 1933 to control fluctuations in the supply and price of potatoes. The scheme was designed to stabilize production and standardize prices by preventing farmers from growing too many potatoes, by preventing wholesalers from selling them at too low a price, and by preventing injurious foreign competition.

The Potato Marketing Board is large. It consists of thirty-one members, twenty-nine of whom are chosen by the producers. There is rotation in membership in the interests of continuity. Good salaries are paid to the chairman, vice-chairman, and an executive committee of seven.

The powers of the board over the industry are extensive. No one may sell potatoes without being licensed. The board has wide powers in the matter of determining size, grades, packing, and similar matters, and it limits the amount any registered producer may sell. This is apportioned to a 'basic acreage' in past production. The producer must pay £5 for each additional acre grown. Producers are forbidden to sell potatoes to any but 'authorized merchants,' and 'authorized merchants' are forbidden to sell below a certain minimum price. This permits the fixing of prices paid to the producers. The Potato Marketing Board, unlike the others, has a share in determining the volume of potatoes imported and this gives it additional influence over the domestic market. The board is authorized to advertise potatoes, and it may buy and sell surplus potatoes. The scheme appears to work satisfactorily from the standpoint of everybody except the consumer, who pays higher prices.

3. APPRAISAL OF THE AGRICULTURAL MARKETING SCHEMES AND THE PRINCIPLE OF GUILD CONTROL

This whole program to stabilize the agricultural market and rehabilitate agricultural industry is very important. Experience with the various techniques employed has been highly instructive. Fifty per cent of English agricultural products is now under these schemes. The experimental nature of the whole program is obvious. It has developed, and is still developing, by a trial and error process. The British farmer was not accustomed to any form of direct government control; like the American farmer he was a rugged individualist, suspicious of any system which placed power over agriculture in the hands of governing bodies not controlled by the farmers themselves. The guild principle was followed in these marketing schemes because, at the outset at least, no higher degree of government intervention was politically possible.

Many criticisms have been urged against these marketing schemes and the results they have produced. These criticisms center mainly around three points:

In the first place, it is charged that the schemes set up producer control at the expense of the consumer. The statute assumes that the producers shall dominate, but also assumes that the consumers will be adequately protected by the consumers' committees and the committees of investigation. They have not been so protected. W. A. Robson has commented on this as follows:

The fundamental defect in this elaborate and cumbersome machinery is that the consumer is organized in parallel with the producer, with the result that he is excluded from the vital processes of decision and policy making. At no stage is the consumer placed in a position to influence policy, at no point is he given an opportunity to get at the facts from the inside, to see the various alternatives which were available to the board, or to obtain an insight into the forces which determined the issue. Instead, he is left outside the ring fence which encircles the happy fraternity of producers, fluttering his wings in a vain attempt to discover grounds for complaint without any right of access to books, statistics, or other relevant information.[28]

The Milk Reorganization Commission in 1936 emphasized the same point, and also made clear that this disregard of consumer interests was an inescapable feature of the marketing schemes:

An examination of the decisions which the Boards have taken in the matter of price-fixing shows that they are no different from what might have been expected from any body of business men engaged in selling a commodity and naturally intent upon obtaining for that commodity the best possible price. Each member must feel it incumbent upon him to have special regard to the views of those who have elected him to represent them: and it is natural for the electors to consider that the chief aim of their representatives should be to secure the best possible price for producers. It would be unreasonable to expect the representatives of producers to give as much consideration to the interests of the 'trade' or to the interests of the consumer, as to their own interests; further, as representatives, they must be tempted to strive after immediate benefits without due regard to the ultimate consequences.

In this assessment of the position we cast no adverse reflection on the Boards; we merely decline to put them on a higher plane than any other body of business men. The simple fact is, in our view, that it is impossible to expect them to fill the dual rôle of advocates and judges.[29]

A second criticism is that the marketing schemes do not adequately take into account the general public interest—an interest broader than that of the consumer. It is here urged that the schemes place a premium upon inefficiency. Weak and in-

28. W. A. Robson, 'The Public Service Board: General Conclusions,' in W. A. Robson (ed.), *Public Enterprise* (1937), 393.
29. Report of Milk Reorganization Commission for Great Britain (1936), 189.

competent producers are kept alive by a sort of artificial respiration. They are given no incentive to improve methods of production or to introduce new ones. The public interest is not served by their survival. This broader public interest would not be protected merely by setting up consumer representation on the marketing boards, a proposal frequently made, since such a change would merely turn the boards into arbitral tribunals to settle the conflicts of interest between producers and consumers.

A third criticism is directed against the inefficiency and ineffective personnel of the boards. There has been a disconcerting lack of interest on the part of many producers; in some cases the number voting upon important matters has been shockingly small. Nor has it been easy to get able businessmen amongst the farmers to make the sacrifices involved in holding positions on the various boards, with the result that the calibre of board members in point of business and administrative ability has not been as high as it should be.

The validity of these criticisms is generally accepted by the British public. The government itself has more than once indicated its dissatisfaction with the present arrangements. The producers' interests, however, have been strong enough thus far to block any substantial changes in the field of agricultural marketing, although new schemes appear to be emerging.

4. THE TREND AWAY FROM GUILD CONTROL

Dissatisfaction with the agricultural marketing schemes has taken shape in various ways. Even in agricultural marketing itself, where individualism is most pronounced, there are signs of a drift away from the principle of guild control toward direct control by the government. This trend has not been abrupt, but it may be clearly observed in various responsible governmental proposals, and also in the nature of the machinery set up for the regulation of other depressed industries besides agriculture.

a. *The proposals of the Milk Reorganization Commission*
of 1936

The sharpest, ablest, and most influential criticism of the
principle of guild control is to be found in the elaborate report
of the Milk Reorganization Commission in 1936. It deserves
comment because of its intrinsic soundness, and because it has
already had an important influence upon government policy.
This is true in spite of the fact that its immediate proposals for
reorganizing the regulation of the milk industry have not yet
been adopted. The report of the commission rejects entirely
the principle of guild control, and proposes regulation through
a wholly independent government body. Its plan is as follows:

The proposed independent milk commission would consist
of a chairman and four members appointed by the Ministry
of Agriculture and the Secretary of State for Scotland, in consultation with certain other members of the government. They
would have five-year staggered terms and be re-eligible. The
members would not be 'representative' of the industry or any
of its parts. The commission would instead be 'composed of
persons of exceptional talent and experience; conspicuous ability in finance, industry, commerce, or administration in the
widest sense would furnish the type required.' It would be paid
from government funds, so that it would not be financially dependent upon the industry.

This milk commission would have broad powers. It would
control policy with respect to price and production, although
these policies would naturally be worked out in consultation
with those whose interests are involved. It would have tight
control over distributors, with power to limit their margin
of profit. It would administer whatever government subsidies
might be desirable. It would promote plans for the general
progress and development of the industry. It would supply information, advice, and recommendations to the Minister of
Agriculture and to Parliament. Provision would be made for
marketing boards, but these would be closely bound by the
decisions of the commission within its jurisdiction and would
have the statutory duty of putting them into effect.

The most important change lies in the relation of the proposed commission to the Minister and to Parliament. This is summed up in the words of the reorganization commission as follows:

> . . . The over-riding control of milk policy, as of every phase of national policy, must, of course, remain with the Government and Parliament, and it will naturally be the Commission's duty to implement the Government's instructions on any matter falling within its province. The establishment of the permanent Commission will thus in no way encroach upon the Government's ultimate responsibility; but the Commission will be a source of informed and disinterested advice upon which the Government can draw for the material needed in making their decisions.[30]

The Minister would act on the recommendations made by the milk commission with respect to the functions and activities of the marketing boards, as he now does on the reports made by the committees of investigation. In view of the changed composition of the commission, no appeal would be allowed from its decisions. Marketing boards would be kept and would exercise many administrative duties of importance: they would register producers, regulate contracts, operate regional pools, collect statistics and information, and generally represent the producers' interests. This, it is believed, would be safe and satisfactory, since the producers would no longer fix prices or exercise any powers in matters of important public policy.

The report of the Milk Reorganization Commission was received with enthusiasm by thoughtful people. Its influence may be traced, it is believed, in some of the recent regulatory statutes we are about to consider, of which a number dealt with depressed industries other than agriculture. Some of these might logically be classified as administrative tribunals, but as they owe their creation to pressures similar to those which produced the marketing boards, there is in some of them enough flavor of guild control to make it appropriate to discuss them in this connection. One wonders, in fact, why these regulatory bodies did not follow more closely the pattern of the agricultural marketing boards. There may be several explanations: In some cases the needed regulation was more closely concerned with the general public interest and less with the problems of mar-

30. Ibid. 243.

keting. In other cases the statutes have been changed since their enactment in ways which indicate a drift away from guild control, a development due perhaps to the unsatisfactory experience with some of the marketing schemes. One or two of the statutes were passed after 1936, and may have been influenced by the convincing report of the Milk Reorganization Commission. Without discussing these bodies in detail, we may mention their chief characteristics and draw attention to what appears to be a rather clearly defined movement away from guild control.

b. *The Wheat Commission of* 1932; *the Sugar Commission of* 1936

These two bodies may be dealt with together. Both are concerned almost exclusively with the administration of large government subsidies to two industries which seem unable to keep afloat without them. The Wheat Commission is composed of nineteen persons appointed by the Minister of Agriculture, and represents in stipulated proportions all relevant interests. Its chief job is to pay to British wheat growers a subsidy raised by a levy on flour millers and importers. This is vaguely reminiscent of the processing taxes levied under the first AAA in the United States. The Minister of Agriculture, in consultation with the Wheat Commission, determines for each season the 'ascertained average price of wheat,' and also fixes with the commission the standard of millable wheat. All by-laws of the commission require the Minister's approval and all by-laws, orders, and regulations must lie in Parliament for twenty-eight days. There is here a closely centralized governmental control.

The Sugar Commission consists of a chairman and four members appointed by the Minister of Agriculture with the consent of the Treasury; none of these may have any interest in the sugar business. Salaries are paid by the government. The main function of the Sugar Commission is to supervise the British Sugar Corporation, a heavily subsidized company formed by the compulsory amalgamation of all the beet-sugar factories in Great Britain. The commission also has some regulatory powers over sugar refiners, including the power to license with a view to preventing inefficiency and uneconomical refining. The commission is subject to the supervision of the Minister of Agriculture. This arrangement is rather like that proposed by the Milk Reorganization Commission. It is expected that a sugar-beet marketing board will shortly be established. General guidance of the industry, as well as power to make important policy decisions, rests in the hands of an impartial commission independent of the industry, appointed by the government and under the control of a responsible Minister to whom it serves as a disinterested adviser.

c. *The Herring Industry Board of* 1935

The herring industry was referred to in the *Economist* as 'perhaps the most depressed of our depressed industries' [31] and the Herring Industry Act was passed in 1935 to rescue it. This created a Herring Industry Board consisting of a chairman and seven members appointed by the Ministers.[32] The chairman and two of these were to be independent and non-expert, the other five were to have special knowledge of the industry. In the beginning the government intended to move still further in the direction of self-government by the industry, with the expectation that this hybrid board would later be changed into a producers' board when the industry had become capable of running itself. This perhaps explains some of the vagueness in the terms of the Act.

The board was to prepare a scheme for the reorganization, development, and regulation of the industry. It was to be somewhat like the agricultural marketing schemes and was to be set up by the same general procedure. The board was given important powers over the industry. These included loans for the equipment of boats, the purchase and disposal of redundant boats, the limitation through a licensing system of the number and operation of boats, curers, salesmen, and the like, the power temporarily to fix prices and prohibit or restrict fishing, the purchase of fish for export, the acquiring and disposal of surplus herring. The expenses of administration were met by a levy on the industry. Government control over the board's ac-

---

31. *The Economist* (1936), vol. cxx, 172.
32. There are several for this and the following boards, and include such Ministers as have concern with the industry.

tivities came mainly through the granting of funds from the Exchequer. A consumers' committee and committee of investigation were set up. The results of the scheme were not impressive, and as time went on sharp criticism was directed against the representation of interests on the board, which resulted in a continuous tug of war between groups having axes to grind.

This dissatisfaction took shape in the Herring Industry Act of 1938. This statute moved sharply away from the principle of guild control or producer representation. It reconstructed the Herring Industry Board so that it now has a chairman and two members appointed by the Ministers and these members must have no financial or commercial interests which might influence the discharge of their duties. The functions of the board are roughly the same as under the Act of 1935, except that it has been given general review of matters relating to the herring industry, including conditions of employment. The expenses of the board are paid by the government. A Herring Industry Advisory Council is created to give advice to the board; this council is appointed by the Minister in consultation with those who will so advise him as to make sure that the industry is adequately represented.

d. *The Livestock Commission of* 1937

The Livestock Industry Act was passed in 1937 to reorganize the industry so that it might become efficient under reasonable import restrictions. It created the Livestock Commission with a chairman and eight members, to be appointed by the Ministers and to have no interests in agriculture or commerce which would influence the discharge of their duties. The chief job of the commission is to prepare schemes for the payment of subsidies to livestock producers. These must have the approval of the Minister, and must lie in Parliament for thirty days before going into effect. The commission also has regulatory powers which extend to markets, market charges, and slaughter house schemes.

The Livestock Commission is subject in every important aspect of its work to the Government of the day. Practically everything it does must receive Ministerial approval. The restriction of imports, a vitally important factor in the picture, is in the hands of the Board of Trade. The finances of the commission are under Treasury control. A Livestock Advisory Committee, appointed by the Minister, keeps the commission in touch with the industry. Some of its members represent special interests. The Act apparently contemplates the formation of a producers' marketing board to stabilize the distribution of the products of the industry. The scheme follows the pattern of the Milk Reorganization Commission's proposals.

e. *The Whitefish Commission of* 1938

The Seafish Industry Act of 1938 created a Whitefish Commission of five members appointed by the Ministers. The chairman is appointed by the commission, but the secretary by the Minister of Agriculture. It is not a representative body, and no one is eligible whose financial or commercial interests might be involved. It is paid by government funds, and this provides Parliament with opportunities for debate. Its functions are chiefly regulatory: it registers all who are engaged in the industry, and this registration is compulsory; and it has control over the marking and grading of fish, over auctions, charges made at auctions, and similar matters. All such regulations must be confirmed by the Ministers.

A Whitefish Industry Joint Council is set up to advise and assist the commission in the discharge of its duties. In the original bill the chairman of this council was to be appointed by the Minister, but the other members were to be chosen by various interest groups. As the bill passed, the chairman is appointed by the Minister and the other members are also appointed by him, 'to represent the interests of every phase of the industry' after consultation with those interests.

The Whitefish Commission in consultation with the industry is to prepare marketing schemes to be administered by marketing boards, one-third of whose members are appointed by the Ministers. Their powers are analogous to those of the agricultural marketing boards. Appeals lie from the decisions of the marketing boards to the commission. Consumers' committees and committees of investigation are created. Here again the whole program follows closely the lines of the Milk Reorganization Commission proposals.

f. *The Cotton Industry Board of* 1939

The position of the British cotton industry has grown increasingly worse. The productive capacity of the industry has been expanded beyond normal market requirements. In 1936 Parliament created the Cotton Spindles Board to function for two years. This board consisted of a chairman and two members appointed by the Board of Trade in consultation with the industry, but the members were to have no direct interests in the industry. Its task was to lay up and scrap surplus spindle productive capacity. Its funds came from levies on producers and from loans approved by the government. It worked under the close control of the Board of Trade and was aided by an advisory committee appointed by the Board of Trade. It was a temporary board set up to restore health to a sick industry by the process of amputation.

In 1939 Parliament passed a more thorough-going statute creating a Cotton Industry Board. This is a corporate body composed of fifteen members appointed by the Board of Trade. Three of these are to be detached and impartial; two must have special knowledge of the industry; the others are to be appointed after consultation with interested bodies and in accordance with an elaborate schedule. The members serve for five years and are re-eligible. Members of Parliament are ineligible.

The functions of the board are important. It registers under penalty all who are engaged in the industry. It supervises the creation and administration of two kinds of schemes. The first are 'redundancy schemes,' set up to effect the elimination of surplus cotton mills; the boards to administer these are appointed by the Board of Trade after consultation with the industry. The second are 'price schemes,' administered by boards similar to the agricultural marketing boards; the members are elected by those who are registered in the industry. Both schemes must be submitted to a Cotton Advisory Committee consisting of three independent members appointed by the Board of Trade. The scheme must then be approved by a poll of those registered in the industry and must thereafter be submitted by the Board of Trade to Parliament for approval. Appeals from the schemes go to the Cotton Industry Board. The board renders certain services to the industry in the field of advertising and in the stimulating of research and experiment.

III. SEMI-INDEPENDENT PUBLIC SERVICE AGENCIES [33]

WE have been discussing the British agencies which regulate or control the various forms of British economic enterprise in private hands. These are roughly analogous to our own independent regulatory commissions. We now turn to a different type of agency, designed for the operation of economic enterprise by governmental power. This is the semi-autonomous public service board, sometimes referred to as the 'Public Trust.' It has characteristics in common with our own government-owned corporations, but it also has certain unique features which have arrested the attention of students of public administration. These public service boards have been set up and given virtual autonomy for two rather different purposes. First, they have been created in order to own and operate important public services. Some of these services are national in scope and the operating boards are therefore parts of the central government; in other cases the services are localized and the boards are limited to definite geographical areas. In either case the autonomous board is used because it seems desirable to remove day-to-day administration of important and highly technical services which are in the nature of business enterprises from the reach of partisan influence or political domination. A second group of autonomous boards has been set up to do what W. A. Robson has happily described as 'taking politics out of politics.' They represent, in other words, a 'buck-passing' technique by which the Government in power is to be relieved of the embarrassment of dealing with problems so highly controversial as to be constant and inevitable causes of attack. This is illustrated by the Unemployment Assistance Board, by the creation of which the Government in power hoped to escape the inescapable odium certain to fall upon whatever official body might be given the difficult and controversial task of administering unemployment assistance.

33. Cf. Robson (ed.), *Public Enterprise, passim;* O'Brien, op. cit. *passim;* Gordon, op. cit. *passim.*

A. Technical or Operating Boards for the Conduct of Nationalized Industries

The public service boards created to own and operate national public services have increased in recent years. They exist in a variety of forms even while the central pattern of organization remains fairly constant. There are four of these boards which operate on a nation-wide scale—the Central Electricity Board, the Forestry Commission, the Coal Commission, and the British Overseas Airways Corporation. Two others, the Port of London Authority and the London Passenger Transport Board, operate equally important services which are local in scope.

1. THE CENTRAL ELECTRICITY BOARD

a. *Background of the Central Electricity Board*

We have already traced the development of electricity control in England which culminated in the Act of 1926, creating the Central Electricity Board and redefining the authority of the Electricity Commissioners. It is suggested by a competent observer, Terence O'Brien, that the creation of the Central Electricity Board was probably not the result of any carefully preconceived plan to nationalize one of the country's great industries, but resulted rather from three immediately practical considerations: First, voluntary consolidations in the electricity industry had failed to develop. Second, the information collected by the Electricity Commission and the Weir committee made it disturbingly plain how backward was the development of this industry in Great Britain. Third, the country was suffering from an acute trade depression, one which had produced the calamitous strike of 1926, and this sharpened the desire of the Government in office to earn the credit for a major piece of economic reconstruction. The setting up of the Central Electricity Board represented a compromise in which the Conservatives, who wanted no nationalization, and the Labour Party, which wanted complete nationalization, agreed on partial nationalization. The purpose of the board was to administer a publicly owned system for the generation and main transmission of electric current. Save in very exceptional cases it was not to own or operate the generating stations, but was to be responsible for the erection of a vast transmission network known as the Grid, and to exercise close control over the operation of individual stations. It was to enjoy wide freedom of action, subject to the supervision of the Electricity Commissioners, who in turn were subject to the Minister of Transport.

b. *Personnel and structure*

The Central Electricity Board has a chairman and seven members appointed by the Minister of Transport after consultation with some of the following interests: local governments, electricity interests, commerce, industry, transportation, agriculture, and labor. The members are not, however, 'representative' of these interests in the sense that they are delegates. The Weir committee had proposed sectional nominations to the board, but this was rejected. The statute sets up no special qualifications for membership. In practice, four members, including the chairman, have been electrical engineers; one has been a barrister; one a trade union secretary; one a railway manager; and one a banker. Members of Parliament are ineligible. The chairman may have no financial interest in the electricity industry and the other members must declare such interests as they have. They are appointed for not less than five or more than ten years, as determined by the Minister. There is no provision as to dismissals. The chairman is a full-time officer and receives a salary of £7,000. Other members give part-time service and receive £750. These salaries are determined by the Minister. There is no bar to the reappointment of members, and few changes in personnel have in fact occurred.

The permanent expert officials of the board, of whom the chairman is chief, are exceedingly important. Under the chairman there is a general manager, a position which Sir Archibald Page, the present chairman, occupied until 1934. The chairman and the general manager have been compared to a chief-of-staff and a commander-in-chief respectively. The other principal officers are a chief engineer, a chief accountant, a secretary and solicitor, a commercial manager, and eight district managers who administer the Grid. All of these officers and the supporting staff are appointed by the board, which fixes salaries and wages. This degree of autonomy is very unusual. The staff has not been recruited through the civil service, but by a different system of selection. The salaries are higher than in the civil service, especially in the upper brackets. There has been sharp criticism of the high salary paid to the chairman. At the same time, many believe that an attempt to organize the board's staff through the civil service would have been unsuccessful.

c. *Powers and functions*

The powers and duties of the Central Electricity Board are highly technical and complicated. It is unnecessary to set them out in detail. In general they comprise the creation and management of a national system of high pressure transmission, based upon a number of large interconnected generating stations selected for their efficiency. The job is essentially that of a wholesaler of electric current. The board has no control over the distribution or price of current to the consumer. As before mentioned, it does not usually own any generating stations, a fact representing part of the political compromise on the electricity bill. We may now summarize the board's more important activities.

The first and most important of the board's tasks was the establishment of the area schemes necessary to get the system going. The country was divided into regions or areas with connecting lines. The initial planning, as we have seen, was confided to the Electricity Commissioners, which worked out these schemes in draft form and passed them on to the board. This is still the procedure followed in making extensions of the present system. The board publishes the schemes, hears objections to them, holds hearings if necessary, and then puts them into effect with any necessary minor changes. The Electricity Commissioners do not present the schemes in great detail, as they do not wish to tie the Central Electricity Board down to an inelastic program. As we have seen before,[34] the actual statutory division of labor between the Electricity Commissioners

34. *Supra,* 537.

and the Central Electricity Board in this field of planning has become somewhat blurred.

A second function of the board is the selection and control of generating stations. Under the schemes just described, the Central Electricity Board 'selects' the stations which appear to be efficient and which are necessary to the program. It pays compensation to any 'displaced' owners, the small people who have lost out in the struggle for survival. The selected stations are under the absolute control of the board, which regulates the amount of current they may produce and the times at which they may produce it. The board may order far-reaching alterations and extensions by station owners, but the owners' interests are carefully safeguarded. The board may not impose 'undue financial burden,' and owners may appeal on this ground to an arbitrator appointed by the Minister. There is little left to the private ownership of the stations but the name, which remains as a concession to certain trends of opinion. The Central Electricity Board is permitted to close down a 'non-selected' station when it can convince the Electricity Commissioners that the board can supply power at a lower cost than the station can. There is, therefore, strictly no legal monopoly, but the board can be under-cut only with difficulty. Some non-selected stations have been retained under arrangement with the board mainly to help supply 'peak' loads. The board itself may own a generating station only if it can convince the Electricity Commissioners that no private owner or agency is able and willing to provide the necessary facilities. The board is under an obligation to supply to all authorized distributors all the current which they may reasonably require. By recent legislation it may supply railways directly. If a station persistently disregards the instructions and requirements of the board, the board may ask the Minister of Transport to issue an order for the compulsory acquisition of the station by another undertaker. Such an order must lie before Parliament for thirty days.

The third major function of the Central Electricity Board is the ownership and operation of the Grid. This was begun in 1928 and finished in 1933. It is a system of high pressure transmission lines linking up the generating stations. The Central Electricity Board buys all of the power generated by all of the stations at a price worked out by a rather complicated formula, but approximating rather roughly the cost of production. It sells this power to distributors, and these distributors are the same old companies and municipalities which were mentioned in connection with the history of the Electricity Commissioners. Some of these companies in cities own 'selected' stations, and therefore still nominally own generating plants. They buy, however, from the board's common pool as do all the others, but they receive from the board a rebate for the amount of current which they contribute to this pool and then repurchase. The board is the sole link between the generating plants and the local distributing agencies. It is, in other words, a wholesaler.

The Central Electricity Board has the power to standardize the generation frequency of electric current—a highly necessary power, in view of the widely existing variations. The cost of this is covered by a levy on all electrical undertakings.

The financial powers of the Central Electricity Board are important and in some respects unique. Its first major task was that of large-scale capital construction for which loans were necessary until operating revenue began to mount. Up to 1939 the board had borrowed about £52,000,000, most of which had gone into the construction of the Grid. Loans by the board may, if the board so desires, be guaranteed by the Treasury. But the board has not availed itself of this Treasury guarantee because it has not wished to be subject to the accompanying Treasury restrictions. Thus between 1930 and 1936 the board was able to borrow at a very low interest rate when money was cheap, and when the Treasury was trying hard to restrict borrowing for large-scale public purposes. The board's loans must be approved by the Electricity Commissioners, and the general terms of the issue must be approved by the Minister. In practice, however, there is little direct interference. There is no outside control over the use by the board of the money borrowed. Revenue comes in from profits made on resale of current. Up to 1936 these had amounted to about £20,000,000, roughly two-thirds of the cost of the Grid. It is generally agreed that the Central Electricity Board has been a financial success.

d. *Procedure*

Procedure is not as important in the case of a board operating a public service as it is in the case of an administrative agency which is making decisions affecting private rights. The procedure of the Central Electricity Board is of the informal character suitable to its task. O'Brien sums it up as follows:

> . . . The Board holds a regular monthly meeting, but has, especially during the early years of its existence, sat in constant session for considerable periods. It has formed a few small sub-committees to deal with special phases of the Corporation's work, which are assisted by leading members of the permanent staff . . . The Board discusses broad questions of policy and finance, sanctions all expenditure and constitutes the final source of authority within the organization upon all matters. Obviously, since all its members with the exception of the Chairman are part-time officials, it does not penetrate the daily functioning and administration of the Corporation . . .[35]

Broadly speaking, the board functions as an agency for the supervision, in a general way and in the public interest, of the policies and the activities of the chairman and the permanent officials who are the day-to-day rulers and operators of the Grid.

e. *Relations with other agencies or departments*

We have referred to the Central Electricity Board as a semi-autonomous agency. We need, therefore, to analyze its relations to other parts of the British government, and determine to what extent it is subject to control and to what extent it is independent.

The board has a number of definite relations with the Minister of Transport. The Minister appoints the board, but this means little in the way of control since there is a tradition of permanent tenure for the board while Ministers of Transport come and go. Also the problem of electricity control is only one of the Minister's many responsibilities. The provisions of the statute are such that the Minister could, if he had the energy and courage, and if he had differing views of policy, make life

35. Op. cit. 55 f.

exceedingly difficult for the Central Electricity Board through his direct authority over the Electricity Commissioners, who supervise the board's major activities. This, however, would be a very up-hill job for the Minister, and he has thus far shown no desire to attempt it. In certain cases, as we have seen, the board must enlist the active co-operation of the Minister in exercising its powers. Only through him may privately owned generating stations be disciplined by compulsory transference to another owner for failure to comply with requirements and regulations of the board. The Minister must also appoint arbitrators to adjust the private property claims of station owners subjected to alleged undue financial burdens by the board's orders for extensions and improvements.

The relations of the board to Parliament are indirect. The Minister of Transport is responsible to Parliament through his control over the Electricity Commissioners for the general policies of the Central Electricity Board. He accordingly answers questions in the House of Commons with reference to the board, but in doing so he refuses to deal with matters which lie 'within the discretion of the Board.' Questions calling for information he refers to the board for answer. This is the substance of normal Parliamentary control over the board. It is true, of course, that if the Central Electricity Board in some manner outraged public opinion, Parliament is fully competent to act, either by the appointment of an investigating commission or by the enactment of corrective legislation. There has been no need for such action.

The relations between the Central Electricity Board and the Electricity Commissioners have already been mentioned. All directions which the board gives to the owners of stations with respect to new construction or alterations require the consent of the Electricity Commissioners. The board may go into the business of generating current through a station of its own only if the Electricity Commissioners agree that this is the only practicable way. The commissioners must also approve the board's action in closing down 'non-selected' stations, an approval based upon finding that the Grid price of supplying current is lower than the local station costs. The major financial operations of the board require the consent of the Electricity Commissioners. It is clear that the Electricity Commissioners could paralyze the board if they set out to do so. Actually, however, the two bodies work together in close and harmonious co-operation. There are constant mutual consultations, wholly 'extra-legal' but very important. The board gives to the commissioners the fullest reports on its work, and the statistical service of the commissioners is always available to the board. The relations between the two bodies and especially the division of labor has been worked out on a thoroughly practical basis rather than by following abstract principles. There is a rough separation of the executive and administrative functions of the board from the judicial and planning functions of the commissioners, but the proposal of the McGowan committee and the Government's bill based upon it would give the Electricity Commissioners important managerial and administrative duties.[36]

f. *Public relations*

Since 1931 there has been attached as an adjunct to the board a special section which is concerned with public relations, statistics, and economic research. Complaints mainly arise from the distributers, and appear to be adequately dealt with. At the same time the board has also undertaken to inform the public of its achievements. A documentary film has been made and shown all over the country. The board is sensitive to public opinion, and, despite its virtual immunity from direct public control, has earned from Mr. Herbert Morrison the name of 'a public institution with a real sense of public accountability.'

g. *Conclusion*

The board has been a striking success, administratively, financially, and technically. With that general judgment few would disagree. In the place of some 600 generating stations of all types, shapes, and descriptions, the board's great national Grid scheme works from 130 linked-up stations, of which a number merely contribute to the peak load, since over half the total energy is provided by fifteen of the 'selected' stations. Capital savings, which are gradually being handed down to the consumer, have been made possible; and despite the nominal

36. *Supra,* 540.

private ownership of the generating stations a real central control for the public good has been decisively established and accepted by all parties.

2. THE FORESTRY COMMISSION

a. *Background of the Forestry Act of* 1919

The need for building up British-grown timber reserves was sharply emphasized by the results of the German submarine blockade of 1917-18. Before the War a Royal Commission (1909) had considered this problem, but no results had ensued. There appeared to be ample supplies of timber available from Canada, Russia, and Scandinavia. During the War the Reconstruction Commission created a forestry sub-commission (Acland Commission), which reported in 1917. The Forestry Act of 1919 was based in the main on the recommendations of this committee.

Both experience and reason made it clear that private landowners had neither the money nor the desire to invest in programs of reforestation (British 'afforestation') from which returns were possible only in the far-distant future. Everyone agreed that if trees were to be planted the government would have to plant them, although it was hoped that private landowners would co-operate to the extent of keeping up existing woodlands and forests. Such being the case, 'nationalization' or 'collectivism' in forestry did not create any serious opposition, since no vested interests would be disturbed or private profits jeopardized. The committee's report proposed an eighty-year program from which no income could be expected for many years to come. The proposal included the creation of a forestry commission to administer the program.

b. *Structure and personnel*

The Forestry Commission at first consisted of eight members, but two more were added by statute in 1927. The members and the chairman are appointed by the Government. They serve for five years and are eligible to reappointment. The need for continuity of policy has resulted in a very small turnover.

Three members are paid, their combined salaries being £4,500, and these give full-time service. The other members, who are unpaid, give only part-time service—an arrangement which has not been wholly satisfactory. One member of the commission must be a member of Parliament, so that he may answer questions concerning the commission in the House of Commons. He customarily belongs to the Government party. He may not receive a salary as a commissioner. This rather unusual arrangement is patterned after the Ecclesiastical Commission and the Charity Commissioners. One member must have 'scientific' attainments and a technical knowledge of forestry. Two members must have knowledge and experience of forestry in Scotland. In practice the commission has been made up mainly of landowners who have practised forestry on their own estates or experimented in agriculture. Two assistant commissioners serve as administrative officers, and to these much of the work of buying and planting land is delegated. The commission has a staff of more than 500 persons working under civil service conditions and rates of pay. It employs over 4,000 laborers.

c. *Powers and functions*

The chief function of the Forestry Commission is 'to create and maintain State forests in order to supply the country's timber requirements.' Concretely, this means buying land and planting trees on it as well as maintaining forests on lands already held by the Crown. The commission is authorized to acquire land by eminent domain, but it has not yet done so in spite of difficulty in getting suitable lands by voluntary sale. It has power to make grants of money to private landowners or to local government authorities to encourage the planting of trees. Beginning in 1925 the commission embarked on a land settlement program which involved the leasing of small holdings of ten acres each in the commission's forests. To those taking up these leases it guaranteed a minimum of 150 days' labor per year. This enterprise has been of help in checking rural depopulation.

Camps for the unemployed have been established in or near the forests, a scheme somewhat similar to the CCC camps in the United States. These camps are run by the Minister of Labour.

They provide labor for the Forestry Commission, although their chief aim is to relieve unemployment rather than to further reforestation. Since 1936 the commission has been required to run tree-planting schemes near certain distressed areas. Finally the commission carries on an extensive program of education and research.

d. *Procedure*

The Forestry Commission meets regularly once a month. It has no quasi-judicial duties, conducts no hearings, and its meetings are informal. It carries on its work through a series of committees. Those which are set up to deal with technical questions, personnel, forest holdings, and so forth, are sub-committees of the commission itself; those dealing with sales, amenities, and housing for timber workers consist of five members of the commission on each committee together with a number of specialists brought in from outside. These committees report to the full commission, which supervises and co-ordinates their efforts, and the commissioners are kept in touch with the work of the subcommittees by written reports circulated by mail. The two assistant commissioners attend the regular meetings and are influential in shaping the commission's policy, but have no votes. Advisory committees, representing county councils, owners of woodlands, forestry associations, and labor, exist in England, Scotland, and Wales, and the commission maintains close contact with them.

e. *Relations to other departments*

The Forestry Commission has no relation to any Ministry or department, but it is represented in Parliament by one of its members selected for that purpose. Through him it is held responsible, and from him the House of Commons may secure information about the commission's work. The chief control over the commission is the financial control exercised by the Treasury. The commission, unlike the Central Electricity Board, is not a corporation with independent borrowing power. It is entirely dependent upon grants of money to carry on its work, and this money it must get from Parliament, which means the Treasury. The Treasury, therefore, exercises the power of life and death over its activities. This arrangement has worked badly. With its finances managed on this hand-to-mouth basis, with its money coming from annual grants, the commission has been wholly dependent on the vicissitudes of national finance. If the Treasury is hard up, the commission may go hungry, and this has sometimes happened. Obviously the successful execution of an eighty-year program of reforestation is impossible without some guarantee of financial stability. If trees are to be set out this year, they must have been planned for and planted several years ago. A liberal grant of money today may be useless if no seedlings are on hand to plant, and seedlings planted five years ago may be wasted if there is no money this year with which to plant them. In 1931-2, 50,000,000 seedlings were destroyed by the commission because it had no money with which to plant them.

f. *Appraisal*

The Forestry Commission is not generally regarded as very successful, although it has probably done as good a job as it has been allowed to do. One reason for describing it in this study is that it affords a striking example of how not to set up an agency to carry on this kind of work. Its experience shows the undesirable results of lack of independence and financial stability in the management of an important public service. It thus stands in contrast to the efficiency and stability of the other public service boards.

3. THE COAL COMMISSION

a. *Background of the Coal Commission*

As in the United States, the coal mining industry in Great Britain has suffered intensely since the first World War. It has been affected by loss of world markets, acute labor troubles, and competition from electricity and oil. Coal production fell and unemployment rose. Some form of reorganization of the industry seemed imperative.

The Sankey Commission reported in 1919 in favor of a scheme of nationalization. It declared that the industry was so highly competitive and the units of production were so small that inefficiency in production and marketing was inevitable; and that the industry could never be made to pay so long as there was uncontrolled production far in excess of any reasonable demand at a reasonable price. The Government, however, was unwilling to accept its far-reaching proposals.

At this time the only legal regulations of the industry were those relating to safety. These were administered by the Department of Mines, set up in 1919 as a division of the Board of Trade, and they embraced merely the issuing of regulations and the conduct of inspections. There was no form of economic control. The mine owners, a highly individualistic group, opposed even these safety regulations. Popular irritation grew at the unwillingness of mine owners to face the problem of the imminent collapse of the industry, and to make concessions of any kind. The coal strike of 1926 accentuated the already desperate situation and brought it more sharply to public attention. As a result the Samuel Commission was set up to investigate the entire problem. It reported in 1926.

The Mining Industry Act of 1926 resulted from the report of the Samuel Commission. It embodied a scheme for the amalgamation of existing undertakings, a cautious experiment coming from a Conservative Government. Realizing that voluntary arrangements would accomplish nothing, the Act created limited powers of compulsion to bring about amalgamations. These compulsory powers could be invoked only on the initiative of the mine owners and in this way: a group of mine owners could plan an amalgamation scheme and submit it to the Board of Trade; this scheme could provide for the compulsory absorption of recalcitrant owners. If the Board of Trade felt that a *prima facie* case was made out for the scheme it could refer it to the Railway and Canal Commission. This body was to hear objections and, if it was satisfied that the scheme was 'in the national interest' and 'fair and equitable to all persons affected thereby,' to confirm it. The mine owners swallowed this as well as they could. The plan was an almost complete failure. Some amalgamations actually took place, affecting, in fact, about one-tenth of the collieries. None of these was brought about by compulsory process, however, though it is possible that the fact of potential compulsion may have had some influence.

b. *The Coal Mines Act of 1930—The Coal Mines Reorganization Commission*

When the Labour Government took over in 1929 it promptly tackled the problems presented by the coal industry. In its campaign it had proposed compulsory amalgamation of the British coal mines through a government commission set up for that purpose. Such a scheme passed the House of Commons, but the House of Lords amended the bill to cut out the separate commission and to refer compulsory amalgamations to the Board of Trade. It also restricted the amalgamations by setting up certain tests which we shall see later made any effective amalgamation impossible. The House of Commons insisted upon keeping the coal commission, but yielded on the other amendments, and the bill passed in that form.

The Act fell into two major parts. The first part contained elaborate provisions for limiting the output of coal and for fixing coal prices. The machinery for doing this comprised a Central Council and District Executive Boards. These were guild bodies chosen by the producers themselves and followed the general pattern of the agricultural marketing boards. The Central Council was composed of representatives of the colliery owners from all of the districts, who were also members of the District Executive Boards. The principal function of the council was to assign to each district an 'allocation' or maximum output which might not be exceeded under penalty of fine. The council was financed by levies on the district boards. These boards were elected by the owners of the district, and varied in size and in the methods of exercising power. They had authority to classify coal, to allocate to individual mines their share of the district allotment, to establish minimum prices for coal, and so forth. The Board of Trade had virtually no direct concern with any of this. It reported to Parliament on the operation of the whole scheme and answered questions on general policy, but had no direct contact with the day-to-day work of the Central Council or the District Executive Boards. As a check the statute provided for the setting up of committees of investigation, one central and one for each district, to be appointed by the Board of Trade; one-half of the members represented the consumers, the others were divided between mine owners and workers. These committees were to investigate complaints and to this end had access to statements and accounts. They reported to the Board of Trade which in turn made recommendations to the Central Council or the District Executive Boards. If relief was not forthcoming the Board of Trade might issue orders which would provide it. The result of the plan was to keep coal prices up, and critics suggest that in effect it subsidized inefficiency.

A Coal Mines Reorganization Commission to bring about compulsory amalgamations was provided for in the second major part of the Act of 1930. This commission consisted of a chairman and four members appointed by the Board of Trade. The chairman was given a salary of £7,000, which stirred up a good deal of criticism. Members of Parliament were not eligible, nor were those who had any financial interest in coal. All of the appointments were excellent.

The chief task of the commission was to prepare schemes of amalgamation which would reduce the number of independent mine undertakings and thus eliminate wasteful competition. Compulsory powers could be used under the following procedure: The amalgamation scheme was referred first to the Board of Trade, and if approved by it was submitted to the Railway and Canal Commission. The commission was instructed by the statute not to approve the scheme unless it met the following tests: (a) it must be in the national interest; (b) it must result in lowering the cost of production and disposal of coal; (c) it must not be financially injurious to any of the undertakings involved in the amalgamation; (d) the terms must be fair and equitable to all persons affected thereby.

This elaborate plan for compulsory amalgamation was a complete failure. The Coal Mines Reorganization Commission began by trying to secure amalgamation by persuasion. The mine owners were not co-operative and it got nowhere. Meanwhile the first part of the statutory plan, with its resulting higher prices, had gone into effect, but without affording the increased efficiency which the amalgamations were supposed to bring. The commission accordingly decided upon a test case in the form of an amalgamation in the Yorkshire area. It worked out a compulsory scheme embracing some sixty undertakings, only four of which refused to co-operate. When this was presented to the Railway and Canal Commission that tribunal held the scheme invalid for failing to meet all of the four tests provided in the statute. It went further and held that the proposed amalgamation was not an amalgamation at all within the meaning of the Act. We cannot go into the technicalities involved here but the upshot of the decision was clear. Any effective action under the statute was impossible. No responsible official believed that any scheme of amalgamation could be devised which would meet the approval of the Railway and Canal Commission. Accordingly in July 1935 the Government asked the Coal Mines Reorganization Commission to cease its activities pending the passage of a new statute redefining its powers.

In 1936 the Government made new proposals relating to the coal industry. These included the repeal of the four tests just discussed to be applied to amalgamations, and the dropping from the picture of the Railway and Canal Commission. The Coal Mines Reorganization Commission was to draw up schemes of amalgamation, hear all objections, and send them to the Board of Trade, which, if it approved them, would send them to Parliament. Unless Parliament disallowed the scheme within twenty-one days the Board of Trade would put it into operation. This proposal was defeated by the vigorous lobbying of the mine owners. The Government retreated all along the line, and there ensued a period of inactivity and uncertainty. This came to an end with the passage of the Coal Act of 1938, under which the British coal mines were completely nationalized.

c. *The Coal Act of* 1938

Over the bitter opposition of many Conservatives and most of the mine owners the Government introduced and passed the Coal Act of 1938. This measure provided for the nationalization of the ownership of British coal mines and supplemented the regulatory statutes at important points. The Act had three important parts, which may be summarized:

The first part provides for the unification of all coal royalties under the ownership and control of a Coal Commission. This

Coal Commission is a corporate body. It assumes the ownership of all the coal in the country, known or unknown, worked or unworked. It replaces by one ownership the separate interests of between four and five thousand individual royalty owners. The commission is charged with the responsibility of exercising its powers of ownership and control so as to promote the interests and more efficient organization of the coal mining industry. The commission itself is not to engage in the business of coal mining, but is to grant leases for that purpose. Minerals other than coal which are located in the various undertakings are also subject to its authority. The Board of Trade may give the commission general directions 'as to the exercise by the Commission of their functions . . . in all matters appearing to the Board to affect the national interest, including all matters affecting the safety of the working of coal.'

The mine owners are to be paid compensation in cash raised by loans secured by the property of the commission and its revenues. A tribunal was set up to value the coal properties. The tribunal set a total value of £66,450,000, of which each owner is to receive a proportionate share. Central and regional boards are to fix individual valuations and to allocate compensation. These are appointed by the Board of Trade, and appeals can be taken to referees appointed by the Board of Trade from a panel set up for that purpose.

The second part of the statute deals with amalgamations. The Coal Mines Reorganization Commission was discontinued and its properties transferred to the new Coal Commission. The commission is charged with the duty of reducing the number of coal undertakings where this is necessary in the interests of efficiency. It was not to begin this, however, before January 1, 1940. Schemes for such compulsory amalgamations are to be drawn by the commission and submitted to the Board of Trade, which may lay them before Parliament, whose approval is necessary to their validity.

The third part of the Act extends to January 1, 1943, and relates to the general arrangements for the organized selling schemes which had been carried on through the Central Council and the District Executive Boards. These provisions were not radically changed, but amendments were added to strengthen in the interest of consumers the committees of investigation provided for in the Act.

d. *Structure of the Coal Commission*

The Coal Commission is a public corporation, consisting of a chairman, deputy-chairman, and three members appointed by the Board of Trade. Two members must have had administrative or other practical experience in the coal mining industry, and one of these two must have been a wage earner in the coal industry. Members of Parliament are ineligible and there are elaborate provisions disqualifying persons having any financial interests in the coal business. Members of the miners' unions are not, however, disqualified. The members are appointed for terms of from five to ten years, as may be determined by the Board of Trade with the approval of the Treasury and subject to such conditions as may be agreed upon. The commission appoints a secretary and such other officers as it may determine. All salaries are fixed by the Board of Trade and the Treasury.

The Coal Commission has not begun functioning, and one can only speculate as to how it will work out. It has not yet taken over ownership of the mines and we do not therefore know what kind of leases will be granted for the actual operation of the mines or what will be the working relations between the commission and the operators. The statute appears to place the commission pretty well under the control of the Board of Trade. It may easily be, however, that if the arrangement has an opportunity to work normally, the Board of Trade will follow the practice which has grown up in similar situations of leaving the commission free from interference in the day-to-day administration of its affairs. The entire project is an experiment in nationalization which will be watched with the keenest interest.

4. THE BRITISH OVERSEAS AIRWAYS CORPORATION OF 1939

The latest British venture in collectivism is the nationalization of the overseas airlines. While the war has prevented the normal development of this enterprise, the statutory foundation of the plan presents features which are unique and interesting.

a. *Background of the British Overseas Airways Act*

The British government began to take an active part in the development of overseas airways in 1924, when it created a corporation known as Imperial Airways, an amalgamation of then existing companies. It was given a ten-year monopoly and was subsidized by the government to aid the development of European services. These subsidies were expected to decrease yearly during the ten-year period, at the end of which the industry was expected to be self-supporting. Things did not work out in this way. Imperial Airways found itself quite unable to survive without substantial aid from the government. It had difficulty in competing with continental airlines which were receiving higher subsidies, and it was required by statute to buy British airplanes which were then inferior to those which could be bought elsewhere.

The situation became increasingly unsatisfactory both to the company and to the government. Public criticism of Imperial Airways and its policies mounted. The government had sunk some £5,000,000 in subsidies to the company, but it had little or no control over it since it appointed but two of the company's ten directors. The company was not developing adequate service to the Empire; this was being neglected in favor of the shorter routes which paid more money. The company's equipment was obsolete. It did not co-operate adequately with the Air Ministry and took a narrow view of its responsibilities to the government. It was charged in certain quarters with arbitrary and unfair dealings with its employees and staff. It was engaged in no adequate planning of air routes, whereas the government felt keenly the necessity of developing strategic routes throughout the Empire.

The Imperial Airways' monopoly expired in 1934, and a number of small companies started up to cover the short European routes, which were the only profitable ones. In 1935 British Airways was chartered to amalgamate these small companies. It was owned mainly by a few large financial concerns and was given a government subsidy for the carriage of mails to Germany. Obviously its creation complicated rather than eased the difficult situation which had been growing up in the industry.

In 1938 the Cadman committee, which had been set up to inquire into civil aviation, reported. It proposed the subsidizing of a number of companies and the allocating of spheres of development amongst them. The Government at first appeared to favor this plan, but in 1939 it decided to buy out the existing companies and create a public corporation with power to operate the industry as a monopoly. Two reasons led to this drastic decision: First was the desire to maintain government control over the substantial subsidies which the industry still needed and which it seemed probable it would continue to need almost indefinitely if necessary expansion was to be achieved. Second, only through direct government control could Great Britain be assured of the proper development of strategic air communication throughout Europe and the Empire. A statute embodying this new policy was accordingly passed in 1939.

b. *Structure and personnel*

The British Overseas Airways Corporation has a chairman, deputy-chairman, and from nine to fifteen members, as the Secretary of State for Air (Air Minister) may determine. The Act has been criticized for creating a body too large to be effective. The Secretary of State for Air appoints all members as well as the chairman and deputy-chairman, but the corporation is authorized to appoint a chief executive member with extra pay. Members of Parliament are ineligible, and no member may have interests in other undertakings operating air transport services or any office which would conflict with his duties. The corporation appoints its own staff and determines pay under the fair wages sections of the Air Navigation Act of 1936. Collective bargaining is permitted.

c. *Powers and duties*

The Airways Corporation is set up to run a great public enterprise as a government monopoly. Its powers and duties are comprehensive and complicated. Some of the more important are as follows: It ratifies and adopts the contracts provisionally made by the Treasury Solicitor for the purchase of the airways owned by Imperial Airways and British Airways. The corporation thus completely buys out the companies. Payment is to be made if desired in the stock of the Airways Corporation. There is no guaranteed return on this stock similar to the 4 per cent guarantee in the case of the stock of the London Passenger Transport Board. The corporation is 'to secure the fullest development consistent with economy, of efficient overseas air transport services to be operated by the corporation, and to secure that such services are operated at reasonable charges.' It is given a long list of specific powers through which to attain this broad objective. These include the acquisition of planes and airports, the lending of money for auxiliary facilities, the appointment of advisory boards and committees and the fixing of their remuneration, the making of agreements with foreign governments, the promoting of bills in Parliament, and the like. The corporation keeps accounts and renders annual reports. Its activities are subject to that part of the Air Navigation Act of 1936 which relates to the licensing of air transport and commercial flying. Its financial powers are very broad. It may issue stock with the consent of the Treasury up to £10,000,000. It creates an Airways Fund for the handling of receipts and payments. The Treasury may guarantee its stock and temporary loans, though as we have seen there is no guarantee of any specified rate of return. The corporation makes capital expenditures with the consent of the Air Minister. It may not engage in the manufacture of airplanes or engines, and it may not use any non-British aircraft without the consent of the Minister.

Criticism has been directed against the price paid to buy out the two companies, which was felt to be excessive. The arrangement is also attacked because it does not include domestic civil aviation within the control of the corporation. The government is still subsidizing certain local British companies.

d. *Relations to the Secretary of State for Air and to Parliament*

In contrast to the other public service boards the British Overseas Airways Corporation operates under the very close control of the government. The Secretary of State for Air has drastic and comprehensive authority over its activities. During the period in which government subsidies or guarantees are in operation it may not undertake any new overseas service without his consent; and he may broadly direct the corporation to perform any activity it has power to undertake, to discontinue any which it may be engaged in, or not to undertake a proposed activity. The Secretary must approve the budget and program of the corporation, and may demand full information and inspection of its books. With regard to the operation of air services between Britain and Eire, and the acquisition and construction of airports in the British Isles, he may issue direct orders to the corporation, orders which must, however, go to Parliament for confirmation. There are other things which the corporation may not do without the specific approval of the Air Minister. These include the acquisition of any type of aircraft not approved by him, and the entering into any agreement with a foreign government. It is clear that the heavy financial operations in which the corporation will be involved are subject to direct government control, and that will bring its affairs to the attention of Parliament at frequent intervals. The corporation's position in this regard differs from that of some of the other public service boards, such as the Central Electricity Board, the Port of London Authority, and the London Passenger Transport Board, which are financially independent.

It is not possible to comment usefully on an enterprise which has had no fair opportunity to get under way. The chief point of interest centers in the fact that the Airways Corporation is not an independent board and was not intended to be. The reason for this is to be found in the fact that aviation, and especially international aviation, impinges at nearly every point upon matters closely connected with defense policy and international relations. No government can afford to relinquish direct supervision of an enterprise lying so near the center of its most vital interests.

5. THE PORT OF LONDON AUTHORITY

The four public service boards which have been discussed are central government bodies operating important national services. We now turn to two local public service agencies set up to do similar work in smaller areas. In England the difference between a metropolitan and a national undertaking is far less sharp than is the case in the United States.

a. *Background of the Port of London Authority*

There had grown up early a need for control and co-operation amongst the numerous private companies which owned and operated the diversified facilities of the Port of London. New docks came into operation from time to time; there ensued periods of cutthroat competition, to be followed in turn by more or less monopolistic combinations. In 1900 the Revelstoke Commission investigated all phases of the port's management. It found the dock accommodations to be inadequate and the credit of the dock companies low. The necessary dredging and upkeep of the river was neglected. New docks were not likely to be built until the river was dredged, and the river was not likely to be dredged until the new docks were built. The things which needed doing could not wisely be turned over to a private corporation. The commission proposed the creation of a non-profitmaking public trust similar to one set up earlier at Liverpool, and in 1903 the Government introduced a bill embodying the recommendations of the Revelstoke Commission. Parliament, however, felt that the London County Council, which was to be actively involved in the new program, was too favorable to labor, and the bill was defeated. Two years later a bill proposed by the London County Council for a municipally appointed port authority was rejected for similar reasons.

In 1906 Lloyd George came to the Board of Trade. He began negotiations with the various dock companies, and two years later introduced a bill following essentially the proposals of the

Revelstoke Commission. This Port of London bill provided for 'a single authority predominantly representative of commercial interests to acquire docks and powers of river conservancy.' This bill was modified only in a few details, and passed in 1908. It has since been amended from time to time and was re-enacted with no very vital changes in the Port of London Act of 1920.

b. *Structure and personnel*

The Port of London Authority is a public corporation with twenty-eight statutory members. Eighteen of these are chosen as representatives by the payers of dues, by wharfingers, and by owners of river craft. Ten are appointed as follows: one by the Admiralty, two by the Minister of Transport, four by the London County Council, two by the Corporation of the City of London, and one by Trinity House (Light Houses). The chairman and vice-chairman are chosen by the members and may come from the outside, which may increase the total membership to thirty. The members serve for three years and are all elected at the same time. They are eligible for re-election and the average tenure has been about eleven years. Aliens and employees of the authority are ineligible, as are also those who are interested in or might profit by Port of London Authority contracts except in the ordinary course of dock or warehousing business. Labor is not directly represented on the authority in spite of many vigorous efforts to bring this about. The nearest approach to labor representation is in the choice of two members by the Minister of Transport and London County Council, after consultation with 'such organizations representative of Labour as they think best qualified to advise them on the matter.' The chairman, vice-chairman, and chairmen of committees may be paid. Actually only the chairman receives a salary, which is £5,000. The most important permanent official is the general manager, with whom are associated a group of chief officers. The ordinary members, however, are not without influence, inasmuch as they actively represent particular interests. Meetings occur every two weeks, but most of the real work devolves upon the committees. There are eight of these, dealing with the main functions of the authority. The administrative staff numbers over 4,000, and there are some 7,000 laborers.

c. *Powers and functions*

The principal activities of the Port of London Authority have been summarized by Lincoln Gordon as follows:

> . . . The P. L. A. exercises a broad statutory jurisdiction over the entire tidal portion of the Thames estuary, a river distance of sixty-nine miles, excluding only the rivers Medway, Swale, and Lee, and the Grand Junction Canal. Its powers may be roughly classified into three divisions. As a quasi-governmental authority it registers and licenses river craft, houseboats, and lightermen and watermen. As a river conservancy it maintains and improves the channel, removes wrecks, formulates by-laws for navigation, licenses the construction of works by other entrepreneurs, ensures the river's flow and purity, and undertakes surveys. As a commercial enterprise, finally, it administers and improves the dock and warehousing system of the former companies, constructs new facilities, and may acquire existing facilities not already within its control. To implement these grants of authority is a host of financial powers, governing the Authority's revenue, expenditure, and borrowing.[37]

The authority does not own or administer all of the services and facilities of the port. Private interests still own some docks and warehouses. General planning and control are, however, in the hands of the authority. Some observers point out that there is still wasteful competition and urge that central control be extended and tightened. The authority does not make a profit. It is financially autonomous, and the capital which it needs for its various activities is raised in the open market.

d. *Relations with other agencies or departments*

The Port of London Authority is subject to control by the Minister of Transport, and in some cases by the Board of Trade. These powers of supervision and direction are listed in the statute and seem very impressive. The maximum charges levied by the authority are fixed in the first instance by Pro-

37. L. Gordon, 'The Port of London Authority,' in W. A. Robson (ed.), *Public Enterprise* (1937), 28 f.

visional Orders, but within this range the Minister may vary them if, after inquiry on application by a trade association or by the Port of London Authority, he sees fit to do so. The authority's power to borrow money is restricted in various ways. In some cases the Minister's permission is necessary, and the conditions of borrowing are partly under his control. In this capacity he serves, as Gordon puts it, as a 'watch dog on behalf of the Treasury.' The compulsory purchase of land or buildings by the authority must be approved by an order of the Minister. He works here through an impartial deputy. The authority may, however, go directly to Parliament in these cases and secure needed authorizations by introducing Private Bills. Fifteen such bills have been passed between 1908 and 1937. The Minister hears appeals on the authority's decisions as to licensing; new works and purchases require his consent; he must confirm all by-laws of the authority; he is empowered to act on complaints of unfairly oppressive action by the authority in any aspect, including the charges of its dock and warehousing business; the finances of the authority are audited annually by an appointee of the Minister, and an annual report is presented to him. Thus the Minister has the broadest kind of control over the work of the Port of London Authority, and could interfere constantly with its normal activities. In practice he does none of these things, nor does he interfere in the day-to-day administration of the authority. Direct political control is negligible. The possibility that it might be exercised probably results in the maintenance of reasonably harmonious conformity on the part of the authority to any general policies which the Government in power might have.

In its relations to Parliament the authority has about the same status as the other public service boards. The Minister of Transport is responsible to Parliament for the Port of London Authority only in a very general way and in matters bearing upon his own relations to the authority. He does not answer questions in the House of Commons on the day-to-day administration of the Port of London Authority. The authority is not discussed in Parliament on the budget vote for the Ministry, since it enjoys financial independence and does not have to ask Parliament for money. The result has been that several years pass at a time without any mention being made of the authority on the floor of the House.

e. *Appraisal and comment*

The Port of London Authority appears to fill adequately the need for what Gordon describes as 'a body combining political independence with direct interest exclusively in the provision of adequate facilities.' It is regarded as an efficient and reasonably impartial body. The representation on its governing board of designated private interests appears to work well. It works well, since the interests of the public as such in the Port of London are fairly indirect and are not such as to compete with those of private interests involved. Were the public interests larger and more sharply defined, such a system of private interest control would be indefensible.

The authority has not escaped criticism. Its policy of letting contracts for dredging, repair, and maintenance work is attacked on the ground that it should do this work itself. It is charged that there is a clash between the authority's administrative responsibilities and its commercial interests, inasmuch as in passing upon applications for licenses from would-be competitors it is judging cases in which it is an interested party—an objection not wholly met by allowing appeals to the Minister of Transport. The chief criticism of the authority is, however, that it lacks effective control over many of the facilities of the Port of London.

6. THE LONDON PASSENGER TRANSPORT BOARD

The London Passenger Transport Board is an interesting experiment in administrative technique for the management of a publicly owned service. It owns, controls, and manages the entire passenger transport system of London and its suburbs. Only the main-line railways are outside its jurisdiction, and even here working arrangements in the form of fare-pool agreements have been made.

a. *Background of the London Passenger Transport Act of* 1933

The history of passenger transport in London is a jumbled story of the multiplication of transport facilities of different kinds in the control of different companies. Four distinct forms of transport emerged: railways (including subways), buses and coaches, tramways, and trolley buses. There were many efforts at amalgamation, and some of these were successful; but none was sufficiently so to unify the entire system. The most important of these amalgamations was the formation in 1912 of the London Traffic Combine, which ultimately brought most of the London subways under one control. The general picture of transport conditions in the metropolitan London area on the eve of the establishment of the London Passenger Transport Board is presented by Terence O'Brien:

. . . The railway services of the Metropolis were being conducted by 9 concerns—the 4 amalgamated Main Line Railways Companies, 4 Companies in the Underground Group, and the Metropolitan Company; the omnibus services were being conducted by 61 concerns—the L. G. O. C. and 5 Companies associated with it, and 55 independent undertakings, and the motor coach services by about 21 concerns; and the tramway services were being operated by 16 concerns—13 municipal undertakings and 3 private undertakings associated with the Underground Company. The number of passengers transported by these different services in 1932 is estimated to be 4,051,500,000.[38]

Proposals that the government should try to consolidate these transport facilities emerged as early as 1905 in the report of a Royal Commission on London Traffic. In 1920 similar proposals were made by the Kennedy Jones Committee on London Traffic. The London Traffic Act of 1924 created a large permanent advisory body to advise the Minister of Transport in respect to his powers and duties relating to the London traffic situation. In 1926 this committee was authorized to discuss with the various companies and municipalities concerned whether further co-operation or combination was possible and desirable. It produced in 1927 the Blue Report, which contained a concrete proposal for co-ordinating the metropolitan

38. Op. cit. 208.

transport facilities by creating a regulated monopoly which would be predominately private. For five years there ensued sharp discussion whether transport consolidation, which everybody agreed was necessary, should be worked out on the basis of private or public ownership of the properties.

In 1929 the Conservative Government introduced bills permitting consolidations of the major interests in the London transport field. This affected largely the transport interests of the London County Council and the London Traffic Combine. These bills were dealt with by private procedure, and the Labour Opposition bitterly attacked them as authorizing private monopoly.

The General Election of May 1929 placed a minority Labour Government in power. Herbert Morrison became the new Minister of Transport, and at his direction the consolidation bills were dropped. Morrison began, however, to work on his proposal for the public ownership of London transport facilities in the hands of a 'Public Trust' appointed by the Minister. This was in 1930-1. He shortly converted his colleagues to his views. In his book on transport[39] he states his reasons for selecting this particular program, as follows: (a) modern Socialist thought, and his own municipal experience; (b) the advocacy of this type of institution (Public Trust) in the Liberal Party's volume *Britain's Industrial Future;* (c) the precedent of the Central Electricity Board with which as Minister of Transport he was familiar. It should be added, however, that there is no evidence in the debates that the ranks of the Labour Party or others looked on the Central Electricity Board or the British Broadcasting Corporation as models to be copied in the transport field.

There was sharp Conservative opposition to Morrison's plan. This attacked the taking away of private property rights and the creation of public ownership. It was pointed out that the establishment of the Central Electricity Board and the Grid had not involved the expropriation of property, nor had it taken from producing concerns the management of their property. The proposed administrative structure was also attacked. It not only placed excessive power in the hands of the Minister of Transport but, through his appointment of the

39. Herbert Morrison, *Socialisation and Transport* (1933).

members of the governing board and his review of their decisions, political considerations would dominate the administration of these vast services. This fear was almost certainly due
to the fact that the Minister of Transport was a representative
of the Labour Party.

Before the transport bill got very far, the Labour Government fell. It was replaced by Ramsay MacDonald's National or
Coalition Government. The new Minister of Transport, P. J.
Pybus, was unable to resist the pressure toward reform of the
London transport situation. It would have been politically
hazardous to drop the Morrison bill, but the new Government
made certain changes in it designed to quiet the fears of those
who foresaw the concentration of power over London transport
in the hands of the Minister. These changes were two in number: First, the new bill called for an electoral college to choose
the board which was to operate London passenger transport;
this was in lieu of appointment by the Minister. Second, the
new bill gave to the Railway Rates Tribunal instead of to the
Minister of Transport the power to compel the operating board
to provide new or better facilities or services and to review
its rates on complaint. Thus modified, the London passenger
transport bill was passed in 1933 under the final sponsorship
of a new Conservative Minister of Transport, Oliver Stanley.
Thus the bill in its final form was the product of the joint
or consecutive effort of all the English parties.

The statute created the London Passenger Transport Board,
which took over the ownership and operation of all the concerns which provided transport facilities within the metropolitan area of nearly 2,000 square miles. The owners were compensated with stock in the new corporation, and a fixed return
was guaranteed by the statute.

b. *Structure and personnel*

The London Passenger Transport Board is a public corporation. It is appointed as we have seen by an electoral body
known as 'appointing trustees,' and it has been said that these
appointing trustees, while no doubt eminent in their own fields
of work, are so very 'non-political' and 'impartial' that they
know nothing whatever about the possible merits and demerits

of possible candidates. These trustees are chosen, one each by the following: the chairman of the London County Council, a representative of the London and Home Counties Traffic Advisory Committee, the chairman of the Committee of London Clearing Bankers, the president of the Law Society, and the president of the Institute of Chartered Accountants.

The London Passenger Transport Board consists of a chairman, a vice-chairman, and five members. The chairman is a full-time officer and to this important post Lord Ashfield, previously head of the Traffic Combine, was appointed. He receives a salary of £12,500. The vice-chairman is also a full-time officer, and to this position Mr. Frank Pick, who had been managing director of the combine, was appointed at a salary of £10,000. Not only are these salaries high, but they are relatively high. The Minister of Transport receives £5,000, while the head of the civil service receives £3,000. The chairman and vice-chairman serve for seven-year terms. The five other members, appointed for terms of three and five years, serve part-time, at an annual salary of £750. Only one of these, Mr. John Cliff, formerly assistant secretary of the Transport and General Workers Union, has any special assignment. He is in charge of labor relations. The statutory qualifications for membership are 'experience and capacity in transport, industrial, commercial or financial matters, or in the conduct of public affairs.' Two members must have had a minimum of six years' experience in local government in the London area. Members of Parliament are ineligible. Dismissal is by the Minister of Transport after consultation with the 'appointing trustees,' but only for incompetence or misconduct.

c. *Powers and functions*

It is unnecessary to set out in detail the comprehensive duties of the London Passenger Transport Board. Their functions fall into three categories: First, they own and operate the great transport system turned over to them. Second, they must make this transport system adequate to the public needs, which means providing necessary extensions and improvements. Third, they must meet the heavy statutory requirement of the payment of a guaranteed interest of 4 per cent on stock held by former owners. This presents a serious problem somewhat reminiscent of the one created by the standard revenue requirement imposed on the rate-making powers of the Railway Rates Tribunal.[40] The statutory interest requirement makes it exceedingly difficult for the London Passenger Transport Board to handle its labor relations fairly and still find money for necessary extensions.

d. *Relations with other agencies or departments*

Under the original Morrison bill the Minister of Transport would have exercised important powers over the London Passenger Transport Board. He would have appointed its members and reviewed on appeal its decisions with respect to rates and facilities. But these powers, as we have seen, went elsewhere. The Minister, therefore, exercises no direct control over the board. He will answer questions in the House of Commons on the London Passenger Transport Board, but he gets his answers from the board, and he disclaims all responsibility for its activities. As a matter of comity the board would be likely to discuss important changes in its broad policies with the Minister of Transport, but it is not obligated to do so. All safety regulations applicable to vehicles and common carriers are under the control of the Minister. These apply automatically to the transport units operated by the board.

Nor does Parliament have any direct contacts with the board, or control over its administration. There is little opportunity for Parliamentary discussion of its affairs. Members may, of course, direct questions to the Minister on the general adequacy of the transport facilities in the various districts, and this may be a means of airing grievances and exerting pressure; but it is not a substitute for direct political responsibility. The board does, however, have to come to Parliament for financial aid from time to time. It could not normally undertake any large-scale scheme, such as the extension of a subway, without financial assistance. Requests for such assistance give Parliament an opportunity to discuss the board's business. There are other matters such as the alteration of subway or tramway routes, for which Parliamentary approval is needed. These mat-

40. *Supra*, 519.

ters turn up in the form of Private Bills or Provisional Orders, and again provide a chance for discussion. In the by and large, however, there is no direct Parliamentary supervision of the board's business, nor does Parliament show any signs of wishing to exercise such control.

The board has some formal contacts with the traffic commissioner of the metropolitan area. Every route upon which it operates within the area of its legal monopoly must be approved by him. It is not necessary, however, for the board's vehicles to be individually licensed.

We have seen that in 1924 the London and Home Counties Traffic Advisory Committee was set up to advise the Minister of Transport with respect to his powers relating to London traffic. This committee was modified by the Act of 1933 and now has two members appointed by the London Passenger Transport Board. It has special duties with reference to the board, 'including the duty of making representations to the Board with respect to any matter connected with the services or facilities provided by the Board in the London Traffic Area which should, in the opinion of the Committee, be considered by the Board, and provision is made for joint meetings of the Advisory Committee and of the Board with a view to facilitating interchange of views with reference to any such representations or with reference to any matter of common interest.' The committee has not, however, been a very efficient ventilator of public opinion.

The board is sensitively alert to the importance of its relations with the public. It has a highly efficient public relations department, which handles with care and studied courtesy the many complaints which pour in. This work has been so skilfully handled that the board has been able to maintain cordial and friendly relations with its patrons. There have sprung up numerous local committees of different classes of transport users, and the board keeps in contact with these.

e. *Appraisal and comment*

Three major criticisms have been directed against the London Passenger Transport Board. The first is aimed at the weird method by which the board is appointed. Few students of public administration approve the institution of 'appointing trustees,' but there is no common agreement on an alternative method. The second criticism is directed against the policy of setting up an agency to operate an important public service and then saddling it with excessive financial obligations. The two tasks of administering the service efficiently and remunerating the former owners ought not to be tied together. The third criticism bears upon the problem of the board's responsibility, and here opinion is sharply divided. In the main it favors the present arrangement under which the problem of political control over the board is solved by having no political control; but there is a feeling in many quarters, and especially in the Labour group, that so important an agency ought not to be free from responsible control. The practical aspects of this irresponsible status of the board were strikingly brought out during the London bus strike of 1937. The efforts of labor to hold the Minister of Transport responsible for the conditions out of which the strike grew completely failed. The Minister, with complete justification, disclaimed any responsibility. The board denied the strikers' demands on the ground that it could not meet those demands in addition to the statutory financial obligations imposed on it. There seemed to be no point at which effective pressure could be brought to bear.

The London Passenger Transport Board is generally regarded as one of the most successful operating agencies in the British government. It has provided an effective solution to a very difficult and complex problem. It seems probable that it will serve as a model for other governing boards which may be set up to take over other socialized enterprises as they may emerge. It is freely predicted that the British main-line railways will sooner or later wind up under this type of public ownership and control.

B. Semi-Autonomous Boards to 'Take Politics out of Politics'

1. THE BRITISH BROADCASTING CORPORATION

The public service boards thus far discussed were made autonomous, or nearly so, in order to protect the day-to-day administration of important public services from political pressure. Autonomy in these cases seems eminently sound and has worked well. There were the same reasons for giving the British Broadcasting Corporation a status of semi-independence, since radio broadcasting is a highly technical enterprise; but in organizing the British Broadcasting Corporation there was also present a strong desire to 'take politics out of politics.' This represents a hopeful effort to inject impartiality and non-partisanship into a field in which the decisions made and policies formulated can hardly escape having political and partisan implications.

a. *Background of the British Broadcasting Corporation*

The first regular daily broadcasting in England began in 1922, and in the same year the British Broadcasting Company was incorporated. By the Postmaster General it was given a license running to January 1, 1925, to operate eight stations with daily programs. This cautious start was colored by the highly experimental state of the broadcasting industry, by the complete chaos into which broadcasting had fallen in the United States under a system of numerous privately owned and competing stations, and by the fact that American companies were producing large surpluses of radio apparatus which British producers feared might be dumped on the British market. The British Broadcasting Company was an association of manufacturers of wireless apparatus. To compensate them for the risks of undertaking national broadcasting they were given a monopoly in providing service and in supplying receiving sets. The company's dividends were limited to 7½ per cent and they were forbidden to broadcast commercial advertising. The Postmaster General licensed all receiving sets at a fee of ten shillings per year; half of this revenue went to the company, and licenses were issued only for apparatus bearing the standard mark of the company. O'Brien points out that three elements in this arrangement were destined to persist: the complete control by the government over the ether; the establishment of a monopoly in broadcasting; and revenue from listeners instead of from commercial advertisers.[41]

41. Op. cit. 99 f.

The British Broadcasting Company experiment was watched with keen interest. Two departmental committees, the Sykes committee in 1923 and the Crawford committee in 1925, studied the operation of the system and made proposals for greater government control. The Crawford committee proposed the creation of a public corporation to serve as a 'trustee for the national interest in broadcasting,' and the committee's report formed the basis of the Government's proposals made in 1926. In proposing the bill with the public corporation at the heart of it, the Minister stated that this governing body ought to have the maximum of freedom which Parliament was prepared to concede. He added that the Government wished that the corporation 'should in every respect be given the greatest possible latitude in respect to the conduct of their own affairs.' Opinion in Parliament and elsewhere supported this view. In fact, it was feared that the new public corporation would be too subservient rather than too irresponsible. With this background the British Broadcasting Corporation was set up with a charter to run for ten years. This charter was not created by act of Parliament, but the corporation was given a Royal Charter of Incorporation.

In 1935, just before this charter expired, the Ullswater committee, composed of persons from all the major parties, was set up to study and report on how broadcasting should be carried on after the ten-year charter had expired. The committee recommended renewal of the charter for ten years with a few rather important changes. The new charter came into effect in 1937, and forms the basis of the present system.

b. *Institutional aspects of the British Broadcasting Corporation*

The British Broadcasting Corporation is managed and operated by a board of seven governors; before 1937 there were five. These are appointed by the Crown for terms of five years, which means that they are in fact chosen by the Prime Minister in consultation with the Postmaster General. They are removable at will by the Crown in Council. The charter does not specify the qualifications of members, but there was an implied understanding that the governors should not be specialists or representatives of particular groups, but should be persons of general good judgment and high ability. There has, in fact, been a heavy proportion of elderly, conservative persons, and the charge is heard that appointments to the board have been used to reward retired politicians. The chairman of the Board of Governors receives £3,000. The governors do not operate the British Broadcasting Corporation, but exercise only general supervision. The director general really manages the corporation. He is reputed to receive a salary of £6,500, and is at the head of a staff of over 2,000 persons. This staff is not unionized nor is it recruited under the Civil Service Act, and there have been criticisms on both these points.

c. *Powers and duties*

The work of the British Broadcasting Corporation need not be described in detail. It is a public corporation set up for the purpose of running as a government monopoly a great public service. It is to perform this duty in the best interests of the nation as a whole. It is responsible for the production, maintenance, and planning of radio programs. It has no shareholders and makes no profits. Its only source of income is from the license duties on receiving sets still fixed at ten shillings per year.

d. *Relations with the government*

The restrictions and requirements which appear in the British Broadcasting Corporation's charter make the corporation appear as a subordinate body. First, it operates under a Royal Charter and a Royal License which run for fixed periods, must be periodically renewed, and are revocable at any time by the Crown. Second, the charter compels the corporation to broadcast anything which any government department requires to be broadcast. Third, it is required to abstain from broadcasting anything to which the Postmaster General objects. Fourth, in times of emergency it must place itself wholly at the disposal of the government. During the General Strike of 1926, before the corporation was set up, the government took over the entire broadcasting system and used it with great effect.

If one turns from these charter provisions to a study of the realities of government control, it becomes clear that the British

Broadcasting Corporation is virtually an independent institution. It is free from interference with its day-to-day administration, and no Government under normal circumstances would dare to interfere with it. The Postmaster General is responsible to Parliament for the British Broadcasting Corporation's 'general policy' and must see that the corporation keeps within its license and its charter; but any vigorous or arbitrary exercise of this general power of supervision is held in check by the consensus of opinion that anything approaching a 'totalitarian' radio system would be a public menace and that no Government should have the chance to exercise partisan censorship. Suspicion of Government domination is most likely to arise in connection with the arrangements for broadcasting political speeches. These political programs have been left entirely in the hands of the corporation. No Government has ever intervened to ask for more political speakers, though the Labour Party has sometimes complained of the small number of speakers allotted to it. Extreme conservatives have protested against what they regard as a 'red' bias in some of the broadcasts, but the British Broadcasting Corporation has fairly successfully handled this difficult problem. In choosing party speakers for political broadcasts it has usually relied upon the advice of the main party organization, and this has sometimes meant that party members who were 'not quite regular,' like Mr. Winston Churchill a few years back, found it difficult to get on the air. These traditions of British Broadcasting Corporation independence do not, of course, mean that hints from Whitehall may not influence informally the policy of the corporation. The corporation is fully aware of the fact that its autonomy depends upon its never outraging the feelings of the Government or Parliament. Within these limits, however, it has very broad freedom of action.

With regard to its finances, the British Broadcasting Corporation is self-contained. 'It makes a contribution to the Treasury each year, but the revenue and expenditure of the broadcasting service do not form part of the national finances under the control of the Chancellor of the Exchequer, nor do they find a place in the Budget.' [42]

42. W. A. Robson, 'The British Broadcasting Corporation,' in W. A. Robson (ed.), *Public Enterprise* (1937), 79.

Parliament has little opportunity to discuss the affairs of the British Broadcasting Corporation. The Postmaster General is responsible only for the corporation's general policy, and the Speaker will rule out of order all questions regarding particular items in programs or routine administrative matters. This taboo extends to nearly the whole field of broadcasting. Parliament does indulge in extended debate on the British Broadcasting Corporation at the time of the renewal of its charter. It then calls for detailed information regarding the corporation's work and future, and it may easily be that this sort of periodical check-up is the most effective way of enforcing the corporation's ultimate responsibility.

The British Broadcasting Corporation maintains only vague and remote contacts with the public. It has a Comptroller of Public Relations, but his job is to organize publicity. It makes no systematic effort to find out whether the broadcasting services are satisfactory or not. 'Fan mail' is, of course, voluminous, but it is notoriously unreliable. Many thoughtful persons believe that the British Broadcasting Corporation should set up an efficient public relations department, like those which have been so successful in some of the other public service boards. The corporation does try to maintain contacts with professional workers and with organizations in special fields. To this end it has set up advisory committees both central and local, which deal with religion, music, charitable appeals, and spoken English; and there is a Central Council for School Broadcasting. There is also a general advisory committee to discuss questions of general policy. Robson states that this body consists of about thirty 'Eminent Victorians leavened with a few Edwardians and presided over by the Archbishop of York.' [43] Nothing very new or startling is likely to emerge from its deliberations.

e. *Appraisal and comment*

Various criticisms have been urged against the British Broadcasting Corporation:

The first turns upon the question of the corporation's responsibility—a matter widely discussed. The Ullswater committee in 1936 approved the general status of the corporation,

43. Ibid. 102.

but contended that the Postmaster General was not the most suitable Minister to be 'responsible for the cultural side of the broadcasting.' It believed that this responsibility should go to a Cabinet Minister, preferably a senior member of the Cabinet who was not burdened by heavy administrative duties. This proposal aroused vigorous protest. It was cogently urged that the Postmaster General is not responsible for the cultural side of broadcasting and that it is highly undesirable that any Minister should be. There is very little fear that the British Broadcasting Corporation will become an arbitrary and irresponsible body. Robson says:

> The B.B.C. is almost overburdened with a sense of responsibility. One sometimes has the impression that because it is not answerable to one particular body, it feels itself to be answerable to everyone for all its actions. Its fits of excessive caution are doubtless due to a belief that nothing must be said or done which would give offençe to powerful institutions or interests which may start a cry of 'Down with the B.B.C.' [44]

Second, there is criticism of the make-up of the governing board on the ground that it is not representative of the tastes and desires of the general mass of the people. It is composed of many aged and highly conservative persons whose influence, even though indirect, is reflected in the character of radio programs.

Third, the financial arrangements between the British Broadcasting Corporation and the Treasury have been attacked. A very substantial amount of money is collected from the taxes on receiving sets. It is felt that the Treasury keeps too much of this, and that the corporation is not allowed sufficient funds for the improvement and expansion of its service and for the carrying on of experimentation. Why, it is asked, should radio listeners be heavily taxed to raise money for general Treasury use?

Fourth, there is sharp criticism of the personnel arrangements in the staff of the corporation. The methods of recruitment are not systematized. They are not governed by the civil service, and the salary scales are irregular. The director general has prevented the unionization of the staff, and other

44. Ibid. 91.

charges of arbitrary treatment have been directed against him. It is urged that if the corporation is not to be made a part of the civil service, and it is generally agreed that there are strong reasons against this, its staff arrangements should at least be standardized and its rates of pay brought into proper relation to normal civil service salaries.

The question is frequently raised whether there ought to be a completely centralized broadcasting monopoly. No one favors private competition with the British Broadcasting Corporation. Robson, however, proposes a plan for decentralization by which autonomy in the matter of radio programs would be given to regional authorities, each one of which would have its own wave lengths. This would permit a wider variety in radio programs and permit a larger and more diversified body of radio talent. Robson emphasizes, however, that these regions should not attempt to rely upon local talent for their programs.[45]

It may be suggested in conclusion that the British Broadcasting Corporation has proved an efficient and on the whole impartial administrator of a service in connection with which individual likes and dislikes loom large. If it has tended to play a bit safe rather than to be unduly venturesome, it has probably thereby escaped serious trouble. Many problems regarding its policies have not been finally settled. There seems, however, to be no serious dissatisfaction with it or any indication that it will be replaced by any other type of agency or form of control.

2. THE POOR LAW COMMISSION 1834-47

A brief comment upon the Poor Law Commission, an unsuccessful experiment of the early nineteenth century, is not wholly irrelevant at this point. It represented the first attempt in England to place an important social statutory power in the hands of a body completely independent of Parliament. It is an early and classic example of an attempt to 'take politics out of politics.' As such it forms an interesting bit of background against which to view the Unemployment Assistance Board, which we shall presently discuss and which stands out as an interesting instance of making the same mistake twice.

45. Ibid. 83 f.

A Royal Commission (1832-4) inquired into the administration of the Poor Law and it accumulated a mass of evidence showing the inconsistency, inefficiency, and maladministration in the local parishes, whose task it was to deal with the poor. There were no common standards; each parish worked quite independently, and there was no central supervision of any kind. The Poor Act of 1834 was based on the report of this Royal Commission. Its chief provisions are described by Sidney and Beatrice Webb:

> The chief operative provision was that for the establishment of a new Government Department, not under a Minister who could answer for it in Parliament, but under three salaried Commissioners with a Secretary, none of whom were permitted to sit in Parliament; they were empowered to appoint assistant commissioners and a clerical staff, and to issue mandatory rules, orders and regulations to the local Poor Law Authorities.[46]

The commissioners were to be appointed by the government, the chairman receiving a salary of £2,000. The commissioners were to be guided by the principles set forth in the report of the Royal Commission. They were given other supervisory powers over local Poor Law bodies, but they were not empowered to intervene in individual cases and order relief. The Royal Commission gave its reasons for creating this independent and irresponsible body rather than placing the administration of the Poor Law in the hands of the goverment itself: (1) Vigilance and economy would be relaxed under direct governmental control; (2) workhouses might be made so comfortable as to cease to be objects of terror; (3) candidates for political power would bid for popularity by promising to be good to the poor. Independence would take the issue of poor relief out of politics. The Royal Commission believed, in other words, that 'political' management would not be strict enough, would not be ruthless enough, would not, in short, carry out the drastic recommendations of the commission with regard to the administration of the Poor Law.

The Poor Law Commissioners were exceedingly unpopular, and although this unpopularity was not due to their status and organization, attack was directed against the whole scheme

46. *English Poor Law History* (1929), Part II, vol. I, 101.

which allowed 'autocratic and tyrannous' practices. In 1841 the commission's powers were due for prolongation; Disraeli led the assault against it, 'eulogizing the superiority of the immemorial local Government of England over the interferences and blunderings characteristic of a centralized bureaucracy.' No one was responsible for the commissioners in the House of Commons. Endless examples of individual cases of hardship were brought up, and no real answer could be given. After a general election, the commissioners' life was finally prolonged till 1847. Then it died, amidst a storm of abuse, unregretted.

During its lifetime it was, as a contemporary commentator put it, 'exposed to the insults of all the refuse of the House of Commons without the power of defending itself; and . . . had as its chief opponent the Secretary [of the commissioners] without the power of dismissing him.' Say the Webbs: 'The case of the Poor Law Commission has become a classic example of the absolute necessity of definite Ministerial responsibility in Parliament for every executive Department without exception.' [47] Says Walter Bagehot: 'The experiment of conducting the administration of a public department by an independent authority has often been tried, and always failed.' [48] In 1847 the administration of the Act of 1834 was placed in the hands of a new Poor Law Board (which, in fact, never met) with a president who was responsible to Parliament. It was later merged into the Local Government Board.

3. UNEMPLOYMENT ASSISTANCE BOARD [49]

a. *Background of the Unemployment Assistance Board*

The Labour Government fell in 1931 in a crisis precipitated by unemployment relief. The Party itself split on the issue, and the National or Coalition Government took office. The question of the 'dole' became acute. The new Government made a 10 per cent cut in the dole and set up a rigid 'family means' test for the payment of 'transitional benefits.' These transitional benefits were payments made to those who had

47. Ibid. 183.
48. W. Bagehot, *English Constitution* (1886), 189.
49. Cf. J. D. Millett, *The British Unemployment Assistance Board* (1940).

exhausted the twenty-six-weeks' statutory payments from the unemployment insurance fund, and by them recipients kept off local public relief for an additional twelve months. This family means test was the cause of fierce Parliamentary arguments as well as of street violence. It produced an acute feeling on the part of the unemployed that they were being unfairly treated. Though paid without central funds, the transitional benefit was administered by the public assistance committees of local authorities who were obliged by the statute to apply the family means test. The normal insurance payments were made at labor exchanges controlled by the Minister of Labour.

The new policy created an acute problem in the field of administration. The policy itself was very unpopular, and its unpopularity was justifiably laid at the door of the central government. Moreover, the policy had to be administered in the main by local bodies, and many of these were controlled by the Labour Party which opposed the policy. The result was unfortunate. There was a striking lack of uniformity in administration. In the areas controlled by the Labour Party the unemployed got more relief than elsewhere. In certain extreme cases the central government had to take over the local public assistance administration in order to get effective enforcement. The local committees were unpaid and proved susceptible to local pressure. Processions and meetings sometimes scared them into granting higher rates.

The Government was forced to centralize the administration of unemployment assistance. The direct way to do this was to give the job to the Ministry of Labour. This, however, would have instantly concentrated popular wrath on the Government and on the very unpopular Minister of Labour, Sir Henry Betterton. Instead of doing this the Government created an independent Unemployment Assistance Board to take over the administration of the transitional benefits system. They sought thereby to do two things: first, to iron out the earlier irregularities; and second, to take the entire controversy over unemployment assistance out of politics. The circumstances under which the new board came into being were such as to arouse all possible suspicion. The board was set up under Part II of the Unemployment Act of 1934, which was bitterly opposed in Parliament by the Opposition. Its chairman was the unpopular Sir Henry Betterton, now thinly disguised as Lord Rushcliffe, and it was very evident that the new 'independent' board was so constituted that it would carry out the highly unpopular policy of the Government in power.

b. *Structure and personnel*

The Unemployment Assistance Board is composed of a chairman, deputy-chairman, and four members. One must be a woman. The chairman is paid £5,000, the deputy-chairman £3,000, and the other members £750. These salaries, determined by the Treasury, must not total over £12,000. The members are appointed by the Government for long terms determined at the time of appointment, and they are eligible to reappointment. Members of Parliament are not eligible. The board determines its own quorum and procedure. It is the central agency in charge of an extensive system of local offices in which transitional benefits are administered by paid officers of the board, in place of the old unpaid public assistance committees of the local authorities. It represents, therefore, a high degree of centralization; some people think too high. The funds dispensed by the board come from the national Exchequer. The costs of administration are paid by the local authorities, who contribute the approximate amount which a centrally administered board saves them.

c. *Functions*

The Unemployment Assistance Board administers transitional relief. This is the relief given to those who are unemployed for from six to eighteen months. The Ministry of Labour's labor exchanges administer insurance payments for the first six months of unemployment, while the local Poor Law authorities take over those who have been unemployed for more than eighteen months. The board accordingly has the duty of relieving a very large group of unemployed persons. It has considerable discretionary power, but this is limited by statutory conditions in regard to who is or is not entitled to receive benefits. The board can alter the scales of allowances to the unemployed only with the consent of Parliament.

The unemployed who are eligible apply to the board for assistance. After estimating their means as well as the resources of their families, the local board officers may grant relief according to the scales approved by Parliament. They may, in addition, require the unemployed person to go to a labor-training camp—dubbed 'slave camps' by some of the unemployed. There has been a great deal of friction and hard feeling over the means test, as well as over the camps. It is clear that the Unemployment Assistance Board is charged with duties of the most controversial, even explosive, type.

Those who are aggrieved by the decisions of the board or its officers may resort to appeal tribunals, of which there are several distributed over the country. These are made up of an impartial chairman nominated by the Minister, a member named by the Minister to represent the workers, and a member of the Unemployment Assistance Board itself. Only the chairman receives a salary. The board determines the procedure of these tribunals.

d. *Relations to other agencies or departments*

The relations of the Unemployment Assistance Board to the Minister of Labour are somewhat confused. The Minister is not legally entitled to interfere with the day-to-day administration of the board, or to direct its decisions. He must, however, approve some of the board's acts and the Treasury must approve payments made for work done by certain classes of workers. Otherwise the board appears free from direct Ministerial interference. Nevertheless the board presents to the Minister of Labour an annual report which he in turn presents to Parliament, and this affords occasion for debate in which the Minister stands as the defender of the board in respect to its general policies. Thus the Minister is placed in a rather anomalous position. He cannot guide the board in any effective way and yet he must defend it in Parliament. This might present no serious difficulties if the board's task were essentially non-controversial; as it is, the Minister has experienced some very unhappy hours as a result of his vague responsibility for the board's all too unpopular activities.

The disadvantages of over-centralization have been mitigated in part by the setting up of some 130 advisory committees throughout England. These are appointed by the Unemployment Assistance Board from a variety of local organizations and groups. They provide some elasticity in the local administration of unemployment assistance, and this has been felt to be helpful.

e. *Appraisal*

Perhaps the best judgment on the Unemployment Assistance Board is to be read in terms of what happened to it. Constituted as it was, it was bound to follow the main principles of the Government's policy. It proceeded to set up a uniform system of administration. It then drew up standard scales for transitional benefit payments, got them approved by Parliament, and in January 1935 put the new scales into effect. These imposed drastic cuts in the payments to families in depressed areas where relatively favorable treatment had previously been meted out by Labour-controlled local authorities. The new scales were greeted with an outburst of popular anger. There were riots, processions, and attacks on local officials; the offices of the Unemployment Assistance Board were stormed. A volume of protests came to Whitehall. Anxious and harassed members of Parliament brought case after case of acute hardship from the new scales to the attention of the Government. No one was foolish enough to assume that the new scales were the 'non-political' output of an impartial expert body. The attack was directed against the Government, and everyone seemed to agree that full responsibility must be assumed by the Ministers.

The political storm was too much for the new Minister of Labour, Mr. Stanley. He was in an exceedingly uncomfortable position, for he had to bear the brunt of the assault on a program for which he was not directly responsible. He tried hard to throw the responsibility onto the Unemployment Assistance Board, but the debates in Parliament showed a very worried and harassed Minister beating a constant retreat. The outcome was complete surrender. The Government brought unofficial pressure to bear on the Unemployment Assistance Board, and the obnoxious rates were withdrawn. Since then the board has been regarded as 'independent' only in name. In practice it works in close collaboration with the Minister; its status of independence is not important.

The whole incident has clearly demonstrated the futility of trying to place the solution of a bitter political controversy 'above politics' in an 'impartial' board. It simply does not work.

IX

SUMMARY AND APPRAISAL OF BRITISH
EXPERIENCE IN THE REGULATION
OF ECONOMIC ENTERPRISE

IT remains to pull together the salient points with regard to British experience in the regulation and management of economic enterprise. This may be done by grouping under separate headings the observations and conclusions which throw light upon the basic problems with which British statesmanship has attempted to deal.

I. TYPES OF AGENCIES AND VARIETIES OF TASKS ASSIGNED TO THEM

WE may begin with the question whether in the British experience under review there has been any conscious effort to select a particular type of governmental agency to handle a particular type of job. Does British experience suggest any clear-cut principles which ought to govern the choice of one kind of governing body rather than another for the doing of particular kinds of work? No one familiar with British institutional history will be surprised to find that no clear and consistent set of conclusions can be drawn in this matter. This does not mean, however, that no correlations exist between the forms of British governing bodies and the jobs assigned to them, or that certain fairly definite trends may not be discerned. In summarizing our conclusions on this it is unnecessary to set up meticulously formulated classifications and definitions which are likely to have clear meaning only to their author. It is enough to say that the kinds of work done by British agencies of regulation and control fall into three rather general divisions: First, in England as in the United States there are a large number of regulatory powers of a narrow variety which we describe as police regulations. The American term 'police power' does not exist in the English political vocabulary, but American students of government are familiar with it. These police regulations comprise the many governmental restraints set up for the protection of health, morals, safety, good order and public convenience, and protection against fraud. These regulatory duties are usually assigned to the British Ministries. In some cases, however, such powers will be given to other governmental bodies which may be handling more impressive kinds of regulation. Second, a substantial body of British regulation may, for want of a better term, be broadly described as economic regulation. Perhaps in its inherent nature it does not differ sharply from police regulation, but it operates with somewhat wider sweeps and in the general field of industry and commerce. It comprises forms of control traditionally applied to public utilities, as well as more general and drastic regulations of economic enterprise. Third, the British government undertakes the ownership and management of certain businesses and industries. The power exercised here is not that of regulating a privately owned enterprise in the public interest, but of operating directly a business which is owned by the government itself.

For the exercise of these kinds of governmental powers there have emerged at least five different kinds of governmental bodies: First, there are the Ministries, the regular executive hierarchies which handle a vast number of the tasks under review. Second, there are the judicialized tribunals, approaching in their structure and functions administrative courts and set up to work in narrow and specialized areas. These have not functioned to the satisfaction of all, and many thoughtful persons believe that even if retained they will not be multiplied. Third, there are administrative tribunals, some inside and some outside the Ministries, which handle the bulk of the work in the field of economic regulation. These are less complicated and less sophisticated than the analogous American regulatory commissions. Fourth, there are what we have called the 'guild' bodies through which various industries are allowed to govern themselves through the sanctions of the law. They perform some of the duties of administrative tribunals, but they are not governmental bodies since they are composed of members chosen by private interests for purposes of industrial self-government. We have seen that the trend is away from this type of agency. Finally, there are the British public service boards, which are increasing in number. They operate the public services which the government feels can no longer be left in private hands and follow roughly the forms of business corporations. In some cases they have been set up for the purpose of 'taking politics out of politics,' in order to relieve the Government of embarrassment in the administering of highly controversial or unpopular policies. It seems safe to predict that sooner or later British regulation and control of economic enterprise will come to be carried on by the Ministries, the administrative tribunals, and the semi-independent public service boards.

A. Factors Determining the Choice of Type of Agency for a Regulatory Task

It would be useful to know with assurance why British government has used one governmental form rather than another for a particular task of economic regulation or control. It has not been possible in this study to trace in detail the legislative history of the various British agencies, as has been done with the American regulatory commissions. Without the information which might have been drawn from Parliamentary debates and similar sources, the following tentative conclusions, based more upon speculation and inference than one might wish, are offered:

First, it is safe to conclude that no very clear-cut or consistent principles have governed the selection of one form of agency rather than another. One does not expect such consistency in British practice. There has been a very large element of opportunism in the choice of British agencies for their particular tasks. They have been set up one at a time to deal with *ad hoc* situations. Sometimes the form of the governmental body set up has been determined by historical or traditional considerations. It is suggested, for instance, that if the British Post Office were being set up now the job would probably be assigned to a semi-independent public service board built along the lines of the British Broadcasting Corporation. When the Post Office was created this form of organization was unknown, and the job was therefore given to a British Ministry. While certain trends are becoming established, it would still be very unsafe to conclude that when a particular kind of regulatory job emerges the British government will automatically assign it to a well-defined type of governmental agency.

Second, pressure from interested groups has led in some cases to the selection of one kind of agency rather than another. In the field of road transport of goods, the Road and Rail Appeal Tribunal was set up as the appeal authority rather than the Minister of Transport simply because the British trucking industry was afraid it would not get a square deal from the Minister. It has since come to regret this decision, and this fact may possibly shorten the life span of the tribunal. We have also seen that the extreme degree of guild control which is embodied in the organization of the agricultural marketing boards was chiefly owing to the political influence of the highly individualistic British farming interests.

Third, the desire of the Government to escape responsibility for the administration of highly controversial policies led to the setting up of the Unemployment Assistance Board with its status of virtual independence of Ministerial or Parliamentary control. In its original form it was to serve as a shock absorber to protect the Government from the inevitable criticism and attack which was bound to strike whatever agency undertook to administer unemployment assistance. The British Broadcasting Corporation was created partly, it is true, to secure the efficient management of a highly technical enterprise, but partly also to relieve the Government in power of the awkward necessity of being held responsible for the particular radio programs which went on the air.

Fourth, the semi-autonomous public service board has been set up to provide efficiency and flexibility in the administration, not of a relatively uncomplicated scheme of regulation, but of an actual industry. Each board has been created to run a business. It has been felt necessary to place these businesses, if they are to succeed, outside the highly stereotyped restrictions of the British Civil Service and what many feel to be the crippling restraints of the normal departmental bureaucracy.

Fifth, there is in British experience, as in our own, an element of copying, of following precedent. This appears in the application to one governmental assignment after another of the formula of the public service board. More recently it looks as if the proposals made in the able report of the Milk Reorganization Commission in 1936 have been followed in the setting up of more than one agency to deal with the problems of a depressed industry.

Sixth, the composition and powers of certain British agencies are the result of a desire to give direct representation in the regulatory process to interest groups, or in some cases to balance these off against the public interest. Thus in many of the depressed industry agencies, as well as in the Railway Rates Tribunal, members must be chosen because they represent producers or workers or railways or shippers or some other particular interest group.

In all this there is to some extent an adjustment of the forms of British agencies to the kinds of work they are asked to do, but the adjustment is still fairly rough. The final decision on the kind of governmental body to be selected will continue to depend on many factors, and amongst these political convenience looms large. There has not yet developed in England any consistent adherence to any carefully worked out theory of administrative structure and organization.

II. MERGER OF DIFFERENT KINDS OF POWERS IN THE SAME AGENCY

We have seen that one of the earliest and most persistent criticisms of the American independent commissions is that they represent a merger in a single body of powers which it is felt ought to be separately administered. They are charged with exercising at the same time the powers of the prosecutor and the judge, and this remains an unsolved problem in American administration. To what extent does a similar problem exist in Great Britain? Do the British agencies of regulation and control merge powers commonly supposed to be incompatible? If they do, has this attracted British public attention, and what efforts or proposals have been made to deal with the problem?

If this problem exists in England, it is not as a constitutional problem. The British Constitution repudiates the principle of the separation of powers, which is so vital a part of our American constitutional system. It is built rather on the principle of legislative supremacy. If we find, therefore, in our analysis of the British agencies that a conscious effort has been made not to place certain kinds of powers in the same hands, we may know that this segregation results from the simple belief that it is expedient. It is not to be explained in terms of constitutional law.

A. To What Extent Are Administrative or Managerial Powers Separated from Judicial or Quasi-Judicial Powers in British Administration?

We look in vain in British governmental practice for any conscious separation of the quasi-judicial functions of regulation from the powers of administration and management. As a general rule they are merged in the same hands, cheerfully and without serious public concern, since any agency to which these supposedly 'incompatible' powers are assigned is felt to be effectively controlled either by Parliament or by the courts of law. Practically every British Minister is responsible for the exercise of many quasi-judicial powers including licensing, price fixing, the regulation of production quotas, and the like, as well as for narrower types of police regulation. These are not felt to be incompatible with the concurrent exercise of all sorts of other powers which are not quasi-judicial.

At the same time the British judicial or quasi-judicial tribunals have not been asked to take on administrative or sub-legislative duties. There seems to be a recognition here that it is desirable to leave these tribunals free from the conflict of interests which might result from giving them other tasks. The Railway and Canal Commission, the Railway Rates Tribunal, and the Road and Rail Appeal Tribunal represent a conscious isolation of the quasi-judicial function from other kinds of governmental responsibility. While each of these agencies in its own field exercises a certain amount of policy-determining power, this part of its assignment is incidental to its quasi-judicial work, and is decently camouflaged.

The principle of segregation of adjudication from administration, which many American students regard as so important, is recognized in British practice by the setting up of appellate procedure to protect private rights which are subject to the jurisdiction of administrative officers in the exercise of judicial or quasi-judicial powers. These appellate tribunals are of three varieties:

First, there are judicial or quasi-judicial appellate bodies created to review the quasi-judicial determinations of the regular administrative officers. Examples of these are the Railway and Canal Commission, to which have been assigned somewhat miscellaneous duties as a sort of appellate administrative court, and the Road and Rail Appeal Tribunal, which functions in the field of British motor trucking regulation. This type of specialized quasi-judicial tribunal is not common. As we have already seen, these two tribunals were each set up as the result of pressure from organized private interests who demanded special protection and were powerful enough to get it. It is unlikely that this kind of tribunal will be multiplied. There is no widespread belief in Great Britain that essential justice in dealing with private rights can be secured only in courts of law or in judicial tribunals set up in imitation of them. Experience with the highly judicialized agencies in England has not been happy, and there is little disposition to allow judicialized agencies to make decisions affecting social and economic policy. Nor has there developed in England the belief, so costly and so paralyzing to the administration of justice in the United States, that fair play requires that a person be given two or three successive trials of the same cause even though each one is essentially correct and fair. An appeal is not allowed in England if the only reason for granting it is to calm the emotions of a litigant. It is virtually impossible to get into the English courts on any matters in the field of economic regulation except on pure questions of law, and it is not always possible to get into a British court even on a question of law.

Secondly, appellate administrative tribunals have been set up in Great Britain to review the decisions and orders of administrative officers. In many cases a Cabinet Minister serves as an appellate tribunal for this purpose. This is true even when the original decision was made by one of his own subordinates, as in the case of appeals in the field of road passenger transport. The findings and decisions of non-departmental agencies are in some cases appealed to the Minister. This is true with respect to decisions made by the Electricity Commissioners and by some of the regulatory bodies set up to deal with depressed industries. In the same way the Electricity Commissioners act as an appellate body to pass upon various decisions made by the Central Electricity Board.

Thirdly, arbitral bodies are very frequently used in British administrative practice and with great success. There are almost countless situations in which the statutes require, permit, or encourage resort to an impartial arbiter. In some cases where appellate jurisdiction lies in a British Minister he may, in order to ensure not only fairness but the appearance of fairness, appoint such an arbiter to hear the appeals and make a recommendation.

We have indicated the extent to which British practice appears to have embodied a formal separation of the quasi-judicial function from other functions which might impair the impartiality or detachment of the adjudicator. While the issue has never been acute, there has been a certain amount of responsible criticism directed against the merger in the same agency of administrative and quasi-judicial powers. This we may now summarize.

B. Criticism Directed against Mergers of Administrative and Quasi-Judicial Powers

There has been desultory criticism directed against certain British agencies on the ground that they act both as judges and litigants in the same case. The Port of London Authority has been criticized for refusing to license new dockyard facilities in the Port of London when those facilities would inevitably compete with the docks owned and operated by the authority itself. It has been urged that the decision should be placed in other hands. Similarly a number of the agricultural marketing boards exercise the quasi-judicial authority to deny licenses to would-be competitors. These accusations of bias have cogency but not great importance, since the alternative to the present arrangement is likely to be complete government monopoly. The rights at stake are precarious, and if they are to some degree sacrificed to the government interest, no serious damage is done.

The most important and conspicuous attack upon the merger of judicial and quasi-judicial powers with other incompatible powers is to be found in Lord Hewart's book, *The New Despotism,* published in 1929. This was a vigorous and well-documented attack on what Lord Hewart regarded as the evils and resulting injustices of British bureaucracy. There were two major counts in the indictment. The first was directed against the delegation of legislative power to the Ministers and to certain other agencies, such as the Electricity Commissioners. This delegation goes to the extent of allowing the Ministers to change by order the provisions of a Parliamentary statute itself. The second attack was against the vesting in public officials 'to the exclusion of the jurisdiction of the courts of law, the power of deciding questions of a judicial nature.' Administrative justice was said to be of a hole-and-corner variety, and justice was denied by giving finality to the judicial or quasi-judicial decisions of administrative officers.

Within a week after the publication of Lord Hewart's book the Committee on Ministers' Powers was set up to explore the entire problem and bring in a report. The report of the committee was made in 1932, and is a document of lasting interest and value to students of public administration and public law. The committee's recommendations were intended to meet the two main points of attack which had been made in *The New Despotism,* at least as far as the committee felt they needed to be met. The first recommendation dealt with the delegation of legislative powers to Ministers or other governmental bodies. It did not propose the abandonment of such delegations, since it believed they were essential to the normal processes of administration. It did, however, suggest a number of safeguards with which delegations of legislative power might be hedged about in 'all but the most exceptional cases.' First, the precise limits of the law-making power which Parliament intends to give to a Minister should be made clear and precise; second, Ministers should not be given power to modify provisions of Acts of Parliament 'except in the most exceptional cases'; third, the validity of Ministerial regulations or orders of a legislative nature should be open to review in the courts, save in exceptional cases of an emergency character; fourth, elaborate and uniform procedure should be followed in issuing rules and regulations so that all relevant rights may be protected; finally, rules and regulations should be laid before Parliament for twenty-eight days to afford opportunity for disallowance.

The second part of the committee's report dealt with the judicial and quasi-judicial powers given to Ministers and other administrative bodies. Here it made five proposals: First, judicial powers should not be conferred on Ministers save in the most exceptional cases. If it is necessary to delegate them, they should be exercised through a Ministerial tribunal rather than through the Minister personally. This procedure should certainly be followed whenever the Minister in exercising such judicial function would also have a 'departmental interest' at stake which might create a bias. Second, quasi-judicial decisions, in contrast to judicial decisions, properly belong to the Ministers rather than to Ministerial tribunals or courts of law. In the committee's terminology, a quasi-judicial decision is characterized by the presence of a major element of discretion, and thereby differs from a judicial decision in which this element of discretion is either lacking or trivial. The committee was conscious, however, that this exercise of quasi-judicial power by the Minister presents a problem. It declared that 'the first and most fundamental principle of natural justice is that a man may not be a judge in his own cause.' It realized that Ministers will occasionally be placed in this position and accordingly made a very interesting proposal to govern the cases where the Minister's interests as a department head would be likely to disqualify him as a judge. This proposal is as follows:

. . . We think, however, that before Parliament entrusts a Minister with the power and duty of giving quasi-judicial decisions as part of a legislative scheme, Parliament ought to consider whether the nature of his interest as Minister in the carrying out of the functions to be entrusted to him by the statute may be such as to disqualify him from acting with the requisite impartiality. The comparative importance of the issues involved in the decision will, of course, be a relevant factor. Where it appears that the policy of the Department might be substantially better served by a decision one way rather than another, the first principle of natural justice will come into play, and the Minister should not be called upon to perform the incongruous task of dealing with the judicial part of the quasi-judicial decision as an impartial judge, when *ex hypothesi* he and his Department want the decision to be one way rather than another. We recognise that this kind of case may be rare, but it is a real possibility. In such a case the judicial functions which must be performed before the ultimate decision is given and on which that decision must be based should be entrusted by Parliament to an independent Tribunal whose decision on any judicial issues should be binding on the Minister when in his discretion he completes the quasi-judicial decision by administrative action.[1]

Third, various procedural safeguards were proposed. These included the holding of open public hearings, the rendering of decisions supported by opinions, and the exercise by the High Court of a supervisory jurisdiction to make sure that the Minister or the Ministerial tribunal has acted within its powers and in good faith. Fourth, the committee proposed an absolute right of appeal to the High Court on any question of law by any party aggrieved. Fifth, there should be no appeal to the courts on any question of fact.

It is difficult to appraise the influence of the report of the Committee on Ministers' Powers. Its immediate concrete influence was probably negligible. Its recommendations were not very drastic, and were not presented as proposals upon which prompt action seemed imperative. It is safe to assume, however, that the report will have influence, if not in the form of concrete legislative action which can be related to it, at least in shaping the thinking of British statesmen and students of government.

We may conclude that the problem presented by the combination of judicial and administrative powers in the same hands

1. Report of Committee on Ministers' Powers, April 1932 (1936), 79.

has not loomed as one of the major problems in the development of British regulatory practice. It has not caused much anxiety or dissatisfaction, and there is no present indication that the form and functions of British agencies are likely to be shaped, except very incidentally, by the influence of this problem.

C. To What Extent Is the Function of Planning Segregated in the British Agencies?

Students of administration are keenly interested in the problem of how best to organize the task of policy planning. In the broad areas of economic regulation, can a body engaged in disciplinary control over business and industry, or in the actual management of a business enterprise, carry on effectively the function of planning? Does British experience indicate that the problem has been appreciated in Great Britain and that steps have been taken to deal with it? Again we find that there is no settled or consistent policy. Although much planning is carried on by the same politically responsible officials who administer the plans if they are adopted, there is some disposition to call in outside assistance and to create planning machinery separate from the mechanism of administration. The variety of devices employed shows the absence of any consistent theory or policy regarding the problem, beyond the simple recognition that it may be desirable to create separate planning agencies, some of them *ad hoc* and some permanent. We shall comment briefly upon the different British agencies to which have been assigned the important task of planning.

The first of these is the Electricity Commissioners. We have already seen that there is an element of confusion and uncertainty about where this job of planning rests and ought to rest. As at first introduced, the Electricity Act of 1926 gave the planning function to the Central Electricity Board, a body of experts, since planning in this field is technical and calls for expert knowledge. The statute as passed, however, gave the planning function to the Electricity Commissioners who were to draw up schemes to be sent to the Central Electricity Board for elaboration. This gave the Electricity Commissioners the function of planning as well as the quasi-judicial duties of supervising the managerial activities of the Central Electricity Board. We have seen that in practice there has been a tendency to reverse this statutory division of labor and to shift the planning job back to the expert operating board and its staff. Certainly no clear principle can be drawn from the experience of these two agencies.

A second type of British planning machinery is the reorganization commission. These bodies may be set up as adjuncts of the Ministries, or attached to non-departmental agencies. They form an important part of the machinery of the agricultural marketing system. A reorganization commission is an *ad hoc* commission of inquiry set up to investigate unsatisfactory conditions and to make recommendations for their improvement. They are appointed by the Minister concerned most closely with the activity involved, and their reports go to him rather than directly to Parliament. In practice they have been staffed by outstanding men, and they have been exceedingly useful agencies. The reorganization commission may be seen at its best in the Milk Reorganization Commission which reported in 1936. Comment has already been made upon the great value and importance of the work done by this commission and the proposals which it made.[2]

The Royal Commission may of course be effectively utilized as a planning agency. Frequently it is set up to investigate unwholesome governmental conditions, but even when investigation is its primary assignment it would be expected to make suggestions for improvement. There is ample evidence in the foregoing pages that many plans and programs in the field of economic control by the government have been based on the proposals of Royal Commissions.

The statutory committee is the most interesting planning device which British ingenuity has evolved. It has proved so useful and has so many potentialities that it merits careful description and analysis. The statutory committee was first set up chiefly to lend aid in the field of administration on tricky points on which it was felt that expert detached judgment ought to be drawn in by the government. This form of it is illustrated by the Import Duties Advisory Committee of 1932. The statute imposed a general 10 per cent *ad valorem* duty

2. *Supra*, 566 ff.

which was to be collected subject to certain exemptions and 'to additional duties.' The advisory committee was set up to pass judgment upon requests for additional duty. If an industry desired an additional duty, as for instance a higher duty on steel, it put its case before the advisory committee which after consideration might then advise the Treasury to take the necessary steps. The Treasury was under no obligation to follow the recommendations of the committee, but it was required to consider them and to publish them whether it followed them or not.

Consideration of the Unemployment Insurance Statutory Committee shows that this type of body may be given much broader and more important duties in the field of planning. This committee was created by the Unemployment Act of 1934, which, it may be observed, was largely based on the report in 1932 of the Royal Commission on Unemployment Insurance. The first part of this Act dealt with unemployment assistance, and set up the ill-fated Unemployment Assistance Board already discussed. The second part of the Act dealt with unemployment insurance, and placed the administration of this insurance, together with the labor exchanges which constitute its indispensable machinery, in the hands of the Ministry of Labour. It was realized that the administration of this Act would create many individual controversies. It was also realized that the statute would have to be left flexible and that wide powers would have to be given to the Minister of Labour, not only to make regulations but also to make alterations in the statutory arrangement to meet the changing needs of the industrial situation. It was felt, however, that these important powers ought not to be exercised by the Minister without his first seeking the advice of an outside and independent authority. A body was needed to consider problems arising out of the administration of the insurance scheme 'outside the arena of party politics.' There was a precedent for this in the advisory committee set up under the so-called Anomalies Act of 1931, a body which had, however, narrowly limited powers.

Accordingly there was created the Unemployment Insurance Statutory Committee,[3] consisting of a chairman and six mem-

3. Cf. W. Beveridge, *The Unemployment Insurance Statutory Committee* (Politica Pamphlet No. 1).

bers appointed by the Minister of Labour. There must be one woman on the committee; there have thus far always been two. Three members must be appointed after consultation with organizations of employers and workers and the Minister of Labour for North Ireland. The members serve for five years and the terms are staggered. They may be removed only for unfitness. The expenses of the committee are paid by the Ministry of Labour, so that the committee comes up for debate on the estimates for the department. It costs about £3,000 per year. The secretary is an official of the Ministry of Labour, and other officials of the Ministry sit with the committee at its request. There has always been the closest harmony between the committee and the Ministry.

The committee has three major functions. First, it must report on all orders or modifying regulations made by the Minister of Labour under the Unemployment Insurance Act. All such orders or regulations must be referred to the committee. It will, as a rule, hold public hearings. It is required to make a report to the Minister either approving or disapproving the order or regulation. The Minister is not required to adopt the report of the committee, but in laying an order or regulation before Parliament for its necessary confirmation he must send also the report of the statutory committee and state whether he has followed the committee's recommendations; and if he has not done so, he must give to Parliament his reasons for disagreement.

Second, the statutory committee must give to the Minister of Labour advice on any question relating to the operation of the statute, including questions on the desirability of amending it, if the Minister requests it to do so. In this way it serves as a sort of continuing Royal Commission for the study not merely of broad problems arising out of the administration of the Act but for the proposal of legislative changes. The procedure here is less rigid. The Minister is not required to submit to Parliament recommendations made by the committee under these circumstances. Actually, legislative suggestions made by the committee have in virtually every instance been enacted into law. This broad planning function of the committee is clearly illustrated by the proposals which it made relating to the extension of the unemployment insurance program to agricultural laborers. The Minister of Labour asked the statutory committee to study and report on this important problem, and the Act of 1936 embodied its recommendations.

The third function of the statutory committee is to report on and to adjust the financial condition of the unemployment fund. As a matter of fact, this is its major responsibility. The preceding unemployment compensation scheme had run up a debt of £115,000,000, and the Government was determined that this should not happen again. Contributions are paid into the unemployment fund by employers, workers, and by the government. The statutory committee must report annually to the Minister of Labour on the existence of a surplus or deficit in this fund and the amount of it. Its findings on these points are conclusive. It then recommends methods, usually changes in the rates of contributory payments, to take care of the surplus or the deficit; but these recommendations need not be followed by the Minister. The committee has no powers of administration whatsoever.

The Unemployment Insurance Statutory Committee got off to an auspicious start, and has been strikingly successful and influential. There are certain fortuitous elements in this success. No small part of it has been due to the influence of Sir William Beveridge, the chairman of the committee. The Ministry of Labour is filled with his friends and former students, so that harmonious relations between the committee and the Ministry are easy to maintain. The committee had the good fortune at the outset to have the Minister of Labour willing to agree with its proposals. As a Ministry official observed to the writer, had the Minister overruled the statutory committee twice in succession at the outset, the committee's influence would have been half gone. It was not, however, pure luck that the committee was not overruled. It has been conscious of the necessity of making proposals which have a fair chance of being approved. As Sir William Beveridge observed: 'If I exercised all the power I have, the committee would very promptly be upset in Parliament.' [4] One of the advantages of the committee is that it affords opportunities in the administration of a complicated statute for the open airing of grievances. The committee regularly holds public hearings and

4. Conversation with the writer, 1937.

persons who feel themselves aggrieved can thus get the attention of the committee, when it might be impossible to get the ear of a preoccupied Minister. Many believe that the committee is able to do a better job of general policy planning than a Royal Commission set up *ad hoc,* since it has a background of experience and thoroughly knows the field of unemployment insurance. It is constantly on the ground and is thus able to deal with objectionable conditions before they become acute. The committee and the principle which it embodies have not escaped criticism. It has been suggested that as time goes on the committee is likely to become the victim of habit and cease to have a fresh point of view. It may, furthermore, fall under the domination of one man. There are those who feel that this has already occurred. Some of the Conservatives in Parliament have charged that the committee has acquired a dangerously powerful position under its present chairman, and they have openly expressed their regret for 'the good old days when laws were made by Parliament, whereas now they are made by Sir William Beveridge.'[5] A different type of criticism argues that a powerful and independent Minister might reduce the committee to a group of nonentities reflecting no points of view except his own. Sir William Beveridge himself believes that the great contribution of the statutory committee is the separating of policy planning from administration. This he believes is essential. He observed to the writer: 'Planning in a democracy is like breathing under water, and the statutory committee is a type of fish which democratic government has invented for this purpose.'[6]

It is not surprising that the statutory committee has attracted a good deal of attention and that it has been thought of as a device which might be used in much broader areas. While it has not so far been duplicated in the British statutes, it seems not unlikely that experiments in this direction on a broader scale may be attempted. The valuable organization P.E.P. (Political and Economic Planning) includes the statutory committee as a major plank in its program for the public regulation of all the social services, a proposal which they frankly

5. Speech delivered by Sir William Beveridge before the Institute of Municipal Treasurers and Accountants, July 1937.
6. Conversation in 1937.

admit was inspired by the highly successful career of the Beveridge committee.

III. THE POLITICAL RESPONSIBILITY OF BRITISH AGENCIES—THE NATURE AND MEASURE OF THEIR INDEPENDENCE

IN turning to the interesting and important problem of the responsibility or independence of the British agencies under discussion, it must be kept in mind that the term independence has at best a somewhat qualified meaning when applied to any part of the British government. Strictly speaking, only the British Parliament is independent. Parliament is supreme. There is no constitutional separation of powers, and therefore no part of the government ever gets wholly beyond the reach of Parliament. Any talk about responsibility and independence must be understood in the light of the fact that Parliament can by law do anything. Any independent or semi-independent British agency lives and works in the full knowledge that if it really outrages public opinion or the majority party something can and probably will be done about it. What we are analyzing here, then, is not this ultimate power of life and death, but the normal type of control exercised over British agencies which are pursuing their customary routine. To what extent are the agencies which we have been reviewing accountable in theory and in practice to somebody else? What are the devices for defining the area of their independence and for enforcing their accountability?

A. MINISTERIAL RESPONSIBILITY FOR DEPARTMENTS

It is enough merely to mention the responsibility of the British Minister for his department. Every officer or body in the department hierarchy is accountable to the Minister and the Minister himself cannot escape the responsibility thus placed upon him. This is roughly similar to the hierarchical arrangements in an American executive department. The striking difference is that while the British Minister is accountable to Parliament, the American department head is accountable to the President of the United States. What has been said does not mean that a British Minister may not utilize the services of Ministerial tribunals, arbiters, and the like, for the purpose of securing impartiality and detachment in the performance of certain duties. But unless Parliament by statute places these Ministerial tribunals beyond the Minister's reach, he remains broadly responsible for the general results of their work even though for reasons of policy he allows them the widest possible measure of independence. Ministerial responsibility and direction, in short, do not necessarily mean partisan or political administration.

B. Responsibility of Non-Departmental Agencies

When we turn to the agencies set up outside the Ministries we face a more complicated problem, and these are the bodies with which this study chiefly deals. What is the measure of their independence or their accountability; by what methods can they be held responsible for what they do? We turn first to the devices at present available in British government for enforcing the responsibility of these agencies.

1. METHODS OF ENFORCING RESPONSIBILITY TO A MINISTER

We shall first review briefly the methods by which a non-departmental agency may be held accountable to a British Minister. These may be grouped under five heads.

a. *The Minister's power of appointment*

Practically every agency or officer in the British government is appointed either by the Prime Minister or by some departmental Minister. The most conspicuous exception to this, the anomalous 'appointing trustees' set up to choose the members of the London Passenger Transport Board, has not met with general approval and is not likely to be copied. Naturally the power of appointment carries with it tremendous influence. It assures initial conformity upon the part of the appointees to the Minister's views, if he has any views and wishes to have them regarded. This is especially important when an agency is being set up, for then all of the members are chosen at the same time. There are in practice certain limitations upon the Minister's freedom of choice in making appointments found in the statutes creating some of the agencies with which we are concerned. If it seems desirable to appoint a lawyer, the Minister will be directed to consult the Lord Chancellor; where the interests of other Ministries may be concerned he will be asked to consult them. In a good many cases the Minister is directed to consult private interest groups or associations, such as producers, employers, workers, and so forth. These directions limit the Minister's otherwise free discretion, and to that extent they restrict the maximum control which he might otherwise have through his power of appointment.

b. *Removal power*

As a tool for enforcing any sort of responsibility upon any British officer beyond the responsibility to be sane, honest, and competent, the power of removal may be disregarded. Neither in theory nor in practice does there appear to be a purely discretionary removal power exercised by a Minister to enforce conformity to his policy. This does not mean that if an officer became antagonistic to the views of his chief he could not be removed. The probabilities are that he would not wait to be removed. But the power of removal is not one of the normal administrative devices for enforcing conformity to policy, and this is a matter governed by custom and practice rather than by clearly defined provisions of statutory law. In connection with the agencies included in this study, there are no clear grants of discretionary removal in the Minister; and if there were it is unlikely that removals would be threatened by the Minister to impose the Minister's own views on a non-departmental agency. The members of the Wheat Commission may be removed 'in a manner prescribed by the Minister.' The Electricity Commissioners may be removed by the Crown at pleasure, which means removal by the Government; but there is no discretionary removal power in the Minister of Transport to whom the commissioners are in many ways accountable. The British statutes contain provisions authorizing the removal of members of British agencies for misbehavior or incompetence; other causes include the acquisition by the member of financial interests thought to be incompatible with the office, prolonged absences from duty, and the release of confidential information. It is safe to conclude, however, that no member of the boards, commissions, and tribunals we are discussing is moved in the making of decisions or the performance of duties by any implied threat of removal from office should he fail to discover and follow the wishes of the Minister.

c. *Supervisory and reviewing power in the Minister—Power to direct*

In a number of cases British regulatory bodies are subject to the power of the Minister to issue orders which they must obey, or they are subject to his authority to pass upon and disallow their decisions or policies. This is true of the Area Traffic Commissioners in the field of passenger transport, the Electricity Commissioners and thus indirectly the Central Electricity Board, the new British Overseas Airways Corporation, the Livestock Commission, and the Whitefish Commission. In all these cases direct and immediate responsibility to the Minister is created. In many other cases the agencies are accountable to the Minister for the performance, not of all of their functions, but of particular duties singled out for this kind of control.

d. *Treasury control of finance*

The grip of the Treasury on the British agencies is very pervasive and hard to escape. It usually extends to the fixing of salaries, to staff arrangements, and to general administrative housekeeping matters. Where the agency receives or manages funds or spends money, Treasury control becomes tighter and more constant. We have seen how crippling it has become in the case of the Forestry Commission, which has sometimes been almost starved to death. The Treasury has been allowed to take for general government use much of the revenue of the British Broadcasting Corporation derived from the license taxes upon radio receiving sets; and this control has cramped the corporation in embarking upon expansions of its service or scientific experimentation. The London Passenger Transport Board has steadily declined to avail itself of the privilege of Treasury guarantee of its loans and stock, because it does not wish to have to carry on its complicated business under the eagle eye and inconvenient restrictions of the Treasury. All agencies which administer government subsidies are subject to Treasury control. Robson has suggested that this Treasury control should not penetrate into the field of policy, but should be limited to seeing that the funds granted have not been wasted or overdrawn.

e. *The 'open letter of instruction'*

Robson has made a further interesting proposal, which would extend the influence of the Minister over Ministerial tribunals or other agencies which are indirectly accountable to the Minister under the statutes, but with the normal routine of which he does not wish to interfere. This method is what Robson calls an open letter of instruction sent by the Minister to the tribunal for the purpose of directing its policy and bringing it into conformity with his own. The value of this device lies in the publicity which would accompany these letters of instruction. They would not be mandatory. The tribunal would reserve its right to ignore them. But if the Minister's case is a strong one, it could be presented in so effective a manner as to make it embarrassing for the tribunal not to comply. We have seen that the Minister of Transport tried something like this in sending certain statements of policy to the Area Traffic Commissioners, which the commissioners ignored. This, however, was done without statutory authorization and without any publicity attending the transaction. The experiment with an open letter would be worth trying, and there seems no good reason why the Ministers should not make their views known in this way to other agencies as well as to the quasi-judicial tribunals in connection with which Robson made his proposal.

2. METHODS OF ENFORCING ACCOUNTABILITY TO PARLIAMENT

Perhaps more important than the agencies' responsibility to the Ministers is their accountability to Parliament. Of course, if an agency is clearly and directly responsible to a Minister it is *ipso facto* responsible to Parliament, because the Minister is responsible to Parliament. This presents no special problem. All the usual machinery through which Ministerial responsibility is enforced is brought into play, and it is unnecessary to describe this routine here. When, however, we turn to the so-called independent or semi-independent bodies set up to handle important tasks of regulation and control, we face a more difficult and complicated problem.

In discussing the responsibility of semi-independent boards, such as the London Passenger Transport Board and the British Broadcasting Corporation, the question arises to what extent these agencies ought to be held responsible. One of the chief reasons for giving them the status which they enjoy is to put them beyond the reach of the deadening effects upon efficiency and initiative which direct accountability to Parliament would be likely to produce. To subject the managers of a big public service enterprise to a constant barrage of Parliamentary questions would make the administrators cautious and would tend to defeat the very objects for which the public control was established. Before venturing an opinion upon just how independent these bodies ought to be we should know how independent they are, and by what methods the responsibility they owe to Parliament is or may be enforced. These methods may be summarized as follows:

First, some of the normal Parliamentary devices for enforcing the responsibility of Cabinet Ministers can be employed with semi-independent agencies. This is true even though no Minister may fairly be held fully and directly responsible for the agency. Perhaps the most useful of these devices is the Parliamentary question. While the unrestricted use of questions to embarrass a public service agency might be undesirable, questions kept within reasonable limits may be exceedingly valuable in giving the public needed information and protection. In practice, questions are not permitted on matters of day-to-day administration with regard to which there is no Ministerial responsibility. But questions with regard to broad policy will not be ruled out, and Ministers will provide information even about matters over which they have no control. Thus Parliament retains the opportunity to speak its mind, while at the same time members do not become serious nuisances or obstruct efficient administration. The experience of the Unemployment Assistance Board shows that where the public mind or some major part of it has been outraged by a government agency, even the statutory independence of that agency will fail to prevent a thorough airing of the controversy in Parliament. In that case the Minister of Labour was put on the spot in the House of Commons on the question of the unemployment assistance rates issued by the board, and no amount of 'passing the buck' to the board appeared to help him. He was obliged to surrender and to agree to focus upon the board the full force of the Government's influence. Thus even if the Minister cannot be made to answer specific questions, it is still possible to create a considerable amount of useful unpleasantness by compelling him to explain why he does not or cannot answer questions on broader issues.

Parliament also makes contacts with the semi-autonomous boards at the time of the debates on the annual estimates. This is true, at least, when the board is financially dependent upon Parliament. There is also a chance to debate the board when its annual report is received, and this is a sound reason for having it make an annual report. In addition there are the various private members' motions which bring before Parliament either matters involving the expenditure of money or matters of administration. These may be directed at the agencies under review.

Second, there are many cases in which the orders or regulations of semi-independent boards must either receive Parliamentary approval or must be laid before Parliament for a period of time to permit disallowance. Under neither of these procedures does Parliamentary debate or active consideration normally occur. The regulations and orders are placed on the legislative calendar as a special item which is reached late at night and the Ministry's recommendations are approved as a matter of routine. While this smacks of rubber-stamping, it nevertheless is valuable. It means in practice that before these orders or regulations are submitted to Parliament their controversial aspects have been so ironed out that no serious risks of Parliamentary disapproval are incurred. It is worth while to keep alive potential Parliamentary action in order to accomplish this useful result.

Third, Parliamentary membership by a member of the agency may be required. We saw in the case of the Forestry Commission that the statute requires that one member of the commission be also a member of Parliament. This provides a channel of contact between Parliament and the commission and was intended to do so. This member is in a position to answer questions in the House of Commons, but apparently the work of the commission is not regarded as sufficiently important to justify making him an under-secretary. In the case of some of the agricultural marketing boards the outside co-opted members are members of Parliament, and are chosen for that reason. This has proved to be an exceedingly feeble device by which to attempt to establish effective responsibility to Parliament. The arrangement has some value, but chiefly in serving as a useful method of propaganda whereby the Forestry Commission may tell its story to the House of Commons. The arrangement was copied from the Ecclesiastical Commission, which similarly contains one member of Parliament.

Fourth, Parliamentary committees or commissions may be set up. There is a growing feeling that the foregoing methods are inadequate, and that more effective machinery could be set up to keep Parliament abreast of what goes on in these areas of complex administration so that accountability can be more intelligently and successfully enforced. Definite proposals have been made to accomplish this purpose. One of these is the setting up of some kind of permanent Parliamentary committee or commission, giving it an adequate staff, and charging it with the duty of following the processes of administration closely enough to provide Parliament with the information it needs. There is one such body, the Public Accounts Committee, which serves as a rough precedent here, while other more sophisticated proposals have been put forward by competent students of British government and administration. The Public Accounts Committee, which dates back to the early nineteenth century, deserves brief comment. It consists of eleven members, and the party division on it is, so far as may be, the same as that in the House of Commons. The chairman is always a member of the Opposition, often a past financial secretary to the Treasury. The committee will normally include a number of former Treasury officials. The committee has several functions. It inspects the accounts and the notes made by the Comptroller and Auditor General, indicating why more or less was spent on each item. It makes precise and thorough inquiries into finances, and gets whatever other information it regards as appropriate. It digs into many matters which have a bearing upon administrative efficiency. Its criticisms of departmental lapses or slackness are embodied in Treasury Minutes, and these are much feared and correspondingly potent. As far as it goes the scheme works admirably, but it has certain shortcomings. It is difficult to get Parliamentary discussion on the committee's reports, since Parliament is apt to be too busy to take up minor details. Furthermore, the committee works on last year's accounts, with the result that by the time it has finished it is dealing with transactions practically two years old. The arrangement does, however, afford a technique whereby a legislative body may, if it cares to, keep itself abreast of the minutia of finance or administration.

Certain proposals have been made for the setting up of Parliamentary administrative committees along lines broad enough to make possible an effective responsibility to Parliament of the British administrator or semi-autonomous board. Without attempting to trace the origin of the idea, we may note that proposals for such committees have been made by Professor Harold Laski and Professor Ivor Jennings. The plans outlined by these two scholars are not very different. The committees are to be standing committees of Parliament, one for each department. While neither Laski nor Jennings specifically suggested it, there might well be one for each major public service board. The membership, if it reflects party lines at all, should reflect the prevailing party strength in Parliament. Laski feels that the members should be chosen for specialized ability rather than for partisan considerations. These committees would not be given the power to make policy or be allowed to perform any of the tasks of administration. They would exist to consult and to scrutinize, so that competent opinion could be laid before Parliament. They should have full power to secure all relevant information. They might be given the task of passing on ordinances or regulations promulgated by the departments, thus providing a solution for the vexed question of delegated legislation. Such a committee would study matters submitted to it by Parliament or by a department, and serve as a general advisory committee. A Minister or his representatives would be present at its deliberations.

Several advantages are claimed for this proposal. The administrator or board would feel a keener sense of responsibility to Parliament by being in closer touch with it through this committee. On the other hand, Parliament could express opinions and make suggestions more intelligently. It would guarantee that in Parliamentary debates there would be present members of the House who thoroughly understood Ministerial policy, whether they agreed with it or not. It would permit a Minister to discover by consultation with such a committee how his policies are likely to strike Parliament or the public. It would provide Parliament with means for watching the results of legislative policies which it sets in motion. Professor Laski, in conversation with the writer, offered the following illustration to show how such a Parliamentary committee might work: The problems of prison reform have long been acute in Great Britain, but it has been virtually impossible for members of Parliament through the ordinary device of questions in the House of Commons to make any substantial headway. If a member suggests that serious abuses have developed in connection with a particular prison, the Home Secretary is very likely to reply that the Honorable Member's information is inaccurate, and it is next to impossible for the individual member to get full information. If there were a standing Parliamentary committee which devoted its attention to the problems of prison administration it could keep itself informed on what was actually going on, and would be able to put the Minister on the spot if abuses were found.

Objections have been urged against this proposal. They rest mainly on the fear that such standing committees might become so powerful that they would overshadow the Ministers and make increasingly difficult the processes of administration. They might come to have very great power without themselves incurring effective responsibility. This was the general result of the French parliamentary commissions, which seriously overshadowed the French ministers and made themselves perhaps the most powerful agencies in the French government. It is said in reply to this that the weakness of the French ministers was due, not to the French parliamentary commissions, but to the inherent looseness of the French party system, and that no such result would be likely to occur in Great Britain. Critics of this plan also allege that a Parliamentary committee would be quite incapable of carrying on an effective examination of the way in which a highly technical administrative job is being handled. The duties of such a committee would be so heavy that they would be incompatible with normal Parliamentary responsibilities.

Fifth, a wholly different proposal is that of a periodical efficiency audit of the activities of the semi-independent public service boards or other highly complicated agencies of public administration. This efficiency audit has been proposed by W. A. Robson, and while Robson does not favor the Parliamentary committee scheme just discussed, there appears to be no real incompatibility between it and the efficiency audit plan. The scheme contemplates a thorough overhauling of the entire field of activity by an outside expert body behaving in many ways like a Royal Commission. It would either function at regular intervals according to some prearranged schedule, or be called into play *ad hoc,* at irregular intervals. It would have the advantage of not burdening members of Parliament with highly technical tasks for which they are not equipped, and it would make it possible for Parliament to secure, when it felt it needed it, the fullest possible information on the administration of any board or department. The plan has been criticized as being ineffective, since the body which would carry on such an efficiency audit would not be composed of members of Parliament and would therefore have no power to enforce its findings or make its criticisms effective. Laski has suggested that any regular efficiency audit would lose its usefulness as a means of disclosing administrative inefficiency, because it would be expected and prepared for. This is one of the weaknesses of the Public Accounts Committee.

Sixth, Professor Herman Finer believes that the best way to hold the semi-autonomous public service boards responsible to Parliament is to subject them to the scrutiny from time to time of a Royal Commission. These Royal Commissions would be set up *ad hoc* as needed, and in many ways the plan is not strikingly different from the Robson proposal of an efficiency audit. It is well known that in many cases Royal Commissions have rendered service of the highest quality. They have uncovered bad administration and they have made effective proposals for reform. Typical of these commissions was the Ullswater committee which investigated the British Broadcasting Corporation when the corporation's charter was about to expire. Its report was of enormous value in bringing before Parliament the facts relating to the corporation's management, together with well-conceived proposals for change. Instances of this sort could be multiplied running back over many years.

There are some, however, who view the Royal Commission with many reservations. It must be admitted that the results depend largely upon the government's good luck in getting the right personnel. Royal Commissions, even the best ones, are likely to show a liberal smattering of stuffed shirts in their membership. Professor Laski ventured the opinion that 30 per cent of the people on these commissions had no business to be there. For example, when a vacancy occurred in the membership of the Committee on Ministers' Powers, Lord Iveagh, the head of Guinness Stout, asked Prime Minister Baldwin to appoint his wife to this vacancy, and this was done. It is clear that there is no incompatibility between the occasional use of a Royal Commission and the use of some of the other devices which have been described. It has been suggested that the Royal Commission is not likely to be very effective unless its assignment is to conduct an inquiry so acutely needed as to command the interest of very able men. It would be virtually impossible to staff Royal Commissions if they were being asked to make investigations of more or less routine nature.

Seventh, it must be remembered that Parliament holds the power of life and death over all British agencies, no matter how independent they may feel that they are. When the Unemployment Assistance Board incurred popular ill will, it was subjected to Parliamentary action which essentially destroyed its independence. In the last analysis all of these bodies exist on sufferance, and any flagrant misconduct or maladministration would result in drastic statutory change.

3. ACCOUNTABILITY OF BRITISH AGENCIES TO THE COURTS

The responsibility which these British agencies owe to the courts presents no major problem, since there is a much more limited view in Great Britain of the proper range of judicial authority in this field than in the United States. The salient facts are as follows: First, there is no judicial review of administrative determinations of fact. It is regarded as neither necessary nor desirable that the courts should undertake to do over again the fact-finding job assigned to the administrator. Second, there is review of administrative decisions on questions of law. These are in the main questions of *ultra vires,* and with the sound British prejudice against frivolous appeals this judicial review of administrative agencies is kept at a minimum. Third, as has been noted, a specialized tribunal has occasionally been set up and utilized in this field. The Railway and Canal Commission is an example. Since appeals go to the regular courts on questions of law, there has been some discussion whether special administrative courts should be set up as branches of the regular judiciary. There is little support for the idea. Some regard the administrative court principle as objectionable in itself, while others feel that there would not be enough business to keep an administrative court busy. It has been suggested, however, that specialized judges might be provided in the regular courts to whom administrative law cases might be assigned.

4. DEGREES OF INDEPENDENCE AND ACCOUNTABILITY

It is clear from the foregoing analysis that the British agencies we are concerned with have varying degrees and kinds of accountability. Some are subject to much more drastic control than others. While these degrees of accountability can hardly be made into sharply defined categories, they may be briefly summarized, even though there is some overlapping and blurring at the edges.

In the first place, there are agencies which are completely accountable for what they do. Here are those which lie wholly within one of the regular Ministries. Here also are the non-departmental agencies which are directly subject to Ministerial direction, such as the Electricity Commissioners, the British Overseas Airways Corporation, and the Area Traffic Commissioners. To say that these agencies are completely responsible to the Minister does not mean that he directs all of their activities. As a matter of policy he may allow them the widest possible range of independence, not only for their own convenience but also for his own; but he cannot in this way escape responsibility for what these agencies do, on the ground that he has allowed them this freedom from his directing control.

In the second place, there are certain bodies which occupy positions of substantial independence. We know that there is no such thing in British government as absolute independence except in the case of Parliament. Substantial independence, however, is enjoyed by judges and judicial bodies. Judicial officers are wholly free from Ministerial or Parliamentary control in any normal sense, and tradition strengthens the independence created by law. But even the courts are responsible to the Treasury with regard to their financial affairs, and the Lord Chancellor is an administrative officer, a member of the Cabinet, and has administrative duties of a wide variety with corresponding responsibilities. The Railway and Canal Commission, the Railway Rates Tribunal, and the Road and Rail Appeal Tribunal are for all practical purposes independent of the policy-determining branch of the government, and are intended to be. They enjoy a degree of independence greater than that of the American regulatory commissions.

In the third place, there is a compromise status which we may call semi-independence. This has been worked out to meet the practical needs of administration. It involves practical independence for the agency in the matters of its day-to-day administration, but accountability to the Government concerning the broad lines of its policies. The status of the public service boards was devised to embody this compromise. There has been created, in short, a sphere of activity with regard to which a governmental body can say 'we are not accountable to you with regard to this,' while at the same time the major purposes and general results of that body's operations are within the area of political control. The experiment has been an interesting one, and the theory involved is fascinating. It is a conscious and intelligent effort to deal with a problem which we have ignored in the United States, but with which sooner or later we may need to come to grips.

IV. STRUCTURE AND PERSONNEL ARRANGEMENTS IN BRITISH AGENCIES

IT remains to comment briefly upon the British agencies with regard to their structure or institutional aspects, and the problems relating to staff and personnel. How are these bodies made up, what kind of men are chosen to man them, and what sort of internal management is employed to secure staff efficiency? These are problems of great practical importance.

A. APPOINTMENT AND REMOVAL METHODS

In discussing the authority which the Minister may exercise over the various British agencies, we have mentioned the method of their appointment. We may now make two or three general observations with regard to the power of appointment and removal.

First, many of these appointments are made by the Minister in consultation with other officials or with the representatives of interest groups. This has become almost a settled policy. It is presumably a policy which a responsible Minister would be likely to follow even if he were not directed by law to do so. The President of the United States not infrequently consults in this manner before making appointments to the major independent commissions, but in no case is he required to do so.

Second, outside independent appointing bodies are not satisfactory, and the drift is very definitely away from them. Few thoughtful observers believe that the device of 'appointing trustees,' by which the members of the London Passenger Transport Board are chosen, is sound and will be used again. An exception to this opinion is that of Sir Gwilym Gibbon of the British Institute of Public Administration, who told the writer that he regarded this method of appointment as highly desirable and believed it should be applied to such agencies as the British Broadcasting Corporation and the Central Electricity Board. It is clear that the appointment of members of the British marketing boards by the producers who are to be regulated has not turned out happily, and we have observed a trend toward official appointment. It seems safe to conclude that the members of the British agencies we are concerned with are likely to be chosen by a responsible Minister.

Third, the removal power in Great Britain is not a method of administrative discipline as in the United States. No one seems to pay any serious attention to it and it has no clear bearing upon the problems under discussion.

B. Calibre of Personnel and Qualifications of Members

One of the important problems connected with the agencies under review is the problem of what kind of people are going to be appointed as members. The measure of statesmanship, integrity, and administrative capacity of a regulatory or public service board is not likely to be greater than that of the individual men and women who compose it. In England and in the United States there is no more difficult or exacting problem than that of getting the kind of people needed into these positions. We may summarize the methods which have been used in England for this purpose.

1. DIRECT REPRESENTATION OF INTERESTS

When boards and tribunals are being set up to deal with economic regulation and control, should they include in their membership persons directly representative of the various interests which will be affected by the policies and activities of the agency? We have several instances of this representative membership in the British agencies. The most conspicuous case is that of the agricultural marketing boards, whose members are chosen directly by the interest groups affected. In other cases, as in the agencies regulating other depressed industries, appointments are made by the Minister, but he is instructed to make them so as to represent particular interests. Sometimes the principle of representation is joined with the principle of appointing impartial members in a sort of mixture. This is frequently a method of tapering off the use of the representation principle, and in certain cases the proportion of detached and impartial members has been increased by successful legislative amendments. In one or two of the agencies dealing with problems of unemployment as, for example, the Unemployment Assistance Board, the statute requires that there be a woman appointed, and this is sometimes done even when it is not required. The setting up of a regulatory body thus made either wholly or partially representative of interests to be affected may be at the outset a necessary political step. This is particularly true where regulation, as in the case of the Agricultural Marketing Acts, is penetrating for the first time into areas which have before been free from control. Thoughtful opinion in Great Britain does not look with favor upon the principle of 'representative' appointments. It feels that what is needed on these governing bodies is a group of trained public-spirited men, not a group of antagonistic partisans each striving to get the most possible for the particular interest group which placed him in office. It seems probable that the principle of representation will ultimately be abandoned.

2. APPOINTMENT OF EXPERTS OR SPECIALLY TRAINED PEOPLE

There is a natural disposition to place on agencies charged with technical and complicated responsibilities men who have the special technical training to discharge those responsibilities efficiently. Some British statutes direct the appointment of persons thus specially trained. This is true in the case of the Central Electricity Board and the Forestry Commission. It is doubtful whether these statutory requirements are much more than pious admonitions, and it is even more doubtful whether they are necessary. It is wholly natural that technically trained men should be chosen for some at least of these positions. The Central Electricity Board has always had on it more electrical engineers than the statute requires. Whether a particular agency ought to be made up of technicians or intelligent laymen will depend in part upon whether the body is to engage directly in administration, as does the Central Electricity Board, or whether it is to serve as a board of directors to supervise a general manager and a technical staff, as in the case of the British Broadcasting Corporation.

Where an agency, particularly a tribunal, is being set up to perform quasi-judicial duties seriously affecting private rights, and where procedure is important, it is customary to require the appointment of one or more lawyers as members. This is the case with the Railway and Canal Commission, the Railway Rates Tribunal, and the Road and Rail Appeal Tribunal. These lawyer-members must be appointed in consultation with the Lord Chancellor. The effect of their presence upon the character of the tribunal and its methods of work is likely to be dominating. Usually the statute requires the lawyer to be chairman, and this puts emphasis upon legal formalities and legal precedents. While there are areas of regulatory activity in which this may be desirable, there is a strong feeling, well supported by experience, that lawyers ought not to dominate any agency from which is desired any high degree of initiative or flexibility. Lawyers are not prone to indulge in innovations of policy; and while the lawyers appointed to these agencies in Great Britain have often been men of high ability and distinction, Professor Laski has pointed out that the policy has its dangers. He observed to the writer that 'decaying K.C.'s not good enough to be judges are likely to be jobbed into these agencies,'[7] a calamity, it may be observed, not wholly unknown in the United States.

3. METHODS DESIGNED TO SECURE DETACHMENT OR IMPARTIALITY

The British statutes contain many specific provisions designed to assure the appointment of persons to British agencies having no axes to grind. The most common device is to describe in the statute various disqualifications for membership; these include the holding of financial or commercial interests in the business to be regulated, or any such interests as would threaten the impartial performance of official duty. In one or two cases the appointing authority is authorized to vacate the office of a member who acquires such interests after his appointment. Except where membership in the House of Commons is required of some one member of a British agency, as in the case of the Forestry Commission, the statutes almost invariably disqualify members of Parliament from serving on these boards

7. Conversation in 1937.

or tribunals. It is easy to see that undesirable results might come from such dual office-holding and the political jobbery which might be engendered. In the main the British regulatory agencies have been manned by persons whose detachment and impartiality are not open to question. This is far from saying, however, that some of these bodies do not reflect a highly conservative point of view, as in the case of the British Broadcasting Corporation, and in some instances British labor feels that the point of view of the British capitalist, if not specifically represented, still remains dominant.

There are few specific disqualifications for membership on the British agencies except those mentioned. It is apparently not considered useful to multiply them. No responsible Minister would appoint an alien, an anarchist, a madman, or an inebriate, and it is not felt to be necessary to forbid such appointments. The question has been raised by some students of administration whether there ought to be an upper age limit for membership on these bodies, for in some cases the public has suffered from the results of superannuation. The problem has not become acute enough to lead to the formulation of any well-shaped policy in regard to the matter.

C. CIVIL SERVICE STATUS

A problem relating to the newer British agencies set up to operate important public services is that of the relations of its staff to the British Civil Service. Ordinarily when a new office or board is added to the British governmental system, it is automatically incorporated into the civil service. Thereafter the appointments, salaries, and other personnel arrangements affecting it are fitted into the normal routine. We have seen, however, that important public service boards and their staffs have been set up outside the civil service. This applies to the British Broadcasting Corporation, the London Passenger Transport Board, the Port of London Authority, and presumably to the new British Overseas Airways Corporation.

The exemption of these important agencies from the civil service has not been inadvertent. In fact, one of the reasons for giving these agencies the form and powers which they have has been to enable them to escape the artificial restrictions and the rigid hierarchical arrangements which are an essential part of the civil service. They have intentionally been left free from the normal forms of bureaucratic control. They have been allowed to use methods of staff recruitment suited to their needs, and they have enjoyed freedom and flexibility all along the line. This exemption of the public service boards from the civil service was certainly necessary and desirable when these agencies were being set up. Wide freedom of action seemed indispensable to their effective inauguration. Existing civil service arrangements would have broken down under the sudden burden of recruiting the large and specially trained staffs required. The question remains open, however, whether bodies of this kind, once they have been established, ought to remain permanently free from civil service control or whether at a later point in their life history they ought to be blanketed into the civil service. This remains a mattery of controversy.

It should not be assumed that the public service boards in question have as a rule followed a hit-or-miss system with regard to their personnel arrangements. No organization employing four or five thousand persons can escape systematizing its personnel system. The British public service boards, with the possible exception of the British Broadcasting Corporation, have developed their own efficient systems for recruitment, promotion, scales of compensation, and similar matters. These have been designed to deal with a personnel differently trained from that which could have been secured through the normal British Civil Service examinations. In most cases the salary scales on these boards have been higher than in the parallel brackets of the civil service. Since the boards have been expanding organizations, opportunities for promotion have been more frequent and alluring than in the civil service. The British Broadcasting Corporation, confronted probably with the most difficult problem of personnel, since there is no common agreement on what qualifications ought to be required, has not standardized its personnel arrangements effectively, and has come in for sharp criticism for its failure to do so.

There are many who urge that it is ruinous to the British Civil Service to have a competing system in which rates of pay and opportunities for promotion are more attractive. They believe that the British Civil Service ought to adjust itself to the new demands presented by the public service boards, and that by making reasonable changes it could adequately perform the work of selecting suitably trained personnel. If, in other words, it is necessary to deviate from the old traditional type of civil service examination, then this should be done. In any event, if independent personnel arrangements are retained in connection with the public service boards, these could and should be administered in close co-operation with the civil service.

In opposition to this, it is urged that development along present lines is necessary and desirable. The civil service is ill equipped to function in an area in which scientifically trained technicians must be selected. Those holding this view do not defend the chaotic and unsystematized arrangements prevailing in the British Broadcasting Corporation. They urge rather that a parallel 'Public Concerns Civil Service' be set up for the recruitment of the new type of public servants needed. There ought to be developed a career service under the public service boards similar to that which prevails in the civil service. This is the position taken by the leaders of the Liberal Party in the interesting and influential document, *Britain's Industrial Future.*[8]

D. SALARIES

Under normal circumstances the salaries of British officials are left to the standardized control of the Treasury. Statutes will occasionally fix the salaries of high officials, but more often Parliament will merely provide that the salaries paid to the members of a new agency shall be fixed by the appointing Minister in consultation with the Treasury. In some cases a maximum sum is specified, within which salary scales are worked out by the Ministers. This does not, of course, mean unlimited discretion. It means, in fact, substantial conformity to civil service classifications and rates of pay. But there is an element of flexibility in dealing with the men at the top, and this is regarded as desirable.

In the case of the non-departmental agencies, and especially the public service boards, the problem of salaries has been handled with even greater flexibility. In getting these new

8. Report of the Liberal Industrial Inquiry (1928).

boards off to a satisfactory start it has been felt necessary to command the services of outstandingly competent and experienced men. In several cases where private enterprises have been made into public services the original managers have been carried over into the new regime. This was done in the case of the London Passenger Transport Board. Here Lord Ashfield and Mr. Frank Pick, the manager and deputy manager respectively of the London Traffic Combine, were appointed as manager and deputy manager of the new board. Lord Ashfield receives a salary of £12,500 and Mr. Pick a salary of £10,000. These particular salaries are recognized as being abnormally high, but there is no widespread feeling that in the case of these two men the government is not getting its money's worth. Upon the retirement of either, however, it is unlikely that anyone would be appointed at anything approaching these salaries. The managing directors of some of the other public service boards are paid much higher salaries than the men in the highest brackets of the civil service. Sharp resentment was felt when Sir Ernest Gowers, who was receiving £3,000 as head of the British Civil Service, was appointed chairman of the newly created Coal Mines Reorganization Commission at a salary of £7,000. The Labour group, especially, felt that his value to the government had not jumped quite so far so suddenly.

While there is lacking in the British tradition the 'democratic' resentment against high official salaries which is so widely felt in this country, there is a growing feeling in England that spectacular salaries ought ultimately to be brought more closely into line with civil service standards of pay. It is felt that the government should not assume that it must compete with private industry on private industry's own terms in bidding for the services of competent administrators and business executives. The distinction of holding an important public post must constitute part of the compensation of any public-spirited servant of the state.

E. Board Organization—Full-Time and Part-Time Membership

One of the devices commonly used in organizing British boards and commissions is to create two types of membership—

a full-time well-paid membership, usually for the chairman or chief executive officer, and a part-time, nominally paid membership. This may have been modeled roughly after the typical organization of the governing board of a private corporation operating through a chief executive officer surrounded by a board of directors drawn in occasionally for consultation or collective decision on important matters. This principle was followed in the organization of most of the agencies we have been studying. Here may be listed the Area Traffic Commissioners, the agricultural marketing boards, the Wheat Commission, the Forestry Commission, the London Passenger Transport Board, the Port of London Authority, the Central Electricity Board, the British Broadcasting Corporation, and the Electricity Commissioners. The precise lines along which this division into full-time and part-time service is made vary from one agency to another. In the Central Electricity Board there is a chairman who is the permanent chief executive, and with whom are associated six part-time members. In the case of the British Broadcasting Corporation there is a highly paid full-time chairman, plus seven part-time governors; but the technical direction of broadcasting is in the hands of a highly paid director general, who works under the chairman and the board of governors. In the case of the Area Traffic Commissioners the chairman is the only full-time officer, and with the aid of a few clerks he performs practically all the administrative work. In matters affecting goods transport he is the sole authority, his part-time associates assisting him only in matters affecting passenger transport.

It is not easy to appraise the actual results of this arrangement. Where the system prevails, the full-time chairman will inevitably dominate the board and is expected to do so, while the part-time members tend to become figure-heads and rubberstamps. The scheme has the advantage of retaining the deliberative aspects of the board form of organization, without dividing administrative responsibility amongst seven or eight men. The advantages of deliberation are retained, however, only in so far as actual deliberation does occur.

There has been criticism of this arrangement, and some proposals for changing it. When the recently established British Overseas Airways Corporation was under discussion it was urged that it ought to be a full-time, highly qualified operating board corresponding in ability to the British Civil Service. Part-time membership on the board was particularly deprecated on the ground that in the past it had proved to be the signal for the receipt of commercial directorships in other companies. Thus the interests of the part-time board member were dissipated and confused, and satisfactory service to the public was sacrificed. It has been suggested that if part-time membership is to be retained as a principle of administrative organization, the part-time service should be completely unpaid. It is claimed in behalf of this proposal that a much higher type of person can be drawn into the public service on a part-time basis, if he receives no compensation and feels himself rewarded by the rendering of service to the government, than can possibly be secured by the payment of a remuneration of £300 or £500 per year. In spite of these criticisms the full-time, part-time scheme for organizing administrative agencies seems to be firmly embedded in British administrative practice. It offers suggestions which might be usefully explored in connection with the organization of some of our American agencies.

F. CO-ORDINATION OF NON-DEPARTMENTAL AGENCIES

A brief comment may be made on the co-ordination, or lack of it, of the non-departmental British agencies we have been discussing. Co-ordination on any broad scale has not been in the minds of British statesmen. There is little evidence of any systematic effort to provide it. There is little direct contact, as we have seen, between the various agencies which are hammering away at the various aspects of the British transportation problem. There are nearly a dozen of these, and they remain for all practical purposes complete strangers to each other. There is no co-ordination between the public control of the electricity industry and the gas industry, although the two are natural competitors. There is no co-ordination between the regulation of the electricity industry and the production of current by water-power. In pointing out these cases in which co-ordination would seem to be desirable but does not exist we may remind ourselves that it is perhaps equally lacking in our own country.

Co-ordination between administrative agencies in Great Britain is not, however, wholly lacking. It exists or may exist in the case of agencies which are responsible either to the same Minister or to any Minister. Besides this there has been a good deal of useful progress in the setting up of interdepartmental committees and advisory committees to bring together administrators dealing with the same problem, and to facilitate the ironing out of difficulties and conflicts.

V. REGULATORY FUNCTIONS OF THE BRITISH MINISTRIES

IT is quite impossible to discuss in detail or even to enumerate the quasi-judicial and regulatory duties which are performed by the British Ministries. They are very numerous and many of them have been exercised for a very long time. Like the analogous duties assigned to American executive departments, they frequently involve very drastic control and in many cases it is impossible to distinguish them, so far as their inherent character goes, from similar functions which have been assigned to non-departmental agencies. To name the Cabinet Ministries to whom such work has been given is to mention most of them; certainly the list would include the Post Office, the Board of Trade, the Home Office, the Ministry of Agriculture, the Ministry of Health, the Ministry of Labour, the Ministry of Transport, and the Air Ministry.

The reasons for assigning tasks of economic regulation to a non-departmental agency rather than to a Ministry are varied. In some cases, as we have seen, the direction of the assignment appears to have a purely historical explanation. This probably explains why the British Post Office is a Cabinet Ministry rather than a semi-autonomous public service board. In some cases there has been apparent a desire to take politics out of technical administration, while in others there has been a reaching after a higher degree of flexibility than Ministerial bureaucracy permits. In other cases the purpose has been to secure complete detachment and impartiality for quasi-judicial activity. It seems clear, however, that there is not the same readiness in Great Britain to assign new jobs to newly created outside agencies as appears to prevail in Washington. A heavy burden of proof all along the line rests upon those who propose the creation of a non-departmental agency. The normal reaction is to assume that a British Ministry is competent to take on a new job, and do it well. The British Ministries enjoy a degree of public and Parliamentary confidence which is not accorded to the executive departments in Washington.

The suitability of the established Ministries to the job of economic control and the degree to which their efficiency and impartiality are recognized even by the interests which would be brought under that control were brought out in the discussion of a recent proposal to establish government control of gas rates. The incident is worth relating for the light which it throws upon the general standing and reputation of the British Ministries. In 1936 a joint committee of the two houses of Parliament was set up to investigate a sudden and very unpopular increase in gas rates by the Southern Metropolitan Gas Company. It reported in 1937. We are not here concerned with its proposals save that it recommended that certain powers of gas price regulation be conferred upon the Board of Trade. During the sessions of the committee the London County Council appeared through its representative and proposed the establishment of a gas prices tribunal to which changes in gas rates might be referred for final settlement, if, on complaint of any local authority, they were first found by the Board of Trade to be unreasonable. This tribunal was to be appointed by the Board of Trade. It was not to fix prices, but merely to determine whether proposed prices were reasonable. It could be either an *ad hoc* or a standing tribunal. Counsel for the Corporation of the City of London also backed the idea of a tribunal, and even proposed that its members should be chosen by 'appointing trustees' after the fashion of the London Passenger Transport Board. The reaction of the gas companies to this proposal was, however, interesting in the extreme. Their representatives before the committee said:

We do not want any tribunal . . . For heaven's sake do not put us under any tribunal which has to be instructed afresh every time. Let us go to the Board of Trade, who know all about these things, who have a department who study these things, who are revising the basic price of gas from time to time, who know what the points are, and who could determine this matter very quickly.[9]

This appears to have taken the counsel for the London County Council by surprise. They had apparently assumed that the proposal of a tribunal so thoroughly rendered impartial would make a strong appeal to the gas companies whose material interests were so vitally at stake. Accordingly they quickly retreated and hastened to say that if the Board of Trade was willing to assume the burden of making these fundamental determinations of gas prices the London County Council would be delighted. They had merely suggested a separate tribunal 'because they did not know whether the Board of Trade would be prepared to assume the burden of acting in an arbitral capacity.' [10] But the incident shows that the Board of Trade has more standing with British industry than any as yet unorganized and unknown non-departmental tribunal.

9. Report by the Joint Committee of the House of Lords and the House of Commons on Gas Prices (1937).

10. Ibid.

X

PROBLEMS OF INDEPENDENCE AND RESPONSIBILITY

At the outset of this study it was stated that when the term 'independent' was applied to our regulatory commissions it meant that they were 'outside the executive departments.' The word did not imply freedom from supervision or control, but merely indicated location in the governmental structure. It now becomes important to discuss the 'independence' of these commissions in the sense of their freedom from accountability to any other department of the government. How free are they from outside control?

In a democratic state we are accustomed to speak of our public officials as servants of the people. We say, somewhat vaguely, that they are responsible to the public will. This is a loose use of the word 'responsible,' for it makes it little more than a description of a state of mind. But responsibility may mean something very specific. Public officers may be responsible to other public officers in the sense that they work under threat of disciplinary action if they are incompetent or dishonest. Not all officers, however, are responsible in this way. Judges owe a general duty to administer justice, but they are not accountable to any other branch of the government in the sense that they must follow its advice and take its orders or else be subject to discipline. They may be removed from office for misconduct by the process of impeachment, but if they decide cases in a way which outrages public opinion all that can be done is to correct by statute or by constitutional amendment the results of the objectionable decisions. Nor is there anything undemocratic about this independence of the judges. It has long since been settled that this particular type of public servant will render better public service if he is independent of outside control than if he were responsible to Congress or to the President. This is a fundamental principle governing the judicial office.

Our principal executive and administrative officers, on the other hand, are responsible to the President, the executive head of the nation. They are his agents, the instruments through whom he works. The President may remove them at will merely to secure men who are more congenial to him or more closely in harmony with his policies and opinions. There is no independence here; the accountability of these officers is absolute.

The members of Congress, and Congress itself, are, of course, not accountable to the President. Superficially they appear to be accountable by the operation of judicial review to the Supreme Court, which will hold void statutes which seem to the Court to violate the Constitution. The Court would probably say that the responsibility of Congress is to the Constitution rather than to the Court, though this does not add much clarity to the analysis. Members of Congress, however, are accountable to their constituents, and that accountability is enforceable through popular elections.

The independent regulatory commissions occupy an anomalous position in the matter of independence and responsibility. Their status is unlike that of any of the three types of officer just mentioned. They are not independent in the highly protected sense in which the courts are. Congress may reduce their pay, cut off their appropriations, or, in extreme cases, reorganize their personnel. Their members may in some cases be removed by the President at will, and in all cases they may be removed for incompetence and misconduct. But the commissions are not directly accountable to the President. They lie outside the executive departments, and, since the Supreme Court's decision in the Humphrey case in 1935, commissioners may be protected by statute against Presidential discipline or removal. Only in very limited circumstances, if at all, can the President compel the commissions to conform to his policies. The commissioners are not popularly elected and therefore have no direct accountability to the voters as do members of Congress. They are accountable to the courts in the sense that they must comply with the mandates of the law under which they operate. The net result of all this is a sort of pluralism in the matter of the responsibility of the independent commissions. They are neither wholly independent nor wholly accountable, and the accountability under which they work is neither simple nor clear, but includes lines of responsibility which move in three different directions—to Congress, to the President, and to the courts.

The purpose of this chapter is to analyze the responsibility of the independent commissions to each of the three departments, and to examine the nature and effectiveness of the machinery available for enforcing that responsibility. What areas are there in which the commissions do or should enjoy independence from all outside control?

I. RESPONSIBILITY OF THE COMMISSIONS TO CONGRESS

A. CONGRESSIONAL INTENTIONS WITH REGARD TO THE INDEPENDENCE OF THE COMMISSIONS

BEFORE dealing with the actual nature and degree of the responsibility of the independent regulatory commissions to Congress, it is useful to try to learn to what extent Congress has intended to leave them independent or to subject them to control. This is not an easy task, as the earlier pages tracing the legislative history of the commissions clearly show. Sometimes Congress has left no record whatever of its intentions, and when it has left one, the record is often inconsistent and vague.

In the first place, Congress has made the commissions independent in order to place the regulatory tasks assigned to them outside of the range of partisan control. During the early period especially, 'independence' meant to the average congressman 'bipartisanship' and the detachment naïvely supposed to result from it. This kind of independence was regarded as vital. Later on, after the Interstate Commerce

Commission had grown up, independence came to be associated in the Congressional mind with the highly creditable achievements of this first great commission. It stood for a measure of impartiality and efficiency rarely prevailing in an executive department, and greatly to be desired. This attitude was clearly reflected when a status of independence was given to the United States Shipping Board and later to the Maritime Commission: the job of regulating and managing our merchant marine was too big and involved too much money for it to be safely left to a politically controlled executive department. Independence would, somehow or other, guarantee efficiency; it may be added that upon this point there has been rather sad disillusionment in some cases. The Congressional preference for making a regulatory body independent was particularly pronounced when the executive department to which the regulatory function would normally go (if not to a commission) was the Department of Commerce. That department, sometimes spoken of as 'the businessman's friend,' is chiefly a promotional department. Its pervading atmosphere is perhaps less suited to the administration of a disciplinary or regulatory job. It seems, rightly or wrongly, to have incurred a substantial measure of Congressional distrust. We may conclude, then, that Congress has had two general aims in creating independent regulatory bodies: first, to secure reasonably impartial and nonpartisan handling of quasi-judicial tasks; second, the honest and efficient handling of tasks too big to be entrusted to the politicians in the executive departments.

Congress has never devoted much serious thought to the matter of the responsibility of the independent commissions. It has left no clear record of just what controls it felt ought to be exercised over the commissions' activities. In certain areas where the commissions' functions are clearly quasi-judicial in nature, Congress seems to have been bent on creating the same kind of irresponsibility or independence which the courts enjoy. The commissions were evidently not intended to be accountable to any other body or department in the rendering of decisions or in their day-to-day administration. In certain other cases the commissions were given assignments on which they were to report back directly to Congress itself. These tasks were usually in the field of planning or recommendations of legislative policy. When a commission received such orders from Congress it carried them out under a sense of accountability to Congress. Congressional ideas, when there is any record of them, have been vague and conflicting concerning the kind and degree of accountability which the independent regulatory commissions owe to the President. In some cases Congress has taken the President to task for what it regarded as the shortcomings or the mistakes of the commissions, implying somewhat vaguely that he was to blame and ought to have done something about it. There is plenty of evidence that Congress feels that the President does have and ought to have certain kinds of authority over the commissions. Our regulatory statutes give to the President many direct powers in connection with the commissions' work. An effort to clear up the general vagueness on the matter of the President's relation to the commissions was made by Mr. Justice Sutherland in the Humphrey decision in 1935, in which he explained to Congress what its legislative intentions had been in creating the Federal Trade Commission and definitely ruled out the idea that the President belonged in the picture at all. Since then Congress has been more consistently certain than before that it does not wish the independent regulatory commissions to be responsible to the President in any effective way.

Congress, however, is fully aware at times that it holds the power of life and death over the commissions. As it creates these bodies so it may destroy them. So also may it starve them to death by limiting or cutting off appropriations, and so may it keep a commission acutely conscious of Congressional supervision by continuing it on a year-by-year footing. At the same time Congress has never been under any illusions regarding its capacity to exercise any steady and direct supervision over the commissions, nor has it shown any desire to do so.

B. Can the Commissions Be Made Effectively Responsible to Congress?

Before considering how far the independent regulatory commissions ought to be responsible to Congress we should try to determine whether they can be made thus responsible and, if so, how. Any real achievement that establishes such responsibility will in the long run be brought about by the will of Congress. Responsibility to Congress will exist in fact only if Congress desires it actively enough to do something about it. There is no evidence that Congress has ever given much thought to the matter save when grave abuses have occurred; and its attention then has been temporary and specialized. Certainly Congress has never taken on as a major responsibility of its own the systematic and effective oversight of the independent commissions.

But if Congress should desire to hold the commissions closely and effectively responsible to itself, what methods are at its disposal for doing so? What methods have been tried? What methods have been proposed? What methods ought to be ruled out? The desire of Congress to exercise control and to enforce accountability might be sharply increased if it were felt that effective machinery could be set up to make this possible.

1. HOW CAN CONGRESS FIND OUT WHAT THE COMMISSIONS ARE DOING?

Any effective control by Congress over the independent regulatory commissions must depend upon the existence of efficient ways of informing Congress about the commissions' work. Successful control depends upon knowledge of the thing controlled. What then are the means or methods at the disposal of Congress for watching the commissions and for securing adequate knowledge how they are managing their jobs?

First as channels of information are the standing committees of the two houses of Congress. Each house has standing committees assigned to the fields of commerce, banking, agriculture, merchant marine, and other areas in which the independent commissions may be operating. Sometimes these standing committees are manned by able and experienced legislators who, through long periods of years, have become experts in the problems with which the independent commissions are dealing. They frequently maintain close and friendly relations with the commissions and their staffs. They are fully competent to pass political judgment on the work being done, to carry on needed investigations, and to bring in constructive proposals. There is, unfortunately, no guarantee that the standing committees of the two houses will have this degree of ability and influence. There are many cases in which they carry negligible weight because of the inexperience of their members, or their lack of interest or capacity. These committees have no assurance of continuity in their personnel: a highly useful member may not be re-elected to Congress and his valuable services may be lost. Furthermore, Congress has never seen fit to equip these committees with permanent staffs competent to carry on the continuing task of supervision over commission activities. This is not a blanket charge of incompetence, but merely a suggestion that the standing committees can be depended upon normally for little more than casual hit-or-miss supervision of the independent commissions.

The standing committees have often rendered valuable service to Congress by conducting special investigations of the independent regulatory commissions. In fact, whenever Congress decides to order such a special investigation the problem is likely to arise whether the job should be assigned to one of the standing committees or whether a special committee should be created for the purpose. The answer may depend upon whether Congress believes that a particular standing committee as constituted at the time may be depended upon to make an effective investigation. In 1939 the Senate Committee on Education and Labor and the House Committee on Labor both undertook investigations of the National Labor Relations Board and took thousands of pages of testimony before the House of Representatives finally decided to create the Smith committee to conduct its special investigation.

In the second place, both houses of Congress have standing committees to deal with appropriations. These are not limited in their fields of authority to any special subject, but must review generally the demands for money which are made upon Congress; they are broken up into subcommittees which deal with appropriations in special fields. In examining with care the budget estimates for the independent regulatory commissions, these committees on appropriations may erect themselves into efficiency auditors to whatever extent time, ability, and inclination may make possible and wise. The study of the actual measure of supervision which these committees exercise over the independent commissions and the appraisal of its influence and value is a colossal undertaking. Competent scholars are beginning to undertake studies in this field. Pending the results of their inquiries one may safely observe that the appropriations committees of Congress have performed useful service in scrutinizing both the finances and general efficiency of the independent commissions, but that these bodies are not at present equipped to carry on a thoroughgoing and effective job in this field.

Third, Congress from time to time creates special investigating committees to inquire into the activities of particular commissions. These are, of course, set up *ad hoc,* and very frequently because Congress believes that the work of a commission is unsatisfactory. The achievements of these special committees depend of course upon the calibre of their personnel and the efficiency and impartiality with which they conduct the inquiry. In contrast to the standing committees of Congress they have the advantage of singleness of purpose. They have no competing responsibilities, at least not as a committee. They are likely to be made up of persons who have a special interest in the problem or commission to be investigated. Yet there is no assurance that they will perform their duties with impartiality and fairness. For example, the Smith committee of the House of Representatives has shown in its methods and procedure unmistakable signs of desiring to build up as strong a case as possible against the National Labor Relations Board. The usefulness of these special committees is likely to be limited to the investigations of situations which have become very bad. The committees are temporary and sporadic; they may effectively aid Congress in dealing with an acute situation, but they do not help keep Congress informed of the regular activities of well-behaved agencies.

Finally, Congress has at its disposal whatever it may wish to ask for in the way of annual reports or special reports from the commissions. These documents give useful facts about past accomplishments and often contain proposals for legislative changes. They cannot be relied upon, however, to provide the kind of information upon which thoroughgoing supervision or control could be based.

2. PRESENT METHODS FOR CONGRESSIONAL CONTROL OF INDEPENDENT COMMISSIONS

We have mentioned the methods by which Congress secures information about the work of the independent regulatory commissions. Assuming that Congress has thus informed itself about a commission, or has decided to do something without informing itself, just what can it do? What modes of control over the commission are available to it?

a. *Congressional control over commission finances*

The most constant and effective control which Congress can exercise over an independent regulatory commission is financial control. Congress holds the nation's purse strings, and enjoys absolute discretion whether to provide money for a particular agency of government, and, if so, how much to provide. Should Congress decide that a particular commission is not worth continuing, it could abolish it entirely, or it could keep it in a state of suspended animation by not giving it any money. Congress has never done this, though members of Congress have sometimes urged such action.

Furthermore, Congress may reduce the activity of an independent regulatory commission by reducing the commission's appropriations. This may be used as a means of controlling commission policy. If the task assigned to a commission is to discover forms of business misconduct and issue corrective orders to deal with them, it is clear that the effectiveness of the results will be governed in large part by the amount of money the commission is allowed to spend. Without questioning the efficiency of the present Federal Trade Commission, it would be generally agreed that if Congress gave the commission five times as much money as it now has, it could do, if not five times as good a job, at least a very much better one than it now does. Conversely, if Congress does not favor the drastic enforcement of disciplinary statutes, but prefers to ease up on big business, it may do so by reducing the appropriations of the regulatory commissions through which these statutes are enforced. It is a well-known fact that Congress never made the slightest pretence of appropriating enough money to enforce the Volstead Act with thoroughness and efficiency, and independent regulatory commissions may be and sometimes have been similarly starved by Congress.

In some cases Congress has seen fit to strike at a given activity carried on by a regulatory commission by specifying in the statute that funds appropriated by Congress shall not be spent for that particular purpose. This may be a weapon of discipline. Congress thus forbade the use of money appropriated to the Federal Trade Commission for the carrying on of certain classes of investigations which the commission had been engaged in.[1] In 1940, in order to get rid of David J. Saposs, the chief economist of the National Labor Relations Board, who had incurred Congressional displeasure, Congress put a provision in the supplemental civil functions appropriations bill forbidding the board to maintain the office.

By earmarking the funds made available for the work of a commission, Congress may of course control the direction of the commission's activities. It may impose a new duty on a commission and provide the funds necessary to perform it. This may have the indirect result of diverting the commission's energy from other activities in which Congress is less interested.

Viewed broadly, the financial control exercised by Congress over the commissions is a necessary and desirable form of supervision. Congress has never made effective enough use of it to enable us to judge the full value which it might have; nor has it always been used wisely or for sound purposes. It makes possible abuses such as Congressional sniping at commissions and the exercise of controls stimulated by outside and illegitimate pressure. In spite of these occasional abuses, this financial control remains essential if Congress is to direct the policy and the balance of the work of an independent regulatory commission, and is to be able to curb particular abuses.

b. *Congressional control over commission personnel*

Congress may, if it wishes, exercise an indirect control over the personnel of the independent regulatory commissions. Since the power of appointment to offices under the Constitu-

1. *Supra*, 220.

tion is given to the President, Congress may not, of course, pass a statute making a given person a member of the Interstate Commerce Commission or of any other body. But there are other methods of influencing the personnel of a commission, devices which Congress may use if it is dissatisfied with the membership of a particular commission. First, with the co-operation of the President it may pack the commission by creating new positions upon it, in the expectation that the new appointees will nullify the influence of the original members. This, however, Congress is not very likely to do since the chief reason for packing a court or any other governmental body lies in the inability of the legislature to get rid of existing members. There are ways by which Congress can get rid of obnoxious commissioners and it is far more likely to use these than to add new members to the commission. While the membership of several of the commissions has been increased by statute, this has always been done for legitimate reasons, and usually at the request of the commission itself.

Second, Congress may keep the question of commission personnel open by giving commissioners year-by-year tenure. This was done when the Federal Radio Commission was set up in 1927. The commission was thus carried along on an annual basis until 1930. This did not mean that a brand new commission was appointed each year, for most of the members were reappointed. It did mean, however, that reappointments had to be made and that objectionable commissioners could have been dropped. As we have already seen, Senator Dill, who was influential in guiding the radio legislation through Congress, definitely urged that during the experimental period in the commission's life Congress ought to keep in its own hands the power to get rid of commissioners who might turn out to be unsatisfactory.[2]

Third, if Congress has the courage of its convictions, or of its emotions, it may employ a more brutal and direct type of control over commission personnel. It may resort to 'ripper legislation,' the simple device of abolishing an existing office by law and creating a new one in its place. This terminates the official tenure of the existing officers who have, of course, no constitutional right to serve out their terms. The appointing

2. *Supra*, 315.

authority may therefore replace them if he so desires. This device was used to reorganize the United States Tariff Commission in 1930. Congress terminated the existence of the old commission and set up a new one. The President carried over only some of the old members. In 1939 and 1940 demand was made in many quarters that 'ripper legislation' be passed to get rid of the members of the National Labor Relations Board, some of whom had become very unpopular; but the proposal was not carried out. The question whether Congress could make ineligible to reappointment the members of a board thus abolished by law raises a constitutional problem with which the Supreme Court has never had to deal. Even if it could not validly declare by law that certain persons may not be appointed, it might still attempt the same result by the careful phrasing of disqualifying characteristics, and the Senate, if it is in sympathy with the enterprise, can, of course, block the reappointments by withholding confirmation.

c. *Congressional orders or directions to commissions*

It is clear that Congress has full authority to control by statute the duties of the independent regulatory commissions. Without Congressional action the commissions would have no duties. If Congress wishes to reduce, increase, or alter these duties, it may do so simply by passing a law. Congress has occasionally gone even further and has undertaken by joint resolution to instruct a commission how to perform its statutory duties. The most conspicuous example of this was the Hoch-Smith resolution of 1925 directing the Interstate Commerce Commission to exercise its rate-making powers with special reference to the needs of farmers. It is generally agreed that this type of Congressional interference with the exercise by the commission of its quasi-judicial authority is highly undesirable from the point of view of commission efficiency and impartiality, and in the case of the Hoch-Smith resolution Congress was found to have exceeded its constitutional powers.[3] We have seen that Congress, in dealing with the Shipping Board after 1920, on several occasions asked the board to delay some projected action, such as the disposal of ships, until Con-

3. *Ann Arbor R. Co.* v. *United States,* 281 U.S. 658 (1930).

gress might study the matter and express its approval or dis-approval.⁴ While the board did not always comply with these requests, it did so in many cases, and the making of the requests represents an effort upon the part of Congress to maintain some control over a part of the commission's major decisions of policy. The practice has not become a general one. It would be entirely possible for Congress either to require Congressional approval of the rules and regulations issued by the regulatory commissions, or to provide for an opportunity for Congressional disallowance of them; it has never seen fit to do so. As we have seen, this procedure, which is generally used by the British government, provides an outside legislative check upon the way in which administrative bodies exercise their sub-legislative powers.⁵ Congress is not at present equipped to exercise this supervision over the commissions' rule making, and it shows no disposition to set up any machinery for such a purpose.

A fair appraisal of the net results of Congressional control over the independent regulatory commissions is that such control is neither continuous nor genuinely efficient. Congress does manage to assure itself that the job given to an independent commission is being carried on along the general lines of the assignment, but Congress has little chance to reach an informed judgment on how efficiently the commissions are doing their work. The upshot is that Congress is likely to content itself with doing nothing for the most part in its dealings with the commissions, and with resorting to some form of drastic action when something approaching a scandal crops up in connection with a commission.

3. POSSIBILITY OF IMPROVING THE CONTROL AND INFLUENCE OF CONGRESS OVER THE COMMISSIONS

It would be foolish to say that Congress could not improve its facilities for informing itself on the activities of the independent regulatory commissions, and for exercising a more intelligent and efficient supervision over them. It would be over-optimistic, however, to predict that Congress is likely to do anything substantial of this sort. We have seen that this

---

4. *Supra,* 249.   5. *Supra,* 645.

problem has become prominent in Great Britain, and that English statesmen and scholars have been struggling with it and have proposed various methods whereby Parliament might maintain more efficient supervision over the semi-independent public service boards.[6] We have also seen that none of these proposals, plausible as they are, has been adopted. A suggestion for reform along somewhat similar lines has been made by scholars on the staff of the Brookings Institution, Messrs. Meriam and Schmeckebier, in a recent analysis of the problem of reorganization of the federal government.[7] They have suggested that the standing committees of Congress ought to be provided with adequate permanent staffs which would permit them to carry on efficiently and continuously the task of supervising administration. The proposal unquestionably is a sound one, but there is little to support the hope that Congress will follow this excellent advice. The conclusion seems inevitable that legislative bodies are not capable of exercising effective control over administration, or even over their own special agencies, the independent regulatory commissions, except the general, sporadic control which has been described. One must further conclude that there may be real danger in encouraging a type of Congressional supervision which lies beyond the capacity of Congress. The temptation to indulge in sniping and various other forms of ulterior pressure is always present, and much of the Congressional activity aimed at the control of the independent commissions in the past has been vicious and misdirected. Congress is fully competent to tell the independent regulatory commissions what they are to do. It is not competent, and is never likely to become competent, to hold them accountable in any effective way for the efficiency of their performance.

II. RESPONSIBILITY OF THE COMMISSIONS TO THE PRESIDENT

THE President's relations with the independent regulatory commissions have been left somewhat confused by the lan-

6. *Supra,* 646 ff.

7. L. Meriam and L. F. Schmeckebier, *Reorganization of the National Government* (1939), 155 ff.

guage of the Supreme Court's decision in the Humphrey case. That decision tends to rule the President out of the picture except in so far as Congress allows him a place in it. It denies him any authority over the commissions against the expressed wishes of Congress. The decision was a narrow one and turned on the nature of the functions performed by the Federal Trade Commission. The decision itself is limited in its impact to quasi-judicial and quasi-legislative commissions—in other words, to commissions not performing executive duties. The status and the relation to the President of those commissions with mixed functions, some of which are clearly executive, have not yet been clarified. These relations were, however, left unchanged by the Humphrey decision, and Congress may by statute permit the President to exercise over the independent commissions a wide and drastic control which he could not validly assert against the wishes of Congress. Congress may thus permit the President to remove commissioners in his discretion, and may give him power to supervise, check, and control their activities. We are concerned here with summarizing the authority which the President has exercised in the past, and does now exercise, over the commissions. How much control ought Congress to allow the President to have? These are problems not of constitutional law but of policy.

A. METHODS AVAILABLE TO THE PRESIDENT FOR CONTROLLING THE COMMISSIONS

1. CONTROL OF COMMISSION POLICY

To those who look upon the independent regulatory commissions exclusively as arms of Congress, the idea may seem shocking that commission policy should be at any point considered to be subject to Presidential supervision or control. The arm-of-Congress theory, however, as we have seen,[8] is only one of several points of view from which to appraise the commissions, and the legislative history of these bodies makes it very obvious that the President has never been regarded either by

8. *Supra,* 450 f.

Congress or by himself as a wholly disinterested onlooker where the commissions are concerned.

Most of our Presidents have from time to time felt that it was necessary for them to control the policies of the independent regulatory commissions, and they have had no serious doubts of the legality and propriety of doing so. In 1908 President Theodore Roosevelt sent to Congress a message urging that all existing independent bureaus and commissions be placed under the jurisdiction of appropriate executive departments. He said:

> It is unwise from every standpoint and results only in mischief to have any executive work done save by executive bodies, under the control of the President; and each such executive body should be under the immediate supervision of a Cabinet minister.[9]

There is not the slightest doubt that he regarded independent commissions as executive bodies. President Wilson made plain his attitude towards the independent commissions on more than one occasion. We are told by Senator Glass that in 1915 he was on the point of removing from office all of the members of the newly created Federal Reserve Board because the board was threatening to eliminate four of the reserve banks created by statute; this the President regarded as a usurpation of power by the board. It was President Wilson who was responsible for placing in the Federal Trade Commission Act the provision giving the President power to order the commission to make investigations.[10] There is no doubt that Wilson with his 'prime minister' theory of the nature of the Presidential office felt that he was entitled to impress his policies on the independent commissions and to expect their conformity to those policies. Presidents Harding and Coolidge made plain on repeated occasions that they believed Presidential domination of certain of the independent commissions to be essential. Harding, as we have seen,[11] engaged in a long and bitter fight to secure control over the Shipping Board and the Fleet Corporation, and it was clear that President Coolidge agreed with his views in the matter. On at least two occasions President Hoover made public statements

9. 43 Cong. Rec. 26.
10. *Supra*, 194 f.

11. *Supra*, 253 ff

indicating how he thought the Interstate Commerce Commission ought to exercise certain of its powers, and the commission somewhat reluctantly yielded to that influence. A member of the Federal Communications Commission told the writer in 1936 that the commission had always complied with all orders and requests made of it by the President, and had never raised any question about its obligation to do so. When Franklin D. Roosevelt became President in 1933, he found most of the independent commissions manned by persons unsympathetic to his general policies. Professor Herring describes what happened:

The President got around this difficulty in his characteristically adroit fashion. Placing his keymen in the departments was a simple matter, but bringing the independent organizations within his control required more ingenuity. The judicial calm of the Interstate Commerce Commission was left undisturbed, but the most able and aggressive commissioner was created Federal Coördinator of Transportation. The United States Tariff Commission was reduced to a harmless condition through the passage of the Reciprocal Tariff act. The Federal Radio Commission was abolished outright and a New Deal commission took its place. The President secured the resignation of Hoover's chairman of the Federal Power Commission and added two appointees of his own.[12]

When President Roosevelt encountered opposition in his efforts to reorganize the Federal Trade Commission, he felt obliged to resort to the drastic procedure of removal; he believed that he had full authority to remove Mr. Humphrey. By June 1, 1934, Mr. Roosevelt had appointed all five members of the Federal Trade Commission, and it was not until a year later that he learned from the Supreme Court that his removal of Mr. Humphrey was illegal.

a. *Presidential control of personnel*

Presidential control of commission policy results largely from the President's power to appoint the members of the commission. This constitutional power may not be taken away from the President. It permits him to place on the independent agencies men who share his views; and when, as with the New Deal

12. E. P. Herring, *Public Administration and the Public Interest* (1936), 222 f.

agencies, the President appoints the entire membership at one time, he can go far towards dominating the commissions' policies. It is partly to mitigate excessive Presidential domination that Congress has almost uniformly provided for staggered terms for the members of the independent commissions. This Presidential prerogative of appointment has been regarded as worth fighting for. We have already commented upon President Hoover's fight with the Senate over his appointments in 1930 to the reorganized Power Commission. Mr. Hoover rightly assumed that the struggle was for control of the policy of the commission, and he won his fight.

In one or two cases Congress has established, and in others considered establishing, ex-officio memberships in some of the independent commissions. Where this has occurred the control of the President has been greatly strengthened, since the ex-officio members have been high executive officers and therefore subject to direct Presidential control. The Federal Power Commission of 1920 was completely ex officio in its membership. Until 1935 the Federal Reserve Board included in its membership the Secretary of the Treasury and the Comptroller of the Currency, thereby greatly increasing Presidential control of its policy. And only after considerable debate did Congress decline to place Cabinet members on the United States Shipping Board.

In addition to appointing the members of the independent regulatory commissions, the President, in the case of about half of them, designates the chairman and sometimes the vice-chairman. This power can be made to strengthen Presidential control over the commissions if the President so desires. There is some variation in the terms for which the President is permitted to name the chairman. Under the Act of 1935 the President appoints for four-year terms the chairman and vice-chairman of the Board of Governors of the Federal Reserve System. These are the executive officers of the board. The President may thus designate his own men, and a new President upon taking office may change them. While there is no judicial decision on this point, it seems fairly clear that an unrestricted grant of power to the President to designate the chairman of a commission carries with it the discretionary power to dismiss the chairman from his chairmanship, even though the President could not validly remove him from membership on the commission except for causes stated in the statute.

Students of administration and federal administrators themselves do not agree on the desirability of giving to the President this important authority. James M. Landis, formerly chairman of the Securities and Exchange Commission, expressed to the writer his belief that the President should have power to name the chairmen of commissions. It creates for the President a direct channel through which he is able to present his ideas and policies to the commission, and Mr. Landis believes that the President is entitled to this privilege. It also makes it more probable that the President, in filling vacancies which may arise in a commission's membership, will consult the commission through the chairman. The commission is also provided in this way with a head through whom contacts and co-operation with other independent agencies may be facilitated, and the President enjoys some indirect authority or influence to see that such inter-commission co-operation does take place. An interesting use of the power to designate the chairman of a commission was the appointment by President Roosevelt of Frank McNinch to the chairmanship of the Federal Communications Commission in 1937. Mr. McNinch was, in fact, borrowed from the Federal Power Commission and was given the chairmanship of the Federal Communications Commission in order to clear up in that agency an exceedingly unsatisfactory internal condition arising mainly from squabbles over the dispensing of spoils. Here the power was used by the President to increase the internal efficiency of the commission, and thereby to ward off a threatened Congressional investigation. Both results were achieved. There is, however, plausible argument against giving the President this power, and it may be noted that the most powerful commissions, the Interstate Commerce Commission and the Federal Trade Commission, choose their own chairmen. It is pointed out that Presidential selection of the chairman gives that officer a position of undue importance and influence and thereby disturbs the equality which should prevail among the members. It also injects Presidential influence, if not domination, into an area which should remain wholly free from outside pressure. It tends, in short, to undermine the independence of the commission.

We have already mentioned the reprehensible efforts of Presidents Harding and Coolidge to control the policy of the independent commissions by holding over the heads of commissioners undated letters of resignation exacted from them at the time of appointment and as the price of appointment. This may in an occasional instance prove an effective device, but few would disagree that if the President is to control commission policy that control should be open and aboveboard and should not operate through such an under-cover arrangement.

The President's control over commission personnel, and, through it, over commission policy, would be complete if the President enjoyed a discretionary power to remove members of the commissions. Presidents Wilson, Harding, and Roosevelt all believed that they had this power and that it could be properly used for dominating the policies of the commissions. The Humphrey decision has changed this view. The President now has discretionary power of removal only in the case of those commissions in which Congress has left the President's power unrestricted by not listing specific causes of removal in the statutes. While the Supreme Court has not ruled squarely on this question, its earlier decisions all indicate that the President may remove at his discretion any officer whom he appoints provided Congress does not restrict by statute that power of removal. It is unlikely, however, that the President's power of removal as it now exists will ever be used as a weapon of control over the independent commissions, except in some case of great emergency.

b. *Presidential directions or orders to commissions*

Presidents have sometimes undertaken to control the policies of independent regulatory commissions by the simple process of telling the commissions what to do. President Hoover told the Interstate Commerce Commission on one occasion that he thought that passenger rates ought to be increased; on another occasion he gave it directions regarding railroad consolidation. In 1925 President Coolidge tried to influence the rediscount policy of the Federal Reserve Board. Professor Corwin tells of a case in which President Wilson 'urgently requested' the Railroad Labor Board to 'expedite' a pending wage decision, and of a recent instance in which President Roosevelt 'instructed the Federal Power Commission, through its chairman, to coöperate with the National Power Policy Committee and the Advisory Commission to the Council of National Defense for certain purposes in connection with national defense.' [13]

Under the statutes the President has no effective means of backing up these orders or directions to the commissions. If, however, the orders are made public they may be exceedingly effective, for the President may be able to invoke a public opinion which the commissions would feel unable to resist. If the President stays on firm ground, and confines his directions to matters in which he clearly has an interest and a responsibility, he may be able to make this a valuable method of control. It is a method not dissimilar in theory and in effect to the 'open letters of instruction' which Robson proposes as a means of allowing a Minister to influence a British administrative tribunal.[14] Such Presidential directions must, of course, be kept at a safe distance from a commission's quasi-judicial work involving matters of individual right; they should be kept clearly within the field of the broad policies which directly impinge on the realm of Presidential duty. Public opinion would be likely to support an independent commission if it refused to comply with an objectionable or inappropriate order or instruction by the President. Since the President must depend upon public opinion to persuade the commission to comply with his orders or directions, the whole arrangement seems to carry with it its own protection against abuse.

2. CONTROL OF ADMINISTRATIVE EFFICIENCY

Many who feel that the President should have no authority over commission policy would be willing to allow him a narrower type of control in the interests of administrative efficiency; and the President does enjoy a certain amount of this authority. It is exercised primarily perhaps through the power of appointment and removal. The President is on safer ground in using the removal power to control administrative efficiency than to control the policy of an independent commission, since

13. E. S. Corwin, *The President: Office and Powers* (1940), 360.
14. *Supra*, 643.

administrative inefficiency may reasonably amount to incompetence and thus constitute a statutory cause for the removal of commissioners.

There are many statutory provisions which give the President power in regard to matters which come before the commissions. The President's approval is sometimes required for the performance of particular acts which relate to the President's own responsibilities. Thus Congress, in regulating the activities of the Shipping Board, required that Presidential approval be secured before certain contracts were entered into by the board.[15]

A limited supervision in the interests of administrative efficiency has been given to the President in one or two cases by placing an otherwise independent commission 'in' an executive department. We have seen that the Interstate Commerce Commission began its career in the Department of the Interior, and remained there in fact until the Secretary of that department asked to have it moved out.[16] The Bituminous Coal Commissions of 1935 and 1937 were both 'in' the Department of the Interior for purposes of administrative housekeeping.[17] When the status of the National Labor Relations Board was being discussed in Congress, Secretary Perkins and several labor leaders urged that it be placed in the Department of Labor.[18] In 1940, by the President's executive order under the Reorganization Act of 1939, the Civil Aeronautics Authority, with its name slightly changed, was placed in the Department of Commerce; yet it remains free from executive supervision with respect to its quasi-judicial and quasi-legislative work.[19] Presidential control over an independent commission which results from placing that commission 'in' an executive department looks more impressive on paper than it proves in practice. Mr. Ickes declared that he knew nothing about the independent Bituminous Coal Commission while it was 'in' his department, except what he read in the newspapers.[20] While such an arrangement may lead to compliance by a commission with uniform bureaucratic routine in many matters, it is not

15. *Supra,* 240, 258 f.
16. *Supra,* 62, 67.
17. *Supra,* 379 ff., 387 f.

18. *Supra,* 360 ff.
19. *Supra,* 415 f.
20. *Supra,* 380.

likely to enlarge the range of Presidential control over a commission in any practically important way.

3. CO-ORDINATION OF COMMISSION ACTIVITY WITH THAT OF OTHER AGENCIES OR DEPARTMENTS

One of the difficult problems of the independent commissions is that in many cases they have no effective machinery for making contacts or co-operating with other independent commissions. Experience has shown that Presidential aid in this area is very necessary and important. The President may move here by creating informal agencies such as advisory or co-ordinating committees in order to facilitate co-operation among the independent commissions. He may also, as we have seen, accomplish similar results through the chairmen of the commissions when the statutes allow him to appoint them. As in many similar situations, these problems of co-ordination are likely to be effectively dealt with by informal methods when there is no machinery for direct control.

4. CONTROL OVER QUASI-JUDICIAL WORK

The President has no authority from any source to influence day-to-day decisions of the independent regulatory commissions in cases in which private and public rights are at issue. This quasi-judicial activity should not be subject to any form of outside control or influence; and it would be a serious abuse of power for the President to intervene in an attempt to control such a decision of a commission. The President does not now possess that power, and it should not be given to him.

B. POSSIBLE METHODS OF INCREASING THE EFFECTIVENESS OF PRESIDENTIAL CONTROL OVER COMMISSIONS

While some students of the problem of the independent regulatory commissions reject the idea that the President ought to have any control over these commissions, the writer is here proceeding on the assumption that the President does in practice enjoy substantial authority in this field and that, so far as administrative supervision is concerned, the President's authority may well be increased. We may summarize here a number of proposals which have been made for strengthening the President's power in this area.

1. OPEN STATEMENTS OF PRESIDENTIAL POLICY

Even if we assume that the President cannot enforce his policies on the independent commissions against their will, and that he ought not to be permitted to do so, there is no reason why he should not openly and frankly state his policies to the commissions and invite their agreement and co-operation. The President may do this with a public letter or statement in which he makes clear the course of action he believes should be followed by the commission and gives his reasons in support thereof. When such a practice came to be sanctioned by tradition, it would lose its present superficial aspect of being a type of unauthorized interference on the part of the President with the commissions' activities. If there are substantial differences in policy between the commissions and the President, there would seem to be great advantage in having these brought into the open in this direct way. Public opinion could thereby act in the matter, should it be disposed to do so. The President should not use this method in an effort to influence or control the strictly quasi-judicial work of the commissions; it is believed that he would be rebuked by public opinion should he attempt to do so.

2. SHARPENED PRESIDENTIAL CONTROL OVER THE ADMINISTRATIVE EFFICIENCY OF WORK OF THE COMMISSIONS BY A MORE EFFECTIVE STATEMENT OF CAUSES OF REMOVAL

The writer believes that careful study of the language of the statutes in which are stated the causes for which commissioners may be removed could be made to result in giving the President desirable authority and responsibility for the efficiency with which the commission does its work, and yet not permit him to interfere through that removal power with the activities with regard to which it ought to be independent. For example, the term 'incompetence' could be substantially elaborated and made more concrete in ways which would extend the range of Presidential supervision over internal efficiency. This has been dealt with more fully in another connection.[21]

3. ENLARGING THE STATUTORY RANGE OF PRESIDENTIAL DIRECTION AND DISALLOWANCE OF COMMISSIONS' ACTS IN FIELDS WHICH IMPINGE ON THE PRESIDENT'S POWERS AND RESPONSIBILITIES

The authority of the President could be substantially extended in order to place under his responsible control certain commission activities which tie in closely with problems for which he is responsible. This could be done either by requiring his approval of specified acts or by allowing him on his initiative to intervene and either to suspend or disallow a commission's act. For example, if the Maritime Commission is to retain the power to approve the transfer of American ships to foreign registry, the President might wisely be authorized to pass upon such transfers in order to make sure in time of international crisis that the President's foreign policy should not be jeopardized by the acts of an independent agency. Congress has occasionally given the President such powers in specific cases; it could probably go considerably farther without sacrificing the independence of the commissions.

4. REQUIRING THE COMMISSIONS TO REPORT TO THE PRESIDENT AT HIS REQUEST

In his recent book on the Presidency, Professor Corwin makes the interesting proposal that Congress might 'require the independent commissions and similar agencies to report to the President at his request. Exaction of such a duty would work beneficially in two ways: (1) would bring divergent tendencies in administration to the light of day and put them on justification; (2) it would inform the legislative judgment of the President. The hierarchical principle, it has been suggested, may be less important for its authoritative than for its communicative aspects.' [22] Corwin does not elaborate this proposal, but it is easy to see that it would tend to draw the President and the commissions closer together and make easier the iron-

21. *Supra,* 464 f.   22. E. S. Corwin, op. cit. 103.

ing out of conflicts of policy between them. There should be substantial value in thus permitting the President to command information from the commissions, even if he has no more power than before to act upon the information he receives.

III. RESPONSIBILITY OF THE COMMISSIONS TO THE COURTS

An earlier chapter has summarized the essential facts with regard to the judicial review of the work of the independent regulatory commissions.[23] It is clear that the courts must review commission decisions on questions of law, that they will supervise commission procedure to make sure that it is fair and orderly, and that they will sometimes review, and at all times keep a watchful eye upon, the commissions' findings of fact. The range of authority which the courts exercise over the commissions is guided, but not always finally controlled, by the statutory directions which Congress gives to the courts. Thus the courts can be required by Congress to review all findings of fact made by commissions, when they otherwise would not review such findings if supported by substantial evidence. At the same time the courts will insist upon exercising the judicial supervision of commission action believed by them to be constitutionally necessary under due process of law, even though Congress may have sought to provide a less drastic review. We have seen that actual range of judicial review, when the courts are left with a free hand, is likely to depend in part upon the courts' impression of the quality of the quasi-judicial job that is being done by the commission.[24] Essential fairness and a sound regular procedure will earn for a commission a substantial degree of immunity from judicial interference, whereas a reputation for biased and shoddy work will sometimes result in the courts doing over again a commission's job.

There are sharply conflicting views on the proper range of judicial control over the independent regulatory commissions and other officers and agencies doing similar work. The controversy is a very old one and it is possible to review here only its major aspects. There is, in the first place, a body of opinion

23. *Supra,* 468 ff.   24. *Supra,* 476 f.

which favors the broadest possible judicial review; every finding and decision of a quasi-judicial tribunal ought to be reviewable on appeal in a court of law. A certain amount of the
vigor with which this view has recently been urged is a result
of the fact that some of the newer independent agencies, such
as the National Labor Relations Board and the Securities and
Exchange Commission, have been created to exercise types of
regulation which are very unpopular in certain quarters. Businessmen subject to these unpopular types of regulation would
in general be glad indeed to have the broadest possible judicial
review in the hope of watering down and delaying the effectiveness of the regulation. Proposals have therefore been made
that all findings of fact as well as rulings of law made by quasi-
judicial bodies should be subject to review by the courts. This
was in substance the proposal made in 1936 by the Committee
on Administrative Law of the American Bar Association. This
proposal rests upon certain assumptions and convictions. First,
it assumes that only a judicial body can fairly and justly determine private rights. It exemplifies, in other words, a belief in
lawyers' justice. Second, it assumes that essential justice requires a second if not a third trial of any given cause, even
though the first one may have been quite fair; it thus assumes
a sort of vested right to keep alive a gambling chance to find
something wrong with the first trial. Third, the proposal rests
upon the conviction supported, it must be admitted, by all too
much concrete evidence, that the findings of fact of administrative officers and quasi-judicial bodies are sometimes reached
by loose and unfair procedure and are not adequately supported by evidence.

There is a strong case, however, for limited judicial review
of the actions of independent regulatory commissions. Justice
does not require that courts dispose of all problems affecting
private rights. The courts themselves have been outspoken in
declaring that essential justice can be dispensed by administrative tribunals or officers. Due process of law does not require
the fullest possible judicial review of administrative rulings.
Left to their own devices the courts have abandoned their
early rigid insistence on the judicial duplication of administrative findings through trials *de novo* on appeal, and they are
quite content to exercise a much milder form of outside super-

vision. We have seen that in England judicial intervention in the administrative process is frowned upon, and that the opportunities to appeal from the findings of a quasi-judicial authority to the courts of law are exceedingly limited. The popular idea that several trials, simply for the sake of repetition, are essential to justice is a vicious and costly fallacy.

The case for limited review is supported by very practical considerations. If the courts must pass upon a large volume of quasi-judicial determinations, the handling of administrative work is seriously retarded. At the same time the dockets of the courts will be crowded with business of a technical and specialized character which the ordinary courts are not well equipped to handle. Excessive judicial review discredits, if it does not actually waste, the expert ability and experience of the administrative officers who have been chosen to handle specialized tasks. Finally, it may be suggested that if an independent regulatory commission is not handling its business in a fair and satisfactory way, the proper solution to the problem is not found by burdening the courts with the responsibility of doing the job over again; instead, the procedure of the commission, or its personnel, or its assignment of work, should be improved so that the specific criticisms are met. That fairness and efficiency can be attained in an independent commission has been demonstrated over many years by the splendid record of the Interstate Commerce Commission.

The Attorney General's Committee on Administrative Procedure made its report in January 1941. The committee studied the problem of judicial review of administrative adjudication and presented recommendations which deserve mention here. These proposals are grounded on the theory that judicial review is 'to check—not to supplant—administrative action.' [25] The courts must exercise the fullest and most searching review of all questions in which constitutional rights are involved, all questions affecting the scope of the agency's authority, and all questions of procedural fairness. On the controversial question of the judicial review of administrative findings of fact, the committee proposes that such findings shall be final and binding if supported by 'substantial evidence.' The Supreme Court has defined substantial evidence as 'such

25. S. Doc. 8, 77th Cong., 1st sess. (1941), 77.

relevant evidence as a reasonable mind might accept as adequate to support a conclusion.' [26] The committee rejected the proposal that these findings of fact be made final only when supported by 'the weight of the evidence,' for the courts would have to 'determine independently which way the evidence preponderates' to apply this test. Such a requirement would 'destroy the values of adjudication of fact by experts or specialists . . . It would divide the responsibility for administrative adjudications.' The committee concluded that the present demand for more drastic judicial review of the work of regulatory agencies arises from 'dissatisfaction with the fact-finding procedures now employed by the administrative bodies.' It made extensive proposals for the improvement of those procedures and expressed the belief that such procedural reforms 'will inspire confidence and will obviate the reasons for change in the scope of judicial review.' [27]

So far then as commission responsibility to the courts is concerned, it seems clear that under favorable conditions judicial review or control of commission activity will not go beyond an outside check upon questions of law, *ultra vires* activities, and commission procedure. Judicial authority cannot and ought not to reach to matters of policy or administrative efficiency. The writer believes that in spite of the recent proposals to enlarge the range of judicial control of quasi-judicial decisions, we are moving steadily in the direction of keeping the courts more and more out of the processes of administration. The trend is toward limiting judicial supervision of the independent regulatory commissions to the lowest point consistent with due process of law.

IV. THE PROBLEM OF DIVIDED RESPONSIBILITY OF THE INDEPENDENT REGULATORY COMMISSIONS

IT is clear from the foregoing analysis that the lines of responsibility which bear upon the independent regulatory commissions are considerably blurred and confused. The commissions

26. *Consolidated Edison Co.* v. *National Labor Relations Board,* 305 U.S. 197, 229 (1938).
27. S. Doc. 8, 77th Cong., 1st sess. (1941), 91 f.

are not clearly aware to whom they are accountable, nor are those to whom they are accountable sharply aware of their own position in the matter. Divergent claims and theories confuse the issue and tend to destroy any sharp sense of accountability.

As a step toward clarifying this confusion on the responsibility of the independent regulatory commissions, the following principles are suggested: First, the commissions owe no responsibility to the courts beyond the obligation to stay within the legal limits of their assignments and to follow fair and orderly procedure. They are in no sense accountable to the courts for any matters of policy or of administrative efficiency. Second, the commissions owe no responsibility either to Congress or to the President concerning the making of individual quasi-judicial decisions. Nothing but abuse and injustice could result from permitting Congress or the President to interfere with or control these decisions affecting private rights. This does not mean, however, that the commissions owe no responsibility either to Congress or to the President for the essential soundness of their quasi-judicial judgments viewed as a whole, or for the general efficiency with which they perform their quasi-judicial tasks. Third, commission accountability to Congress can extend only to matters of policy in the broad sense. It does not extend to day-to-day adjudication or day-to-day administration. We have seen that Congress has developed no machinery for making this accountability with regard to policy surely and consistently effective. The attention which it gives to the commissions has usually been *ad hoc* and inadvertent, but Congress cannot escape its own responsibility for supervising the way in which the independent commissions handle the broad policies confided to their discretion. Fourth, the responsibility of the commissions to the President is limited to two areas. It does not extend to day-to-day adjudication. A commission may be accountable to the President for policy decisions within limits blocked out by statute, and for matters directly impinging upon the President's own obligations and duties. There is a sharper responsibility to the President for efficient administration; it is the President's duty under the Constitution to see that the laws are faithfully executed—and this includes the execution of the laws by an independent commission.

We may therefore conclude that the responsibility of the

independent regulatory commission is a divided one. We are faced here with a practical and not a theoretical problem; there is no reason why an agency must serve only one master. There may be lines of control and corresponding lines of accountability which move in different directions. Congress is the creator of the independent commissions and it would do well frankly to recognize this principle of divided responsibility and to direct more effectively and define more clearly its nature and limits.

The idea that the independent commission or other administrative agency may owe a divided allegiance is by no means new. There is an interesting precedent in the field of English administration. In 1911 a Treasury minute was issued by the Chancellor of the Exchequer clarifying the status of the Insurance Commissioners under the National Health Insurance scheme. This minute distinguished between the executive and judicial functions of the commissioners. The judicial functions, though not numerous, were said to be very important and the independence necessary for their proper handling was secured by making them free from Treasury control. It was felt there should be definite responsibility for the executive acts performed by the commissioners. These accordingly would have to be defined by the Board of the Treasury in Parliament. The government here shows an unwillingness to assume any control over the judicial activities of administrative agencies, while at the same time it recognizes that an agency may be politically responsible for part of its work but not all of it.

Another attempt to embody the principle of divided responsibility in the form of a Congressional statute was made in some of the early drafts of the civil aeronautics bill of 1937.[28] The proposal by the interdepartmental committee called for the creation of a civil aeronautics authority with regard to which the following arrangement was proposed: 'the exercise or performance of any other power or duty of the board which is not subject to review by courts of law shall be subject to the general direction of the President.' Here was a frank attempt to create an agency which would have both executive and quasi-judicial duties, and to make that agency effectively responsible to the President for its administrative work, while

28. *Supra*, 396, 413 f.

its quasi-judicial activities were subject to review by the courts alone. The line of division attempted here is difficult to draw, and in actual practice the proposal embodied in the bill might have resulted in litigation and confusion, especially since there is no assured way of telling beforehand just where the courts are going to draw the lines which limit their own authority. There should, however, be no difficulty whatever in dividing the responsibility of the commissions between Congress and the President, for Congress itself has full power to draw that line of division and to make it sharp and clear.

V. GENERAL CONCLUSIONS REGARDING THE RESPONSIBILITY OF THE COMMISSIONS

THE following conclusions are ventured with regard to the problem of commission responsibility. The writer believes these are supported by the foregoing analysis and summary of experience.

1. The present situation with regard to commission responsibility is vague, confused, and unsatisfactory.

2. Congress should establish by law an effective division of commission responsibility which will sharpen and clarify the areas of control and accountability. This division should run along the following lines:

a. Judicial control over commissions and their corresponding accountability to the courts should be kept at a minimum. It should extend to questions of law and all issues of *ultra vires,* and to the fairness and regularity of the procedure of the commissions in performing quasi-judicial work. It should not extend to determinations of fact which are supported by substantial evidence and under no circumstances should it extend to matters of policy.

b. Save for the judicial review described above, there should be complete freedom from outside control from any source of individual decisions rendered in the exercise of quasi-judicial power.

c. Congress must retain ultimate policy control over the commissions through its basic statutory direction and by its provision of financial support. The resulting responsibility is of a broad and general sort, since Congress is not equipped to exercise control in detail over the commissions. While improvements such as the establishment of well-staffed standing committees may increase the ability of Congress to keep itself informed of commission activities, these must not be expected to change substantially the area of control possible to a legislative body.

d. Congress should clarify by statute the areas within which the commissions should be responsible to the President. These areas will have to be larger than would be necessary or desirable if Congress could exercise effective control over an administrative or quasi-judicial agency. The areas of Presidential control over commissions should include the following: First, there should be a range of policy control allotted to the President. There are many points at which commission policies impinge upon the general policies of the President, policies for which the President as head of the nation is responsible. Commission policies impinge also upon other commission policies. In these areas the President should be given directing authority; it is possible to establish suitable devices by which this control and responsibility may be implemented. Second, it should be clearly and·definitely recognized that the commissions are accountable to the President in the field of administrative efficiency. While it is not clear that Congress could constitutionally prevent the President from exercising control in this area, it should certainly not attempt to do so but should facilitate in every possible way this accountability of the commissions to the President for the efficiency with which they do their work.

XI

MERGER OF POWERS IN COMMISSIONS—
SEGREGATION OF ADJUDICATION
FROM ADMINISTRATION

I. NATURE OF THE PROBLEM

FROM the time our first independent regulatory commission was set up in 1887 down through the report of the Attorney General's Committee on Administrative Procedure in 1941, there has been constant criticism of the fact that the independent agencies place in the hands of the same men governmental powers thought to be incompatible. Sometimes these attacks have been explicit and have been accompanied by reasoned proposals to separate the functions thus merged. In other cases the criticisms have been largely expressions of resentment against unwelcome forms of regulation. So long standing a problem justifies careful analysis. This chapter, therefore, attempts to summarize the character and extent of these much-criticized mergers of power in the commissions and to describe and appraise the more important plans which have been either tried or proposed for the segregation of these powers. The mergers which have been most seriously attacked are those in which powers of adjudication are given to independent commissions which at the same time exercise powers of prosecution, policy determination, or business management.

A. MERGER OF POLICY-DETERMINING FUNCTIONS WITH ADJUDICATION

In most of the independent regulatory commissions, important quasi-judicial work in which private rights are directly affected is supplemented by the responsibility of making broad policy decisions and carrying on administrative activities of a general nature. It is believed by many that the combination of these two kinds of duties in the hands of the same agency tends to destroy the atmosphere of neutrality and detachment in which the work of adjudication ought to be carried on. Our constitutional courts have from the beginning protected their judicial impartiality by refusing to perform any non-judicial duties; yet our independent commissions are compelled by law to perform the duties of the lawmaker and the administrator along with those of the judge. The policy determinations which independent commissions are obliged to make are often controversial, and are sometimes controversial in a partisan sense. The result is that the commissions are subject actually or potentially to pressures from various official and unofficial sources. These pressures may not be in and of themselves illegitimate, but they are clearly not compatible with the complete impartiality with which private rights ought to be adjudicated. It is urged, therefore, that policy determination and adjudication ought to be kept as far apart as possible.

B. Merger of the Powers of Prosecutor and Judge

Much sharper criticism is directed against some of the commissions on the ground that they both prosecute and judge those within their jurisdiction. Agencies like the Federal Trade Commission and the National Labor Relations Board perform a task comprising three elements: First, they determine what constitutes a violation of some legislative standard, such as 'unfair competition' or 'unfair labor practice.' Second, they discover through the methods of a prosecutor that a person has violated this legislative standard. Third, they issue an order restraining the conduct thus found objectionable. Elsewhere the writer referred to this aspect of the work of the Federal Trade Commission: 'The business man learns from the same act of the commission what the law of unfair competition is and that he has violated it.' [1] The commissioners through their

1. R. E. Cushman's memorandum for the President's Committee on Administrative Management, Report with Special Studies (1937), 219.

subordinates work up from the initial complaint the cases which they later present to themselves for decision. Here again is lacking the atmosphere of detachment and impartiality in which private rights ought to be adjudicated. The temptation on the part of the commission to decide that it has proved its case is very strong. Gerard Henderson said of the Federal Trade Commission, 'The crux of the matter is that the commission has not been able to overcome the handicap of a procedure which makes it both complainant and judge, and to impress upon its findings that stamp of impartiality and disinterested justice which alone can give them weight and authority.' [2] While Henderson was referring to the commission's early days, there are many who feel that the defect he points out still exists and that the commission continues inescapably to violate the long-standing principle that one ought not be a judge in his own cause.

C. Long-Standing Criticisms of These Mergers of Powers

The concrete results of the merging of these allegedly incompatible powers in the same hands are exceedingly difficult to measure. There have no doubt been cases in which a commission has been guilty of merely rubber-stamping by its decision the complaint brought by its staff against particular defendants. As we have seen, the Federal Trade Commission during its earlier years created a rather general impression that its final decisions were largely rationalizations of the conclusions with which it had started out.[3] The Supreme Court seems to have felt that the commission was not unbiased in its quasi-judicial work and accordingly subjected its decisions to the most rigorous type of judicial supervision. It would be difficult, however, to prove how far substantial abuses have actually resulted from these mergers of powers.

Also, there is a psychological factor which may not be safely forgotten and the actual results of these mergers of powers may in the long run be less important than the popular impression

2. G. C. Henderson, *The Federal Trade Commission* (1924), 328.
3. *Supra*, 477.

which they create. Many years ago a wise British judge observed that 'important as it was that the people should get justice, it was even more important that they should be made to see and feel that they were getting it.' If an independent regulatory commission is so organized and so administers its powers of adjudication that those subject to its authority honestly feel that they are being denied essential justice by having their rights adjudicated by a tribunal not fully impartial, this is a very serious indictment whether injustice is actually done or not.

There can be no doubt of the persistence of this criticism of the regulatory commissions or of the sincerity of most of those who have voiced it. Evidence of dissatisfaction with this aspect of commission work and procedure is seen throughout the entire legislative history of nearly every commission studied. In some cases, as in that of the National Labor Relations Board, these criticisms of the so-called prosecutor-judge combination are to some extent smoke screens to cover up more fundamental resentments against the regulatory agency and the statute which it is enforcing. But the criticism is also voiced by numerous able and responsible people who have no personal axes to grind, and who are merely disturbed by what appears to them to be the adjudication of private rights by officers occupying also the role of prosecutor. We have seen that this was one of the main charges brought against British agencies by Lord Hewart in *The New Despotism,* and that the reality and seriousness of the complaint and the situation out of which it grew were recognized and carefully considered by the Committee on Ministers' Powers.[4]

II. METHODS OF SEGREGATING ADJUDICATION FROM OTHER COMMISSION FUNCTIONS

THOSE who have criticized our independent regulatory commissions for the mergers of powers just described have not stopped with criticism; they have made numerous proposals either for eliminating the objectionable mergers of powers completely, or for minimizing their unfortunate effects. We

4. *Supra,* 630 ff.

turn now to an analysis of these proposals for segregating the job of adjudication from the other kinds of commission activity believed to be incompatible with it.

A. Segregation of Executive and Managerial Functions

There are a number of cases in which the independent regulatory commissions have been given executive or managerial jobs which have little or no connection with the quasi-judicial tasks of regulation. Such tasks have often been imposed on the commission because there was no other existing body to which they might suitably be assigned, and in some cases their performance in no way threatens the impartiality of the commission's quasi-judicial work. They do, however, create difficulties and there are major objections to imposing such duties upon commissions which must carry a heavy assignment of administrative adjudication. These objections may be stated as follows: First, there is a loss of effective executive responsibility for work which is executive in character. Second, these duties impose upon a body equipped to do quasi-judicial work executive or managerial functions which call for different abilities and attitudes of mind. President Hoover summarized his views upon this problem in a message to Congress in December 3, 1929, dealing with departmental reorganization. He said:

It seems to me that the essential principles of reorganization are two in number. First, all administrative activities of the same major purpose should be placed in groups under single-headed responsibility; second, all executive and administrative functions should be separated from boards and commissions and placed under individual responsibility; while quasi-legislative and quasi-judicial and broadly advisory functions should be removed from individual authority and assigned to boards and commissions. Indeed, these are the fundamental principles upon which our Government was founded, and they are the principles which have been adhered to in the whole development of our business structure, and they are the distillation of the common sense of generations.[5]

The earliest example of this combination of duties is found in the Interstate Commerce Commission; the commission's im-

5. 72 Cong. Rec. 27.

portant executive functions under the Safety Appliance Acts
have little or nothing to do with rate making or with the commission's other powers of regulation. The commission, through
its agents, conducts safety appliance inspection of railroad
equipment, discovers violations of the statutes, and reports
these for appropriate penal action to the federal district attorneys. These duties were given to the commission before
the Department of Commerce was created and there was no
very appropriate executive department to which they could be
assigned. They have been left where they are partly through
inertia, but mainly because the commission has established in
regard to these executive duties what amounts to an internal
segregation of functions or division of labor by which the enforcement of the Safety Appliance Acts is entrusted to a corps
of men who are not charged with other quasi-judicial duties.
The task is carried on, it is true, under the supervision of one
of the commissioners, but the control which he exercises is
casual to the point of being almost nominal. Certainly the
possession of these executive powers in no way threatens the
complete impartiality with which the commission handles its
quasi-judicial work. The situation is open to criticism solely
on the ground of the absence of direct responsibility for the
handling of an executive task, and under the circumstances
this objection is more theoretical than practical. There seems
no sound reason for making a change in this concrete situation,
but the arrangement ought not to be copied in setting up new
agencies or in revising old ones.

A somewhat similar combination of duties was given in 1936
to the United States Maritime Commission. This body has
highly important executive and managerial duties with regard
to shipping subsidies and the management of our merchant
marine; it also has quasi-judicial powers over shipping rates
and services. Here the managerial job overshadows the regulatory job. This merger of tasks in the new commission put in
the same hands duties which had formerly been exercised by
the United States Shipping Board, a quasi-judicial body, and
the Emergency Fleet Corporation, a managerial body. The
duties of the Maritime Commission involve an internal conflict
of interests since the commission is charged with the regula-

tion of the rates and service of shipping carried on in competition with the commission's own merchant shipping business. This is open to the same criticism which we have seen has been directed against the Port of London Authority because it passes on applications for licenses for new docks to be operated in competition with the authority's own docks.[6] The Transportation Act of 1940 took away from the Maritime Commission a good deal of its regulatory work—that dealing with domestic shipping—and transferred it to the Interstate Commerce Commission.[7] It is doubtful whether the commission now retains enough quasi-judicial work to justify on any sound theory a continued status of independence.

The Civil Aeronautics Act of 1938 embodied the most carefully considered attempt thus far made in a regulatory statute to segregate executive functions from duties of administrative adjudication. The Civil Aeronautics Authority was created as an independent quasi-judicial body. In addition, there was set up a separate Civil Aeronautics Administrator directly responsible to the President for the performance of important executive and promotional functions. While the authority could give directions to the Administrator, it could not remove him from office. The Act also created a separate Air Safety Board subject to the President's discretionary power of removal but wholly independent of the authority; its duty was to report on air accidents and to make recommendations to the authority to prevent further accidents.

In the status of the Federal Co-ordinator of Transportation we again see a groping after a somewhat similar segregation of duties. The analogy is not so close because the Co-ordinator was created chiefly to assume the functions of transportation planning. He did, however, have important administrative and promotional powers in the field of railroad co-ordination, although all of his orders were subject to review by the commission. The line of cleavage here was blurred since the Co-ordinator was also a member of the commission.

These few cases represent the attempts which have been made to segregate executive and managerial duties from the quasi-judicial duties of the independent regulatory commis-

---

6. *Supra*, 600.   7. *Supra*, 142.

sions. With the exception of the Civil Aeronautics Act, these attempts at segregation were not motivated by any clearly conceived theories on the impropriety of the original mergers. We turn now to a number of proposals which have been made for this kind of segregation. Some of these are still receiving active consideration.

The most important of these proposals have arisen in the field of transportation, and several were presented during the discussions which culminated in the passage of the Transportation Act of 1920. It was clear at that time that the forthcoming railroad legislation would establish much more comprehensive and drastic control of railroad affairs by the government than had existed before. The statute was being drawn to place in the hands of a regulatory body, either the Interstate Commerce Commission or some other agency, the responsibility of developing and maintaining an efficient and self-supporting system of railway transportation. This was bound to take the government into problems of management, co-ordination, and promotion. Proposals came from many responsible quarters that the new managerial and executive duties ought not to be placed in the hands of a quasi-judicial independent commission charged with the adjudication of private rights. As early as 1916 the Railway Executives proposed a separate federal railroad commission to be set up parallel to the Interstate Commerce Commission to handle the new executive and managerial functions which the government might assume.[8] By 1919, the Railroad Executives had modified their proposals so as to call for a separate Cabinet department of transportation in addition to the Interstate Commerce Commission.[9] At about the same time a National Transportation Conference called under the auspices of the United States Chamber of Commerce brought in a proposal for a separate transportation board of five members to function parallel to the Interstate Commerce Commission.[10] This board would be responsible for financial regulation, consolidations, approval of new capital expenditures, and the general promotion of a national system of railway, water, and highway transportation. This proposal was endorsed not only by the United States Chamber of Commerce,

8. *Supra,* 119.
9. *Supra,* 119.

10. *Supra,* 119 f.

but by the Senate Committee on Interstate Commerce. It was incorporated in the Cummins bill as it passed the Senate, and was discussed at some length. It was urged against it that the Interstate Commerce Commission was greatly aided in the performance of its regulatory duties by its exercise of collateral administrative functions in transportation, that the commission was entirely competent to perform efficiently all of these new functions, and that to give them to separate bodies would sacrifice efficiency and co-ordination. It was argued in reply that the qualifications needed for the different kinds of work, executive and quasi-judicial, were entirely different, and that the tasks therefore ought not to be conferred on the same body.[11]

The proposals of 1919 and 1920 were not adopted, but in the Omnibus Transportation bill introduced by Chairman Lea of the House Committee on Interstate and Foreign Commerce in 1939 we find a provision for an administrator of transportation. This officer would be given substantial executive and promotional duties to be taken away from the Interstate Commerce Commission. There have been other similar proposals, and there is a continuing if not a growing body of opinion that some such segregation of duties as this ought to be worked out in the field of transportation.

We have already seen that during the checkered career of the United States Shipping Board numerous proposals were made to effect a sharp separation between the board and the Fleet Corporation which was by statute placed under its direction.[12] It was urged that the Shipping Board should remain an independent regulatory body and confine itself to quasi-judicial activities, while the Fleet Corporation should be cut loose from it and be made responsible to the President for the executive task of managing the fleet. Promotional and managerial work would thus be kept separate from the work of adjudication. Such a segregation was favored by Mr. Hoover, who, as Secretary of Commerce, served as chairman of the interdepartmental committee on shipping during the 69th Congress.[13]

11. Hearings before the House Committee on Interstate and Foreign Commerce on H. R. 4378, 66th Cong., 1st sess. (1919), vol. 1, 288 ff.

12. *Supra,* 249 ff.

13. *Supra,* 262 f.

Such a segregation of functions was strongly urged when federal radio regulation was first being discussed. Secretary Hoover, in making his influential recommendations with regard to radio control during the '20's, kept insisting that a sharp line should be drawn between what he called the 'traffic problems' which needed executive control and the problems of licensing which called for quasi-judicial action. He believed that there ought to be separate machinery to handle these two jobs. The White bill of 1925 worked out such a segregation of functions; [14] Congress, however, unfamiliar with such an arrangement but very familiar with the ordinary independent regulatory commission, set up in the Radio Act of 1927 an independent commission to deal with the problems of radio control. Yet the Act did not rule out the possibility of such segregation, for it created a radio commission for only one year. At the end of the year, when the commission would have solved all the important problems of radio policy, the segregation of functions was to have gone into effect. The major tasks of radio control, except the revocation of station licenses, were to revert to the Secretary of Commerce; and the radio commission was to be transformed into an appellate board to which the Secretary's decisions might be appealed. We have already indicated why this plan was not carried out.[15]

B. SEGREGATION OF PROSECUTION FROM ADJUDICATION

1. CREATION OF SEPARATE BODIES

The most sharply criticized merger of powers in the independent regulatory commissions is that commonly referred to as the 'prosecutor-judge' combination. Much ingenuity has been expended to devise ways for breaking down this unpopular merger. Many students of the problem feel strongly that this ought to be accomplished, even though they are unable to suggest any specific plan for producing the desired result. They consider that some segregation ought to be worked out to restore administrative adjudication to a level of complete impartiality by preventing the 'quasi-judges' from passing on cases which they have prepared or which have been prepared

14. *Supra*, 301.   15. *Supra*, 311 ff.

by their subordinates. By the same process responsibility would be restored for the performance of the commissions' non-judicial work for which there is now no effective supervision or accountability. We may summarize therefore the more important proposals which have been made to segregate the duties of the prosecutor from the duties of the judge.

Such a proposal was incorporated in the report of the President's Committee on Administrative Management in 1937, the Brownlow committee, and was explained and supported in an accompanying memorandum prepared by the writer.[16] This committee's proposal did not attempt to segregate the functions of the independent regulatory commissions by creating categories of duties which were clearly legislative, clearly executive, or clearly judicial. It attempted rather a horizontal division of the processes involved in quasi-judicial regulation into a preliminary group of administrative functions, and a later group of judicial functions. The essence of the proposal is found in the following paragraphs of the Brownlow committee's report:

The following proposal is put forward as a possible solution of the independent commission problem, present and future. Under this proposed plan the regulatory agency would be set up, not in a governmental vacuum outside the executive departments, but within a department. There it would be divided into an administrative section and a judicial section. The administrative section would be a regular bureau or division in the department, headed by a chief with career tenure and staffed under civil service regulations. It would be directly responsible to the Secretary and through him to the President. The judicial section, on the other hand, would be 'in' the department only for purposes of 'administrative housekeeping,' such as the budget, general personnel administration, and matériel. It would be wholly independent of the department and the President with respect to its work and its decisions. Its members would be appointed by the President with the approval of the Senate for long, staggered terms and would be removable only for causes stated in the statute.

The division of work between the two sections would be relatively simple. The first procedural steps in the regulatory process as now carried on by the independent commissions would go to the administrative section. It would formulate rules, initiate action, inves-

16. Report with Special Studies (1937), 39-42, 203-43.

tigate complaints, hold preliminary hearings, and by a process of sifting and selection prepare the formal record of cases which is now prepared in practice by the staffs of the commissions. It would, of course, do all the purely administrative or sublegislative work now done by the commissions—in short all the work which is not essentially judicial in nature. The judicial section would sit as an impartial, independent body to make decisions affecting the public interest and private rights upon the basis of the records and findings presented to it by the administrative section. In certain types of cases where the volume of business is large and quick and routine action is necessary, the administrative section itself should in the first instance decide the cases and issue orders, and the judicial section should sit as an appellate body to which such decisions could be appealed on questions of law.[17]

It is unnecessary to include here any elaborate analysis or defense of this proposal. In the memorandum referred to above, the writer claimed four chief advantages for the plan: First, by turning back to the executive departments the functions of policy determination and administration now handled by the commissions, there would be an 'increase in the coherence and unity of the national administrative structure,' together with a 'tightening of the lines of responsibility so necessary to effective administrative management.' Second, the plan would protect and improve the handling of the judicial and quasi-judicial work now carried on by the commissions. The judicial sections proposed would 'be free from those subtle pressures that menace the judicial neutrality of the independent commission, and that are the inevitable result of its important policy-determining duties'; the proposal would also result in the abandonment of 'the vicious principle of merging in one body the role of prosecutor and judge.' Third, the plan is flexible and could be readily adapted to varying conditions. 'With the Administrative Section and the Judicial Section under the roof of the same department, the details of their organization can be worked out experimentally by Executive order. The division of labor between them can also be modified in the light of experience . . . Furthermore, the principle of the plan does not have to be applied with relentless thoroughness in order to be applied at all to advantage.' Finally,

17. Ibid. 41.

the proposal does not rest upon any revolutionary principle but rather extends and crystallizes divisions of labor which have already been made the subjects of experiment. Such experiments have been made not only within the staffs of some of the commissions, but also in adjusting the relations between regulatory agencies and some of the legislative courts.

The Brownlow committee's proposal relating to the independent regulatory commissions was not incorporated into the ill-fated reorganization bill which was so bitterly debated in Congress during the early months of 1938. It was, however, widely discussed by students of administration and administrative law, as well as by administrators. Many of these disapproved of the proposal, but there is much unevenness in the cogency and objectivity with which they stated their objections. We cannot here analyze this discussion in detail; probably the most impartial and telling criticism of the Brownlow committee's plan is found in the majority report of the Attorney General's Committee on Administrative Procedure issued in January 1941.[18] This criticism has additional persuasiveness because of the committee's agreement with some of the main purposes of the Brownlow committee's plan. The Attorney General's committee was acutely aware of the problems presented by the prosecutor-judge combination of functions in our regulatory agencies; it rejected the Brownlow committee's principle of complete separation of the functions of prosecution and adjudication in favor of the less drastic plan of working out this segregation inside the internal structure of the commission. This plan will be discussed later.[19] The committee stated its reasons for rejecting complete segregation as follows: First, the prosecutor-judge combination of functions in regulatory agencies can be adequately broken up by means of internal segregation of duties within the commission; the more drastic method of the Brownlow committee proposal is therefore not necessary. Second, complete segregation would result in the 'multiplication of separate governmental organizations. If the proposal were rigorously carried out, two agencies would grow in each case where one grew before.' The relations between these two agencies would be varied and confused and in many cases one would greatly overshadow the other in im-

18. S. Doc. 8, 77th Cong., 1st sess. (1941), 55 ff.   19. *Infra*, 718.

portance. Third, such a division would destroy the internal consistency of regulatory policy. The job carried on by a regulatory agency needs to be regarded as a whole, and there should be harmony between the quasi-legislative and quasi-judicial elements in the common task. The placing of these functions in different hands would jeopardize that harmony. Fourth, to set up a body solely engaged in prosecuting cases and without any responsibility for deciding them would inevitably increase litigation. 'A body devoted solely to prosecuting often is intent upon "making a record." . . . At present the added responsibility of deciding exercises a restraining influence which limits the activities of the agency as a whole. If only to save itself time and expense an agency will not prosecute cases which it knows are defective on the facts or on the law—which it knows, in short, it will dismiss after hearing.' Fifth, 'a separation of functions would seriously militate against what this Committee has already noted as being, numerically and otherwise, the lifeblood of the administrative process—negotiations and informal settlements.' An amicable and informal disposition of cases would be much more difficult to negotiate with officials concerned only with prosecution and having no close relations with those holding the power of final decision. Furthermore, the prosecuting agency would have to litigate, and keep on litigating, in order to sharpen and clarify the meaning and policy of the regulatory statutes, whereas now this clarification can be achieved by mutual consultation and agreement within the unitary agency itself. Finally, the complete separation of prosecution from decision would not necessarily prevent bias. Lack of fairness and detachment results from personal and psychological factors rather than from the form of administrative structure; these evils may be eliminated without changing that structure. These were the views of eight of the twelve members of the Attorney General's committee—Chairman Dean Acheson, Francis Biddle, Ralph F. Fuchs, Lloyd K. Garrison, Henry M. Hart, Jr., James W. Morris, Harry Shulman, and Director Walter Gellhorn.

These criticisms of complete segregation were not left unanswered. Four members of the Attorney General's committee, while not disapproving of the majority's proposal for segregation within the regulatory agency of the functions of advocacy and decision, felt that this plan was inadequate and came out squarely for complete separation of functions along the lines proposed by the Brownlow committee.[20] A minority report was presented by Carl McFarland, E. Blythe Stason, and Arthur T. Vanderbilt. Mr. Chief Justice D. Lawrence Groner agreed with both the majority and the minority, but felt that neither proposed a sufficiently complete segregation. The minority's answer to the majority's criticism of the plan is summed up in the following paragraph.

The report of the present Committee . . . reaches the conclusion that the adjudication of contested cases by agencies which do not also investigate and prosecute them would be unwise if not definitely harmful to both the Government and the citizen. It is said that 'an administrative agency is not one man or a few men but many,' that an agency is not 'a collective person,' and that it is not true that 'the same person is doing both' the job of prosecuting and judging. But every agency is actually controlled by a few officials, who work in close cooperation. It is said, in the Committee report, that there would be a division of responsibility for policy if one agency could settle cases by consent but only a separate agency could decide disputed cases, yet this is what the Department of Justice and the courts do in the judicial system as we know it and it is what takes place in the administration of the tax, customs, and criminal law. It is said that separation would mean hindrance of 'amicable disposition of cases' and 'a break-down of responsibility.' But this has not been true of the Department of Justice, which must go to the courts with contested cases, nor of the Bureau of Internal Revenue, which must go to the Board of Tax Appeals with contested tax matters. Finally, it is argued that the prosecuting agency would have to litigate to find out what policy to pursue. But, as a matter of fact, through possession of the rule-making power and the guidance of statutes, the prosecuting agency may, in the same way as the Commissioner of Internal Revenue does, so prescribe policies that any separate adjudicating tribunal will chiefly do no more than apply those policies to the facts.of individual cases.[21]

To keep the record straight, it should be stated that the writer in proposing his plan for the segregation of commission functions to the Brownlow committee, and the Brownlow committee in proposing it to the President, viewed it as a tentative and experimental device. It was not intended or expected that

20. S. Doc. 8, 77th Cong., 1st sess. (1941), 203 ff.   21. Ibid. 206 f.

the plan would be applied forthwith to long-established and successful commissions. It was not regarded as a mathematical formula for solving all administrative equations, and was not intended to be applied uniformly to all regulatory commissions. The agencies and the problems they present differ widely. The proposal for complete segregation was to be applied with realistic caution, and with wide flexibility. In their endorsement of the principle, the minority of the Attorney General's committee took exactly the same position. They disclaim any intention to apply mechanically to all cases a single formula for segregation. Different methods are needed to meet different concrete problems; but the principle of complete segregation is not to be ruled out on the basis of speculative objections, or because in certain instances a less drastic method of segregation may prove effective.

Throughout the 76th Congress, which expired December 1940, a vigorous drive was made to bring about a reorganization of the National Labor Relations Board. This agency has been steadily and sharply criticized on the ground that it combines in the same body the functions of the prosecutor and the judge. A number of proposals were made for the complete segregation of these functions so that the obnoxious combination of duties might be ended. One or two of these proposals may be very briefly mentioned. Representative Anderson of Missouri introduced a bill to confine the powers of the National Labor Relations Board to those of investigation and prosecution. It would cease to be a quasi-judicial body, and its present powers of decision would be transferred to the federal courts. Senator Holman of Oregon proposed the creation of a labor relations commissioner and a labor relations division in the Department of Labor to which sublegislative and prosecuting functions would be assigned; there would also be an independent labor board of appeals consisting of nine members to exercise quasi-judicial functions under the National Labor Relations Act. This plan bears superficial resemblance to the proposal of the Brownlow committee, which was almost certainly unintentional.

The Smith committee of the House of Representatives conducted an extensive investigation of the National Labor Relations Board and proposed another plan for segregating the functions of the present board. This plan called for a labor administrator, not in any executive department, to be appointed by the President and to hold office at his discretion. This administrator would exercise all of the functions of the present board except the actual decision of cases and the conduct of labor elections. No charges could be filed unless the administrator so decided and no appeal would lie from his decision on this point. A critic of the plan observed that all forward motion depends on the administrator's discretion. A new labor relations board of three members was to be created —a neat device for getting rid of the three men composing the existing three-member board. This board would hear and determine complaints filed with it by the administrator, and would hold and supervise elections; but it would have power to afford only the relief specifically asked for, and its procedure would embody 'so far as practicable' the rules of evidence which prevail in the United States District Courts. It is too early to know whether these proposals will command any effective support in the 77th Congress. It is, however, perfectly clear that they are the product of hostility to the National Labor Relations Board on political and economic grounds, and are not primarily the result of loyalty to any abstract theory of the segregation of the functions of an independent regulatory commission.

2. SEGREGATION WITHIN A COMMISSION

We have already mentioned [22] a less revolutionary method of segregating the functions of prosecution from those of adjudication in the independent regulatory commissions—to segregate these functions within the commission itself by assigning each to a separate body of men and keeping the two groups effectively quarantined from each other. This plan seems to be wholly safe and sensible. It is questionable whether it really solves the basic problem of the prosecutor-judge merger, since the power to make final decisions will have to rest with the full commission to which any such separately organized subdivisions are subordinate. But even if such internal segregation should be inadequate, there is no sound reason why it

22. *Supra,* 711.

should not be worked out as thoroughly as possible in order to secure such benefits as may result. This in fact seems to be going on in many cases. While more drastic proposals for the segregation of commission functions are being considered, some of the independent commissions are scrutinizing their own internal arrangements in an effort to see how far the evils of the prosecutor-judge merger can be mitigated by this less drastic method.

For example, the Securities and Exchange Commission has from the beginning been conscious of the problem and has made efforts to meet it by an effective adjustment of its internal arrangements. Not only does the commission separate the groups which handle complaints and present cases to trial examiners from those which reach the decisions, but there is also a separate section to write opinions so that the commission's decisions are put into writing by men who have had no contact with the earlier stages of the regulatory process. Both James M. Landis and William O. Douglas as chairmen of the commission were acutely aware of the problem involved and sought to meet it as effectively as possible. Mr. Landis's convictions on this point had been strengthened by his earlier experience on the Federal Trade Commission where no such carefully worked out program for internal segregation was in force.

And the National Labor Relations Board has been made acutely aware of the problem by continual outside attack. There has been a good deal of effort upon the part of the board's critics and a hostile press to convince the public that the board is exercising its drastic powers by unfair procedure and that the board's decisions are dictated, if not written, by a staff of aggressive and wholly biased investigators and attorneys working in different parts of the country. The facts do not support these sweeping charges, but the board has nevertheless made a definite effort to be sure that the charges of unfairness against its procedure are not justified. It has carefully segregated various parts of the regulatory task in the hands of different groups of subordinate officers and has tried to protect those who decide cases from the pressures which might naturally come from an enthusiastic investigator. In its third annual report the board describes its present procedure in the following paragraph:

Inasmuch as the decision of the Supreme Court in the *Morgan case* during the spring of 1938 also gave rise to a wide revival of popular and professional interest as to the nature of quasi judicial agencies and in their methods of administration, it may be helpful to describe in a general way the manner in which the Board performs its several functions. When charges are filed by individuals or labor organizations they are investigated by the Board's field agents who are subject to the general supervision of the Secretary of the Board. The Board itself decides whether complaints should be issued in only a very small proportion of the cases, and then only if the preliminary investigation indicates that the case involves a particularly difficult question of fact or law or an important new application of the statutory policy. The members of the Board themselves are therefore rarely familiar with the details of the case in its investigative stages, and never at first-hand. When a complaint is issued, the case is tried by an attorney permanently assigned to a field office who is directly responsible to an Associate General Counsel. Neither the attorney nor the Associate General Counsel is in direct consultation with the Board in connection with the particular case except when there is an extraordinary development which concerns the policy of the Board as a whole. Even in the exceptional case, however, the members of the Board take no further direct interest in the case after the question of policy has been decided. The hearing on the complaint is presided over by a trial examiner who is designated in each case by the Chief Trial Examiner. Again there is no consultation in the particular case between the Board, on the one hand, and the trial examiner or the Chief Trial Examiner, on the other unless, again, some new question of policy is involved. More significant are the instructions to the staff that there must be no relationship between the attorney for the Board trying the case and the trial examiner sitting on it except that which normally exists between judge and counsel. After the trial examiner issues his intermediate report, and exceptions thereto are taken by the parties, the case comes to the Board on the formal record for the making of the statutory findings of fact, conclusions of law, and appropriate order. In this work the Board is assisted, as the Supreme Court has expressly said administrative agencies may be, by a staff of lawyers under the supervision of an Assistant General Counsel. In deciding a particular case on the record there is no consultation between the Board or its assistants, on the one hand, and the attorney who tried the case or the trial examiner who heard it, on the other.[23]

23. Third Ann. Rept. of the N. L. R. B. (1939), 5.

The most carefully devised plan for the internal segregation of the functions of advocacy and decision within a regulatory agency is that proposed by the Attorney General's Committee on Administrative Procedure in 1941, and already
mentioned.[24] The committee was unanimous in its disapproval
of the prosecutor-judge merger and in its conviction that something ought to be done about it. The majority believed that
the complete separation of the two functions in the hands of
separate bodies was unnecessary and objectionable; its reasons
for this conclusion have been summarized. It proposed an entirely new plan which would keep intact the general form and
functions of the regulatory agencies but which would rear-
range their internal structure and procedure. The crux of it
is the creation of special hearing commissioners. These would
be appointed for seven-year terms by a three-man 'Office of
Federal Administrative Procedure,' would be removable only
upon formal charges of fraud, neglect of duty, incompetence,
or other impropriety, and would be paid substantial salaries.
The hearing commissioners would be a separate unit in each
regulatory agency, and would have no functions except the
holding of hearings and the making of findings of fact, conclusions of law, and orders for the disposition of matters presented to them. The decision of the hearing commissioner
would thus be an initial adjudication of all the cases coming
before the agency, and a final adjudication of many of them.
Appeals from the decisions of the hearing commissioner could
be taken to the full commission by the parties to the case, including the agency's trial attorney, and the agency itself could
review such decision on its own motion.

The central purpose of the committee's plan seems to be
first, to preserve the unity and coherence of the action of the
regulatory commission; and second, to guarantee the judicial
impartiality of the hearing commissioner—a sort of glorified
trial examiner—by rigidly limiting his duties, by placing his
appointment in non-political hands, and by giving him a high
salary and secure tenure. The dissenting members of the committee agreed that these aims are desirable and that the committee's plan ought to be put into operation where complete
segregation of prosecution from adjudication might prove im-

24. *Supra,* 711.

practicable. They denied, however, that anything short of such complete segregation can place the deciding authority in a position of complete neutrality and independence. They state:

> . . . So long as both investigators and prosecutors, on the one hand, and hearing and deciding officers, on the other, are subject to the same superior authority, there is an inevitable commingling of all these functions. Hearing and deciding officers cannot be wholly independent so long as their appointments, assignments, personnel records, and reputations are subject to control by an authority which is also engaged in investigating and prosecuting. Of course, this dependence may be diminished by various devices, as the Committee has very rightly attempted. We think it clear, however, that such dependence cannot be eliminated by measures short of complete segregation into independent agencies.[25]

The kernel of their objection is found in a remark made during the committee's hearings that 'you cannot wean a calf if you leave it in the same pasture with its mother.'

It may be recalled that the Committee on Ministers' Powers, in its report in 1932, proposed an internal segregation of functions in British Ministries which might be called upon to make quasi-judicial decisions on matters in which as departments they had a direct interest. The committee suggested that when such a situation arose the Minister ought to refer the decision to an arbiter or some disinterested officer or group to advise him so that he might not justly be charged with departmental bias in rendering his decision.[26]

C. APPELLATE TRIBUNALS AND ADMINISTRATIVE COURTS AS PART OF THE MOVEMENT FOR SEGREGATION

Part at least of the current urge to set up special appellate tribunals or administrative courts to review the decisions of the regulatory agencies results from an awareness of the fact that these agencies usually place the functions of prosecution and adjudication in the same hands. This merger of functions calls for an appellate revision of some sort by a body which is dissociated from the task of making the initial decision. If powers are improperly merged in the agency which has original

---

25. S. Doc. 8, 77th Cong., 1st sess. (1941), 209.   26. *Supra,* 631 f.

jurisdiction, at least they are not merged in the appellate body, for there is a complete segregation in personnel of the prosecuting from the final adjudicating agencies. While this is not the only reason for the proposal of appellate tribunals and administrative courts, it nevertheless makes relevant a discussion of such appellate bodies as part of the movement toward segregation, or at least as a movement to secure some of the results expected from segregation.

1. APPELLATE ADMINISTRATIVE BODIES

We turn first to a substantial group of appellate bodies set up throughout our governmental system simply as reviewing agencies in the field of administration. They are not courts and in many instances they function without the formalities of judicial procedure. Most of them are to be found in the executive departments. F. F. Blachly in his *Working Papers on Administrative Adjudication* lists some forty of these differing widely in functions and importance.[27] Their tasks are in the main simple and routine. In many fields of regulation vast numbers of minor quasi-judicial decisions must be made and made speedily by many different officers. There is no need for elaborate judicial review of such decisions, and the courts would be overburdened if they were obliged to review them. What is needed is a cheap and simple way of making it possible to correct mistakes and this is accomplished by setting up an appellate administrative body to review on appeal the officer's initial decision.

Such an arrangement exists within some of the independent regulatory commissions. Sometimes the commission itself acts as an appellate administrative tribunal to review decisions made by individual commissioners or subdivisions to which initial regulatory powers have been delegated. This is likely to prevail in any commission which has the right thus to delegate its authority to its members or to its staff. The Interstate Commerce Commission does this in some measure, and the Federal Communications Commission also delegates the making of initial decisions to individual commissioners. The proposals for the reorganization of the Interstate Commerce Com-

27. *Supra,* 17

mission made by Co-ordinator Eastman in 1934 called for an elaborate arrangement embodying this general principle. There were to be a number of separate sections set up within the commission to which particular duties would be assigned and from which appeals in specified cases would go to a central board of control. The proposal was not adopted.

The *reductio ad absurdum* of this principle was embodied in the Logan-Walter bill vetoed by President Roosevelt in December 1940. This was a comprehensive scheme for setting up numerous appellate administrative tribunals within every department, agency, or commission. To these tribunals, 'any person . . . aggrieved by a decision of any officer or employee of any agency' may appeal for 'hearing and determination.' In the case of executive departments or agencies these boards were to consist of three persons, one of whom, the chairman, must be a lawyer. In the independent regulatory commissions the purpose of the bill was to be attained through a trial examiner who was to report his decision to the full commission or to three members thereof. The Logan-Walter bill specifically exempted from its provisions the Federal Reserve Board, the Interstate Commerce Commission, and the Federal Trade Commission. Of course, the bill included much more than the provisions here summarized, but this provision for mandatory review of all administrative action by these appellate tribunals incurred sharp criticism from a large proportion of those most familiar with the problems of administration and administrative law.

2. APPELLATE LEGISLATIVE COURTS

Another type of reviewing agency in the field of administration is the appellate legislative court. These courts are set up by Congress in the exercise of various delegated powers such as the commerce power or the taxing power, and not in exercise of the authority granted by Article III of the Constitution. The distinction between a legislative court and constitutional court lies chiefly in the fact that non-judicial duties may be imposed on legislative courts and in the fact that Congress does not have to accord them the protection regarding the tenure and compensation of the judges with which Article III surrounds the constitutional courts. The legislative courts sometimes serve a useful purpose in permitting the judicial review on appeal of the decisions of regulatory agencies involving very wide administrative discretion—much wider discretion, in fact, than could constitutionally be reviewed by a constitutional court. This point was emphasized during the early history of the Federal Radio Commission.[28] Congress desired to have the decisions of the commission reviewed by the courts not only on questions of law and procedure but also on the essential soundness and fairness of the discretion involved in making the decisions. The reviewing court was directed to scrutinize the findings and issue an order which in the premises seemed to it just and right. The Supreme Court declined to review on appeal this broad discretionary power, on the ground that it was an administrative and not a judicial power. But while this duty could not validly be imposed on a constitutional court, it could be imposed upon a legislative court which may with complete propriety exercise non-judicial power. The Federal Radio Act was accordingly modified to meet the Supreme Court's decision.

There are at present three legislative courts, none of which deals with problems connected with this study. These are the Customs Court, the Court of Customs and Patent Appeals, and the Court of Claims. The United States courts in the District of Columbia occupy an anomalous position in this regard. The Supreme Court has held that they are constitutional courts in the sense that they enjoy the protections which Article III gives to the tenure and compensation of judges, but that they are also legislative courts created in the exercise of the delegated power of Congress to govern the District of Columbia and that therefore non-judicial duties may validly be imposed upon them. This has proved convenient for it relieves Congress from worry about the exact scope of the review which the courts of the District are asked to exercise over the decisions of regulatory agencies.

We have discussed earlier in some detail the interesting but ill-fated experiment of the United States Commerce Court of 1910.[29] This was a specialized legislative court composed, however, of judges drawn from the constitutional courts, and empowered to decide all appeals taken from the decisions and

---

28. *Supra,* 313 f.   29. *Supra,* 84 ff.

orders of the Interstate Commerce Commission. There were many reasons for the failure of the Commerce Court and most of them had nothing to do with the actual merits of the principle upon which the court was set up. The experience had practical importance because the bad reputation of the court, justly or unjustly earned, has proved a powerful deterrent against repeating the experiment.

There have been proposals for the creation of appellate legislative courts in the field of administration. One of the most conspicuous of these proposals was made in 1936 by the Committee on Administrative Law of the American Bar Association. The writer has elsewhere summarized this proposal as follows:

1. There is to be an administrative court of 40 judges, under the judicial superintendence of the Chief Justice, 35 of whom would be the members of the existing Court of Claims, Customs Court, Board of Tax Appeals, and Court of Customs and Patent Appeals.

2. The court would have a trial division of at least four sections and an appellate division with enough sections to handle its work.

3. The sections of the trial division would take over the present jurisdiction of the legislative courts over claims customs, and tax matters. This division would have original jurisdiction to revoke and suspend all licenses, permits, registrations, or other grants for regulatory purposes. The Committee found 54 cases in which administrative agencies now do this. The trial division would also take over the present jurisdiction of the courts of the District of Columbia to issue extraordinary writs against Federal officers and employees.

4. The appellate division would review the decisions of the various trial sections and would take over the present jurisdiction of the Court of Customs and Patent Appeals. This review would extend to all issues of law and fact.

5. The decisions of this administrative court would be final, subject only to review by the Supreme Court on certiorari.[30]

There is a certain irony in the fact that this interesting proposal was defeated by the American Bar Association's Section on Administrative Law at its annual meeting in 1936 not because of any objections urged against the new administrative court, but because the organized bars which practice before

30. *Supra,* note 1, op. cit. 239.

the existing legislative courts feared the practical effects of the new arrangement on their professional activities. In the judgment of the writer the proposal was essentially unsound, for it would have brought the court into the field of administration by compelling it to decide cases involving wide administrative discretion. The court would tend to do again the work of the administrator, and this is highly undesirable.

3. CONSTITUTIONAL ADMINISTRATIVE COURTS

It would be quite possible to set up an administrative court under the provisions of Article III of the Constitution. It would be a full-fledged constitutional court, but with specialized or limited jurisdiction. As has been pointed out, the courts of the District of Columbia have jurisdiction which makes them in part administrative constitutional courts; they review the decisions of many regulatory agencies, including some of the independent commissions, and a substantial part of their work falls in the field of administrative law. It was recently proposed, in a bill introduced in 1939 by Senator Logan of Kentucky, to set up a United States Court of Appeals for Administration. The plan was simple and provided merely for the segregation of appeals from quasi-judicial officers or commissions to a special United States court of appeals; the other circuit courts of appeals which at present handle a share of this business would be relieved of the necessity of deciding such cases. The proposed court would, however, have no powers not enjoyed by an ordinary circuit court of appeals or be in any other way different from them except in the content of its jurisdiction. The point of the entire plan lies in the segregation of a stream of specialized judicial business.

The question whether we are to have administrative courts and if so what is to be their exact structure and jurisdiction concerns the independent regulatory commissions only indirectly. What does concern them is the scope of judicial review of the findings of quasi-judicial officers and commissions by whatever court may be given this power. The writer believes that this judicial review should be kept to the narrowest point consistent with due process of law. Then it will not make much practical difference whether that judicial review is exercised by a legislative court or a constitutional court.

III. CONCLUSIONS

THE following conclusions may be suggested with regard to the combinations of functions exercised by the independent regulatory commissions and the problem of their possible segregation.

First, there is no constitutional restriction upon these mergers of powers in the same hands. The courts have had ample opportunity to hold that the prosecutor-judge combination of functions denies due process of law. They have not so held.

Second, there is a growing awareness of the prevalence of the prosecutor-judge combination in our regulatory agencies, and increasing dissatisfaction with it. Part of this criticism serves to cover a general resentment against the entire regulatory policy assigned to the agency under attack, and part of it comes from an objective appreciation of the inherent vice of the arrangement.

Third, study is being devoted by students of public administration to this problem and to possible plans for a segregation of functions in the regulatory process. The writer's proposal to the Brownlow committee was made as a contribution to this experimental approach. The reports of the majority and minority of the Attorney General's Committee on Administrative Procedure have given fresh emphasis to the issue and focused attention upon methods of dealing with it.

Fourth, one form of segregation should be effectively and consistently applied if new regulatory agencies are created or old ones reorganized. That is, regulatory agencies should have no extraneous duties which are clearly managerial, promotional, or executive. The commissions must not be treated as dumping grounds for miscellaneous jobs which Congress is too lazy or too indifferent to classify and allocate properly. This type of segregation of function involves no debatable principles and would promote both efficiency and responsibility.

Fifth, it seems clear that we shall continue to experiment with the internal segregation of functions within the commissions themselves in order to mitigate the evils of the prosecutor-judge combination. Impetus will be given to this kind of reform by the report of the Attorney General's committee and valuable results should follow. Such internal segregation of functions should be given wide publicity in order to allay public criticism and to enhance as much as possible the reputation of the regulatory agencies for complete impartiality.

Sixth, complete separation of the functions of prosecution and adjudication along the lines of the Brownlow committee proposal or some similar plan merits continued study and experimentation. Nothing short of complete separation goes to the root of the evil of the prosecutor-judge combination. Of course some inconveniences may attend the making of such a complete separation; most administrative reforms involve compromise. The criticisms urged against the plan still lie in the realm of prophecy. Only by fair-minded and intelligent experimentation under carefully controlled conditions can we reach any reliable conclusion on whether the incidental inconveniences of complete segregation outweigh the important gains in responsibility and impartiality which it promises. The writer believes the plan ought not to be rejected before it has had a fair trial.

Seventh, no plan for segregating the functions of the regulatory commissions should be applied as a rule of thumb. There should be the greatest flexibility not only in the details of the plan itself, but in its application to particular agencies. The commissions vary widely in the kinds of regulatory work they do; those variations may well determine which plan of segregation is to be applied, and how it is to be applied.

XII

THE INDEPENDENT COMMISSIONS AND
PLANNING

In dealing with the activities of the independent regulatory
commissions in the field of planning we are not referring to
the narrow administrative planning by which a commission
may seek to improve the efficiency of its internal mechanism,
but to broad policy planning, the kind of planning, for example, by which the Interstate Commerce Commission might
seek to evolve a national transportation policy. The problems
relating to such planning by the commissions might logically
have been dealt with as part of the problem of the segregation
of commission functions, since we are here mainly concerned
with schemes for separating the planning functions from the
other activities which the commissions carry on. Planning, however, has in recent years become so important in the field of
public administration that separate treatment of the subject
is justified.

A. The Need for Policy Planning in the Regulatory Field

The broad field of economic regulation is one in which
sound policy planning is acutely needed. It is a field which
includes some of the most important phases of the nation's
economic life; such planning ought, therefore, to provide an
intelligent approach to some of our more pressing problems.
Furthermore, if there is to be regulation of business and industry by the national government, it is no more than fair to
those who are to be regulated to let them know in a broad way
what are the government's aims in the field of regulation, and

how the achievement of these ends is likely to affect private rights. For its own sake, and for the sake of those affected by its regulatory policies, the government ought to know where it is going and how it expects to get there. This is planning.

B. CONGRESSIONAL USE OF THE INDEPENDENT REGULATORY AGENCIES FOR PLANNING

Congress may not have been long accustomed to the use of the word planning, since that word has but recently come into our political vocabulary, but Congress has long been aware with varying degrees of acuteness that the job which we now label planning must be done. While Congress has not been steadily conscious of this need, it has, however, sporadically at least, felt obliged to call for expert assistance in the formulation of its policies of economic regulation.

The legislative history of the independent regulatory commissions makes it very clear that in setting them up Congress intended in practically every case that they should undertake the duty of exploring, investigating, and recommending legislative changes in the fields of regulation assigned to them. As early as 1874 the Windom committee reported to the Senate a proposal for creating a body to investigate railroad problems and to propose legislation to Congress.[1] The Federal Trade Commission was given the general assignment of policing interstate commerce in order to break up unfair competitive trade practices.[2] Congress here conceived the commission's job to be that of careful investigation of the field and the problem, and the determination in concrete cases what unfair competition actually meant; viewed broadly, it was a planning job of the first magnitude. It was due neither to the commission nor to Congress that this planning assignment was withdrawn from the commission by the Supreme Court in the Gratz case,[3] in a decision which served notice that the meaning of 'unfair competition' would be determined by the Court in terms of common law precedents. We have seen that Congress was driven into the regulation of radio broadcasting by the sheer physical necessities which had arisen in the radio industry.[4] It was

1. *Supra,* 41.
2. *Supra,* 187.
3. *Supra,* 472.
4. *Supra,* 298 f.

obliged to act before it had a fair chance to work out any general policies for the control of that industry. The legislative history of the Radio Commission shows that one of the major purposes of Congress in setting it up, and particularly in first setting it up on a one-year basis, was to create a body which could bring order out of chaos, and which could do some major policy planning for the regulation of the industry.

Not only did Congress expect the independent commissions to carry on a steady job of investigation and policy planning, but in many cases it gave to the commissions specific assignments, in the form of statutory commands, to investigate and present proposals for legislation. The Radio Commission of 1927 was set up under such a general mandate. When the Federal Communications Commission was created in 1934 it was not only directed to report legislative recommendations annually, but was specifically ordered to bring in such recommendations on a definite date. The Federal Trade Commission has occasionally been ordered by Congress to investigate particular industries and to make reports which would aid Congress in planning appropriate action for the regulation of those industries. It is clear that Congress expected planning assistance from the United States Shipping Board, and it repeatedly called upon the board for advice and recommendations in the field of maritime policy. Some of the proposals made in Congress for the reorganization of the board were aimed at making it a more effective planning agency. The Interstate Commerce Commission is constantly called upon for such service; the broadest type of planning was demanded of it in the Congressional instructions to the commission to develop a satisfactory scheme of railroad consolidations. It is, in short, abundantly clear that Congress looks longingly to the commissions for substantial expert aid in the important tasks of economic policy planning.

C. Failure of the Independent Commissions as Planning Agencies

In spite of Congressional hopes and expectations for policy planning by the independent commissions, the commissions have not achieved much success in this field. They have proved themselves competent to explore small areas and make relatively specific and narrow recommendations. They have handled efficiently many of the *ad hoc* assignments which have been given them, and many valuable and constructive plans and programs have emerged from their conscientious efforts. But there has been no long-time policy planning worthy of the name or adequate to the major problems in the fields of regulatory action, and, in the opinion of some of the ablest men connected with the independent commissions, we are not likely to get from them this kind of planning. This is not hostile criticism of the commissions; it is merely a realistic appraisal of their inherent limitations. Such a conclusion is not based on speculation, but is supported by evidence. For example, no one considers the Interstate Commerce Commission to be the agency from which we can hope to get a broad, far-reaching plan for our entire national transportation system. We have never got it so far, and neither Congress nor the President appears to believe the commission able to render this service. In 1915 President Wilson proposed in a message to Congress the creation of a commission of inquiry to investigate the entire transportation problem. Thus the Newlands committee was created, a joint committee of the two houses of Congress; no one seemed to feel that the assignment ought to be given to the Interstate Commerce Commission. In 1919 Mr. Alba B. Johnson, in his testimony before a House committee, expressed 'incredulous amazement that any group of eight men having to do with transportation in the United States could have lived and worked through these last few years and come before you without apparently the faintest realization that the country is confronted with a railroad problem requiring heroic measures.' [5] Neither the Radio Commission nor its successor, the Federal Communications Commission, has come to grips with the major policy problems which are involved in the regulation of the radio industry. The two commissions have followed the line of least resistance and have assumed that what is best for the radio industry as a business enterprise must also

5. Hearings before the House Committee on Interstate and Foreign Commerce on H. R. 4378, 66th Cong., 1st sess. (1919), vol. II, 1536.

be best for the country. No serious attempt has been made to analyze the problems of newspaper ownership of broadcasting stations or the death grip which commercial advertisers have on the radio industry. The commission of course is aware of these problems, but it has formulated no policies with regard to them nor has it made any recommendations to Congress which could be dignified by the name of policy planning. Nothing comparable to the report of the Ullswater committee [6] in England has come or could come from the Federal Communications Commission. In short, the planning of the independent regulatory commissions has been sporadic and has usually been carried on because of some particular crisis.

There are many reasons why the independent commissions have failed as effective policy-planning agencies. First, the commissions do not have time to engage in planning. The members are kept busy deciding cases and carrying on other detailed and exhausting assignments. Their minds are occupied not with broad and general ideas, but with concrete situations and specific tasks. Mr. Eastman, one of the most experienced commissioners in Washington, declared emphatically that no member of the Interstate Commerce Commission has any fair chance to do anything in the field of broad planning. His testimony on this point is especially persuasive since he has not only served for many years as a member of the commission but also occupied the post of Co-ordinator of Transportation; in this position he was relieved of the duties of a commissioner in order to undertake large-scale planning. A member of the Federal Communications Commission told the writer in 1936, 'I have fewer ideas about the whole radio problem now than when I first came down to Washington.' This was not a confession of want of intelligence, but a commentary on the pressure under which a commissioner has to work.

A second reason why the commissions cannot plan effectively is that they are not usually made up of the kind of men from whom broad policy planning could reasonably be expected; there are individual exceptions, but in the by and large the statement stands. Many men are appointed to the commissions for reasons which have no connection with any possible ability

6. *Supra,* 609, 650.

on their part to administer, to judge, or to plan; the reasons have, instead, been personal or political. Furthermore, even the ablest commissioners would not necessarily make good planners, for the task of planning calls for a very different kind of ability from that which the efficient commissioner acting in a quasi-judicial or administrative capacity has or ought to have. A commissioner's attention is riveted upon individuals and how their rights and interests are affected in concrete cases. He is not likely to see the town for the houses, and it is not his business to do so. Experience indicates that broad policy planning is often best done by laymen rather than by experts, by men who view things against a broader background than that of the technician.

Third, the commissions, for the most part, are not equipped with research staffs either adequate or competent to handle the broad planning jobs. They may have much research assistance, but it is and must be technical and highly specialized.

Fourth, in its broader aspects, the job of planning often calls for the co-ordination of interests lying in the areas of several independent regulatory commissions. It thus lies beyond the scope of any one of these agencies and can be dealt with effectively only by a body which straddles commission or departmental lines. The final report of the National Planning Board in 1934 indicated that nineteen separate agencies and departments exercised some kind of authority over the development and regulation of transportation in the United States. Clearly, even under ideal conditions, the effective planning of a national transportation policy is not likely to come from any one of these bodies. When the large-scale investigation of monopoly which the Temporary National Economic Committee is now conducting was being originally discussed, it was suggested that this inquiry and the resulting policy planning should be assigned to the Federal Trade Commission. The suggestion was not followed and it seems clear that the commission is not equipped to plan in an area of such breadth, even if it were not overburdened with other work.

Finally, the independent regulatory commissions are not abstractions, but are composed of people with human impulses and interests. They have a substantial stake in the status quo; they do not wish to be disrupted, and it is natural for them to feel that wise planning should avoid radical changes. They cannot be wholly impartial in their judgment of possible policy changes which might affect their own standing and powers. One would hardly expect the Interstate Commerce Commission, even if it were a more useful planning agency than it is, to plan a broad transportation policy which did not have the continuance of that commission firmly embedded in its provisions.

D. Alternative Planning Machinery in the Field of Economic Regulation

It seems to be rather generally agreed that we are not going to get from the independent regulatory commissions the broad policy planning which we need, and that this failure is the result of factors inherent in the nature and status of the commissions. Accordingly, much thought has been devoted in recent years to the problem of how to set up agencies or devices from which effective policy planning may be secured. The studies which have been carried on by the National Resources Committee show clearly the need for broad over-all planning in areas by no means confined within the jurisdictional lines of the regulatory commissions. Perhaps we shall ultimately create broadly conceived, well-integrated, national planning machinery which, while using the regulatory commissions and keeping in contact with them, will fit them as minor pieces into a much broader pattern. This does not seem imminent, and in the meantime it is well to examine some of the less ambitious schemes for the carrying on of policy planning in the narrower fields of economic regulation. Some of these have been tried, others merely proposed. These schemes do not assume that we should deprive our present independent commissions of all responsibility in the planning field, but they aim to supplement our present unsatisfactory planning machinery and in some cases they draw the independent commissions into new relations. We may summarize the more important of these practices and proposals.

1. PLANNING AGENCIES NOT CONNECTED WITH THE COMMISSIONS

It is by no means a new policy for Congress to set up completely separate and independent boards or committees to carry on planning in some field of economic regulation. England has followed the same policy through the technique of the Royal Commission. In nine cases out of ten these separate planning agencies are created on a temporary basis to deal with some concrete situation or problem that has forced itself upon the attention of the public or of Congress. The report of the National Resources Committee for December 1938 contains a long list of many of these independent investigations; most of them, so far as their subjects go, might logically have been assigned to the independent regulatory commissions. Congress has occasionally created separate planning agencies intended to be permanent. The Mann-Elkins Act of 1910 set up a Railway Securities Commission to function broadly in the area of railroad finance.[7] It was wholly separate from the Interstate Commerce Commission and Senator Newlands sharply criticized its creation on the ground that the planning job assigned to it should have been given to the Interstate Commerce Commission. It had a short and uneventful life. The Federal Reserve Act of 1914 created an Advisory Council which was authorized to advise the Federal Reserve Board and recommend fiscal policy. As we have already seen, it was created in order to placate the bankers for the failure of the statute to give them direct representation on the Federal Reserve Board.[8] The council still exists and still may make what it can of its position as an advisory and planning agency.

The committee of six appointed by President Roosevelt on September 20, 1937, to submit recommendations upon the general transportation situation proposed the creation of a transportation board to serve as an independent planning agency. This board was to be entirely independent of the Interstate Commerce Commission; it would investigate and report to Congress on the general development of the national system of transportation in regard to modes of transportation,

7. *Supra*, 87, 102.　　　　　　8. *Supra*, 151, 160 f.

consolidations, certificates of convenience and necessity for new construction, financing of new ventures, mergers, leases, and the like. A somewhat analogous scheme, worked out in less detail, was proposed by the Transportation Conference of 1919.[9]

Congress has not tended to favor the creation of wholly separate planning agencies as permanent entities. It has been willing enough to set them up from time to time to carry on specific investigations or to make recommendations on some definite problem. It has not been willing to set up permanent planning bodies to function year after year more or less in a vacuum.

2. 'AD HOC' PLANNING BODIES AS ADJUNCTS TO THE INDEPENDENT COMMISSIONS

Another effective planning device is the temporary or *ad hoc* planning body created to carry on policy planning in the area in which a regulatory commission is at work, and to serve as an adjunct to such a commission. This relation between the two agencies is not an inadvertent one; it is the result of the conviction that while adequate policy planning in the fields of economic regulation will probably have to be done outside the regulatory commissions themselves, those who do the planning will have to be closely associated with the commissions and must clear their proposals through them in order to take advantage of the experience and practical wisdom of the administrators. We have had one clear example of such a planning device in connection with the Securities and Exchange Commission. This was explained to the writer by Mr. William O. Douglas while he was still chairman of the commission. When the Securities and Exchange Act was set up it was definitely intended that it would be expanded and perhaps modified in the light of legislative recommendations which the commission would present to Congress. Congress blocked out in the statute the immediately essential phases of the regulatory program, but made no attempt to extend control to certain other complex problems in the field, on which its data were

9. *Supra,* 120.

neither adequate nor reliable. It was agreed that these problems demanded attention and the commission was given the mandate to inform itself adequately about them and to propose appropriate extensions of the law. The commission accordingly faced the problem of providing itself with suitable machinery for carrying on this major planning activity. It did not assume these important and highly technical tasks itself, but set up separate *ad hoc* planning bodies to investigate particular problems and to bring in reports to the commission. Mr. Douglas himself first came to Washington to direct one of these major planning enterprises. The group of which he was the head conducted an elaborate investigation, and submitted its results in eight volumes for the scrutiny and approval of the Securities and Exchange Commission. The problem under inquiry was that of protective and reorganization committees, and upon the basis of the recommendations of this separate temporary planning body the Chandler Act relating to reorganizations in bankruptcy was passed. Mr. Douglas pointed out that the policy of setting up an outside group to do this sort of planning job was followed because the problems themselves were so highly specialized and technical that it seemed necessary to draw in the services of persons who were clearly expert in the field. This promised better results than to establish as adjunct to the commission a permanent planning agency to which all such problems would be referred. The method has been employed on several occasions by the Securities and Exchange Commission. It may be that the uniquely specialized nature of the problems in this area justifies the use of temporary *ad hoc* planning bodies, whereas permanent planning bodies might successfully cope with the planning needs in other regulatory fields. It should be noted that in each case the planning task was turned over to a group of men not submerged in the details of administration. At the same time the plans and recommendations proposed by the planning agency sifted through the commission itself because of the requirement of its approval. This guaranteed their careful appraisal in the light of the actual experience of the commission.

A similar proposal to deal with the problems of radio regulation was made in 1935 by Mr. Scott, a representative from

Maine, in a bill for the creation of a broadcasting research commission.[10]

3. PERMANENT PLANNING BODIES AS ADJUNCTS TO THE COMMISSIONS

It is only a short logical step from the creation of a temporary *ad hoc* planning body to function as an adjunct to an independent regulatory commission to the setting up of such a planning body on a permanent basis. A very notable experiment of this kind was the creation in 1933 of the office of Federal Co-ordinator of Transportation, a position most appropriately assigned to Mr. Eastman. The details of this arrangement have already been summarized and need not be repeated here.[11] The essence of the plan was to relieve the Co-ordinator, selected by the President from the members of the Interstate Commerce Commission, from his routine duties as a member of the commission. Thus set free he was to study the major problems affecting the development of a national transportation system. He was to explore the problems connected with railroad consolidations and to formulate plans which would eliminate needless duplication of service and increase national railroad efficiency. Mr. Eastman took this planning assignment seriously and presented reports which contained recommendations of policy so wisely conceived that most of them were enacted into law. There may be some question whether the exact status given to the Co-ordinator of Transportation was the one best conceived to produce the most satisfactory results; some believe that the Co-ordinator should not have been a member of the commission, but a person dissociated from it. Mr. Eastman himself felt that it was necessary for the Co-ordinator to be intimately familiar with the work of the commission but not absorbed in its routine duties. He urged the continuance of the arrangement.

There have been several recent proposals for the establishment of permanent planning agencies connected with the regulatory commissions. Early in 1938 President Roosevelt asked three members of the Interstate Commerce Commission, Messrs. Splawn, Eastman, and Mahaffie, to bring in within a

10. *Supra,* 325 f. 11. *Supra,* 132 ff.

week recommendations for 'the immediate relief of railroads.' An interesting division of the report of this group is entitled 'The Long-Term Program.' Here is proposed the creation of a federal transportation authority of three men appointed by the President and reporting to him. The functions of this authority would be to explore and formulate plans for the general improvement and increased efficiency of the national transportation system through such means as consolidations, mergers, and various other devices for increasing co-ordination and eliminating waste. The authority would have no power to issue orders, to hold public hearings, or to follow any formal procedure. It was felt that its functions should be kept quite sharply separate and distinct from the quasi-judicial activities of the commission. Although the report is not explicit upon this point, it seems to imply that there would be informal contacts between the two bodies at all times and definite co-operation if necessary.

Following the same principle, the Omnibus Transportation bill introduced into the House by Chairman Lea of the House Committee on Interstate and Foreign Commerce in 1939 proposed the creation of a transportation administrator. The duties of this officer would be to plan consolidations or pass on those which might be initiated by the railroads, and to clear these proposals, together with recommendations for legislative changes, through the Interstate Commerce Commission to Congress; this officer would be somewhat similar to the Federal Co-ordinator of Transportation.

These various proposals finally bore some fruit. As we have already seen,[12] the Transportation Act of 1940[13] created a board of investigation and research. This is not a fly-by-night committee, but a body of three men appointed by the President and the Senate at salaries of $10,000. It is adequately staffed and has power to command information. Its assignment is important and comprehensive. The board is directed to investigate: (1) 'the relative economy and fitness of carriers by railroad, motor carriers, and water carriers for transportation service, or any particular classes or descriptions thereof, with the view to determining the service for which each type of carrier is especially fitted or unfitted; the methods by which each type

12. *Supra,* 143.   13. Act of September 18, 1940.

can and should be developed so that there may be provided a national transportation system adequate to meet the needs of the commerce of the United States, of the Postal Service and of the national defense'; (2) the extent to which these classes of carriers have received public financial support; (3) the forms of taxation, federal, state, or local, to which they are subjected. The board is further directed 'in its discretion, to investigate or consider any other matter relating to rail carriers, motor carriers, or water carriers, which it may deem important to effectuate the national transportation policy declared in the Interstate Commerce Act, as amended.' The board is to make a preliminary report in 1941, and subsequent annual and final reports. Its tenure is for two years unless the President extends it for two years more. The board has no formal relations with the Interstate Commerce Commission, nor is it required to clear its reports and proposals through that body. The results of this interesting experiment in transportation planning will be watched with very keen interest.

In this connection we may note again the successful experience in Great Britain with the Unemployment Insurance Statutory Committee.[14] As we have seen, this interesting body is a permanent agency attached to the Ministry of Labour and is available at all times for planning assignments in the general field of unemployment insurance. Such an arrangement set up in connection with our own regulatory commissions might also render effective service. One of the most valuable features of the statutory committee scheme is the requirement upon the Minister of Labour to present to Parliament the committee's reports upon matters referred to it, and to explain publicly the reasons for rejecting the committee's proposals if the Minister is unwilling to endorse them. This has the important and valuable effect of bringing the issues between the committee and the Minister out into the open and of permitting Parliament and the public to judge between them on the merits of the controversy. A somewhat similar result was attained, perhaps inadvertently, in connection with the reports of the Federal Co-ordinator of Transportation. In one notable case Mr. Eastman was unable to carry his colleagues on the Interstate

14. *Supra*, 635 ff.

Commerce Commission with him in support of his proposals for the internal reorganization of the commission. The Coordinator's plan was presented to the Interstate Commerce Commission for transmission to the President and Congress. The commission was therefore put under the necessity of justifying its opposition to Mr. Eastman's proposals in as plausible an argument as it could formulate. Those responsible for making the final decisions were thus given the advantage of a frank and public presentation of all the issues involved.

4. CONCLUSIONS

We may venture some conclusions on planning in the fields in which lie the functions of the independent regulatory commissions. First, it is highly important that planning activities in particular fields be carefully co-ordinated. Narrow and provincial points of view must be kept as far as possible out of the picture, and every effort should be made to avoid piecemeal work carried on at cross-purposes or in mutual ignorance.

Second, the problem of fitting planning activities together into some kind of over-all scheme for planning on broad national lines is an important and compelling one. We have not yet achieved anything so ambitious, and we may be slow in achieving it; such broad national planning may remain something of an air castle for some time to come.

Third, pending this happy consummation we should continue to promote the development of planning methods and planning machinery on a less cosmic scale so long as they produce helpful results.

Fourth, it must be kept in mind that there is always danger of getting the planning function too far up in the air by failure to keep the planners closely enough in touch with the administrators who will have to implement the plans.

Fifth, the independent regulatory commissions cannot carry on continuous long-time policy planning and they ought not to be asked to do so. We should continue to ask of them plans and proposals with regard to narrow and specific problems well within the areas of their experience, but we should not burden them with responsibilities which they cannot effectively assume.

Finally, planning bodies ought to be organized as adjuncts

to our independent regulatory commissions. These should be set up *ad hoc* or as permanent bodies, depending upon particular conditions; in most cases they should be permanent. They should be available to the commissions, to Congress, and to the President, to investigate broad policy problems in their several areas and to bring in reports and proposals with regard to them. They should also have a general roving commission to embark upon planning projects on their own initiative and report upon the results. The plans and proposals coming from such planning bodies should go first to the independent commissions to which they are attached. A commission receiving such a plan should carefully study it, conduct public hearings upon it if its character makes this appropriate, and reach a conclusion supporting, rejecting, or modifying it. The commission's conclusions should be carefully explained and supported by argument. The commission should then transmit the report of the planning agency, together with the report embodying its own views thereon, to the President and to Congress for such action as either department may see fit to take.

XIII

PROBLEMS OF STRUCTURE AND
PERSONNEL

We now turn to what may be called the institutional aspects of the independent regulatory commissions—such matters as their size, structure, internal mechanism, and the vastly important problems connected with getting the right kind of men to serve on them. Probably no dogmatic statements can be made about these subjects, but it is worth while to draw attention to them and to review the experiments which have been made in an effort to find the right solutions. Most of the naked facts about these matters are presented in convenient form in the chart appended to this chapter.

A. Size of Boards and Commissions

The size of an independent regulatory body is not intrinsically a matter of importance. There is no ideal size. When Lincoln was asked how long a soldier's legs ought to be, he replied that they should be long enough to reach from his body to the ground; and so a commission ought to be big enough or small enough to perform efficiently the task assigned to it. The present commissions vary in size from three to eleven members. It will be generally agreed, however, that it is better to keep a commission as small as possible. Mr. Eastman observes that a body of eleven men partakes somewhat of the nature of a town meeting. It is inevitably unwieldy and slow in many of its movements and it invites debate and divergence of opinion.

There are certain factors which appear to influence the size of our independent commissions. The first factor is the kind and complexity of the job to be done. A fairly simple quasi-judicial task can be readily handled by three members. If the commission is saddled with complicated and diversified incidental functions or if the job of regulation is inherently complex—and both of these conditions prevail in the Interstate Commerce Commission—more members will be necessary to handle the business. Secondly, size will depend in some measure upon whether the members of a commission are to act as administrators in addition to serving as a quasi-judicial body. This depends partly upon whether the commission has statutory power to delegate its authority or whether it is obliged to exercise it directly. If it may not delegate it, the total volume of work may be so large as to make it imperative that a considerable number of members share in its performance. Third, the size of a commission will vary with the degree to which members of the commission 'represent' various groups or interests. We may recall the agitation in 1922 to enlarge the Federal Reserve Board in order to add to it a 'dirt farmer' [1]; and there has always been a rather general belief that the Federal Reserve Board, the Interstate Commerce Commission, and the Federal Communications Commission ought to be large enough to permit the representation of all major geographical sections of the country.

B. Appointment of Members

There are no problems about the methods of appointing federal commission members since the Constitution explicitly vests that power in the President. It is true that Congress could by law vest the appointment of the members of an independent commission in the head of an executive department. There is, however, no disposition anywhere to give to the commissions this subordinate status, and since the heads of executive departments are subordinates of the President, the net results of the two methods would be much the same. We have seen that it is rather common in Great Britain to direct a Minister to make appointments 'in consultation with' other officials, and this

1. *Supra,* 161 ff.

appears to serve a useful purpose.[2] Such a direction given by Congress to the President could be only advisory in effect, for the President could not constitutionally be compelled to hold such consultations although he might in practice be very willing to do so. We may conclude that the members of independent regulatory commissions will always be appointed by the President, though probably always with the advice and consent of the Senate.

C. TENURE AND REMOVAL

The constitutional aspects of the President's power to remove the members of the independent commissions have already been discussed.[3] There are, however, several questions of policy relating to the tenure of commissioners and the circumstances governing their removal. These may be considered separately.

1. OVERLAPPING TERMS

The desirability of securing continuity of personnel and policy in the independent regulatory commissions will be readily granted. One of the reasons for creating the independent commission has been that its status of freedom from normal partisan or political tenure makes it easier to secure such continuity. The most direct method of accomplishing this is by making the terms of the commissioners overlap. In the case of every independent commission, except the Bituminous Coal Commission of 1935, the policy has been followed of staggering the terms of the members so that there will always be a substantial number of experienced commissioners in office at any given time.[4] The same rule is followed in practice, even if it is not always required by statute, in the setting up of British agencies.

2. LENGTH OF TERMS

Unless Congress definitely intends to create a temporary body when it sets up an independent commission, it usually makes the terms of the members either five or seven years. The members of the Board of Governors of the Federal Reserve

2. *Supra*, 653.
3. *Supra*, 454 ff.

4. See chart at end of book.

System serve for fourteen years. One purpose of these longer terms is to assure experience on the part of commissioners by allowing a man to remain in office long enough to acquire it. Another purpose for the long term is to place a limitation upon the number of members on any commission which a President in a single four-year term would have the opportunity to appoint.

The question of the length of commissioners' terms and the President's influence over the commissions is one on which opinions differ sharply. Some favor keeping at a minimum the President's power to influence the independent commission through the power of appointment, and they favor therefore long terms of office for the commissioners. This view prevails most strongly with regard to the commissions whose functions are predominately judicial in character. On the other hand it is argued that the commissioners should be appointed for short terms so that the President will have frequent opportunities through appointment to influence the commission by placing on it men sympathetic to his ideas. When President Roosevelt took office in 1933 he found on the Federal Trade Commission a majority of members whose views on commission policy were very acceptable to Presidents Coolidge and Hoover, but who were definitely not in sympathy with Mr. Roosevelt's ideas. Many of our regulatory commissions are engaged in policy-determining activities in areas in which conditions are constantly changing and with regard to which the President also has important responsibilities. It is less easy to defend long terms of office for such commissioners. The members of regulatory commissions are not as a rule, and probably should not be, technical experts whose continuing services are indispensable to the smooth functioning of the commission's job. They are administrators or quasi-judicial officers and in many instances, though not in all, it would be wise to give them terms of office short enough to keep open the opportunity to inject new blood into the membership of the commission.

3. RE-ELIGIBILITY

The members of the Board of Governors of the Federal Reserve System are ineligible by law to reappointment. In the case of no other regulatory commission does this rule apply. The National Labor Relations Act specifically states that the members of the board are re-eligible, strongly implying that Congress hoped that competent commissioners would be re-appointed. Congress cannot constitutionally go beyond such an expression of approval of the policy of reappointment. Compulsory reappointment would merely lengthen the statutory term of office. The appointing power retains full discretion in the matter, and circumstances do arise in which it is highly important that certain commissioners should not be reappointed. All that can be done is to further in every possible way the growth of a tradition in favor of reappointing competent commissioners. Professor E. P. Herring's valuable study, *Federal Commissioners,* shows down to 1936 to what extent we have built up such a tradition. The evidence is not heartening; for such a tradition apparently prevails only in the case of the Interstate Commerce Commission, and even here it is not very robust. Down to 1936 forty-three men have been appointed to the commission and of these twenty-six were reappointed. In the other commissions reappointments have been much less frequent. Obviously the problem here is no different in theory from that affecting other appointive public officers charged with important administrative or quasi-judicial duties. In England, where traditions respecting the public service are very different from our own, the presumption is always in favor of the reappointment of competent officers.

4. CAUSES OF REMOVAL

It has already been pointed out that Congress has never considered with care the possibilities bound up in the statutory listing of causes for removal from office.[5] It has been content to follow the old formula which permits removal for incompetence and misconduct, or some similar grouping of words. The writer believes that the formulation of causes of removal could be used effectively by Congress for blocking out a substantial range of accountability on the part of the independent commissions to the President in those areas in which his supervision and control is wholly justifiable. At a minimum Congress

5. *Supra,* 465.

could make the President effectively responsible, through a more concrete statement of causes for removal, for the administrative efficiency of the commissions. This deserves closer study than it has received. The President himself has never fully explored the possibilities of his present power to remove commissioners for cause, perhaps for the reason that he has had no occasion to do so.

D. Selection and Status of Chairmen of the Commissions

While the precise method of selecting the chairman of an independent commission may seem a trivial matter, it actually has great practical importance and has caused a good deal of discussion.

1. method of selection

There are two methods by which the chairmen of independent commissions are chosen. By far the most common is choice by the commission itself; then the chairman usually serves as the presiding officer when the commission meets together. He remains, however, equal among equals. There may be minor perquisites attached to the chairmanship under these circumstances, but in the by and large the chairman's position in relation to his colleagues is rather like that of the Chief Justice to the other members of the United States Supreme Court. It certainly does not give him any important powers of control. He is not, for instance, thereby made the executive officer of the commission, as is so commonly the case in Great Britain. When he is selected by the commission, the chairman's term of office varies. Usually the chairmanship rotates annually, as in the Securities and Exchange Commission or the Federal Trade Commission. Such rotation of course rules out any possibility that the chairman has any real pre-eminence over his colleagues. The Interstate Commerce Commission adopted the policy of rotation many years ago upon the resignation of Chairman Knapp. Mr. Knapp had been re-elected year after year by the commission for so long that, though they felt that it would be desirable to make a change, they felt embarrassment in doing so. Mr. Knapp was appointed to the Commerce Court in 1910 and after that the commission rotated its chairmanship until 1939 when it established a three-year term for the chairmanship.

In other cases commission chairmen are appointed by the President. This seems to be the current tendency. When the President has this power he probably also has the power to remove the chairman from his chairmanship at discretion, even though he cannot remove him from the commission. There is, however, no court decision on this point. The implications arising from Presidential designation of commission chairmen are exceedingly important. They were explained to the writer by James M. Landis, who strongly favors this policy. Mr. Landis's membership on two commissions and chairmanship of one of these lend substantial weight to his judgment on the matter. He believes that the extra prestige which the chairman gets from Presidential appointment, and it is not unsubstantial, is useful and desirable. It may be used by the chairman to improve the efficiency of the commission. The plan allows the President a clear channel of communication through which his own policies may be effectively made known to the commission and through which the President himself may be kept informed on matters of commission policy and action. The President needs this kind of contact with the commissions. Furthermore, if the President has appointed the chairman of a commission, he is very likely to consult him on the matter of appointments to fill commission vacancies when they arise. This is highly desirable, since the commission itself is probably the group most competent to give advice on this point. The system also provides an effective method for securing co-ordination and inter-commission co-operation. A group of Presidentially appointed commission chairmen can meet together and are likely to feel disposed to do so. They may, in fact, be definitely told to do so by the President. When the chairman is selected by the commission itself, he looms much less as a leader and he is usually much less effective and accessible when inter-commission co-operation is needed. Mr. Landis also believes that when the chairman is appointed by the commission there is usually a tendency for power, though without effective responsibility, to be vested in the permanent secretary of the commission—a result which has proved highly undesirable.

2. STATUS AND POWER OF CHAIRMEN

We have not in general followed the policy of singling out the chairman of an independent regulatory commission and making him substantially more powerful and important than his colleagues. Where the job of the commission is closely limited to quasi-judicial regulation it would be difficult to do so even if it were felt to be desirable. In the commissions where there are important assignments of administrative or managerial work, the chairman, by being made chief executive officer, could if desired be made a dominating figure. But Congress has not felt disposed to do this. In the main the power and influence of the chairman has been kept at a minimum and we have done much less experimenting with the possibilities of the situation than we might.

We have not followed in this country the plan so often used in Great Britain of creating a full-time highly paid chairman to work along with a group of part-time and nominally paid board or commission members.[6] There are two reasons for this: first, most of our commissions have heavy quasi-judicial duties which call for the full-time service of all the members; and second, the idea runs counter to our democratic ideas of equality of status. We have already seen from our analysis of the English practice that it too has disadvantages.

E. CIVIL SERVICE AND ITS APPLICATION TO COMMISSIONS

The question whether the staff of an independent regulatory commission should be part of the Federal Civil Service is quite different from the question whether civil service regulations should apply to the British Public Service Boards. The British Civil Service from the days of Lord Macaulay has operated frankly on the principle that men should be recruited for the public services on the basis of their general education. The system does not lend itself easily to the selection of highly specialized technicians. The American civil service on the contrary has always equally frankly undertaken to devise methods of selecting men specially qualified to hold particular jobs.

6. *Supra,* 660 f.

There is therefore no sound reason why we should not success-fully recruit the staffs of the independent commissions by civil service methods. This in fact is customarily done save when emergency conditions have prevailed. The liabilities and diffi-culties incident to our civil service arrangements affect the regulatory commissions no more seriously than they do the other branches of the government.

The creation of new and large agencies on short notice may create special problems. When some of the New Deal commis-sions were set up, such as the Securities and Exchange Com-mission and the Social Security Board, it would have been very difficult to build the initial organization through then existing civil service facilities. The staff had to be somewhat uniquely trained and available in large numbers; these commissions were therefore staffed without regard to civil service require-ments, though not without regard to generally sound personnel standards. It may be that the best solution for the problem presented by such a situation is to set up the new agencies under flexible personnel arrangements designed to secure the kind of ability specifically needed. After the staff of the com-mission has been organized and standardized, it may then be blanketed into the civil service under a non-competitive testing arrangement by which incompetents may be dismissed and the others kept; recruitments should thereafter be made through the Civil Service Commission. In time the federal civil service system may be developed to the point where it will be adequate to meet even emergency demands of this kind.

F. SALARIES

No unique problem exists regarding the salaries of commis-sioners. The salaries range from ten to fifteen thousand dollars a year and compare favorably with those paid to officers of comparable responsibility and importance. It will always be true that the government cannot command by these salaries the services of some able men whom it might wish to enlist. This problem is, however, by no means peculiar to the com-missions. The salary level must of course be considered in the light of the fact that the work demanded is full-time work and that commissioners are required by law in most cases to give up business associations which might influence their official duties. In 1935 Mr. Eccles, the chairman of the Federal Reserve Board, proposed a bill including a provision that the members of the Board of Governors of the Federal Reserve System be given pensions upon retirement. He argued that the fourteen-year term was so long that when a man had served it he might find it difficult to re-establish himself in business, and he therefore deserved a pension. The plan did not commend itself to Congress.

G. QUALIFICATIONS OF MEMBERS

Here is a problem of tremendous importance. Ours may be a government of laws and not of men, but the success of the regulatory commission rests with the men who compose it. If our commissions could be manned throughout with men of the calibre of Mr. Eastman and one or two of his colleagues, many of the troublesome problems relating to the commissions would become largely academic. One of the reasons which influenced Congress to set up independent commissions was the belief, not fully justified by later experience, that abler and more independent men could be secured for the commissions than are usually found in the executive departments. When we have struggled to improve everything else about the commissions, we still come back to the problem of personnel. Water does not rise above its own level. If we man our regulatory agencies with decayed politicians who have political claims on the President we need not be shocked if the commissions do not rise to the higher levels of statesmanship.

It is unnecessary to set out here or even to summarize the facts relating to the background, education, experience, and general ability of the men who have served on our independent regulatory commissions. This has been admirably done in Professor Herring's little volume *Federal Commissioners*. We may, however, discuss the problems which arise with regard to the qualifications of the members of the independent commissions.

1. POLITICAL APPOINTMENTS

As long as members of the independent commissions are appointed by the President, and as long as the President is the head of his party, we shall get a substantial number of appointments made for frankly political reasons. We have never succeeded in ruling politics out of the appointment of the federal judiciary, and we are not any more likely to accomplish it with regard to the commissions. But political appointments are not *ipso facto* and inevitably bad; many officers chosen for bad or irrelevant reasons have proved competent and high-minded. There is no solution to this problem except to use pressure and education to develop a tradition against playing politics with the independent commissions.

2. BIPARTISANSHIP ON THE COMMISSIONS

In setting up our independent regulatory commissions Congress has imposed upon them the bipartisan rule for membership, except in the cases of the Federal Reserve Board, the Bituminous Coal Commission, and the National Labor Relations Board. This rule requires that no more than a bare majority of the members of any commission be members of the same political party. The rule is defensible only on the supposition that the President, unless otherwise restrained, would make his appointments to the commissions along strictly partisan lines. Unfortunately that is by no means an incorrect assumption. The bipartisan rule focuses attention upon the party affiliation of prospective candidates. Professor Harvey Mansfield observes: 'There is nothing in the words to prohibit nonpartisanship, but in a world where it is inconceivable, bipartisanship has been looked upon as the summit of virtue.' [7] The evidence seems to indicate that, as in the case of the courts, partisanship is a negligible factor in the functioning of commissions which are well established and which are administering the less controversial regulatory statutes. Mansfield states that the Interstate Commerce Commission has never divided along party lines in any decision. There might, however, in reality be a substantial difference between the Republican and Democratic way of administering the affairs of either the Federal Trade Commission or the National Labor Relations Board. Mansfield says, 'Indeed the best thing that can be said for the bi-partisan provision in the statute now is that it

7. H. C. Mansfield, *The Lake Cargo Coal Rate Controversy* (1932), 143.

enables the President, if he so chooses, to disregard partisan considerations in appointing nearly half the commission.'[8]

We may conclude that the bipartisan requirement is obsolete and unnecessary. It is neither sound nor relevant to the actual work of the commissions, but it remains to insure an equitable division of spoils between the two major parties. It is just as logical to require a similar bipartisan division on the Supreme Court of the United States.

3. GEOGRAPHICAL REPRESENTATION ON COMMISSIONS

The regulatory jobs assigned to some of the independent commissions are of such a nature that geographical sections feel themselves keenly concerned. This, of course, is not always the case. Geography has little to do with the problems coming before the Federal Trade Commission, the Securities and Exchange Commission, or the National Labor Relations Board, and sectional claims could hardly extend beyond a demand for a fair share of any federal patronage being distributed. In some cases, however, geographical representation on the commissions is required by statute; in other cases it is demanded and often secured by political pressure at the time of making and confirming the appointments of members.

Sectional representation, which was embodied in the Federal Reserve Board when it was set up in 1914, is still retained. Of the appointive members on the board, no more than one, unless it be the Governor, may come from any single federal reserve district. In this case there is rather definite justification for applying the geographical principle. In the organization of the board the reserve districts are the basic units upon which the entire structure is built; they are the lower levels of an administrative hierarchy and it is appropriate that they be represented as such on the board itself. There were other reasons for sectional representation in this case, for there was great concern in Congress during the debates on the Federal Reserve System that the entire organization might fall into the hands of the eastern banking interests. The board as a whole is not overburdened with administrative duties. It operates largely as an advisory or consultative body, so that possible

8. Ibid. 144.

clashes of sectional interest upon it are not likely to interfere with efficiency. An attempt made in 1935 to eliminate the sectional requirement did not succeed.

The United States Shipping Board was set up in 1916 under a requirement for 'fair geographical representation.' The statute was never more specific, but sectional pressures insisted upon geographical representation; our legislative history has shown that this frequently resulted in a deadlock between the interests thus represented.[9]

The Federal Radio Commission of 1927 had five members who, under the law, must be each a resident of one of the five zones created by the Act. There was great jealousy between various sections of the country with regard to the allocation of broadcasting stations which many felt ought to be distributed with an even hand. As one observer remarked, 'Congress looks upon radio as a sort of pie to be divided into five equal parts.' This geographical requirement was a source of continuous friction and inefficiency. It prevented the board from functioning effectively as a harmonious group and seriously retarded the normal development of radio policy. It was not until the Federal Communications Act was passed in 1934 that Congress could be persuaded to abandon the requirement.

There is no statutory requirement for geographical representation on the Interstate Commerce Commission, but there has been almost constant political pressure throughout the commission's history to secure some degree of sectional representation. Senators have engaged in determined and sometimes successful fights to prevent the appointment of able men for no other reason than to bring about the selection of a commissioner from their state or section. Professor Mansfield has set forth in detail the dramatic story of the long-continued but unsuccessful fight of Senator Reed of Pennsylvania to place a Pennsylvania man on the commission.[10] The admitted motive in all of these cases is to secure, in addition to the immediate patronage involved, the kind of representation which would be likely to influence the rate-making decision of the commission to the advantage of geographical sections.

The disadvantages of geographical representation are beyond dispute. It tends in the first place to increase unnecessarily the

9. *Supra*, 273, 318.   10. Op. cit. 166 ff.

size of the commission. Second, it almost invariably results in intersectional logrolling or intersectional deadlock. It distracts attention from the merit of the appointee and focuses it upon the place from which he comes. Thus the appointment of the President's first choices to these important posts is often prevented. Finally, such representation injects into the work of the commission itself the idea of representation, instead of leaving the commission free from pressure to serve the best interests of the public irrespective of local interests. Furthermore, all of the advantages, if they be such, which sectional representation is supposed to produce can be secured through the wise use of the President's appointing power unhampered by statutory requirements.

4. REPRESENTATION OF GROUP INTERESTS

In the statutes setting up two of our independent regulatory commissions Congress sought to give 'fair representation' to certain economic interests felt to be intimately concerned with the regulatory process set in motion. The first of these was the Federal Reserve Board. We have already related the interesting account given by Senator Glass of the desperate effort made by the banking fraternity to secure direct representation on the Federal Reserve Board.[11] Not only did the bankers want to be represented on the board, but they wanted themselves to choose their representatives. President Wilson firmly rejected this idea and the bankers and others had to be content with the provision in the statute that the President in making his appointments was to see that 'fair representation' was given to 'financial, industrial, agricultural, and commercial interests.' When the second Bituminous Coal Commission was set up in 1937, the Act contained a provision demanded by the mine workers that the agency should include 'two experienced coal mine workers, two producers, and three disinterested members.' When the Securities Act in 1933 was under discussion, Mr. Richard Whitney proposed before the committees of Congress and on behalf of the stock exchanges that two members out of seven on the governing board set up to administer the Act should be directly chosen by the stock exchanges. While

11. *Supra,* 155 ff.

no Congressional committee was willing to sanction the choice of these public officials by the private interests concerned, the Roper interdepartmental committee, which had been considering the entire problem, did propose that the stock exchange authority should have on it one representative of the stock exchanges.[12] This, however, was not adopted.

All of the earlier national labor boards were organized on a representative basis. The members here were chosen to represent labor, employers, and the public. It is generally admitted that this is one of the main reasons why they worked so badly. They served a useful purpose as long as all they were supposed to do was to arbitrate disputes, for an arbitral tribunal must, of necessity, be representative in character. The boards broke down completely, however, as soon as any regulatory functions were assigned to them. The authors of the Wagner Act and the Railway Labor Act profited by this earlier experience and abandoned entirely the idea of representation. The Wagner Act says nothing whatever about it, while the Railway Labor Act forbids the members to have any connection either with employers or with unions. It may be concluded that representation of group interests is highly undesirable in the case of any governing body charged with duties of administration or regulation. We have already noted the present tendency in Great Britain to abandon this form of organization in setting up the agricultural marketing boards and the agencies to control depressed industries, and to replace the so-called guild authorities with governmentally appointed, non-representative boards.[13]

5. TECHNICAL OR EXPERT PROFESSIONAL QUALIFICATIONS

There are no statutory requirements that the members of any of the regulatory commissions have technical or professional qualifications. Congress has been content with an occasional pious admonition to the President to appoint men 'with due regard to efficiency and ability,' or 'with regard to special fitness.' It may be recalled in this connection that neither the United States Constitution nor our federal statutes require any of our federal judges to be learned in the law. The failure of Congress to set up requirements of this type may be due to a

12. *Supra,* 332. 13. *Supra,* 565 ff.

variety of reasons. First, there may be some doubt whether Congress may constitutionally control the President's discretion in the exercise of his appointing power. Second, it is probably felt that such requirements would accomplish little which could not be accomplished through senatorial confirmation. Finally, there is a good deal of honest disagreement about just what technical or professional equipment may be needed on any particular regulatory commission. British practice, as we have seen, leans in the direction of stipulating such qualifications and the British statutes will often require that members be appointed who are electrical engineers, lawyers, etc. The facts regarding the technical and professional experience of the members of our major commissions from the beginning are set out in detail in Professor Herring's book mentioned above.[14]

The problem is one for the President's own discretion. Should he in appointing commissioners select experts and technicians, or should he appoint able men of general background and broad interests? This is of course not a problem confined to the commissions. The weight of opinion both in England and in this country leans toward the selection of able laymen who will work through, and be advised by, an expert staff. It is not a question of doing without the services of experts; it is rather the question of where to put these experts. Too often the expert or the technician is too narrowly trained and too specialized in his approach to the problems of regulation to make a good general administrator or member of a quasi-judicial commission.

6. DISQUALIFICATIONS

It is an almost invariable policy both in England and in this country to disqualify for membership on a regulatory commission anyone who has any financial or business connections or interests in the business which is to be regulated. These disqualifications are stated with varying degrees of precision; some are very rigidly and comprehensively drawn. One of the criticisms directed against the British part-time board membership arrangement is that these nominally paid part-time members of some of the British boards and agencies are not dis-

14. *Supra,* 751.

qualified from holding other commercial directorships, and they very often do.[15] This criticism seems aimed quite as much against the resulting diversion of time and interest as against any possible impairment of impartiality. This, however, is not a problem in the United States. Many years ago Representative Grosvenor of Ohio caustically attacked the disqualification set up in the Interstate Commerce Act. He charged that the effect of the rule was to guarantee complete ignorance on the part of the commissioners, since it automatically barred from membership everyone who knew anything about the railroad business. Grosvenor stands alone in this opinion, for there is almost unanimous agreement that the principle underlying these disqualifications is sound. It is sound in the first place because it prevents people from being appointed who are disqualified by reason of bias. There have been times when we could not safely rely on Presidential discretion to appoint wholly disinterested persons. There may be such times again. The rule is sound in the second place because of its valuable effect on public opinion. The regulatory commissions must be jealous of their reputations; it is necessary and desirable that they have all possible external earmarks of impartiality, and one of the most conspicuous of these is the absence from their membership of persons clearly biased.

H. SENATORIAL CONFIRMATION OF APPOINTMENTS

The question whether the Senate improves the quality of appointments to federal offices by exercising its prerogative of confirmation is a difficult one to answer upon the basis of evidence. But while we may not have statistics, we may have reasonably settled convictions on the matter, and the writer believes that the results of the requirement of Senatorial confirmation have been thoroughly bad in very many more cases than those in which the public interest has been protected by it. The usual consequence of the requirement is to subject the appointments to the customary tugging and hauling by which intersectional logrolling and partisan spoils are manipulated. It makes it much more difficult to establish a sound tradition for the appointment of able non-political officials, or a tradi-

15. *Supra*, 661 f.

tion of reappointing able members whose services ought to be retained.

There are two clear reasons why we retain a system which is so open to attack. First, it provides an outside check against thoroughly bad appointments on the part of the President. Unfortunately there are just enough cases where objectionable appointments have been blocked by the Senate to prove this point. Second, we are faced with the complete political impossibility of doing anything else. Congress shows no disposition to relinquish its grip on major federal appointments and even if it did there is no organized public opinion to bring about an amendment to the Constitution to eliminate Senatorial confirmation. The net result appears to be that the best we can hope for is the slow development of sounder traditions to govern the making of Presidential appointments and the confirmation of them by the Senate.

Comment upon the problems relating to the personnel of the independent regulatory commissions has been placed at the end of this volume because, in the judgment of the writer, those problems overshadow all others in importance. If by some combination of intelligence and good fortune we are able to develop personnel practices and traditions which will place and keep on the regulatory commissions men of genuinely high calibre, we need not worry unduly about problems of commission structure and procedure, although those problems are important and their solution will require great wisdom. But the soundest commission organization and the fairest and most efficient commission procedure will avail little against the disintegrating influence of biased, incompetent, or corrupt men sitting as the members of a commission. If the vastly important tasks assigned to our regulatory commissions are ever handled on a level of maximum efficiency and statesmanship, it will be because we have found the formula for manning the commissions with men of outstanding ability and unquestioned integrity.

Agency	Date Created	Number of Members	Tenure of Office	Method of Removal	Qualifications and Disqualifications	Salaries	Chairman Appointed by
Interstate Commerce Commission	Feb. 4, 1887	5,[1] 7,[2] 9,[3] 11[4]	7 years staggered; until successor chosen	By the President for inefficiency, neglect of duty, or malfeasance in office	1. No more than 6 members from same political party 2. Members must not be interested in any carrier under the commission 3. No other employment	$10,000	Members of commission, for three-year term
Federal Reserve Board, now the Board of Governors of the Federal Reserve System	Dec. 23, 1913 Aug. 23, 1935	7,[3] 8,[7] 7[10]	10 years staggered;[3] 12 years staggered;[8] 14 years staggered; until successor chosen[10]	By the President for cause	1. No more than 1 member from same Federal Reserve District 2. President shall give due regard to fair representation of financial, industrial, agricultural,[7] and commercial interests, and geographical divisions of the country 3. No other employment 4. Ineligible while members or two years after to hold office in member bank, except after expiration of full term 5. Ineligible to reappointment for second full term	12,000 15,000[10]	President, for four-year term
Federal Trade Commission	Sept. 26, 1914	5	7 years staggered	By the President for inefficiency, neglect of duty, or malfeasance in office	1. No more than 3 members from same political party 2. No other business or employment	10,000	Members of commission
United States Shipping Board[5]	Sept. 17, 1916 Mar. 3, 1933	5,[6] 7,[4] 3[9]	6 years staggered;[6] 3 years staggered;[8] hold till successor[9]	By the President for inefficiency, neglect of duty, or malfeasance in office	1. Due regard to efficiency and ability 2. Fair geographical representation 3. No more than 3 members from same political party 4. No other employment or financial interest in shipping companies	7,500[6] 12,000[4]	Members of board[6] President[4]
Federal Radio Commission[5]	Feb. 23, 1927	5	6 years staggered	No comment	1. Members must be residents—1 from each of 5 zones 2. No financial interest in any radio concern 3. No more than 3 members from same political party	30 per day while at work	Members of commission
Federal Power Commission	June 23, 1930	5	5 years staggered	No comment	1. No more than 3 members from same political party 2. No employment or financial interest in power company	10,000	Members of board; to expiration of his term of office
Securities and Exchange Commission	June 6, 1934	5	5 years staggered	No comment	1. No more than 3 members from same political party; to be appointed from alternate parties as nearly as practicable 2. No other employment or stock market operations	10,000	No comment

[1] 1887.　[2] 1906.　[3] 1917.　[4] 1920.　[5] Extinct.　[6] 1916.　[7] 1922.　[8] 1932.　[9] 1933.　[10] 1935.

Agency	Date Created	Number of Members	Tenure of Office	Method of Removal	Qualifications and Disqualifications	Salaries	Chairman Appointed by
Federal Communications Commission	June 19, 1934	7	7 years staggered	No comment	1. No more than 4 members from same political party. 2. No financial interest in products or services controlled 3. No other employment 4. Citizenship	$10,000	President
National Labor Relations Board	July 5, 1935	3	5 years staggered	By the President, upon notice and hearing, for neglect of duty or malfeasance in office, but for no other cause	1. No other business or employment 2. Eligible to reappointment	10,000	President
Bituminous Coal Commission [11]	August 30, 1935 April 26, 1937	5 [12] 7 [13]	4 years	By the President for inefficiency, neglect of duty, or malfeasance in office	1. No financial interest in mining, gas, transportation, or associated industries [12] 2. No other business or employment 3. Two experienced bituminous coal mine workers; two with previous experience as producers; no other financial interest, direct or indirect, in mining, gas, transportation, or associated industries [13]	10,000	Members, annually
United States Maritime Commission	June 29, 1936	5	6 years staggered	By the President for neglect of duty or malfeasance in office	1. No more than 3 members from same political party 2. Appointed with regard to special fitness 3. No financial interest in any shipping company for three years prior to appointment; no such current financial interest 4. No other employment	12,000	President
Civil Aeronautics Authority [14]	June 23, 1938	5	6 years staggered	By the President for inefficiency, neglect of duty, or malfeasance in office	1. No more than 3 members from same political party 2. Appointed with due regard to fitness 3. No financial interest in civil aviation industry 4. No other business or employment 5. Citizenship	12,000	President, annually

[11] Extinct; functions transferred to Department of the Interior.
[14] Transferred to Department of Commerce, but remaining independent as to quasi-legislative and quasi-judicial duties.

[12] 1935.

[13] 1937.

CHART OF ESSENTIAL FACTS ABOUT THE INDEPENDENT REGULATORY COMMISSIONS

TABLE OF CASES

INDEX

765